PLUNKETT'S FINTECH, CRYPTOCURRENCY & ELECTRONIC PAYMENTS INDUSTRY ALMANAC 2022

The only comprehensive guide to fintech, cryptocurrency and electronic payments companies & trends

Jack W. Plunkett

Published by:
Plunkett Research®, Ltd., Houston, Texas
www.plunkettresearch.com

PLUNKETT'S FINTECH, CRYPTOCURRENCY & ELECTRONIC PAYMENTS INDUSTRY ALMANAC 2022

Editor and Publisher:
Jack W. Plunkett

Executive Editor and Database Manager:
Martha Burgher Plunkett

Senior Editor and Researchers:
Isaac Snider
Michael Cappelli

Editors, Researchers and Assistants:
Annie Paynter
Gina Sprenkel

Information Technology Manager:
Rebeca Tijiboy

Special Thanks to:
ETFGI LLC
Federal Deposit Insurance Corporation (FDIC)
Federal Reserve Bank of Atlanta
FT Partners
Gartner
International Data Corporation (IDC)
Investment Company Institute (ICI)
McKinsey & Co.
National Association of Realtors (NAR)
PricewaterhouseCoopers
Securities Industry and Financial Markets
Association
Stanford University
Token Insight
U.S. Bureau of Labor Statistics
U.S. Census Bureau
U.S. Department of the Treasury
World Federation of Exchanges (WFE)

Plunkett Research®, Ltd.
P. O. Drawer 541737, Houston, Texas 77254 USA
Phone: 713.932.0000 Fax: 713.932.7080
www.plunkettresearch.com

Copyright © 2022, Plunkett Research®, Ltd. All rights reserved. Except as provided for below, you may not copy, resell, reproduce, distribute, republish, download, display, post, or transmit any portion of this book in any form or by any means, including, but not limited to, electronic, mechanical, photocopying, recording, or otherwise, without the express prior written permission of Plunkett Research, Ltd. Additional copyrights are held by other content providers, including, in certain cases, Morningstar, Inc. The information contained herein is proprietary to its owners and it is not warranted to be accurate, complete or timely. Neither Plunkett Research, Ltd. nor its content providers are responsible for any damages or losses arising from any use of this information. Market and industry statistics, company revenues, profits and other details may be estimates. Financial information, company plans or status, and other data can change quickly and may vary from those stated here. **Past performance is no guarantee of future results**.

Plunkett Research®, Ltd.
P. O. Drawer 541737
Houston, Texas 77254-1737
Phone: 713.932.0000, Fax: 713.932.7080 www.plunkettresearch.com

ISBN13 # 978-1-62831-632-2 (eBook Edition # 978-1-62831-957-6)

Limited Warranty and Terms of Use:

Users' publications in static electronic format containing any portion of the content of this book (and/or the content of any related Plunkett Research, Ltd. online service to which you are granted access, hereinafter collectively referred to as the "Data") or Derived Data (that is, a set of data that is a derivation made by a User from the Data, resulting from the applications of formulas, analytics or any other method) may be resold by the User only for the purpose of providing third-party analysis within an established research platform under the following conditions: (However, Users may not extract or integrate any portion of the Data or Derived Data for any other purpose.)

a) Users may utilize the Data only as described herein. b) User may not export more than an insubstantial portion of the Data or Derived Data, c) Any Data exported by the User may only be distributed if the following conditions are met:

   i)   Data must be incorporated in added-value reports or presentations, either of which are part of the regular services offered by the User and not as stand-alone products.
   ii) Data may not be used as part of a general mailing or included in external websites or other mass communication vehicles or formats, including, but not limited to, advertisements.
   iii) Except as provided herein, Data may not be resold by User.

"Insubstantial Portions" shall mean an amount of the Data that (1) has no independent commercial value, (2) could not be used by User, its clients, Authorized Users and/or its agents as a substitute for the Data or any part of it, (3) is not separately marketed by the User, an affiliate of the User or any third-party source (either alone or with other data), and (4) is not retrieved by User, its clients, Authorized Users and/or its Agents via regularly scheduled, systematic batch jobs.

LIMITED WARRANTY; DISCLAIMER OF LIABILITY: While Plunkett Research, Ltd. ("PRL") has made an effort to obtain the Data from sources deemed reliable, PRL makes no warranties, expressed or implied, regarding the Data contained herein. This book and its Data are provided to the End-User "AS IS" without warranty of any kind. No oral or written information or advice given by PRL, its employees, distributors or representatives will create a warranty or in any way increase the scope of this Limited Warranty, and the Customer or End-User may not rely on any such information or advice. Customer Remedies: PRL's entire liability and your exclusive remedy shall be, at PRL's sole discretion, either (a) return of the price paid, if any, or (b) repair or replacement of a book that does not meet PRL's Limited Warranty and that is returned to PRL with sufficient evidence of or receipt for your original purchase.

NO OTHER WARRANTIES: TO THE MAXIMUM EXTENT PERMITTED BY APPLICABLE LAW, PRL AND ITS DISTRIBUTORS DISCLAIM ALL OTHER WARRANTIES AND CONDITIONS, EITHER EXPRESSED OR IMPLIED, INCLUDING, BUT NOT LIMITED TO, IMPLIED WARRANTIES OR CONDITIONS OF MERCHANTABILITY, FITNESS FOR A PARTICULAR PURPOSE, TITLE AND NON-INFRINGEMENT WITH REGARD TO THE BOOK AND ITS DATA, AND THE PROVISION OF OR FAILURE TO PROVIDE SUPPORT SERVICES. LIMITATION OF LIABILITY: TO THE MAXIMUM EXTENT PERMITTED BY APPLICABLE LAW, IN NO EVENT SHALL PRL BE LIABLE FOR ANY SPECIAL, INCIDENTAL OR CONSEQUENTIAL DAMAGES WHATSOEVER (INCLUDING, WITHOUT LIMITATION, DAMAGES FOR LOSS OF BUSINESS PROFITS, BUSINESS INTERRUPTION, ABILITY TO OBTAIN OR RETAIN EMPLOYMENT OR REMUNERATION, ABILITY TO PROFITABLY MAKE AN INVESTMENT, OR ANY OTHER PECUNIARY LOSS) ARISING OUT OF THE USE OF, OR RELIANCE UPON, THE BOOK OR DATA, OR THE INABILITY TO USE THIS DATA OR THE FAILURE OF PRL TO PROVIDE SUPPORT SERVICES, EVEN IF PRL HAS BEEN ADVISED OF THE POSSIBILITY OF SUCH DAMAGES. IN ANY CASE, PRL'S ENTIRE LIABILITY SHALL BE LIMITED TO THE AMOUNT ACTUALLY PAID BY YOU FOR THE BOOK.

PLUNKETT'S FINTECH, CRYPTOCURRENCY & ELECTRONIC PAYMENTS INDUSTRY ALMANAC 2022

CONTENTS

Introduction	**1**
How to Use This Book	**3**
<u>Chapter 1:</u> **Major Trends Affecting the Fintech, Cryptocurrency & Electronic Payments Industry**	**7**
1) Introduction to the FinTech, Cryptocurrency & Electronic Payments Industry	**7**
2) Cryptocurrencies and Blockchain Explained	**9**
3) The Difference Between Cryptocurrencies and Stable Coins/National Treasuries Consider Issuing Stable Digital Currencies	**10**
4) BNPL (Buy Now Pay Later) Options Gain Payments Market Share	**11**
5) Digital Wallets Gain Payments Market Share	**11**
6) The SuperApp Begins to Develop in FinTech	**12**
7) Real Time Payments (RTP)/Instant Payments to Grow	**12**
8) Neobanks/Virtual Banks Explained/Top Competitors	**12**
9) A Brief History of Artificial Intelligence (AI) and the State of the Industry Today	**13**
10) Voice, Face & Image Recognition Change the Wireless World, Enhanced Through Artificial Intelligence (AI)	**14**
11) Insurance Underwriting Uses Artificial Intelligence (AI)/Policy Holders Allow Their Habits to Be Tracked for Lower Insurance Rates	**15**
12) Robotic Process Automation (RPA) Is Replacing Human Workers	**17**
13) Digital Assistants Include Amazon's Echo and Google's Home/Alexa and Similar Software Power Third-Party Developers	**17**
14) Growth in Big Data Supported by Expansion of Cloud Computing and Predictive Analytics	**18**
15) Artificial Intelligence (AI) Powers Hedge Fund Investment Strategies	**20**
16) Banks and Mobile Apps Vie for Previously Underserved Markets, Including Hispanics	**20**
17) China Sees Growth in Online Payments, Banking and Lending/Alipay Soars	**21**
18) The Internet, Smartphones and ATMs Replace Bank Branches and Tellers	**22**
19) Smartphones and Financial Technology (FinTech) Enable New Mobile Payment Methods	**23**
20) Peer-to-Peer (P2P) Payment Systems, such as Zelle and Venmo, Soar in Popularity	**24**
21) In Emerging Nations, mChek and M-PESA Enable Remote Banking via Smartphone	**24**
22) Online Competition Changes the Mortgage Industry	**25**
23) Open Banking May Revolutionize the World of Banking and Finance	**26**
24) The Future of Banking, Credit Cards, Mobile Payments and Mortgages	**26**
<u>Chapter 2:</u> **Fintech, Cryptocurrency & Electronic Payments Industry Statistics**	**29**
FinTech, Cryptocurrency & Electronic Payments Industry Statistics and Market Size Overview	**30**
Artificial Intelligence Industry Statistics and Market Size Overview	**31**
Investment & Securities Industry Statistics and Market Size Overview	**32**
U.S. Banking, Mortgages & Credit Industry Statistics and Market Size Overview	**33**

Continued on next page

Continued from previous page

Global Credit Card Industry Statistics and Market Size Overview	**34**
FDIC Insured Institution Statistics: 2nd Quarter 2021	**35**
Employment in the Banking Industry, U.S.: 2015-July 2021	**36**

<u>Chapter 3:</u> **Important Fintech, Cryptocurrency & Electronic Payments Industry Contacts** 37
(Addresses, Phone Numbers and Internet Sites)

<u>Chapter 4:</u> **THE FINTECH 235:**

Who They Are and How They Were Chosen	**63**
Index of Companies Within Industry Groups	**64**
Alphabetical Index	**71**
Index of Headquarters Location by U.S. State	**73**
Index of Non-U.S. Headquarters Location by Country	**76**
Individual Data Profiles on Each of THE FINTECH 235	**77**

<u>Additional Indexes</u>

Index of Hot Spots for Advancement for Women/Minorities	**322**
Index by Subsidiaries, Brand Names and Selected Affiliations	**323**

A Short Fintech, Cryptocurrency & Electronic Payments Industry Glossary   **329**

INTRODUCTION

PLUNKETT'S FINTECH, CRYPTOCURRENCY & ELECTRONIC PAYMENTS INDUSTRY ALMANAC is designed to be used as a general source for researchers of all types.

The data and areas of interest covered are intentionally broad, from the various types of businesses involved in FinTech, to the evolution of cryptocurrency and electronic payments, to an in-depth look at the major for-profit firms (which we call "THE FINTECH 235") within the many industry sectors that make up the FinTech arena.

This reference book is especially intended to assist with market research, strategic planning, employment searches, contact or prospect list creation and financial research, and as a data resource for executives and students of all types.

PLUNKETT'S FINTECH, CRYPTOCURRENCY & ELECTRONIC PAYMENTS INDUSTRY ALMANAC takes a rounded approach for the general reader. This book presents a complete overview of the entire FinTech industry (see "How To Use This Book"). For example, financial technology or "FinTech" is explained, as are cryptocurrencies, blockchain, neobanks and payments platforms.

THE FINTECH 235 is our unique grouping of the fastest growing, most successful corporations in all segments of the FinTech industry. Tens of thousands of pieces of information, gathered from a wide variety of sources, have been researched and are presented in a unique form that can be easily understood. This section includes thorough indexes to THE FINTECH 235, by geography, industry, sales, brand names, subsidiary names and many other topics. (See Chapter 4.)

Especially helpful is the way in which PLUNKETT'S FINTECH, CRYPTOCURRENCY & ELECTRONIC PAYMENTS INDUSTRY ALMANAC enables readers who have no business background to readily compare the financial records and growth plans of FinTech companies and major industry groups. You'll see the mid-term financial record of each firm, along with the impact of earnings, sales and strategic plans on each company's potential to fuel growth, to serve new markets and to provide investment and employment opportunities.

No other source provides this book's easy-to-understand comparisons of growth, expenditures, technologies, corporations and many other items of great importance to people of all types who may be studying this, one of the most complex industries in the world today.

By scanning the data groups and the unique indexes, you can find the best information to fit your personal research needs. The major companies in the FinTech industry are profiled and then ranked using several different groups of specific criteria. Which firms are the biggest employers? Which companies earn the most profits? These things and much more are easy to find.

In addition to individual company profiles, an overview of FinTech, markets and trends is provided. This book's job is to help you sort through easy-to-understand summaries of today's trends in a quick and effective manner.

Whatever your purpose for researching the FinTech field, you'll find this book to be a valuable guide. Nonetheless, as is true with all resources, this volume has limitations that the reader should be aware of:

- Financial data and other corporate information can change quickly. A book of this type can be no more current than the data that was available as of the time of editing. Consequently, the financial picture, management and ownership of the firm(s) you are studying may have changed since the date of this book. For example, this almanac includes the most up-to-date sales figures and profits available to the editors as of early-2022. That means that we have typically used corporate financial data as of the end of 2021.

- Corporate mergers, acquisitions and downsizing are occurring at a very rapid rate. Such events may have created significant change, subsequent to the publishing of this book, within a company you are studying.

- Some of the companies in THE FINTECH 235 are so large in scope and in variety of business endeavors conducted within a parent organization, that we have been unable to completely list all subsidiaries, affiliations, divisions and activities within a firm's corporate structure.

- This volume is intended to be a general guide to a quickly changing industry. That means that researchers should look to this book for an overview and, when conducting in-depth research, should contact the specific corporations or industry associations in question for the very latest changes and data. Where possible, we have listed contact names, toll-free telephone numbers

and internet site addresses for the companies, government agencies and industry associations involved so that the reader may get further details without unnecessary delay.

- Tables of industry data and statistics used in this book include the latest numbers available at the time of printing, generally through mid-2021. In a few cases, the only complete data available was for earlier years.

- We have used exhaustive efforts to locate and fairly present accurate and complete data. However, when using this book or any other source for business and industry information, the reader should use caution and diligence by conducting further research where it seems appropriate. We wish you success in your endeavors, and we trust that your experience with this book will be both satisfactory and productive.

Jack W. Plunkett
Houston, Texas
June 2022

HOW TO USE THIS BOOK

The two primary sections of this book are devoted first to the FinTech industry as a whole and then to the "Individual Data Listings" for THE FINTECH 235. If time permits, you should begin your research in the front chapters of this book. Also, you will find lengthy indexes in Chapter 4 and in the back of the book.

THE FINTECH, CRYPTOCURRENCY & ELECTRONIC PAYMENTS INDUSTRY

Chapter 1: Major Trends Affecting the FinTech, Cryptocurrency & Electronic Payments Industry. This chapter presents an encapsulated view of the major trends that are creating rapid changes in the FinTech industry today.

Chapter 2: FinTech, Cryptocurrency & Electronic Payments Industry Statistics. This chapter presents in-depth statistics on revenue, employment and more.

Chapter 3: Important FinTech, Cryptocurrency & Electronic Payments Industry Contacts – Addresses, Telephone Numbers and Internet Sites. This chapter covers contacts for important government agencies, FinTech organizations and trade groups. Included are numerous important internet sites.

THE FINTECH 235

Chapter 4: THE FINTECH 235: Who They Are and How They Were Chosen. The companies compared in this book were carefully selected from the FinTech industry, largely in the United States. Many of the firms are based outside the U.S. For a complete description, see THE FINTECH 235 indexes in this chapter.

Individual Data Listings:

Look at one of the companies in THE FINTECH 235's Individual Data Listings. You'll find the following information fields:

Company Name:

The company profiles are in alphabetical order by company name. If you don't find the company you are seeking, it may be a subsidiary or division of one of the firms covered in this book. Try looking it up in the Index by Subsidiaries, Brand Names and Selected Affiliations in the back of the book.

Industry Code:

Industry Group Code: An NAIC code used to group companies within like segments.

Types of Business:

A listing of the primary types of business specialties conducted by the firm.

Brands/Divisions/Affiliations:

Major brand names, operating divisions or subsidiaries of the firm, as well as major corporate affiliations—such as another firm that owns a significant portion of the company's stock. A complete Index by Subsidiaries, Brand Names and Selected Affiliations is in the back of the book.

Contacts:

The names and titles up to 27 top officers of the company are listed, including human resources contacts.

Growth Plans/ Special Features:

Listed here are observations regarding the firm's strategy, hiring plans, plans for growth and product development, along with general information regarding a company's business and prospects.

Financial Data:

Revenue (2021 or the latest fiscal year available to the editors, plus up to five previous years): This figure represents consolidated worldwide sales from all operations. These numbers may be estimates.

R&D Expense (2021 or the latest fiscal year available to the editors, plus up to five previous years): This figure represents expenses associated with the research and development of a company's goods or services. These numbers may be estimates.

Operating Income (2021 or the latest fiscal year available to the editors, plus up to five previous years): This figure represents the amount of profit realized from annual operations after deducting operating expenses including costs of goods sold, wages and depreciation. These numbers may be estimates.

Operating Margin % (2021 or the latest fiscal year available to the editors, plus up to five previous years): This figure is a ratio derived by dividing operating income by net revenues. It is a measurement of a firm's pricing strategy and operating efficiency. These numbers may be estimates.

SGA Expense (2021 or the latest fiscal year available to the editors, plus up to five previous years): This figure represents the sum of selling, general and administrative expenses of a company, including costs such as warranty, advertising, interest, personnel, utilities, office space rent, etc. These numbers may be estimates.

Net Income (2021 or the latest fiscal year available to the editors, plus up to five previous years): This figure represents consolidated, after-tax net profit from all operations. These numbers may be estimates.

Operating Cash Flow (2021 or the latest fiscal year available to the editors, plus up to five previous years): This figure is a measure of the amount of cash generated by a firm's normal business operations. It is calculated as net income before depreciation and after income taxes, adjusted for working capital. It is a prime indicator of a company's ability to generate enough cash to pay its bills. These numbers may be estimates.

Capital Expenditure (2021 or the latest fiscal year available to the editors, plus up to five previous years): This figure represents funds used for investment in or improvement of physical assets such as offices, equipment or factories and the purchase or creation of new facilities and/or equipment. These numbers may be estimates.

EBITDA (2021 or the latest fiscal year available to the editors, plus up to five previous years): This figure is an acronym for earnings before interest, taxes, depreciation and amortization. It represents a company's financial performance calculated as revenue minus expenses (excluding taxes, depreciation and interest), and is a prime indicator of profitability. These numbers may be estimates.

Return on Assets % (2021 or the latest fiscal year available to the editors, plus up to five previous years): This figure is an indicator of the profitability of a company relative to its total assets. It is calculated by dividing annual net earnings by total assets. These numbers may be estimates.

Return on Equity % (2021 or the latest fiscal year available to the editors, plus up to five previous years): This figure is a measurement of net income as a percentage of shareholders' equity. It is also called the rate of return on the ownership interest. It is a vital indicator of the quality of a company's operations. These numbers may be estimates.

Debt to Equity (2021 or the latest fiscal year available to the editors, plus up to five previous years): A ratio of the company's long-term debt to its shareholders' equity. This is an indicator of the overall financial leverage of the firm. These numbers may be estimates.

Address:

The firm's full headquarters address, the headquarters telephone, plus toll-free and fax numbers where available. Also provided is the internet address.

Stock Ticker, Exchange: When available, the unique stock market symbol used to identify this firm's common stock for trading and tracking purposes is indicated. Where appropriate, this field may contain "private" or "subsidiary" rather than a ticker symbol. If the firm is a publicly-held company headquartered outside of the U.S., its international ticker and exchange are given.

Total Number of Employees: The approximate total number of employees, worldwide, as of the end of 2021 (or the latest data available to the editors).

Parent Company: If the firm is a subsidiary, its parent company is listed.

Salaries/Bonuses:

(The following descriptions generally apply to U.S. employers only.)

Highest Executive Salary: The highest executive salary paid, typically a 2021 amount (or the latest year available to the editors) and typically paid to the Chief Executive Officer.

Highest Executive Bonus: The apparent bonus, if any, paid to the above person.

Second Highest Executive Salary: The next-highest executive salary paid, typically a 2021 amount (or the latest year available to the editors) and typically paid to the President or Chief Operating Officer.

Second Highest Executive Bonus: The apparent bonus, if any, paid to the above person.

Other Thoughts:

Estimated Female Officers or Directors: It is difficult to obtain this information on an exact basis, and employers generally do not disclose the data in a public way. However, we have indicated what our best efforts reveal to be the apparent number of women who either are in the posts of corporate officers or sit on the board of directors. There is a wide variance from company to company.

Hot Spot for Advancement for Women/Minorities: A "Y" in appropriate fields indicates "Yes." These are firms that appear either to have posted a substantial number of women and/or minorities to high posts or that appear to have a good record of going out of their way to recruit, train, promote and retain women or minorities. (See the Index of Hot Spots For Women and Minorities in the back of the book.) This information may change frequently and can be difficult to obtain and verify. Consequently, the reader should use caution and conduct further investigation where appropriate.

Glossary: A short list of FinTech industry terms.

Chapter 1

MAJOR TRENDS AFFECTING THE FINTECH, CRYPTOCURRENCY & ELECTRONIC PAYMENTS INDUSTRY

1) Introduction to the FinTech, Cryptocurrency & Electronic Payments Industry
2) Cryptocurrencies and Blockchain Explained
3) The Difference Between Cryptocurrencies and Stable Coins/National Treasuries Consider Issuing Stable Digital Currencies
4) BNPL (Buy Now Pay Later) Options Gain Payments Market Share
5) Digital Wallets Gain Payments Market Share
6) The SuperApp Begins to Develop in FinTech
7) Real Time Payments (RTP)/Instant Payments to Grow
8) Neobanks/Virtual Banks Explained/Top Competitors
9) A Brief History of Artificial Intelligence (AI) and the State of the Industry Today
10) Voice, Face & Image Recognition Change the Wireless World, Enhanced Through Artificial Intelligence (AI)
11) Insurance Underwriting Uses Artificial Intelligence (AI)/Policy Holders Allow Their Habits to Be Tracked for Lower Insurance Rates
12) Robotic Process Automation (RPA) Is Replacing Human Workers
13) Digital Assistants Include Amazon's Echo and Google's Home/Alexa and Similar Software Power Third-Party Developers
14) Growth in Big Data Supported by Expansion of Cloud Computing and Predictive Analytics

15) Artificial Intelligence (AI) Powers Hedge Fund Investment Strategies
16) Banks and Mobile Apps Vie for Previously Underserved Markets, Including Hispanics
17) China Sees Growth in Online Payments, Banking and Lending/Alipay Soars
18) The Internet, Smartphones and ATMs Replace Bank Branches and Tellers
19) Smartphones and Financial Technology (FinTech) Enable New Mobile Payment Methods
20) Peer-to-Peer (P2P) Payment Systems, such as Zelle and Venmo, Soar in Popularity
21) In Emerging Nations, mChek and M-PESA Enable Remote Banking via Smartphone
22) Online Competition Changes the Mortgage Industry
23) Open Banking May Revolutionize the World of Banking and Finance
24) The Future of Banking, Credit Cards, Mobile Payments and Mortgages

1) Introduction to the FinTech, Cryptocurrency & Electronic Payments Industry

One of the fastest growing global business sectors in recent years is the financial technology or "FinTech" sector. Innovation by this field has been extremely challenging to traditional financial services giants while at the same time offering exceptional opportunities for new business models and startups that bring much-needed change. Ventura capital has been pouring into FinTech at a tremendous rate.

Looked at in a broad manner, FinTech is now the driving force in financial services, accounts and transactions of all types, including bank accounts, lending, investment accounts/trading, insurance, mortgages, credit cards, and wealth management. Also, a fast growing, vital part of FinTech today comprises online payments and mobile payments, enabling consumers to easily pay for online purchases and to send each other money for business or personal purposes.

Another branch of FinTech is cryptocurrencies such as Bitcoin. An estimate by CoinCapMarket was that global cryptocurrencies (sometimes called "crypto") had soared to nearly $3 trillion in market value in November 2021. However, this number plummeted to $0.9 trillion by mid-June 2022 during a market rout. That was not the first time that cryptocurrencies had shown extreme instability.

Only a few decades ago, virtually all financial services relationships were managed in person—at banks' branch offices, insurance agents' desks and investment company offices. During the 1970s and 1980s, a slowly expanding number of financial products could be reasonably well managed by telephone. During this period, ATMs started to displace bank tellers in large numbers.

The internet era launched very rapid adoption of online banking, investments and insurance. Discount stock brokerages gained so much market share that they forced traditional brokerages to provide more customer-friendly services and lower fees—so much so that today, many stock trades can be executed on a no-commission basis. Companies like Charles Schwab soared old-line firms like Merrill Lynch were forced to adapt.

Insurance became much more competitive and easier to obtain as the internet grew to mass market scale. Consumers could easily compare rates, apply for insurance and make claims online. This was extremely disruptive to the traditional insurance industry, and value-priced companies like Geico boomed.

The convenience and cost-effectiveness brought about by the early foundation of financial technologies (such as the push-button telephone, the ATM and the internet) were extremely important. However, these early applications pale in comparison to the total FinTech revolution that was launched soon after the January 2007 introduction of the iPhone and the smartphone era, followed by the mid-2000s emergence of ubiquitous, remote computer power in the cloud.

Smartphone apps are relatively easy to create and scale thanks to the flexibility of cloud computing platforms such as Microsoft's Azure and Amazon's AWS. At the same time, a reasonable estimate would be that well over 6 billion consumers worldwide have access to smartphones. More than 1.5 billion new smartphones are sold yearly. Portability, reasonably good security and cost-effectiveness make smartphones a nearly-ideal platform for financial account management, and the cloud has vastly boosted this trend.

Not surprisingly, emerging/developing nations where the economy is expanding rapidly have been among locales to most readily adopt FinTech innovations. If a shortage of bank branches existed in India, for example, mobile banking solved the problem. If a modern insurance industry was not fully developed in Vietnam or Thailand, online insurance expanded the market. If consumers had few credit cards or checking accounts anywhere in the world, then payment platforms like Paypal solved a major need. The market in Asia is a perfect example. A late-2019 study by Bain/Google/Temasek found that 50% of Southeast Asians (home to 600 million people) are underbanked, 90%+ are under-insured and about 80% lack investment accounts. FinTech is rapidly solving those problems.

FinTech innovation has been exceptional. For example:

- Square's tiny credit card reader plugs into smartphones to enable the phone to be a portable card reader and POS (point of sale) device. (Square's parent company recently changed its name to Block.)
- Paypal's online payment system makes it simple to make and manage payments, 24/7, on a worldwide basis.
- Plaid's connections to bank account data in real-time makes it possible to verify account balances and ownership, while enabling thousands of app-based financial and payments firms to grow and prosper. (Plaid is known as a financial account information aggregator, a vital function underlying many FinTech services. These aggregators also offer sophisticated, artificial intelligence-driven analysis of consumers' spending and account histories.)
- Nubank is revolutionizing the convenience of mobile banking across Latin America.

- Walmart is leveraging its massive, global customer base to expand into financial services and FinTech.

Fortunes have been made by many FinTech company founders, while convenience is soaring, costs are plummeting, and delays in making and receiving payments are disappearing. At the same time, traditional financial companies are adapting and modernizing their own services while launching new innovations.

- Zelle, the popular peer-to-peer payments system, was launched by a technology-driven company that partners with America's leading banks.
- Marcus, an online banking and investment platform intended for the mass market, was launched by upscale investment bank Goldman Sachs, a firm that previously focused on very wealthy clients.
- Merrill Lynch, owned by traditional banking giant Bank of America, offers no-fee online trading for many types of trades.
- Capital One, a massive bank that is one of the world's leading credit card issuers, is a hotbed of financial technologies development and investment.
- Both Visa and Mastercard, the world's leading credit card processing firms, are making immense and continuing investments in FinTech startups, while developing their own improved technologies for rapid payments and other innovations.

2) Cryptocurrencies and Blockchain Explained

Simply put, Bitcoin and similar cryptocurrencies are "mined" by fast computers (or servers) that run algorithms 24/7. When an algorithm successfully solves a given mathematical puzzle, a new Bitcoin is unlocked, and the value is credited to the miner. These "mines" can be massive enterprises. One analysis found that a firm called Bitfarms was generating over $300,000 in gross profit daily from such an operation.

While profits may be high for certain companies and people (nearly all of the cryptocurrency wealth is held by a relatively small number of people—most of whom got in on the bottom floor), the industry is not without high levels of risk and controversy. On a global basis, this mining activity is eating up enough electricity to power an entire nation of modest population size. It's ironic that many young consumers who lean towards green

products and sustainability are, at the same time, big boosters of and investors in power-hungry cryptocurrencies.

In fact, this mining of cryptocurrencies like Bitcoin is extremely dubious from an ecological point of view, despite the fact that mine owners are attempting to locate in areas with low energy costs and reduced-emission generation infrastructure. Servers guzzle electricity.

Blockchain Technology Enables Crypto

Blockchain software makes it possible for groups to share, track and store data. Blockchain tracks and links transactions in "chains," which are verified cryptographically into lists (known as "blocks"). The result is a consistently verifiable record of when and how transactions occurred, and thereby which account holds what assets as of a certain date. Blockchain is the technology that records ownership of Bitcoin and similar cryptocurrencies. Assuming that the system or network hosting the blockchain is secure (which is not always the case), there is potential here to increase efficiencies. An open-source collaborative known as Hyperledger (associated with the Linux Foundation) encourages the use of blockchain in a wide variety of industries beyond the financial sector, such as manufacturing and distribution. Hyperledger envisions blockchain used in advanced industrial and information systems in order to create "smart contracts and other assistive technologies."

Until 2019, China was the world's largest operator of crypto mines by far—one analysis found that China was, at one time, generating 75% of all Bitcoins. However, China's government shut down all mining in response to this immense power drain in a nation that is still generating much of its electricity from plants that are burning coal under very dirty, undesirable conditions. (Much, but not all, of China's crypto mining was done in regions with significant levels of clean, hydroelectric power).

Cryptocurrency fans often consider crypto and blockchain technologies to be revolutionary. In fact, the nickname DeFi, a popular nickname for this sector, (which stands for decentralized finance) sounds a lot like "defiance." Crypto can be universal in nature (not controlled by any one institution), cross-border (not controlled by any one nation) and theoretically transparent in operation.

At the same time, however, crypto is unfortunately subject to vast losses to hacking and account takeover. Recent hacks of cryptocurrency accounts include incidents such as the 2022 Ronin Network heist totaling $614 million, the Coincheck hack of 2018 totaling $547 million and the 2021 Poly Network hack totaling $611 million. Funds are sometimes recovered—and sometimes not. A single hack may enable a thief to access the assets of thousands of users at once.

Since cryptocurrencies are virtual—exist only in the cloud, they are accessed and controlled only by the account owner's username and password. The true identity of the account owner is generally not recorded or known, and the password or key to an account is vital for accessing its assets. There have been multiple stories of users who have lost their account information and therefore their assets, sometimes in the millions of dollars.

Cryptocurrencies are not only popular with millennials and people looking for alternative investments. They are also wildly popular with thieves, crooks and scammers. For example, they are the preferred method of payment for perpetrators of computer network ransomware—the practice whereby thieves, often located in Russia or North Korea, remotely lockup (encrypt) computer operations, even those of massive enterprises like hospitals and electric utilities, and hand over the decryption keys only after they have been paid off—sometimes to the tune of multiple millions of dollars in cryptocurrency.

3) The Difference Between Cryptocurrencies and Stable Coins/National Treasuries Consider Issuing Stable Digital Currencies

Cryptocurrencies are subject to significant fluctuations in market value. Cryptos, such as Bitcoin, have suffered extremely large declines in value from time to time, although the long-term trend through recent years was a substantial climb in value.

Some "stablecoins," in contrast, are theoretically backed by a reserve asset that acts as collateral, such as dollar-denominated bonds or currency accounts, and should therefore be relatively stable in value. The idea is that they should be able to be utilized in financial transactions and payments without concerns about swings in their value. Tether is an example of a stablecoin. However, investors and payees need to be aware that not all stablecoins are equal in nature, and some are actually backed, at least to some extent, by baskets of cryptocurrencies—which are not at all stable in value. It gets worse. Some stablecoins are actually just based on computer code (algorithmic) that is supposed to keep the system at a level value. Infamously, TerraUSD fell by 82% in one 24-hour period during May 2022. The somewhat related cryptotoken, Luna, fell from more than $60 to less than one cent over a very short period as well.

To date, cryptocurrencies have been largely unregulated by governments. However, they are gathering large amounts of scrutiny by various government agencies worldwide, and significant levels of regulation and disclosure are likely to evolve.

Stablecoins, due to their claim to be inherently stable, may act to some extent as a substitute for dollars, Euros and other currencies. They are extremely likely to come under very high levels of regulation. In late 2021, the International Organization of Securities Commissions declared that stablecoins should be regulated in a manner similar to the regulation of financial clearinghouses and payment systems.

More government control of, and participation in, digital currencies is likely inevitable. Many government officials believe that cryptocurrencies may become a useful part of national banking systems. Others think they are completely unnecessary. In March 2022, President Biden, wanting to encourage the U.S. Government to stay on top of digital currency developments, including a study of needed regulations, signed an executive order aimed at "ensuring responsible development of digital assets." At that time, the White House estimated that "over 100 countries are exploring or piloting Central bank Digital Currencies (CNDCs), a digital form of a country's sovereign currency."

In September 2021, the Central American nation of El Salvador made history by officially making Bitcoin legal tender within that nation. Citizens were encouraged to sign up for the government-created digital wallet (the "Chivo") that enables anyone to use the cryptocurrency. Chivo users can make payments to each other, in Bitcoin. A small number of Bitcoin ATMs were established. Stated goals included decreasing dependency on the U.S. Dollar, helping the local economy to digitize and lowering remittance costs for funds that are transferred home to relatives in El Salvador by people who are working in the U.S. and elsewhere abroad. (However, many very successful FinTech startups are making such remittance payments faster, easier and much less expensive to transact online, without the need for Bitcoins. The outcome of El

Salvador's experiment remains to be seen. Meanwhile, other nations are running their own crypto programs, including the Sand Dollar in the Bahamas, the eNaira in Nigeria, DCash for use in a group of several cooperating nations in the Eastern Caribbean Union, and China, with its e-CNY or digital yuan. India, the European Central Bank, Jamaica and Sweden are likewise already active in, or seriously considering an experiment with, digital currencies.

4) BNPL (Buy Now Pay Later) Options Gain Payments Market Share

Consumers who want to conserve their cash for a few months are making use of a new checkout option. Companies like Affirm that enable short-term installment purchases for consumers to use at the point of sale, have partnered with both online and in-store retailers. These partnerships provide customers the ability to make credit-style purchases without the need for a credit card. This new checkout option is known as "Buy Now Pay Later" (BNPL).

Typically, consumers are enabled to pay for their purchases in four equal monthly installments, with no interest fees and no late fees (although consumers who run late in payments may be blocked from further BNPL purchases until they catch up). Retailers, on the other hand, pay a percentage of the total sale as a fee to the BNPL platform. In general, vendors are motivated to participate, because many see significant increases in the level of sales to their online customers.

Leaders in the payments space, such as PayPal and Block (the parent company of Square) have made sizable investments in BNPL companies. Block acquired the Australian BNPL provider Afterpay for $29 billion. PayPal snapped up Japanese BNPL provider Paidy for $2.1 billion. This is part of an overall goal of FinTech: to make both purchasing and payments as convenient as possible for the consumer.

5) Digital Wallets Gain Payments Market Share

Many consumers don't write paper checks at all, thanks to modern payment technologies, and many others never use a physical credit card. For these consumers, the advent of the digital wallet makes payments faster, more convenient and paperless. Many people are switching all or part of their payment processes to their smartphone apps and related online tools.

The digital wallet is a type of smartphone app/online account that enables consumers to a) make payments at cash registers or online, b) securely store all needed bank account, debit card and credit card information and c) communicate wirelessly with cash registers/point-of-sale systems in stores. Most wallets also enable peer-to-peer (P2P) payments directly to the accounts of personal friends or family members.

Apple's digital wallet is one of the most popular in this sector. This app comes included with Apple devices such as the iPhone. Users store their payment accounts' information within the app. Then, their credit and debit accounts can be easily used with participating sellers, without the need for cash, paper checks or physical credit/debit cards. The digital wallet has the capacity to store other items for convenience, such as transit or concert tickets, student identification cards, boarding passes and/or loyalty cards (such as Walgreens rewards).

Apple's own popular credit card is often used in conjunction with the digital wallet. Digital security is very high. When a user receives an Apple Card, they are given a unique iPhone identifier number. Every purchase made on the Apple Card requires both this device number and a one-time code that the iPhone's digital wallet creates when the purchase is authorized. Purchases are authorized via Face ID, Touch ID or by inputting the password on the iPhone.

Security: Google's popular Google Pay digital wallet offers another good example of the high level of security utilized in these systems, referred to as tokenization. First, a Google Pay user adds credit and/or debit cards to the Google Pay app. The app will request, from the bank issuing the cards, a token (a unique identification number) to represent the account, creating a "virtual" credit card. Google Pay then encrypts the newly tokenized card, making it ready for use. When a user taps the mobile device on a POS terminal or pays within a mobile app, Google Pay responds with the token and a cryptogram which acts as a one-time-use password. Google Pay can also store reward cards, transportation passes and other vital information. Users can also send and request money with Google Pay through email. Google Pay does not store a user's physical credit card number in the app, and it requires a PIN for purchases over $100. If the phone is lost or stolen, a user can use the Android Device Manager online to instantly lock the device or wipe it clean of personal information.

6) The SuperApp Begins to Develop in FinTech

The SuperApp is a strategy where financial apps and related digital wallets expand their roster of services and functions, to the extent that they encompass nearly all of a consumer's (or small business's) day-to-day financial activities. For example, Square started out as a mobile credit card reader. Then, the company began offering Cash App accounts as a convenient place for small businesses to deposit and access the funds that come in from those credit card payments. Over a period of time, Square added a long list of vital services for the small businesses that rely on the Square card processor. Since small businesses lack specialized management, HR and accounting departments, these services conveniently automate certain vital, routine business tasks, including:

- Credit card processing services
- Mobile payment processing and services
- Customer loyalty rewards
- Customer relations management (CRM) and email marketing solutions
- Invoicing and Inventory
- Peer-to-peer payments
- Cash accounts and debit cards (replacing, or supplementing, traditional bank accounts)
- Payroll, HR and contractor management solutions, including timecards
- Small business lending

Square also expanded Cash App's features for consumers as well as small businesses, so that the smartphone app offers:

- Stock investments
- Cryptocurrency investments
- Debit cards
- Peer-to-peer payments

Leading FinTech apps and SuperApps offering wide ranges of services are often seeing the fastest growth in markets outside of the U.S. Firms like Paytm, Go Jek and WeChat (part of Tencent). Paypal and many other leading payment companies are trending in the SuperApp direction.

7) Real Time Payments (RTP)/Instant Payments to Grow

Increasingly, companies are searching for new and innovative ways to process payments faster. Real-Time Payments (RTP, or Instant Payments) will become more widespread over the near future. The name refers to the speed at which a payment is credited to a payee's account.

These real-time payments are each part of a "payment rail," or a specific type of network. The networks generally close their transactions almost instantaneously, operate 24/7 and are considered "open loop."

"Closed loop" systems are operated by a single central provider or institution at which both the payer and the payee must have an account. Thus, these in-house transfers can be prompt. However, the receiver of the funds may want to transfer the money to another system, such as a traditional bank, which takes time and may involve fees, because the transaction is no longer in-house. An "open loop" strategy, in contrast, enables much wider groups of payees and payors (and their financial institutions) to interact instantly and conveniently.

The Automated Clearing House (ACH) in the United States, a funds transfer institution that has operated for decades, launched its own "RTP" in November 2017. This network can be used by any federally insured institution to process payments 24/7. It facilitates payments such as direct payroll deposits, account-to-account (A2A) transfers, etc. Recent changes in its rules are enabling many transactions to clear through the ACH system on the same business day.

National banking systems worldwide, including those in India and China, have been slowly rolling out instant payments systems. This is a massive improvement over traditional bank wire and bank transfers, which can take many days to complete.

In the U.S., FedNow is a new instant payment service that the Federal Reserve bank system is creating to enable all of its member institutions throughout America to provide instant payments. The service's launch is anticipated in 2023.

8) Neobanks/Virtual Banks Explained/Top Competitors

Neobanks, sometimes called challenger banks, were typically launched as non-bank entities. That is, they provide technology that acts as a middleman or enabling layer within financial transactions, but don't have bank charters. Instead of having their own authorized and government-insured bank operations, they partnered with true banks in order to be able to offer debit cards and depository accounts. These traditional banks charge a fee for providing such services, while the neobanks operate under their own new brands, including branded credit and debit cards. The neobanks provide easy-to-use smartphone apps that seamlessly connect the consumers to their accounts.

However, well-established and well-funded neobanks have been seeking their own bank charters so that they can expand services and offer their own FDIC insurance (in the U.S.), along with other banking services, without having to pay fees or share financial assets with third-party banks. This neobank business model has generally been designed to appeal to younger (millennial) consumers. The strategy is focused on:

- Online account opening, with extreme ease signing up (e.g., "Takes less than 2 minutes" to apply).
- Easy-to-understand fee and service rules.
- Low-to-no additional fees for basic services (often a "No Fees" positioning).
- Generous cash-back rewards on debit card transactions (e.g., 1.0% "unlimited" cash-back).
- Rapid availability of funds from direct deposits such as payroll deposits.
- No minimum balance fees.
- No overdraft fees.

Neobanks have slowly begun to eat away at the market share of traditional banks. These newer banks offer services akin to those of their larger, established traditional competitors, like checking, savings, debit, credit cards, and sometimes even loans. However, neobanks do not typically possess physical locations in the manner of giant banking firms like JP Morgan or Wells Fargo. From banking accounts and debit cards, the firm is expanding into payday loans, home equity loans and many other types of credit. It is also adopting a SuperApp-like strategy, by offering ecommerce, gaming and insurance via the app, often in conjunction with well-established partners. It has plans to expand into many Latin American nations and could easily become a serious contender in the U.S. market. It gained a large and rapidly growing customer base in Mexico shortly after establishing operations there.

NuBank: Revolutionizing Consumer Banking in Latin America

A highly successful example of neobanks is NuBank, which was launched in Brazil and is now a major online bank there. The firm was an instant success because it reduced fees, increased convenience, is smartphone-based and made it much simpler for consumers to open accounts. In contrast, traditional banks in Brazil tended to be stodgy and not user-friendly. Warren Buffet's U.S.-based investment firm, Berkshire Hathaway, acquired $1 billion in NuBank's stock in late 2021.

---

9) A Brief History of Artificial Intelligence (AI) and the State of the Industry Today

The concept of artificial intelligence (often referred to as "AI") continues to evolve, as scientists and software engineers gain a greater understanding of reasonably possible goals for this technology. In 1956, John McCarthy may have been the first to use the phrase, describing artificial intelligence as "the science and engineering of making intelligent machines." This was a pretty dramatic statement, considering the barely advanced state of computers and robotics at the time.

In 1950, computer pioneer Alan Turing proposed, in a paper titled *Computing Machinery and Intelligence*, a test that could determine whether or not a machine could "think." Essentially, he suggested that, in a situation where a person asked the same questions of both a machine and a human being, if he couldn't tell the difference between text answers coming from the machine and the human in blind results, then it might be reasonable to call the machine "intelligence." The Turing Test clearly avoids any discussion of what "consciousness" is.

Gary Marcus, a scientist at New York University, proposed another test, the Ikea Construction Challenge, to see whether or not a machine could assemble a piece of Ikea furniture when provided with a pile of parts and related instructions.

Near the end of 2015, a group of well-known Silicon Valley investors, including Elon Musk and Peter Thiel, announced a long-term commitment to raise funds of as much a $1 billion for a new organization to be known as OpenAI, www.openai.com. OpenAI is a nonprofit group, dedicated to moving AI ahead to the point that it "will benefit humanity."

Another well-funded AI organization is the Allen Institute for Artificial Intelligence (AI2).

Located in Seattle, the group was co-founded by Paul Allen, one of the co-founders of Microsoft, and scientist Oren Etzioni. AI2 has developed its own complex test for artificial intelligence called a GeoSolver.

The rapid growth of cloud computing at reasonable cost has been among the biggest accelerators to the development of AI. The extension of the internet of things (IoT) will likewise boost AI. However, one of the most interesting boosters has been the advent of an open-source software coding language known as Python. Hundreds of thousands of pre-written parcels of code are available to Python developers via a simple online portal known as the "CheeseShop." Among them are a large number of code packs that enable users to rapidly create neural networks and other AI tools with limited effort.

Massive investments in research, development and applications of AI and machine learning are being made by government and industry on a global scale. Global spending on AI has been estimated for 2021 at $85.3 billion by analysts at IDC. This amount could triple by 2022. For example, in 2018 Samsung announced it would invest more than $22 billion over the following three years in development of advanced technologies, including AI. It planned to create a staff of at least 1,000 researchers and engineers dedicated to artificial intelligence by 2020.

Elsewhere, the semiconductor industry is especially focused on creating advanced chips capable of delivering on the full potential of AI. An ever-accelerating amount of data to be filtered and analyzed via machine learning and AI will require ever more powerful chips that can operate at blinding speed. Leading chip makers are in a race to create the industry's best semiconductors for AI computing. (Consider, for example, the processing power required to learn from the billions of internet searches conducted by business and consumers daily, or to analyze the billions of photos and comments posted to social media and other web sites each month.) Nvidia is considered to be the leading maker of high-powered chips for AI, with its competitors trying hard to keep pace. Other companies, such as startup Run:AI are developing software that will help AI chips run more efficiently.

Today, a serious battle is in place between the United States and China for long-term dominance of the AI sector. While the U.S. has long made the highest total investments in AI research, China, in July 2017, announced that it wants to grow the output of its AI-based industries to 10 trillion yuan (about $1.5 trillion in U.S. currency) by 2030. Firms based in China with very significant and growing reliance on AI include Alibaba, Baidu, Tencent, Huawei and iFlyTek, along with specialty firms Megvii and SenseTime that have superb capabilities in applying AI to facial recognition. In 2020, AI proved its use in rapid development of Coronavirus vaccines and in tracking the disease.

10) Voice, Face & Image Recognition Change the Wireless World, Enhanced Through Artificial Intelligence (AI)

With the advent of voice recognition via Siri, Apple's virtual personal iPhone assistant, the wireless market changed irrevocably. Siri not only translates spoken words into text in the form of e-mails, text messages and reminders, it responds to voice commands for such tasks as making phone calls, and it searches the internet for answers to spoken questions. Siri created a major boost to both business and consumer interest in voice recognition.

Significant advancements in voice recognition on the latest smartphone software from Microsoft, Apple and other leading firms continue to be introduced. Using technology originally developed by Nuance Communications as an app, Siri and similar technologies turn voice recognition capability into a mobile everyday tool. It understands natural language including colloquialisms and some nuances of context. For example, ask Siri "Will the weather be nice?" and the response might be "No, probably not so nice today through this Wednesday," along with the display of the local weather forecast for the next six days. Ask it to find the calorie count in a Big Mac and Siri searches online for nutritional information from McDonald's and displays it.

Siri continues to evolve with subsequent updates to Apple's mobile operating system. Siri's voice can now be either male or female, there are new animations and the system has faster response times. In addition, Siri checks more sources for answers to queries, and performs more tasks such as returning calls, voicemail playback and controlling iTunes Radio. This technology has been incorporated in Apple's HomePod digital assistant, intended to compete with similar products pioneered by Google and Amazon. Most importantly, these technologies rely on artificial intelligence and machine learning in order to continuously improve accuracy and capabilities.

Smartphones are only the beginning of the voice recognition revolution. This capability is rapidly being added to all types of electronics, appliances and much more. Voice recognition is already available in advanced entertainment systems in many automobiles. The fuel for this trend will be state-of-the-art technologies that are available to third-party developers, including Microsoft's Cortana, Google's Home and Amazon's Lex (Alexa, which powers the extremely popular Amazon Echo digital assistant device.)

The newest smartphones have cutting-edge cameras capable of scanning 3-D objects. Samsung and Apple both offer models (the Galaxy and the iPhone respectively) with cameras that can scan faces to unlock phone screens, rather than relying on fingerprint recognition or a manually typed passcode. In the near future, smartphone cameras will be able to scan text and translate it into different languages. Apple acquired PrimeSense, a company that developed depth-sensing camera systems used in Microsoft's Kinect motion-sensitive devices, to help build its face recognition technology.

OpenAI (openai.com) created GPT-3, or Generative Pre-trained Transformer 3. It uses language-processing algorithms mined from roughly 570 gigabytes of data gathered by internet crawling, enabling it to answer questions, write essays and summaries, translate languages, create memos or program computer code. More recently, the Allen Institute for Artificial Intelligence (AI2, allenai.org) developed a model that can create images from a text caption. In the same vein, the University of North Carolina, Chapel Hill's scientists came up with a method that combines images with existing language models, resulting in amped-up reading comprehension. These are breakthroughs that will greatly enhance machines' ability to perform complex tasks.

11) Insurance Underwriting Uses Artificial Intelligence (AI)/Policy Holders Allow Their Habits to Be Tracked for Lower Insurance Rates

Like other financial services sectors, the insurance industry has undergone major changes due to the internet and advanced data networks. The internet and the development of e-commerce have delivered more expedient operations and cost efficiency to the insurance industry, while enabling customers to get pricing and to order policies online. Now, very fast cellphone networks, smartphones and tablets will be the biggest drivers of change in terms of interfacing with customers and with agents in the field. At the same time, the advent of "big data," that is, vast databases of customer activity, claims data, environmental data and more, is enabling underwriters to better evaluate risks and thereby adjust pricing correctly on an individual customer basis.

State of the art software, often based on machine learning or artificial intelligence (AI), is also providing powerful risk modeling and management tools to insurance underwriters. Such software makes it easier and faster for underwriters to rate customers according to risk and thereby quickly determine the most appropriate (and profitable) price for a given policy. Adopting risk modeling technology can enable an underwriter to confidently enter new areas of risk and write new types of specialty insurance.

In California, Farmers Insurance now offers wildfire coverage through a partnership with startup Zesty.ai. The new firm offers high-resolution aerial imagery and other cutting-edge AI to analyze potential property risk due to wildfires.

Meanwhile, savvy underwriters are utilizing advanced communications systems and software to make their sales systems—both direct- and agency-based—more efficient. Their goals are faster response to the customer and higher productivity. The benefits of getting all agents onto an underwriter's computer network are worth the expense. The internet makes it possible for an agent to log in, submit a request for an underwriting, a binder (a preliminary agreement to provide immediate coverage), or a firm quote, and then receive the fastest possible response. It wasn't very long ago that such functions were handled by snail mail and printed forms. Advanced communications systems enable both underwriters and agents to achieve much greater productivity. As a result, profits can be improved, and savings can be passed along to the consumer.

One rapidly emerging technology is called the Internet of Things ("IoT"), a concept of communications between devices and central databases. This concept has been underway for decades in tracking the movement of specially equipped commercial trucks, and lately, automobiles. This usage is often referred to as telematics. Growing numbers of drivers are choosing to install data-logging devices into ports in their cars that transmit information about driving habits from car computers to insurance companies via cellphone networks. Sometimes called "user-based insurance," the technology affords insurance companies the ability to offer drivers individualized pricing based on data collected. The IoT Insurance Observatory reported that the number of personal autos in the U.S. with telematic connections to an insurer rose from 2 million in 2013 to more than 8 million in 2020.

The Progressive Corporation offers a program called Snapshot (formerly called MyRate), which utilizes on-board telematics. Drivers receive periodic reports about their driving habits and those who drive cautiously and log fewer miles are offered discounts, depending on which state they are in. Progressive collects and analyzes data for a period of six months, after which the customer can remove the device. GMAC Insurance, a subsidiary of American Capital Acquisition Corporation, offers a similar program using the OnStar telematics system. Unlike Progressive's Snapshot program, the GMAC version includes GPS data on a driver's whereabouts.

Conversely, drivers who opt into telematic measurements of their driving habits can face surcharges for reckless driving (such as excessive miles, high speeds and hard braking) in some states. Using smartphones while driving is also leading to soaring insurance rates. Star Farm Mutual Auto Insurance Co. conducted a survey which found that 36% of those surveyed admitted to texting while driving and 29% access the internet. The percentages are even higher for Millennials, of which 64% reported that they text while driving and 54% use the internet.

At present, careful drivers are the customers who will be the most motivated to participate in monitoring programs. As the use of telematics grows by car insurance underwriters, all drivers may eventually be required to participate in programs like Snapshot in order to obtain insurance. This would essentially be forced, automatic, ever-present surveillance of driving habits.

SPOTLIGHT: Car Insurance by the Mile

San Francisco-based Metromile (www.metromile.com) offers pay-as-you drive auto insurance measured through an onboard sensor called Metronome that plugs into a vehicle's data port. Drivers who log more miles pay higher rates than those who drive less. Policies are underwritten by National General Insurance Group.

Teenaged and young adult drivers are also eligible for special rate programs that utilize telematics. Although these age groups have traditionally been difficult and costly to insure, programs such as Safeco Corp.'s Teen Safety Rewards (formerly called Teensurance) and American Family Mutual Insurance Co.'s Teen Safe Driver Program use on-board surveillance technology to track driver locations and driving habits. Young drivers who consistently drive safely get a substantial break on their auto insurance premiums. Teen Safety Rewards, for example, is GPS-based and offers drivers up to age 25 as much as a 15% discount. Other companies such as Nationwide Mutual Insurance Co. and State Farm Mutual Automobile Insurance Co. offer discounts to young drivers who complete safety courses (some may be taken online). Also of note is Fireman's Fund Insurance Co.'s offer to independent young adults up to age 27 who can qualify for their parents' multiline, multicar and long-term customer discounts of between 35% and 50%.

SPOTLIGHT: Lytx

In an effort to monitor commercial vehicle drivers, Lytx (formerly DriveCam, Inc.), www.lytx.com is marketing a video camera with audio that records activity both inside and outside moving vehicles. Sudden movements trigger the DriveCam device to send digital feed to the company's central monitoring station for analysis. Alerts are e-mailed to parents within 24 hours and weekly reports on driving skills are sent as well. The cost for the camera and a one-year monitoring contract is relatively expensive, but many insurance companies are willing to pay for in order to attract new business. The company also offers products that assist in truck fleet fuel management and tracking.

In a similar vein, life insurance premiums may be discounted for certain policy holders who agree to have their habits tracked by smartphone or wearable devices such as the Fitbit. John Hancock was the first U.S. insurer to institute such a policy, which it calls Vitality, in 2015. Under the policy, customers earn points for healthy habits such as not smoking, maintaining low cholesterol levels and regular exercise. There are three point levels: silver, gold and platinum. Gold level participants, for example, enjoy about a 9% discount on a 20-year, $500,000 term life insurance policy.

Another twist on habit-tracking is the use of algorithms to analyze a variety of data, including customer survey responses, data pulled from prescription pharmaceutical databases and motor vehicle records. Startup Haven Life (which is owned by Massachusetts Mutual Life Insurance Co.) offers some of the lowest rates available for life insurance to individuals who rate highly in healthy habits, spend less on prescription drugs and have clean driving records.

Meanwhile, technology is now on the market to assist corporate insurance buyers in managing the purchasing process and attempting to receive the best prices. For example, HighRoads, www.highroads.com, sells software that enables corporate health insurance purchasing managers to bypass brokers and send requests for bids directly to major companies. The insurance firms are able to submit their bids online. The software has been used by customers including Dell, Pfizer, IBM, Bristol-Myers Squibb and Verizon.

12) Robotic Process Automation (RPA) Is Replacing Human Workers

Robotic Process Automation (RPA) is a category of software that operates in a "robotic" manner to repeatedly complete basic tasks that might otherwise have been done by human workers. Examples include editing electronic files or forms and checking them for completeness or accuracy. This technology is being widely applied to back-office tasks in such departments as human resources, insurance claims and expense reimbursement. RPA has very broad implications for many types of office work. In a 2017 survey, Accenture PLC found that 74% of participating executives said they planned to use AI to automate tasks by 2020.

Amelia, formerly IPSoft, Inc., an automation software company, developed a white-collar robot named Amelia that is used for help desk, customer service and a variety of other call-desk operations. The unit speaks 20 languages and has the appearance of a young, blonde blue-eyed woman. Allstate Insurance Co. uses Amelia to handle 82% of its in-house IT service desk requests. The company's 350 call-center employees use it to help them solve customer inquiries faster and more efficiently. Telefonica also uses Amelia to handle 4.5 million customer calls per month. In 2020, Amelia launched the Amelia HyperAutomation Platform and custom consumer facing avatars, as well as Amelia v4 and Digitalworkforce.ai for cloud-sourced pre-trained digital employees.

Accenture Strategy reported that less than one-half of global companies' accounts payable activity was automated as of 2019. This kind of automation is expected to rise to 80% by 2025, particularly in the areas of invoice processing and expense reports. For example, Airbus SE recently invested in software from AppZen, Inc. to automate expense report processing. The technology matches reports against a database of accepted vendors, expense types and amounts to find anomalies. It also checks for receipts and is capable of recognizing more than 100 languages.

The banking industry is spending an estimated $150 billion annually on technology including RPA. An industry analyst at Wells Fargo estimated that all U.S. banks in total will cut more than 200,000 jobs between 2019 and 2029. The analyst expects artificial intelligence to reduce mortgage processing costs by 10% to 20% while cloud-based computing will also yield major savings in expenses. Global banks, such as UBS, are also following this trend, investing heavily in labor-reducing technologies such as RPA.

Amazon introduced five new cloud-based call center tools in late 2020. One utilizes artificial intelligence to assist call center agents in answering questions quickly, while another speeds the customer authentication process. Amazon Web Services offers Amazon Connect, a cloud-based contact center product, that enables customer services over voice and chat; manages follow up tasks; and provides contact center automation services.

The net result of the growing use of RPA will be a significant reduction of human employees. This will be particularly true in call centers and other BPO (business process outsourcing) centers.

13) Digital Assistants Include Amazon's Echo and Google's Home/Alexa and Similar Software Power Third-Party Developers

Apple, Google, Amazon and Microsoft are competing to offer the best voice-activated systems that can do anything from reporting the time and weather, to playing music on request, to performing web searches, to telling jokes, to making purchases from internet sites. These platforms utilize the latest in artificial intelligence in order to become more useful over time. Apple's Siri is available on iPhones, iPads, Apple Watches and through an app in some vehicles. Google Now is an app available on a variety of mobile devices as is Microsoft's Cortana app. Amazon's Alexa web app is installed on a gadget called Amazon Echo that sits on a countertop, desk or shelf. Alexa software can be installed on other devices as well. Google offers a similar device called Google Home. All of these apps and platforms are voice-activated, and use connections to other apps and systems to find information such as directions, time, date, weather and trivia, or make purchases, which are reported audibly (users can choose their device's voice gender and language). The next step for these handy assistants is the ability to connect with apps relating to climate control, lighting and/or security enabling users to simply say, for example, "Set home temperature to 72 degrees," or "Activate alarm system," and have the action performed, even from remote locations.

Importantly, most systems are open to third-party developers. For example, Amazon has opened "Lex" to developers, which is the artificial intelligence engine behind the Alexa and Echo platforms. Lex is tied into Amazon's AWS cloud computing system. Software and product developers can incorporate Lex, enabling voice-activated or click-activated responsiveness (often in the form of specific task-oriented icons or apps known as "bots"). This gives these developers instant access to extremely powerful cloud computing, artificial intelligence and voice-activation in one easy-to-launch package. Amazon charges a modest fee per thousand uses or data accesses. This ease-of-use has spurred a tidal wave of new product development worldwide, with the potential to revolutionize the manner in which consumers interface with their digital devices and the internet.

Top Voice-Activated Technology Platforms and their Unique Advantages:

Alexa: Owned by Amazon. Connects to Amazon AWS Cloud services, making it easy to embed Alexa software in third-party products.
Siri: Owned by Apple. Siri, already familiar to hundreds of millions of iPhone users worldwide, has evolved into a very sophisticated digital assistant.
Cortana: Owned by Microsoft. Microsoft had deep partnerships and experience with third-party corporate software and technology firms, making this an easy platform for others to embed.
Google Assistant: Owned by Google. Assistant capitalizes on Google's constantly evolving expertise in search and artificial intelligence.
Source: Plunkett Research, Ltd.

---

14) Growth in Big Data Supported by Expansion of Cloud Computing and Predictive Analytics

"Big data" refers to the massive sets of digital information that are generated and captured at an accelerating rate by a wide variety of enterprises. For example, the digitization of health care records for hundreds of millions of patients is creating massive data sets. Likewise, the recording of activities of billions of monthly users of Facebook creates big data that is key to Facebook's ability to generate advertising revenues. Today, advertising of all types is being adjusted on a continuous basis due to the analysis of big data, often in real-time. Top technology companies such as IBM are seeing tremendous growth in this segment.

A growing trend is the generation of big data sets by remote wireless sensors in heavy industry, transportation and agriculture. The analysis of big data is creating enormous opportunities for greater efficiency in such areas as manufacturing, energy, finance, and marketing, as well as the development of intelligent transportation systems and better outcomes in health care. At the same time, challenges in the big data trend include the capture, storage, visualization and analysis of immense amounts of information in a rapid and cost-effective manner. Security and privacy are additional concerns.

The hand-in-hand partner of big data is analytical software, sometimes referred to as "predictive analytics." Gaining advantage from increasing amounts of data is accomplished via extremely powerful software algorithms that can parse reams of data at extremely high speed. That software then must present results, predictions and viewpoints that solve the needs of the organization in question. Statisticians and other professionals who can manage these tasks are in very high demand. Big data is also closely linked to the rapidly developing field of artificial intelligence (AI), and the related study of machine learning.

SAS, a global corporation known for its analytical software, recently wrote about the power of this trend at work in a major retail chain that is able to analyze data gathered from past customer transactions to determine the optimum prices to set in each of its stores. By using the latest data capture and analysis tools, the company reduced the amount of time for this weekly project from 30 hours of work to only two hours. Another example from SAS discusses a major bank that was able to reduce its regularly scheduled analysis of loan portfolios, looking for potential loan default, from 96 hours of work to only 4 hours. Such savings in time can represent very large boosts to productivity and profits.

The online advertising industry has been a prime beneficiary of the big data trend. As search engines, e-commerce sites and social media have been able to capture immense amounts of information about people who are online (often extending to consumers' locations, tastes and demographics), they have developed highly targeted advertising opportunities for firms that want to reach specific types of consumers. Media networks including Comcast Corp.'s NBCUniversal are offering advertisers data analytics tools to target ads more effectively. Called Audience Targeting Platform, it links data in set-top boxes to buying patterns of the people who use them.

The global financial industry is also a key player in big data. Now that all types of banking, investment, insurance and trading activities have been digitized and globalized, the amount of data that financial institutions must deal with offers both headaches and opportunities. On the challenges side, financial companies are faced with an ever-increasing need to fend off hackers, scam artists and major fraud schemes from their digital repositories, while providing highly regulated levels of consumer privacy. At the same time, having access to reams of information about their customers enables these institutions to better tailor targeted advertising and marketing, and to make better credit and lending decisions. On the investment side, big data enables traders, hedge fund managers and mutual funds, as well as financial analysts and money managers, to conduct real-time analysis of big data sets to maximize return on investment while minimizing risk. Insurance underwriters likewise benefit greatly from the risk analysis and risk management afforded by the proper analysis of big data.

The health care industry is beginning to rely heavily on big data. One of the major initiatives within the industry is the digitization of patient records. Similarly, the compilation of massive databases containing the outcomes of all types of treatments, drug therapies and surgeries will increase reliance on big data analysis. The goals include making patient records portable and readily accessible by any caregiver, along with using state-of-the-art analysis tools to determine the most effective treatments for specific types of patients and illnesses. In addition, big data will be used to pinpoint the most effective health care organizations

based on cost of care, mortality, readmission to the hospital and other factors. Such studies will help identify best practices and potentially increase cost-effectiveness. At the same time, the industry will be able to create incentives for organizations shown to provide the best care.

An excellent example of a big data project is NEON, the National Ecological Observatory Network. The $434 million project is being overseen by the U.S. National Science Foundation. NEON became fully operational in 2019. It has 15,000 sensors across the U.S. will collect more than 500 types of daily data from 81 field sites (47 terrestrial and 34 aquatic) such as temperature, air pressure, wind speed and direction, ozone levels and soil and water nutrients. The data not only helps boost the effectiveness of government programs, it also is available to the public free of charge, as an aid to weather forecasting and agriculture. The system generates 200 terabytes of data each year, or four times that collected and transmitted by the Hubble telescope.

Technologies that have Synergies with Big Data:
- Artificial Intelligence (AI)
- Autonomous vehicles
- Cloud computing
- Data visualization software
- Drug and vaccine development
- E-Commerce product recommendations
- ERP (Enterprise Resource Planning) software
- Health care technologies
- IoT (Internet of Things)
- M2M (Machine-to-Machine) communications
- Online advertising
- Predictive analytics software
- Remote wireless sensors
- Search engines
- Semiconductor manufacturing
- Social media
- Software-as-a-Service (SaaS)

Source: Plunkett Research, Ltd.

The rapidly escalating trend of big data across a broad range of industries is a perfect fit with the expansion of cloud computing. Now, massive databases can be hosted by remote databases (in the cloud) and then accessed via the internet for analysis and action.

Network technology leader Cisco Systems publishes the Cisco Global Cloud Index. In its latest release, it forecast that data center internet-based traffic will grow more than threefold, or a 27%

compound annual growth rate, from 2017-2022. Traffic will reach 20.6 zettabytes (a zettabyte is about 909 million terabytes) in 2021. By 2021, 95% of all traffic will come from cloud systems.

Self-Driving Cars and the IoT Require Edge Computing as an Adjunct to Cloud Computing

While computing via the cloud is clearly a dominant trend today, a concept called edge computing is also growing in popularity as a supplement to cloud-based data processing. Edge computing is a local technology strategy whereby digital processing is done near the point where the data is first acquired. For example, a self-driving car generates vast amounts of data constantly. Sending that data to the cloud to be processed would create small delays in analyzing road conditions and safety threats. Such delays, even if tiny, could imperil the car and its occupants.

In contrast, computing at the "edge" of the in-car laser detection system (LIDAR) and other devices would be nearly instantaneous, and portions of the data could still be transmitted via wireless networks to the cloud for further analysis. (Recent analysis shows that autonomous vehicles could generate as much as 25 gigabytes of data hourly.)

Many other technology trends will drive the use of edge computing forward. M2M (machine-to-machine) communications is rapidly emerging in the form of IoT (the Internet of Things). Here, remote sensors gather vast amounts of data from machinery, aircraft, trucks, ships, infrastructure and other vital components of day-to-day life. The intent is to capture data that can be rapidly analyzed in order to optimize both safety and operating efficiencies. Here, too, sending the data to the cloud may not be fast or efficient enough for the intended purpose. For example, conducting edge computing of data continuously gathered from industrial machinery, and later sending the resulting analysis on to a cloud computing center, may save factories from breakdowns and significantly reduce maintenance costs.

---

15) Artificial Intelligence (AI) Powers Hedge Fund Investment Strategies

While algorithms are being used by "FinTech" (financial technology) firms to offer asset management at very low fees to everyday investors, a much more sophisticated trend is emerging at hedge funds that service some of the world's largest investors. Mathematicians, statisticians and experts in machine learning and artificial intelligence at select hedge funds are operating massive investment software and data platforms that seek to maximize investment returns with split-second timing. Each of these hedge funds tries to establish a unique competitive advantage through such artificial intelligence-driven computer systems. Many use their computers to analyze vast troves of historical market data to identify the cause and effect of patterns, and then attempt to forecast when such events will recur. Others include massive datasets of non-financial data, such as employment, household income, weather or international trade, and build automated investment strategies based on such data.

These AI systems are designed to continuously learn and to hopefully improve investment returns over time. Thus, this practice is often referred to as machine learning. Innovative companies in this field include Quantitative Investment Management LLC (www.quantitative.com) and Teza Capital Management LLC (www.tezacapital.com).

16) Banks and Mobile Apps Vie for Previously Underserved Markets, Including Hispanics

In the U.S., there are an estimated 15.3 million adults without bank accounts (6% of all Americans over 18), according to a Federal Deposit Insurance Corp. (FDIC) survey in 2019. An additional 40.8 million (16%) were estimated to be "underbanked," meaning individuals with very low credit scores or no access to credit at all. Until recently, this market was not actively pursued by banks.

In the U.S., hundreds of millions of dollars are paid yearly by employers or other sources, to people with no bank accounts, as well as the underbanked and undocumented immigrants. Those with no bank accounts must seek financial services from check-cashing services, sellers of money orders, so-called "payday lenders" which charge exorbitant interest rates and fees, along with Western Union and other firms that wire money ("remittances") to the immigrants' family members back home.

The remittance of money from the United States to family members in Latin America is one of the most active payment corridors. There is good profit potential in providing simple financial services to consumers who have historically spurned traditional bank accounts.

Financial technologies are being developed to serve the needs of consumers outside of the traditional banking system via smartphone apps. For example, in China, WeChat Payment (owned by Tencent) enables peer-to-peer payments and money transfers, without the assistance of banks. Venmo, owned by PayPal, provides similar services as does competitor Zelle. Several mobile apps are competing to assist consumers, including the unbanked, to easily pay the rent, pay utility bills and make other recurring payments.

As of mid-2021, major U.S. banks including JPMorgan Chase & Co., Wells Fargo & Co. and U.S. Bancorp were considering data relating to credit card applicants' checking and savings accounts, as an alternative to making judgements based solely on traditional credit scores. People who pay with cash or with debit cards only, or those who are new to the U.S., often do not have credit scores and were unlikely to be approved for credit cards in the past. Today, these individuals have a better chance of approval if they keep positive bank account balances over time and avoid overdrafts.

In the U.S., the Hispanic population is rapidly expanding. At the same time, it is growing in household wealth and buying power. By as early as 2037, Hispanics in America will total 100 million (up from 49 million in 2010) and make up about 25% of the population.

The 2019 FDIC survey found that 10% of Hispanic adults in the U.S. are unbanked, down from 17.9% in 2013. (This is partly a result of strong economic growth from 2015 through 2019, reducing unemployment and lifting household incomes.) Marketing to the Hispanic segment involves a number of special initiatives and new services, including signage in Spanish and Spanish-speaking employees at hand. Special marketing campaigns aimed at Hispanic consumers are evolving as well.

17) China Sees Growth in Online Payments, Banking and Lending/Alipay Soars

A significant number of Chinese consumers are enjoying upper class incomes equal to those found in wealthy households in America or Europe. That means tens of millions of additional Chinese will be purchasing imported food brands, driving luxury automobiles, buying jewelry from Tiffany and Cartier and wearing designer clothes. China is a ripe market for a broad array of financial outlets, products and services, from credit cards to insurance to mortgages and personal loans.

Many banks in China are hoping to use mortgages, automobile loans, credit cards and other kinds of modern financial products to stimulate consumer spending. The government's official policy is to boost household spending, and modern

lending will be required to meet this goal. Mortgages have been available only since the late 1990s.

In October 2014, the Chinese State Council announced that qualified domestic and foreign credit card companies may apply to create bank card clearing operations in China, effectively opening the country to foreign credit card firms.

Online banking via smartphone is a regular practice in China. Financial-technology companies such as Ant Financial Services Group and Tencent Holdings are working hard to tap this enormous market. Ant's Alipay phone app had exceeded 1.3 billion users as of mid-2020. With the app, shoppers call up a QR code on their phones for retailers to scan (similar to Apple Pay) for payment. Users can also send money to other users. In addition, Alipay offers investment services through its online only bank called MyBank. Tencent, the company behind China's wildly popular WeChat messaging system, has a similar online only bank called WeBank. Although online banking is convenient, it is susceptible to fraud, and the Chinese government is taking steps to regulate payment platforms and set limits on online lending.

SPOTLIGHT: Industrial & Commercial Bank of China

Industrial and Commercial Bank of China Ltd. (ICBC) is a leading bank in China, with global locations including Asia, Europe, the UAE, the U.K., the U.S. and Australia. ICBC provides financial service in renminbi and foreign currencies to wholesale, retail, ecommerce and international businesses. The firm has more than 8.6 million corporate clients and 680 million individual clients, serving domestic institutions, overseas institutions as well as correspondent banks in over 140 countries and regions. ICBC offers corporate banking and personal banking. Corporate banking offers loans, trade financing, deposit services, eBanking/mobile banking, bank cards and corporate wealth management services to corporations, financial institutions and government agencies. Personal banking involves services to individual clients including personal loans, deposits, eBanking/mobile banking, wealth management and card services. During 2021, ICBC (49%) announced the establishment of a joint venture with Goldman Sachs Asset Management (51%) to help provide more diversified and professional wealth management services to customers.

Products and services include wealth management to the public, investment and management services to property investors, private placement of wealth management products to investors, and related financial advisory and consulting services.

SPOTLIGHT: Ant Group

Ant Group (formerly Ant Financial Services Group) is the financial services affiliate of Alibaba Group Holding Limited. Ant Group operates Alipay.com, a third-party online payment platform that charges no transaction fees. Alipay's payment platform has a market share of about 1.3 billion users worldwide, and controls about half of the overall online payment market in China. Alipay operates with hundreds of financial institution partners, offering payment services for around 10 million small and micro merchants. Yu'e Bao is an online spare cash management platform that invests spare cash from over 600 million users in a money market fund. Huabei is a consumer credit platform that offers small loans to individual users. Xiang Hu Bao is an online mutual aid platform that provides basic health plans. Mybank is a private online bank that serves small and micro enterprises, as well as individual entrepreneurs. Zhima Credit is an independent third-party credit filing and scoring service provider. It offers beta services for individuals and enterprises via cloud computing and machine learning technologies. In October 2020, Ant Group was set to raise approximately $34 billion in the largest initial public offering (IPO) to date. However, in November 2020 the Chinese government halted the IPO.

18) The Internet, Smartphones and ATMs Replace Bank Branches and Tellers

Banks have learned that combining the convenience of online banking with a chain of branch locations and ATMs allows them to fill the entire range of many customers' needs. This is similar to the trend among major retailers of combining ecommerce and physical storefronts, thereby creating synergies between bricks and clicks. Virtually all banks now have web sites where customers can monitor the status of their accounts, including checking, savings, investments and loans; make money-transfers to pay bills; and apply for services online. Online banking has been an enormous success, and was boosted even further by the Coronavirus pandemic, as people curtailed trips to physical bank offices.

Thousands of U.S. branch locations have closed in recent years. Online banking, in combination with ATMs, goes a long way to fill the gap left by fewer brick and mortar bank locations. The end result is greater operating efficiency for banks. Nonetheless, online banking presents a long list of costs and challenges, including security and hacking issues.

A number of financial firms are targeting America's massive Generation Y as a growth sector for new customers (referring to 85+ million people born between 1982 and 2002). Strategies include updated financial sites that offer services such as bill paying, fund transfers, multiple accounts management and investment options. Mint.com, a site from Intuit, Inc., is quickly becoming one of the most popular financial tools in the internet. It offers account management and investment tracking.

Another formerly online-only bank, GoBank, targets young 20-somethings in the U.S. who prefer to perform some banking tasks (such as checking balances) on their smartphones. Fees are minimal, and there are no minimum balance requirements. GoBank is owned by Green Dot Corporation, which also owns Green Dot Bank where assets deposited by GoBank users are held. Green Dot partnered with Walmart to launch GoBank checking accounts. Other online-only banks, including Simple and Moven, are actually banking service providers that depend on brick-and-mortar banks to hold assets and provide additional banking functions.

E*Trade Financial, a major online stockbroker, entered the online and electronic banking field in a big way. It owns a nationwide system of ATMs under the E*Trade brand and has a rapidly growing base of online bank deposits.

Companies that offer a network of ATMs and physical branches, as well as online services, find the combination to be extremely effective. It costs a modest amount to service a customer who primarily relies on online services to manage accounts and relies on ATMs to get cash. The extremely rapid growth of fast internet access in U.S. homes and businesses, along with the now-massive number of people accessing the internet via smartphones, encouraged banks to fill their internet sites with robust features. Brick and mortar branches still offer a few services that online banks cannot, such as cashier's checks and safe deposit boxes, and a large percentage of customers want to know they can walk into a branch for assistance when needed. Bank of

America has opened a small number of employee-free branches, where customers can use ATMs and converse with remote tellers via video phones.

Bank of America offers SafePass, a 6-digit, one-time passcode sent as a text message to customers' smartphones which can then be used to authorize fund transfers, administer the online payment system and receive higher transfer limits. Major security software providers include RSA, the security division of EMC Corporation (www.rsa.com/en-us), Broadcom, which acquired Symantec in 2019 (www.broadcom.com) and Entrust (www.entrust.com).

Biometrics are becoming more common with regard to smartphone security. Customers by the millions at Wells Fargo, Bank of America and JP Morgan Chase use fingerprints to log into their bank accounts via smartphone. Retinal scans are also in use at Wells Fargo for corporate accounts. In addition, Citigroup uses voice recognition to verify its credit card customers.

In 2018, banks including HSBC and OCBC Bank of Singapore instituted facial recognition technology for corporate customers to speed log-in times and increase security (see www.nec.com/en/global/solutions/safety/face_recog nition/index.html for more about facial recognition technology). In September 2019, the EU required multi-factor identification ("MFA") for online payments greater than €30 (about $35), which may include biometric data in addition to a password and/or a digital device such as a USB token.

As for the future, many analysts expect tools known as chatbots to quickly grow in use for mobile and online banking. Chatbots are computer programs that simulate conversation with customers via ATM screens and smartphones. Already in use to answer simple questions about recent transactions and spending limits, chatbots will likely become full-scale automated financial assistants capable of making payments and tracking budgets.

19) Smartphones and Financial Technology (FinTech) Enable New Mobile Payment Methods

A wide variety of services, technologies and strategies are now competing with conventional cash and credit cards for consumers' payment needs.

Smartphones as Credit Card Terminals: Smartphones are being used by merchants and service companies as credit card readers, thanks to technology from companies like Square. Using a small scanner that plugs into a smartphone, users can process credit cards for a small fee. Square, for example, makes a device that plugs into the earphone jack of an iPhone or iPad (as well as some other smartphones). Square quickly developed into one of the world's most innovative payments companies, adding many levels of tools and services for small business, including debit cards and marketing assistance. Likewise, PayPal has an iPhone app with transactions for bank accounts or PayPal accounts. The technology is a boon for small businesses that previously worked only on a cash or check basis. For example, a plumber can get paid by credit card, on-the-spot, after completing a job. Like Square, PayPal has also added numerous important tools for business.

Mobile Commerce: Payments via Smartphones (Digital Wallets): The Google Wallet is an app that enables smartphones to be used to pay for goods and services by waving the phones across readers at checkout counters. Related apps are available on both the Apple App Store and Google Play. Users with a Google Wallet account also are able to take advantage of Buy With Google icons on online shopping sites. Google Wallet account holders simply log into Google, and then do not have to enter shipping addresses or credit card numbers that are already stored in Google Wallet. Around the world, multiple other mobile payment systems compete with Google and Apple, including Alipay (which originated in China) and Paytm (which originated in India).

Payment via smartphone is fostered by the fact a vast number of consumers are already managing their banking and investment accounts on their phones, keeping tabs on account balances and making transfers as needed. However, Americans have been slower than people in Asia and parts of Europe in adopting mobile payments. Challenges include the facts that typical American smartphone users are wary of security issues, and there are already hundreds of millions of credit and debit cards in widespread use across the nation. U.S. households are very comfortable with using debit cards for day-to-day purchases, and it has been difficult for wireless payment firms to change their habits.

There are also questions about the fees generated by using mobile phones as payment devices. Every business involved in a transaction, from the credit card company to the smartphone service provider, wants a piece of the immense potential revenue. On the other side of the transactions, many retailers and restaurants are anxious to control mobile payments themselves and reduce their transaction costs.

In the U.S., consumers were barely aware of the payment by smartphone concept until 2014, when Apple announced Apple Pay. Apple Pay users wave their iPhones over sales terminals and their accounts are charged. (Touchless payment features like this are highly desirable due to the Coronavirus.) Money can also be sent by text message or by using Apple's Siri voice-controlled assistant. Banks pay Apple a tiny fraction of every transaction made. The technology behind it, developed by Visa and MasterCard, replaces credit card information such as account numbers and expiration dates with unique series of numbers that validates the user's identity. Credit card accounts may be linked to Apple Pay by taking a photo of a card or manually entering card information. Apple promises that credit card information will not be stored on iPhones or on the company's servers. The technology also works with the Apple Watch. Apple has been growing rapidly in popularity on a global basis.

By working with existing payment networks such as MasterCard, Apple is seamlessly entering the payment market. It doesn't need to invent a new network or new technology. It is simply adapting it into the iPhone and pushing it to its vast base of very enthusiastic Apple fans. The recent introduction of the Apple Card credit card is a logical extension of its brand.

Digital wallets are also evolving to assist the rapidly growing number of consumers who make payments online. For example, MasterCard offers MasterPass. This service enables users to set up credit or debit card and shipping information in one secure electronic wallet. Once a user has filled out a shopping cart at a participating online store, he or she then clicks the "Buy With MasterPass" icon, logs in, and completes the purchase and payment. The intent is to increase convenience while reducing fraud.

In China, the potential of the mobile payment market is staggering. Social media giant Alibaba's Alipay mobile payment system holds a major share of the Chinese market. A number of other contenders are attempting to challenge Alipay's hold, notably major gaming and social media firm Tencent's Tenpay. WeChat, a multi-service platform in China that has more than 1 billion users, offers a number of simple payment apps accepted by individuals and businesses throughout the country.

20) Peer-to-Peer (P2P) Payment Systems, such as Zelle and Venmo, Soar in Popularity

One of the biggest areas of growth in payments technology lies in making it easier and faster for consumers to digitally transfer money to their friends and family. For example, six friends go out to dinner. One person pays for the meal. The other five digitally remit their proportionate share to the person who paid. Platforms like Zelle (owned by Early Warning LLC) and Venmo (owned by PayPal) make it easy to accomplish this instantly—before they leave the table. Square Cash (owned by credit card processing firm Square) is another, but less popular, example.

Venmo enables users to transfer money that's existing in their Venmo accounts. They can also link to their bank accounts or debit cards. Money can be moved effortlessly from their Venmo accounts to their bank accounts. Venmo is also usable as something of a digital debit card, as many websites and apps accept it as a payment method.

Zelle is closely linked to the user's bank account. It is set up easily by the consumer, particularly if the Zelle service is already available in a particular bank's mobile app. Otherwise, the consumer can download the Zelle mobile app and link to the consumer's bank account.

These services were designed primarily as a way for consumers to easily and safely interact with family and friends. (They have been adopted to a minor degree by small businesses.) They were launched without guarantees regarding the trustworthiness of the party you are paying. Unfortunately, some scammers have preyed on Zelle users. For example, unscrupulous third parties advertising a product or service on Craigslist or some other web site have been known to ask to be paid via Venmo and then never delivered the product or service that was promised. Zelle and Venmo have consistently encouraged their users to send payments only to parties that they know and trust.

21) In Emerging Nations, mChek and M-PESA Enable Remote Banking via Smartphone

Mobile phones have the unique ability to leap past barriers. No highways? No landlines? No internet connections? No problem. Smartphones create instant links to modern civilization that can be carried around in subscribers' pockets. Low-cost, easy to erect service towers solve the logistics problem instantly. State-of-the-art telecommunications equipment made by companies like China's Huawei provides the network systems at relatively low cost. This is true even in the deepest, darkest corners of the world, from Nigeria to New Guinea, from Cambodia to the Congo. By mid-2021, according to Plunkett Research estimates, there were already more than 9.0 billion wireless service subscriptions on Planet Earth. Even people living the simplest lives imaginable, with no running water, dirt floors in their homes and cooking over wood fires, have smartphones. Soon enough, virtually every adult on Earth who wants one will have at least one smartphone, as will a vast number of their children.

In India, for example, innovative business practices have created the world's most efficient smartphone companies, bringing the wireless world to subscribers at rock bottom prices. In rural India, a one-man, smartphone-based banking stand can take deposits from customers, who are now able to establish formal savings accounts for the first time in their lives. Their accounts are credited by the banker via a code sent to a main bank by secure text message. The account's owner has a secure user name and password to enter via smartphone, enabling the customer to identify herself and track account balances. Payments can be sent by the same methods to another bank customer's account. These mobile bank customers are able to purchase and pay for goods or services via long distance. Next, using their smartphones for internet access, they can view and order online, purchasing, for example, a ticket on one of the developing world's many new, ultra-cheap airlines.

Mobile consumers are suddenly enabled to view government information, health care assistance, news, entertainment and educational material online via their smartphones. They are connected to the modern world. They can save and spend money. They can engage in trade and commerce in order to boost their own incomes. With a little luck, they can climb up the first steps of the ladder to the middle class. Their children who have left the villages to go to the cities or distant lands in order to find work can use smartphones to stay in touch with family members back home via text and smartphone messages. Even more important from an economic point of view, they can send remittances back home to parents who now have mobile banking accounts.

Significant, sustained economic progress is not possible without widespread access to a stable, reliable consumer banking system. Consequently, the biggest single contribution that smartphones make to economic growth in the developing world may be mobile banking—enabling people in remote villages to have access to bank accounts for the first time in their lives, including the ability to safely build savings, make remote payments and send money transfers by wireless means.

Companies tapping this potential goldmine include M-PESA in Kenya, which is run by Safaricom, a mobile service provider partly owned by Vodaphone. East African company Airtel Nigeria (formerly Zain) offers the Airtel Money mobile money transfer service app, and South Africa's MTN deployed Mobile Money accounts in several African countries. mChek is a very innovative company to watch in India. It has partnered with Airtel to create a mobile payment system that is rapidly gaining ground in rural India, where physical banks are hard to find, and is also providing mobile convenience to city dwellers. mChek is able to link a customer's debit card, credit card or bank account to a mobile phone, enabling customers to make payments, as well as pay certain bills and make purchases such as airline tickets and movie tickets via smartphone. The firm uses state-of-the-art security technology.

22) Online Competition Changes the Mortgage Industry

The internet has created a much more competitive landscape for home mortgages. Sites such as LendingTree, Better.com and Quicken Loans offer low origination fees and make it simple to complete applications online, while the internet itself makes it much simpler for consumers to compare interest rates and mortgage options. At Bank of America's user-friendly web site, prospective borrowers can apply online, view a breakdown of proposed fees, compare mortgage options and check the status of a loan in progress. By 2020, non-bank lenders issued 68.1% of all U.S. home mortgages.

Mortgage competition online is really part of a much larger, global trend: fierce competition among financial services providers of all types. Firms throughout the consumer finance sector, from banks to insurance companies to stock brokerages, are fiercely battling to attract, retain and cross-market new services to consumers.

> **Internet Research Tip: Online Mortgage Tools**
> For mortgage loan and loan provider advice, see
> 1) www.mtgprofessor.com, a site run by Jack M. Guttentag, Professor of Finance Emeritus at the Wharton School of the University of Pennsylvania.
> 2) www.myfico.com, a site operated by the credit analysis firm Fair Isaac Corp.
> 3) www.bankrate.com, a site that provides financial rate information.
> 4) www.hsh.com, a site run by financial publisher HSH Associates.

23) Open Banking May Revolutionize the World of Banking and Finance

To understand the concept of "open banking," you have to start by understanding "APIs." An API (application programming interface) is a programmer's tool that makes it easy for a software or website designer to link to data. An API receives requests for data, and then serves up that data on demand. For designers, API's offer drag-and-drop convenience, where the website designer can simply drag the API code for the desired data, place it in their own software, and make the needed data appear when desired.

APIs are the enabler of many rapidly emerging, exciting banking and financial tools (FinTech), accessed by consumers and businesses either online or through their mobile apps. They save software designers hundreds of hours of design time and effort. Equally important is the fact that data aggregators that have access to financial information can make certain that data is passed along, via their APIs, in a manner that meets today's stringent regulatory environment.

Let's say that a new web-based service wants to help consumers monitor balances and expenses of all of their bank, credit card, debit card and investment accounts. They might add visual data such as graphs that show where and how the consumer is spending money, and further add alerts that appear when balances get too low or spending at bars, restaurants and stores gets too high. API-based systems like Sila can enable designers to have immediate access to all of this data at thousands of financial institutions, and do so in a way that meets regulatory, privacy and cybersecurity needs.

Another example is MicroBilt. Its APIs provide secure access to a consumer's credit files, bank performance history and risk assessment profiles. They can enable a web-based service to verify bank information on-the-fly before a business accepts a check, makes a loan or transfers money. It can also help verify that a new customer relationship is not fraudulent by confirming a consumer's address, social security number and other vital information.

In 2021, the state-owned Central Bank of Brazil launched an open banking system, forcing it (and rival privately-owned banks such as Banco do Brasil, Bradesco and Santander) to share data on a more open basis. The Central Bank also set up its own touchless pay system called Pix, which offers consumers and merchants a simple, cost-effective payment method that is not controlled by the major private banks.

Online payment processor Stripe is partnering with Goldman Sachs Group and Citigroup to offer services such as bank accounts, credit cards and other cash management services to Stripe's merchants and vendors. Stripe's goal is to automate a wide range of its business customers' banking needs within the Stripe platform. Shopify, Inc. has partnered with Stripe to offer Shopify Balance accounts to its massive base of merchants who use Shopify's highly popular ecommerce platform and software.

Simply put, open banking speeds up transactions. At the same time, it reduces fraud and increases customer convenience. There are endless ways that it can be applied in a very cost-effective manner to develop revolutionary credit, mortgage, payment, leasing and transfer platforms. As a result, competition and investment in the FinTech arena is soaring.

24) The Future of Banking, Credit Cards, Mobile Payments and Mortgages

Banking and related financial services, such as mortgages and credit cards, will see sweeping future changes due to continuing developments in technology and in the way consumers utilize technology to interact with financial business of all types. Companies with advanced ideas for the use of online platforms have proven that they can quickly disrupt the banking industry and rapidly gather market share. An outstanding example is PayPal, which promptly developed very significant market share in enabling the transfer of payments outside of traditional banks. Meanwhile, emerging blockchain technologies (such as that used to power virtual currencies such as Bitcoin), may eventually take market share from banks, unless the banks themselves become blockchain innovators.

Credit card processing is likewise open to stiff competition from innovators, such as the simple, mobile platform called Square that enables businesses to accept and process cards in a store, at a restaurant, online or on the go, whether they are operating a booth at a craft fair, or providing home repairs from the back of a plumber's truck.

Online lending platforms for small businesses, student loans and certain types of consumer loans will continue to enjoy very rapid growth. This will include the efforts of loan companies like OnDeck and its competitors, as well as new online loan offerings by larger firms such as American Express and PayPal. (In 2020, American Express acquired small business online lending platform Kabbage.)

The rapid growth of smartphones on a global basis opened the banking industry to countless types of competition. Banks will continue to respond but will also continue to be subject to big competitive challenges. As consumers and businesses become more comfortable with banking online, they are more likely to respond to financial services offered by alternative online firms that are competing against traditional banks.

This level of competition, driven by evolving technologies, will open both challenges and opportunities that will drive significant changes. The biggest challenge is cybersecurity. Consumers, businesses and their financial accounts are under constant attack by hackers, phishers and con artists. This may become worse before it gets better. Technologies are struggling to outpace criminals, through the development of innovative ways to store and protect passwords and better ways to verify identities online, along with more secure log in methods (including biometrics such as facial, iris and fingerprint recognition).

Payment systems and credit cards will continue to evolve quickly, sometimes for convenience and sometimes for vital improvements to security. Thanks to Apple Pay and other advanced mobile payments platforms, Americans are finally becoming accustomed to using their smartphones to make payments at cash registers—something that has been popular and Europe and Asia for years. The stunning success of Alipay, a mobile payments and financial services platform launched by Alibaba in China, shows just how quickly a clever firm can turn a traditional market upside-down.

The mortgage market is also ripe for change and innovation by smart competitors. The best example is Quicken Loans, an easy-to-use, online way for consumers to apply for home mortgages. Fees may be lower and response times much faster than those of traditional mortgage brokers. The fact that closing costs, upfront fees and title insurance typically are extremely expensive makes the entire home mortgage market ripe for disruption by providers who can provide convenience while lowering costs.

Also, for the future, shadow banking will play an increasingly major role in lending and credit. Hedge funds and other companies are making corporate loans, thus taking market share away from commercial banks. Walmart now offers a variety of financial services in its stores. The retail giant's financial offerings are especially robust in its Mexico stores, but it also is making a significant stand in financial services in its U.S. locations. This is illustrative of a major trend: traditional banks finding themselves more and more often facing competition from alternative companies outside the banking industry.

Chapter 2

FINTECH, CRYPTOCURRENCY & ELECTRONIC PAYMENTS INDUSTRY STATISTICS

Contents:	
FinTech, Cryptocurrency & Electronic Payments Industry Statistics and Market Size Overview	**30**
Artificial Intelligence Industry Statistics and Market Size Overview	**31**
Investment & Securities Industry Statistics and Market Size Overview	**32**
U.S. Banking, Mortgages & Credit Industry Statistics and Market Size Overview	**33**
Global Credit Card Industry Statistics and Market Size Overview	**34**
FDIC Insured Institution Statistics: 2nd Quarter 2021	**35**
Employment in the Banking Industry, U.S.: 2015-July 2021	**36**

FinTech, Cryptocurrency & Electronic Payments Industry Statistics and Market Size Overview

	Amount	Units	Date	Source
Global				
Global Payments Industry Revenue	1.9	Tril. US$	2021	McKinsey
Financing Volume for FinTech Companies, Annual	141.6	Bil. US$	2021	FT
M&A Volume in FinTech Acquisitions, Annual	348.5	Bil. US$	2021	FT
Spot Trading Volume of Cryptocurrency, Annual	49.0	Tril. US$	2021	TI
Total Cryptocurrency Market Cap	1.4	Tril. US$	10-May-22	CoinCapMarket
Global IT Spending*	4.4	Tril. US$	2022	Gartner
Global Credit Cards & Debit Cards				
Number of Visa Cards	3.7	Bil	2021	Visa
Visa Payments Volume	10.4	Tril. US$	2021	Visa
Number of Mastercards	2.6	Bil	2021	MasterCard
MasterCard Gross Dollar Volume (GDV)	7.7	Tril. US$	2021	MasterCard
United States				
Number of FDIC-Insured Institutions	4,839	Thous.	2021	FDIC
Number of FDIC-Supervised Institutions	3,122	Thous.	2021	FDIC
Avg. Number of Electronic Payments per Month per U.S. Citizen	4		2020	FRATL
Avg. Value of Electronic Payments per Month per U.S. Citizen	1,572	Thous. US$	2020	FRATL
Total Payments processed by NACHA	29.1	Bil.	2021	NACHA
Total Value of All Payments processed by NACHA	72.6	Tril. US$	2021	NACHA
Total Retail Sales, U.S.[1] (includes Ecommerce)	5,638	Bil. US$	2020	PRE
Employment				
Total Employment in the U.S. Banking & Credit Industries[2]	2,706.4	Thous.	2021	BLS
Employment in Software Publishing (NAICS 5112)	529	Thous.	2021	BLS
Employment in Electronic Shopping & Mail Order Houses (4541)	315.0	Thous.	2021	BLS
Employment in Business to Business Electronic Markets (42511)	27.6	Thous.	2021	BLS
Employment In Companies Involved In Securities, Commodity Contracts, Investments, and funds and trusts, U.S. (523,5)	989.6	Thousand	2021	BLS

[1] Including food services

[2] Preliminary estimates

*Forecast

McKinsey = McKinsey & Co.

FT = FT Partners

TI = Token Insight

PwC = PricewaterhouseCoopers

FRATL = Federal Reserve Bank of Atlanta;

NACHA = National Automated Clearing House Association;

BLS = U.S. Bureau of Labor Statistics

Plunkett Research, ® Ltd. Copyright© 2022, All Rights Reserved

www.plunkettresearch.com

Artificial Intelligence Industry Statistics and Market Size Overview

Global Market:	Amount	Unit	Date	Source
Global Business Value Derived from AI	2.9	Tril. US$	2021	Gartner
Global Investment in AI Startups	42.2	Tril. US$	2020	Stanford
Artificial Intelligence Spending (Software, Hardware, and Services)	341.8	Bil. US$	2021	IDC
Artificial Intelligence Spending (Software, Hardware, and Services)	500.0	Bil. US$	2025	IDC
Potential Business Value Added of AI and Analytics to Global GDP by 2030	16.0	%	2018	McKinsey
Potential Business Value Added of AI and Analytics to Global GDP by 2030	13.0	Tril. US$	2018	McKinsey

U.S. Market:	Amount	Unit	Date	Source
U.S. Artificial Intelligence Spending (Software, Hardware, and Services)	80.0	Bil. US$	2021	PRE
U.S. IT Spending	4.2	Tril. US$	2021	Gartner
Software Publishing Industry Revenue	357.0	Bil. US$	2021	PRE
Data Processing, Hosting, and Related Services Industry Revenue	230.4	Bil. US$	2021	PRE

IDC = International Data Corporation

PRE = Plunkett Research Estimate

Plunkett Research, ® Ltd. Copyright© 2022, All Rights Reserved
www.plunkettresearch.com

Investment & Securities Industry Statistics and Market Size Overview

	Amount	Units	Date	Source
Global				
Total Value (Market Cap.) of Stocks on Global Exchanges	110.4	Tril. US$	2020	WFE
Total Number of Listed Companies, Global	55,316	Companies	2020	WFE
U.S.				
Estimated Total Assets of 401(k) Plans, U.S.	7.3	Tril. US$	Q2-21	ICI
Estimated Active Participants in 401(k) Plans	60.0	Million	Q2-21	ICI
Interest Rate on 3-Month Treasuries (Average)	0.04	%	Nov-21	UST
Interest Rate on 10-Year Treasuries (Average)	1.44	%	Nov-21	UST
Total Corporate Bond Issuance, U.S.	1,714.9	Bil. US$	2021	sifma
Total Municipal Bond Issuance, U.S.	397.3	Bil. US$	2020	sifma
Total Mutual Fund Assets, U.S.	25,918.5	Tril. US$	Sep-21	ICI
ETF Assets, U.S.	6.3	Tril. US$	Jun-21	ETFGI
Average Daily Stock Market Volume				
NYSE	1,915.1	Mil. Shares	Nov-20	NYSE
NASDAQ	1,611.2	Mil. Shares	Nov-20	NASDAQ
Average Daily Value Traded on the Stock Market				
NYSE	88.4	Bil. US$	Nov-20	NYSE
NASDAQ	91.1	Bil. US$	Nov-20	NASDAQ
Employment In Companies Involved In Securities, Commodity Contracts, Investments, and funds and trusts, U.S. (NAICS 523,5)	996.0	Thousand	Sep-21	BLS

ICI = Investment Company Institute

PRE = Plunkett Research Estimate

sifma = Securities Industry and Financial Markets Association

NAICS = North American Industry Classification System

ETFGI = ETFGI LLC

WFE = World Federation of Exchanges

UST = U.S. Department of the Treasury

ETF = Exchange Traded Funds

BLS = U.S. Bureau of Labor Statistics

Plunkett Research, ® Ltd. Copyright© 2022, All Rights Reserved

www.plunkettresearch.com

U.S. Banking, Mortgages & Credit Industry Statistics and Market Size Overview

	Amount	Units	Year	Source
Banks				
Total Number U.S. FDIC-Insured Banks & Savings Assocs.	4,951	Companies	Jun-21	FDIC
Commercial Banks	4,336	Companies	Jun-21	FDIC
Total Assets	21.36	Tril. US$	Jun-21	FDIC
Total Deposits	17.54	Tril. US$	Jun-21	FDIC
Total Liabilities	19.20	Tril. US$	Jun-21	FDIC
Equity Capital	2.16	Tril. US$	Jun-21	FDIC
Savings Associations	615	Companies	Jun-21	FDIC
Total Assets	1.43	Tril. US$	Jun-21	FDIC
Total Liabilities	1.28	Tril. US$	Jun-21	FDIC
Total Deposits	1.19	Bil. US$	Jun-21	FDIC
Number of U.S. Credit Unions	5,029	Companies	Jun-21	NCUA
Total Assets	1.98	Tril. US$	Jun-21	NCUA
Total Loans	2,670.8	Thous.	Jul-21	BLS
Total Members	1,334.3	Thous.	Jul-21	BLS
Total Employment in the U.S. Banking & Credit Industries[1]	93.3	Thous.	Jul-21	BLS
Commercial Banks[1]	296.3	Thous.	Jul-21	BLS
Savings Institutions[1]	612.5	Thous.	Jul-21	BLS
Credit Unions & Other Depository Credit Intermediation[1]	4,951	Companies	Jun-21	FDIC
Nondepository Credit Intermediation[1]	4,336	Companies	Jun-21	FDIC
Housing & Mortgages				
Homeownership Rate, U.S.	66.6	%	2020	Census
Total Privately-Owned Housing Starts, U.S.	1,380	Thousand	2020	Census
Total Mortgages Outstanding, U.S.	17.62	Tril. US$	2021 (Q2)	Fed
1-4 Family Home Mortgages Outstanding, U.S.	12.03	Tril. US$	2021 (Q2)	Fed
Existing Home Sales (Units), U.S.	6.29	Million	Sep-21	NAR
Median Asking Sales Price for Vacant for Sale Units, U.S.	238.6	Thous. US$	2021 (Q2)	Census
Total Mortgage Delinquency Rate, U.S.[2]	5.47	%	2021 (Q2)	MBA
Consumer Debt				
Total Consumer Credit Outstanding, U.S. (Non-housing debt)	4.19	Tril. US$	2021 (Q2)	FRBNY
Credit Card Balances Outstanding	0.79	Tril. US$	2021 (Q2)	FRBNY
Total Number of Open Credit Card Accounts, U.S.	365	Million	2021 (Q2)	ABA
Student Loan Debt Outstanding, U.S.	1.57	Tril. US$	2021 (Q2)	FRBNY
Student Loan 90+day Delinquency Rate	5.2	%	2021 (Q2)	FRBNY

[1] Preliminary estimates. [2] Refers to 1-4 unit residential properties, seasonally adjusted annual rate.

FDIC = Federal Deposit Insurance Corporation; NCUA = National Credit Union Administration; BLS = U.S. Bureau of Labor Statistics; Census = U.S. Census Bureau; Fed = U.S. Federal Reserve Board; NAR = National Association of Realtors; MBA = Mortgage Bankers Association; FRBNY = Federal Reserve Bank of New York; ABA = American Bankers Association.

Plunkett Research, ® Ltd. Copyright© 2022, All Rights Reserved
www.plunkettresearch.com

Global Credit Card Industry Statistics and Market Size Overview

	Amount	Units	Year	Source
Global Credit Cards & Debit Cards				
Visa				
Number of Visa Cards	3.9	Bil	Q1, 2022	Visa
Visa Payments Transactions	164.7	Bil	2021	Visa
Visa Payments Volume	10.4	Tril. US$	2021	Visa
MasterCard				
Number of MasterCards	2.5	Bil	2021	MasterCard
MasterCard Gross Dollar Volume (GDV)	7.7	Tril. US$	2021	MasterCard
American Express				
Number of American Express Cards	71.4	Mil	2021	American Express

Source: Plunkett Research, Ltd. Copyright © 2022, All Rights Reserved

www.plunkettresearch.com

FDIC Insured Institution Statistics: 2nd Quarter 2021

(Dollar Amounts In US$ Billions)

	All Insured Institutions	Commercial Banks	Savings Institutions
Number of FDIC-Insured	4,951	4,336	615
Number of FDIC-Supervised	3,194	2,887	307
Total Assets $	22,789	21,359	1,430
Total Loans$	10,858	10,193	665
Domestic Deposits$	17,164	15,972	1,192
Bank Net Income (QTR)$	70.38	66.09	4.29
Percent Profitable (QTR)%	95.8	96.4	91.5
Average Return on Assets (QTR)%	1.24	1.25	1.20
Average Return on Equity (QTR)%	12.37	12.39	12.07
Net Interest Margin (QTR)%	2.50	2.48	2.75
Equity to Assets%	10.12	10.11	10.26
Noncurrent Loan Rate - Total Loans*%	1.01	0.91	2.52
Real Estate Loans%	1.45	1.26	3.48
C&I Loans%	0.82	0.81	0.91
Loans to Individuals%	0.63	0.62	0.73
Coverage Ratio**%	177.98	194.78	85.04
Net Charge-Off Rate - All Loans (QTR)%	0.27	0.26	0.46
Real Estate Loans (QTR)%	0.00	0.00	0.01
C&I Loans (QTR)%	0.21	0.21	0.16
Loans to Individuals (QTR)%	1.30	1.22	2.30

* Nonaccruing loans and loans past due 90+ days. ** Loss reserve as a percentage of noncurrent loans.

FDIC = Federal Deposit Insurance Corporation

Source: Federal Deposit Insurance Corporation (FDIC)

Plunkett Research, ® Ltd. Copyright© 2022, All Rights Reserved

www.plunkettresearch.com

Employment in the Banking Industry, U.S.: 2015-July 2021

(Annual Estimates in Thousands of Employed Workers)

NAICS Code[1]	Industry Sector	2015	2016	2017	2018	2019	2020	Jul-21[2]
521	Monetary authorities - central bank	18.0	18.6	19.2	19.6	19.7	20.2	20.6
522	**Credit intermediation & related activities**	**2,570.7**	**2,609.7**	**2,644.9**	**2,651.2**	**2,651.5**	**2,655.1**	**2,670.8**
5221	Depository credit intermediation	1,683.8	1,697.8	1,713.3	1,759.1	1,776.2	1,768.2	**1,733.9**
52211	Commercial banking	1,284.7	1,309.5	1,323.6	1,381.4	1,391.2	1,382.9	1,344.3
52212	Savings institutions	140.2	121.5	116.1	96.9	95.2	92.9	93.3
52213,9	Credit unions & other depository credit intermediation	259.0	266.8	273.6	280.8	289.8	292.4	296.3
5222	Nondepository credit intermediation	594.6	610.7	622.1	588.8	574.1	582.4	612.5
52221	Credit card issuing	88.3	88.8	85.9	71.7	72.1	70.5	72.5
52222	Sales financing	92.8	94.7	96.0	94.9	95.2	90.9	93.1
52229	Other nondepository credit intermediation	413.5	427.2	440.2	422.1	406.8	421.0	446.9
522291	Consumer lending	104.1	104.5	104.3	102.5	102.5	98.3	90.7
522292	Real estate credit	217.4	231.7	244.0	227.6	211.5	231.8	265.9
522293,4,8	Miscellaneous nondepository credit intermediation	92.0	90.9	91.9	92.4	92.9	91.0	90.3
5223	Activities related to credit intermediation	292.3	301.2	309.4	303.3	301.2	304.5	324.4
52231	Mortgage & nonmortgage loan brokers	79.8	85.8	90.7	88.6	85.1	100.3	124.4
52232	Financial transaction processing & clearing	127.8	130.7	133.8	130.0	131.2	124.5	124.1
52239	Other credit intermediation activities	84.8	84.8	84.9	84.7	84.9	79.7	75.9

Note: Numbers are not seasonally adjusted.

[1] For a full description of the NAICS codes used in this table, see www.census.gov/epcd/www/naics.html.

[2] Preliminary estimates.

Source: U.S. Bureau of Labor Statistics

Plunkett Research, ® Ltd. Copyright© 2022, All Rights Reserved

www.plunkettresearch.com

Chapter 3

IMPORTANT FINTECH INDUSTRY CONTACTS

Addresses, Telephone Numbers and Internet Sites

Contents:

1) Artificial Intelligence Associations
2) Banking & Finance Ministries
3) Banking Industry Associations
4) Banking Industry Resources
5) Blockchain Associations
6) Canadian Government Agencies-Finance
7) Canadian Government Agencies-General
8) Careers-Banking
9) Careers-Computers/Technology
10) Careers-First Time Jobs/New Grads
11) Careers-General Job Listings
12) Careers-Job Reference Tools
13) Chinese Government Agencies-General
14) Computer & Electronics Industry Associations
15) Computer & Electronics Industry Resources
16) Conference Calls with Corporate Management
17) Consulting Industry Associations
18) Corporate Information Resources
19) Ecommerce and Data Interchange Technology Associations
20) Economic Data & Research
21) Engineering, Research & Scientific Associations
22) EU Agencies-Banking
23) Financial Industry Resources
24) Financial Technology Associations, FinTech
25) FinTech Resources
26) Foreign Exchange Industry Associations

27) Government Agencies-Hong Kong
28) Government Agencies-Singapore
29) Identity Theft Resources
30) Industry Research/Market Research
31) Insurance Industry Associations
32) Insurance Industry Resources
33) International Regulatory Body
34) Internet Industry Associations
35) Internet Industry Resources
36) Internet Usage Statistics
37) Investment Industry Associations
38) Investment Industry Resources
39) Investment Information-Funds
40) IPOs (Initial Public Offerings)
41) Magazines, Business & Financial
42) MBA Resources
43) Mortgage Industry Associations
44) Patent Organizations
45) Payments Industry Associations
46) Payments Industry Resources
47) Pensions, Benefits & 401(k) Associations
48) Pensions, Benefits & 401(k) Resources
49) Privacy & Consumer Matters
50) Privacy Associations
51) Retirement Planning Resources
52) Robotic Process Automation (RPA) Associations
53) Securities Industry Associations
54) Securities Industry Resources
55) Singaporean Government & Agencies - Finance

56) Software Industry Associations
57) Software Industry Resources
58) Stocks & Financial Markets Data
59) Technology Transfer Associations
60) Telecommunications Industry Associations
61) Trade Associations-General
62) Trade Associations-Global
63) Trade Resources
64) U.S. Government Agencies
65) Wireless & Cellular Industry Associations

1) Artificial Intelligence Associations

Allen Institute for Artificial Intelligence (AI2)
2157 N. Northlake Way, Ste. 110
Seattle, WA USA 98103
Phone: 206-548-5600
E-mail Address: ai2-info@allenai.org
Web Address: allenai.org
AI2 was founded in 2014 with the singular focus of
conducting high-impact research and engineering in
the field of artificial intelligence, all for the common
good. AI2 was the creation of late Paul Allen,
Microsoft co-founder. Situated on the shores of Lake
Union, AI2 employs over 40 of the world's best
scientific talent in the field of AI, attracting
individuals of varied interests and backgrounds from
across the globe.

OpenAI
E-mail Address: info@openai.com
Web Address: www.openai.com
Near the end of 2015, a group of well-known Silicon
Valley investors, including Elon Musk and Peter
Thiel, announced a long-term commitment to raise
funds of as much a $1 billion for a new organization
to be known as OpenAI, www.openai.com. OpenAI
is a nonprofit research organization consisting of 60
people focused on long-term, fundamental AI
projects.

2) Banking & Finance Ministries

Banco Central do Brasil (Central Bank of Brazil)
Setor Bancario Sul (SBS)
Quadra 3, Bloco B, Ed. Sede
Brasilia, DF Brazil 70074-900
Phone: 55-61-3414-1414
Web Address: www.bcb.gov.br
The Central Bank of Brazil, created in 1964, serves
as the Brazilian monetary authority and acts as an
autonomous federal institution and part of Brazil's

National Financial System. The bank regulates
foreign exchange operations on behalf of government
and public sector entities, while also regulating
interest rates, the issue of new currency and other
related matters.

Finance Ministry-Gov. of India (The)
North Block
New Delhi, India 110 001
Phone: 011-23093881
Fax: 011-23092024
Web Address: www.finmin.nic.in
The Government of India's Finance Ministry website
includes information about the financial situation in
India and provides information regarding economic
data, statistics and related links.

3) Banking Industry Associations

American Bankers Association (ABA)
1120 Connecticut Ave. NW
Washington, DC USA 20036
Toll Free: 800-226-5377
E-mail Address: custserv@aba.com
Web Address: www.aba.com
The American Bankers Association (ABA) represents
banks of all sizes on issues of national importance for
financial institutions and their customers. The site
offers financial information and solutions, financial
news and member access to further advice and
content.

Association of Banks in Singapore (The)
10 Shenton Way #12-08
MAS Bldg.
Singapore, Singapore 079117
Phone: 65-6224-4300
Fax: 65-6224-1785
E-mail Address: banks@abs.org.sg
Web Address: www.abs.org.sg
The Association of Banks in Singapore (ABS) is
made up of member banks drawn from a wide
spectrum of banking entities ranging from major
global giants to smaller financial niche service
providers. In February 2011, Singapore Investment
Banking Association was incorporated into ABS.
The combined membership of both associations, over
158 member banks, will allow ABS to better
represent the interests of the banking industry.

British Bankers' Association (BBA)
105-108 Old Broad St.
Pinners Hall

London, UK EC2N 1EX
Phone: 44-20-7216-8800
Fax: 44-20-7216-8811
E-mail Address: info@bba.org.uk
Web Address: www.bba.org.uk
The BBA is a leading trade association for the UK banking and financial services sector. It speaks for over 200 member banks from 50 countries on a range of UK and international banking issues.

Indian Banks' Association
World Trade Ctr. Complex, Cuff Parade
Fl. 6, Ctr. 1 Bldg.
Mumbai, MH India 400 005
Phone: 91-22-22174040
Fax: 91-22-22184222
E-mail Address: webmaster@iba.org.in
Web Address: www.iba.org.in
The Indian Banks' Association is composed of members of public, private and foreign banks which have offices in India.

4) Banking Industry Resources

American Banker
One State St. Plz., Fl. 27
New York, NY USA 10004
Phone: 212-803-8200
Fax: 212-843-9600
Toll Free: 800-221-1809
E-mail Address:
Christopher.Wood@sourcemedia.com
Web Address: www.americanbanker.com
American Banker publishes an online magazine and offers news, reports and research tools on a broad spectrum of business and financial topics on a subscriber basis.

Brazilian National Bank for Economic & Social Development
Av. Republica do Chile, 100
Rio de Janeiro, RJ Brazil 20031-917
Phone: 55-21-3747-7447
Web Address: www.bndes.gov.br
The Brazilian National Bank for Economic & Social Development (Banco Nacional de Desenvolvimento Economico e Social, or BNDES) is a government organization founded in 1952 and affiliated with the Ministry of Development, Industry and Foreign Trade. BNDES focuses in particular on providing long-term business financing to help develop the overall Brazilian economy. BNDES has worked with small, medium and large-scale organizations, and

investment areas include large-scale infrastructure projects, agriculture, trade, education, film and music, public transportation and sanitation.

5) Blockchain Associations

Enterprise Ethereum Alliance
401 Edgewater Pl., Ste. 600
Wakefield, MA USA 01880
Web Address: https://entethalliance.org/
The Enterprise Ethereum Alliance connects Fortune 500 enterprises, startups, academics and technology vendors with Ethereum virtual currency network subject matter experts. Members learn from and build upon the blockchain network to define enterprise-grade software capable of handling complex, highly demanding applications at the speed of business.

Hyperledger
E-mail Address: info@hyperledger.org
Web Address: www.hyperledger.org
Hyperledger is an open source collaborative effort created to advance cross-industry blockchain technologies. It is a global collaboration, hosted by The Linux Foundation, including leaders in finance, banking, Internet of Things, supply chains, manufacturing and technology.

6) Canadian Government Agencies-Finance

Bank of Canada (The)
234 Laurier Ave. W.
Ottawa, ON Canada K1A 0G9
Phone: 613-782-8111
Fax: 613-782-7713
Toll Free: 800-303-1282
E-mail Address: info@bankofcanada.ca
Web Address: www.bankofcanada.ca
The Bank of Canada is the national bank belonging to the Canadian government. Its responsibilities include Canada's monetary policy, designing and issuing currency, providing liquidity to financial systems and federal funds management.

Department of Finance Canada (DFC)
90 Elgin St.
Ottawa, ON Canada K1A 0G5
Phone: 613-369-3710
Fax: 613-369-4065
E-mail Address: finpub@fin.gc.ca
Web Address: www.fin.gc.ca

The Department of Finance Canada (DFC) governs federal financial institutions; insurance companies and credit unions; and manages the debt and reserves of the Canadian government.

Financial Transactions and Reporting Analysis Centre of Canada (FINTRAC)
234 Laurier Ave. W., Fl. 24
Ottawa, ON Canada K1P 1H7
Fax: 613-943-7931
Toll Free: 866-346-8722
E-mail Address: guidelines-lignesdirectrices@fintrac-canafe.gc.ca
Web Address: www.fintrac.gc.ca
The Financial Transactions and Reporting Analysis Centre of Canada (FINTRAC) analyzes financial intelligence to safeguard against money laundering and the financing of threats to the security of Canada.

7) Canadian Government Agencies-General

Canadian Centre for Cyber Security
Toll Free: 1-833-292-3788
E-mail Address: contact@cyber.gc.ca
Web Address: https://cyber.gc.ca/en/
The Canadian Centre for Cyber Security leads the government's response to cyber security events. They have united existing operational cyber security expertise from Public Safety Canada, Shared Services Canada, and the Communications Security Establishment in to one high-functioning, responsive organization.

8) Careers-Banking

National Banking & Financial Service Network (NBFSN)
3075 Brickhouse Ct.
Virginia Beach, VA USA 23452-6860
Phone: 757-463-5766
Fax: 757-340-0826
E-mail Address: smurrell@nbn-jobs.com
Web Address: www.nbn-jobs.com/
The National Banking & Financial Service Network (NBFSN) is made up of recruiting firms in the banking and financial services marketplace. The web site provides job listings.

9) Careers-Computers/Technology

ComputerJobs.com, Inc.
675 Alpha Dr., Ste. E
Highland Heights, OH USA 44143
Toll Free: 800-850-0045
Web Address: www.computerjobs.com
ComputerJobs.com, Inc. is an employment web site that offers users a links to computer-related job opportunities organized by skill and market.

Institute for Electrical and Electronics Engineers (IEEE) Job Site
445 Hoes Ln.
Piscataway, NJ USA 08855-1331
Phone: 732-981-0060
Toll Free: 800-678-4333
E-mail Address: candidatejobsite@ieee.org
Web Address: careers.ieee.org
The Institute for Electrical and Electronics Engineers (IEEE) Job Site provides a host of employment services for technical professionals, employers and recruiters. The site offers job listings by geographic area, a resume bank and links to employment services.

Pencom Systems, Inc.
152 Remsen St.
Brooklyn, NY USA 11201
Phone: 718-923-1111
Fax: 718-923-6065
E-mail Address: tom@pencom.com
Web Address: www.pencom.com
Pencom Systems, Inc., an open system recruiting company, hosts a career web site geared toward high-technology and scientific professionals, featuring an interactive salary survey, career advisor, job listings and technology resources. Its focus is the financial services industry within the New York City area.

10) Careers-First Time Jobs/New Grads

CollegeGrad.com, Inc.
950 Tower Ln., Fl. 6
Foster City, CA USA 94404
E-mail Address: info@quinstreet.com
Web Address: www.collegegrad.com
CollegeGrad.com, Inc. offers in-depth resources for college students and recent grads seeking entry-level jobs.

National Association of Colleges and Employers (NACE)
62 Highland Ave.
Bethlehem, PA USA 18017-9085
Phone: 610-868-1421
E-mail Address: customerservice@naceweb.org
Web Address: www.naceweb.org
The National Association of Colleges and Employers (NACE) is a premier U.S. organization representing college placement offices and corporate recruiters who focus on hiring new grads.

11) Careers-General Job Listings

CareerBuilder, Inc.
200 N La Salle Dr., Ste. 1100
Chicago, IL USA 60601
Phone: 773-527-3600
Fax: 773-353-2452
Toll Free: 800-891-8880
Web Address: www.careerbuilder.com
CareerBuilder, Inc. focuses on the needs of companies and also provides a database of job openings. The site has over 1 million jobs posted by 300,000 employers, and receives an average 23 million unique visitors monthly. The company also operates online career centers for 140 newspapers and 9,000 online partners. Resumes are sent directly to the company, and applicants can set up a special e-mail account for job-seeking purposes.
CareerBuilder is primarily a joint venture between three newspaper giants: The McClatchy Company, Gannett Co., Inc. and Tribune Company.

CareerOneStop
Toll Free: 877-872-5627
E-mail Address: info@careeronestop.org
Web Address: www.careeronestop.org
CareerOneStop is operated by the employment commissions of various state agencies. It contains job listings in both the private and government sectors, as well as a wide variety of useful career resources and workforce information.
CareerOneStop is sponsored by the U.S. Department of Labor.

eFinancialCareers
1040 Ave. of the Americas, Ste. 16B
New York, NY USA 10018
Phone: 212-370-8502
Web Address: www.efinancialcareers.com
eFinancialCareers.com provides employment listings in the finance industry, as well as job tools such as

salary surveys, resume writing assistance and industry news. It is owned DHI Group, Inc.

LaborMarketInfo (LMI)
Employment Development Dept.
P.O. Box 826880, MIC 57
Sacramento, CA USA 94280-0001
Phone: 916-262-2162
Fax: 916-262-2352
Web Address: www.labormarketinfo.edd.ca.gov
LaborMarketInfo (LMI) provides job seekers and employers a wide range of resources, namely the ability to find, access and use labor market information and services. It provides statistics for employment demographics on both a local and regional level, as well as career searching tools for California residents. The web site is sponsored by California's Employment Development Office.

Recruiters Online Network
E-mail Address: rossi.tony@comcast.net
Web Address: www.recruitersonline.com
The Recruiters Online Network provides job postings from thousands of recruiters, Careers Online Magazine, a resume database, as well as other career resources.

USAJOBS
USAJOBS Program Office
1900 E St. NW, Ste. 6500
Washington, DC USA 20415-0001
Phone: 818-934-6600
Web Address: www.usajobs.gov
USAJOBS, a program of the U.S. Office of Personnel Management, is the official job site for the U.S. Federal Government. It provides a comprehensive list of U.S. government jobs, allowing users to search for employment by location; agency; type of work; or by senior executive positions. It also has special employment sections for individuals with disabilities, veterans and recent college graduates; an information center, offering resume and interview tips and other information; and allows users to create a profile and post a resume.

12) Careers-Job Reference Tools

Vault.com, Inc.
132 W. 31st St., Fl. 16
New York, NY USA 10001
Fax: 212-366-6117
Toll Free: 800-535-2074
E-mail Address: customerservice@vault.com

Web Address: www.vault.com
Vault.com, Inc. is a comprehensive career web site for employers and employees, with job postings and valuable information on a wide variety of industries. Its features and content are largely geared toward MBA degree holders.

13) Chinese Government Agencies-General

Ministry of Commerce the People's Republic of China
No. 2 Dong Chang'an Ave.
Beijing, China 100731
Phone: 86-10-5377-1360
Fax: 86-10-5377-1311
Web Address: english.mofcom.gov.cn
The Ministry of Commerce the People's Republic of China (MOFCOM) has links to general information regarding trade and commerce in China as well as links to other related governmental departments.

14) Computer & Electronics Industry Associations

Canadian Advanced Technology Alliances (CATAAlliance)
207 Bank St., Ste. 416
Ottawa, ON Canada K2P 2N2
Phone: 613-236-6550
E-mail Address: info@cata.ca
Web Address: www.cata.ca
The Canadian Advanced Technology Alliances (CATAAlliance) is one of Canada's leading trade organizations for the research, development and technology sectors.

Information Technology Association of Canada (ITAC)
5090 Explorer Dr., Ste. 801
Mississauga, ON Canada L4W 4T9
Phone: 905-602-8345
Fax: 905-602-8346
E-mail Address: dwhite@itac.ca
Web Address: www.itac.ca
The Information Technology Association of Canada (ITAC) represents the IT, software, computer and telecommunications industries in Canada.

Information Technology Industry Council (ITI)
700 K St. NW, Ste. 600
Washington, DC USA 20001

Phone: 202-737-8888
Fax: 202-638-4922
E-mail Address: info@itic.org
Web Address: www.itic.org
The Information Technology Industry Council (ITI) is a premier group of the nation's leading high-tech companies and widely recognized as one of the tech industry's most effective lobbying organization in Washington, in various foreign capitals and the World Trade Organization (WTO).

Retail Solutions Providers Association (RSPA)
9920 Couloak Dr., Ste. 120
Charlotte, NC USA 28216
Phone: 704-357-3124
Fax: 704-357-3127
Toll Free: 800-782-2693
E-mail Address: Info@GoRSPA.org
Web Address: www.gorspa.org
The Retail Solutions Providers Association (RSPA) is a trade association composed of businesses involved in the purchase, resale, enhancement, installation and maintenance of point-of-sale systems to and for end users.

Singapore Computer Society
53/53A Neil Rd.
Singapore, Singapore 088891
Phone: 65-6226-2567
Fax: 65-6226-2569
E-mail Address: scs.secretariat@scs.org.sg
Web Address: www.scs.org.sg
The Singapore Computer Society is a membership society for infocomm professionals in Singapore.

15) Computer & Electronics Industry Resources

EETimes
Web Address: www.eetimes.com
The EETimes is an online magazine devoted to electronic engineers in the semiconductor, systems and software design fields.

Information Technology and Innovation Foundation (ITIF)
700 K St. NW, Ste. 600
Washington, DC USA 20001
Phone: 202-449-1351
E-mail Address: mail@itif.org
Web Address: www.itif.org
Information Technology and Innovation Foundation (ITIF) is a non-partisan research and educational

institute (a think tank) with a mission to formulate and promote public policies to advance technological innovation and productivity internationally, in Washington, and in the States. Recognizing the vital role of technology in ensuring American prosperity, ITIF focuses on innovation, productivity, and digital economy issues.

16) Conference Calls with Corporate Management

Vcall, Inc.
9011 Arboretum Pkwy., Ste. 295
c/o PrecisionIR Group
Richmond, VA USA 23236
Fax: 804-327-3400
Toll Free: 804-327-3400
E-mail Address: info@precisionir.com
Web Address:
www.investorcalendar.com/vcall/index.aspx
Vcall, Inc. provides live and archived web casts, special events and conference broadcasts of investor relations events. Vcall is part of the PrecisionIR Group.

17) Consulting Industry Associations

Investment Management Consultant Association (IMCA)
5619 DTC Pkwy., Ste. 500
Greenwood Village, CO USA 80111
Phone: 303-770-3377
Fax: 303-770-1812
E-mail Address: imca@imca.org
Web Address: www.imca.org
The Investment Management Consultant Association (IMCA) provides information and communication for investment management consultants.

18) Corporate Information Resources

Business Journals (The)
120 W. Morehead St., Ste. 400
Charlotte, NC USA 28202
Toll Free: 866-853-3661
E-mail Address: gmurchison@bizjournals.com
Web Address: www.bizjournals.com
Bizjournals.com is the online media division of American City Business Journals, the publisher of dozens of leading city business journals nationwide. It provides access to research into the latest news regarding companies both small and large. The

organization maintains 42 websites and 64 print publications and sponsors over 700 annual industry events.

Business Wire
101 California St., Fl. 20
San Francisco, CA USA 94111
Phone: 415-986-4422
Fax: 415-788-5335
Toll Free: 800-227-0845
E-mail Address: info@businesswire.com
Web Address: www.businesswire.com
Business Wire offers news releases, industry- and company-specific news, top headlines, conference calls, IPOs on the Internet, media services and access to tradeshownews.com and BW Connect On-line through its informative and continuously updated web site.

Edgar Online, Inc.
35 W. Wacker Dr.
Chicago, IL USA 60601
Phone: 301-287-0300
Fax: 301-287-0390
Toll Free: 800-823-5304
Web Address: www.edgar-online.com
Edgar Online, Inc. is a gateway and search tool for viewing corporate documents, such as annual reports on Form 10-K, filed with the U.S. Securities and Exchange Commission.

PR Newswire Association LLC
200 Vesey St., Fl. 19
New York, NY USA 10281
Fax: 800-793-9313
Toll Free: 800-776-8090
E-mail Address: mediainquiries@cision.com
Web Address: www.prnewswire.com
PR Newswire Association LLC provides comprehensive communications services for public relations and investor relations professionals, ranging from information distribution and market intelligence to the creation of online multimedia content and investor relations web sites. Users can also view recent corporate press releases from companies across the globe. The Association is owned by United Business Media plc.

Silicon Investor
E-mail Address: si.admin@siliconinvestor.com
Web Address: www.siliconinvestor.com
Silicon Investor is focused on providing information about technology companies. Its web site serves as a

financial discussion forum and offers quotes, profiles and charts.

---

19) Ecommerce and Data Interchange Technology Associations

Center for Research in Electronic Commerce
McCombs School of Business
CBA 6.426, 2100 Speedway, Stop B6500
Austin, TX USA 78712-1170
Phone: 512-471-7962
Fax: 512-471-3034
E-mail Address: abw@uts.cc.utexas.edu
Web Address: cism.mccombs.utexas.edu/
The Center for Research in Electronic Commerce at the University of Texas is a leading research institution in generating critical knowledge and understanding in the fields of information systems and management, electronic commerce and the digital economy.

RosettaNet
7877 Washington Village Dr., Ste. 300
Dayton, OH USA 45459
Phone: 937-435-3870
E-mail Address: info@gs1us.org
Web Address: www.resources.gs1us.org/rosettanet
RosettaNet, a subsidiary of GS1 US, is a nonprofit organization whose mission is to develop e-business process standards that serve as a frame of reference for global trading networks. The organization's standards provide a common language for companies within the global supply chain.

---

20) Economic Data & Research

Centre for European Economic Research (The, ZEW)
L 7, 1
Mannheim, Germany 68161
Phone: 49-621-1235-01
Fax: 49-621-1235-224
E-mail Address: empfang@zew.de
Web Address: www.zew.de/en
Zentrum fur Europaische Wirtschaftsforschung, The Centre for European Economic Research (ZEW), distinguishes itself in the analysis of internationally comparative data in a European context and in the creation of databases that serve as a basis for scientific research. The institute maintains a special library relevant to economic research and provides external parties with selected data for the purpose of scientific research. ZEW also offers public events and seminars concentrating on banking, business and other economic-political topics.

Economic and Social Research Council (ESRC)
Polaris House
North Star Ave.
Swindon, UK SN2 1UJ
Phone: 44-01793 413000
E-mail Address: esrcenquiries@esrc.ac.uk
Web Address: www.esrc.ac.uk
The Economic and Social Research Council (ESRC) funds research and training in social and economic issues. It is an independent organization, established by Royal Charter. Current research areas include the global economy; social diversity; environment and energy; human behavior; and health and well-being.

Eurostat
5 Rue Alphonse Weicker
Joseph Bech Bldg.
Luxembourg, Luxembourg L-2721
Phone: 352-4301-1
E-mail Address: eurostat-pressoffice@ec.europa.eu
Web Address: ec.europa.eu/eurostat
Eurostat is the European Union's service that publishes a wide variety of comprehensive statistics on European industries, populations, trade, agriculture, technology, environment and other matters.

Federal Statistical Office of Germany
Gustav-Stresemann-Ring 11
Wiesbaden, Germany D-65189
Phone: 49-611-75-2405
Fax: 49-611-72-4000
Web Address: www.destatis.de
Federal Statistical Office of Germany publishes a wide variety of nation and regional economic data of interest to anyone who is studying Germany, one of the world's leading economies. Data available includes population, consumer prices, labor markets, health care, industries and output.

India Brand Equity Foundation (IBEF)
Fl. 20, Jawahar Vyapar Bhawan
Tolstoy Marg
New Delhi, India 110001
Phone: 91-11-43845500
Fax: 91-11-23701235
E-mail Address: info.brandindia@ibef.org
Web Address: www.ibef.org

India Brand Equity Foundation (IBEF) is a public-private partnership between the Ministry of Commerce and Industry, the Government of India and the Confederation of Indian Industry. The foundation's primary objective is to build positive economic perceptions of India globally. It aims to effectively present the India business perspective and leverage business partnerships in a globalizing marketplace.

National Bureau of Statistics (China)
57, Yuetan Nanjie, Sanlihe
Xicheng District
Beijing, China 100826
Fax: 86-10-6878-2000
E-mail Address: info@gj.stats.cn
Web Address: www.stats.gov.cn/english
The National Bureau of Statistics (China) provides statistics and economic data regarding China's economy and society.

Organization for Economic Co-operation and Development (OECD)
2 rue Andre Pascal
Cedex 16
Paris, France 75775
Phone: 33-1-45-24-82-00
Fax: 33-1-45-24-85-00
E-mail Address: webmaster@oecd.org
Web Address: www.oecd.org
The Organization for Economic Co-operation and Development (OECD) publishes detailed economic, government, population, social and trade statistics on a country-by-country basis for over 30 nations representing the world's largest economies. Sectors covered range from industry, labor, technology and patents, to health care, environment and globalization.

Statistics Bureau, Director-General for Policy Planning (Japan)
19-1 Wakamatsu-cho
Shinjuku-ku
Tokyo, Japan 162-8668
Phone: 81-3-5273-2020
E-mail Address: toukeisoudan@soumu.go.jp
Web Address: www.stat.go.jp/english
The Statistics Bureau, Director-General for Policy Planning (Japan) and Statistical Research and Training Institute, a part of the Japanese Ministry of Internal Affairs and Communications, plays the central role of producing and disseminating basic

official statistics and coordinating statistical work under the Statistics Act and other legislation.

Statistics Canada
150 Tunney's Pasture Driveway
Ottawa, ON Canada K1A 0T6
Phone: 514-283-8300
Fax: 514-283-9350
Toll Free: 800-263-1136
E-mail Address: STATCAN.infostats-infostats.STATCAN@canada.ca
Web Address: www.statcan.gc.ca
Statistics Canada provides a complete portal to Canadian economic data and statistics. Its conducts Canada's official census every five years, as well as hundreds of surveys covering numerous aspects of Canadian life.

21) Engineering, Research & Scientific Associations

Center for Innovative Technology (CIT)
2214 Rock Hill Rd., Ste. 600
Herndon, VA USA 20170-4228
Phone: 703-689-3000
Fax: 703-689-3041
E-mail Address: info@cit.org
Web Address: www.cit.org
The Center for Innovative Technology is a nonprofit organization designed to enhance the research and development capabilities by creating partnerships between innovative technology start-up companies and advanced technology consumers.

Indian Institute of Technology - Roorkee
Indian Institute of Technology Roorkee
Roorkee, Uttarakhand India 247 667
Phone: 91-1332-285311
E-mail Address: registar@iitr.ernet.in
Web Address: www.iitr.ac.in
Indian Institute of Technology - Roorkee is among the foremost institutes in higher technological education and engineering in India for basic and applied research.

Institute of Electrical and Electronics Engineers (IEEE)
3 Park Ave., Fl. 17
New York, NY USA 10016-5997
Phone: 212-419-7900
Fax: 212-752-4929
Toll Free: 800-678-4333
E-mail Address: society-info@ieee.org

Web Address: www.ieee.org
The Institute of Electrical and Electronics Engineers (IEEE) is a nonprofit, technical professional association of more than 430,000 individual members in approximately 160 countries. The IEEE sets global technical standards and acts as an authority in technical areas ranging from computer engineering, biomedical technology and telecommunications to electric power, aerospace and consumer electronics.

Institution of Engineering and Technology (The) (IET)
Michael Faraday House
Six Hills Way
Stevenage, Herts UK SG1 2AY
Phone: 44-1438-313-311
Fax: 44-1438-765-526
E-mail Address: postmaster@theiet.org
Web Address: www.theiet.org
The Institution of Engineering and Technology (IET) is an innovative international organization for electronics, electrical, manufacturing and IT professionals.

22) EU Agencies-Banking

European Banking Authority (EBA)
One Canada Sq., Fl. 46
Canary Wharf
London, UK E14 5AA
Phone: 44-207-382-1776
Fax: 44-207-382-1771
E-mail Address: info@eba.europa.eu
Web Address: www.eba.europa.eu
The European Banking Authority (EBA) officially opened in early 2011 and has taken over all existing and ongoing tasks and responsibilities from the Committee of European Banking Supervisors (CEBS). The EBA acts as a network of EU and national bodies safeguarding values such as the stability of the financial system, the transparency of markets and financial products and the protection of depositors and investors.

23) Financial Industry Resources

SNL Financial
1 SNL Plz., 212 7th St. NE
Charlottesville, VA USA 22902
Phone: 434-977-1600
Fax: 434-977-4466
Toll Free: 866-296-3743

E-mail Address: SNLInfo@SNL.com
Web Address: www.snl.com
SNL Financial provides industry-specific research and statistics in the banking, financial services, insurance, real estate and energy sectors.

24) Financial Technology Associations, FinTech

Association for Financial Technology
3525 Piedmont Rd. NE, Ste. 300
Atlanta, GA USA 30305
Phone: 404-789-3154
Fax: 404-240-0998
E-mail Address: aft@aftweb.com
Web Address: www.aftweb.com
Association for Financial Technology (AFT) is a premier resource for networking and professional development for those companies and executives serving U.S. financial institutions (FI's), including banks, credit unions, lenders and payment companies. Founded in 1972, the organization members represent virtually every area of technology, data or services needed to help FI's succeed.

Consumer Bankers Association
1225 New York Ave., NW, Ste. 100
Washington, DC USA 20005
Web Address: www.consumerbankers.com
The Consumer Bankers Association (CBA) is a US trade organization representing financial institutions offering retail lending products and services. The CBA is a retail banking interest group; it also provides educational courses, industry research and federal and state-level representation on issues relating to consumer banking.

Electronic Transactions Association
1620 L St. NW, Ste. 1020
Washington, DC USA 20036
Phone: 202-828-2635
Fax: 202-828-2639
Toll Free: 800-695-5509
Web Address: www.electran.org
The Electronic Transactions Association is the leading trade association for the payments industry, representing 550 companies worldwide involved in electronic transaction processing products and services. The purpose of ETA is to influence, monitor and shape the payments industry by providing leadership through education, advocacy and the exchange of information. ETA's membership spans the breadth of the payments industry to include

independent sales organizations (ISOs), payments networks, financial institutions, transaction processors, mobile payments products and services, payments technologies, and software providers (ISV) and hardware suppliers.

FinTech Professionals Association
Phone: (512) 981-7293
E-mail Address: info@fintechpros.org
Web Address: https://fintechpros.org/
FinTech Professionals Association's mission is to bring the traditional financial services world together with new and emerging financial technology companies to expand opportunities, share ideas, network and shape the future of the industry. Its goal is to create an online community that aggregates FinTech-centric events, news and resources from around the globe while creating a vast network of established and emerging professionals. The Fintech Professionals Association was founded by Cyfeon as a nonprofit organization dedicated to building a robust community for financial service technology companies.

National Automated Clearing House Association (NACHA)
2550 Wasser Ter., Suite 400
Hendon, VA USA 20171
Phone: 703-561-1100
Fax: 703-787-0996
Web Address: www.nacha.org
National Automated Clearing House Association manages the administration, development, and governance of the ACH network, which is the electronic system that facilitates the movement of money in the United States via ACH transfers.

Wall Street Technology Association
620 Shrewsbury Ave., Ste. C
Tinton Falls, NJ USA 07701
Phone: 732-530-8808
Fax: 732-530-0020
E-mail Address: info@wsta.org
Web Address: www.wsta.org
The Wall Street Technology Association (WSTA), founded in 1967, is a not-for-profit educational organization that focuses on technologies, operational approaches, and business issues for the global financial community. Initially New York Tri-State Area focused, the WSTA also hosts events in Boston since 2010. The WSTA is comprised of financial firm members, vendor affiliates and sponsors. Additionally, the WSTA has a tremendous database

of other technology professionals that are not currently members.

---

25) FinTech Resources

Cambridge Centre for Alternative Finance (CCAF)
10 Trumpington St.
University of Cambridge
Cambridge, UK CB2 1QA
Phone: 44 (0)1223-339111
E-mail Address: ccaf@jbs.cam.ac.uk
Web Address: www.jbs.cam.ac.uk/faculty-research/centres/alternative-finance/
The Cambridge Centre for Alternative Finance (CCAF) is a research arm of Cambridge University that conducts studies on alternative finance channels such as virtual currency and the shadow banking industry.

Crowdfund Insider
P.O. Box 221196
Beachwood, OH USA 44122
Phone: 917-818-3443
E-mail Address: info@crowdfundinsider.com
Web Address: www.crowdfundinsider.com
Crowdfund Insider is a news and information website covering investment crowdfunding, blockchain/distributed ledger technology, digital banking, and other FinTech sectors.

Finextra Research
77 Shaftesbury Ave.
London, UK W1D 5DU
Phone: 44 (0) 20-3100-3670
E-mail Address: contact@finextra.com
Web Address: www.finextra.com
Finextra Research is a news site that publishes research articles, white papers, and case studies about the FinTech community. Finextra covers news from the wholesale and retail banking sector, capital markets, and insurance. Finextra also provides advertising and promotional opportunities to support marketing campaigns.

FinTech Breakthrough
E-mail Address: info@fintechbreakthrough.com
Web Address: https://fintechbreakthrough.com/
FinTech Breakthrough runs an annual technology awards program that recognizes outstanding technology platforms and executives in areas such as payments, mortgages, banking and investments. Its

website is an excellent source for learning about outstanding companies in this field.

Global System for Mobile Communications (GSMA)
25 Walbrook
London, UK EC4N 8AF
Phone: 44 (0)207-356-0600
Fax: 44 (0)20-7356-0601
E-mail Address: info@gsma.com
Web Address: www.gsma.com
The GSMA represents the interests of mobile operators worldwide. About 400 companies in the broader mobile ecosystem, including handset and device makers, software companies, equipment providers and internet companies, as well as organizations in adjacent industry sectors.

Money 20/20
229 W. 43rd St., Fl. 7
New York, NY USA 10036
Phone: 212-682-8000
E-mail Address: info@money2020.com
Web Address: www.money2020.com
Money 20/20 is a networking platform for businesses and individuals to share content, ideas, and insight for the global money ecosystem. Money 20/20 hosts events that feature data analysts, expert speakers, and company leaders.

26)	Foreign Exchange Industry Associations

Foreign Exchange Dealers' Association of India
Cuffe Parade
173, Maker Twr. 'F', Fl. 17
Mumbai, MH India 400 005
Phone: 91-22-22184432
Fax: 91-22-22189946
E-mail Address: mail@fedai.org.in
Web Address: www.fedai.org.in
Foreign Exchange Dealers' Association of India represents an association of banks dealing in the foreign exchange market in India.

27)	Government Agencies-Hong Kong

GovHK
Phone: 852-183-5500
E-mail Address: enquiry@1835500.gov.hk
Web Address: www.gov.hk

GovHK is the one-stop portal of the Hong Kong Special Administrative Region (HKSAR) Government. GovHK features links to governmental agencies, information and services. It also organizes them by user groups (transport, business, trade) and subjects (education, youth, etc.).

28)	Government Agencies-Singapore

Singapore Government Online (SINGOV)
E-mail Address: singov_webmaster@mci.gov.sg
Web Address: www.gov.sg
Singapore Government Online (SINGOV) is the default homepage for the Singapore Government and is a portal for governmental information. The web site lists governmental agencies, news, information, policies and initiatives.

29)	Identity Theft Resources

Identity Theft Resource Center (ITRC)
3625 Ruffin Rd., Ste. 204
San Diego, CA USA 92123
Toll Free: 888-400-5530
E-mail Address: itrc@idtheftcenter.org
Web Address: www.idtheftcenter.org
The Identity Theft Resource Center (ITRC) is a nonprofit organization established to support victims of identity theft in resolving their cases, and to broaden public education and awareness in the understanding of identity theft, data breaches, cyber security, scams/fraud and privacy issues.

30)	Industry Research/Market Research

Forrester Research
60 Acorn Park Dr.
Cambridge, MA USA 02140
Phone: 617-613-5730
Toll Free: 866-367-7378
E-mail Address: press@forrester.com
Web Address: www.forrester.com
Forrester Research is a publicly traded company that identifies and analyzes emerging trends in technology and their impact on business. Among the firm's specialties are the financial services, retail, health care, entertainment, automotive and information technology industries.

Gartner, Inc.
56 Top Gallant Rd.
Stamford, CT USA 06902

Phone: 203-964-0096
E-mail Address: info@gartner.com
Web Address: www.gartner.com
Gartner, Inc. is a publicly traded IT company that provides competitive intelligence and strategic consulting and advisory services to numerous clients worldwide.

MarketResearch.com
6116 Executive Blvd., Ste. 550
Rockville, MD USA 20852
Phone: 240-747-3093
Fax: 240-747-3004
Toll Free: 800-298-5699
E-mail Address:
customerservice@marketresearch.com
Web Address: www.marketresearch.com
MarketResearch.com is a leading broker for professional market research and industry analysis. Users are able to search the company's database of research publications including data on global industries, companies, products and trends.

Plunkett Research, Ltd.
P.O. Drawer 541737
Houston, TX USA 77254-1737
Phone: 713-932-0000
Fax: 713-932-7080
E-mail Address:
customersupport@plunkettresearch.com
Web Address: www.plunkettresearch.com
Plunkett Research, Ltd. is a leading provider of market research, industry trends analysis and business statistics. Since 1985, it has served clients worldwide, including corporations, universities, libraries, consultants and government agencies. At the firm's web site, visitors can view product information and pricing and access a large amount of basic market information on industries such as financial services, InfoTech, ecommerce, health care and biotech.

31) Insurance Industry Associations

General Insurance Association of Singapore
Bangkok Bank Building
180 Cecil St., 15-01
Singapore, Singapore 069546
Phone: 65-6221-8788
Fax: 65-6227-2051
Web Address: www.gia.org.sg

General Insurance Association of Singapore represents companies providing non-life insurance services.

Life Insurance Association (LIA)
79 Anson Rd., #11-05
Singapore, Singapore 048422
Phone: 65-6438-8900
Fax: 65-6438-6989
Web Address: www.lia.org.sg
Founded in the 1950s, the Life Insurance Association (LIA) is the trade association of life insurance companies that are licensed by the Monetary Authority of Singapore (MAS) to issue life insurance products in Singapore. LIA has 22 life insurance member companies, and five associate members comprising life reinsurance companies.

32) Insurance Industry Resources

Insurance Information Institute
110 William St.
New York, NY USA 10038
Phone: 212-346-5500
Toll Free: 800-331-9146
E-mail Address: members@iii.org
Web Address: www.iii.org
The Insurance Information Institute works to improve public understanding of what insurance does and how it works. The group's web site provides information on all types of insurance, as well as facts, statistics, interviews and hot topics and issues. It also provides excellent statistics on financial services, banking and investment sectors. See the Facts and Statistics area.

33) International Regulatory Body

European Banking Authority
Tour Europlaza
20 ave. Andre Prothin
Courbevoie, France 92400
Phone: +33 1 86 52 70 00
E-mail Address: info@eba.europa.eu
Web Address: www.eba.europa.eu
A regulatory body that works to maintain financial stability in the EU banking industry. It was established in 2010 by the European Parliament and replaced the Committee of European Banking Supervisors (CEBS).

European Securities and Markets Authority
201-203 Rue de Bercy

Paris, France 75012
Phone: +33 1 58 36 43 21
E-mail Address: info@esma.europa.eu
Web Address: www.esma.europa.eu
EU securities and markets regulatory body that sets
out to ensure integrity, transparency, efficiency and
orderly functioning of securities markets, as well as
investor protection. Esma fosters supervisory
convergence amongst securities regulators, and
across financial sectors by working closely with EBA
and EIOPA.

Global Financial Markets Association (GFMA)
1099 New York Ave., NW 6th Fl.
Washington, DC USA 20005
Phone: 202-962-7300
E-mail Address: inquiry@gfma.org
Web Address: www.gfma.org
A finance industry body which includes some of the
world's largest financial trade associations to develop
strategies for global policy issues in the financial
markets and promote coordinated advocacy efforts.
GFMA currently has three members: The Association
for Financial Markets in Europe (AFME), the Asia
Securities Industry & Financial Markets Association
(ASIFMA), and, in the United States, the Securities
Industry and Financial Markets Association
(SIFMA).

34) Internet Industry Associations

**Cooperative Association for Internet Data
Analysis (CAIDA)**
9500 Gilman Dr., Mail Stop 0505
La Jolla, CA USA 92093-0505
Phone: 858-534-5000
E-mail Address: info@caida.org
Web Address: www.caida.org
The Cooperative Association for Internet Data
Analysis (CAIDA), representing organizations from
the government, commercial and research sectors,
works to promote an atmosphere of greater cohesion
in the engineering and maintenance of the Internet.
CAIDA is located at the San Diego Supercomputer
Center (SDSC) on the campus of the University of
California, San Diego (UCSD).

35) Internet Industry Resources

**Congressional Internet Caucus Advisory
Committee (CICA)**
1440 G St. NW

Washington, DC USA 20005
Phone: 202-638-4370
E-mail Address: tlordan@netcaucus.org
Web Address: www.netcaucus.org
The Congressional Internet Caucus Advisory
Committee (ICAC) works to educate the public, as
well as a bipartisan group from the U.S. House and
Senate about Internet-related policy issues.

Web3 Foundation
Zug, Switzerland 6300
Web Address: web3.foundation
Web3 Foundation funds research and development
teams building the technology stack of the
decentralized web. It was established in Zug,
Switzerland by Ethereum co-founder Gavin Wood.
Polkadot is the Foundation's flagship project

36) Internet Usage Statistics

Pew Internet & American Life Project
1615 L St. NW, Ste. 800
Washington, DC USA 20036
Phone: 202-419-4300
Fax: 202-857-8562
E-mail Address: info@pewinternet.org
Web Address: www.pewinternet.org
The Pew Internet & American Life Project, an
initiative of the Pew Research Center, produces
reports that explore the impact of the Internet on
families, communities, work and home, daily life,
education, health care and civic and political life.

37) Investment Industry Associations

ACI - The Financial Markets Association
ACI 8, Rue du Mail
Paris, France F-75002
Phone: 33-1-4297-5115
Fax: 33-1-4297-5116
Web Address: www.aciforex.com
ACI - The Financial Markets Association is the
global umbrella body of national associations. The
Paris-based body, founded as Association Cambiste
Internationale (ACI), has more than 13,000 members
worldwide in more than 60 countries. This makes
ACI the largest international association in the
wholesale financial markets. ACI - The Financial
Markets Association was founded in France in 1955
following an agreement between foreign exchange
dealers in Paris and London.

American Finance Association (AFA)
Tepper School of Business
Carnegie Mellon University
Pittsburgh, PA USA 15213-3890
E-mail Address: jim.schallheim@business.utah.edu
Web Address: www.afajof.org
The American Finance Association is a membership organization focused on financial economics. The group publishes The Journal of Finance.

Asia Securities Industry & Financial Markets Association
Lippo Centre 89 Queensway
Unit 3603, Tower 2
Hong Kong, China
Phone: +852 2531 6500
E-mail Address: wwong@asifma.org
Web Address: www.asifma.org
ASIFMA (Asia Securities Industry & Financial Markets Association) is an independent, regional trade association comprising a diverse range of over 150 leading financial institutions from both the buy and sell side, including banks, asset managers, professional services firms and market infrastructure service providers.

Association for Financial Markets in Europe (AFME)
25 Canada SQ., Fl. 39
London, UK E14 5LQ
Phone: +44 (0) 20 3828 2700
E-mail Address: londonreception@afme.eu
Web Address: www.afme.eu
AFME advocates for deep and integrated European capital markets, which serve the needs of companies and investors, supporting economic growth and benefiting society. It aims to act as a bridge between market participants and policy makers across Europe.

Institute for Private Investors (IPI)
17 State St.
New York, NY USA 10004
Phone: 212-693-1300
Web Address: https://memberlink.net
The IPI, owned by Campden Wealth, provides educational resources for high wealth individuals. It does not endorse individual products, and it does not sell consulting services. Its annual conferences and publications serve advisors, managers and high net worth investors.

Institute of Banking & Finance, Singapore (IBF)
10 Shenton Way

13-07/08 MAS Bldg.
Singapore, Singapore 079117
Phone: 65-6220-8566
Fax: 65-6224-4947
Web Address: www.ibf.org.sg
The Institute of Banking & Finance (IBF) was established to serve the banking and finance industry in Singapore. IBF now administers part of the Capital Markets and Financial Advisory Services (CMFAS) examination series on behalf of the Monetary Authority of Singapore (MAS). It is also the national accreditation and certification agency for financial competency under the Financial Industry Competency Standards (FICS) framework.

Investment Industry Association of Canada (IIAC)
11 King St. W., Ste. 1600
Toronto, Ontario Canada M5H 4C7
Phone: 416-364-2754
Fax: 416-364-4861
E-mail Address: P
Web Address: www.iiac.ca
The Investment Industry Association of Canada (IIAC) is the trade organization for the Canadian investment industry, representing around 189 investment and investment-related firms.

Investment Management Association of Singapore (IMAS)
One Phillip St.
Royal One Phillip #10-02
Singapore, Singapore 048692
Phone: 65-6223-9353
Fax: 65-6223-9352
E-mail Address: enquiries@imas.org.sg
Web Address: www.imas.org.sg
The Investment Management Association of Singapore (IMAS) is a representative body of investment managers spearheading the development and growth of the industry in Singapore.

Securities Industry and Financial Markets Association (SIFMA)
120 Broadway, Fl. 35
New York, NY USA 10271
Phone: 212-313-1200
E-mail Address: inquiry@sifma.org
Web Address: www.sifma.org
SIFMA is the leading trade association for broker-dealers, investment banks and asset managers operating in the U.S. and global capital markets. SIFMA advocates on legislation, regulation and

business policy affecting retail and institutional investors, equity and fixed income markets and related products and services.

38) Investment Industry Resources

Committee on Capital Markets Regulation (CCMR)
125 Mt. Auburn St., Fl. 3
Cambridge, MA USA 02138
Phone: 617-496-2217
E-mail Address: info@capmktsreg.org
Web Address: www.capmktsreg.org
The Committee on Capital Markets Regulation (CCMR) is an independent and bipartisan group comprised of 33 leaders from the investor community, business, finance, law, accounting, and academia. The CCMR issues interim report, highlighting areas of concern about the competitiveness of U.S. capital markets and outlining recommendations in four key areas to enhance that competitiveness. It continues to study issues in such areas as derivatives, mutual funds and shareholder rights.

Economic Times, The
DLF Phase III
Ecstasy IT Park Plot, 391 Udyog Vihar
Gurgaon, Haryana India 122 016
Phone: 91-124-4518550
Web Address: www.economictimes.indiatimes.com
The Economic Times, a site operated by India Times, provides economic news, industry specific headlines and market advice. The site has stock market updates, indices and statistics for the Indian and global markets.

39) Investment Information-Funds

iShares
525 Washington Blvd., Ste. 1405
Jersey City, NJ USA 07310
Toll Free: 800-474-2737
E-mail Address: isharesetfs@blackrock.com
Web Address: www.ishares.com
iShares, owned by BlackRock, offers investors a wide range of investment opportunities through exchange traded funds (ETF), and provides online tools and information in order to meet specific investment goals.

40) IPOs (Initial Public Offerings)

OpenIPO
909 Montgomery St., Fl. 3
San Francisco, CA USA 94133
Phone: 415-551-8600
Fax: 415-551-8686
Toll Free: 877-828-5200
E-mail Address: info@wrhambrecht.com
Web Address: www.wrhambrecht.com
OpenIPO is an auction process for distributing stock individuals and institutional investors in initial public offerings. It is a service of WR Hambrecht & Co.

41) Magazines, Business & Financial

Economist (The)
25 St. James's St.
London, UK SW1A 1HG
Phone: 44-20-7830-7000
Fax: 44-20-7839-2968
Web Address: www.economist.com
The Economist, operating in print and online, tracks global and domestic economic, political and technological trends, and is full of informative articles and commentary.

Financial Times
1 Southwark Bridge
London, UK SE1 9HL
Phone: 44-207-775-6248
Toll Free: 800-0705-6477
E-mail Address: help@ft.com
Web Address: www.ft.com
Financial Times covers news and stock information, allows users to maintain a profile and provides specific company information. The company offers a newspaper, FT.com, alerts and news feeds.

Forbes Online
60 5th Ave.
New York, NY USA 10011
Phone: 212-620-2200
E-mail Address: customerservice@forbes.com
Web Address: www.forbes.com
Forbes Online offers varied stock information, news and commentary on business, technology and personal finance, as well as financial calculators and advice.

Fortune
1271 Ave. of the Americas

Rockefeller Ctr.
New York, NY USA 10020-1393
Phone: 212-522-8528
Web Address: http://fortune.com/
Fortune, one of the world's premiere business magazines, contains news, business profiles and information on investing, careers, small business, technology and other details of U.S. and international business. Fortune is a publication of Cable News Network (CNN), a Time Warner company.

Investor's Business Daily (IBD)
12655 Beatrice St.
Los Angeles, CA USA 90066
Phone: 310-448-6000
Toll Free: 800-831-2525
Web Address: www.investors.com
Investor's Business Daily (IBD) offers subscribers information and articles on the stock market, educational resources, advice from analyst William O'Neil, personal portfolios and updates on events and workshops.

Wall Street Journal Online (The)
1211 Ave. of the Americas
New York, NY USA 10036
Phone: 609-514-0870
Toll Free: 800-568-7625
E-mail Address: support@wsj.com
Web Address: www.wsj.com
The outstanding resources of The Wall Street Journal are available online for a nominal fee.

42) MBA Resources

MBA Depot
Web Address: www.mbadepot.com
MBA Depot is an online community and information portal for MBAs, potential MBA program applicants and business professionals.

43) Mortgage Industry Associations

Mortgage Bankers Association (MBA)
1919 M St. NW, Fl. 5
Washington, DC USA 20036
Phone: 202-557-2700
Toll Free: 800-793-6222
Web Address: www.mbaa.org
The Mortgage Bankers Association (MBA) serves the real estate finance industry by representing its legislative and regulatory interests before Congress

and federal agencies; providing educational programs, periodicals and publications; and supporting its business interests with research initiatives, products and services.

44) Patent Organizations

European Patent Office
Bob-van-Benthem-Platz 1
Munich, Germany 80469
Phone: 49 89 2399-0
Toll Free: 08-800-80-20-20-20
E-mail Address: press@epo.org
Web Address: www.epo.org
The European Patent Office (EPO) provides a uniform application procedure for individual inventors and companies seeking patent protection in up to 38 European countries. It is the executive arm of the European Patent Organization and is supervised by the Administrative Council.

45) Payments Industry Associations

The Payments Association
20 St Thomas Street
London, UK SE1 9RS
Phone: 44 20 7378 9890
Web Address: www.thepaymentsassociation.org
The Payments Assoociation operates as an independent representative for the payments industry and its interests, and drive collaboration within the payments sector in order to bring about meaningful change and innovation.

46) Payments Industry Resources

Finextra
77 Shaftesbury Ave.
London, UK W1D 5DU
Phone: 44 20 3100 9670
E-mail Address: contact@finextra.com
Web Address: www.finextra.com
Finextra is a FinTech-focused news site that covers covers payments, startups, banking, the capital markets and insurance. Finextra also publishes a wide range of research articles, features, white papers and case studies.

Pymnts.com
E-mail Address: information@pymnts.com
Web Address: www.pymnts.com

Pymnts is a payments-focused industry news site. It covers global industry news.

47) Pensions, Benefits & 401(k) Associations

Plan Sponsor Council of America (PSCA)
20 N. Wacker Dr., Ste. 3164
Chicago, IL USA 60606
Phone: 312-419-1863
Fax: 312-419-1864
E-mail Address: psca@psca.org
Web Address: www.psca.org
The Plan Sponsor Council of America (PSCA), formerly the Profit Sharing/401(k) Council of America (PSCA). is a national nonprofit association of 1,200 companies and their 6 million employees. The group expresses its members' interests to federal policymakers and offers practical, cost-effective assistance with profit sharing and 401(k) plan design, administration, investment, compliance and communication. Its web site offers a thorough glossary, statistics and educational material.

48) Pensions, Benefits & 401(k) Resources

Employee Benefits Security Administration (EBSA)
200 Constitution Ave. NW
Washington, DC USA 20210
Toll Free: 866-444-3272
Web Address: www.dol.gov/ebsa
The Employee Benefits Security Administration (EBSA) is a division of the U.S. Department of Labor, whose web site features a wealth of benefits information for both employers and employees. Included are the answers to such questions as to how a company's bankruptcy will affect its employees and what one should know about pension rights.

49) Privacy & Consumer Matters

Get Safe Online
Clifton House
Four Elms Rd.
Cardiff, UK CF24 1LE
E-mail Address: info@getsafeonline.org
Web Address: www.getsafeonline.org
Get Safe Online is a joint initiative between the U.K. government, law enforcement, leading businesses and the public sector. Its aim is to provide computer users

and small businesses with free, independent, user-friendly advice that will allow them to use the internet confidently, safely and securely. It provides videos and online advice about such subjects as identify theft, computer security and safe purchasing practices for products, services and travel.

TRUSTe
111 Sutter St., Ste. 600
San Francisco, CA USA 94104
Phone: 415-520-3490
Fax: 415-520-3420
Toll Free: 888-878-7830
E-mail Address: trustarc-info@trustarc.com
Web Address: trustarc.com/consumer-info/privacy-certification-standards/
TRUSTe formed an alliance with all major portal sites to launch the Privacy Partnership campaign, a consumer education program designed to raise the awareness of Internet privacy issues. The organization works to meet the needs of business web sites while protecting user privacy.

50) Privacy Associations

International Association of Privacy Professionals (IAPP)
75 Rochester Ave.
Portsmouth, NH USA 03801
Phone: 603-427-9200
Fax: 603-427-9249
Toll Free: 800-266-6501
Web Address: www.iapp.org
The International Association of Privacy Professionals (IAPP) is a resource for companies and individuals to learn best practices, advance privacy management issues, and provide education on information privacy. The IAPP aides in providing credentialing programs to privacy information professionals.

51) Retirement Planning Resources

Financial Engines
1050 Enterprise Way, Fl. 3
Sunnyvale, CA USA 94089
Phone: 408-498-6000
Fax: 408-498-6010
Toll Free: 888-443-8577
E-mail Address: support@financialengines.com
Web Address: www.financialengines.com

The Financial Engines web site assists visitors by forecasting what investments might be worth in the future. The site provides users with unbiased advice in order to assist in making better and more informed financial decisions. Users can also monitor investments and read news features.

52) Robotic Process Automation (RPA) Associations

Institute for Robotic Process Automation & Artificial Intelligence
E-mail Address: helpdesk@irpanetwork.com
Web Address: www.irpaai.com
Founded in 2013, the Institute for Robotic Process Automation and Artificial Intelligence (IRPA AI) is an independent professional association and knowledge forum for the buyers, sellers, influencers and analysts of robotic process automation, cognitive computing and artificial intelligence.

53) Securities Industry Associations

Bombay Stock Exchange Limited (BSE)
Phiroze Jeejeebhoy Twrs.
Dalal St.
Mumbai, MH India 400 001
Phone: 91-22-22721233
Fax: 91-22-22721919
E-mail Address: corp.comm@bseindia.com
Web Address: www.bseindia.com
The Bombay Stock Exchange Limited (BSE) in India is now one of the largest exchanges. The BSE Index, the SENSEX, is one of India's first stock market indexes.

Financial Industry Regulatory Authority, Inc. (FINRA)
1735 K St.
Washington, DC USA 20006
Phone: 301-590-6500
Web Address: www.finra.org
The Financial Industry Regulatory Authority, Inc. (FINRA) is one of the largest non-governmental regulators for security firms in the United States. The organization was created in July 2007 through the consolidation of the National Association of Security Dealers (NASD) and the member functions of the New York Stock Exchange, and is dedicated to protecting investors and maintaining market integrity.

Investment Company Institute (ICI)
1401 H St. NW, Ste. 1200
Washington, DC USA 20005
Phone: 202-326-5800
E-mail Address: memberservices@ici.org
Web Address: www.ici.org
The Investment Company Institute (ICI) is a national association of U.S. investment companies. It represents its members in matters of legislation, regulation, taxation, public information, economic and policy research, business operations and statistics.

London Stock Exchange
10 Paternoster Sq.
London, UK EC4M 7LS
Phone: 44-20-7797-1000
E-mail Address: events@londonstockexchange.com
Web Address: www.londonstockexchange.com
The London Stock Exchange is one of most international of all the world's stock exchanges with companies from over 70 countries admitted to trading on its markets.

NASDAQ
165 Broadway, 1 Liberty Plz.
New York, NY USA 10006
Phone: 212-401-8700
Web Address: www.nasdaq.com
NASDAQ is an electronic U.S. stock market which plays host to about 3,900 companies. It is home to companies in technology, retail, communications, financial services, transportation, media and biotechnology. The exchange is owned by NASDAQ OMX.

National Securities Clearing Corp. (NSCC)
55 Water St., Fl. 26
New York, NY USA 10041
Phone: 212-635-5910
E-mail Address: infor@dtcc.com
Web Address:
http://www.dtcc.com/about/businesses-and-subsidiaries/nscc.aspx
National Securities Clearing Corp. (NSCC) is a leading provider of centralized clearance, settlement and information services to the financial services industry. NSCC is a subsidiary of The Depository Trust & Clearing Corporation.

North American Securities Administrators Association (NASAA)
750 First St. NE, Ste. 1140

Washington, DC USA 20002
Phone: 202-737-0900
Fax: 202-783-3571
E-mail Address: jo@nasaa.org
Web Address: www.nasaa.org
The North American Securities Administrators
Association (NASAA) is the oldest international
organization devoted to investor protection. It is a
voluntary association of securities administrators.

NYSE Euronext
11 Wall St.
New York, NY USA 10005
Phone: 212-656-3000
Fax: 212-656-5549
E-mail Address: eryan@nyx.com
Web Address: www.nyse.com
The NYSE Euronext, the result of the resent merger
between the New York Stock Exchange and Euronext
N.V., is the world's largest equities exchange group.
Its web site features extensive market information,
listed company information, international viewpoints,
market regulation data, educational information and
more.

Securities Association of China (SAC, The)
Fl. 2, Bldg. B, Focus Plaza
No. 19 Jinrong St., Xicheng District
Beijing, China 100033
E-mail Address: icd@sac.net.cn
Web Address: www.sac.net.cn
SAC is an organization that represents China's fund
managers, investment banks, stock exchanges and
investment consulting firms.

Securities Investor Protection Corp. (SIPC)
1667 K St. NW, Ste. 1000
Washington, DC USA 20006-1620
Phone: 202-371-8300
Fax: 202-223-1679
E-mail Address: asksipc@sipc.org
Web Address: www.sipc.org
Securities Investor Protection Corp. (SIPC) acts as a
trustee and works with an independent court-
appointed trustees in missing asset cases to recover
funds.

Security Traders Association (STA)
1115 Broadway
New York, NY USA 10010
Phone: 646-699-5996
E-mail Address: sta@securitytraders.org
Web Address: www.securitytraders.org

The Security Traders Association (STA) is a
professional trade organization that works to improve
the ethics, business standards and working
environment for members, who are engaged in the
buying, selling and trading of securities.

Singapore Exchange Limited (SGX)
2 Shenton Way
02-02 SGX Ctr. 1
Singapore, Singapore 068804
Phone: 65-6236-8888
Fax: 65-6535-6994
E-mail Address: asksgx@sgx.com
Web Address: www.sgx.com
The Singapore Exchange Limited (SGX) was formed
from the merger of the Stock Exchange of Singapore
(SES) and the Singapore International Monetary
Exchange (SIMEX) in 1999.

World Federation of Exchanges (WFE)
125 Old Broad St.
London, UK EC2N 1AR
Phone: 44-0-207151-4150
Web Address: www.world-exchanges.org
The World Federation of Exchanges (WFE) is an
organization that represents all of the world's most
significant stock exchanges. It publishes in-depth
statistics on market capitalization, share turnover and
investment flows for exchanges worldwide.

54) Securities Industry Resources

China Securities Regulatory Commission
Focus Pl. 19
Jin Rong St., W. District
Beijing, China 100033
Fax: 010-66210205
E-mail Address: consult@csrc.gov.cn
Web Address: www.csrc.gov.cn
The China Securities Regulatory Commission
(CSRC), directly under the State Council, was
authorized to supervise and regulate the securities
and futures markets in order to ensure their orderly
and legitimate operation.

Securities & Exchange Board of India
Bandra Kurla Complex, Bandra E.
Plot No. C4-A, G Block
Mumbai, MH India 400 051
Phone: 91-22-26449000
Fax: 91-22-26449019-22
Toll Free: 800-22-7575
E-mail Address: sebi@sebi.gov.in

Web Address: www.sebi.gov.in
The Securities & Exchange Board of India serves to promote and regulate the securities market in India.

Securities and Futures Commission
35/F, Cheung Kong Ctr.
2 Queen's Rd. Central
Hong Kong, Hong Kong Hong Kong
Phone: 852-2231-1222
Fax: 852-2521-7836
E-mail Address: enquiry@sfc.hk
Web Address: www.sfc.hk
The Securities and Futures Commission (SFC) is non-governmental and independent statutory body responsible for regulating the securities and futures markets in Hong Kong.

55) Singaporean Government & Agencies – Finance

Ministry of Finance (MOF)
100 High St.
#06-03 The Treasury
Singapore, Singapore 179434
Fax: 65-6332-7435
Toll Free: 800-226-0806
E-mail Address: mof_qsm@mof.gov.sg
Web Address: www.mof.gov.sg
The Ministry of Finance (MOF) designs the regulatory policies and statutes of Singapore with an towards sound public finances, fiscal growth and effective and efficient use of government resources.

Monetary Authority of Singapore (MAS)
10 Shenton Way MAS Building
Singapore, Singapore 079117
Phone: 65-6225-5577
Fax: 65-6229-9229
E-mail Address: webmaster@mas.gov.sg
Web Address: www.mas.gov.sg
The Monetary Authority of Singapore (MAS) is the central bank of Singapore. Its mission is to promote sustained non-inflationary economic growth, and a sound and progressive financial center.

56) Software Industry Associations

Business Software Alliance (BSA)
20 F St. NW, Ste. 800
Washington, DC USA 20001
Phone: 202-872-5500
Fax: 202-872-5501

E-mail Address: info@bsa.org
Web Address: www.bsa.org
The Business Software Alliance (BSA) is a leading global software industry association. BSA educates consumers regarding software management, copyright protection, cyber security, trade, ecommerce and other Internet-related issues.

Enterprise Data Management Council (EDM)
Phone: 646-722-4381
E-mail Address: info@edmcouncil.org
Web Address: www.edmcouncil.org
The EDM Council is a non-profit trade association created by leading financial industry participants. Its primary purpose is to address the issues and challenges associated with managing data content as a business and operational priority.

European Software Institute (ESI)
Parque Tecnologico de Bizkaia
Edificio 202
Zamudio, Bizkaia Spain E-48170
Phone: 34-946-430-850
Fax: 34-901-706-009
Web Address: www.esi.es
The European Software Institute (ESI) is a nonprofit foundation launched as an initiative of the European Commission, with the support of leading European companies working in the information technology field.

Korea Software Industry Association (KOSA)
IT Venture Tower W., 12F
135 Jung-daero, Songpa-gu
Seoul, South Korea 05717
Phone: 82-2-2188-6900
Fax: 82-2-2188-6901
E-mail Address: choicy@sw.or.kr
Web Address: www.sw.or.kr
The Korea Software Industry Association (KOSA) is Korea's nonprofit trade organization representing more than 1,200 member companies in the software industry.

Software & Information Industry Association (SIIA)
1090 Vermont Ave. NW, Fl. 6
Washington, DC USA 20005-4095
Phone: 202-289-7442
Fax: 202-289-7097
Web Address: www.siia.net

The Software & Information Industry Association (SIIA) is a principal trade association for the software and digital content industry.

57) Software Industry Resources

Software Engineering Institute (SEI)-Carnegie Mellon
4500 5th Ave.
Pittsburgh, PA USA 15213-2612
Phone: 412-268-5800
Fax: 412-268-5758
Toll Free: 888-201-4479
E-mail Address: info@sei.cmu.edu
Web Address: www.sei.cmu.edu
The Software Engineering Institute (SEI) is a federally funded research and development center at Carnegie Mellon University, sponsored by the U.S. Department of Defense through the Office of the Under Secretary of Defense for Acquisition, Technology, and Logistics [OUSD (AT&L)]. The SEI's core purpose is to help users make measured improvements in their software engineering capabilities.

58) Stocks & Financial Markets Data

Corporate Information Online
177 W Putnam Ave.
Greenwich, CT USA 06830
Phone: 203-783-4343
Fax: 203-783-4401
Web Address: www.corporateinformation.com
Corporate Information Online, operating on a subscription basis and pay-per-report basis, profiles 39,000 publicly-held companies on a worldwide basis.

SiliconValley.com
4 N. Second St., Ste. 700
San Jose, CA USA 95113
Phone: 408-920-5000
Fax: 408-228-8060
E-mail Address: svfeedback@mercurynews.com
Web Address: www.siliconvalley.com
SiliconValley.com, run by San Jose Mercury News and owned by MediaNews Group, offers a summary of current financial news and information regarding the field of technology.

59) Technology Transfer Associations

Licensing Executives Society (USA and Canada), Inc.
11130 Sunrise Valley Dr., Ste. 350
Reston, VA USA 20191
Phone: 703-234-4058
Fax: 703-435-4390
E-mail Address: info@les.org
Web Address: www.lesusacanada.org
Licensing Executives Society (USA and Canada), Inc., established in 1965, is a professional association composed of about 3,000 members who work in fields related to the development, use, transfer, manufacture and marketing of intellectual property. Members include executives, lawyers, licensing consultants, engineers, academic researchers, scientists and government officials. The society is part of the larger Licensing Executives Society International, Inc. (same headquarters address), with a worldwide membership of some 12,000 members from approximately 80 countries.

60) Telecommunications Industry Associations

DigitalEurope
Rue de la Science 14
Brussels, Belgium 1040
Phone: 32-2-609-5310
Fax: 32-2-609-5339
E-mail Address: info@digitaleurope.org
Web Address: www.digitaleurope.org
DigitalEurope is dedicated to improving the business environment for the European information and communications technology and consumer electronics sector. Its members include 57 leading corporations and 37 national trade associations from across Europe.

61) Trade Associations-General

Associated Chambers of Commerce and Industry of India (ASSOCHAM)
5, Sardar Patel Marg
Chanakyapuri
New Delhi, India 110 021
Phone: 91-11-4655-0555
Fax: 91-11-2301-7008
E-mail Address: assocham@nic.in
Web Address: www.assocham.org

The Associated Chambers of Commerce and Industry of India (ASSOCHAM) has a membership of more than 300 chambers and trade associations and serves members from all over India. It works with domestic and international government agencies to advocate for India's industry and trade activities.

BUSINESSEUROPE
168 Ave. de Cortenbergh 168
Brussels, Belgium 1000
Phone: 32-2-237-65-11
Fax: 32-2-231-14-45
E-mail Address: main@businesseurope.eu
Web Address: www.businesseurope.eu
BUSINESSEUROPE is a major European trade federation that operates in a manner similar to a chamber of commerce. Its members are the central national business federations of the 34 countries throughout Europe from which they come. Companies cannot become direct members of BUSINESSEUROPE, though there is a support group which offers the opportunity for firms to encourage BUSINESSEUROPE objectives in various ways.

United States Council for International Business (USCIB)
1212 Ave. of the Americas
New York, NY USA 10036
Phone: 212-354-4480
Fax: 212-575-0327
E-mail Address: azhang@uscib.org
Web Address: www.uscib.org
The United States Council for International Business (USCIB) promotes an open system of world trade and investment through its global network. Standard USCIB members include corporations, law firms, consulting firms and industry associations. Limited membership options are available for chambers of commerce and sole legal practitioners.

62) Trade Associations-Global

International Chamber of Commerce (ICC)
33-43 avenue du President Wilson
Paris, France 75116
Phone: 33-0-1-4953- 3072
E-mail Address: andreia.furtado@iccwbo.org
Web Address: www.iccwbo.org
International Chamber of Commerce (ICC) represents the interests of the globalized business community, ensuring the voice of international business is heard among the world's governments. It provides international intergovernmental bodies such as the UN with information concerning business interests and sets standards for global commerce. ICC's Uniform Customs and Practice for Documentary Credits (UCP 600) are the rules that banks apply to finance billions of dollars' worth of world trade every year.

World Trade Organization (WTO)
Centre William Rappard
Rue de Lausanne 154
Geneva 21, Switzerland CH-1211
Phone: 41-22-739-51-11
Fax: 41-22-731-42-06
E-mail Address: enquiries@wto.og
Web Address: www.wto.org
The World Trade Organization (WTO) is a global organization dealing with the rules of trade between nations. To become a member, nations must agree to abide by certain guidelines. Membership increases a nation's ability to import and export efficiently.

63) Trade Resources

Enterprise Singapore
1 Fusionopolis Walk
#01-02 S. Tower, Solaris
Singapore, Singapore 138628
Phone: 65-6898-1800
Fax: 65-6278-6667
E-mail Address: enquiry@enterprisesg.gov.sg
Web Address: www.spring.gov.sg
International Enterprise Singapore and SPRING came together on 1 April 2018 as a single agency to form Enterprise Singapore. Enterprise Singapore is an enterprise development agency for growing, innovative companies. It works with partners to help small and medium enterprises with financing; capabilities and management development; technology and innovation; and access to markets.

64) U.S. Government Agencies

Board of Governors of the Federal Reserve System (FRB)
20th St. and Constitution Ave. NW
Washington, DC USA 20551
Phone: 202-452-3000
Fax: 877-888-2520
Toll Free: 888-851-1920
Web Address: www.federalreserve.gov
The Board of Governors of the Federal Reserve System (FRB) regulates the national banking system

to promote a more stable monetary and financial system.

Bureau of Economic Analysis (BEA)
4600 Silver Hill Rd.
Washington, DC USA 20233
Phone: 301-278-9004
E-mail Address: customerservice@bea.gov
Web Address: www.bea.gov
The Bureau of Economic Analysis (BEA), is an agency of the U.S. Department of Commerce, is the nation's economic accountant, preparing estimates that illuminate key national, international and regional aspects of the U.S. economy.

Bureau of Labor Statistics (BLS)
2 Massachusetts Ave. NE
Washington, DC USA 20212-0001
Phone: 202-691-5200
Fax: 202-691-7890
Toll Free: 800-877-8339
E-mail Address: blsdata_staff@bls.gov
Web Address: stats.bls.gov
The Bureau of Labor Statistics (BLS) is the principal fact-finding agency for the Federal Government in the field of labor economics and statistics. It is an independent national statistical agency that collects, processes, analyzes and disseminates statistical data to the American public, U.S. Congress, other federal agencies, state and local governments, business and labor. The BLS also serves as a statistical resource to the Department of Labor.

Consumer Financial Protection Bureau (CFPB)
P. O. Box 4503
Iowa City, IA USA 52244
Phone: 855-411-2372
Fax: 855-237-2392
E-mail Address: info@consumerfinance.gov
Web Address: www.consumerfinance.gov
The Consumer Financial Protection Bureau oversees and regulates the issuance of consumer financial products like mortgages, credit cards, personal loans and retirement plans.

Cybersecurity & Infrastructure Security Agency (CISA)
245 Murray Ln.
Washington, D.C. USA 20528-0380
Phone: 888-282-0870
E-mail Address: central@cisa.gov
Web Address: www.cisa.gov
The Cybersecurity & Infrastructure Security Agency (CISA) is the U.S. government agency focused on defending against cyber attacks and the development of new cybersecurity tools. The CISA also responds to attacks against the U.S. Government.

Federal Deposit Insurance Corporation (FDIC)
550 17th St. NW
Washington, DC USA 20429
Toll Free: 877-275-3342
E-mail Address: publicinfo@fdic.gov
Web Address: www.fdic.gov
The Federal Deposit Insurance Corporation (FDIC) preserves and promotes public confidence in the U.S. financial system by insuring deposits in banks and thrift institutions for at least $250,000; by identifying, monitoring and addressing risks to the deposit insurance funds; and by limiting the effect on the economy and the financial system when a bank or thrift institution fails. It is funded by premiums that banks and thrift institutions pay for deposit insurance coverage and from earnings on investments in U.S. Treasury securities.

FedStats
Web Address: fedstats.sites.usa.gov/
FedStats compiles information for statistics from over 100 U.S. federal agencies. Visitors can sort the information by agency, geography and topic, as well as perform searches.

U.S. Census Bureau
4600 Silver Hill Rd.
Washington, DC USA 20233-8800
Phone: 301-763-4636
Toll Free: 800-923-8282
E-mail Address: pio@census.gov
Web Address: www.census.gov
The U.S. Census Bureau is the official collector of data about the people and economy of the U.S. Founded in 1790, it provides official social, demographic and economic information. In addition to the Population & Housing Census, which it conducts every 10 years, the U.S. Census Bureau conducts numerous other surveys annually.

U.S. Department of Commerce (DOC)
1401 Constitution Ave. NW
Washington, DC USA 20230
Phone: 202-482-2000
E-mail Address: publicaffairs@doc.gov
Web Address: www.commerce.gov

The U.S. Department of Commerce (DOC) regulates trade and provides valuable economic analysis of the economy.

U.S. Department of Labor (DOL)
200 Constitution Ave. NW
Washington, DC USA 20210
Phone: 202-693-4676
Toll Free: 866-487-2365
E-mail Address: m-DOLPublicAffairs@dol.gov
Web Address: www.dol.gov
The U.S. Department of Labor (DOL) is the government agency responsible for labor regulations. The Department of Labor's goal is to foster, promote, and develop the welfare of the wage earners, job seekers, and retirees of the United States; improve working conditions; advance opportunities for profitable employment; and assure work-related benefits and rights.

U.S. Securities and Exchange Commission (SEC)
100 F St. NE
Washington, DC USA 20549
Phone: 202-942-8088
Fax: 202-772-9295
Toll Free: 800-732-0330
E-mail Address: help@sec.gov
Web Address: www.sec.gov
The U.S. Securities and Exchange Commission (SEC) is a nonpartisan, quasi-judicial regulatory agency responsible for administering federal securities laws. These laws are designed to protect investors in securities markets and ensure that they have access to disclosure of all material information concerning publicly traded securities. Visitors to the web site can access the EDGAR database of corporate financial and business information.

---

65) Wireless & Cellular Industry Associations

NFC Forum (Near Field Communications Forum)
401 Edgewater Pl., Ste. 600
Wakefield, MA USA 01880
Phone: 781-876-8955
Fax: 781-610-9864
E-mail Address: info@nfc-forum.org
Web Address: www.nfc-forum.org
The NFC Forum is an industry organization that promotes standards for Near Field Communication (NFC) technology. NFC is used by smart cards, smart phones and similar devices to exchange information and make payments wirelessly, with a touch.

Chapter 4

THE FINTECH 235:
WHO THEY ARE AND HOW THEY WERE
CHOSEN

Includes Indexes by Company Name, Industry & Location

The companies chosen to be listed in PLUNKETT'S FINTECH, CRYPTOCURRENCY & ELECTRONIC PAYMENTS INDUSTRY ALMANAC comprise a unique list. THE FINTECH 235 were chosen specifically for their dominance in the many facets of the FinTech industry in which they operate. Complete information about each firm can be found in the "Individual Profiles," beginning at the end of this chapter. These profiles are in alphabetical order by company name.

THE FINTECH 235 companies are from all parts of the United States, Canada, Europe, Asia/Pacific and beyond. THE FINTECH 235 includes companies that are deeply involved in the technologies, services and trends that keep the entire industry forging ahead.

Simply stated, THE FINTECH 235 contains the largest, most successful, fastest growing firms in FinTech and related industries in the world. To be included in our list, the firms had to meet the following criteria:

1) Generally, these are corporations based in the U.S., however, the headquarters of many firms are located in other nations.
2) Prominence, or a significant presence, in FinTech, services, equipment and supporting

fields. (See the following Industry Codes section for a complete list of types of businesses that are covered).

3) The companies in THE FINTECH 235 do not have to be exclusively in the FinTech field.
4) Financial data and vital statistics must have been available to the editors of this book, either directly from the company being written about or from outside sources deemed reliable and accurate by the editors. A small number of companies that we would like to have included are not listed because of a lack of sufficient, objective data.

INDEXES TO THE FINTECH 235, AS FOUND IN THIS CHAPTER AND IN THE BACK OF THE BOOK:

Index of Rankings Within Industry Groups	**p. 64**
Alphabetical Index	**p. 71**
Index of Headquarters Location by U.S. State	**p. 73**
Index of Non-U.S. Headquarters Location by Country	**p. 76**
Index of Firms Noted as "Hot Spots for Advancement" for Women/Minorities	**p. 322**
Index by Subsidiaries, Brand Names and Selected Affiliations	**p. 323**

INDEX OF COMPANIES WITHIN INDUSTRY GROUPS

The industry codes shown below are based on the 2012 NAIC code system (NAIC is used by many analysts as a replacement for older SIC codes because NAIC is more specific to today's industry sectors, see www.census.gov/NAICS). Companies are given a primary NAIC code, reflecting the main line of business of each firm.

Industry Group/Company	Industry Code	2020 Sales	2020 Profits
Asset Management			
Acorns Grow Inc	523920	71,000,000	-65,000,000
Betterment LLC	523920		
Cadre (RealCadre LLC)	523920		
Digit (Hello Digit LLC)	523920		
Fidelity Investments Inc	523920	21,000,000,000	7,200,000,000
Fundrise LLC	523920		
Guideline Inc	523920		
OpenInvest	523920		
Paxos Technology Solutions LLC	523920		
Wealthfront Corporation	523920		
Cloud, Data Processing, Business Process Outsourcing (BPO) and Internet Content Hosting Services			
Creek Road Miners Inc	518210	4,518,163	-1,940,401
Singularity Future Technology Ltd	518210	6,535,956	-16,452,894
Commercial Banks (Banking)			
Aspiration Partners Inc	522110	14,714,000	-66,000,000
Bank of America Corporation	522110	85,528,002,560	17,894,000,640
Barclays PLC	522110	28,780,474,368	2,031,876,224
Citigroup Inc	522110	75,493,998,592	11,047,000,064
Citizens Financial Group Inc	522110	6,904,999,936	1,057,000,000
Cross River Bank (CRB Group Inc)	522110		
Fifth Third Bancorp	522110	7,232,999,936	1,427,000,064
JPMorgan Chase & Co Inc	522110	119,475,003,392	29,130,999,808
M&T Bank Corporation	522110	5,954,761,216	1,353,152,000
Monzo Bank Limited	522110	69,158,178	-146,217,139
PNC Financial Services Group Inc	522110	16,798,000,128	7,517,000,192
Qonto (Olinda SAS)	522110		
Regions Financial Corporation	522110	6,224,999,936	1,094,000,000
SVB Financial Group	522110	3,919,848,960	1,208,368,000
Truist Financial Corporation	522110	22,705,000,448	4,481,999,872
US Bancorp (US Bank)	522110	23,225,999,360	4,959,000,064
Varo Money NA	522110		
Wells Fargo & Company	522110	72,339,996,672	3,300,999,936
Commodities and Futures Contracts Investors and Traders			
Binance	523130		
bitFlyer Inc	523130		
Bitkub Online Co Ltd	523130		
Circle Internet Financial Limited	523130	15,441,000	3,790,000
Coinbase Global Inc	523130	1,277,480,960	322,316,992
FTX Trading Ltd	523130		
Gemini Trust Company LLC	523130		

Industry Group/Company	Industry Code	2020 Sales	2020 Profits
Huobi Global Ltd	523130		
Kraken (Payward Inc)	523130		
KuCoin (Mek Global Limited)	523130		
UAB JM Trading (Cryptomate)	523130		
Computer Software: Accounting, Banking & Financial			
9F Inc	511210Q	196,650,208	-353,670,720
Accelitas Inc	511210Q		
ACI Worldwide Inc	511210Q	1,294,322,048	72,660,000
Addepar Inc	511210Q		
Agile Payments	511210Q		
Akoya LLC	511210Q		
Anchorage Labs Inc	511210Q		
AppTech Payments Corp	511210Q	329,500	-4,187,317
authID.ai (Ipsidy Inc)	511210Q	2,140,644	-11,298,558
BIGG Digital Assets Inc	511210Q		
BillGO Inc	511210Q		
Billtrust (BTRS Holdings Inc)	511210Q	145,684,992	-17,027,000
Blend Labs Inc	511210Q	96,029,000	-74,617,000
Bottomline Technologies Inc	511210Q	442,220,992	-9,229,000
Calero-MDSL	511210Q		
Chime Financial Inc	511210Q		
Concur Technologies Inc	511210Q	1,848,510,000	69,273,000
CoreCard Corp	511210Q	35,873,000	8,161,000
CSG Forte Payments Inc	511210Q		
Current (Finco Services Inc)	511210Q		
Dave Inc	511210Q	121,796,000	-6,957,000
Divvy Homes Inc	511210Q		
DocuSign Inc	511210Q	973,971,008	-208,359,008
Doxo Inc	511210Q		
Early Warning Services LLC	511210Q		
Enfusion Ltd LLC	511210Q	79,565,000	4,061,000
Esusu Financial Inc	511210Q		
Even (Even Responsible Finance Inc)	511210Q		
Feedzai Inc	511210Q		
Finicity a Mastercard Company	511210Q		
Greenlight Financial Technology Inc	511210Q		
Guaranteed Rate Inc	511210Q		
Industrial & Financial Systems AB (IFS)	511210Q	880,312,000	
Intuit Inc	511210Q	7,679,000,064	1,826,000,000
Jack Henry & Associates Inc	511210Q	1,697,067,008	296,668,000
Kabbage Inc	511210Q		
Katipult Technology Corp	511210Q	1,035,484	-1,473,544
MANTL (Fin Technologies Inc)	511210Q		
MicroBilt Corporation	511210Q		
MoCaFi (Mobility Capital Finance Inc)	511210Q		
MX Technologies Inc	511210Q		
One Finance Inc	511210Q		
OppFi Inc	511210Q	291,014,000	77,516,000
Payfare Inc	511210Q	10,558,575	-20,665,758

Industry Group/Company	Industry Code	2020 Sales	2020 Profits
PitchBook Data Inc	511210Q		
Plaid Inc	511210Q	220,000,000	
Prodigy Ventures Inc	511210Q	12,536,118	411,975
Propel Inc	511210Q		
Q2 Holdings Inc	511210Q	402,751,008	-137,620,000
Real Matters Inc	511210Q	455,944,992	41,991,000
RIBBIT (Cash Flow Solutions Inc)	511210Q		
Suplari Inc	511210Q		
Tala	511210Q		
TrueAccord Corp	511210Q		
Truebill Inc	511210Q		
Truework (Zethos Inc)	511210Q		
Trumid Financial LLC	511210Q		
ValidiFI LLC	511210Q		
Voyager Digital Ltd	511210Q	1,149,903	-10,170,259
Yodlee Inc	511210Q		
Computer Software: Business Management & Enterprise Resource Planning (ERP)			
Microsoft Corporation	511210H	143,015,002,112	44,280,999,936
Workday Inc	511210H	3,627,205,888	-480,673,984
Computer Software: E-Commerce, Web Analytics & Applications Management			
BigCommerce Holdings Inc	511210M	152,368,000	-37,560,000
Computer Software: Operating Systems, Languages & Development Tools, Artificial Intelligence (AI)			
Alchemy Insights Inc	511210I		
Computer Software: Sales & Customer Relationship Management			
Bolt Financial Inc	511210K		
Q4 Inc	511210K	40,381,180	-13,118,534
Verifi Inc	511210K		
Computer Software: Security & Anti-Virus			
Behavox Ltd	511210E		
Chainalysis Inc	511210E		
Coalition Inc	511210E		
Ekata Inc	511210E		
Fireblocks Inc	511210E		
Forter Inc	511210E		
Giact Systems LLC	511210E		
Immutable Holdings Inc	511210E	391,399	-85,979
Orum (Project Midas Inc)	511210E		
Revelock (Buguroo Offensive Security SL)	511210E		
Riskified Ltd	511210E	169,740,000	-11,347,000
Socure Inc	511210E		
Spring Labs (Springcoin Inc)	511210E		
Trulioo Inc	511210E		
Veriff Inc	511210E		
Consumer Loans and Consumer Lending			
Affirm Holdings Inc	522291	509,528,000	-112,598,000

Industry Group/Company	Industry Code	2020 Sales	2020 Profits
Avant Inc	522291	451,143,000	
Billd LLC	522291		
Bread Financial (Lon Operations LLC)	522291		
CommonBond Inc	522291		
Du Xiaoman Financial	522291		
Enova International Inc	522291	1,083,709,952	377,844,000
Forward Financing LLC	522291		
GreenSky Inc	522291	525,648,992	9,965,000
Klarna Bank AB	522291	1,220,800,000	-167,958,000
LendingClub Corporation	522291	243,508,992	-187,538,000
On Deck Capital Inc	522291	425,000,000	
SoFi (SoFi Technologies Inc)	522291	565,532,032	-224,052,992
Upgrade Inc	522291		
Credit & Debit Card Issuing			
Brex Inc	522210		
Capital One Financial Corporation	522210	28,522,999,808	2,713,999,872
Deserve Inc	522210		
Discover Financial Services	522210	11,088,000,000	1,140,999,936
NetSpend Holdings Inc	522210	836,403,750	
Nu Holdings Ltd (NuBank)	522210		
Petal Card Inc	522210		
Ramp Business Corporation	522210		
Synchrony Financial	522210	15,456,000,000	1,384,999,936
Credit Bureaus and Credit Rating Agencies			
Credit Karma Inc	561450	8,200,000,000	
Equifax Inc	561450	4,127,500,032	520,100,000
Experian plc	561450	5,178,999,808	675,000,000
LexisNexis	561450	3,000,000,000	
TransUnion	561450	2,716,600,064	343,200,000
Credit Card Processing, Online Payment Processing, EFT, ACH and Clearinghouses			
ACHQ Inc	522320		
ACHWorks	522320		
Actum Processing LLC	522320		
Aeropay (Aero Payments Inc)	522320		
AffiniPay LLC	522320	68,580,000	
Alacriti Inc	522320		
American Express Company	522320	36,087,001,088	3,135,000,064
Arcus Financial Intelligence Inc	522320		
Autoscribe Corporation	522320		
BitPay Inc	522320		
Braintree	522320		
Certegy Payments Solutions LLC Certegy Payments Solutions LLC	522320		
Checkbook Inc	522320		
Checkout.com (Checkout Ltd)	522320	252,719,000	-25,932,000
Clover Network Inc	522320		
DailyPay Inc	522320		
Dwolla Inc	522320		

Industry Group/Company	Industry Code	2020 Sales	2020 Profits
Finix Payments Inc	522320		
Fiserv Inc	522320	14,851,999,744	958,000,000
Flywire Corporation	522320	131,783,000	-11,107,000
Gravity Payments Inc	522320		
Headnote Inc	522320		
iCheckGateway.com	522320		
KakaoPay Corp	522320	3,818,970,780	159,269,247
Marqeta Inc	522320	290,292,000	-47,695,000
MasterCard Incorporated	522320	15,301,000,192	6,410,999,808
Modern Treasury Corp	522320		
National Cash Management Systems	522320		
NationalACH	522320		
Nivelo Tech Inc	522320		
Obopay Inc	522320		
Payliance	522320		
PayPal Holdings Inc	522320	21,454,000,128	4,201,999,872
Plastiq Inc	522320		
Poynt Company	522320		
Remitly Inc	522320	256,956,000	-32,564,000
Ripple Labs Inc	522320		
Secure Payment Systems Inc	522320		
SpotOn Transact LLC	522320		
Square (Block Inc.)	522320	9,497,578,496	213,104,992
Stripe Inc	522320	7,400,000,000	
Trustly Group AB	522320	241,963,280	
Veem Inc	522320		
Venmo	522320		
Visa Inc	522320	21,845,999,616	10,865,999,872
Wise Ltd	522320	375,000,076	18,588,900
Yapstone Inc	522320		
Zelle	522320		
Financial Investment Activities Including Securities Transfers, Quotes and Holders Protective Services; Deposit Brokers; and Clearinghouses			
Carta Inc (eShares Inc)	523999		
Insurance Agencies, Risk Management Consultants and Insurance Brokers			
ABD Insurance and Financial Services Inc (Newfront)	524210		
Clyde Technologies Inc	524210		
Hippo Holdings Inc	524210	50,100,000	-125,000,000
Insurify Inc	524210		
Policygenius Inc	524210		
Internet Search Engines, Online Publishing, Sharing, Gig and Consumer Services, Online Radio, TV and Entertainment Sites and Social Media			
Alphabet Inc (Google)	519130	182,527,000,576	40,269,000,704
NerdWallet Inc	519130	245,300,000	5,300,000
Refinitiv Limited	519130	2,418,099,320	-43,447,040
Zillow Group Inc	519130	3,339,816,960	-162,115,008

Industry Group/Company	Industry Code	2020 Sales	2020 Profits
Investment Advisors and Wealth Management			
Envestnet Inc	523930	998,230,016	-3,110,000
Personal Capital Corporation	523930		
Roofstock Inc	523930		
Investment Banking, and Related Stock Brokerage and Investment Services			
Goldman Sachs Group Inc (The)	523110	44,558,999,552	9,459,000,320
Hudson River Trading LLC	523110		
Morgan Stanley	523110	45,269,000,192	10,995,999,744
Optiver	523110		
Magazine Publishing and Financial Information Publishing			
Morningstar Inc	511120	1,389,500,032	223,600,000
Market Research, Business Intelligence and Opinion Polling			
IHS Markit Ltd	541910	4,287,800,064	870,700,032
Mortgage Lending, Underwriting and Investment			
LoanSnap Inc	522292		
Pawn Shops and Specialty Short-Term Financing			
BlockFi Inc	522298		
Property and Casualty (P&C) Insurance Underwriters (Direct Carriers)			
Lemonade Inc	524126	94,400,000	-122,300,000
Next Insurance Inc	524126		
Real Estate Brokers and Agents, Including Property Management, RealtorsÂ® and Leasing Agents			
KE Holdings Inc	531210	11,035,067,392	434,882,080
Sales Financing			
Ally Financial Inc	522220	6,960,999,936	1,084,999,936
Securities Brokerage, Discount Brokers and Online Stock Brokers			
Boursorama	523120	276,412,500	
Charles Schwab Corporation (The)	523120	11,690,999,808	3,299,000,064
COL Financial Group Inc	523120	22,597,300	8,782,500
E*Trade from Morgan Stanley	523120	3,030,300,134	
Groww (Nextbillion Technology Pvt Ltd)	523120	385,448	-10,547,976
M1 Holdings Inc	523120		
MarketAxess Holdings Inc	523120	689,124,992	299,376,992
Moomoo Inc	523120		
Public.com (Public Holdings Inc)	523120		
Robinhood Markets Inc	523120	958,833,024	7,449,000
Stash Financial Inc	523120	75,000,000	
TD Ameritrade Holding Corporation	523120	6,113,000,000	
Tornado (Nvstr Technologies Inc)	523120		
TradeStation Group Inc	523120	188,639,000	10,277,000
UP Fintech Holding Limited	523120	138,496,688	16,064,793
Virtu Financial Inc	523120	3,239,331,072	649,196,992
Webull Financial LLC	523120		

Industry Group/Company	Industry Code	2020 Sales	2020 Profits
Venture Capital, Private Equity Investment and Hedge Funds			
iCapital Network Inc	523910		
Wireless Communications and Radio and TV Broadcasting Equipment Manufacturing, including Cellphones (Handsets) and Internet of Things (IoT)			
Apple Inc	334220	274,515,001,344	57,410,998,272

ALPHABETICAL INDEX

9F Inc
ABD Insurance and Financial Services Inc (Newfront)
Accelitas Inc
ACHQ Inc
ACHWorks
ACI Worldwide Inc
Acorns Grow Inc
Actum Processing LLC
Addepar Inc
Aeropay (Aero Payments Inc)
AffiniPay LLC
Affirm Holdings Inc
Agile Payments
Akoya LLC
Alacriti Inc
Alchemy Insights Inc
Ally Financial Inc
Alphabet Inc (Google)
American Express Company
Anchorage Labs Inc
Apple Inc
AppTech Payments Corp
Arcus Financial Intelligence Inc
Aspiration Partners Inc
authID.ai (Ipsidy Inc)
Autoscribe Corporation
Avant Inc
Bank of America Corporation
Barclays PLC
Behavox Ltd
Betterment LLC
BigCommerce Holdings Inc
BIGG Digital Assets Inc
Billd LLC
BillGO Inc
Billtrust (BTRS Holdings Inc)
Binance
bitFlyer Inc
Bitkub Online Co Ltd
BitPay Inc
Blend Labs Inc
BlockFi Inc
Bolt Financial Inc
Bottomline Technologies Inc
Boursorama
Braintree
Bread Financial Holdings Inc
Bread Pay (Lon Operations LLC)
Brex Inc
Cadre (RealCadre LLC)
Calero-MDSL
Capital One Financial Corporation
Carta Inc (eShares Inc)
Certegy Payments Solutions LLC
Chainalysis Inc
Charles Schwab Corporation (The)

Checkbook Inc
Checkout.com (Checkout Ltd)
Chime Financial Inc
Circle Internet Financial Limited
Citigroup Inc
Citizens Financial Group Inc
Clover Network Inc
Clyde Technologies Inc
Coalition Inc
Coinbase Global Inc
COL Financial Group Inc
CommonBond Inc
Concur Technologies Inc
CoreCard Corp
Credit Karma Inc
Creek Road Miners Inc
Cross River Bank (CRB Group Inc)
CSG Forte Payments Inc
Current (Finco Services Inc)
DailyPay Inc
Dave Inc
Deserve Inc
Digit (Hello Digit LLC)
Discover Financial Services
Divvy Homes Inc
DocuSign Inc
Doxo Inc
Du Xiaoman Financial
Dwolla Inc
E*Trade from Morgan Stanley
Early Warning Services LLC
Ekata Inc
Enfusion Ltd LLC
Enova International Inc
Envestnet Inc
Equifax Inc
Esusu Financial Inc
Even (Even Responsible Finance Inc)
Experian plc
Feedzai Inc
Fidelity Investments Inc
Fifth Third Bancorp
Finicity a Mastercard Company
Finix Payments Inc
Fireblocks Inc
Fiserv Inc
Flywire Corporation
Forter Inc
Forward Financing LLC
FTX Trading Ltd
Fundrise LLC
Gemini Trust Company LLC
Giact Systems LLC
Goldman Sachs Group Inc (The)
Gravity Payments Inc
Greenlight Financial Technology Inc
GreenSky Inc
Groww (Nextbillion Technology Pvt Ltd)

Guaranteed Rate Inc
Guideline Inc
Headnote Inc
Hippo Holdings Inc
Hudson River Trading LLC
Huobi Global Ltd
iCapital Network Inc
iCheckGateway.com
IHS Markit Ltd
Immutable Holdings Inc
Industrial & Financial Systems AB (IFS)
Insurify Inc
Intuit Inc
Jack Henry & Associates Inc
JPMorgan Chase & Co Inc
Kabbage Inc
KakaoPay Corp
Katipult Technology Corp
KE Holdings Inc
Klarna Bank AB
Kraken (Payward Inc)
KuCoin (Mek Global Limited)
Lemonade Inc
LendingClub Corporation
LexisNexis
LoanSnap Inc
M&T Bank Corporation
M1 Holdings Inc
MANTL (Fin Technologies Inc)
MarketAxess Holdings Inc
Marqeta Inc
MasterCard Incorporated
MicroBilt Corporation
Microsoft Corporation
MoCaFi (Mobility Capital Finance Inc)
Modern Treasury Corp
Monzo Bank Limited
Moomoo Inc
Morgan Stanley
Morningstar Inc
MX Technologies Inc
National Cash Management Systems
NationalACH
NerdWallet Inc
NetSpend Holdings Inc
Next Insurance Inc
Nivelo Tech Inc
Nu Holdings Ltd (NuBank)
Obopay Inc
On Deck Capital Inc
One Finance Inc
OpenInvest
OppFi Inc
Optiver
Orum (Project Midas Inc)
Paxos Technology Solutions LLC
Payfare Inc
Payliance

PayPal Holdings Inc
Personal Capital Corporation
Petal Card Inc
PitchBook Data Inc
Plaid Inc
Plastiq Inc
PNC Financial Services Group Inc
Policygenius Inc
Poynt Company
Prodigy Ventures Inc
Propel Inc
Public.com (Public Holdings Inc)
Q2 Holdings Inc
Q4 Inc
Qonto (Olinda SAS)
Ramp Business Corporation
Real Matters Inc
Refinitiv Limited
Regions Financial Corporation
Remitly Inc
Revelock (Buguroo Offensive Security SL)
RIBBIT (Cash Flow Solutions Inc)
Ripple Labs Inc
Riskified Ltd
Robinhood Markets Inc
Roofstock Inc
Secure Payment Systems Inc
Singularity Future Technology Ltd
Socure Inc
SoFi (SoFi Technologies Inc)
SpotOn Transact LLC
Spring Labs (Springcoin Inc)
Square (Block Inc.)
Stash Financial Inc
Stripe Inc
Suplari Inc
SVB Financial Group
Synchrony Financial
Tala
TD Ameritrade Holding Corporation
Tornado (Nvstr Technologies Inc)
TradeStation Group Inc
TransUnion
TrueAccord Corp
Truebill Inc
Truework (Zethos Inc)
Truist Financial Corporation
Trulioo Inc
Trumid Financial LLC
Trustly Group AB
UAB JM Trading (Cryptomate)
UP Fintech Holding Limited
Upgrade Inc
US Bancorp (US Bank)
ValidiFI LLC
Varo Money NA
Veem Inc
Venmo

Veriff Inc
Verifi Inc
Virtu Financial Inc
Visa Inc
Voyager Digital Ltd
Wealthfront Corporation
Webull Financial LLC
Wells Fargo & Company
Wise Ltd
Workday Inc
Yapstone Inc
Yodlee Inc
Zelle
Zillow Group Inc

INDEX OF HEADQUARTERS LOCATION BY U.S. STATE

To help you locate the firms geographically, the city and state of the headquarters of each company are in the following index.

ALABAMA
Regions Financial Corporation; Birmingham

ARIZONA
Early Warning Services LLC; Scottsdale
Zelle; Scottsdale

CALIFORNIA
ABD Insurance and Financial Services Inc (Newfront); San Francisco
Accelitas Inc; Petaluma
ACHWorks; Rancho Cordova
Acorns Grow Inc; Irvine
Addepar Inc; Mountain View
Affirm Holdings Inc; San Francisco
Alchemy Insights Inc; San Francisco
Alphabet Inc (Google); Mountain View
Anchorage Labs Inc; San Francisco
Apple Inc; Cupertino
AppTech Payments Corp; Carlsbad
Aspiration Partners Inc; Marina Del Rey
Blend Labs Inc; San Francisco
Bolt Financial Inc; San Francisco
Carta Inc (eShares Inc); San Francisco
Checkbook Inc; San Mateo
Chime Financial Inc; San Francisco
Clover Network Inc; Sunnyvale
Coalition Inc; San Francisco
Credit Karma Inc; Oakland
Dave Inc; Los Angeles
Deserve Inc; Palo Alto
Digit (Hello Digit LLC); San Francisco
Divvy Homes Inc; San Francisco
DocuSign Inc; San Francisco
Even (Even Responsible Finance Inc); Oakland
Feedzai Inc; San Mateo
Finix Payments Inc; San Francisco
Headnote Inc; San Francisco
Hippo Holdings Inc; Palo Alto
Intuit Inc; Mountain View
Kraken (Payward Inc); San Francisco
LendingClub Corporation; San Francisco
LoanSnap Inc; Costa Mesa
Marqeta Inc; Oakland
Modern Treasury Corp; San Francisco
Moomoo Inc; Palo Alto
NerdWallet Inc; San Francisco
Next Insurance Inc; Palo Alto
One Finance Inc; Sacramento
OpenInvest; San Francisco

PayPal Holdings Inc; San Jose
Personal Capital Corporation; Redwood City
Plaid Inc; San Francisco
Plastiq Inc; San Francisco
Poynt Company; Palo Alto
Ripple Labs Inc; San Francisco
Robinhood Markets Inc; Menlo Park
Roofstock Inc; Oakland
SoFi (SoFi Technologies Inc); San Francisco
SpotOn Transact LLC; San Francisco
Spring Labs (Springcoin Inc); Marina Del Rey
Square (Block Inc.); San Francisco
Stripe Inc; San Francisco
SVB Financial Group; Santa Clara
Tala; Santa Monica
Truework (Zethos Inc); San Francisco
Upgrade Inc; San Francisco
Varo Money NA; San Francisco
Veem Inc; San Francisco
Venmo; San Jose
Verifi Inc; Los Angeles
Visa Inc; San Francisco
Wealthfront Corporation; Palo Alto
Wells Fargo & Company; San Francisco
Workday Inc; Pleasanton
Yapstone Inc; Walnut Creek
Yodlee Inc; San Mateo

COLORADO
BillGO Inc; Fort Collins

CONNECTICUT
Synchrony Financial; Stamford

DELAWARE
Coinbase Global Inc; Wilmington

DISTRICT OF COLUMBIA
Fundrise LLC; Washington

FLORIDA
ACHQ Inc; Sarasota
ACI Worldwide Inc; Naples
Autoscribe Corporation; Jacksonville
Certegy Payments Solutions LLC; Clearwater
iCheckGateway.com; Fort Myers
TradeStation Group Inc; Plantation
ValidiFI LLC; Boca Raton

GEORGIA
BitPay Inc; Atlanta
CoreCard Corp; Norcross
Equifax Inc; Atlanta
Greenlight Financial Technology Inc; Atlanta
GreenSky Inc; Atlanta
Kabbage Inc; Atlanta
MicroBilt Corporation; Kennesaw

ILLINOIS
Aeropay (Aero Payments Inc); Chicago
Avant Inc; Chicago
Braintree; Chicago
Discover Financial Services; Riverwoods
Enfusion Ltd LLC; Chicago
Enova International Inc; Chicago
Envestnet Inc; Chicago
Guaranteed Rate Inc; Chicago
M1 Holdings Inc; Chicago
Morningstar Inc; Chicago
OppFi Inc; Chicago
TransUnion; Chicago

IOWA
Dwolla Inc; Des Moines

KANSAS
TrueAccord Corp; Lenexa

MARYLAND
Truebill Inc; Silver Spring

MASSACHUSETTS
Akoya LLC; Boston
Circle Internet Financial Limited; Boston
Fidelity Investments Inc; Boston
Flywire Corporation; Boston
Forward Financing LLC; Boston
Insurify Inc; Cambridge

MICHIGAN
Ally Financial Inc; Detroit

MINNESOTA
US Bancorp (US Bank); Minneapolis

MISSOURI
Jack Henry & Associates Inc; Monett

NEBRASKA
TD Ameritrade Holding Corporation; Omaha

NEVADA
NationalACH; Las Vegas
Secure Payment Systems Inc; Las Vegas
Socure Inc; Incline Village

NEW HAMPSHIRE
Bottomline Technologies Inc; Portsmouth

NEW JERSEY
Alacriti Inc; Piscataway
Billtrust (BTRS Holdings Inc); Lawrenceville
BlockFi Inc; Jersey City

Cross River Bank (CRB Group Inc); Fort Lee

NEW YORK
Agile Payments; Saratoga Springs
American Express Company; New York
Arcus Financial Intelligence Inc; New York
authID.ai (Ipsidy Inc); Long Beach
Behavox Ltd; New York
Betterment LLC; New York
Bread Pay (Lon Operations LLC); New York
Cadre (RealCadre LLC); New York
Calero-MDSL; Rochester
Chainalysis Inc; New York
Citigroup Inc; New York
Clyde Technologies Inc; New York
CommonBond Inc; New York
Current (Finco Services Inc); New York
DailyPay Inc; New York
Esusu Financial Inc; New York
Fireblocks Inc; New York
Forter Inc; New York
Gemini Trust Company LLC; New York
Goldman Sachs Group Inc (The); New York
Hudson River Trading LLC; New York
iCapital Network Inc; New York
JPMorgan Chase & Co Inc; New York
Lemonade Inc; New York
LexisNexis; New York
M&T Bank Corporation; Buffalo
MANTL (Fin Technologies Inc); New York
MarketAxess Holdings Inc; New York
MasterCard Incorporated; Purchase
MoCaFi (Mobility Capital Finance Inc); New York
Morgan Stanley; New York
Nivelo Tech Inc; New York
On Deck Capital Inc; New York
Orum (Project Midas Inc); New York
Paxos Technology Solutions LLC; New York
Petal Card Inc; New York
Policygenius Inc; New York
Propel Inc; Brooklyn
Public.com (Public Holdings Inc); New York
Ramp Business Corporation; New York
Singularity Future Technology Ltd; Great Neck
Stash Financial Inc; New York
Tornado (Nvstr Technologies Inc); New York
Trumid Financial LLC; New York
Virtu Financial Inc; New York
Voyager Digital Ltd; New York
Webull Financial LLC; New York

NORTH CAROLINA
Bank of America Corporation; Charlotte
Truist Financial Corporation; Charlotte

OHIO
Bread Financial Holdings Inc; Columbis
Fifth Third Bancorp; Cincinnati

Payliance; Columbus
RIBBIT (Cash Flow Solutions Inc); Oxford

PENNSYLVANIA
PNC Financial Services Group Inc; Pittsburgh

RHODE ISLAND
Citizens Financial Group Inc; Providence

TEXAS
Actum Processing LLC; Austin
AffiniPay LLC; Austin
BigCommerce Holdings Inc; Austin
Billd LLC; Austin
Charles Schwab Corporation (The); Westlake
CSG Forte Payments Inc; Allen
Giact Systems LLC; Allen
Guideline Inc; Austin
National Cash Management Systems; McKinney
NetSpend Holdings Inc; Austin
Q2 Holdings Inc; Austin

UTAH
Brex Inc; Draper
Creek Road Miners Inc; Park City
Finicity a Mastercard Company; Salt Lake City
MX Technologies Inc; Lehi

VIRGINIA
Capital One Financial Corporation; McLean
E*Trade from Morgan Stanley; Arlington

WASHINGTON
Concur Technologies Inc; Bellevue
Doxo Inc; Seattle
Ekata Inc; Seattle
Gravity Payments Inc; Seattle
Microsoft Corporation; Redmond
PitchBook Data Inc; Seattle
Remitly Inc; Seattle
Suplari Inc; Seattle
Zillow Group Inc; Seattle

WISCONSIN
Fiserv Inc; Brookfield

INDEX OF NON-U.S. HEADQUARTERS LOCATION BY COUNTRY

ANTIGUA
FTX Trading Ltd; Saint John's

BRAZIL
Nu Holdings Ltd (NuBank); Sao Paulo

CANADA
BIGG Digital Assets Inc; Vancouver
Immutable Holdings Inc; Vancouver
Katipult Technology Corp; Vancouver
Payfare Inc; Toronto
Prodigy Ventures Inc; Toronto
Q4 Inc; Toronto
Real Matters Inc; Markham
Trulioo Inc; Vancouver

CAYMAN ISLANDS
Binance; George Town

CHINA
9F Inc; Beijing
Du Xiaoman Financial; Beijing
KE Holdings Inc; Beijing
UP Fintech Holding Limited; Beijing

ESTONIA
Veriff Inc; Tallinn, Harjumaa

FRANCE
Boursorama; Boulogne-Billancourt
Qonto (Olinda SAS); Paris

INDIA
Groww (Nextbillion Technology Pvt Ltd); Bengaluru
Obopay Inc; Bangalore

IRELAND
Experian plc; Dublin

ISRAEL
Riskified Ltd; Tel Aviv

JAPAN
bitFlyer Inc; Tokyo

KOREA
KakaoPay Corp; Seongnam-si

LITHUANIA
UAB JM Trading (Cryptomate); Vilnius

PHILIPPINES
COL Financial Group Inc; Pasig City

SEYCHELLES
Huobi Global Ltd; Mahe

SINGAPORE
KuCoin (Mek Global Limited); Singapore

SPAIN
Revelock (Buguroo Offensive Security SL); Alcobendas

SWEDEN
Industrial & Financial Systems AB (IFS); Linkoping
Klarna Bank AB; Stockholm
Trustly Group AB; Stockholm

THE NETHERLANDS
Optiver; Amsterdam

THAILAND
Bitkub Online Co Ltd; Bangkok

UNITED KINGDOM
Barclays PLC; London
Checkout.com (Checkout Ltd); London
IHS Markit Ltd; London
Monzo Bank Limited; London
Refinitiv Limited; London
Wise Ltd; London

Individual Profiles
On Each Of
THE FINTECH 235

9F Inc

NAIC Code: 511210Q

ir.9fgroup.com

TYPES OF BUSINESS:
Computer Software: Accounting, Banking & Financial

GROWTH PLANS/SPECIAL FEATURES:
9F Inc is a financial account platform integrating and personalizing financial services in China. It provides a range of financial products and services across loan products, online wealth management products, and payment facilitation. The company generates the majority of the revenue from Loan facilitation services. All of its revenues are generated from the People's Republic of China.

BRANDS/DIVISIONS/AFFILIATES:

CONTACTS: *Note: Officers with more than one job title may be intentionally listed here more than once.*
Lei Liu, CEO
Li Zhang, CFO
Lei Sun, Chmn.

FINANCIAL DATA: *Note: Data for latest year may not have been available at press time.*

In U.S. $	2021	2020	2019	2018	2017	2016
Revenue		196,650,200	692,807,700	869,967,400	1,055,547,000	353,945,800
R&D Expense						
Operating Income		-200,747,400	-369,547,700	345,728,500	144,128,800	62,090,180
Operating Margin %						
SGA Expense		257,850,100	547,858,900	454,592,700	832,518,800	265,548,400
Net Income		-353,670,700	-338,120,500	310,287,100	93,581,340	24,430,560
Operating Cash Flow		-273,148,400	-67,175,040	367,291,700	448,659,700	64,814,780
Capital Expenditure			8,875,841	7,605,292	7,467,042	3,144,825
EBITDA		-196,955,800	-363,681,200	348,666,200	145,990,100	63,555,970
Return on Assets %						
Return on Equity %						
Debt to Equity						

CONTACT INFORMATION:
Phone: 86 1085276996   Fax:
Toll-Free:
Address: 5 W. Laiguangying Rd., Beijing, 100012 China

STOCK TICKER/OTHER:
Stock Ticker: JFU   Exchange: NAS
Employees: Fiscal Year Ends: 12/31
Parent Company:

SALARIES/BONUSES:
Top Exec. Salary: $ Bonus: $
Second Exec. Salary: $ Bonus: $

OTHER THOUGHTS:
Estimated Female Officers or Directors:
Hot Spot for Advancement for Women/Minorities:

Sales, profits and employees may be estimates. Financial information, benefits and other data can change quickly and may vary from those stated here.

ABD Insurance and Financial Services Inc (Newfront)

www.newfront.com
NAIC Code: 524210

TYPES OF BUSINESS:
Business Insurance Brokerage
Insurance Brokerage Solutions
Insurance Software
Insurance Services
Business Insurance
Business Retirement Solutions
Employee Benefits
Private Client Insurance

BRANDS/DIVISIONS/AFFILIATES:

CONTACTS: Note: Officers with more than one job title may be intentionally listed here more than once.
Spike Lipkin, CEO
Brian Hetherington, Pres.
Alex Ip, CFO
Aaron Forth, Chief Product Officer
Amy Steadman, Chief People Officer
Mike Brown, COO
Kurt de Grosz, Chmn.

GROWTH PLANS/SPECIAL FEATURES:

ABD Insurance and Financial Services, Inc. is an insurance brokerage that offers products and services under the Newfront brand name. The company serves more than 10,000 clients across 20+ industry and service groups. Newfront leverages technology to simplify the insurance-buying process for clients and the selling process for brokers. The Newfront insurance platform delivers risk management, employee experience, insurance and retirement solutions. Data is transparent, seamless and delivered in real-time. Areas of industry expertise include agriculture, aviation, blockchain/cryptocurrency, cannabis, construction, digital health/telemedicine, entertainment, fintech, food and beverage, life science, maritime, non-profit, private equity and venture capital, public sector, real estate, schools/school districts, sharing economy and technology. Newfront partners with businesses to provide employee benefits, financial management, retirement services and employee experience solutions and services, including online tools, projection analysis data, long-term cost containment strategies, summary reports and more. Newfront provides comprehensive solutions for private clients. Headquartered in San Francisco, California, Newfront has additional U.S. offices in Illinois, New York and Washington, but serves clients domestically and globally.

FINANCIAL DATA: Note: Data for latest year may not have been available at press time.

In U.S. $	2021	2020	2019	2018	2017	2016
Revenue						
R&D Expense						
Operating Income						
Operating Margin %						
SGA Expense						
Net Income						
Operating Cash Flow						
Capital Expenditure						
EBITDA						
Return on Assets %						
Return on Equity %						
Debt to Equity						

CONTACT INFORMATION:
Phone: 415 754-3635   Fax:
Toll-Free:
Address: 450 Sansome St., Ste. 300, San Francisco, CA 94111 United States

STOCK TICKER/OTHER:
Stock Ticker: Private   Exchange:
Employees: 750   Fiscal Year Ends:
Parent Company:

SALARIES/BONUSES:
Top Exec. Salary: $ Bonus: $
Second Exec. Salary: $ Bonus: $

OTHER THOUGHTS:
Estimated Female Officers or Directors:
Hot Spot for Advancement for Women/Minorities:

Sales, profits and employees may be estimates. Financial information, benefits and other data can change quickly and may vary from those stated here.

Accelitas Inc

NAIC Code: 511210Q

www.accelitas.com

TYPES OF BUSINESS:
Computer Software: Accounting, Banking & Financial
Identity Intelligence Services
Financial Technology Solutions
Data Intelligence and Prediction
Bank Account Validation
Predictive Financial Scoring
Credit Analytic Solutions
Lending

BRANDS/DIVISIONS/AFFILIATES:
Ai Validate
Ai Lift
Ai Extract
Ai Life Save

CONTACTS: *Note: Officers with more than one job title may be intentionally listed here more than once.*
Greg Cote, CEO
Mark Smith, COO
Monika Salquist, Dir.-Finance
Scott Mullins, Sr. VP-Mktg.
James Cook, Sr. Dir.-Product Mgmt..
Steve Krawczyk, CTO
Jimmy Williams, Sr. VP-Sales

GROWTH PLANS/SPECIAL FEATURES:
Accelitas, Inc. develops and delivers financial technology products and solutions that serve both financial services companies and customers, providing loans for those unable to obtain one through traditional approaches. With expertise in identity intelligence, predictive analytics, alternative data and payment reconciliation, Accelitas removes the barriers to financial access. The company's data, analytics, artificial intelligence (AI) and machine learning techniques identify predictive signals that other services miss, and they identify performance indicators that improve outcomes for businesses. Products by Accelitas include: Ai Validate, offering real-time bank account validation; Ai Lift, offering customizable predictive scoring tools for seeing and accepting credit-worthy borrowers; Ai Extract reads government-issued identifications such as driver's licenses and passports, extracts barcodes and text data, and uses extracted data to automatically fill account applications; and Ai Life Save applies AI techniques to analyze rejected financial applications for overlooked indications of creditworthiness, enabling companies to approve profitable applicants that would have otherwise been rejected.

FINANCIAL DATA: *Note: Data for latest year may not have been available at press time.*

In U.S. $	2021	2020	2019	2018	2017	2016
Revenue						
R&D Expense						
Operating Income						
Operating Margin %						
SGA Expense						
Net Income						
Operating Cash Flow						
Capital Expenditure						
EBITDA						
Return on Assets %						
Return on Equity %						
Debt to Equity						

CONTACT INFORMATION:
Phone: 415 842-7700   Fax: 415 532-1994
Toll-Free:
Address: 201 1st St., Ste. 300, Petaluma, CA 94952 United States

STOCK TICKER/OTHER:
Stock Ticker: Private   Exchange:
Employees: 35   Fiscal Year Ends:
Parent Company:

SALARIES/BONUSES:
Top Exec. Salary: $ Bonus: $
Second Exec. Salary: $ Bonus: $

OTHER THOUGHTS:
Estimated Female Officers or Directors:
Hot Spot for Advancement for Women/Minorities:

Sales, profits and employees may be estimates. Financial information, benefits and other data can change quickly and may vary from those stated here.

ACHQ Inc

achq.com

NAIC Code: 522320

TYPES OF BUSINESS:

Financial Transactions Processing, Reserve, and Clearinghouse Activities
Electronic Payment ACH Processing
Payment Technology
Account Verification
Payment Gateway Solutions
Payment Portal Customization

BRANDS/DIVISIONS/AFFILIATES:

CONTACTS: *Note: Officers with more than one job title may be intentionally listed here more than once.*

Chad Willard, CEO

GROWTH PLANS/SPECIAL FEATURES:

ACHQ, Inc. has developed and delivers an electronic payment automated clearing house (ACH) processing solution, serving more than 5,000 business customers across all 50 U.S. states. The company's payment technology enables a swift and easy way to take one-off and recurring eCheck and ACH payments. Solutions span ACH processing, account verification, remotely-created checks, credit cards, recurring payments and payment gateway. ACHQ's payment solutions can improve cashflow, lower transaction fees, save time and process more types of payments, and is secure and cloud-based, enabling access to free 24/7 online reporting in multiple file formats. The firm's technology tools allow businesses to manage payments, reduce workloads and increase profitability. ACHQ's payment portal is primarily designed for executives and teams of small- to medium-sized businesses who can create recurring invoices, match transaction activity to bank deposits, offer live notifications, automatically bill customers at ongoing intervals, host payment pages, detect fraud and more. ACHQ's integrated payment services are customizable. Prices range from $29 per month to more than $99 per month. Headquartered in Florida, ACHQ has an additional office located in Colorado.

FINANCIAL DATA: *Note: Data for latest year may not have been available at press time.*

In U.S. $	2021	2020	2019	2018	2017	2016
Revenue						
R&D Expense						
Operating Income						
Operating Margin %						
SGA Expense						
Net Income						
Operating Cash Flow						
Capital Expenditure						
EBITDA						
Return on Assets %						
Return on Equity %						
Debt to Equity						

CONTACT INFORMATION:

Phone: Fax:
Toll-Free: 877 743-1551
Address: 1990 Main St., Ste. 750, Sarasota, FL 34236 United States

SALARIES/BONUSES:

Top Exec. Salary: $ Bonus: $
Second Exec. Salary: $ Bonus: $

STOCK TICKER/OTHER:

Stock Ticker: Private   Exchange:
Employees: Fiscal Year Ends:
Parent Company:

OTHER THOUGHTS:

Estimated Female Officers or Directors:
Hot Spot for Advancement for Women/Minorities:

ACHWorks

ww3.achworks.com

NAIC Code: 522320

TYPES OF BUSINESS:

Financial Transactions Processing, Reserve, and Clearinghouse Activities
Payments Technology Platform
Commercial Transaction Processing
ACH Payment Processing
Credit Card Transaction
Payment Tracking
ACH File Verification
Bank Account Verification

BRANDS/DIVISIONS/AFFILIATES:

VeriCheck Inc
ACHWorks Virtual Terminal
ACHWorks Checkout
ACHFileChex

CONTACTS: *Note: Officers with more than one job title may be intentionally listed here more than once.*

Ryan McCurry, Pres.
Greg Bahry, Mngr.-Oper.
Lisa Pezzi-Forres, Mngr.-Accounting & Human Resources
Dave Kirk, Mngr. - Sales

GROWTH PLANS/SPECIAL FEATURES:

ACHWorks is a bank-sponsored provider of payment technology for the facilitation of processing commercial transactions via the Automated Clearing House (ACH) network. The company is sponsored by Commercial Bank of California and owned and powered by VeriCheck, Inc. ACHWorks' proprietary systems and software provide businesses secure access to the ACH network via interface or by integrating to existing accounting platforms. The firm's systems facilitate a full menu of ACH payments applicable to a number of business environments. ACHWorks was primarily designed to serve small- to medium-sized businesses. Products of the firm include: ACHWorks Virtual Terminal, for creating, tracking and reporting on ACH and credit card transactions through the firm's secure portal; ACHWorks Checkout, a payment system that allows customers to send businesses a payment through their website; and ACHFileChex, which automatically verifies ACH files and reporting errors. Other products include real-time bank account verification, and a variety of integration solutions for organizations of all sizes and technical capabilities.

FINANCIAL DATA: *Note: Data for latest year may not have been available at press time.*

In U.S. $	2021	2020	2019	2018	2017	2016
Revenue						
R&D Expense						
Operating Income						
Operating Margin %						
SGA Expense						
Net Income						
Operating Cash Flow						
Capital Expenditure						
EBITDA						
Return on Assets %						
Return on Equity %						
Debt to Equity						

CONTACT INFORMATION:

Phone: 916 638-8811   Fax: 888 400-1658
Toll-Free: 866 463-2439
Address: 4022 Sunrise Blvd., Ste. 120-360, Rancho Cordova, CA 95742 United States

STOCK TICKER/OTHER:

Stock Ticker: Subsidiary   Exchange:
Employees: Fiscal Year Ends:
Parent Company: VeriCheck Inc (VCI)

SALARIES/BONUSES:

Top Exec. Salary: $ Bonus: $
Second Exec. Salary: $ Bonus: $

OTHER THOUGHTS:

Estimated Female Officers or Directors:
Hot Spot for Advancement for Women/Minorities:

Sales, profits and employees may be estimates. Financial information, benefits and other data can change quickly and may vary from those stated here.

ACI Worldwide Inc

NAIC Code: 511210Q

www.aciworldwide.com

TYPES OF BUSINESS:
Computer Software-Electronic Funds Transfer
Information Management Solutions
Electronic Banking & Smart Card Solutions
International Payments & Message Processing Software

BRANDS/DIVISIONS/AFFILIATES:
Universal Payments (UP)
Speedpay

GROWTH PLANS/SPECIAL FEATURES:
ACI Worldwide Inc develops, markets, and installs a portfolio of software products primarily focused on facilitating electronic payments. The firm also leverages its distribution network in the Americas; Europe, the Middle East, and Africa, or EMEA; and Asia-Pacific regions to sell software developed by third parties. ACI software products process payment transactions for retail banking clients, billers such as utilities and healthcare providers, and community banks and credit unions. ACI's customers are financial institutions all over the world, but most of the revenue is generated in the United States and EMEA regions.

CONTACTS: *Note: Officers with more than one job title may be intentionally listed here more than once.*
Odilon Almeida, CEO
Scott Behrens, CFO
Dennis Byrnes, Chief Legal Officer
Carolyn Homberger, Chief Risk Officer
Jeremy Wilmot, Executive VP
Michael Braatz, Executive VP
Raj Vaidyanathan, Other Corporate Officer
Evanthia Aretakis, Other Executive Officer

FINANCIAL DATA: *Note: Data for latest year may not have been available at press time.*

In U.S. $	2021	2020	2019	2018	2017	2016
Revenue		1,294,322,000	1,258,294,000	1,009,780,000	1,024,191,000	1,005,701,000
R&D Expense		139,293,000	146,573,000	143,630,000	136,921,000	169,900,000
Operating Income		144,744,000	123,756,000	125,911,000	84,640,000	69,667,000
Operating Margin %						
SGA Expense		256,035,000	258,980,000	225,303,000	260,917,000	231,699,000
Net Income		72,660,000	67,062,000	68,921,000	5,135,000	129,535,000
Operating Cash Flow		336,302,000	137,649,000	183,932,000	146,197,000	99,830,000
Capital Expenditure		46,633,000	48,014,000	43,893,000	54,414,000	63,080,000
EBITDA		319,020,000	274,746,000	230,679,000	184,809,000	329,219,000
Return on Assets %						
Return on Equity %						
Debt to Equity						

CONTACT INFORMATION:
Phone: 239-403-4600   Fax:
Toll-Free:
Address: 3520 Kraft Rd., Ste. 3000, Naples, FL 34105 United States

STOCK TICKER/OTHER:
Stock Ticker: ACIW
Employees: 3,768
Parent Company:

Exchange: NAS
Fiscal Year Ends: 12/31

SALARIES/BONUSES:
Top Exec. Salary: $547,355   Bonus: $
Second Exec. Salary: $450,000   Bonus: $

OTHER THOUGHTS:
Estimated Female Officers or Directors: 1
Hot Spot for Advancement for Women/Minorities:

Sales, profits and employees may be estimates. Financial information, benefits and other data can change quickly and may vary from those stated here.

Acorns Grow Inc

www.acorns.com

NAIC Code: 523920

TYPES OF BUSINESS:
Portfolio Management
Investment Strategy

BRANDS/DIVISIONS/AFFILIATES:
Round-Ups
Acorns Later
Acorns Early
Acorns Sustainable Portfolios

CONTACTS: *Note: Officers with more than one job title may be intentionally listed here more than once.*
Noah Kerner, CEO
Manning Field, COO
Jasmine Lee, CFO
Roma Vakil, VP-Mktg.
Patricia Gonzales, VP-Human Resources
Hugh Tamassia, CTO

GROWTH PLANS/SPECIAL FEATURES:

Acorns Grow, Inc. has developed an application platform in which users invest their spare change to invest, save and spend more responsibly. Fees range from $3 to $5 per month until the user has $1 million invested. The platform provides easy-to-understand articles and videos from financial experts about growing one's money. Leftover change from everyday purchases is set aside through the app's automatic Round-Ups technology. This small change savings strategy is referred to as micro-investing. Set-up through Acorns Grow usually takes less than five minutes' time, with the capability to automatically add money to the diversified portfolio. A portfolio is a select combination of investments, often stocks or bonds that the user owns. Stocks are shares of ownership in a business; and bonds are a debt investment where an investor loans money to a business or government for a defined period of time and interest rate. Portfolios are created by entering present financial situation and future goals, with Acorns Grow recommending a mix of exchange-traded funds (ETFs) that become a portfolio. Portfolios range from conservative to aggressive. Every Acorns Grow portfolio is structured with ETFs from well-known investment management companies. Investments can be made automatically, whether daily, weekly or monthly, every purchase can become an investment. All data is protected by bank-level security and 256-bit encryption. For retirement goals, Acorns Later offers an individual retirement account (IRA) specifically-designed for the customers. The IRAs are updated regularly to match goals. Support is offered via telephone or email. The firm also offers Acorns Early investment accounts for kids and Acorns Sustainable Portfolios that focus on environmental, social and corporate governance (ESG) investments.

FINANCIAL DATA: *Note: Data for latest year may not have been available at press time.*

In U.S. $	2021	2020	2019	2018	2017	2016
Revenue	126,000,000	71,000,000	44,000,000			
R&D Expense						
Operating Income						
Operating Margin %						
SGA Expense						
Net Income	-85,000,000	-65,000,000				
Operating Cash Flow						
Capital Expenditure						
EBITDA						
Return on Assets %						
Return on Equity %						
Debt to Equity						

CONTACT INFORMATION:
Phone: 949-478-5064   Fax:
Toll-Free: 855-739-2859
Address: 19900 Macarthu Blvd., Ste. 400, Irvine, CA 92612-8434 United States

STOCK TICKER/OTHER:
Stock Ticker: Private   Exchange:
Employees: Fiscal Year Ends: 12/31
Parent Company:

SALARIES/BONUSES:
Top Exec. Salary: $ Bonus: $
Second Exec. Salary: $ Bonus: $

OTHER THOUGHTS:
Estimated Female Officers or Directors:
Hot Spot for Advancement for Women/Minorities:

Sales, profits and employees may be estimates. Financial information, benefits and other data can change quickly and may vary from those stated here.

Actum Processing LLC

www.actumprocessing.com

NAIC Code: 522320

TYPES OF BUSINESS:

Financial Transactions Processing, Reserve, and Clearinghouse Activities
ACH Payment Solutions
Identity Verification
Payment Processing Solutions
Payment Dashboards
Data Protection Solutions

BRANDS/DIVISIONS/AFFILIATES:

AuthenteCheck
Accelerated Payouts
Simplify
Peace of Mind

CONTACTS: Note: Officers with more than one job title may be intentionally listed here more than once.

Daniel Parodi, CEO
Vincent Lipari, Pres.

GROWTH PLANS/SPECIAL FEATURES:

Actum Processing, LLC operates as a third-party sender of automated clearing house (ACH) transactions, working directly with the Originating Depository Financial Institution. Actum has offered ACH payment solutions since 2011 and serves a wide range of industries, including lending, schools/camps, non-profits, religious organizations, startups, media/entertainment, marketplaces, medical, cryptocurrency, real estate, fitness, utilities, local governments, supply chain management, collections, law firms, gaming/wagering and payroll. Actum's AuthenteCheck product offers rapid verification across identity verification, account balance and account numbers, in real-time. Accelerated Payouts offers processing options, including same day ACH, late-night processing, weekend and holiday processing, recurring payments scheduling, all of which can be tailored to the business' preferences. Simplify is Actum's real-time dashboard, allowing users to access detailed and consolidated reports, review past and upcoming transactions, manage returns and exposure limits with real-time analytics, and choose between daily or monthly fee assessments. Peace of Mind is the company's privacy and data protection solution for safeguarding data, utilizing TLS 1.2 data encryption, reading tokenized bank account numbers, identifying account verifications and detecting/preventing fraud. ACH processing methods include web-based, batch upload and application programming interface (API) integration. Software companies can integrate with Actum's payment technology to facilitate payments for their customers and streamline operations. Current customers can resell Actum's ACH solution to their own customers, thus expanding their own solution offerings, and improving profitability and retention rate.

FINANCIAL DATA: Note: Data for latest year may not have been available at press time.

In U.S. $	2021	2020	2019	2018	2017	2016
Revenue						
R&D Expense						
Operating Income						
Operating Margin %						
SGA Expense						
Net Income						
Operating Cash Flow						
Capital Expenditure						
EBITDA						
Return on Assets %						
Return on Equity %						
Debt to Equity						

CONTACT INFORMATION:

Phone: 512 402-0082   Fax:
Toll-Free:
Address: 7004 Bee Caves Rd., Bldg. 3, Ste. 312, Austin, TX 78746
United States

STOCK TICKER/OTHER:

Stock Ticker: Private
Employees: 15
Parent Company:

Exchange:
Fiscal Year Ends:

SALARIES/BONUSES:

Top Exec. Salary: $ Bonus: $
Second Exec. Salary: $ Bonus: $

OTHER THOUGHTS:

Estimated Female Officers or Directors:
Hot Spot for Advancement for Women/Minorities:

Sales, profits and employees may be estimates. Financial information, benefits and other data can change quickly and may vary from those stated here.

Addepar Inc

addepar.com

NAIC Code: 511210Q

TYPES OF BUSINESS:
Computer Software: Accounting, Banking & Financial
Wealth Management Solutions
Wealth Management Online Platform
Analytics
Data Aggregation

BRANDS/DIVISIONS/AFFILIATES:
AdvisorPeak

GROWTH PLANS/SPECIAL FEATURES:
Addepar, Inc. offers a technology platform for wealth management purposes. The Addepar platform specializes in data aggregation, analytics and reporting for even the most complex of investment portfolios. Addepar aggregates portfolio, market and client data in a single place, and provides asset owners and advisors a financial picture at every level, enhancing informed investment decision making. Addepar works with hundreds of leading financial advisors, family offices and large financial institutions that manage data for over $3 trillion of assets on the company's platform. Based in California, Addepar has additional offices in Illinois, New York and Utah, as well as in the U.K. In late-2021, Addepar acquired AdvisorPeak, which offers investment professionals enterprise-class portfolio management tools that support portfolio trading and rebalancing.

Addepar offers its employees comprehensive health benefits.

CONTACTS: *Note: Officers with more than one job title may be intentionally listed here more than once.*
Eric Poirier, CEO
David Obrand, Pres.
Eric Daniels, CFO
Peter O'Brien, Head-Global Sales
Don Nilsson, Chief Product Officer
Karen Brooks, CIO
Joe Lonsdale, Chmn.

FINANCIAL DATA: *Note: Data for latest year may not have been available at press time.*

In U.S. $	2021	2020	2019	2018	2017	2016
Revenue						
R&D Expense						
Operating Income						
Operating Margin %						
SGA Expense						
Net Income						
Operating Cash Flow						
Capital Expenditure						
EBITDA						
Return on Assets %						
Return on Equity %						
Debt to Equity						

CONTACT INFORMATION:
Phone: 650 279-8847   Fax:
Toll-Free: 855 464-6268
Address: 303 Bryant St., Mountain View, CA 94041 United States

STOCK TICKER/OTHER:
Stock Ticker: Private   Exchange:
Employees: 500   Fiscal Year Ends:
Parent Company:

SALARIES/BONUSES:
Top Exec. Salary: $ Bonus: $
Second Exec. Salary: $ Bonus: $

OTHER THOUGHTS:
Estimated Female Officers or Directors:
Hot Spot for Advancement for Women/Minorities:

Sales, profits and employees may be estimates. Financial information, benefits and other data can change quickly and may vary from those stated here.

Plunkett Research, Ltd.

Aeropay (Aero Payments Inc)

www.aeropay.com

NAIC Code: 522320

TYPES OF BUSINESS:

Financial Transactions Processing, Reserve, and Clearinghouse Activities
ACH Transfers
Financial Technology
Digital Payment Solution
Business Payment Solutions
Software Development Kit
Ecommerce

BRANDS/DIVISIONS/AFFILIATES:

CONTACTS: *Note: Officers with more than one job title may be intentionally listed here more than once.*

Dan Muller, CEO
Jerry Cole, CFO
Analisa Thompson, CMO
P.J. Caraher, CTO

GROWTH PLANS/SPECIAL FEATURES:

Aero Payments, Inc. is a financial technology company that has developed the Aeropay platform for moving money via bank-to-bank Automated Clearing House (ACH) transfers. Aeropay enables businesses to accept compliant, cashless and contactless payments, and is equipped with technology focused on compliance. Consumers link their bank information with the Aeropay platform, which connects to over 2,000 banks, and Aeropay transfers funds from the bank to the entity being paid. Consumers are not charged a fee. Businesses with an Aeropay account allow consumers to pay them digitally, and the business can also use the platform to make their own purchases as well. Businesses do pay a fee for transactions. For business developers, the company offers an easy-to-implement software development kit (SDK), an extensive application programming interface (API) library for customizable integrations, and connections with many point-of-sale and ecommerce platforms.

FINANCIAL DATA: *Note: Data for latest year may not have been available at press time.*

In U.S. $	2021	2020	2019	2018	2017	2016
Revenue						
R&D Expense						
Operating Income						
Operating Margin %						
SGA Expense						
Net Income						
Operating Cash Flow						
Capital Expenditure						
EBITDA						
Return on Assets %						
Return on Equity %						
Debt to Equity						

CONTACT INFORMATION:

Phone: 773 739-9061   Fax:
Toll-Free:
Address: 4619 N Ravenswood, Ste. 202, Chicago, IL 60640 United States

STOCK TICKER/OTHER:

Stock Ticker: Private   Exchange:
Employees: Fiscal Year Ends:
Parent Company:

SALARIES/BONUSES:

Top Exec. Salary: $ Bonus: $
Second Exec. Salary: $ Bonus: $

OTHER THOUGHTS:

Estimated Female Officers or Directors:
Hot Spot for Advancement for Women/Minorities:

Sales, profits and employees may be estimates. Financial information, benefits and other data can change quickly and may vary from those stated here.

AffiniPay LLC

www.affinipay.com

NAIC Code: 522320

TYPES OF BUSINESS:

Financial Transactions Processing, Reserve, and Clearinghouse Activities
Industry Specific Payment Processing
Financial Technology
Digital Payments
Payment Compliance
Application Programming Interface Solutions
Integration Solutions

BRANDS/DIVISIONS/AFFILIATES:

LawPay
CPA Charge
ClientPay
AffiniPay For Associations
MedPay

CONTACTS: Note: Officers with more than one job title may be intentionally listed here more than once.

Dru Armstrong, CEO
Greg Haney, Exec. VP-Oper.
Christian Fadel, CFO
Greg Kattawar, Exec. VP-Product & Engineering
Erin Brooks, Exec. VP-People Resources
Bryan Thompson, CTO

GROWTH PLANS/SPECIAL FEATURES:

AffiniPay, LLC develops financial technology for completing payment transactions across a range of industries. The company processes more than 17 billion transactions each year, and has a 97% customer satisfaction rate. Products of AffiniPay include: LawPay, a digital way for paying lawyers; CPA Charge, an online payments and reporting solution designed for accountants; ClientPay, a payment solution designed for architecture, engineering, design and construction professionals; AffiniPay For Associations, in which the company partners with associations and non-profit organizations to offer a way to accept member payments; and MedPay, an online payment solution for medical professionals. AffiniPay's solutions allow business customers to accept Visa, MasterCard, Discover, American Express and ACH/eCheck in person and online, and maintain compliance and compatibility per industry field. AffiniPay offers application programming interface (API) documentation and integration solutions for technology developers, to advance their business' platform.

FINANCIAL DATA: Note: Data for latest year may not have been available at press time.

In U.S. $	2021	2020	2019	2018	2017	2016
Revenue	74,760,000	68,580,000	62,400,000	47,000,000	35,600,000	
R&D Expense						
Operating Income						
Operating Margin %						
SGA Expense						
Net Income						
Operating Cash Flow						
Capital Expenditure						
EBITDA						
Return on Assets %						
Return on Equity %						
Debt to Equity						

CONTACT INFORMATION:

Phone: 512 716-8561   Fax:
Toll-Free: 855 656-4684
Address: 3700 N Capital of Texas Hwy, Ste. 300, Austin, TX 78746 United States

STOCK TICKER/OTHER:

Stock Ticker: Private   Exchange:
Employees: 215   Fiscal Year Ends:
Parent Company:

SALARIES/BONUSES:

Top Exec. Salary: $ Bonus: $
Second Exec. Salary: $ Bonus: $

OTHER THOUGHTS:

Estimated Female Officers or Directors:
Hot Spot for Advancement for Women/Minorities:

Sales, profits and employees may be estimates. Financial information, benefits and other data can change quickly and may vary from those stated here.

Plunkett Research, Ltd.

Affirm Holdings Inc

www.affirm.com

NAIC Code: 522291

TYPES OF BUSINESS:
Consumer Lending

BRANDS/DIVISIONS/AFFILIATES:
PayBright
Returnly

GROWTH PLANS/SPECIAL FEATURES:
Affirm Holdings Inc offers a platform for digital and mobile-first commerce. It comprises a point-of-sale payment solution for consumers, merchant commerce solutions, and a consumer-focused app. The firm generates its revenue from merchant networks, and through virtual card networks among others. Geographically, it generates a major share of its revenue from the United States.

Affirm offers its employees comprehensive health benefits, including medical, dental, vision, life and disability insurance.

CONTACTS: Note: Officers with more than one job title may be intentionally listed here more than once.
Max Levchin, CEO
Michael Linford, CFO
Siphelele Jiyane, Chief Accounting Officer
Katherine Adkins, Chief Legal Officer
Libor Michalek, Director
Silvija Martincevic, Other Executive Officer

FINANCIAL DATA: Note: Data for latest year may not have been available at press time.

In U.S. $	2021	2020	2019	2018	2017	2016
Revenue	870,464,000	509,528,000	264,367,000			
R&D Expense						
Operating Income	-326,493,000	-75,474,000	-101,546,000			
Operating Margin %						
SGA Expense	554,530,000	146,274,000	105,765,000			
Net Income	-430,923,000	-112,598,000	-120,455,000			
Operating Cash Flow	-193,130,000	-71,302,000	-87,649,000			
Capital Expenditure	20,252,000	21,019,000	21,250,000			
EBITDA	-306,514,000	-66,030,000	-96,280,000			
Return on Assets %						
Return on Equity %						
Debt to Equity						

CONTACT INFORMATION:
Phone: 415 984-0490   Fax:
Toll-Free: 855 423-3729
Address: 650 California St., San Francisco, CA 94108 United States

STOCK TICKER/OTHER:
Stock Ticker: AFRM
Employees: 1,641
Parent Company:

Exchange: NAS
Fiscal Year Ends: 12/31

SALARIES/BONUSES:
Top Exec. Salary: $410,833   Bonus: $128,941
Second Exec. Salary: $431,667   Bonus: $

OTHER THOUGHTS:
Estimated Female Officers or Directors:
Hot Spot for Advancement for Women/Minorities:

Sales, profits and employees may be estimates. Financial information, benefits and other data can change quickly and may vary from those stated here.

Agile Payments

NAIC Code: 511210Q

www.agilepayments.com

TYPES OF BUSINESS:
Computer Software: Accounting, Banking & Financial
SaaS/PaaS - Integrated Payment Solutions
Payment Software Solutions
Funds Transfer Solutions
Payment Compliance
Billing Statement Creation
Transaction Reports
Payment Website Solutions

BRANDS/DIVISIONS/AFFILIATES:

CONTACTS: *Note: Officers with more than one job title may be intentionally listed here more than once.*
Wayne Akey, CEO

GROWTH PLANS/SPECIAL FEATURES:
Agile Payments offers payment integration solutions for software application partners, facilitating the payment process via software as a service. Agile Payments is a single solution for Automated Clearing House (ACH) and Canadian electronic funds transfers. The firm's payment card industry (PCI) compliant platform provides a gateway for credit card, ACH/EFT, anti-fraud and risk management. Businesses can build a credit card processing solution that encompasses both U.S. and Canadian transactions. Application programming interface (API) integration tools allow developers to schedule recurring transactions and reports. Agile's web-based API enables consumers to view billing statements and make payments. Payment facilitation spans hybrid payments, managed payments, ACH payments, text/SMS payments and payment facilitation as a service. Payment tools by Agile address website solutions, account verification, checking account owner authentication, anti-fraud, virtual terminal, IVR solutions and ACH tokenization, among others.

FINANCIAL DATA: *Note: Data for latest year may not have been available at press time.*

In U.S. $	2021	2020	2019	2018	2017	2016
Revenue						
R&D Expense						
Operating Income						
Operating Margin %						
SGA Expense						
Net Income						
Operating Cash Flow						
Capital Expenditure						
EBITDA						
Return on Assets %						
Return on Equity %						
Debt to Equity						

CONTACT INFORMATION:
Phone: 518 580-0098   Fax:
Toll-Free: 888 729-4968
Address: 15 Ingersoll Rd., Saratoga Springs, NY 12866 United States

STOCK TICKER/OTHER:
Stock Ticker: Private   Exchange:
Employees: Fiscal Year Ends:
Parent Company:

SALARIES/BONUSES:
Top Exec. Salary: $ Bonus: $
Second Exec. Salary: $ Bonus: $

OTHER THOUGHTS:
Estimated Female Officers or Directors:
Hot Spot for Advancement for Women/Minorities:

Sales, profits and employees may be estimates. Financial information, benefits and other data can change quickly and may vary from those stated here.

Plunkett Research, Ltd.

Akoya LLC

akoya.com

NAIC Code: 511210Q

TYPES OF BUSINESS:
Computer Software: Accounting, Banking & Financial

BRANDS/DIVISIONS/AFFILIATES:

GROWTH PLANS/SPECIAL FEATURES:
Akoya, LLC is jointly owned by more than 10 member banks, and operates a secure application programming interface (API)-based network that creates a safe and transparent way for consumers to grant access to their personal financial data to third-party financial apps. The network acts as a bridge between financial institutions and data recipients, such as financial technology data aggregators, and is available to the entire financial services industry. Akoya provides this network-based option for sharing financial data between financial institutions and data recipients in a way that can improve transparency and reduce cybersecurity, privacy and financial risks compared to data-sharing methods that rely on consumer-provided online credentials. Akoya operates separately from its owners. Its API is aligned with the Financial Data Exchange (FDX) standard.

CONTACTS: *Note: Officers with more than one job title may be intentionally listed here more than once.*
Joe Branca, CFO

FINANCIAL DATA: *Note: Data for latest year may not have been available at press time.*

In U.S. $	2021	2020	2019	2018	2017	2016
Revenue						
R&D Expense						
Operating Income						
Operating Margin %						
SGA Expense						
Net Income						
Operating Cash Flow						
Capital Expenditure						
EBITDA						
Return on Assets %						
Return on Equity %						
Debt to Equity						

CONTACT INFORMATION:
Phone: 617-655-4279   Fax:
Toll-Free:
Address: 245 Summer St., V8C, Boston, MA 02210 United States

STOCK TICKER/OTHER:
Stock Ticker: Private   Exchange:
Employees: 65   Fiscal Year Ends:
Parent Company:

SALARIES/BONUSES:
Top Exec. Salary: $ Bonus: $
Second Exec. Salary: $ Bonus: $

OTHER THOUGHTS:
Estimated Female Officers or Directors:
Hot Spot for Advancement for Women/Minorities:

Sales, profits and employees may be estimates. Financial information, benefits and other data can change quickly and may vary from those stated here.

Alacriti Inc

NAIC Code: 522320

www.alacriti.com

TYPES OF BUSINESS:

Financial Transactions Processing, Reserve, and Clearinghouse Activities
Payments Platform
Financial Technology
Cloud-based Platform
Electronic Billing
Electronic Payments
Digital Disbursements
Consulting Services

BRANDS/DIVISIONS/AFFILIATES:

Orbipay

GROWTH PLANS/SPECIAL FEATURES:

Alacriti, Inc. is a financial technology company that designs platforms, software and related tools in regards to digital payments. The firm's cloud-based platform, Orbipay, delivers solutions across the payments strategy, including The Clearing House's real-time payment (RTP) network, electronic billing, electronic payments and digital disbursements. Alacriti also provides technology outsourcing services for clients, including AWS cloud consulting. Other services by Alacriti include bank account validation, chatbot and bank reselling. The company primarily serves the auto finance, banking, healthcare, insurance, mortgage and utility industries.

Alacriti offers its employees comprehensive health benefits, 401(k) and short-/long-term disability insurance.

CONTACTS: *Note: Officers with more than one job title may be intentionally listed here more than once.*

Manish Gurukula, CEO

FINANCIAL DATA: *Note: Data for latest year may not have been available at press time.*

In U.S. $	2021	2020	2019	2018	2017	2016
Revenue						
R&D Expense						
Operating Income						
Operating Margin %						
SGA Expense						
Net Income						
Operating Cash Flow						
Capital Expenditure						
EBITDA						
Return on Assets %						
Return on Equity %						
Debt to Equity						

CONTACT INFORMATION:

Phone: 908 791-2916   Fax: 908 822-8558
Toll-Free:
Address: 1551 South Washington Ave., Ste. 130, Piscataway, NJ 08854 United States

STOCK TICKER/OTHER:

Stock Ticker: Private   Exchange:
Employees: 250   Fiscal Year Ends:
Parent Company:

SALARIES/BONUSES:

Top Exec. Salary: $ Bonus: $
Second Exec. Salary: $ Bonus: $

OTHER THOUGHTS:

Estimated Female Officers or Directors:
Hot Spot for Advancement for Women/Minorities:

Sales, profits and employees may be estimates. Financial information, benefits and other data can change quickly and may vary from those stated here.

Alchemy Insights Inc

www.alchemy.com

NAIC Code: 511210I

TYPES OF BUSINESS:

Computer Software: Operating Systems, Languages & Development Tools
Blockchain Development Platform
Technology Development
Artificial Intelligence
Blockchain API
Developer Tools
App Behavior Alerts
Product Launch and Marketing

BRANDS/DIVISIONS/AFFILIATES:

Alchemy Supernode
Alchemy Build
Alchemy Monitor
Alchemy Notify
Alchemy Amplify
NFT API

CONTACTS: Note: Officers with more than one job title may be intentionally listed here more than once.

Nikil Viswanathan, CEO
Joe Lau, CTO

GROWTH PLANS/SPECIAL FEATURES:

Alchemy Insights, Inc. provides a blockchain development platform that powers millions of users in nearly 200 countries. The platform was designed so that developers could continuously create technology, and is equipped with massively scalable infrastructure, artificial intelligence (AI) and blockchain capabilities. Alchemy Supernode is the company's blockchain application programming interface (API) product for Ethereum, Polygon, Arbitrum, Optimism, Flow and Crypto.org. It comes with the functionality of a node, including JSON-RPC support, but with the data correctness and scalability needed to run world-class applications on the blockchain. Alchemy Build is a no-configuration in-house suite of developer tools to prototype, debug and ship products. It enables users to instantly search through millions of historical requests, view real-time transactions, make JSON-RPC calls directly from the dashboard and scan recent requests and errors. Alchemy Monitor is an all-in-one dashboard that provides automated alerts concerning app performance, user behavior, privacy and more. Alchemy Notify allows developers to send real-time push notifications to users for mined, delayed and dropped transactions, as well as for interest earned, tokens burned and other events. Alchemy Amplify is a launch solution that enables instant visibility to content or products across Amplify partner sites, reaching and connecting with more than 10,000 users. Last, NFT API enables users to instantly find, verify and display any non-fungible token (NFT) across all major blockchains.

FINANCIAL DATA: Note: Data for latest year may not have been available at press time.

In U.S. $	2021	2020	2019	2018	2017	2016
Revenue						
R&D Expense						
Operating Income						
Operating Margin %						
SGA Expense						
Net Income						
Operating Cash Flow						
Capital Expenditure						
EBITDA						
Return on Assets %						
Return on Equity %						
Debt to Equity						

CONTACT INFORMATION:

Phone: 415 320-6550   Fax:
Toll-Free:
Address: 1550 Bryant St., Ste. 750, San Francisco, CA 94103 United States

STOCK TICKER/OTHER:

Stock Ticker: Private   Exchange:
Employees: 65   Fiscal Year Ends:
Parent Company:

SALARIES/BONUSES:

Top Exec. Salary: $ Bonus: $
Second Exec. Salary: $ Bonus: $

OTHER THOUGHTS:

Estimated Female Officers or Directors:
Hot Spot for Advancement for Women/Minorities:

Sales, profits and employees may be estimates. Financial information, benefits and other data can change quickly and may vary from those stated here.

Ally Financial Inc

www.ally.com

NAIC Code: 522220

TYPES OF BUSINESS:
Automobile Financing
Online Banking
Corporate Financial Services
Investment Brokering
Investment Advisory
Loans

BRANDS/DIVISIONS/AFFILIATES:
Ally Bank
Ally Invest Securities LLC
Ally Invest Forex LlC
Ally Invest Advisors Inc
Ally Ventures
Ally Lending
Ally Corporate Finance

GROWTH PLANS/SPECIAL FEATURES:
Ally Financial Inc is a diversified financial services firm that services automotive dealers and their retail customers. The company operates as a financial holding company and a bank holding company. Its banking subsidiary, Ally Bank, caters to the direct banking market through Internet, mobile, and mail. The company reports four business segments including Automotive Finance operations, Insurance operations, Mortgage Finance operations and Corporate Finance operations.

CONTACTS: *Note: Officers with more than one job title may be intentionally listed here more than once.*
Jeffrey Brown, CEO
Jennifer LaClair, CFO
Franklin Hobbs, Chairman of the Board
David Debrunner, Chief Accounting Officer
Jason Schugel, Chief Risk Officer
Scott Stengel, General Counsel
Douglas Timmerman, President, Divisional
Diane Morais, President, Subsidiary

FINANCIAL DATA: *Note: Data for latest year may not have been available at press time.*

In U.S. $	2021	2020	2019	2018	2017	2016
Revenue		6,961,000,000	6,838,000,000	6,343,000,000	6,587,000,000	6,804,000,000
R&D Expense						
Operating Income						
Operating Margin %						
SGA Expense		1,910,000,000	1,723,000,000	1,622,000,000	1,560,000,000	1,446,000,000
Net Income		1,085,000,000	1,715,000,000	1,263,000,000	929,000,000	1,067,000,000
Operating Cash Flow		3,739,000,000	4,050,000,000	4,150,000,000	4,079,000,000	4,567,000,000
Capital Expenditure		4,320,000,000	4,023,000,000	3,709,000,000	4,052,000,000	3,274,000,000
EBITDA						
Return on Assets %						
Return on Equity %						
Debt to Equity						

CONTACT INFORMATION:
Phone: 866-710-4623   Fax: 815-282-6156
Toll-Free: 877-247-2559
Address: 500 Woodward Ave., Fl. 10, Ally Detroit Center, Detroit, MI 48226 United States

STOCK TICKER/OTHER:
Stock Ticker: ALLY   Exchange: NYS
Employees: 10,500   Fiscal Year Ends: 12/31
Parent Company:

SALARIES/BONUSES:
Top Exec. Salary: $1,000,000   Bonus: $3,675,000
Second Exec. Salary: $600,000   Bonus: $1,280,000

OTHER THOUGHTS:
Estimated Female Officers or Directors: 7
Hot Spot for Advancement for Women/Minorities: Y

Sales, profits and employees may be estimates. Financial information, benefits and other data can change quickly and may vary from those stated here.

Plunkett Research, Ltd.

Alphabet Inc (Google)

abc.xyz/investor

NAIC Code: 519130

TYPES OF BUSINESS:

Search Engine-Internet
Paid Search Listing Advertising Services
Online Software and Productivity Tools
Online Video and Photo Services
Travel Booking
Web Analytical Tools
Venture Capital
Online Ad Exchanges

BRANDS/DIVISIONS/AFFILIATES:

Google LLC
Android
YouTube
GooglePlay
Gmail
Google Ad Manager
AdSense
AdMob

GROWTH PLANS/SPECIAL FEATURES:

Alphabet is a holding company, with Google, the Internet media giant, as a wholly owned subsidiary. Google generates 99% of Alphabet revenue, of which more than 85% is from online ads. Google's other revenue is from sales of apps and content on Google Play and YouTube, as well as cloud service fees and other licensing revenue. Sales of hardware such as Chromebooks, the Pixel smartphone, and smart homes products, which include Nest and Google Home, also contribute to other revenue. Alphabet's moonshot investments are in its other bets segment, where it bets on technology to enhance health (Verily), faster Internet access to homes (Google Fiber), self-driving cars (Waymo), and more. Alphabet's operating margin has been 25%-30%, with Google at 30% and other bets operating at a loss.

CONTACTS: *Note: Officers with more than one job title may be intentionally listed here more than once.*

Sundar Pichai, CEO
Ruth Porat, CFO
John Hennessy, Chairman of the Board
Amie OToole, Chief Accounting Officer
Sergey Brin, Co-Founder
Larry Page, Co-Founder
Kent Walker, Other Executive Officer
Philipp Schindler, Other Executive Officer
Prabhakar Raghavan, Senior VP, Subsidiary

FINANCIAL DATA: *Note: Data for latest year may not have been available at press time.*

In U.S. $	2021	2020	2019	2018	2017	2016
Revenue		182,527,000,000	161,857,000,000	136,819,000,000	110,855,000,000	90,272,000,000
R&D Expense		27,573,000,000	26,018,000,000	21,419,000,000	16,625,000,000	13,948,000,000
Operating Income		41,224,000,000	35,928,000,000	31,392,000,000	28,882,000,000	23,716,000,000
Operating Margin %						
SGA Expense		28,998,000,000	28,015,000,000	24,459,000,000	19,765,000,000	17,470,000,000
Net Income		40,269,000,000	34,343,000,000	30,736,000,000	12,662,000,000	19,478,000,000
Operating Cash Flow		65,124,000,000	54,520,000,000	47,971,000,000	37,091,000,000	36,036,000,000
Capital Expenditure		22,281,000,000	23,548,000,000	25,139,000,000	13,184,000,000	10,212,000,000
EBITDA		61,914,000,000	51,506,000,000	44,062,000,000	34,217,000,000	30,418,000,000
Return on Assets %						
Return on Equity %						
Debt to Equity						

CONTACT INFORMATION:

Phone: 650 253-0000   Fax: 650 253-0001
Toll-Free:
Address: 1600 Amphitheatre Pkwy., Mountain View, CA 94043 United States

STOCK TICKER/OTHER:

Stock Ticker: GOOGL   Exchange: NAS
Employees: 135,301   Fiscal Year Ends: 12/31
Parent Company:

SALARIES/BONUSES:

Top Exec. Salary: $2,015,385   Bonus: $
Second Exec. Salary: $655,000   Bonus: $

OTHER THOUGHTS:

Estimated Female Officers or Directors: 3
Hot Spot for Advancement for Women/Minorities: Y

Sales, profits and employees may be estimates. Financial information, benefits and other data can change quickly and may vary from those stated here.

American Express Company

NAIC Code: 522320

www.americanexpress.com

TYPES OF BUSINESS:
Credit Card Processing and Issuing
Travel-Related Services
Lending & Financing
Transaction Services
Bank Holding Company
International Banking Services
Expense Management
Magazine Publishing

BRANDS/DIVISIONS/AFFILIATES:
American Express Travel Related Services Co Inc
American Express Global Business Travel
Kabbage Inc

GROWTH PLANS/SPECIAL FEATURES:
American Express is a global financial institution, operating in about 130 countries, that provides consumers and businesses charge and credit card payment products. The company also operates a highly profitable merchant payment network. Since 2018, the company has operated in three segments: global consumer services, global commercial services, and global merchant and network services. In addition to payment products, the company's commercial business offers expense management tools, consulting services, and business loans.

CONTACTS:
Note: Officers with more than one job title may be intentionally listed here more than once.

Anre Williams, CEO, Subsidiary
Stephen Squeri, CEO
Jeffrey Campbell, CFO
Jessica Quinn, Chief Accounting Officer
Marc Gordon, Chief Information Officer
Laureen Seeger, Chief Legal Officer
Elizabeth Rutledge, Chief Marketing Officer
David Nigro, Chief Risk Officer
Mohammed Badi, Chief Strategy Officer
Monique Herena, Other Executive Officer
Jennifer Skyler, Other Executive Officer
Denise Pickett, President, Divisional

FINANCIAL DATA:
Note: Data for latest year may not have been available at press time.

In U.S. $	2021	2020	2019	2018	2017	2016
Revenue		36,087,000,000	43,556,000,000	40,315,000,000	33,471,000,000	33,337,000,000
R&D Expense						
Operating Income						
Operating Margin %						
SGA Expense		12,465,000,000	13,025,000,000	11,720,000,000	8,475,000,000	8,909,000,000
Net Income		3,135,000,000	6,759,000,000	6,921,000,000	2,736,000,000	5,408,000,000
Operating Cash Flow		5,591,000,000	13,632,000,000	8,930,000,000	13,540,000,000	8,224,000,000
Capital Expenditure		1,478,000,000	1,645,000,000	1,310,000,000	1,062,000,000	1,375,000,000
EBITDA						
Return on Assets %						
Return on Equity %						
Debt to Equity						

CONTACT INFORMATION:
Phone: 212 640-2000   Fax: 212 640-2458
Toll-Free: 800-528-4800
Address: 200 Vesey St., New York, NY 10285 United States

STOCK TICKER/OTHER:
Stock Ticker: AXP   Exchange: NYS
Employees: 63,700   Fiscal Year Ends: 12/31
Parent Company:

SALARIES/BONUSES:
Top Exec. Salary: $1,500,000   Bonus: $3,960,000
Second Exec. Salary: $1,083,333   Bonus: $3,600,000

OTHER THOUGHTS:
Estimated Female Officers or Directors: 4
Hot Spot for Advancement for Women/Minorities: Y

Sales, profits and employees may be estimates. Financial information, benefits and other data can change quickly and may vary from those stated here.

Plunkett Research, Ltd.

Anchorage Labs Inc

www.anchorage.com

NAIC Code: 511210Q

TYPES OF BUSINESS:

Computer Software: Accounting, Banking & Financial
Digital Asset Platform-Crypto Custody, Trading , Staking, Governance
Cryptocurrency

BRANDS/DIVISIONS/AFFILIATES:

Anchorage Digital Bank NA
Anchorage Hold LLC
Anchorage Lending CA LLC
Anchorage Custody
Anchorage Trading
Anchorage Staking
Anchorage Governance
Anchorage Financing

CONTACTS: Note: Officers with more than one job title may be intentionally listed here more than once.

Nathan McCauley, CEO
Diogo Monica, Pres.

GROWTH PLANS/SPECIAL FEATURES:

Anchorage Labs, Inc. developed the Anchorage Digital platform, which deals in the holding, investing and infrastructure for cryptocurrency and related products. Anchorage Digital helps institutions participate securely in digital assets. Services include: Anchorage Custody, a digital asset custody that adapts to, interfaces with and evolves alongside the user's fund; Anchorage Trading, which enables crypto trading via application programming interface (API), web-based interface or with the help of Anchorage traders; Anchorage Staking, enables users to hold and delegate digital assets from the Anchorage vault; Anchorage Governance, in which the user determines their on-chain participation instead of relying on community governance mechanisms within other blockchain protocols; and Anchorage Financing, using digital assets as collateral for crypto loans or lines of credit in US dollars, which can be repaid, drawn on and traded with the loan balance from a single, intuitive interface. Custody and settlement services are offered through Anchorage Digital Bank NA; digital asset trading services are provided by Anchorage Hold LLC; lending services are provided by Anchorage Lending CA, LCC. These entities are wholly owned by Anchorage Labs. Headquartered in California, Anchorage Labs has additional offices in South Dakota, Portugal and Singapore. The firm is a member of the Blockchain Association, the Crypto Rating Council and ADAM.

Anchorage Labs offers its employees comprehensive health benefits, 401(k), FSA account and time-off plans, among other benefits.

FINANCIAL DATA: Note: Data for latest year may not have been available at press time.

In U.S. $	2021	2020	2019	2018	2017	2016
Revenue						
R&D Expense						
Operating Income						
Operating Margin %						
SGA Expense						
Net Income						
Operating Cash Flow						
Capital Expenditure						
EBITDA						
Return on Assets %						
Return on Equity %						
Debt to Equity						

CONTACT INFORMATION:

Phone: 415 610-0179   Fax:
Toll-Free:
Address: 221 Pine St., Fl. 6, San Francisco, CA 94104 United States

STOCK TICKER/OTHER:

Stock Ticker: Private
Employees:
Parent Company:

Exchange:
Fiscal Year Ends:

SALARIES/BONUSES:

Top Exec. Salary: $ Bonus: $
Second Exec. Salary: $ Bonus: $

OTHER THOUGHTS:

Estimated Female Officers or Directors:
Hot Spot for Advancement for Women/Minorities:

Sales, profits and employees may be estimates. Financial information, benefits and other data can change quickly and may vary from those stated here.

Apple Inc

NAIC Code: 334220

www.apple.com

TYPES OF BUSINESS:
Electronics Design and Manufacturing
Software
Computers and Tablets
Retail Stores
Smartphones
Online Music Store
Apps Store
Home Entertainment Software & Systems

BRANDS/DIVISIONS/AFFILIATES:
iPhone
iPad
Apple Watch
Apple TV
iOS
watchOS
HomePod
AirPods

CONTACTS: *Note: Officers with more than one job title may be intentionally listed here more than once.*
Timothy Cook, CEO
Luca Maestri, CFO
Arthur Levinson, Chairman of the Board
Chris Kondo, Chief Accounting Officer
Jeffery Williams, COO
Katherine Adams, General Counsel
Deirdre OBrien, Senior VP, Divisional

GROWTH PLANS/SPECIAL FEATURES:
Apple designs a wide variety of consumer electronic devices, including smartphones (iPhone), tablets (iPad), PCs (Mac), smartwatches (Apple Watch), AirPods, and TV boxes (Apple TV), among others. The iPhone makes up the majority of Apple's total revenue. In addition, Apple offers its customers a variety of services such as Apple Music, iCloud, Apple Care, Apple TV+, Apple Arcade, Apple Card, and Apple Pay, among others. Apple's products run internally developed software and semiconductors, and the firm is well known for its integration of hardware, software and services. Apple's products are distributed online as well as through company-owned stores and third-party retailers. The company generates roughly 40% of its revenue from the Americas, with the remainder earned internationally.

Apple offers employees comprehensive health benefits, retirement plans and various employee assistance programs.

FINANCIAL DATA: *Note: Data for latest year may not have been available at press time.*

In U.S. $	2021	2020	2019	2018	2017	2016
Revenue	365,817,000,000	274,515,000,000	260,174,000,000	265,595,000,000	229,234,000,000	215,639,000,000
R&D Expense	21,914,000,000	18,752,000,000	16,217,000,000	14,236,000,000	11,581,000,000	10,045,000,000
Operating Income	108,949,000,000	66,288,000,000	63,930,000,000	70,898,000,000	61,344,000,000	60,024,000,000
Operating Margin %						
SGA Expense	21,973,000,000	19,916,000,000	18,245,000,000	16,705,000,000	15,261,000,000	14,194,000,000
Net Income	94,680,000,000	57,411,000,000	55,256,000,000	59,531,000,000	48,351,000,000	45,687,000,000
Operating Cash Flow	104,038,000,000	80,674,000,000	69,391,000,000	77,434,000,000	63,598,000,000	65,824,000,000
Capital Expenditure	11,085,000,000	7,309,000,000	10,495,000,000	13,313,000,000	12,795,000,000	13,548,000,000
EBITDA	123,136,000,000	81,020,000,000	81,860,000,000	87,046,000,000	76,569,000,000	73,333,000,000
Return on Assets %						
Return on Equity %						
Debt to Equity						

CONTACT INFORMATION:
Phone: 408 996-1010   Fax: 408 974-2483
Toll-Free: 800-692-7753
Address: One Apple Park Way, Cupertino, CA 95014 United States

STOCK TICKER/OTHER:
Stock Ticker: AAPL   Exchange: NAS
Employees: 147,000   Fiscal Year Ends: 09/30
Parent Company:

SALARIES/BONUSES:
Top Exec. Salary: $3,000,000   Bonus: $
Second Exec. Salary: $1,000,000   Bonus: $

OTHER THOUGHTS:
Estimated Female Officers or Directors:
Hot Spot for Advancement for Women/Minorities:

Sales, profits and employees may be estimates. Financial information, benefits and other data can change quickly and may vary from those stated here.

AppTech Payments Corp

apptechcorp.com

NAIC Code: 511210Q

TYPES OF BUSINESS:
Computer Software: Accounting, Banking & Financial

BRANDS/DIVISIONS/AFFILIATES:

GROWTH PLANS/SPECIAL FEATURES:
AppTech Corp is a FinTech company providing electronic payment processing technologies and merchant services. This includes credit card processing, Automated Clearing House (ACH) processing, gift and loyalty cards and e-commerce. Its core services include global Short Messaging Service (SMS) patented text messaging and secure mobile payments based on multi-factor authentication technologies. Other services include digital marketing, lead generation, mobile app development and intellectual property rights development.

CONTACTS: Note: Officers with more than one job title may be intentionally listed here more than once.
Luke DAngleo, CEO
Gary Wachs, CFO
Bobby Bedi, President

FINANCIAL DATA: Note: Data for latest year may not have been available at press time.

In U.S. $	2021	2020	2019	2018	2017	2016
Revenue		329,500	256,138	291,285	255,103	282,040
R&D Expense						
Operating Income						
Operating Margin %						
SGA Expense						
Net Income		-4,187,317	-1,343,210	-2,128,868	-1,549,500	-2,172,815
Operating Cash Flow						
Capital Expenditure						
EBITDA						
Return on Assets %						
Return on Equity %						
Debt to Equity						

CONTACT INFORMATION:
Phone: 760 707-5955   Fax:
Toll-Free:
Address: 5876 Owens Ave., Ste. 100, Carlsbad, CA 92008 United States

STOCK TICKER/OTHER:
Stock Ticker: APCX
Employees: 18
Parent Company:

Exchange: NAS
Fiscal Year Ends: 12/31

SALARIES/BONUSES:
Top Exec. Salary: $ Bonus: $
Second Exec. Salary: $ Bonus: $

OTHER THOUGHTS:
Estimated Female Officers or Directors:
Hot Spot for Advancement for Women/Minorities:

Sales, profits and employees may be estimates. Financial information, benefits and other data can change quickly and may vary from those stated here.

Arcus Financial Intelligence Inc

www.arcusfi.com

NAIC Code: 522320

TYPES OF BUSINESS:

Financial Transactions Processing, Reserve, and Clearinghouse Activities
Payments as a Service - Digital Wallets/Online Payments
Technology Innovation
Bill Pay Solutions
Payment Checkout Solutions
Gift Card Solutions
Application Programming Interface (API) Solutions
Billing Statements

BRANDS/DIVISIONS/AFFILIATES:

Mastercard Incorporated

CONTACTS: *Note: Officers with more than one job title may be intentionally listed here more than once.*

Inigo Rumayor, Co-CEO
Lucia Lopez, Dir.-Finance
Ana Sofia Lara, Mngr.-Mktg. & Communications
Betty Eguiarte, Dir.-People
Omar Vargas, Sr. VP-Engineering

GROWTH PLANS/SPECIAL FEATURES:

Arcus Financial Intelligence, Inc. is a business-to-business company that offers payment solutions across the many applications used by people every day. Arcus' payment network comprises all the major banks, fintech billers and retailers, which saves clients time and cost in building those connections themselves. The Arcus pay network offers bill pay, cash-in, cash-out, top-ups, gift cards and checkout. Payments can be sent and received in real-time. The firm's payments-as-a-service platform offers payments solutions via application programming interfaces (APIs), allowing clients to offer their users a wide range of payment functionalities. Financial data solutions are also offered by Arcus, including bill presentment and liabilities data. As an innovator of technology, Arcus has generated an information security culture as part of its daily activities through the adoption of international standard certifications such as PCI DSS Level 1 and SOC 1 Type 2. Arcus operates in six countries across the Americas, including the U.S., Mexico, the Dominican Republic, Colombia, Peru and Chile. The firm is part of Mastercard Incorporated.

Arcus offers its employees medical insurance, professional development opportunities and a variety of company perks.

FINANCIAL DATA: *Note: Data for latest year may not have been available at press time.*

In U.S. $	2021	2020	2019	2018	2017	2016
Revenue						
R&D Expense						
Operating Income						
Operating Margin %						
SGA Expense						
Net Income						
Operating Cash Flow						
Capital Expenditure						
EBITDA						
Return on Assets %						
Return on Equity %						
Debt to Equity						

CONTACT INFORMATION:

Phone: 212 904-1849   Fax:
Toll-Free:
Address: 214 W 29th St., Ste. 1007, New York, NY 10001 United States

STOCK TICKER/OTHER:

Stock Ticker: Subsidiary   Exchange:
Employees: 100   Fiscal Year Ends: 12/31
Parent Company: MasterCard Inc

SALARIES/BONUSES:

Top Exec. Salary: $ Bonus: $
Second Exec. Salary: $ Bonus: $

OTHER THOUGHTS:

Estimated Female Officers or Directors:
Hot Spot for Advancement for Women/Minorities:

Sales, profits and employees may be estimates. Financial information, benefits and other data can change quickly and may vary from those stated here.

Aspiration Partners Inc

www.aspiration.com

NAIC Code: 522110

TYPES OF BUSINESS:
Retail Banking and Investing Services

BRANDS/DIVISIONS/AFFILIATES:
Aspiration Zero
Cargon Insights
InterPrivate III Financial Partners Inc

GROWTH PLANS/SPECIAL FEATURES:
Aspiration Partners, Inc. is a global Sustainability as a Service (SaaS) provider for consumers and enterprises, offering a variety of financial services. These services include cash management and savings accounts, managed investment portfolios and IRAs. It also offers the Aspiration Zero credit card, which pays awards for purchases in the form of cash back or in tree planting initiatives. Aspiration Partners focuses on rewarding its 6 million customers with cash back for purchases made from companies that promote social and environmental change. In January 2022, the company acquired Carbon Insights, a technology firm specializing in carbon measurement and scoring. As of mid-2022, Aspiration was in the process of merging with InterPrivate III Financial Partners, Inc., a publicly traded special purpose acquisition company. Upon completion of the merger, Aspiration Partners will become a publicly listed company called Aspiration, Inc.

CONTACTS: Note: Officers with more than one job title may be intentionally listed here more than once.
Andrei Cherny, CEO

FINANCIAL DATA: Note: Data for latest year may not have been available at press time.

In U.S. $	2021	2020	2019	2018	2017	2016
Revenue	95,000,000	14,714,000				
R&D Expense						
Operating Income						
Operating Margin %						
SGA Expense						
Net Income		-66,000,000				
Operating Cash Flow						
Capital Expenditure						
EBITDA						
Return on Assets %						
Return on Equity %						
Debt to Equity						

CONTACT INFORMATION:
Phone: Fax:
Toll-Free: 800-683-8529
Address: 4640 Admiralty Way, Ste. 725, Marina Del Rey, CA 90292 United States

STOCK TICKER/OTHER:
Stock Ticker: Private
Employees:
Parent Company:

Exchange:
Fiscal Year Ends: 12/31

SALARIES/BONUSES:
Top Exec. Salary: $ Bonus: $
Second Exec. Salary: $ Bonus: $

OTHER THOUGHTS:
Estimated Female Officers or Directors:
Hot Spot for Advancement for Women/Minorities:

Sales, profits and employees may be estimates. Financial information, benefits and other data can change quickly and may vary from those stated here.

authID.ai (Ipsidy Inc)

NAIC Code: 511210Q

www.ipsidy.com

TYPES OF BUSINESS:
Computer Software: Accounting, Banking & Financial

BRANDS/DIVISIONS/AFFILIATES:

GROWTH PLANS/SPECIAL FEATURES:
Ipsidy Inc is a provider of an Identity as a Service (IDaaS) platform that delivers a suite of secure, mobile, biometric identity solutions. The company provides secure, biometric, identity verification and electronic transaction authentication services. The firm has developed an IDaaS platform for businesses, residences, governments, or other organizations. Geographically, it has operational footprints in North America, South America, and Africa. The firm's products and services operate in two reportable segments: identity management and payment processing. It generates a majority of its revenue from the Identity Management segment.

CONTACTS: *Note: Officers with more than one job title may be intentionally listed here more than once.*
Thomas Thimot, CEO
Stuart Stoller, CFO
Phillip Kumnick, Chairman of the Board
Cecil Smith, Chief Technology Officer
Thomas Szoke, Other Executive Officer

FINANCIAL DATA: *Note: Data for latest year may not have been available at press time.*

In U.S. $	2021	2020	2019	2018	2017	2016
Revenue		2,140,644	2,552,045	3,828,993	2,303,606	1,929,938
R&D Expense		1,161,416	1,614,054	208,311	222,068	340,317
Operating Income		-7,676,199	-8,413,945	-9,323,219	-12,009,120	-13,567,470
Operating Margin %						
SGA Expense		6,743,258	7,892,046	11,193,350	13,026,190	14,243,360
Net Income		-11,298,560	-10,500,360	-10,027,610	-17,481,630	-9,851,403
Operating Cash Flow		-4,668,461	-6,055,078	-5,950,425	-6,541,160	-3,788,974
Capital Expenditure			27,364	59,091	907,681	42,765
EBITDA		-9,042,297	-9,271,462	-8,745,873	-15,640,560	-5,800,979
Return on Assets %						
Return on Equity %						
Debt to Equity						

CONTACT INFORMATION:
Phone: 516 274-8700   Fax:
Toll-Free:
Address: 670 Long Beach Blvd., Long Beach, NY 11561 United States

STOCK TICKER/OTHER:
Stock Ticker: AUID   Exchange: NAS
Employees: 60   Fiscal Year Ends: 12/31
Parent Company:

SALARIES/BONUSES:
Top Exec. Salary: $275,000   Bonus: $2,857
Second Exec. Salary: $262,315   Bonus: $

OTHER THOUGHTS:
Estimated Female Officers or Directors:
Hot Spot for Advancement for Women/Minorities:

Sales, profits and employees may be estimates. Financial information, benefits and other data can change quickly and may vary from those stated here.

Autoscribe Corporation

www.autoscribe.com

NAIC Code: 522320

TYPES OF BUSINESS:
Financial Transactions Processing, Reserve, and Clearinghouse Activities
Financial Services
Payment Processing
Electronic Payment Processing Solutions
Payment Card Processing
Telephone Payment Processing
Data Verification Solutions
Transaction Processing Solutions

BRANDS/DIVISIONS/AFFILIATES:
PaymentVision
Lyons Commercial Data

GROWTH PLANS/SPECIAL FEATURES:

Autoscribe Corporation is a financial services company and payment processor, processing more than $2 billion transactions annually and servicing thousands of financial institutions and corporate billers throughout the U.S. The firm's PaymentVision brand is a biller-direct, payment card industry (PCI)-certified, electronic payment gateway solution that offers clients the ability to accept Automated Clearing House (ACH) electronic funds, check and credit or debit card payments, by phone, or through internet channels. The Lyons Commercial Data brand provides U.S. financial institution data that includes all current ABA routing numbers and other information in regards to transaction processing. Headquartered in Jacksonville, Florida, Autoscribe has additional offices in Fort Lauderdale, Florida and in Gaithersburg, Maryland.

Autoscribe offers its employees comprehensive health benefits, 401(k), health savings account, life and long-term disability insurance, continuing education reimbursement and other company benefits and perks.

CONTACTS: *Note: Officers with more than one job title may be intentionally listed here more than once.*
Rob Pollin, CEO

FINANCIAL DATA: *Note: Data for latest year may not have been available at press time.*

In U.S. $	2021	2020	2019	2018	2017	2016
Revenue						
R&D Expense						
Operating Income						
Operating Margin %						
SGA Expense						
Net Income						
Operating Cash Flow						
Capital Expenditure						
EBITDA						
Return on Assets %						
Return on Equity %						
Debt to Equity						

CONTACT INFORMATION:
Phone: 301 987-0700   Fax:
Toll-Free: 855 289-2815
Address: 12276 San Jose Blvd., Ste. 624, Jacksonville, FL 32258 United States

STOCK TICKER/OTHER:
Stock Ticker: Private
Employees: 50
Parent Company:

Exchange:
Fiscal Year Ends:

SALARIES/BONUSES:
Top Exec. Salary: $ Bonus: $
Second Exec. Salary: $ Bonus: $

OTHER THOUGHTS:
Estimated Female Officers or Directors:
Hot Spot for Advancement for Women/Minorities:

Sales, profits and employees may be estimates. Financial information, benefits and other data can change quickly and may vary from those stated here.

Avant Inc

NAIC Code: 522291

www.avant.com

TYPES OF BUSINESS:

Personal Loans
Online Lending
Credit Card
Credit Building

BRANDS/DIVISIONS/AFFILIATES:

Avant Credit Card

GROWTH PLANS/SPECIAL FEATURES:

Avant, Inc. is an online lending marketplace. The Chicago-based company partners with WebBank to offer access to personal loans for middle-income borrowers for solving issues such as high-interest debt, home improvement, unexpected expenses, etc. In addition, the Avant Credit Card helps customers pay for what they need while building their credit at the same time. The card comes with a $300 to $1000 credit limit, no hidden fees and benefits such as MasterCard ID theft protection. Since the company's launch in 2012, more than $6.5 billion has been borrowed (as of October 2021). Customer support services are provided through the company's website as well as via email and telephone. Investors of Avant include August Capital, QED Investors, KKR, RRE Ventures, DFJ, TigerGlobal, General Atlantic and Victory Park Capital.

CONTACTS:
Note: Officers with more than one job title may be intentionally listed here more than once.

Matt Bochenek, CEO
Kevin Friedrich, CFO
Paul Zhang, CTO
Al Goldstein, Chmn.

FINANCIAL DATA:
Note: Data for latest year may not have been available at press time.

In U.S. $	2021	2020	2019	2018	2017	2016
Revenue	469,188,720	451,143,000	485,100,000	462,000,000	440,000,000	438,000,000
R&D Expense						
Operating Income						
Operating Margin %						
SGA Expense						
Net Income						
Operating Cash Flow						
Capital Expenditure						
EBITDA						
Return on Assets %						
Return on Equity %						
Debt to Equity						

CONTACT INFORMATION:

Phone: 312 448-8685   Fax: 866-625-0930
Toll-Free: 800-712-5407
Address: 222 N. LaSalle St., Ste. 1600, Chicago, IL 60601 United States

STOCK TICKER/OTHER:

Stock Ticker: Private
Employees: 600
Parent Company:

Exchange:
Fiscal Year Ends: 12/31

SALARIES/BONUSES:

Top Exec. Salary: $ Bonus: $
Second Exec. Salary: $ Bonus: $

OTHER THOUGHTS:

Estimated Female Officers or Directors:
Hot Spot for Advancement for Women/Minorities:

Sales, profits and employees may be estimates. Financial information, benefits and other data can change quickly and may vary from those stated here.

Plunkett Research, Ltd.

Bank of America Corporation

www.bankofamerica.com

NAIC Code: 522110

TYPES OF BUSINESS:

Banking
Asset Management
Investment & Brokerage Services
Mortgages
Credit Cards
Insurance Agency

BRANDS/DIVISIONS/AFFILIATES:

CONTACTS: Note: Officers with more than one job title may be intentionally listed here more than once.

Brian Moynihan, CEO
Ross Jeffries, Other Corporate Officer
Paul Donofrio, CFO
Rudolf Bless, Chief Accounting Officer
Andrea Smith, Chief Administrative Officer
Geoffrey Greener, Chief Risk Officer
Catherine Bessant, Chief Technology Officer
Thomas Montag, Co-COO
David Leitch, General Counsel
Sheri Bronstein, Other Executive Officer
Dean Athanasia, President, Divisional
Kathleen Knox, President, Divisional

GROWTH PLANS/SPECIAL FEATURES:

Bank of America is one of the largest financial institutions in the United States, with more than $2.5 trillion in assets. It is organized into four major segments: consumer banking, global wealth and investment management, global banking, and global markets. Bank of America's consumer-facing lines of business include its network of branches and deposit-gathering operations, home mortgage lending, vehicle lending, credit and debit cards, and small-business services. The company's Merrill Lynch operations provide brokerage and wealth-management services, as does U.S. Trust private bank. Wholesale lines of business include investment banking, corporate and commercial real estate lending, and capital markets operations. Bank of America has operations in several countries.

Bank of America offers its employees benefits including tuition and adoption reimbursement; medical, dental and vision insurance plans; employee assistance programs; and health care and dependent care flexible spending accounts.

FINANCIAL DATA: Note: Data for latest year may not have been available at press time.

In U.S. $	2021	2020	2019	2018	2017	2016
Revenue		85,528,000,000	91,244,000,000	91,247,000,000	87,352,000,000	83,701,000,000
R&D Expense						
Operating Income						
Operating Margin %						
SGA Expense		46,378,000,000	46,715,000,000	45,911,000,000	47,154,000,000	46,408,000,000
Net Income		17,894,000,000	27,430,000,000	28,147,000,000	18,232,000,000	17,906,000,000
Operating Cash Flow		37,993,000,000	61,777,000,000	39,520,000,000	10,403,000,000	18,306,000,000
Capital Expenditure						
EBITDA						
Return on Assets %						
Return on Equity %						
Debt to Equity						

CONTACT INFORMATION:

Phone: 704 386-5681   Fax:
Toll-Free: 800-432-1000
Address: 100 N. Tryon St., Charlotte, NC 28255 United States

STOCK TICKER/OTHER:

Stock Ticker: BAC
Employees: 208,000
Parent Company:

Exchange: NYS
Fiscal Year Ends: 12/31

SALARIES/BONUSES:

Top Exec. Salary: $1,250,000   Bonus: $7,100,000
Second Exec. Salary: $1,000,000   Bonus: $4,400,000

OTHER THOUGHTS:

Estimated Female Officers or Directors: 8
Hot Spot for Advancement for Women/Minorities: Y

Sales, profits and employees may be estimates. Financial information, benefits and other data can change quickly and may vary from those stated here.

Barclays PLC

NAIC Code: 522110

www.barclays.com

TYPES OF BUSINESS:
Banking
Mortgages & Consumer Loans
Asset & Investment Management Services
Credit Cards
Business Finance & Risk Management Services

BRANDS/DIVISIONS/AFFILIATES:
Barclays UK
Barclays International

GROWTH PLANS/SPECIAL FEATURES:
Barclays is a universal bank headquartered in the United Kingdom. It operates via two principal segments; U.K. (38% of profit before tax) and International (62% of PBT). In its U.K. segment, the bank provides current accounts, mortgages, savings and investment management services, credit cards, and business banking services to retail clients and small and medium-size enterprises. The international segment includes a corporate bank offering banking solutions to large corporates, a bulge-bracket global investment bank, and a credit card and payments business. In 2018, Barclays generated roughly 52% of its income from the U.K. and 34% from the United States.

The company offers employees health benefits, an employee assistance program, a share purchase program and discounts on Barclays' products and services.

CONTACTS: *Note: Officers with more than one job title may be intentionally listed here more than once.*
Jes Staley, CEO
Paul Compton, Pres.
Tushar Morzaria, Dir.-Finance
Tristram Roberts, Dir.-Human Resources
Mark Harding, Group General Counsel
Hector Sants, Head-Compliance & Govt Regulatory Rel.
Robert Le Blanc, Chief Risk Officer
Eric Bommensath, Co-Chief Exec.-Corp. & Investment Banking
Thomas King, Co-Chief Exec.-Corp. & Investment Banking
Nigel Higgins, Chmn.

FINANCIAL DATA: *Note: Data for latest year may not have been available at press time.*

In U.S. $	2021	2020	2019	2018	2017	2016
Revenue		28,780,470,000	28,793,790,000	28,137,360,000	28,058,800,000	28,534,150,000
R&D Expense						
Operating Income						
Operating Margin %						
SGA Expense		2,681,650,000	2,761,541,000	2,913,332,000	3,837,396,000	3,338,082,000
Net Income		2,031,876,000	3,276,833,000	1,856,118,000	-2,559,152,000	2,161,032,000
Operating Cash Flow		76,568,180,000	-16,370,850,000	11,323,120,000	80,836,980,000	15,027,360,000
Capital Expenditure		1,762,912,000	2,387,388,000	1,866,770,000	1,938,671,000	2,272,879,000
EBITDA						
Return on Assets %						
Return on Equity %						
Debt to Equity						

CONTACT INFORMATION:
Phone: 44 2071161000   Fax: 44 2071167665
Toll-Free:
Address: 1 Churchill Pl., London, E14 5HP United Kingdom

STOCK TICKER/OTHER:
Stock Ticker: BCS   Exchange: NYS
Employees: 81,600   Fiscal Year Ends: 12/31
Parent Company:

SALARIES/BONUSES:
Top Exec. Salary: $3,129,036   Bonus: $1,122,459
Second Exec. Salary: $2,196,983   Bonus: $762,952

OTHER THOUGHTS:
Estimated Female Officers or Directors: 2
Hot Spot for Advancement for Women/Minorities: Y

Sales, profits and employees may be estimates. Financial information, benefits and other data can change quickly and may vary from those stated here.

Behavox Ltd

www.behavox.com

NAIC Code: 511210E

TYPES OF BUSINESS:

Computer Software: Network Security, Managed Access, Digital ID,
Cybersecurity & Anti-Virus
Compliance Software
Artificial Intelligence
Workplace Analytics
Risk Management

BRANDS/DIVISIONS/AFFILIATES:

GROWTH PLANS/SPECIAL FEATURES:

Behavox Ltd. is a people analytics company that helps organizations transform behavior in the workplace via artificial intelligence (AI). The firm's AI-based software reveals insights to protect reputation and maximize revenue generation by analyzing vast amounts of structured and unstructured data. The platform delivers benefits across the enterprise, including; reducing the costs of compliance, increasing the effectiveness of systems and controls, optimizing the performance of teams, enhancing levels of customer services, and tracking/measuring corporate culture to strengthen teams and companies. Behavox's processes, products and technology continuously incorporate regulatory updates and adapt to identify leading indicators of risk. Behavox is headquartered in New York City, with offices in Abu Dhabi, Dallas, London, Montreal, San Francisco, Seattle, Singapore and Tokyo.

CONTACTS:
Note: Officers with more than one job title may be intentionally listed here more than once.

Erkin Adylov, CEO
Kiryl Trembovolski, COO
Daniel Strathearn, VP-Finance
Neil Wu Becker, CMO
Joseph Benjamin, CTO

FINANCIAL DATA:
Note: Data for latest year may not have been available at press time.

In U.S. $	2021	2020	2019	2018	2017	2016
Revenue						
R&D Expense						
Operating Income						
Operating Margin %						
SGA Expense						
Net Income						
Operating Cash Flow						
Capital Expenditure						
EBITDA						
Return on Assets %						
Return on Equity %						
Debt to Equity						

CONTACT INFORMATION:

Phone: 212-634-9362 Fax:
Toll-Free:
Address: 180 Maiden Ln., New York, NY 10038 United States

SALARIES/BONUSES:

Top Exec. Salary: $ Bonus: $
Second Exec. Salary: $ Bonus: $

STOCK TICKER/OTHER:

Stock Ticker: Private Exchange:
Employees: 207 Fiscal Year Ends:
Parent Company:

OTHER THOUGHTS:

Estimated Female Officers or Directors:
Hot Spot for Advancement for Women/Minorities:

Sales, profits and employees may be estimates. Financial information, benefits and other data can change quickly and may vary from those stated here.

Betterment LLC

www.betterment.com

NAIC Code: 523920

TYPES OF BUSINESS:
Portfolio Management
Investment Management
Financial Advisory

BRANDS/DIVISIONS/AFFILIATES:
Betterment Holdings Inc

CONTACTS: *Note: Officers with more than one job title may be intentionally listed here more than once.*
Sarah Kirshbaum Levy, CEO

GROWTH PLANS/SPECIAL FEATURES:

Betterment, LLC offers online financial advisory services in the U.S. The company takes investing strategies and combines them with personalized guidance and tax-related technology to provide opportunities for saving money for specific goals such as purchasing a home, paying for college, saving for retirement, etc., or to merely invest. Two main questions are asked: how much is hoped to save and when will that money be needed. From that point, Betterment builds a personalized portfolio with a risk level and investment mix that suits each investor's goal, which can be adjusted as desired. The firm's technology manages the money, and as investments produce dividends, Betterment reinvests them. When it is time to sell a portion of a portfolio, it is done so in a tax-efficient way. Portfolios are automatically rebalanced in order to maintain an optimal level of risk. Auto-deposits are seamlessly transferred into the investor's account. There are no hidden fees, and no additional trading and transfer fees; but there is a one annual fee that amounts to about $25 per year for every $10,000 invested. To get started, investors need to create an online account and provide information that will help Betterment create a personalized investment portfolio. Portfolios can benefit from growth in both developed and emerging markets, including stock exchange-traded funds (ETFs) and bond ETFs, as well as other strategies. In addition, Betterment offers interest-bearing checking and savings accounts. The firm had more than 700,000 customers as of May 2022, and over $33 billion in assets under management. Betterment is privately-held by Betterment Holdings, Inc.

FINANCIAL DATA: *Note: Data for latest year may not have been available at press time.*

In U.S. $	2021	2020	2019	2018	2017	2016
Revenue						
R&D Expense						
Operating Income						
Operating Margin %						
SGA Expense						
Net Income						
Operating Cash Flow						
Capital Expenditure						
EBITDA						
Return on Assets %						
Return on Equity %						
Debt to Equity						

CONTACT INFORMATION:
Phone: 203 518-6993   Fax:
Toll-Free: 888-428-9482
Address: 8 West 24th St., Fl. 6, New York, NY 10010 United States

STOCK TICKER/OTHER:
Stock Ticker: Subsidiary   Exchange:
Employees: Fiscal Year Ends: 12/31
Parent Company: Betterment Holdings Inc

SALARIES/BONUSES:
Top Exec. Salary: $ Bonus: $
Second Exec. Salary: $ Bonus: $

OTHER THOUGHTS:
Estimated Female Officers or Directors:
Hot Spot for Advancement for Women/Minorities:

Sales, profits and employees may be estimates. Financial information, benefits and other data can change quickly and may vary from those stated here.

BigCommerce Holdings Inc

NAIC Code: 511210M

www.bigcommerce.com

TYPES OF BUSINESS:
Computer Software: E-Commerce & Web Analytics
Ecommerce Platform
Business Website
Business Commerce
Online
Application Programming Interface
Marketplace

BRANDS/DIVISIONS/AFFILIATES:
BigCommerce Pty Ltd

GROWTH PLANS/SPECIAL FEATURES:
BigCommerce Holdings Inc is engaged in offering Software-as-a-service (SaaS) e-commerce platform. The company's SaaS platform engages in the creation of online stores by delivering a combination of ease-of-use, enterprise functionality, and flexibility. It powers both the customers' branded ecommerce stores and their cross-channel connections to popular online marketplaces, social networks, and offline point-of-sale systems. The group operates in a single segment covering geographical areas of Americas-U.S.; Americas-other; EMEA; and APAC, of which a majority of revenue is generated from Americas-U.S.

CONTACTS:
Note: Officers with more than one job title may be intentionally listed here more than once.

Brent Bellm, CEO
Robert Alvarez, CFO
Thomas Aylor, Chief Accounting Officer
Jeff Mengoli, Chief Legal Officer
Lisa Pearson, Chief Marketing Officer
Brian Dhatt, Chief Technology Officer
Marc Ostryniec, Other Executive Officer
Paul Vaillancourt, Other Executive Officer
Jimmy Duvall, Other Executive Officer
Russell Klein, Other Executive Officer

FINANCIAL DATA:
Note: Data for latest year may not have been available at press time.

In U.S. $	2021	2020	2019	2018	2017	2016
Revenue		152,368,000	112,103,000	91,867,000		
R&D Expense		48,332,000	43,123,000	42,485,000		
Operating Income		-38,697,000	-40,987,000	-37,980,000		
Operating Margin %						
SGA Expense		108,607,000	82,944,000	65,425,000		
Net Income		-37,560,000	-42,590,000	-38,878,000		
Operating Cash Flow		-26,529,000	-39,969,000	-30,591,000		
Capital Expenditure		1,964,000	5,579,000	3,326,000		
EBITDA		-31,348,000	-38,381,000	-35,535,000		
Return on Assets %						
Return on Equity %						
Debt to Equity						

CONTACT INFORMATION:
Phone: 512-758-7588   Fax:
Toll-Free: 888-699-8911
Address: 11305 Four Points Dr., Bldg. 2, 3/Fl, Austin, TX 78726 United States

STOCK TICKER/OTHER:
Stock Ticker: BIGC
Employees: 813
Parent Company:

Exchange: NAS
Fiscal Year Ends: 12/31

SALARIES/BONUSES:
Top Exec. Salary: $404,167   Bonus: $
Second Exec. Salary: $363,542   Bonus: $

OTHER THOUGHTS:
Estimated Female Officers or Directors:
Hot Spot for Advancement for Women/Minorities:

Sales, profits and employees may be estimates. Financial information, benefits and other data can change quickly and may vary from those stated here.

BIGG Digital Assets Inc

biggdigitalassets.com

NAIC Code: 511210Q

TYPES OF BUSINESS:
Computer Software: Accounting, Banking & Financial

BRANDS/DIVISIONS/AFFILIATES:
Netcoins
Blockchain Intelligence Group
TerraZero Technologies Inc

GROWTH PLANS/SPECIAL FEATURES:
BIGG Digital Assets Inc. owns, operates and invests in crypto businesses that support and enhance a compliant and regulated ecosystem. BIGG owns Netcoins, an online cryptocurrency brokerage for Canadians; and Blockchain Intelligence Group, a developer of blockchain technology search, risk-scoring and data analytics services. In February 2022, BIGG made a $7.6 million investment in TerraZero Technologies, Inc., a vertically integrated metaverse development group and web 3.0 technology group.

CONTACTS: Note: Officers with more than one job title may be intentionally listed here more than once.
Mark Binns, CEO
Lance Morginn, Pres.
Kim Evans, CFO

FINANCIAL DATA: Note: Data for latest year may not have been available at press time.

In U.S. $	2021	2020	2019	2018	2017	2016
Revenue						
R&D Expense						
Operating Income						
Operating Margin %						
SGA Expense						
Net Income						
Operating Cash Flow						
Capital Expenditure						
EBITDA						
Return on Assets %						
Return on Equity %						
Debt to Equity						

CONTACT INFORMATION:
Phone: 778 819-8704   Fax:
Toll-Free:
Address: 1220 - 1130 W. Pender St., Vancouver, BC V6E 4A4 Canada

STOCK TICKER/OTHER:
Stock Ticker: BBKCF   Exchange: OTC
Employees: Fiscal Year Ends: 12/31
Parent Company:

SALARIES/BONUSES:
Top Exec. Salary: $ Bonus: $
Second Exec. Salary: $ Bonus: $

OTHER THOUGHTS:
Estimated Female Officers or Directors:
Hot Spot for Advancement for Women/Minorities:

Sales, profits and employees may be estimates. Financial information, benefits and other data can change quickly and may vary from those stated here.

Billd LLC

billd.com

NAIC Code: 522291

TYPES OF BUSINESS:

Consumer Lending
Payment & Finance Solutions - Construction Industry

BRANDS/DIVISIONS/AFFILIATES:

GROWTH PLANS/SPECIAL FEATURES:

Billd, LLC offers payment solutions for subcontractors, having worked with more than 2,600 suppliers. The Billd platform works like this: material suppliers or commercial contractors enroll with Billd's online or mobile app; contractors purchase materials from any supplier through the Billd platform; and suppliers get paid for materials prior to shipping when transacting with Billd. Billd offers the flexibility of paying back within 120 days. This solution enables contractors to continue projects and not have to miss out due to cash flow. Suppliers can expand business by providing a payment solution where materials are paid for upfront and customers receive flexible terms to pay for them over time. Partners and integrations of Billd include Procure, Autodesk, Stack and StructShare. Tools and resources on Billd's site include a payment estimator, cash flow estimator, contractor financing, contractor lines of credit and 2022 subcontractor market report.

CONTACTS: *Note: Officers with more than one job title may be intentionally listed here more than once.*

Christopher Doyle, CEO
Devon Choo, COO
Andres Morin, VP-Finance
Jesse Weissburg, CCO
Francisco Michel, Dir.-Talent
Russ Briscoe, VP-Sales
Michael Scallan, VP-Engineering

FINANCIAL DATA: *Note: Data for latest year may not have been available at press time.*

In U.S. $	2021	2020	2019	2018	2017	2016
Revenue						
R&D Expense						
Operating Income						
Operating Margin %						
SGA Expense						
Net Income						
Operating Cash Flow						
Capital Expenditure						
EBITDA						
Return on Assets %						
Return on Equity %						
Debt to Equity						

CONTACT INFORMATION:

Phone: 512 270-4805   Fax:
Toll-Free:
Address: 2700 W Anderson Lane, Ste. 206, Austin, TX 78757 United States

STOCK TICKER/OTHER:

Stock Ticker: Private
Employees:
Parent Company:

Exchange:
Fiscal Year Ends:

SALARIES/BONUSES:

Top Exec. Salary: $ Bonus: $
Second Exec. Salary: $ Bonus: $

OTHER THOUGHTS:

Estimated Female Officers or Directors:
Hot Spot for Advancement for Women/Minorities:

Sales, profits and employees may be estimates. Financial information, benefits and other data can change quickly and may vary from those stated here.

BillGO Inc

NAIC Code: 511210Q

www.billgo.com

TYPES OF BUSINESS:
Computer Software: Accounting, Banking & Financial
Bill Management & Payments Platform
Financial Platform
Realtime Payment Solution
Bill Payment Notification

BRANDS/DIVISIONS/AFFILIATES:

GROWTH PLANS/SPECIAL FEATURES:

BillGO, Inc. has developed a financial platform through which users manage and pay their bills. BillGo's real-time bill management and payments platform is used by more than 30 million consumers in the U.S., as well as thousands of financial institutions, fintechs and billers. Each entity within the platform therefore becomes connected in order to bill, make and receive payments. The mobile or online platform displays all bills in one place and sends reminders about due dates so that payments are not missed. The platform also offers a whole view of account balances, income and expenses. Billers don't have to send paper bills, and the entire payment process is streamlined digitally through the BillGO platform. Paper checks are transformed into digital payments that pay companies in real time rather than days. Payments are seamlessly made to over 170,000 supplier endpoints.

CONTACTS: Note: Officers with more than one job title may be intentionally listed here more than once.
Dan Holt, CEO
Jerod Sands, CFO
Mary Anne Keegan, CMO

FINANCIAL DATA: Note: Data for latest year may not have been available at press time.

In U.S. $	2021	2020	2019	2018	2017	2016
Revenue						
R&D Expense						
Operating Income						
Operating Margin %						
SGA Expense						
Net Income						
Operating Cash Flow						
Capital Expenditure						
EBITDA						
Return on Assets %						
Return on Equity %						
Debt to Equity						

CONTACT INFORMATION:
Phone: 970-829-0809   Fax:
Toll-Free:
Address: PO Box 272390, Fort Collins, CO 80527 United States

STOCK TICKER/OTHER:
Stock Ticker: Private   Exchange:
Employees: Fiscal Year Ends:
Parent Company:

SALARIES/BONUSES:
Top Exec. Salary: $ Bonus: $
Second Exec. Salary: $ Bonus: $

OTHER THOUGHTS:
Estimated Female Officers or Directors:
Hot Spot for Advancement for Women/Minorities:

Sales, profits and employees may be estimates. Financial information, benefits and other data can change quickly and may vary from those stated here.

Billtrust (BTRS Holdings Inc)

www.billtrust.com

NAIC Code: 511210Q

TYPES OF BUSINESS:
Computer Software: Accounting, Banking & Financial

GROWTH PLANS/SPECIAL FEATURES:
BTRS Holdings Inc is a provider of cloud-based software and integrated payment processing solutions. The company is at the forefront of the digital transformation of AR, providing mission-critical solutions that span credit decisioning and monitoring, online ordering, invoice delivery, payments and remittance capture, cash application and collections.

BRANDS/DIVISIONS/AFFILIATES:
BTRS Holdings Inc
South Mountain Merger Corp

CONTACTS: *Note: Officers with more than one job title may be intentionally listed here more than once.*
Flint Lane, CEO
Mark Shifke, CFO
Andrew Herning, Chief Accounting Officer
Joe Eng, Chief Information Officer
Jeanne O'Connor, Other Executive Officer
Steven Pinado, President

FINANCIAL DATA: *Note: Data for latest year may not have been available at press time.*

In U.S. $	2021	2020	2019	2018	2017	2016
Revenue		145,685,000	136,468,000	120,515,000		
R&D Expense		36,468,000	34,285,000	23,606,000		
Operating Income		-11,662,000	-21,116,000	-17,062,000		
Operating Margin %						
SGA Expense		45,608,000	45,395,000	40,420,000		
Net Income		-17,027,000	-22,803,000	-18,231,000		
Operating Cash Flow		-217,000	-7,275,000	-6,289,000		
Capital Expenditure		1,756,000	4,317,000	7,936,000		
EBITDA		-6,538,000	-15,255,000	-11,308,000		
Return on Assets %						
Return on Equity %						
Debt to Equity						

CONTACT INFORMATION:
Phone: 609 235-1010   Fax:
Toll-Free:
Address: 1009 Lenox Dr., Ste. 101, Lawrenceville, NJ 08648 United States

STOCK TICKER/OTHER:
Stock Ticker: BTRS
Employees: 566
Parent Company:

Exchange: NAS
Fiscal Year Ends: 12/31

SALARIES/BONUSES:
Top Exec. Salary: $400,000   Bonus: $37,500
Second Exec. Salary: $350,000   Bonus: $26,250

OTHER THOUGHTS:
Estimated Female Officers or Directors:
Hot Spot for Advancement for Women/Minorities:

Sales, profits and employees may be estimates. Financial information, benefits and other data can change quickly and may vary from those stated here.

Binance

NAIC Code: 523130

www.binance.com/en

TYPES OF BUSINESS:

Virtual Currency Exchange Services
Cryptocurrency Platform
Crypto Trading
Crypto Buying and Holding
Crypto Auto-Burn Solutions
Financial Payments
Blockchain Investment

BRANDS/DIVISIONS/AFFILIATES:

BNB
Binance Chain
Binance Smart
Binance Labs

CONTACTS: *Note: Officers with more than one job title may be intentionally listed here more than once.*

Changpeng Zhao, CEO

GROWTH PLANS/SPECIAL FEATURES:

Binance has developed and operates a financial exchange platform on which users can buy, trade and hold more than 600 types of cryptocurrencies. Binance comprises approximately 90 million registered users, who are offered 24/7 support. BNB is the cryptocurrency coin and native asset on Binance Chain, a blockchain software system developed by Binance and the community. BNB has multiple forms of utility tokenization, which can not only be traded but can also be used in a wide range of applications and use cases. BNB can be used to pay for goods and services, settle transaction fees on Binance Smart Chain, participate in exclusive token sales and more. BNB uses an auto-burn system to reduce its total supply to 100,000,000 BNB. The auto-burn mechanism adjusts the amount of BNB to be burned based on BNB's price and the number of blocks generated on the BNB Smart Chain during the quarter. BNB can be used for payments, travel, entertainment, services and financial purposes. Binance Labs invests in blockchain entrepreneurs, startups and communities that provide financing to industry products that help grow the blockchain ecosystem. Services offered by Binance span downloads, desktop applications, execution solutions, over-the-counter trading, listing and merchant applications, historical market data and many other services and products.

Binance offers its employees health insurance and a variety of company options and perks.

FINANCIAL DATA: *Note: Data for latest year may not have been available at press time.*

In U.S. $	2021	2020	2019	2018	2017	2016
Revenue						
R&D Expense						
Operating Income						
Operating Margin %						
SGA Expense						
Net Income						
Operating Cash Flow						
Capital Expenditure						
EBITDA						
Return on Assets %						
Return on Equity %						
Debt to Equity						

CONTACT INFORMATION:

Phone: 345 769-1314   Fax:
Toll-Free:
Address: 23 Lime Tree Bay Ave., George Town, KY1-1100 Cayman Islands

STOCK TICKER/OTHER:

Stock Ticker: Private   Exchange:
Employees: Fiscal Year Ends:
Parent Company:

SALARIES/BONUSES:

Top Exec. Salary: $ Bonus: $
Second Exec. Salary: $ Bonus: $

OTHER THOUGHTS:

Estimated Female Officers or Directors:
Hot Spot for Advancement for Women/Minorities:

Sales, profits and employees may be estimates. Financial information, benefits and other data can change quickly and may vary from those stated here.

bitFlyer Inc

bitflyer.com/en-jp

NAIC Code: 523130

TYPES OF BUSINESS:
Virtual Currency Exchange Services
Cryptocurrency Exchange Platform
Cryptocurrency Buying and Selling
Cryptocurrency Trading
Cryptocurrency Wire Transfer Services
Credit Card

BRANDS/DIVISIONS/AFFILIATES:

GROWTH PLANS/SPECIAL FEATURES:
bitFlyer, Inc. is a Japanese company that developed and operates a cryptocurrency asset exchange platform called bitFlyer. The platform offers financial capabilities such as buying, selling, trading and wire transferring, which is done through Sumitomo Mitsui Banking Corporation. A number of cryptocurrencies can be purchased in very small amounts through bitFlyer, including Bitcoin, Ripple (XRP), Ethereum and Bitcoin Cash, and fees may or may not apply. Accounts can be opened on the platform in as little as 10 minutes after identification documents have been submitted. How it works: users enter an email address, register information once the email has been confirmed, submit ID verification documents and deposit Japanese Yen (JPY) from their bank accounts in order to purchase virtual currency. Automatic virtual currency purchases can be scheduled on bitFlyer. The bitFlyer credit card offers Bitcoin cash back rewards.

CONTACTS: *Note: Officers with more than one job title may be intentionally listed here more than once.*
Masaaki Seki, Pres.

FINANCIAL DATA: *Note: Data for latest year may not have been available at press time.*

In U.S. $	2021	2020	2019	2018	2017	2016
Revenue						
R&D Expense						
Operating Income						
Operating Margin %						
SGA Expense						
Net Income						
Operating Cash Flow						
Capital Expenditure						
EBITDA						
Return on Assets %						
Return on Equity %						
Debt to Equity						

CONTACT INFORMATION:
Phone: 813-6434-5864   Fax:
Toll-Free:
Address: Midtown Tower, 9-7-1 Akasaka, Minato-ku, Tokyo, 107-6233 Japan

STOCK TICKER/OTHER:
Stock Ticker: Private
Employees:
Parent Company:

Exchange:
Fiscal Year Ends:

SALARIES/BONUSES:
Top Exec. Salary: $ Bonus: $
Second Exec. Salary: $ Bonus: $

OTHER THOUGHTS:
Estimated Female Officers or Directors:
Hot Spot for Advancement for Women/Minorities:

Sales, profits and employees may be estimates. Financial information, benefits and other data can change quickly and may vary from those stated here.

Bitkub Online Co Ltd

NAIC Code: 523130

www.bitkub.com

TYPES OF BUSINESS:
Virtual Currency Exchange Services
Cryptocurrency Platform
Cryptocurrency Buying and Selling
Cryptocurrency Trading
Cryptocurrency Investment

BRANDS/DIVISIONS/AFFILIATES:
Bitkub Capital Group Holdings

GROWTH PLANS/SPECIAL FEATURES:
Bitkub Online Co., Ltd. is a Thailand-based company that has developed and operates a digital asset exchange under the bitkub moniker. Opening an account is free, and users can buy, sell and store Bitcoin, Ethereum and other cryptocurrencies with Thai Baht. How it works: users enter their email address and set a bitkub password, they deposit money or cryptocurrency using a local bank account or crypto wallet, and are then free to utilize the platform. Users have privacy and control over their money, and cryptocurrencies can be sent anywhere in the world and can be used to purchase goods online. Users can diversify their account digital currency portfolio for both long- and short-term investments. Bitkub offers 24/7 support and can be used across multiple devices and operating systems. Bitkub Online is privately owned by Bitkub Capital Group Holdings.

CONTACTS: Note: Officers with more than one job title may be intentionally listed here more than once.
Topp Jirayut Srupsrisopa, CEO

FINANCIAL DATA: Note: Data for latest year may not have been available at press time.

In U.S. $	2021	2020	2019	2018	2017	2016
Revenue						
R&D Expense						
Operating Income						
Operating Margin %						
SGA Expense						
Net Income						
Operating Cash Flow						
Capital Expenditure						
EBITDA						
Return on Assets %						
Return on Equity %						
Debt to Equity						

CONTACT INFORMATION:
Phone: 66-2-032-9555   Fax:
Toll-Free:
Address: 2525, FYI Ctr., Twr. 2, Fl. 11, Unit 2/1101-2/1107, Rama 4 Rd., Klongtoei Sub-district, Klongtoei District, Bangkok, 10110 Thailand

STOCK TICKER/OTHER:
Stock Ticker: Private   Exchange:
Employees: Fiscal Year Ends:
Parent Company: Bitkub Capital Group Holdings

SALARIES/BONUSES:
Top Exec. Salary: $ Bonus: $
Second Exec. Salary: $ Bonus: $

OTHER THOUGHTS:
Estimated Female Officers or Directors:
Hot Spot for Advancement for Women/Minorities:

Sales, profits and employees may be estimates. Financial information, benefits and other data can change quickly and may vary from those stated here.

BitPay Inc

bitpay.com

NAIC Code: 522320

TYPES OF BUSINESS:

Financial Transactions Processing, Reserve, and Clearinghouse Activities
Bitcoin Payment Solutions
Technology Innovation
Cryptocurrency
Blockchain Payment Processing
Crypto Digital Wallet
Crypto Payment Acceptance
Crypto Mobile App

BRANDS/DIVISIONS/AFFILIATES:

GROWTH PLANS/SPECIAL FEATURES:

BitPay, Inc. builds enterprise-grade tools for cryptocurrency acceptance and spending. Founded in 2011, BitPay is a pioneer in blockchain payment processing. Products for individuals include cryptocurrency cards, crypto digital wallet and crypto mobile app, all of which enables users to spend crypto like cash. BitPay also offers a browser extension in which Amazon and hundreds of other brands enable users to purchase through ecommerce sites with crypto. Businesses connected with BitPay can accept or send payments globally. BitPay has offices in North America, Europe and South America, and has raised more than $70 million in funding (as of April 2022) from investment firms including Founders Fund, Index Ventures, Virgin Group, and Aquiline Technology Growth.

BitPay offers its employees health insurance and a variety of employee options and company perks.

CONTACTS:
Note: Officers with more than one job title may be intentionally listed here more than once.

Stephen Pair, CEO
Jim Lester, COO
Jagruti Solanki, CFO
Bill Zielke, CMO
Michelle Jager, Chief People Officer
Justin Langston, CTO

FINANCIAL DATA:
Note: Data for latest year may not have been available at press time.

In U.S. $	2021	2020	2019	2018	2017	2016
Revenue						
R&D Expense						
Operating Income						
Operating Margin %						
SGA Expense						
Net Income						
Operating Cash Flow						
Capital Expenditure						
EBITDA						
Return on Assets %						
Return on Equity %						
Debt to Equity						

CONTACT INFORMATION:

Phone: 404 907-2055   Fax:
Toll-Free:
Address: 3423 Piedmont Rd. NE, Ste 516, Atlanta, GA 30305 United States

STOCK TICKER/OTHER:

Stock Ticker: Private   Exchange:
Employees: Fiscal Year Ends:
Parent Company:

SALARIES/BONUSES:

Top Exec. Salary: $ Bonus: $
Second Exec. Salary: $ Bonus: $

OTHER THOUGHTS:

Estimated Female Officers or Directors:
Hot Spot for Advancement for Women/Minorities:

Sales, profits and employees may be estimates. Financial information, benefits and other data can change quickly and may vary from those stated here.

Blend Labs Inc

NAIC Code: 511210Q

blend.com

TYPES OF BUSINESS:
Computer Software: Accounting, Banking & Financial
Digital Lending Platform
Digital Banking
Digital Insurance
Financial Services
Cloud-based Software
Software Development
Technology

BRANDS/DIVISIONS/AFFILIATES:

GROWTH PLANS/SPECIAL FEATURES:

Blend Labs Inc is a cloud based platform. It supports and simplifies applications for mortgages, consumer loans, and deposit accounts.

Blend offers its employees comprehensive health benefits, 401(k), work development opportunities and a variety of employee assistance plans/programs and company perks.

CONTACTS: *Note: Officers with more than one job title may be intentionally listed here more than once.*

Erin Collard, Co-Founder
Nima Ghamsari, Co-Founder
Timothy Mayopoulos, Director
Marc Greenberg, Other Corporate Officer
Crystal Sumner, Other Corporate Officer

FINANCIAL DATA: *Note: Data for latest year may not have been available at press time.*

In U.S. $	2021	2020	2019	2018	2017	2016
Revenue		96,029,000	50,671,000			
R&D Expense		55,503,000	48,597,000			
Operating Income		-75,291,000	-81,722,000			
Operating Margin %						
SGA Expense		81,528,000	64,249,000			
Net Income		-74,617,000	-81,452,000			
Operating Cash Flow		-65,013,000	-58,939,000			
Capital Expenditure		1,322,000	620,000			
EBITDA		-71,298,000	-76,958,000			
Return on Assets %						
Return on Equity %						
Debt to Equity						

CONTACT INFORMATION:
Phone: 650-550-4810   Fax:
Toll-Free:
Address: 415 Kearny St., San Francisco, CA 94108 United States

STOCK TICKER/OTHER:
Stock Ticker: BLND   Exchange: NYS
Employees: 1,689   Fiscal Year Ends:
Parent Company:

SALARIES/BONUSES:
Top Exec. Salary: $500,000   Bonus: $
Second Exec. Salary: $350,000   Bonus: $25,000

OTHER THOUGHTS:
Estimated Female Officers or Directors:
Hot Spot for Advancement for Women/Minorities:

Sales, profits and employees may be estimates. Financial information, benefits and other data can change quickly and may vary from those stated here.

Plunkett Research, Ltd. 119

BlockFi Inc

blockfi.com

NAIC Code: 522298

TYPES OF BUSINESS:

Crypto-Backed Loans
Cryptocurrency Technology
Crypto Financial Products and Solutions
Crypto Buying, Selling and Storing
Cryptocurrency Exchange
Crypto Rewards Card
Equipment-Backed Loans
Cryptocurrency Trusts

BRANDS/DIVISIONS/AFFILIATES:

BlockFi Wallet
BlockFi Rewards
BlockFi Bitcoin Trust
BlockFi Ethereum Trust
BlockFi Litecoin Trust

CONTACTS: *Note: Officers with more than one job title may be intentionally listed here more than once.*

Zac Prince, CEO
Flori Marquez, Sr. VP-Oper.
Tona Lauro, CFO
Andrew Tam, CMO
Laura Cooper, Chief People Officer
Alex Grigoryan, CTO
David Spack, Chief Compliance Officer

GROWTH PLANS/SPECIAL FEATURES:

BlockFi, Inc. has developed technology and products that provide credit services to markets with limited access to financial products. The company's BlockFi Wallet product enables users to buy, sell and store cryptocurrency and stablecoins. It requires no minimum balance and users can trade and exchange crypto immediately after setting up a free account. The BlockFi Rewards Visa Signature Card lets card holders earn crypto rewards on every purchase. Money can be borrowed at rates as low as 4.5% via BlockFi, and the funds can be borrowed against one's crypto assets. BlockFi's personalized yield product offers exclusive benefits for high net-worth clients, in which they can negotiate crypto interest rates, fiat borrowing and trading costs. Blockfi offers equipment-backed loans for miners, exchanges and automated teller machines (ATMs) through its relationships with manufacturers and hosting providers to assist in scaling up projects. Underwriting and structuring capabilities enable the borrowing of cash or crypto. BlockFi offers trusts, the BlockFi Bitcoin Trust, Ethereum Trust and Litecoin Trust, in which institutional and accredited investors can access as an investment vehicle. The goal of each trust is to enable investors to implement asset allocation strategies that use Bitcoin, Ethereum and Litecoin by using the shares of that trust instead of directly purchasing and holding the underlying cryptocurrency. BlockFi is an independent lender with institutional backing from investors such as Valar Ventures, Galaxy Digital, Fidelity, Akuna Capital, SoFi, and Coinbase Ventures. Gemini Trust Company, LLC is BlockFi's primary custodian.

FINANCIAL DATA: *Note: Data for latest year may not have been available at press time.*

In U.S. $	2021	2020	2019	2018	2017	2016
Revenue						
R&D Expense						
Operating Income						
Operating Margin %						
SGA Expense						
Net Income						
Operating Cash Flow						
Capital Expenditure						
EBITDA						
Return on Assets %						
Return on Equity %						
Debt to Equity						

CONTACT INFORMATION:

Phone: 646 779-9688   Fax:
Toll-Free:
Address: 201 Montgomery St., Ste. 263, Jersey City, NJ 07302 United States

STOCK TICKER/OTHER:

Stock Ticker: Private
Employees:
Parent Company:

Exchange:
Fiscal Year Ends:

SALARIES/BONUSES:

Top Exec. Salary: $ Bonus: $
Second Exec. Salary: $ Bonus: $

OTHER THOUGHTS:

Estimated Female Officers or Directors:
Hot Spot for Advancement for Women/Minorities:

Sales, profits and employees may be estimates. Financial information, benefits and other data can change quickly and may vary from those stated here.

Bolt Financial Inc

www.bolt.com

NAIC Code: 511210K

TYPES OF BUSINESS:

Computer Software: Sales & Customer Relationship Management (CRM)
Ecommerce
Online Payment Solution
Blockchain
Machine Learning
Fraud Protection

BRANDS/DIVISIONS/AFFILIATES:

CONTACTS: *Note: Officers with more than one job title may be intentionally listed here more than once.*

Ryan Breslow, CEO

GROWTH PLANS/SPECIAL FEATURES:

Bolt Financial, Inc. has developed an ecommerce platform that provides an online checkout solution for retailers. Bolt's payment solution offers one-click checkout, post-purchase order management, real-time data approval signals, chargeback representment, micro-authorization verification, direct payments, payment processor integrations, alternative payment methods, international payments, fraud protection, plug & play integrations, shoppers analytics, dedicated support and personalization for shoppers. For developers, Bolt's platform offers plugins, custom checkout, webhooks, payment testing, full application programming interface (API) reference, release notes, status page and support. Technologies and specialties used by Bolt include blockchain, machine learning, data science and more. In October 2021, Bolt Financial announced $393 million in new funding via Untitled Investments, Willoughby Capital and Soma Capital who joint existing investors General Atlantic, Tribe Capital, Activant Capital and Moore Strategic Venture that participated in the round. The funding helps Bolt to end guest checkout on the internet and a secure way for shoppers to shop and checkout securely across marketplaces, no matter where they are, with a single identity.

Bolt Financial offers its employees comprehensive health benefits, 401(k) and a variety of company incentives and perks.

FINANCIAL DATA: *Note: Data for latest year may not have been available at press time.*

In U.S. $	2021	2020	2019	2018	2017	2016
Revenue						
R&D Expense						
Operating Income						
Operating Margin %						
SGA Expense						
Net Income						
Operating Cash Flow						
Capital Expenditure						
EBITDA						
Return on Assets %						
Return on Equity %						
Debt to Equity						

CONTACT INFORMATION:

Phone: 415-226-9630   Fax:
Toll-Free:
Address: 588 Sutter St., Ste. 509, San Francisco, CA 94102 United States

STOCK TICKER/OTHER:

Stock Ticker: Private   Exchange:
Employees: 550   Fiscal Year Ends:
Parent Company:

SALARIES/BONUSES:

Top Exec. Salary: $ Bonus: $
Second Exec. Salary: $ Bonus: $

OTHER THOUGHTS:

Estimated Female Officers or Directors:
Hot Spot for Advancement for Women/Minorities:

Sales, profits and employees may be estimates. Financial information, benefits and other data can change quickly and may vary from those stated here.

Plunkett Research, Ltd.

Bottomline Technologies Inc

www.bottomline.com

NAIC Code: 511210Q

TYPES OF BUSINESS:
Software-Electronic Banking
Online Billing, Payment & Invoicing Software
Software-as-a-Service (SaaS)

BRANDS/DIVISIONS/AFFILIATES:
Paymode-X

GROWTH PLANS/SPECIAL FEATURES:
Bottomline Technologies Inc provides financial oriented solutions. It is a trusted and easy-to-use set of cloud-based digital banking, fraud prevention, payment, financial document, and healthcare solutions. Bottomline consists of four operating segments: Cloud Solutions segment provides customers predominately with SaaS technology offerings that facilitate electronic payment, electronic invoicing and spend management; Digital Banking segment provides solutions that are specifically designed for banking and financial institution customers; Payments and Transactional Documents segment is a supplier of software products that provide a range of financial business process management solutions; and Other segment consists of healthcare and cyber fraud and risk management operating segments.

CONTACTS: *Note: Officers with more than one job title may be intentionally listed here more than once.*
Robert Eberle, CEO
Stephanie Lucey, Other Exec. Officer
Adam Bowden, CFO
Joseph Mullen, Chairman of the Board
Jonathan Dack, Chief Information Officer
Christine Nurnberger, Chief Marketing Officer
Eric Morgan, Controller
Andrew Mintzer, Executive VP, Divisional
David Sweet, Executive VP, Divisional
Danielle Sheer, General Counsel
John Kelly, General Manager, Divisional
Tom Dolan, General Manager, Divisional
Paul Fannon, Managing Director, Divisional
Norman Deluca, Managing Director, Divisional
Brian McLaughlin, Other Executive Officer
Nigel Savory, Other Executive Officer
Kimberly Hannemann, Other Executive Officer
Angela White, Vice President, Divisional

FINANCIAL DATA: *Note: Data for latest year may not have been available at press time.*

In U.S. $	2021	2020	2019	2018	2017	2016
Revenue	471,403,000	442,221,000	421,962,000	394,096,000	349,412,000	343,274,000
R&D Expense	78,090,000	73,019,000	67,364,000	57,310,000	53,002,000	47,355,000
Operating Income	-7,548,000	-3,432,000	3,079,000	5,831,000	-13,659,000	-3,551,000
Operating Margin %						
SGA Expense	183,236,000	163,178,000	147,464,000	135,749,000	123,997,000	123,392,000
Net Income	-16,288,000	-9,229,000	9,432,000	9,328,000	-33,137,000	-19,648,000
Operating Cash Flow	76,116,000	97,171,000	78,277,000	76,028,000	60,975,000	67,157,000
Capital Expenditure	31,859,000	46,650,000	53,783,000	21,376,000	28,173,000	27,717,000
EBITDA	48,496,000	44,057,000	54,924,000	54,365,000	22,559,000	39,143,000
Return on Assets %						
Return on Equity %						
Debt to Equity						

CONTACT INFORMATION:
Phone: 603 436-0700   Fax: 603 436-0300
Toll-Free: 800-243-2528
Address: 325 Corporate Dr., Portsmouth, NH 03801 United States

STOCK TICKER/OTHER:
Stock Ticker: EPAY
Employees: 2,000
Parent Company:

Exchange: NAS
Fiscal Year Ends: 06/30

SALARIES/BONUSES:
Top Exec. Salary: $397,800   Bonus: $35,880
Second Exec. Salary: $300,179   Bonus: $

OTHER THOUGHTS:
Estimated Female Officers or Directors: 2
Hot Spot for Advancement for Women/Minorities:

Sales, profits and employees may be estimates. Financial information, benefits and other data can change quickly and may vary from those stated here.

Boursorama

NAIC Code: 523120

groupe.boursorama.fr

TYPES OF BUSINESS:
Online Brokerage Services
Online Banking Services
Online Brokerage Services
Insurance
Wealth Management
Financial Information Services

BRANDS/DIVISIONS/AFFILIATES:
Societe Generale Group
Boursorama Banque

CONTACTS: *Note: Officers with more than one job title may be intentionally listed here more than once.*
Benoit Grisoni, Gen. Mgr.
Nicole Viviand, Dir-Oper.
Jean-Philippe Lavenir, Dir.-Finance
Xavier Prin, Dir.-Mktg.
Isabelle Pla, Dir.-Human Resources
Bertrand Le Bras, Dir.-Information Systems
Diane-Charlotte Kermorgant, Head-Press Rel.
Diane-Charlotte Kermorgant, Head-Investor Rel.
Ralf Oetting, Managing Dir.-Onvista AG Germany
Xavier Prin, Portal Dir.
Benoit Grisoni, Managing Dir.-Boursorama Banque
Patrick Sommelet, Deputy CEO
Philippe Aymerich, Chmn.
Alberto Navarro, Managing Dir.-Selftrade Bank, Spain

GROWTH PLANS/SPECIAL FEATURES:

Boursorama, a subsidiary of the Societe Generale Group, is a leading European online financial and insurance services provider which operates through Boursorama Banque. The company has three main areas of activity: online banking, online brokerage and financial information on the internet. The online banking division has more than 3 million customers, providing several services areas free of charge. Boursorama Banque offers account banking, mortgage lending and other money-related services all online. The online brokerage division provides access to major exchanges with rates tailored to the investor's profile. Its products include equities, options, futures, warrants, turbos, certificates, bonds and trackers. The internet portal division comprises the boursorama.com website, which offers a wide array of financial information and averages more than 50 million monthly visits every year. The website disseminates market and economic news and offers general information, as well as video content and discussion forums. In addition, Boursorama's customers can use the Google Assistant (including connected Google Home speakers) on all compatible devices for managing their bank accounts autonomously and securely. Boursorama's mobile platform is compatible with Samsung Pay, Apple Pay and Google Pay.

FINANCIAL DATA: *Note: Data for latest year may not have been available at press time.*

In U.S. $	2021	2020	2019	2018	2017	2016
Revenue	287,469,000	276,412,500	283,500,000	270,000,000	255,000,000	251,000,000
R&D Expense						
Operating Income						
Operating Margin %						
SGA Expense						
Net Income						
Operating Cash Flow						
Capital Expenditure						
EBITDA						
Return on Assets %						
Return on Equity %						
Debt to Equity						

CONTACT INFORMATION:
Phone: 33-1-46-09-50-00   Fax:
Toll-Free:
Address: 18 Quai du Point du Jour, Boulogne-Billancourt, 92659 France

STOCK TICKER/OTHER:
Stock Ticker: Subsidiary   Exchange:
Employees: 810   Fiscal Year Ends: 12/31
Parent Company: Societe Generale Group

SALARIES/BONUSES:
Top Exec. Salary: $ Bonus: $
Second Exec. Salary: $ Bonus: $

OTHER THOUGHTS:
Estimated Female Officers or Directors: 5
Hot Spot for Advancement for Women/Minorities: Y

Sales, profits and employees may be estimates. Financial information, benefits and other data can change quickly and may vary from those stated here.

Braintree

www.braintreepayments.com

NAIC Code: 522320

TYPES OF BUSINESS:

Financial Transactions Processing, Reserve, and Clearinghouse Activities
Ecommerce Payments Solutions
Ecommerce Transactions
Point of Sale Payment Solutions
Payment Development Kits

BRANDS/DIVISIONS/AFFILIATES:

PayPal Holdings Inc

CONTACTS: *Note: Officers with more than one job title may be intentionally listed here more than once.*

Bill Ready, CEO

GROWTH PLANS/SPECIAL FEATURES:

Braintree, a subsidiary of PayPal Holdings, Inc., specializes in mobile and web payment systems for ecommerce companies. Braintree provides global ecommerce tools needed for building businesses, enabling transactions and accepting payments. Braintree's technology works across any device and through almost any payment method. Merchants in more than 45 countries worldwide can accept, split and enable payments in 130+ currencies via Braintree. Business-builders will need to know what kind of operation they are running: direct, which means selling a product or service directly to consumers; subscription-based, which bills users regularly without service interruption; marketplace, which splits payments between sub merchants; shopping cart, which connects Braintree merchants for data insight, analytics and marketing purposes; or contextual commerce, which provides on-the-spot commerce. A variety of payment options for ecommerce sites include credit/debit cards, PayPal, Apple Pay, Android Pay, Venmo, Visa Checkout, Masterpass and Amex Express Checkout. The transaction lifecycle contains two components: client-side integration, which handles online and mobile payment method collection from users; and server-side integration, which authenticates payment methods, and passes tokens back and forth between Braintree servers and the ecommerce business' client. SDKs are available in programming languages such as Ruby, Python, PHP, Node.js, Java and .NET. Braintree also offers in-store payment services in the U.S., U.K. and Australia.

FINANCIAL DATA: *Note: Data for latest year may not have been available at press time.*

In U.S. $	2021	2020	2019	2018	2017	2016
Revenue						
R&D Expense						
Operating Income						
Operating Margin %						
SGA Expense						
Net Income						
Operating Cash Flow						
Capital Expenditure						
EBITDA						
Return on Assets %						
Return on Equity %						
Debt to Equity						

CONTACT INFORMATION:

Phone: 312 822-0709   Fax:
Toll-Free: 877-434-2894
Address: 222 W. Merchandise Mast Plaza, Ste. 800, Chicago, IL 60654 United States

STOCK TICKER/OTHER:

Stock Ticker: Subsidiary   Exchange:
Employees: 500   Fiscal Year Ends:
Parent Company: PayPal Holdings Inc

SALARIES/BONUSES:

Top Exec. Salary: $ Bonus: $
Second Exec. Salary: $ Bonus: $

OTHER THOUGHTS:

Estimated Female Officers or Directors:
Hot Spot for Advancement for Women/Minorities:

Sales, profits and employees may be estimates. Financial information, benefits and other data can change quickly and may vary from those stated here.

Bread Pay (Lon Operations LLC)

payments.breadfinancial.com

NAIC Code: 522291

TYPES OF BUSINESS:

Consumer Lending
Payments Platform
Buy Now Pay Later
Merchant API
Financial Services
Financial Mobile App

BRANDS/DIVISIONS/AFFILIATES:

Bread Financial
Bread Pay

CONTACTS: *Note: Officers with more than one job title may be intentionally listed here more than once.*

Josh Abramowitz, CEO

GROWTH PLANS/SPECIAL FEATURES:

Lon Operations, LLC operates through subsidiary Bread Financial, which developed and operates Bread Pay, a flexible payments platform for shoppers and merchants. Bread Pay enables consumers to buy now and pay later through its flexible payment methods, paying for purchases over time. Automatic payments can be set up. Each transaction does require Bread's approval, which occurs in seconds. Merchants can expand their point-of-sale footprint by partnering with Bread Pay, of which merchants get paid immediately and Bread Pay takes on the financial risk. Brands that utilize Bread Pay include Hublot, Digital Storm, Create Room, Newton and BBQ Guys. Bread offers a seamless plug-in and direct application programming interface (API) that integrates with merchant's existing platforms and can be customized to fit specific requirements. Platforms and integrations include Salesforce, Volusion, Miva, 3dcart, WooCommerce, Kibo, BigCommerce, NetSuite, Magento and Shopify.

FINANCIAL DATA: *Note: Data for latest year may not have been available at press time.*

In U.S. $	2021	2020	2019	2018	2017	2016
Revenue						
R&D Expense						
Operating Income						
Operating Margin %						
SGA Expense						
Net Income						
Operating Cash Flow						
Capital Expenditure						
EBITDA						
Return on Assets %						
Return on Equity %						
Debt to Equity						

CONTACT INFORMATION:

Phone: Fax:
Toll-Free: 844 992-7323
Address: 156 5th Ave., New York, NY 10010-7002 United States

STOCK TICKER/OTHER:

Stock Ticker: Subsidiary   Exchange:
Employees: Fiscal Year Ends:
Parent Company: Bread Financial Holdings Inc

SALARIES/BONUSES:

Top Exec. Salary: $ Bonus: $
Second Exec. Salary: $ Bonus: $

OTHER THOUGHTS:

Estimated Female Officers or Directors:
Hot Spot for Advancement for Women/Minorities:

Sales, profits and employees may be estimates. Financial information, benefits and other data can change quickly and may vary from those stated here.

Plunkett Research, Ltd.

Brex Inc

brex.com

NAIC Code: 522210

TYPES OF BUSINESS:

Business Credit Card Issuing
Financial Services
Technology
Business Management
Cash Management
Application Programming Interface

BRANDS/DIVISIONS/AFFILIATES:

Brex Cash
Brex Card
Brex API

CONTACTS: *Note: Officers with more than one job title may be intentionally listed here more than once.*

Henrique Dubugras, Co-CEO
Pedro Franceschi, Co-CEO

GROWTH PLANS/SPECIAL FEATURES:

Brex, Inc. is a financial service and technology company based in California, USA, that helps thousands of businesses to manage their finances. Solutions by Brex include cash management, expense management, ERP and accounting integrations, fraud protection, virtual card, higher limits, instant card, no personal liability, no interest and no foreign transaction fees. Brex Cash is a bank account alternative that companies of any size can use to deposit cash, send payments and track spend. Brex Card can be used as a corporate credit card. Reward points are earned on all card spend, and extra points are given for daily payments. Points can be redeemed for cash back, gift cards or miles. Brex serves startups, established tech companies, life sciences companies, and eCommerce brands. Its customers include Y Combinator, Airbnb, carta, classpass, Mircoculus, Sonoma, Spiral Therapeutics, CLSA, Vouched, NUMI, Bounce and Mutiny. Investors of Brex is Y Combinator, Kleiner Perkins, DST Global, PayPal co-founders, Lone Pine Capital and Ribbit Capital. In late-2021, Brex announced the Brex API (application programming interface), which is available to all Brex customers, free of charge. The Brex API allows customers to seamlessly manage financial information in a customizable interface, saving time, reducing errors and better meeting the needs of their own customers and vendors. With Brex API developers can build customizable workflows. The API facilitates transactions across processes such as payments, teams and transactions.

Brex offers its employees health, dental, vision, life and disability insurance coverage, 401(k) and company perks.

FINANCIAL DATA: *Note: Data for latest year may not have been available at press time.*

In U.S. $	2021	2020	2019	2018	2017	2016
Revenue						
R&D Expense						
Operating Income						
Operating Margin %						
SGA Expense						
Net Income						
Operating Cash Flow						
Capital Expenditure						
EBITDA						
Return on Assets %						
Return on Equity %						
Debt to Equity						

CONTACT INFORMATION:

Phone: 650 250-6428   Fax:
Toll-Free: 833 228 2044
Address: 12832 Frontrunner Blvd., Ste. 500, Draper, UT 84020 United States

STOCK TICKER/OTHER:

Stock Ticker: Private   Exchange:
Employees: Fiscal Year Ends:
Parent Company:

SALARIES/BONUSES:

Top Exec. Salary: $ Bonus: $
Second Exec. Salary: $ Bonus: $

OTHER THOUGHTS:

Estimated Female Officers or Directors:
Hot Spot for Advancement for Women/Minorities:

Sales, profits and employees may be estimates. Financial information, benefits and other data can change quickly and may vary from those stated here.

Cadre (RealCadre LLC)

cadre.com

NAIC Code: 523920

TYPES OF BUSINESS:

Private Real Estate Investment Management
Investment Brokerage
Real Estate Investment
Online Platform
Investment Fund
Property Renovation
Real Estate Operations

BRANDS/DIVISIONS/AFFILIATES:

Cadre
RealCadre
Cadre Fund Co-Investments
Opportunity Zones
Secondary Market

CONTACTS: *Note: Officers with more than one job title may be intentionally listed here more than once.*

Ryan Williams, CEO
Allen Smith, Pres.
Josephine Scesney, Head-Finance & Oper.
Dustin Cohn, CMO
Rita Ramakrishnan, VP-People & Talent
Skand Gupta, VP-Engineering

GROWTH PLANS/SPECIAL FEATURES:

RealCadre, LLC offers financial brokerage services through its online Cadre platform. Cadre provides access to a diversified portfolio of real estate investments spanning multi-family, industrial, office and hotel properties in the U.S. Members can create an account and invest on the platform within minutes. Cadre works with partners to select each fund investment and to build a balanced portfolio. The fund targets established properties that range in total value from $50 million to $200 million. Assets are purchased at a discount but have stable in-place tenants that are generating cash flows for investors. Once an investment is selected, RealCadre actively manages it through any renovation project and/or operational improvement to enhance value. Cadre also offers deal-by-deal investing in regards to commercial real estate assets. This strategy offers transparency, lower fees and a secondary market for investors that want more control over their portfolio. Once a deal-by-deal investment is secured to syndicate, a majority of its equity is allocated to the Fund and the remainder is allocated to deal-by-deal investors. Allocations are typically granted on a first-come, first-served basis while equity is available. When the syndication is complete, Cadre closes the deal. There are three deal-by-deal investment types: Cadre Fund Co-Investments, which secures a new asset; Opportunity Zones, designed to offer tax benefits; and Secondary Market, which allows investors to purchase positions from sellers on Cadre's platform.

FINANCIAL DATA: *Note: Data for latest year may not have been available at press time.*

In U.S. $	2021	2020	2019	2018	2017	2016
Revenue						
R&D Expense						
Operating Income						
Operating Margin %						
SGA Expense						
Net Income						
Operating Cash Flow						
Capital Expenditure						
EBITDA						
Return on Assets %						
Return on Equity %						
Debt to Equity						

CONTACT INFORMATION:

Phone: 646 661-7677   Fax:
Toll-Free: 800-356-4951
Address: 419 Park Ave. S., Fl. 12, New York, NY 10016 United States

STOCK TICKER/OTHER:

Stock Ticker: Private   Exchange:
Employees: Fiscal Year Ends:
Parent Company:

SALARIES/BONUSES:

Top Exec. Salary: $ Bonus: $
Second Exec. Salary: $ Bonus: $

OTHER THOUGHTS:

Estimated Female Officers or Directors:
Hot Spot for Advancement for Women/Minorities:

Sales, profits and employees may be estimates. Financial information, benefits and other data can change quickly and may vary from those stated here.

Plunkett Research, Ltd.

Calero-MDSL
www.caleromdsl.com

NAIC Code: 511210Q

TYPES OF BUSINESS:
Financial Software for the Telecommunications Industry
Software
Expense Management
Telecom Solutions
Mobility Solutions
Software-as-a-Service Solutions

BRANDS/DIVISIONS/AFFILIATES:

CONTACTS: *Note: Officers with more than one job title may be intentionally listed here more than once.*
Scott Gilbert, CEO
Andrew Taylor, Pres.
Brian Brady, CFO
David Bliss, Exec. VP-Product Mgmt..
Kris Sleeper, VP-Human Resources
James Jones, Dir.-R&D
Simon Mendoza, CTO
Kristie Shanks, Dir.-Prod. Management & Quality Assurance
Brian Martin, Pres., Telesoft Recovery Corp.
Robert Sullivan, Exec. VP-Telesoft Recovery Corp.
Joan Lara, Dir.-Managed Services
Devin Gentry, Dir.-Implementation
Patrick Mulvehill, Exec. VP-Oper.

GROWTH PLANS/SPECIAL FEATURES:
Calero-MDSL is a software provider, with a focus on expense management for the technology industry. The firm's solutions are designed to offer clarity, control, compliance and cost savings. Solutions are grouped into three categories: telecom, mobility and software-as-a-service (SaaS). The telecom solutions category provides an easy-to-use platform that enables order management, usage analysis, call accounting and expense management for telecom environments, spanning a wide range of applications such as inventory tracking, automating expenses and gaining insight. The mobility solution category offers managed mobility services, which centralizes enterprise mobility across global carriers from a single platform. This division support customer's teams with resources for all mobile hardware, software and carrier-related issues. It prepares and delivers devices for immediate use, including pre-loading of apps, configuration and customized packaging. Calero-MDSL verifies device eligibility and places orders with carriers around the world to keep mobile inventory up-to-date, which also offering a centralized view of everything. The SaaS solution category provides expense management across all unified communications spend, including subscriptions, variable teleconferencing and call usage. Turn-key integrations are provided for enabling end-to-end invoice, subscription (phone, webinar, rooms, etc.), call accounting, contract and renewals management. Based in the U.S., Calero-MDSL has offices worldwide, including North America, Europe and Asia.

FINANCIAL DATA: *Note: Data for latest year may not have been available at press time.*

In U.S. $	2021	2020	2019	2018	2017	2016
Revenue						
R&D Expense						
Operating Income						
Operating Margin %						
SGA Expense						
Net Income						
Operating Cash Flow						
Capital Expenditure						
EBITDA						
Return on Assets %						
Return on Equity %						
Debt to Equity						

CONTACT INFORMATION:
Phone: 866-769-5992   Fax:
Toll-Free:
Address: 1040 University Ave., Ste. 200, Rochester, NY 14607 United States

STOCK TICKER/OTHER:
Stock Ticker: Private
Employees: 140
Parent Company:

Exchange:
Fiscal Year Ends: 11/30

SALARIES/BONUSES:
Top Exec. Salary: $ Bonus: $
Second Exec. Salary: $ Bonus: $

OTHER THOUGHTS:
Estimated Female Officers or Directors: 2
Hot Spot for Advancement for Women/Minorities:

Sales, profits and employees may be estimates. Financial information, benefits and other data can change quickly and may vary from those stated here.

Capital One Financial Corporation

www.capitalone.com

NAIC Code: 522210

TYPES OF BUSINESS:
Credit Card Issuing
Credit Card Products & Services
Mortgage Services
Consumer Lending
Health Care Financing
Small Business Loans
Mortgages
Commercial Banking

BRANDS/DIVISIONS/AFFILIATES:
Capital One Bank (USA) National Association
Capital One National Association

GROWTH PLANS/SPECIAL FEATURES:
Capital One is a diversified financial services holding company headquartered in McLean, Virginia. Originally a spin-off of Signet Financial's credit card division in 1994, the company is now primarily involved in credit card lending, auto loans, and commercial lending.

CONTACTS: *Note: Officers with more than one job title may be intentionally listed here more than once.*
Richard Fairbank, CEO
Christopher Newkirk, Pres., Divisional
Andrew Young, CFO
Timothy Golden, Chief Accounting Officer
Robert Alexander, Chief Information Officer
Sheldon Hall, Chief Risk Officer
Matthew Cooper, General Counsel
Kevin Borgmann, Other Corporate Officer
Frank LaPrade, Other Corporate Officer
John Finneran, Other Corporate Officer
Jory Berson, Other Executive Officer
Celia Karam, Other Executive Officer
Michael Wassmer, President, Divisional
Lia Dean, President, Divisional
Sanjiv Yajnik, President, Divisional

FINANCIAL DATA: *Note: Data for latest year may not have been available at press time.*

In U.S. $	2021	2020	2019	2018	2017	2016
Revenue		28,523,000,000	28,593,000,000	27,577,000,000	27,237,000,000	25,501,000,000
R&D Expense						
Operating Income						
Operating Margin %						
SGA Expense		9,630,000,000	9,952,000,000	9,161,000,000	8,746,000,000	8,182,000,000
Net Income		2,714,000,000	5,546,000,000	6,015,000,000	1,982,000,000	3,751,000,000
Operating Cash Flow		16,699,000,000	16,639,000,000	12,978,000,000	14,182,000,000	11,856,000,000
Capital Expenditure		710,000,000	887,000,000	874,000,000	1,018,000,000	779,000,000
EBITDA						
Return on Assets %						
Return on Equity %						
Debt to Equity						

CONTACT INFORMATION:
Phone: 703 720-1000   Fax:
Toll-Free: 800-801-1164
Address: 1680 Capital One Dr., McLean, VA 22102 United States

STOCK TICKER/OTHER:
Stock Ticker: COF   Exchange: NYS
Employees: 50,767   Fiscal Year Ends: 12/31
Parent Company:

SALARIES/BONUSES:
Top Exec. Salary: $ Bonus: $3,000,000
Second Exec. Salary: Bonus: $1,383,000
$1,144,846

OTHER THOUGHTS:
Estimated Female Officers or Directors: 3
Hot Spot for Advancement for Women/Minorities: Y

Sales, profits and employees may be estimates. Financial information, benefits and other data can change quickly and may vary from those stated here.

Carta Inc (eShares Inc)

carta.com

NAIC Code: 523999

TYPES OF BUSINESS:

Transfer Agency
Ownership Management
Online Securities Brokering
Transfer Agency
Financial Investments

BRANDS/DIVISIONS/AFFILIATES:

Carta Securities LLC

GROWTH PLANS/SPECIAL FEATURES:

eShares, Inc. does business as Carta, Inc., which is a transfer agent registered with the U.S. Securities and Exchange Commission that offers an ownership management platform. Subsidiary Carta Securities, LLC is a broker-dealer. Carta's products and solutions for private companies include cap table management, 409A valuations, scenario modeling, ASC 718 reporting, private company liquidity, Carta for LLCs, Carta for healthcare/life sciences, and more. Products and solutions for investors include fund administration, ASC 820, capital call line of credit, scenario modeling, portfolio insights, Carta for emerging managers, and more. Products and solutions for public companies include an employee stock purchase plan (ESPP) and transfer agency. Carta comprises over 28,000 companies, and more than one million investors, law firms and employees on its platform. Headquartered in California, USA, the company has additional office locations in the U.S., Canada, Brazil, Singapore and Australia.

CONTACTS: *Note: Officers with more than one job title may be intentionally listed here more than once.*

Henry Ward, CEO

FINANCIAL DATA: *Note: Data for latest year may not have been available at press time.*

In U.S. $	2021	2020	2019	2018	2017	2016
Revenue						
R&D Expense						
Operating Income						
Operating Margin %						
SGA Expense						
Net Income						
Operating Cash Flow						
Capital Expenditure						
EBITDA						
Return on Assets %						
Return on Equity %						
Debt to Equity						

CONTACT INFORMATION:

Phone: 650 669-8381   Fax:
Toll-Free:
Address: 333 Bush St., Fl. 23, Ste. 2300, San Francisco, CA 94104 United States

STOCK TICKER/OTHER:

Stock Ticker: Private   Exchange:
Employees: Fiscal Year Ends:
Parent Company:

SALARIES/BONUSES:

Top Exec. Salary: $ Bonus: $
Second Exec. Salary: $ Bonus: $

OTHER THOUGHTS:

Estimated Female Officers or Directors:
Hot Spot for Advancement for Women/Minorities:

Sales, profits and employees may be estimates. Financial information, benefits and other data can change quickly and may vary from those stated here.

Certegy Payments Solutions LLC

certegy.com

NAIC Code: 522320

TYPES OF BUSINESS:

Financial Transactions Processing, Reserve, and Clearinghouse Activities
Payment Transaction Services
Online and Mobile Transaction Processing
Payment Acceptance or Decline
Payroll Processing
Automatic Deposit Services
Identity Screening Technologies
Check Verification Solutions

BRANDS/DIVISIONS/AFFILIATES:

Variant Equity Advisors

CONTACTS: *Note: Officers with more than one job title may be intentionally listed here more than once.*

Farhadd Wadia, Managing Dir.-Variant

GROWTH PLANS/SPECIAL FEATURES:

Certegy Payments Solutions, LLC enables low-risk, low-cost transactions between consumers and businesses. The company's products are designed to pass transactions securely whether it be receiving electronic payments through a bank account, accepting checks at point-of-sale terminals or processing payroll, government or personal checks. Certegy's verification process scans its database of consumer account histories, screens transactions through proprietary data science and risk analytics tools, and processes transactions in real-time, sending instant accept/decline recommendations. Certegy is available for a variety of industries, including retail, casinos/gaming, health and wellness, services, hospitality and leisure, automotive, transportation, financial institutions, ecommerce/subscriptions, government and utilities. Products offered include bank pay, buy now/pay later, virtual terminal, mobile pay, Automated Clearing House (ACH) services, retail check verification, check cashing and depositing, and warranty coverage. Certegy is privately owned by Variant Equity Advisors.

FINANCIAL DATA: *Note: Data for latest year may not have been available at press time.*

In U.S. $	2021	2020	2019	2018	2017	2016
Revenue						
R&D Expense						
Operating Income						
Operating Margin %						
SGA Expense						
Net Income						
Operating Cash Flow						
Capital Expenditure						
EBITDA						
Return on Assets %						
Return on Equity %						
Debt to Equity						

CONTACT INFORMATION:

Phone: Fax:
Toll-Free: 800 437-5120
Address: 17757 US Hwy 19 N., Ste. 375, Clearwater, FL 33764 United States

STOCK TICKER/OTHER:

Stock Ticker: Private Exchange:
Employees: Fiscal Year Ends:
Parent Company: Variant Equity Advisors

SALARIES/BONUSES:

Top Exec. Salary: $ Bonus: $
Second Exec. Salary: $ Bonus: $

OTHER THOUGHTS:

Estimated Female Officers or Directors:
Hot Spot for Advancement for Women/Minorities:

Sales, profits and employees may be estimates. Financial information, benefits and other data can change quickly and may vary from those stated here.

Chainalysis Inc

www.chainalysis.com

NAIC Code: 511210E

TYPES OF BUSINESS:

Computer Software: Network Security, Managed Access, Digital ID, Cybersecurity & Anti-Virus
Investigation, Compliance and Market Intelligence Software
Blockchain Data Platform
Cryptocurrency Protection
Security Software
Compliance Solutions
Digital Economy Solutions
Research and Data Analytics

BRANDS/DIVISIONS/AFFILIATES:

Chainalysis
Chainalysis Business Data
Chainalysis KYT
Chainalysis Kryptos
Chainalysis Market Intel
Chianalysis Reactor

CONTACTS: *Note: Officers with more than one job title may be intentionally listed here more than once.*

Michael Gronager, CEO
Thomas Stanley, Pres.
Rakib Azad, VP-Finance
Ian Andrews, CMO
Jaclyn Mack, VP-People
Gerd Behrmann, CTO
Pratima Arora, Chief Product Officer

GROWTH PLANS/SPECIAL FEATURES:

Chainalysis, Inc. has developed and delivers the blockchain data platform known as Chainalysis. The company provides data, software, services and research to government agencies, exchanges, financial institutions, and insurance and cybersecurity companies in more than 60 countries worldwide. Chainalysis' data powers investigation, compliance and market intelligence software, and has been used to solve criminal cases as well as to grow consumer access to cryptocurrency safely. The firm develops regulations, establishes standard audit practices and implements compliance controls for cryptocurrency to help customers sustain growth, integrate into the global financial infrastructure and thrive in the digital economy. Chainalysis Business Data is a product that provides a layer of customer intelligence to cryptocurrency businesses for understanding customers better, tailoring products and identifying new revenue streams. Chainalysis KYT (know your transaction) combines blockchain intelligence and a real-time application programming interface (API) for reducing manual workflows, staying compliant and interacting with emerging technologies safely. Chainalysis Kryptos provides on-chain metrics of cryptocurrency businesses based on the industry's blockchain data so that firms can navigate the cryptocurrency landscape and discover opportunities. Chainalysis Market Intel leverages blockchain transparency to provide data and insights for decision-making purposes. Chainalysis Reactor is an investigation software that connects cryptocurrency transactions to global entities, and is primarily used for examining criminal activity such as stolen funds and for examining legitimate activity such as flash loans and non-fungible token (NFT) transfers. Chainalysis, Inc. has certification programs that teach how investigators, compliance officers, analysists, regulators and more can be certified in cryptocurrency fundamentals, Ethereum and other related areas.

FINANCIAL DATA: *Note: Data for latest year may not have been available at press time.*

In U.S. $	2021	2020	2019	2018	2017	2016
Revenue						
R&D Expense						
Operating Income						
Operating Margin %						
SGA Expense						
Net Income						
Operating Cash Flow						
Capital Expenditure						
EBITDA						
Return on Assets %						
Return on Equity %						
Debt to Equity						

CONTACT INFORMATION:

Phone: 888-254-9670   Fax:
Toll-Free:
Address: 114 Fifth Ave. Fl. 18, New York, NY 10011-5668 United States

STOCK TICKER/OTHER:

Stock Ticker: Private   Exchange:
Employees: Fiscal Year Ends:
Parent Company:

SALARIES/BONUSES:

Top Exec. Salary: $ Bonus: $
Second Exec. Salary: $ Bonus: $

OTHER THOUGHTS:

Estimated Female Officers or Directors:
Hot Spot for Advancement for Women/Minorities:

Sales, profits and employees may be estimates. Financial information, benefits and other data can change quickly and may vary from those stated here.

Charles Schwab Corporation (The)

www.schwab.com

NAIC Code: 523120

TYPES OF BUSINESS:

Stock Brokerage-Retail, Online & Discount
Investment Services
Physical Branch Investment Offices
Mutual Funds
Wealth Management
Financial Information
Retail Banking
Online Trading Platform

BRANDS/DIVISIONS/AFFILIATES:

Charles Schwab & Co Inc
Charles Schwab Bank
Charles Schwab Investment Management Inc
TD Ameritrade Holding Corporation
TD Ameritrade Inc
TD Ameritrade Clearing Inc

GROWTH PLANS/SPECIAL FEATURES:

Charles Schwab operates in the brokerage, banking, and asset-management businesses. The company runs a large network of brick-and-mortar brokerage branch offices and a well-established online investing website. It also operates a bank and a proprietary asset management business and offers services to independent investment advisors. The company is among the largest firms in the investment business, with over $6.5 trillion of client assets at the end of 2020. Nearly all of its revenue is from the United States.

CSC offers employees health benefits; 401(k) and savings plans; education reimbursement; and on-the-job training and support.

CONTACTS: *Note: Officers with more than one job title may be intentionally listed here more than once.*

Walter Bettinger, CEO
Jonathan Craig, Sr. Exec. VP
Peter Crawford, CFO
Charles Schwab, Chairman of the Board
Nigel Murtagh, Chief Risk Officer
Joseph Martinetto, COO
Bernard Clark, Executive VP, Divisional
Peter Morgan, Executive VP
Richard Wurster, President

FINANCIAL DATA: *Note: Data for latest year may not have been available at press time.*

In U.S. $	2021	2020	2019	2018	2017	2016
Revenue		11,691,000,000	10,721,000,000	10,132,000,000	8,618,000,000	7,473,000,000
R&D Expense						
Operating Income						
Operating Margin %						
SGA Expense		4,796,000,000	4,002,000,000	3,801,000,000	3,415,000,000	2,968,000,000
Net Income		3,299,000,000	3,704,000,000	3,507,000,000	2,354,000,000	1,889,000,000
Operating Cash Flow		6,852,000,000	9,325,000,000	12,456,000,000	1,263,000,000	2,662,000,000
Capital Expenditure		631,000,000	708,000,000	570,000,000	400,000,000	346,000,000
EBITDA						
Return on Assets %						
Return on Equity %						
Debt to Equity						

CONTACT INFORMATION:

Phone: 817 859-5000   Fax:
Toll-Free: 800-648-5300
Address: TX-114 Circle T Ranch, Westlake, TX 76262 United States

STOCK TICKER/OTHER:

Stock Ticker: SCHW   Exchange: NYS
Employees: 19,700   Fiscal Year Ends: 12/31
Parent Company:

SALARIES/BONUSES:

Top Exec. Salary: $1,383,333   Bonus: $
Second Exec. Salary: $741,667   Bonus: $

OTHER THOUGHTS:

Estimated Female Officers or Directors: 6
Hot Spot for Advancement for Women/Minorities: Y

Sales, profits and employees may be estimates. Financial information, benefits and other data can change quickly and may vary from those stated here.

Plunkett Research, Ltd.

Checkbook Inc

checkbook.io

NAIC Code: 522320

TYPES OF BUSINESS:
Financial Transactions Processing, Reserve, and Clearinghouse Activities
Digital Checks
Payment Technology
Sending and Receiving Digital Checks
Digital Invoicing
Digital Recurring Billing Solutions

BRANDS/DIVISIONS/AFFILIATES:

GROWTH PLANS/SPECIAL FEATURES:
Checkbook, Inc. is engaged in payment innovation technology and has developed a payouts platform for the digital age. The Checkbook platform offers everything needed to disburse payments at scale. How it works: create an account by using name and email, verify banking information, choose between manual or instant verification, once bank is verified, checks can be sent. Through the Checkbook platform senders enter the recipient's name and email, as well as the amount to be sent and click the send button. Integrations offered by Checkbook can also be used when sending online checks. Checkbook offers an invoicing solution, enabling users to get paid through the platform's digital check solution, which would be deposited directly into their bank accounts. Checkbook's digital invoicing system allows businesses to manage payments and invoices in a single place. Recurring billing options for obtaining payments is also offered. Checkbook is compliant with PCI DSS, SOC 1 and 2, and HIPAA.

CONTACTS: *Note: Officers with more than one job title may be intentionally listed here more than once.*
P.J. Gupta, CEO
Sam Garcia, Dir.-Oper.
Clark R. Spink, VP-Sales
Anthony Sanchez, Dir.-Communications

FINANCIAL DATA: *Note: Data for latest year may not have been available at press time.*

In U.S. $	2021	2020	2019	2018	2017	2016
Revenue						
R&D Expense						
Operating Income						
Operating Margin %						
SGA Expense						
Net Income						
Operating Cash Flow						
Capital Expenditure						
EBITDA						
Return on Assets %						
Return on Equity %						
Debt to Equity						

CONTACT INFORMATION:
Phone: 650 761-0008   Fax:
Toll-Free:
Address: 1500 Fashion Island Blvd., Ste. 103, San Mateo, CA 94404 United States

STOCK TICKER/OTHER:
Stock Ticker: Private   Exchange:
Employees: Fiscal Year Ends:
Parent Company:

SALARIES/BONUSES:
Top Exec. Salary: $ Bonus: $
Second Exec. Salary: $ Bonus: $

OTHER THOUGHTS:
Estimated Female Officers or Directors:
Hot Spot for Advancement for Women/Minorities:

Sales, profits and employees may be estimates. Financial information, benefits and other data can change quickly and may vary from those stated here.

Checkout.com (Checkout Ltd)

www.checkout.com

NAIC Code: 522320

TYPES OF BUSINESS:
Financial Transactions Processing, Reserve, and Clearinghouse Activities
Global Payments Platform
Payment and Payout Solutions
Fraud Protection
Reporting and Data
Cryptocurrency
Payment Compliance Management

BRANDS/DIVISIONS/AFFILIATES:
Checkout LLC
Checkout SAS
Checkout MENA FZ LLC

CONTACTS: *Note: Officers with more than one job title may be intentionally listed here more than once.*
Guillaume Pousaz, CEO
Celine Dufetel, COO
Nick Worswick, Chief Revenue Officer
Leela Srinivasan, CMO
Kerry Van Voris, Chief Human Resources Officer
Ott Kaukver, CTO
Meron Colbeci, Chief Product Officer

GROWTH PLANS/SPECIAL FEATURES:

Checkout Ltd. is a technology company that has developed a global payments solution for the digital economy. The checkout.com platform offers payment and payout solutions, with features spanning fraud protection, integrations, international coverage, a variety of payment methods, reporting and data, unified payments and cryptocurrency. Payments can be processed anywhere through the checkout.com platform, which processes more than 150 currencies and 20+ settlement currencies. Payment methods include local cards, alternative payment methods (APMs) and digital wallets. Payouts can be seamlessly sent, including card and bank payouts, locally or globally. Checkout.com offers built-in compliance management, advanced detection, precision flagging and dedicated customer service. Headquartered in London, U.K., Checkout Ltd. has office locations in Berlin, Paris, Porto, Dubai, Hong Kong, Singapore, Mauritius, Sao Paulo, Karachi, Barcelona, New York and San Francisco. Global subsidiaries of the firm include Checkout LLC, Checkout SAS and Checkout MENA FZ LLC.

FINANCIAL DATA: *Note: Data for latest year may not have been available at press time.*

In U.S. $	2021	2020	2019	2018	2017	2016
Revenue	262,827,760	252,719,000	146,384,000	74,826,000	46,767,000	
R&D Expense						
Operating Income						
Operating Margin %						
SGA Expense						
Net Income		-25,932,000	-9,743,000	2,361,000	6,653,000	
Operating Cash Flow						
Capital Expenditure						
EBITDA						
Return on Assets %						
Return on Equity %						
Debt to Equity						

CONTACT INFORMATION:
Phone: 44207-323-3888 Fax:
Toll-Free:
Address: Wenlock Works, Shepherdess Walk, London, N1 7BQ United Kingdom

STOCK TICKER/OTHER:
Stock Ticker: Private
Employees:
Parent Company:

Exchange:
Fiscal Year Ends: 12/31

SALARIES/BONUSES:
Top Exec. Salary: $ Bonus: $
Second Exec. Salary: $ Bonus: $

OTHER THOUGHTS:
Estimated Female Officers or Directors:
Hot Spot for Advancement for Women/Minorities:

Sales, profits and employees may be estimates. Financial information, benefits and other data can change quickly and may vary from those stated here.

Chime Financial Inc

www.chime.com

NAIC Code: 511210Q

TYPES OF BUSINESS:
Computer Software: Accounting, Banking & Financial
Financial Technology
Financial App Development
Credit Building
Debit Cards
Savings Account
Mobile Payments
Mobile Banking

BRANDS/DIVISIONS/AFFILIATES:

CONTACTS: Note: Officers with more than one job title may be intentionally listed here more than once.
Chris Britt, CEO
Mark Troughton, COO
Matt Newcomb, CFO
Melissa Alvarado, CMO
Beth Steinberg, VP-People
Ryan King, CTO
Dennis Yu, Chief of Staff

GROWTH PLANS/SPECIAL FEATURES:
Chime Financial, Inc. is a financial technology company that has developed an online banking platform that helps members get ahead through a transparent, simplified money management process. Chime partners with regional banks to design its financial products, which enables lower-cost options versus traditional banks. Chime is not a bank and does not profit from its members, but it does profit alongside them. For example, every time a Chime app member uses their debit card, Chime earns a small fee from Visa, paid by the merchant. Three kinds of accounts are offered to Chime members: spending account, credit builder and savings account. The spending account comes with a debit card, no monthly fees and no maintenance fees. The credit builder account offers ways to build credit by charging no fees and a 0% annual percentage rate (APR), and no credit checks nor minimum security deposits are required to apply. Credit can be increase by an average of 30 points using Chime's credit builder credit card. The savings account offers a 1.00% annual percentage yield, and offers automatic savings features for setting money aside, all for no bank fees. Chime accounts feature online banking, fee-free overdraft protection, no hidden fees, mobile banking, automatic savings, mobile payments and security.

FINANCIAL DATA: Note: Data for latest year may not have been available at press time.

In U.S. $	2021	2020	2019	2018	2017	2016
Revenue						
R&D Expense						
Operating Income						
Operating Margin %						
SGA Expense						
Net Income						
Operating Cash Flow						
Capital Expenditure						
EBITDA						
Return on Assets %						
Return on Equity %						
Debt to Equity						

CONTACT INFORMATION:
Phone: 415 603-6030   Fax:
Toll-Free: 844 244-6363
Address: 77 Maiden Ln., San Francisco, CA 94108 United States

STOCK TICKER/OTHER:
Stock Ticker: Private
Employees:
Parent Company:

Exchange:
Fiscal Year Ends:

SALARIES/BONUSES:
Top Exec. Salary: $ Bonus: $
Second Exec. Salary: $ Bonus: $

OTHER THOUGHTS:
Estimated Female Officers or Directors:
Hot Spot for Advancement for Women/Minorities:

Sales, profits and employees may be estimates. Financial information, benefits and other data can change quickly and may vary from those stated here.

Circle Internet Financial Limited

NAIC Code: 523130

www.circle.com/en

TYPES OF BUSINESS:
Foreign Currency Exchange Services (i.e. Selling to the Public)
Financial Technology
Digital Currencies
Public Blockchains
Commerce Platforms
Financial Applications
Accounts
Payment Services

BRANDS/DIVISIONS/AFFILIATES:
USD Coin
SeedInvest

CONTACTS:
Note: Officers with more than one job title may be intentionally listed here more than once.
Jeremy Allaire, CEO
Elizabeth Carpenter, COO
Jeremy Fox-Green, CFO

GROWTH PLANS/SPECIAL FEATURES:
Circle Internet Financial Limited is a global financial technology firm that enables businesses of all sizes to utilize digital currencies and public blockchains for payments, commerce and financial applications worldwide. Circle is the principal operator of USD Coin (USDC), a regulated, fully-reserved dollar digital currency. USDC in circulation is greater than $30 billion and has supported over $1 trillion in on-chain transactions (as of October 2021). Circle's transactional services, business accounts and platform application programming interfaces (APIs) help to raise global economic prosperity for all via programmable internet commerce. Products and services offered via Circle include circle accounts for global financial transactions (including express accounts), payments and payouts. In addition, Circle operates SeedInvest, an equity crowdfunding platform in the U.S., and is a registered broker dealer. A range of banking and financial solutions are offered in regards to banks, corporate treasuries, exchanges, wallets, fintechs, institutional traders and non-fungible token (NFT) platforms. During 2021, Circle began the process of becoming a public company, trading on the New York Stock Exchange under ticker symbol CRCL.

FINANCIAL DATA:
Note: Data for latest year may not have been available at press time.

In U.S. $	2021	2020	2019	2018	2017	2016
Revenue	84,877,000	15,441,000	9,423,000			
R&D Expense						
Operating Income						
Operating Margin %						
SGA Expense						
Net Income	-310,393,000	3,790,000	-178,565,000			
Operating Cash Flow						
Capital Expenditure						
EBITDA						
Return on Assets %						
Return on Equity %						
Debt to Equity						

CONTACT INFORMATION:
Phone: 617 326-8326   Fax:
Toll-Free: 800 398-7172
Address: 332 Congress St., Fl. 4, Boston, MA 02210 United States

STOCK TICKER/OTHER:
Stock Ticker: Private   Exchange:
Employees: 404   Fiscal Year Ends: 12/31
Parent Company:

SALARIES/BONUSES:
Top Exec. Salary: $ Bonus: $
Second Exec. Salary: $ Bonus: $

OTHER THOUGHTS:
Estimated Female Officers or Directors:
Hot Spot for Advancement for Women/Minorities:

Sales, profits and employees may be estimates. Financial information, benefits and other data can change quickly and may vary from those stated here.

Citigroup Inc

www.citigroup.com

NAIC Code: 522110

TYPES OF BUSINESS:

Banking
Commercial, Residential & Consumer Lending
Credit Cards
Investment Banking
Insurance
Brokerage Services
Equity
Cash Management

BRANDS/DIVISIONS/AFFILIATES:

GROWTH PLANS/SPECIAL FEATURES:

Citigroup is a global financial services company doing business in more than 100 countries and jurisdictions. Citigroup's operations are organized into two primary segments: the global consumer banking segment, which provides basic branch banking around the world, and the institutional clients group, which provides large customers around the globe with investment banking, cash management, and other products and services.

CONTACTS: Note: Officers with more than one job title may be intentionally listed here more than once.

Paco Ybarra, CEO, Divisional
Anand Selvakesari, CEO, Divisional
David Livingstone, CEO, Geographical
Peter Babej, CEO, Geographical
Ernesto Torres Cantu, CEO, Geographical
Jane Fraser, CEO
Mark Mason, CFO
Barbara Desoer, Chairman of the Board, Subsidiary
John Dugan, Chairman of the Board
Johnbull Okpara, Chief Accounting Officer
Karen Peetz, Chief Administrative Officer
Mary McNiff, Chief Compliance Officer
Zdenek Turek, Chief Risk Officer
Rohan Weerasinghe, General Counsel
Mike Whitaker, Other Corporate Officer

FINANCIAL DATA: Note: Data for latest year may not have been available at press time.

In U.S. $	2021	2020	2019	2018	2017	2016
Revenue		75,494,000,000	75,067,000,000	74,036,000,000	72,698,000,000	71,020,000,000
R&D Expense						
Operating Income						
Operating Margin %						
SGA Expense		32,130,000,000	30,880,000,000	31,175,000,000	31,038,000,000	30,636,000,000
Net Income		11,047,000,000	19,401,000,000	18,045,000,000	-6,798,000,000	14,912,000,000
Operating Cash Flow		-20,621,000,000	-12,837,000,000	36,952,000,000	-8,587,000,000	53,932,000,000
Capital Expenditure		3,446,000,000	5,336,000,000	3,774,000,000	3,361,000,000	2,756,000,000
EBITDA						
Return on Assets %						
Return on Equity %						
Debt to Equity						

CONTACT INFORMATION:

Phone: 212 559-1000   Fax: 212 816-8913
Toll-Free: 800-285-3000
Address: 388 Greenwich St., New York, NY 10013 United States

STOCK TICKER/OTHER:

Stock Ticker: C   Exchange: NYS
Employees: 210,000   Fiscal Year Ends: 12/31
Parent Company:

SALARIES/BONUSES:

Top Exec. Salary: $8,355,669   Bonus: $
Second Exec. Salary: $500,000   Bonus: $6,660,000

OTHER THOUGHTS:

Estimated Female Officers or Directors: 5
Hot Spot for Advancement for Women/Minorities: Y

Sales, profits and employees may be estimates. Financial information, benefits and other data can change quickly and may vary from those stated here.

Citizens Financial Group Inc

www.citizensbank.com

NAIC Code: 522110

TYPES OF BUSINESS:

Banking
Insurance
Business Finance
Loans
Wholesale Banking
Online Stock Brokerage
Investment Management

BRANDS/DIVISIONS/AFFILIATES:

GROWTH PLANS/SPECIAL FEATURES:

Citizens Financial Group is a retail bank holding company operating primarily in the New England, Mid-Atlantic, and Midwest regions of the United States. The bank operates through two segments: consumer and commercial banking. Citizens' strategy emphasizes differentiation through customer service. Net interest income is the largest source of the bank's net revenue. Most net interest income is derived from commercial loans, securities, home equity lines of credit, automobile loans, and residential mortgages. Some of CFG's higher-yielding products include credit cards, home equity loans, and other retail loans.

Citizens offers comprehensive employee benefits, retirement options and assistance programs.

CONTACTS: *Note: Officers with more than one job title may be intentionally listed here more than once.*

Bruce Van Saun, CEO
John Woods, CFO
Jack Read, Chief Accounting Officer
Stephen Gannon, Chief Legal Officer
Malcolm Griggs, Chief Risk Officer
Mary Baker, Executive VP
Brendan Coughlin, Executive VP
Elizabeth Johnson, Executive VP
Susan LaMonica, Executive VP
Donald McCree, Other Corporate Officer

FINANCIAL DATA: *Note: Data for latest year may not have been available at press time.*

In U.S. $	2021	2020	2019	2018	2017	2016
Revenue		6,905,000,000	6,485,000,000	6,123,000,000	5,707,000,000	5,253,000,000
R&D Expense						
Operating Income						
Operating Margin %						
SGA Expense		2,289,000,000	2,200,000,000	2,113,000,000	2,003,000,000	1,927,000,000
Net Income		1,057,000,000	1,791,000,000	1,721,000,000	1,652,000,000	1,045,000,000
Operating Cash Flow		111,000,000	1,697,000,000	1,767,000,000	1,883,000,000	1,490,000,000
Capital Expenditure		118,000,000	366,000,000	485,000,000	440,000,000	303,000,000
EBITDA						
Return on Assets %						
Return on Equity %						
Debt to Equity						

CONTACT INFORMATION:

Phone: 401-456-7000   Fax: 401-456-7819
Toll-Free:
Address: One Citizens Plaza, Providence, RI 02903 United States

STOCK TICKER/OTHER:

Stock Ticker: CFG   Exchange: NYS
Employees: 18,000   Fiscal Year Ends: 12/31
Parent Company:

SALARIES/BONUSES:

Top Exec. Salary: $1,487,000   Bonus: $2,268,900
Second Exec. Salary: $700,000   Bonus: $864,000

OTHER THOUGHTS:

Estimated Female Officers or Directors: 3
Hot Spot for Advancement for Women/Minorities: Y

Sales, profits and employees may be estimates. Financial information, benefits and other data can change quickly and may vary from those stated here.

Plunkett Research, Ltd.

Clover Network Inc

www.clover.com

NAIC Code: 522320

TYPES OF BUSINESS:
Financial Transactions Processing, Reserve, and Clearinghouse Activities
Point of Sale Platform
Cloud-Based Payment Solutions
Transaction Services
Sales Tracking Solutions
Point of Sales Systems
Payment Software and Hardware Products

BRANDS/DIVISIONS/AFFILIATES:
Clover
Clover Online Ordering
Clover Dashboard

CONTACTS: *Note: Officers with more than one job title may be intentionally listed here more than once.*
John Beatty, CEO

GROWTH PLANS/SPECIAL FEATURES:
Clover Network, Inc. has developed a cloud-based point of sale platform called Clover. The all-in-one system for businesses enables them to accept any type of payment, including in-person, card, app and online. All purchases are secure and trackable and transaction history is easily accessible. Online orders can be managed with Clover Online Ordering, and online invoicing capabilities are provided. Sales tracking and reporting features reveal trends, analytics, sales, employee performance and customer loyalty. Clover offers modern and fast point of sale systems for small businesses, and payments can be accepted easily and securely through the business' computer with the Clover Dashboard. The Clover platform is payment card industry (PC)I-compliant. Clover primarily serves the dining, retail, personal services, professional services, home services and field services industries. A variety of integrations are obtainable through Clover, including developer, apps, links, strategic connections and other integration services. Headquartered in California, the company has additional offices in New York, Colorado and Georgia.

Clover offers its employees comprehensive health benefits, 401(k) and a variety of other benefits and company perks.

FINANCIAL DATA: *Note: Data for latest year may not have been available at press time.*

In U.S. $	2021	2020	2019	2018	2017	2016
Revenue						
R&D Expense						
Operating Income						
Operating Margin %						
SGA Expense						
Net Income						
Operating Cash Flow						
Capital Expenditure						
EBITDA						
Return on Assets %						
Return on Equity %						
Debt to Equity						

CONTACT INFORMATION:
Phone: 650 210-7888   Fax:
Toll-Free: 800-368-1000
Address: 415 N. Mathilda Ave., Sunnyvale, CA 94085 United States

STOCK TICKER/OTHER:
Stock Ticker: Private   Exchange:
Employees: Fiscal Year Ends:
Parent Company:

SALARIES/BONUSES:
Top Exec. Salary: $ Bonus: $
Second Exec. Salary: $ Bonus: $

OTHER THOUGHTS:
Estimated Female Officers or Directors:
Hot Spot for Advancement for Women/Minorities:

Sales, profits and employees may be estimates. Financial information, benefits and other data can change quickly and may vary from those stated here.

Clyde Technologies Inc

www.joinclyde.com

NAIC Code: 524210

TYPES OF BUSINESS:
Insurance Agencies and Brokerages
Extended Warranties & Accident Protection Plans Online Platform
Product Registration
Product Purchasing

BRANDS/DIVISIONS/AFFILIATES:
Clyde

CONTACTS: *Note: Officers with more than one job title may be intentionally listed here more than once.*
Brandon Gell, CEO

GROWTH PLANS/SPECIAL FEATURES:
Clyde Technologies, Inc. is a technology company that has developed and operates a product lifecycle platform called Clyde. Founded in 2017, Clyde helps merchants manage product warranties and registrations, and therefore helps provide resolutions for purchasers who cannot find their warranties or did not register products. Clyde also enables merchants to offer extended warranties on many branded products. Clyde unites brands with the customers, which could help brands and merchants retain customers who are happy with specific brands or merchant services. How it works: when customers purchase a product, through Clyde they are prompted to scan a QR code which takes them directly to the merchant's website to register; and Clyde's registration technology provides a short-form to fill out along with auto-populating product features, making the process swift and easy. Clyde's dashboard enables users to manage their purchases, add coverage, file claims and buy more products, all from a single place. Clyde can be installed on any existing customer touchpoint with one line of code. With a fully integrated checkout, the registration flow includes a seamless warranty buying experience for customers as well as potential extended warranty plans. Merchants can follow the customer's journey, including price, location and purchase data from third-party channels, and can sent post-purchase offers and other announcements.

FINANCIAL DATA: *Note: Data for latest year may not have been available at press time.*

In U.S. $	2021	2020	2019	2018	2017	2016
Revenue						
R&D Expense						
Operating Income						
Operating Margin %						
SGA Expense						
Net Income						
Operating Cash Flow						
Capital Expenditure						
EBITDA						
Return on Assets %						
Return on Equity %						
Debt to Equity						

CONTACT INFORMATION:
Phone: Fax:
Toll-Free: 888 585-8504
Address: 579 Broadway Ste. 2C, New York, NY 10012 United States

STOCK TICKER/OTHER:
Stock Ticker: Private Exchange:
Employees: Fiscal Year Ends:
Parent Company:

SALARIES/BONUSES:
Top Exec. Salary: $ Bonus: $
Second Exec. Salary: $ Bonus: $

OTHER THOUGHTS:
Estimated Female Officers or Directors:
Hot Spot for Advancement for Women/Minorities:

Coalition Inc

www.coalitioninc.com

NAIC Code: 511210E

TYPES OF BUSINESS:

Computer Software: Network Security, Managed Access, Digital ID,
Cybersecurity & Anti-Virus
Cyber Insurance and Security Company
Cybersecurity Tools
Technology Errors & Omissions Insurance
Executive Risks Insurance
Live Industry Data
Compliance Solutions

BRANDS/DIVISIONS/AFFILIATES:

CONTACTS: *Note: Officers with more than one job title may be intentionally listed here more than once.*

Joshua Motta, CEO

GROWTH PLANS/SPECIAL FEATURES:

Coalition, Inc. provides cyber insurance and security products and services. The firm combines comprehensive insurance and cybersecurity tools to protect organizations from cyberattacks. Coalition's cyber insurance covers up to $15 million in financial, tangible and intangible damage to businesses, including stolen funds, lost business income, breach response costs, cyber extortion, computer replacement and bodily injury. Coalition offers technology errors and omissions (E&O) insurance for tech businesses, with coverage including privacy attorneys, IT forensic investigation, state-by-state notification to impacted individuals and other defense costs. Coalition's next-generation executive risks insurance helps brokers and their clients stay ahead of important policy changes. It provides notifications concerning law changes and public relations events, and offers live data on industry, corporate structure, news, mergers/acquisitions, social media sentiment and more. Coalition is backed by global insurers Swiss Re Corporate Solutions, Arch Insurance, Lloyd's of London, and Zurich North America. Based in the U.S., Coalition has operations throughout the U.S., Canada, the U.K., Switzerland and Portugal.

Coalition offers its employees comprehensive health benefits, 401(k), life and disability benefits and more.

FINANCIAL DATA: *Note: Data for latest year may not have been available at press time.*

In U.S. $	2021	2020	2019	2018	2017	2016
Revenue						
R&D Expense						
Operating Income						
Operating Margin %						
SGA Expense						
Net Income						
Operating Cash Flow						
Capital Expenditure						
EBITDA						
Return on Assets %						
Return on Equity %						
Debt to Equity						

CONTACT INFORMATION:

Phone: 833 866-1337   Fax:
Toll-Free:
Address: 1160 Battery St., Ste. 350, San Francisco, CA 94111 United States

STOCK TICKER/OTHER:

Stock Ticker: Private   Exchange:
Employees: 400   Fiscal Year Ends:
Parent Company:

SALARIES/BONUSES:

Top Exec. Salary: $ Bonus: $
Second Exec. Salary: $ Bonus: $

OTHER THOUGHTS:

Estimated Female Officers or Directors:
Hot Spot for Advancement for Women/Minorities:

Sales, profits and employees may be estimates. Financial information, benefits and other data can change quickly and may vary from those stated here.

Coinbase Global Inc

NAIC Code: 523130

www.coinbase.com

TYPES OF BUSINESS:
Digital Currency Exchange
Digital Currency Platform
Digital Currency Wallet

BRANDS/DIVISIONS/AFFILIATES:

GROWTH PLANS/SPECIAL FEATURES:
Founded in 2012, Coinbase is the leading cryptocurrency exchange platform in the United States. The company intends to be the safe and regulation-compliant point of entry for retail investors and institutions into the cryptocurrency economy. Users can establish an account directly with the firm, instead of using an intermediary, and many choose to allow Coinbase to act as a custodian for their cryptocurrency, giving the company breadth beyond that of a traditional financial exchange. While the company still generates the majority of its revenue from transaction fees charged to its retail customers, Coinbase uses internal investment and acquisitions to expand into adjacent businesses, such as prime brokerage, data analytics, and collateralized lending.

CONTACTS: Note: Officers with more than one job title may be intentionally listed here more than once.
Brian Armstrong, CEO
Alesia Haas, CFO
Paul Grewal, Chief Legal Officer
Emilie Choi, COO
Surojit Chatterjee, Other Executive Officer

FINANCIAL DATA: Note: Data for latest year may not have been available at press time.

In U.S. $	2021	2020	2019	2018	2017	2016
Revenue		1,277,481,000	533,735,000			
R&D Expense		271,732,000	185,044,000			
Operating Income		408,951,000	-35,643,000			
Operating Margin %						
SGA Expense		336,662,000	256,079,000			
Net Income		322,317,000	-30,387,000			
Operating Cash Flow		3,004,070,000	-80,594,000			
Capital Expenditure		18,802,000	40,471,000			
EBITDA		439,913,000	-18,765,000			
Return on Assets %						
Return on Equity %						
Debt to Equity						

CONTACT INFORMATION:
Phone: 302-777-0200   Fax:
Toll-Free:
Address: 1209 Orange St., Wilmington, DE 19801 United States

STOCK TICKER/OTHER:
Stock Ticker: COIN   Exchange: NAS
Employees: 3,730   Fiscal Year Ends: 12/31
Parent Company:

SALARIES/BONUSES:
Top Exec. Salary: $1,000,000   Bonus: $
Second Exec. Salary: $616,435   Bonus: $300,000

OTHER THOUGHTS:
Estimated Female Officers or Directors:
Hot Spot for Advancement for Women/Minorities:

Sales, profits and employees may be estimates. Financial information, benefits and other data can change quickly and may vary from those stated here.

COL Financial Group Inc

www.colfinancial.com

NAIC Code: 523120

TYPES OF BUSINESS:

Securities Brokerage
Online Trading
Investment Strategies
Online Tools
Stock Market Trading
Education and Support
Short-Term Investment
Long-Term Investment

BRANDS/DIVISIONS/AFFILIATES:

COL Easy Investment Program
COL Margin Account

CONTACTS: Note: Officers with more than one job title may be intentionally listed here more than once.

Conrado F. Bate, CEO
Edward K. Lee, Chmn.

GROWTH PLANS/SPECIAL FEATURES:

COL Financial Group, Inc. is a Filipino investment company helping customers take control of their financial future by providing online innovative solutions and accessible tools. The company operates an online trading platform that enables clients to manage their stock portfolios, and offers access to COL Fund source, an online mutual fund supermarket in the Philippines. COL also helps investors take advantage of stock market opportunities by sharing knowledge and market expertise, and by offering access to opinions and research information through the company's website. COL offers continuous education and guidance to clients via seminars, events and customer support. The COL Easy Investment Program is a way for individuals to begin investing in the stock market. COL Margin Account offers short-term market opportunities for increased profit potential, and requires a minimum credit line. COL Financial's equity advisors take a disciplined and active investment approach to managing client long-term investments via asset allocation, risk management and stock selection services.

FINANCIAL DATA: Note: Data for latest year may not have been available at press time.

In U.S. $	2021	2020	2019	2018	2017	2016
Revenue	25,846,926	22,597,300	21,718,600	22,373,400	19,404,000	16,791,000
R&D Expense						
Operating Income						
Operating Margin %						
SGA Expense						
Net Income	11,361,630	8,782,500	9,021,790	9,721,430	7,575,120	6,615,600
Operating Cash Flow						
Capital Expenditure						
EBITDA						
Return on Assets %						
Return on Equity %						
Debt to Equity						

CONTACT INFORMATION:

Phone: 632 865 15888   Fax: 632 863 3512
Toll-Free:
Address: Fl. 24, E. Tower, Exchange Rd., Ortigas Center, Pasig City, 1605 Philippines

STOCK TICKER/OTHER:

Stock Ticker: COL
Employees: 147
Parent Company:

Exchange: Manila
Fiscal Year Ends: 12/31

SALARIES/BONUSES:

Top Exec. Salary: $ Bonus: $
Second Exec. Salary: $ Bonus: $

OTHER THOUGHTS:

Estimated Female Officers or Directors:
Hot Spot for Advancement for Women/Minorities:

Sales, profits and employees may be estimates. Financial information, benefits and other data can change quickly and may vary from those stated here.

CommonBond Inc

www.commonbond.co

NAIC Code: 522291

TYPES OF BUSINESS:
Consumer Lending
Student Loan Refinancing
Homeowner Solar Loans
Lending Investments
Online Loan Platform

BRANDS/DIVISIONS/AFFILIATES:

GROWTH PLANS/SPECIAL FEATURES:

CommonBond, Inc. Is a financial and technology company that has developed an online platform that offers loans, primarily student loans and homeowner solar product loans. CommonBond enables students to simplify their loans and pay off debt more quickly through its refinancing plan, and offers residential solar financing options to help make going solar more accessible and affordable. Investors provide funds and receive a stake in the company in return. In addition, CommonBond has a partnership with Pencils of Promise, which together have provided schools, teachers and technology to thousands of young students in developing countries. More than 470 schools have been built through Pencils of Promise programs.

CONTACTS: *Note: Officers with more than one job title may be intentionally listed here more than once.*

David Klein, CEO
Robb Granado, Pres.
Pete Wylie, COO
Steve Balik, VP-Oper.
Keryn Koch, VP-People
Jeremy Hodges, VP-Engineering
Cara Phillips, Chief Creative Officer

FINANCIAL DATA: *Note: Data for latest year may not have been available at press time.*

In U.S. $	2021	2020	2019	2018	2017	2016
Revenue						
R&D Expense						
Operating Income						
Operating Margin %						
SGA Expense						
Net Income						
Operating Cash Flow						
Capital Expenditure						
EBITDA						
Return on Assets %						
Return on Equity %						
Debt to Equity						

CONTACT INFORMATION:
Phone: Fax:
Toll-Free: 800 975-7812
Address: 524 Broadway, Fl. 6, New York, NY 10012 United States

STOCK TICKER/OTHER:
Stock Ticker: Private   Exchange:
Employees: Fiscal Year Ends:
Parent Company:

SALARIES/BONUSES:
Top Exec. Salary: $ Bonus: $
Second Exec. Salary: $ Bonus: $

OTHER THOUGHTS:
Estimated Female Officers or Directors:
Hot Spot for Advancement for Women/Minorities:

Sales, profits and employees may be estimates. Financial information, benefits and other data can change quickly and may vary from those stated here.

Concur Technologies Inc

www.concur.com

NAIC Code: 511210Q

TYPES OF BUSINESS:

Software Manufacturer-Expense Reporting
Corporate Expense Management Solutions
Invoice Management
Travel Management
Software
Data Analysis
Data Capture

BRANDS/DIVISIONS/AFFILIATES:

SAP SE
SAP Concur

CONTACTS: *Note: Officers with more than one job title may be intentionally listed here more than once.*

Jim Lucier, Pres.
Tom Lavin, CFO
Chris Juneau, CMO
Kyile Stair, VP-Human Resources
Saju Pillai, CTO
John Torrey, Executive VP, Divisional
Robert Cavanaugh, Executive VP
Elena Donio, Executive VP
Ed Kim, Sr. VP-Strategic Programs & Oper.

GROWTH PLANS/SPECIAL FEATURES:

Concur Technologies, Inc. does business as SAP Concur, and provides travel, expense and invoice management tools that simplify processes and creates enhanced experiences. SAP Concur's travel management solutions enable employees to book business travel on their own. The software along with an extensive network of travel suppliers combine to provide an automated, integrated corporate travel system for achieving travel and expense goals. SAP Concur's expense management solutions automate and integrate so that employee travel spending can be planned and captured through multiple devices to a single source. Business settings can be configured, spending policies can be adjusted and receipts can be automatically captured. Reimbursement to employees is swift and the expense reporting process is simplified across each business trip. SAP Concur's invoice solutions automate accounts payable and invoices, reducing tedious tasks. The invoice software increases compliance, reduces fraud, and captures data for business decision purposes. Its mobile tools enable employees to work from anywhere. Industries served by SAP Concur's products and solutions include financial services, healthcare, higher education, legal services, professional services, life sciences, manufacturing, non-profits, oil and gas, mining, retail, restaurant, technology and more. Concur Technologies is owned by German software giant SAP SE. The company is headquartered in Washington, USA, with global locations spanning the Americas, Europe, Asia Pacific, Middle East and Africa.

FINANCIAL DATA: *Note: Data for latest year may not have been available at press time.*

In U.S. $	2021	2020	2019	2018	2017	2016
Revenue	1,836,653,149	1,848,510,000	2,139,255,800	1,767,980,000	1,743,120,000	1,381,972,534
R&D Expense						
Operating Income						
Operating Margin %						
SGA Expense						
Net Income	213,644,246	69,273,000	2,166,597	2,043,960	155,798,000	1,291,875,652
Operating Cash Flow						
Capital Expenditure						
EBITDA						
Return on Assets %						
Return on Equity %						
Debt to Equity						

CONTACT INFORMATION:

Phone: 425 590-5000   Fax: 425 590-5999
Toll-Free: 800-401-8412
Address: 601 108th Ave. NE, Suite 1000, Bellevue, WA 98004 United States

STOCK TICKER/OTHER:

Stock Ticker: Subsidiary
Employees: 3,485
Parent Company: SAP SE

Exchange:
Fiscal Year Ends: 12/31

SALARIES/BONUSES:

Top Exec. Salary: $ Bonus: $
Second Exec. Salary: $ Bonus: $

OTHER THOUGHTS:

Estimated Female Officers or Directors: 2
Hot Spot for Advancement for Women/Minorities:

Sales, profits and employees may be estimates. Financial information, benefits and other data can change quickly and may vary from those stated here.

CoreCard Corp

www.corecard.com

NAIC Code: 511210Q

TYPES OF BUSINESS:
Computer Software: Accounting, Banking & Financial

BRANDS/DIVISIONS/AFFILIATES:
ChemFree Corp
CoreCard Software Inc
CoreCard SRL
ISC Software
SmartWasher
CoreENGINE

CONTACTS: *Note: Officers with more than one job title may be intentionally listed here more than once.*
J. Strange, CEO
Matthew White, CFO

GROWTH PLANS/SPECIAL FEATURES:

CoreCard Corp. is a holding company with subsidiaries involved in information technology products & services and industrial Products. The principal operating company in the information technology products and services segment is CoreCard Software, Inc. CoreCard Software designs, develops and markets a comprehensive suite of software solutions to accounts receivable businesses, financial institutions, retailers and processors to manage their credit and debit cards, prepaid cards, private label cards, fleet cards, loyalty programs and accounts receivable and small loan transactions. The software solutions of CoreCard Software are based upon its financial transaction processing platform, CoreENGINE. The CoreENGINE addresses the unique requirements of customers and program managers that issue or process credit/debit cards and prepaid cards. The firm also owns CoreCard Software's software development and testing firms CoreCard SRL, in Romania and ISC Software, in India.

FINANCIAL DATA: *Note: Data for latest year may not have been available at press time.*

In U.S. $	2021	2020	2019	2018	2017	2016
Revenue		35,873,000	34,303,000	20,100,000	9,302,000	8,178,000
R&D Expense						
Operating Income						
Operating Margin %						
SGA Expense						
Net Income		8,161,000	10,969,000	6,244,000	473,000	-1,112,000
Operating Cash Flow						
Capital Expenditure						
EBITDA						
Return on Assets %						
Return on Equity %						
Debt to Equity						

CONTACT INFORMATION:
Phone: 770 381-2900   Fax: 770 381-2808
Toll-Free:
Address: 4355 Shackleford Rd., Norcross, GA 30093 United States

STOCK TICKER/OTHER:
Stock Ticker: CCRD   Exchange: NYS
Employees: 570   Fiscal Year Ends: 12/31
Parent Company:

SALARIES/BONUSES:
Top Exec. Salary: $ Bonus: $
Second Exec. Salary: $ Bonus: $

OTHER THOUGHTS:
Estimated Female Officers or Directors: 1
Hot Spot for Advancement for Women/Minorities:

Sales, profits and employees may be estimates. Financial information, benefits and other data can change quickly and may vary from those stated here.

Plunkett Research, Ltd.

Credit Karma Inc
www.creditkarma.com
NAIC Code: 561450

TYPES OF BUSINESS:
Consumer Credit Counseling Services
Credit Management Platform
Financial Management Platform
Credit Scoring
Credit Report Data
Tax Preparation Services

BRANDS/DIVISIONS/AFFILIATES:
Intuit Inc
Credit Score Simulator

CONTACTS: Note: Officers with more than one job title may be intentionally listed here more than once.
Kenneth Lin, CEO
Joseph Kauffman, Pres.
Nichole Mustard, Chief Revenue Officer
Greg Lull, CMO
Colleen McCreary, Chief Product Officer
Ryan Graciano, CTO

GROWTH PLANS/SPECIAL FEATURES:
Credit Karma, Inc. is the creator and distributor of a free credit and financial management platform, with more than 100 million members across the U.S. and Canada. The company provides a way for people to obtain a free credit score and credit report with no hidden costs or obligations. Based on the score, the user gains access to targeted offers from companies that value the individual's creditworthiness. The platform offers credit report data, including an overview of accounts, payment history, credit inquiries and public records, personalized information and options, credit report details, credit monitoring and savings recommendations. Credit Karma provides free weekly updated credit scores and reports from national credit bureaus TransUnion and Equifax, as well as daily credit monitoring from TransUnion. The firm's website also provides credit tools such as a simulator that displays the effect potential financial actions may have on a user's credit score; home affordability calculator; debt repayment calculator; loan calculator; and amortization calculator. Credit Karma Tax is a tax preparation online service allowing most Americans to file federal and state taxes completely free of charge. Credit Karma, Inc. is a subsidiary of Intuit, Inc., and has offices in California and North Carolina, USA, as well as in London, England.

Credit Karma offers its employees health benefits, a retirement plan and professional development opportunities.

FINANCIAL DATA: Note: Data for latest year may not have been available at press time.

In U.S. $	2021	2020	2019	2018	2017	2016
Revenue	864,000,000	820,000,000	770,000,000	700,000,000	650,000,000	500,000,000
R&D Expense						
Operating Income						
Operating Margin %						
SGA Expense						
Net Income						
Operating Cash Flow						
Capital Expenditure						
EBITDA						
Return on Assets %						
Return on Equity %						
Debt to Equity						

CONTACT INFORMATION:
Phone: 415-692-5722   Fax:
Toll-Free:
Address: 1100 Broadway, Oakland, CA 94607 United States

STOCK TICKER/OTHER:
Stock Ticker: Subsidiary   Exchange:
Employees: 210   Fiscal Year Ends: 07/31
Parent Company: Intuit Inc

SALARIES/BONUSES:
Top Exec. Salary: $ Bonus: $
Second Exec. Salary: $ Bonus: $

OTHER THOUGHTS:
Estimated Female Officers or Directors:
Hot Spot for Advancement for Women/Minorities:

Sales, profits and employees may be estimates. Financial information, benefits and other data can change quickly and may vary from those stated here.

Creek Road Miners Inc

creekroadminers.com

NAIC Code: 518210

TYPES OF BUSINESS:
Virtual Currency Mining

BRANDS/DIVISIONS/AFFILIATES:
Wizard Brands Inc
Wizard Entertainment Inc
Wizard World Inc
GoEnergy Inc

GROWTH PLANS/SPECIAL FEATURES:
Creek Road Miners, Inc. (formerly known as Wizard Brands, Inc., Wizard Entertainment, Inc., Wizard World, Inc. and GoEnergy, Inc.) is a cryptocurrency mining company. Creek Road Miners deals exclusively in Bitcoin, which is strategically held or sold at beneficial prices and times. The firm uses special cryptocurrency mining computers (known as miners) to solve complex cryptographic algorithms to support the Bitcoin blockchain and, in return, receives Bitcoin as a reward. Miners measure their processing power, which is known as hashing power, in terms of the number of hashing algorithms solved (or hashes) per second, which is the miner's hash rate. Creek Road Miners participates in mining pools that pool the resources of groups of miners and split cryptocurrency rewards earned according to the hashing capacity each miner contributes to the pool.

CONTACTS:
Note: Officers with more than one job title may be intentionally listed here more than once.

John Maatta, CEO
Paul Kessler, Director

FINANCIAL DATA:
Note: Data for latest year may not have been available at press time.

In U.S. $	2021	2020	2019	2018	2017	2016
Revenue		4,518,163	10,578,316	13,901,603	15,067,613	22,701,534
R&D Expense						
Operating Income						
Operating Margin %						
SGA Expense						
Net Income		-1,940,401	-2,161,855	-2,615,419	-5,732,814	-8,516,144
Operating Cash Flow						
Capital Expenditure						
EBITDA						
Return on Assets %						
Return on Equity %						
Debt to Equity						

CONTACT INFORMATION:
Phone: 435 900-1949   Fax:
Toll-Free:
Address: 2700 Homestead Rd., Ste. 50, Park City, UT 84098 United States

STOCK TICKER/OTHER:
Stock Ticker: CRKR
Employees: 5
Parent Company:

Exchange: OTC
Fiscal Year Ends: 12/31

SALARIES/BONUSES:
Top Exec. Salary: $ Bonus: $
Second Exec. Salary: $ Bonus: $

OTHER THOUGHTS:
Estimated Female Officers or Directors:
Hot Spot for Advancement for Women/Minorities:

Sales, profits and employees may be estimates. Financial information, benefits and other data can change quickly and may vary from those stated here.

Cross River Bank (CRB Group Inc)

www.crossriver.com

NAIC Code: 522110

TYPES OF BUSINESS:

Commercial Banking
Financial Services
Financial Technology Solutions
Banking Services
Cryptocurrency Services
Payments Services
Lending Services
Capital Markets

BRANDS/DIVISIONS/AFFILIATES:

Cross River
Cross River Bank

CONTACTS: *Note: Officers with more than one job title may be intentionally listed here more than once.*

Camilo Concha, CEO

GROWTH PLANS/SPECIAL FEATURES:

CRB Group, Inc. is a financial and technology company that has developed the Cross River platform, which provides financial products and services. Through partnerships, Cross River offers banking, cryptocurrency, payments and lending services. Directly, Cross River offers capital markets, deposits, certificates of deposit, commercial lending, small business lending and lender financing services. All loans and deposit products are provided by Cross River Bank. The company operates through a compliance management system, utilizing technology for research and analysis to stay abreast with due diligence, as well as risk assessments, testing and monitoring via audits/process controls/compliance and evaluating the effectiveness of compliance procedures. Internally, the compliance management system includes background checks, federal and state licensure reviews, daily review of files, site visits, marketing/advertising/website reviews, underwriting, policy and procedure reviews, sample transaction reviews, annual reviews of relationships and regulatory risk assessments. Cross River is a member of the Federal Deposit Insurance Corporation (FDIC), is an Equal Housing Lender, and is an Online Lending Policy Institute (OLPI) founder. Headquartered in New Jersey, the company has branch locations in New Jersey and New York.

FINANCIAL DATA: *Note: Data for latest year may not have been available at press time.*

In U.S. $	2021	2020	2019	2018	2017	2016
Revenue						
R&D Expense						
Operating Income						
Operating Margin %						
SGA Expense						
Net Income						
Operating Cash Flow						
Capital Expenditure						
EBITDA						
Return on Assets %						
Return on Equity %						
Debt to Equity						

CONTACT INFORMATION:

Phone: 201 808-7000   Fax:
Toll-Free:
Address: 400 Kelby St., Fl. 14, Fort Lee, NJ 07024 United States

STOCK TICKER/OTHER:

Stock Ticker: Private   Exchange:
Employees: 800   Fiscal Year Ends:
Parent Company:

SALARIES/BONUSES:

Top Exec. Salary: $ Bonus: $
Second Exec. Salary: $ Bonus: $

OTHER THOUGHTS:

Estimated Female Officers or Directors:
Hot Spot for Advancement for Women/Minorities:

Sales, profits and employees may be estimates. Financial information, benefits and other data can change quickly and may vary from those stated here.

CSG Forte Payments Inc

NAIC Code: 511210Q

www.forte.net

TYPES OF BUSINESS:

Computer Software: Accounting, Banking & Financial
SaaS - Enterprise-Class Payment Solutions
Finance Software
Finance Technology
Payment Compliance
Payments Management
Payment Processing

BRANDS/DIVISIONS/AFFILIATES:

CSG Systems International Inc

CONTACTS: *Note: Officers with more than one job title may be intentionally listed here more than once.*

Jeff Thorness, CEO
Jeff Kump, Pres.

GROWTH PLANS/SPECIAL FEATURES:

CSG Forte Payments, Inc. is a finance and technology company that has developed a payments platform to help businesses accept payments. CSG Forte's unified payments platform seamlessly adapts to meet each business' evolving needs, and comprises a vast ecosystem of software-providing partners across a range of industries. This network enables comprehensive payment processing, business automation and other solutions. CSG Forte partners include Accela, Chargify, CivicPlus, Easy Manage Software, gWorks, Kofile and Rentvine. The cloud-based platform enables businesses to streamline payments management, including transaction monitoring, dispute management, reporting and analytics, as well as addressing customer needs, granting refunds, canceling charges, changing payment methods and more. Everything is managed and visible in one location. Its reporting dashboards offer real-time insight into sales performance, including transaction breakdowns and payment methods, and can be viewed either as general data or as individual transactions. CSG Forte uses high technology standards and protocols, with solutions spanning secure payment acceptance and processing across any application or payment channel. Security capabilities include tokenization, end-to-end encryption, hosted payment pages and data privacy/security. The firm is ISO 27001:2013 certified and SSAE SOC 1, PCI DSS and HIPAA compliant. CSG Forte primarily serves integrated software vendors, small/medium businesses, enterprises and government entities. The company operates as a subsidiary of CSG Systems International, Inc.

CSG offers its employees comprehensive benefits.

FINANCIAL DATA: *Note: Data for latest year may not have been available at press time.*

In U.S. $	2021	2020	2019	2018	2017	2016
Revenue						
R&D Expense						
Operating Income						
Operating Margin %						
SGA Expense						
Net Income						
Operating Cash Flow						
Capital Expenditure						
EBITDA						
Return on Assets %						
Return on Equity %						
Debt to Equity						

CONTACT INFORMATION:

Phone: 866 290-5400   Fax:
Toll-Free:
Address: 500 W Bethany Dr., Ste. 200, Allen, TX 75013 United States

SALARIES/BONUSES:

Top Exec. Salary: $ Bonus: $
Second Exec. Salary: $ Bonus: $

STOCK TICKER/OTHER:

Stock Ticker: Subsidiary   Exchange:
Employees: 120   Fiscal Year Ends:
Parent Company: CSG Systems International Inc

OTHER THOUGHTS:

Estimated Female Officers or Directors:
Hot Spot for Advancement for Women/Minorities:

Sales, profits and employees may be estimates. Financial information, benefits and other data can change quickly and may vary from those stated here.

Current (Finco Services Inc)

current.com

NAIC Code: 511210Q

TYPES OF BUSINESS:

Computer Software: Accounting, Banking & Financial
Online Banking Platform
Banking Services
Automated Savings
Cash Back Program
Overdraft Protection
Money Management Solutions
Financial Technology

BRANDS/DIVISIONS/AFFILIATES:

Current Core

CONTACTS: Note: Officers with more than one job title may be intentionally listed here more than once.

Stuart Sopp, CEO

GROWTH PLANS/SPECIAL FEATURES:

Finco Services, Inc. is a financial technology company that has developed the Current online platform of banking services. Current offers savings accounts with interest, automated savings, a cash back program, overdraft protection services, free automated teller machines (ATMs), money management solutions, direct deposits, mobile banking, mobile deposits, teen banking and more. The firm's custom-built technology is referred to as Current Core, and is designed to provide enhanced financial stability and swift access to money management, affordably to everyone. Current does not have: hidden fees, overdraft fees, minimum balance fees nor transfer fees when transferring money to other members on Current using the Current ~tag. Current is a financial technology company and not a bank. Banking services are provided by Choice Financial Group, which is a member of the Federal Deposit Insurance Corporation (FDIC).

Current offers its employees comprehensive health benefits, equity opportunities and other company incentives and perks.

FINANCIAL DATA: Note: Data for latest year may not have been available at press time.

In U.S. $	2021	2020	2019	2018	2017	2016
Revenue						
R&D Expense						
Operating Income						
Operating Margin %						
SGA Expense						
Net Income						
Operating Cash Flow						
Capital Expenditure						
EBITDA						
Return on Assets %						
Return on Equity %						
Debt to Equity						

CONTACT INFORMATION:

Phone: Fax:
Toll-Free: 888-851-1172
Address: 217 Centre St., Ste. 180, New York, NY 10013 United States

STOCK TICKER/OTHER:

Stock Ticker: Private   Exchange:
Employees: Fiscal Year Ends:
Parent Company:

SALARIES/BONUSES:

Top Exec. Salary: $ Bonus: $
Second Exec. Salary: $ Bonus: $

OTHER THOUGHTS:

Estimated Female Officers or Directors:
Hot Spot for Advancement for Women/Minorities:

Sales, profits and employees may be estimates. Financial information, benefits and other data can change quickly and may vary from those stated here.

DailyPay Inc

NAIC Code: 522320

www.dailypay.com

TYPES OF BUSINESS:

Financial Transactions Processing, Reserve, and Clearinghouse Activities
Electronic Funds Transfer Services
On-Demand Pay
Digital Wallet Solution
Earned Wages Payment Transfers
Employee Bonus Pay Program
Financial Technology
Savings and Investment Solutions

BRANDS/DIVISIONS/AFFILIATES:

DailyPay
REWARD

CONTACTS: Note: Officers with more than one job title may be intentionally listed here more than once.

Jason Lee, CEO
Rob Law, CTO
Scot Parnell, CFO
Konstantin Getmanchuk, Sr. VP-Product
Irene Hendricks, Chief People Officer
John Abel, CIO
Jane Levine, Chief Compliance Officer

GROWTH PLANS/SPECIAL FEATURES:

DailyPay, Inc. is a financial services company engaged in providing software as a service, primarily on-demand pay. DailyPay manages over $2 billion in earnings to support millions of employees when they need to be paid sooner rather than later. The proprietary DailyPay online platform is designed as a digital wallet and encompasses many applications, enabling employers to provide employees with instant access to the money they've earned. Employees have 24/7/365 access to earned pay, and can have the money sent directly to any bank account, debit card or prepaid card, and can also use it to pay bills, build savings, invest money, buy goods and services, and more. DailyPay technology integrates with existing human capital management (HCM) systems with no changes to any element of the payroll process. DailyPay also offers REWARD, an on-the-spot incentive program that enables employers to give employees instant monetary bonus awards for acknowledging hard work, commitment and/or accomplishments. REWARD runs on the employer's unique program parameters and ensures tracking to monitor program success via employee experiences. REWARD payments are reported back to payroll transparently through a reporting dashboard, to ensure tax compliance. Industries served by DailyPay primarily include hospitals and health care entities, retail, restaurants (including quick service restaurants/QSRs), travel, hospitality, grocers and supermarkets, call centers and contact centers. DailyPay is PCI DSS Level 1, SOC 2 Type 2, ISO 27001 and ANAB Accredited certified.

DailyPay offers its employees comprehensive health benefits, 401(k), stock options and a variety of company incentives and perks.

FINANCIAL DATA: Note: Data for latest year may not have been available at press time.

In U.S. $	2021	2020	2019	2018	2017	2016
Revenue						
R&D Expense						
Operating Income						
Operating Margin %						
SGA Expense						
Net Income						
Operating Cash Flow						
Capital Expenditure						
EBITDA						
Return on Assets %						
Return on Equity %						
Debt to Equity						

CONTACT INFORMATION:

Phone: 646-435-2791   Fax:
Toll-Free:
Address: 55 Water St., New York, NY 10041 United States

STOCK TICKER/OTHER:

Stock Ticker: Private   Exchange:
Employees: 570   Fiscal Year Ends:
Parent Company:

SALARIES/BONUSES:

Top Exec. Salary: $ Bonus: $
Second Exec. Salary: $ Bonus: $

OTHER THOUGHTS:

Estimated Female Officers or Directors:
Hot Spot for Advancement for Women/Minorities:

Sales, profits and employees may be estimates. Financial information, benefits and other data can change quickly and may vary from those stated here.

Dave Inc

dave.com

NAIC Code: 511210Q

TYPES OF BUSINESS:
Computer Software: Accounting, Banking & Financial
Online Banking Platform

BRANDS/DIVISIONS/AFFILIATES:
Dave
ExtraCash
Side Hustle
FTX Ventures

GROWTH PLANS/SPECIAL FEATURES:
Dave, Inc. is a developer of an affordable, integrated financial services online platform. Dave offers a suite of innovative financial products in the form of the Dave app, including a budgeting tool that helps the company's members manage their upcoming bills and avoid overspending. To help members avoid punitive overdraft fees and access short-term liquidity, Dave offers cash advances through its flagship 0% interest ExtraCash product. The firm also offers its Side Hustle product, where members can access information about supplemental work opportunities. Through Dave Banking, it provides a modern checking account experience with valuable tools for building long-term financial health. In March 2022, FTX Ventures invested $100 million in the company.

CONTACTS:
Note: Officers with more than one job title may be intentionally listed here more than once.

Jason Wilk, CEO
Kyle Beilman, CFO
Michael Goodbody, Chief Mktg. Officer
Shannon Sullivan, Chief People Officer
Paras Chitrakar, CTO

FINANCIAL DATA:
Note: Data for latest year may not have been available at press time.

In U.S. $	2021	2020	2019	2018	2017	2016
Revenue		121,796,000	76,227,000			
R&D Expense						
Operating Income						
Operating Margin %						
SGA Expense						
Net Income		-6,957,000	787,000			
Operating Cash Flow						
Capital Expenditure						
EBITDA						
Return on Assets %						
Return on Equity %						
Debt to Equity						

CONTACT INFORMATION:
Phone: 323 452-9809   Fax:
Toll-Free: 844 857-3283
Address: 1265 S. Cochran Ave., Los Angeles, CA 90019 United States

STOCK TICKER/OTHER:
Stock Ticker: DAVE   Exchange: NAS
Employees: 200   Fiscal Year Ends: 12/31
Parent Company:

SALARIES/BONUSES:
Top Exec. Salary: $ Bonus: $
Second Exec. Salary: $ Bonus: $

OTHER THOUGHTS:
Estimated Female Officers or Directors:
Hot Spot for Advancement for Women/Minorities:

Sales, profits and employees may be estimates. Financial information, benefits and other data can change quickly and may vary from those stated here.

Deserve Inc

NAIC Code: 522210

www.deserve.com

TYPES OF BUSINESS:

Credit Card Issuing
Financial Technology
Digital Credit Card Services
University Student Credit Services
Commercial Credit Cards
Machine Learning Technology

BRANDS/DIVISIONS/AFFILIATES:

CONTACTS: *Note: Officers with more than one job title may be intentionally listed here more than once.*

Kalpesh Kapadia, CEO

GROWTH PLANS/SPECIAL FEATURES:

Deserve, Inc. is a financial technology company that has developed the Deserve digital credit card platform. Deserve's software-as-a-service (SaaS) solutions provide customized branded and co-branded credit card programs, with capabilities spanning issuance, processing, marketing, offer management, customizable underwriting, customer experience, compliance, risk management, servicing, customer relations management and portfolio analytics. The firm's motive is to help individuals, primarily university students, build good credit for financial success. Deserve's machine learning and alternative data offers individuals a simple path to credit, with cards including consumer education, tips and tools to help keep them on track. The company supports 5,000 university campuses throughout the U.S., to help them gain access to credit, including Berkeley University of California, Caltech, Carnegie Mellon University and Fresno State University. Moreover, Deserve helps all kinds of companies integrate cryptocurrency in their card programs, including VISA, Mastercard, Silvergate and Zero Hash. In addition to student credit cards, Deserve offers a commercial credit card platform designed to help companies that serve small/medium businesses launch co-branded credit and charge cards. Pre-qualification and card activation can be made on the Deserve platform, as well as comparing cards and rates and reading reviews. Investors of Deserve include Goldman Sachs, SallieMae, Accel, Pelion, Aspect Ventures, and Mission Holdings.

FINANCIAL DATA: *Note: Data for latest year may not have been available at press time.*

In U.S. $	2021	2020	2019	2018	2017	2016
Revenue						
R&D Expense						
Operating Income						
Operating Margin %						
SGA Expense						
Net Income						
Operating Cash Flow						
Capital Expenditure						
EBITDA						
Return on Assets %						
Return on Equity %						
Debt to Equity						

CONTACT INFORMATION:

Phone: Fax:
Toll-Free: 800 418-2362
Address: 195 Page Mill Rd., Ste. 109, Palo Alto, CA 94306 United States

STOCK TICKER/OTHER:

Stock Ticker: Private   Exchange:
Employees: 165   Fiscal Year Ends:
Parent Company:

SALARIES/BONUSES:

Top Exec. Salary: $ Bonus: $
Second Exec. Salary: $ Bonus: $

OTHER THOUGHTS:

Estimated Female Officers or Directors:
Hot Spot for Advancement for Women/Minorities:

Sales, profits and employees may be estimates. Financial information, benefits and other data can change quickly and may vary from those stated here.

Digit (Hello Digit LLC)

digit.co

NAIC Code: 523920

TYPES OF BUSINESS:
Portfolio Management
Automatic Savings/Investment
Financial Technology
Money Management App
Deposit Services
Savings Services
Investment Services

BRANDS/DIVISIONS/AFFILIATES:
Oportun Financial Corporation
digit

CONTACTS: *Note: Officers with more than one job title may be intentionally listed here more than once.*
Ethan Bloch, CEO

GROWTH PLANS/SPECIAL FEATURES:

Hello Digit, LLC is a financial technology company that has developed an all-in-one money app called digit, which budgets, saves and invests on behalf of its users. The firm designed the app to help individuals obtain financial stability and reach goals. Hello Digit designed a smart bank account that continuously guides money in opportunistic directions, including strategy for current needs as well as needs in the near and distant future. The digit platform causes spending, bills, savings and investments to work together by splitting deposits for each category. Users can see how much is okay to spend and how much is needed/spent for expenses and goals, keeping them on track with money management. Money used for bills such as rent, utilities and subscriptions are kept separate so users are less apt to spend it. Digit saves a little every day, but more money can be added as desired. No fees are charged at more than 55,000 automated teller machines (ATMs) through digit. Digit is Federal Deposit Insurance Corporation (FDIC)-insured up to $250,000, and offers end-to-end encryption and remote card locking features for security purposes. Hello Digit operates as a subsidiary of public company Oportun Financial Corporation.

Hello Digit offers its employees comprehensive health benefits, 401(k), life/AD&D/disability benefits and a variety of other benefits and company perks.

FINANCIAL DATA: *Note: Data for latest year may not have been available at press time.*

In U.S. $	2021	2020	2019	2018	2017	2016
Revenue						
R&D Expense						
Operating Income						
Operating Margin %						
SGA Expense						
Net Income						
Operating Cash Flow						
Capital Expenditure						
EBITDA						
Return on Assets %						
Return on Equity %						
Debt to Equity						

CONTACT INFORMATION:
Phone: 415 260-2684   Fax:
Toll-Free: 888-322-3103
Address: 100 Pine St., Fl. 20, San Francisco, CA 94111 United States

STOCK TICKER/OTHER:
Stock Ticker: Subsidiary   Exchange:
Employees: Fiscal Year Ends:
Parent Company: Oportun Financial Corporation

SALARIES/BONUSES:
Top Exec. Salary: $ Bonus: $
Second Exec. Salary: $ Bonus: $

OTHER THOUGHTS:
Estimated Female Officers or Directors:
Hot Spot for Advancement for Women/Minorities:

Sales, profits and employees may be estimates. Financial information, benefits and other data can change quickly and may vary from those stated here.

Discover Financial Services

www.discover.com/company

NAIC Code: 522210

TYPES OF BUSINESS:
Credit Card Issuer
Credit Cards
Loans
Deposit Products
Electronic Funds Transfer Services
Payments Services

BRANDS/DIVISIONS/AFFILIATES:
Discover
Discover Network
PULSE
Diners Club
Network Partners

GROWTH PLANS/SPECIAL FEATURES:

Discover Financial Services is a bank operating in two distinct segments: direct banking and payment services. The company issues credit and debit cards and provides other consumer banking products including deposit accounts, students loans, and other personal loans. It also operates the Discover, Pulse, and Diners Club networks. The Discover network is the fourth-largest payment network in the United States as ranked by overall purchase volume, and Pulse is one of the largest ATM networks in the country.

DFS offers its employees health care, dental and vision coverage; life and disability insurance; an employee stock purchase plan; a 401(k) plan; access to a fitness center and health service center; and flexible spending accounts.

CONTACTS:
Note: Officers with more than one job title may be intentionally listed here more than once.

Roger Hochschild, CEO
John Greene, CFO
Thomas Maheras, Chairman of the Board
Shifra Kolsky, Chief Accounting Officer
Robert Eichfeld, Chief Administrative Officer
Amir Arooni, Chief Information Officer
Wanjiku Walcott, Chief Legal Officer
Brian Hughes, Chief Risk Officer
Keith Toney, Executive VP, Divisional
Diane Offereins, Executive VP
Carlos Minetti, Executive VP
Daniel Capozzi, Executive VP

FINANCIAL DATA:
Note: Data for latest year may not have been available at press time.

In U.S. $	2021	2020	2019	2018	2017	2016
Revenue		11,088,000,000	11,459,000,000	10,709,000,000	9,897,000,000	9,099,000,000
R&D Expense						
Operating Income						
Operating Margin %						
SGA Expense		2,553,000,000	2,621,000,000	2,484,000,000	2,288,000,000	2,110,000,000
Net Income		1,141,000,000	2,957,000,000	2,742,000,000	2,099,000,000	2,393,000,000
Operating Cash Flow		6,196,000,000	6,196,000,000	5,191,000,000	5,208,000,000	4,425,000,000
Capital Expenditure		261,000,000	284,000,000	254,000,000	218,000,000	179,000,000
EBITDA						
Return on Assets %						
Return on Equity %						
Debt to Equity						

CONTACT INFORMATION:
Phone: 224 405-0900   Fax:
Toll-Free: 800-347-2683
Address: 2500 Lake Cook Rd., Riverwoods, IL 60015 United States

STOCK TICKER/OTHER:
Stock Ticker: DFS   Exchange: NYS
Employees: 16,700   Fiscal Year Ends: 11/30
Parent Company:

SALARIES/BONUSES:
Top Exec. Salary: $1,118,539   Bonus: $
Second Exec. Salary: Bonus: $
$1,118,539

OTHER THOUGHTS:
Estimated Female Officers or Directors: 2
Hot Spot for Advancement for Women/Minorities: Y

Sales, profits and employees may be estimates. Financial information, benefits and other data can change quickly and may vary from those stated here.

Divvy Homes Inc

NAIC Code: 511210Q

www.divvyhomes.com

TYPES OF BUSINESS:
Computer Software: Accounting, Banking & Financial
Rent-to-Own Real Estate Platform
Financial Technology
Online Prequalification Application
Down Payment Saving Strategy

BRANDS/DIVISIONS/AFFILIATES:

CONTACTS: *Note: Officers with more than one job title may be intentionally listed here more than once.*
Adena Hefets, CEO

GROWTH PLANS/SPECIAL FEATURES:
Divvy Homes, Inc. is a financial technology company that has developed a rent-to-own platform for potential homebuyers. Divvy enables individuals to rent the home they want to purchase until they've saved enough for a down payment to purchase the home. How it works: fill out a pre-qualification application online, with no commitment and no impact to current credit score; find a qualifying rent-to-own home on the market through a real estate agent or through Divvy; Divvy buys the home in cash, covering all fees, closing costs, taxes and insurance while the applicant makes an initial payment of 1% or 2% of the selling price, which goes directly to savings for the final down payment; move in and live in the home, making monthly payments that include savings that grow the down payment over time (primarily within three years); and either purchase the home when the savings is complete or walk away from the purchase while keeping the savings. Pricing varies by home, the initial payment and the monthly savings amount. Becoming qualified for the process is free. Divvy is beneficial for those who need help saving up for a down payment, who have a FICO credit score of 550 or higher, who are self-employed or obtained a new job, and who want to try to have a home before buying it. Divvy makes money from monthly rents and the home's appreciation over time. About one-fourth of every monthly payment goes toward the down payment saving strategy. When rent-to-owners move in with Divvy, they are provided an option to buy the home at a pre-set price in the future, and if the home's value is higher, the pre-set price remains the same. Divvy Homes operates in several U.S. states.

FINANCIAL DATA: *Note: Data for latest year may not have been available at press time.*

In U.S. $	2021	2020	2019	2018	2017	2016
Revenue						
R&D Expense						
Operating Income						
Operating Margin %						
SGA Expense						
Net Income						
Operating Cash Flow						
Capital Expenditure						
EBITDA						
Return on Assets %						
Return on Equity %						
Debt to Equity						

CONTACT INFORMATION:
Phone: 530 734-8890   Fax:
Toll-Free:
Address: 633 Folsom St., Fl. 7, San Francisco, CA 94107 United States

STOCK TICKER/OTHER:
Stock Ticker: Private   Exchange:
Employees: 195   Fiscal Year Ends:
Parent Company:

SALARIES/BONUSES:
Top Exec. Salary: $ Bonus: $
Second Exec. Salary: $ Bonus: $

OTHER THOUGHTS:
Estimated Female Officers or Directors:
Hot Spot for Advancement for Women/Minorities:

Sales, profits and employees may be estimates. Financial information, benefits and other data can change quickly and may vary from those stated here.

DocuSign Inc

NAIC Code: 511210Q

www.docusign.com

TYPES OF BUSINESS:
Online Signature Management Software
Cloud
Electronic Signature

GROWTH PLANS/SPECIAL FEATURES:
DocuSign offers the Agreement Cloud, a broad cloud-based software suite that enables users to automate the agreement process and provide legally binding e-signatures from nearly any device. The company was founded in 2003 and completed its IPO in May 2018.

BRANDS/DIVISIONS/AFFILIATES:
DocuSign Agreement Cloud
DocuSign eSignature
Seal Software Group Limited
Liveoak Technololgies Inc

CONTACTS: *Note: Officers with more than one job title may be intentionally listed here more than once.*
Daniel Springer, CEO
Cynthia Gaylor, CFO
Mary Agnes Wilderotter, Chairman of the Board
Scott Olrich, COO
Tram Phi, General Counsel
Loren Alhadeff, Other Executive Officer
Michael Sheridan, President, Divisional

FINANCIAL DATA: *Note: Data for latest year may not have been available at press time.*

In U.S. $	2021	2020	2019	2018	2017	2016
Revenue	1,453,047,000	973,971,000	700,969,000	518,504,000	381,459,000	250,481,000
R&D Expense	271,522,000	185,552,000	185,968,000	92,428,000	89,652,000	62,255,000
Operating Income	-173,855,000	-193,509,000	-426,323,000	-51,653,000	-115,817,000	-119,304,000
Operating Margin %						
SGA Expense	991,322,000	738,694,000	748,903,000	359,456,000	305,147,000	233,675,000
Net Income	-243,267,000	-208,359,000	-426,458,000	-52,276,000	-115,412,000	-122,559,000
Operating Cash Flow	296,954,000	115,696,000	76,086,000	54,979,000	-4,790,000	-67,995,000
Capital Expenditure	82,395,000	72,046,000	30,413,000	18,929,000	43,330,000	28,305,000
EBITDA	-129,801,000	-126,098,000	-379,337,000	-16,798,000	-85,976,000	-101,684,000
Return on Assets %						
Return on Equity %						
Debt to Equity						

CONTACT INFORMATION:
Phone: 866-219-4318   Fax:
Toll-Free:
Address: 221 Main St., Ste. 1550, San Francisco, CA 94105 United States

STOCK TICKER/OTHER:
Stock Ticker: DOCU
Employees: 5,630
Parent Company:

Exchange: NAS
Fiscal Year Ends: 01/31

SALARIES/BONUSES:
Top Exec. Salary: $424,999   Bonus: $
Second Exec. Salary: $387,692   Bonus: $

OTHER THOUGHTS:
Estimated Female Officers or Directors:
Hot Spot for Advancement for Women/Minorities:

Sales, profits and employees may be estimates. Financial information, benefits and other data can change quickly and may vary from those stated here.

Doxo Inc

www.doxo.com

NAIC Code: 511210Q

TYPES OF BUSINESS:

Computer Software: Accounting, Banking & Financial
Bill Management & Payments Platform
Financial Technology
Identity Theft Production Services
Late Fee Protection Services
Payment Behavior Analytics

BRANDS/DIVISIONS/AFFILIATES:

Doxo
doxoPLUS
doxoDIRECT
doxoINSIGHTS

CONTACTS: *Note: Officers with more than one job title may be intentionally listed here more than once.*

Steve Shivers, CEO
Roger Parks, VP-Bus. Dev.
Mark Goris, CTO

GROWTH PLANS/SPECIAL FEATURES:

Doxo, Inc. is a financial technology company that has developed an all-in-one household bill management platform for enhancing financial health. Doxo helps more than 7 million people manage their recurring bills and due dates in a single place, paying their bills anytime on any device, with free payment delivery options. Users across 97% of U.S. zip codes have their bills paid through the payment network, including more than 45 different service categories. The Doxo platform comprises over 120,000 payable billers, enabling users to manage all their bills from a single source. Those who upgrade to doxoPLUS get additional protections across credit, identity theft and late fees. doxoDIRECT is a payment platform for businesses, enabling bill payments to come from a single source instead of multiple channels such as mail, bank payments, cash payments and others. doxoINSIGHTS provides analysis of U.S., bill pay statistics and bill payer behavior so that payment insights across validated payment behaviors can be attained, including infographic expenses per state and actual household payment activity. Types of bills paid via Doxo include alarm/security, healthcare, home service, insurance, loans, credit card, phone, mortgage, television and internet, toll roads, travel and utility.

Doxo offers its employees comprehensive health benefits, long-term disability and life insurance, pet insurance, 401(k), employee stock options, tuition reimbursement, hybrid and remote options and a variety of other benefits and company perks.

FINANCIAL DATA: *Note: Data for latest year may not have been available at press time.*

In U.S. $	2021	2020	2019	2018	2017	2016
Revenue						
R&D Expense						
Operating Income						
Operating Margin %						
SGA Expense						
Net Income						
Operating Cash Flow						
Capital Expenditure						
EBITDA						
Return on Assets %						
Return on Equity %						
Debt to Equity						

CONTACT INFORMATION:

Phone: 206-319-0097   Fax:
Toll-Free:
Address: 1420 5th Ave., Fl. 22, Seattle, WA 98101 United States

STOCK TICKER/OTHER:

Stock Ticker: Private   Exchange:
Employees: 100   Fiscal Year Ends:
Parent Company:

SALARIES/BONUSES:

Top Exec. Salary: $ Bonus: $
Second Exec. Salary: $ Bonus: $

OTHER THOUGHTS:

Estimated Female Officers or Directors:
Hot Spot for Advancement for Women/Minorities:

Sales, profits and employees may be estimates. Financial information, benefits and other data can change quickly and may vary from those stated here.

Du Xiaoman Financial

www.duxiaoman.com

NAIC Code: 522291

TYPES OF BUSINESS:

Consumer Lending
Wealth Management Services

GROWTH PLANS/SPECIAL FEATURES:

Du Xiaoman Financial is a financial services company based in Beijing, China. The company's services include risk management, econometric models analysis, money management, short-term loans and other financial services such as data analysis relating to assets. Du Xiaoman is owned by Baidu, Inc.

BRANDS/DIVISIONS/AFFILIATES:

Baidu Inc

CONTACTS: *Note: Officers with more than one job title may be intentionally listed here more than once.*

Guang Zhu, CEO

FINANCIAL DATA: *Note: Data for latest year may not have been available at press time.*

In U.S. $	2021	2020	2019	2018	2017	2016
Revenue						
R&D Expense						
Operating Income						
Operating Margin %						
SGA Expense						
Net Income						
Operating Cash Flow						
Capital Expenditure						
EBITDA						
Return on Assets %						
Return on Equity %						
Debt to Equity						

CONTACT INFORMATION:

Phone: Fax:
Toll-Free:
Address: Bldg. 4, West Dist., 10 NW. Wangdong Rd., Haidian Dist., Beijing, 100089 China

STOCK TICKER/OTHER:

Stock Ticker: Private
Employees:
Parent Company: Baidu Inc

Exchange:
Fiscal Year Ends:

SALARIES/BONUSES:

Top Exec. Salary: $ Bonus: $
Second Exec. Salary: $ Bonus: $

OTHER THOUGHTS:

Estimated Female Officers or Directors:
Hot Spot for Advancement for Women/Minorities:

Sales, profits and employees may be estimates. Financial information, benefits and other data can change quickly and may vary from those stated here.

Dwolla Inc

www.dwolla.com

NAIC Code: 522320

TYPES OF BUSINESS:

Financial Transactions Processing, Reserve, and Clearinghouse Activities
Financial Technology
Digital Payments Platform
Developer Integrations and Tools

BRANDS/DIVISIONS/AFFILIATES:

Dwolla
Dwolla Balance

GROWTH PLANS/SPECIAL FEATURES:

Dwolla, Inc. is a financial technology company that has developed an accessible and affordable digital payments platform for innovators and individuals. Dwolla offers a full suite of solutions through a single application programming interface (API). The platform enables a broad range of account-to-account payment types and flows. It is scalable, reliable and flexible, being able to programmatically handle five or 5,000 transactions with a single click, having a 99.99% uptime rate with billions in payments being processed, and offering real-time webhooks and more. Businesses can add wallet-like functionality via Dwolla Balance so that verified users can access funds and initiate payments instantly. Integrations can be built in Dwolla's test environment, and the process of transferring funds to and from external parties can be obtained through the Dwolla Balance feature.

Dwolla offers its employees comprehensive health benefits, a retirement savings plan, stock options and a variety of other company programs and perks.

CONTACTS: *Note: Officers with more than one job title may be intentionally listed here more than once.*

Joe Edgar, CEO

FINANCIAL DATA: *Note: Data for latest year may not have been available at press time.*

In U.S. $	2021	2020	2019	2018	2017	2016
Revenue						
R&D Expense						
Operating Income						
Operating Margin %						
SGA Expense						
Net Income						
Operating Cash Flow						
Capital Expenditure						
EBITDA						
Return on Assets %						
Return on Equity %						
Debt to Equity						

CONTACT INFORMATION:

Phone: 515 280-1000   Fax:
Toll-Free: 888 289-8744
Address: 909 Locust St., Ste. 201, Des Moines, IA 50309 United States

STOCK TICKER/OTHER:

Stock Ticker: Private   Exchange:
Employees: 115   Fiscal Year Ends:
Parent Company:

SALARIES/BONUSES:

Top Exec. Salary: $ Bonus: $
Second Exec. Salary: $ Bonus: $

OTHER THOUGHTS:

Estimated Female Officers or Directors:
Hot Spot for Advancement for Women/Minorities:

Sales, profits and employees may be estimates. Financial information, benefits and other data can change quickly and may vary from those stated here.

E*Trade from Morgan Stanley

www.etrade.com

NAIC Code: 523120

TYPES OF BUSINESS:

Stock Brokerage/Investment Management-Online
Financial Services
Banking Services
Stock Services
Online Banking
Online Trading
Retirement Financial Solutions

BRANDS/DIVISIONS/AFFILIATES:

Morgan Stanley
ETRADE Securities LLC
ETRADE Capital Management LLC
ETRADE Futures LLC

CONTACTS: Note: Officers with more than one job title may be intentionally listed here more than once.

Chad Turner, CFO
Michael Curcio, Executive VP, Divisional
James P Gorman, Chmn.-Morgan Stanley

GROWTH PLANS/SPECIAL FEATURES:

E*TRADE from Morgan Stanley is a financial services company that offers banking and stock plans to retail customers. The firm provides access digital resources for its online services, as well as market insights, webinars and answers to a variety of questions. Types of accounts include brokerage, retirement, core portfolios, managed portfolios, small business and bank. Investment choices span stocks, options, mutual funds, exchange traded funds (ETFs), futures, bonds, certificates of deposit (CDs) and pre-built portfolios. The trading division encompasses platforms, margin trading and execution. E*TRADE offers information for those new to trading. Trading prices range from free to $1.50, depending on the stock, option, contract and/or bond. Prices for other services are listed on the company's website and mobile app. Securities products and services are offered by E*TRADE Securities LLC; investment advisory services by E*TRADE Capital Management LLC; and commodity futures and options on futures products and services by E*TRADE Futures LLC. E*TRADE from Morgan Stanley is a wholly-owned subsidiary of Morgan Stanley.

FINANCIAL DATA: Note: Data for latest year may not have been available at press time.

In U.S. $	2021	2020	2019	2018	2017	2016
Revenue	3,151,512,140	3,030,300,134	2,886,000,128	2,872,999,936	2,366,000,128	1,940,999,936
R&D Expense						
Operating Income						
Operating Margin %						
SGA Expense						
Net Income			955,000,000	1,052,000,000	614,000,000	552,000,000
Operating Cash Flow						
Capital Expenditure						
EBITDA						
Return on Assets %						
Return on Equity %						
Debt to Equity						

CONTACT INFORMATION:

Phone: 646 521-4300   Fax:
Toll-Free: 800-387-2331
Address: 671 N. Glebe Rd., Arlington, VA 22203 United States

SALARIES/BONUSES:

Top Exec. Salary: $ Bonus: $
Second Exec. Salary: $ Bonus: $

STOCK TICKER/OTHER:

Stock Ticker: Subsidiary   Exchange:
Employees: 4,100   Fiscal Year Ends: 12/31
Parent Company: Morgan Stanley

OTHER THOUGHTS:

Estimated Female Officers or Directors: 3
Hot Spot for Advancement for Women/Minorities: Y

Sales, profits and employees may be estimates. Financial information, benefits and other data can change quickly and may vary from those stated here.

Early Warning Services LLC

www.earlywarning.com

NAIC Code: 511210Q

TYPES OF BUSINESS:
Computer Software: Accounting, Banking & Financial
Financial Technology Solutions
Payment Solutions
Identity Fraud Solutions
Banking Technologies
Instant Payments
Financial Accounts

BRANDS/DIVISIONS/AFFILIATES:
Zelle Network
Identity Chek
Deposit Chek

CONTACTS: *Note: Officers with more than one job title may be intentionally listed here more than once.*
Al Ko, CEO
Jose Resendiz, COO
Mark Travi, CFO
Melissa Lowry, CMO
Natalie Schwimer, Chief Human Resources Officer
Milind Nagnur, CTO
Lou Anne Alexander, Chief Product Officer

GROWTH PLANS/SPECIAL FEATURES:
Early Warning Services, LLC is a financial technology company owned by seven U.S. banks. The firm provides identity, risk and payment solutions for financial institutions so they can make decisions, mitigate fraud and enable payments. More than 2,500 companies rely on Early Warning's technology for opening new accounts, recognizing fraud and moving payments (sending/receiving). Financial account solutions span credit insights, deposit account data, identity theft protection, account location, asset search and more. Early Warning's Identity Chek service utilizes bank intelligence to validate customer identity, retrieve account scores and access information concerning fraud and account mismanagement. Deposit Chek offers high-risk deposit notifications and checking account authentication services in real-time. The Zelle Network is owned and operated by Early Warning, and is a financial services network focused on transforming payment experiences. Zelle offers person-to-person payment services, corporate or government disbursement payments, payment movement for small businesses, digital payment solutions via email or mobile app, and risk insight concerning fraud and scams.

Early Warning offers its employees comprehensive health and retirement benefits, paid time off, parental leave, life and disability insurance and more.

FINANCIAL DATA: *Note: Data for latest year may not have been available at press time.*

In U.S. $	2021	2020	2019	2018	2017	2016
Revenue						
R&D Expense						
Operating Income						
Operating Margin %						
SGA Expense						
Net Income						
Operating Cash Flow						
Capital Expenditure						
EBITDA						
Return on Assets %						
Return on Equity %						
Debt to Equity						

CONTACT INFORMATION:
Phone: 480 483-4610   Fax:
Toll-Free: 800 745-1560
Address: 16552 N. 90th St., Scottsdale, AZ 85260 United States

STOCK TICKER/OTHER:
Stock Ticker: Joint Venture   Exchange:
Employees: 1,600   Fiscal Year Ends:
Parent Company:

SALARIES/BONUSES:
Top Exec. Salary: $ Bonus: $
Second Exec. Salary: $ Bonus: $

OTHER THOUGHTS:
Estimated Female Officers or Directors:
Hot Spot for Advancement for Women/Minorities:

Sales, profits and employees may be estimates. Financial information, benefits and other data can change quickly and may vary from those stated here.

Ekata Inc

ekata.com

NAIC Code: 511210E

TYPES OF BUSINESS:

Computer Software: Network Security, Managed Access, Digital ID,
Cybersecurity & Anti-Virus
Global Identity Verification Data
SaaS - Digital Risk Assessment
Machine Learning
Behavioral Technology
Application Programming Interfaces
Artificial Intelligence

BRANDS/DIVISIONS/AFFILIATES:

Mastercard Incorporated
Ekata Identity Engine
ADVANCE.AI

CONTACTS: *Note: Officers with more than one job title may be intentionally listed here more than once.*

Rob Eleveld, CEO
Kushai Shah, COO
Jason Eglit, CFO
Beth Shulkin, Sr. VP-Global Mktg.
Samantha Rist, VP-People
Varun Kumar, Sr. VP-Engineering
Spencer McLain, Sr. VP-global Sales

GROWTH PLANS/SPECIAL FEATURES:

Ekata, Inc., a Mastercard Incorporated company, offers digital identity verification solutions. The firm enables businesses worldwide to link digital interactions with the individuals involved, enabling businesses to perform secure transactions and mitigate fraud. The Ekata Identity Engine leverages proprietary data sets, identity elements and machine learning models to correlate behaviors with identity. Its high-scale and low-latency application programming interfaces (APIs) are utilized in transaction, monitoring and customer onboarding alongside its software-as-a-service solution that scans possibilities of fraud. Ekata's solutions are used by more than 2,000 businesses and partners, including Alipay, Equifax and Microsoft. Industries served by Ekata primarily consist of ecommerce, financial services and payments. In late-2021, Ekata announced a partnership with Singapore-based artificial intelligence and big data company ADVANCE.AI to offer business-to-business digital identity solutions and risk products across southern and southeastern Asian markets.

Ekata offers its employees health and wellness benefits, a retirement savings plan, career and professional development opportunities and more.

FINANCIAL DATA: *Note: Data for latest year may not have been available at press time.*

In U.S. $	2021	2020	2019	2018	2017	2016
Revenue						
R&D Expense						
Operating Income						
Operating Margin %						
SGA Expense						
Net Income						
Operating Cash Flow						
Capital Expenditure						
EBITDA						
Return on Assets %						
Return on Equity %						
Debt to Equity						

CONTACT INFORMATION:

Phone: 888 308-2549 Fax:
Toll-Free:
Address: 1301 Fifth Ave., Ste. 1600, Seattle, WA 98101 United States

STOCK TICKER/OTHER:

Stock Ticker: Subsidiary Exchange:
Employees: 250 Fiscal Year Ends:
Parent Company: Mastercard Incorporated

SALARIES/BONUSES:

Top Exec. Salary: $ Bonus: $
Second Exec. Salary: $ Bonus: $

OTHER THOUGHTS:

Estimated Female Officers or Directors:
Hot Spot for Advancement for Women/Minorities:

Sales, profits and employees may be estimates. Financial information, benefits and other data can change quickly and may vary from those stated here.

Enfusion Ltd LLC

www.enfusion.com

NAIC Code: 511210Q

TYPES OF BUSINESS:
Computer Software: Accounting, Banking & Financial
SaaS - Investment Management

BRANDS/DIVISIONS/AFFILIATES:

GROWTH PLANS/SPECIAL FEATURES:
Enfusion Inc is a software-as-a-service (SaaS) provider focused on transforming the investment management industry. Its solutions are designed to eliminate technology and information barriers, empowering investment managers to make and execute better-informed investment decisions in real-time. It simplifies investment and operational workflows by unifying mission-critical systems and coalescing data into a single dataset resulting in a single source of truth.

CONTACTS: Note: Officers with more than one job title may be intentionally listed here more than once.
Thomas Kim, CEO

FINANCIAL DATA: Note: Data for latest year may not have been available at press time.

In U.S. $	2021	2020	2019	2018	2017	2016
Revenue		79,565,000	59,027,000			
R&D Expense						
Operating Income		6,074,000	13,869,000			
Operating Margin %						
SGA Expense		52,133,000	28,197,000			
Net Income		4,061,000	12,656,000			
Operating Cash Flow		1,665,000	12,306,000			
Capital Expenditure		5,068,000	4,429,000			
EBITDA		8,447,000	15,023,000			
Return on Assets %						
Return on Equity %						
Debt to Equity						

CONTACT INFORMATION:
Phone: 312 253-9800   Fax:
Toll-Free:
Address: S. Clark St., Ste. 750, Chicago, IL 60603 United States

STOCK TICKER/OTHER:
Stock Ticker: ENFN
Employees: 639
Parent Company:

Exchange: NYS
Fiscal Year Ends: 12/31

SALARIES/BONUSES:
Top Exec. Salary: $504,735   Bonus: $271,100
Second Exec. Salary: $283,878   Bonus: $141,000

OTHER THOUGHTS:
Estimated Female Officers or Directors:
Hot Spot for Advancement for Women/Minorities:

Sales, profits and employees may be estimates. Financial information, benefits and other data can change quickly and may vary from those stated here.

Enova International Inc

NAIC Code: 522291

www.enova.com

TYPES OF BUSINESS:

Consumer Lending
Online Lending Services
Secured Loans
Finance Receivable Products
Line of Credit
Receivable Purchase Agreements

BRANDS/DIVISIONS/AFFILIATES:

CashNetUSA
NetCredit
Simplic
Pangea

GROWTH PLANS/SPECIAL FEATURES:

Enova International Inc provides online financial services, including short-term consumer loans, line of credit accounts, and installment loans to customers primarily in the United States and the United Kingdom. Consumers apply for credit online, receive a decision almost immediately, and can receive funds within one day. Enova acts as either the lender or a third-party facilitator between borrowers and other lenders. The company earns revenue from interest income, finance charges, and other fees, including fees on the transactions between borrowers and third-party lenders. Nearly 80% of all revenue comes from the United States. The company realizes similar amounts of revenue from each of its three different products: short-term loans, lines of credit, and installment loans.

CONTACTS:
Note: Officers with more than one job title may be intentionally listed here more than once.

David Fisher, CEO
Steven Cunningham, CFO
James Lee, Chief Accounting Officer
Sean Rahilly, Chief Compliance Officer
Kirk Chartier, Chief Marketing Officer

FINANCIAL DATA:
Note: Data for latest year may not have been available at press time.

In U.S. $	2021	2020	2019	2018	2017	2016
Revenue		1,083,710,000	1,174,757,000	1,114,074,000	843,741,000	745,569,000
R&D Expense						
Operating Income		357,797,000	248,210,000	183,072,000	134,414,000	121,477,000
Operating Margin %						
SGA Expense		210,380,000	224,336,000	232,329,000	203,152,000	195,360,000
Net Income		377,844,000	36,612,000	70,098,000	29,240,000	34,602,000
Operating Cash Flow		740,871,000	848,639,000	684,840,000	447,173,000	393,373,000
Capital Expenditure		29,491,000	20,062,000	16,079,000	16,528,000	14,396,000
EBITDA		541,843,000	260,728,000	170,951,000	126,291,000	138,603,000
Return on Assets %						
Return on Equity %						
Debt to Equity						

CONTACT INFORMATION:

Phone: 312 568-4200   Fax:
Toll-Free:
Address: 175 West Jackson Blvd., Chicago, IL 60604 United States

STOCK TICKER/OTHER:

Stock Ticker: ENVA   Exchange: NYS
Employees: 1,463   Fiscal Year Ends: 12/31
Parent Company:

SALARIES/BONUSES:

Top Exec. Salary: $805,692   Bonus: $232,696
Second Exec. Salary: $486,539   Bonus: $155,085

OTHER THOUGHTS:

Estimated Female Officers or Directors:
Hot Spot for Advancement for Women/Minorities:

Sales, profits and employees may be estimates. Financial information, benefits and other data can change quickly and may vary from those stated here.

Envestnet Inc

www.envestnet.com

NAIC Code: 523930

TYPES OF BUSINESS:
Investment Advisory Services
Portfolio Management
Investment Research & Due Diligence Services
Software

BRANDS/DIVISIONS/AFFILIATES:
Envestnet | Enterprise
Envestnet | Tamarac
Envestnet | Retirement Solutions
Envestnet | MoneyGuide
Envestnet | PMC
Envestnet | Yodlee
Envestnet | Analytics

GROWTH PLANS/SPECIAL FEATURES:
Envestnet provides wealth-management technology and solutions to registered investment advisors, banks, broker/dealers, and other firms. Its Tamarac platform provides trading, rebalancing, portfolio accounting, performance reporting, and client relationship management software to high-end RIAs. Envestnet's portfolio management consultants provides research services and consulting services to assist advisors, including vetted third-party managed account products. In November 2015, Envestnet acquired Yodlee, a provider of data aggregation.

CONTACTS: *Note: Officers with more than one job title may be intentionally listed here more than once.*
William Crager, CEO
Peter DArrigo, CFO
James Fox, Chairman of the Board
Matthew Majoros, Chief Accounting Officer
Shelly OBrien, Chief Legal Officer
Scott Grinis, Chief Technology Officer
Stuart DePina, President

FINANCIAL DATA: *Note: Data for latest year may not have been available at press time.*

In U.S. $	2021	2020	2019	2018	2017	2016
Revenue		998,230,000	900,127,000	812,363,000	683,679,000	578,164,000
R&D Expense						
Operating Income		19,441,000	-16,073,000	14,165,000	16,420,000	-23,444,000
Operating Margin %						
SGA Expense		559,199,000	536,118,000	457,172,000	385,402,000	357,019,000
Net Income		-3,110,000	-16,782,000	5,755,000	-3,280,000	-55,567,000
Operating Cash Flow		169,836,000	108,726,000	117,385,000	108,607,000	76,815,000
Capital Expenditure		66,996,000	53,943,000	44,592,000	27,569,000	22,576,000
EBITDA		132,928,000	81,198,000	90,242,000	73,775,000	36,893,000
Return on Assets %						
Return on Equity %						
Debt to Equity						

CONTACT INFORMATION:
Phone: 312 827-2800   Fax: 312 827-2801
Toll-Free: 866-924-8912
Address: 35 E. Wacker Dr., Ste. 2400, Chicago, IL 60601 United States

STOCK TICKER/OTHER:
Stock Ticker: ENV
Employees: 4,375
Parent Company:

Exchange: NYS
Fiscal Year Ends: 12/31

SALARIES/BONUSES:
Top Exec. Salary: $490,646   Bonus: $493,287
Second Exec. Salary: $480,000   Bonus: $10,000

OTHER THOUGHTS:
Estimated Female Officers or Directors: 2
Hot Spot for Advancement for Women/Minorities: Y

Sales, profits and employees may be estimates. Financial information, benefits and other data can change quickly and may vary from those stated here.

Equifax Inc

NAIC Code: 561450

www.equifax.com

TYPES OF BUSINESS:
Credit Reporting
Information Database Management
Marketing Information
Business Credit Information
Decisioning & Analytical Tools
Consumer Credit Information
Identify Verification Services

BRANDS/DIVISIONS/AFFILIATES:
Appriss Insights

GROWTH PLANS/SPECIAL FEATURES:
Along with Experian and TransUnion, Equifax is one of the leading credit bureaus in the United States. Equifax's credit reports provide credit histories on millions of consumers, and the firm's services are critical to lenders' credit decisions. In addition, about a third of the firm's revenue comes from workforce solutions, which provides income verification and employer human resources services. Equifax generates over 20% of its revenue from outside the United States.

CONTACTS:
Note: Officers with more than one job title may be intentionally listed here more than once.

Mark Begor, CEO
John Gamble, CFO
Mark Feidler, Chairman of the Board
James Griggs, Chief Accounting Officer
Jamil Farshchi, Chief Information Officer
John Kelley, Chief Legal Officer
Bryson Koehler, Chief Technology Officer
Julia Houston, Other Executive Officer
Prasanna Dhore, Other Executive Officer
Carla Chaney, Other Executive Officer
John Hartman, President, Divisional
Rodolfo Ploder, President, Divisional
Beverly Anderson, President, Divisional
Sid Singh, President, Geographical
Sunil Bindal, Senior VP, Divisional

FINANCIAL DATA:
Note: Data for latest year may not have been available at press time.

In U.S. $	2021	2020	2019	2018	2017	2016
Revenue		4,127,500,000	3,507,600,000	3,412,100,000	3,362,200,000	3,144,900,000
R&D Expense						
Operating Income		676,600,000	-335,400,000	448,000,000	824,600,000	817,900,000
Operating Margin %						
SGA Expense		1,322,500,000	1,990,200,000	1,213,300,000	1,039,100,000	948,200,000
Net Income		520,100,000	-398,800,000	299,800,000	587,300,000	488,800,000
Operating Cash Flow		946,200,000	313,800,000	672,200,000	816,000,000	795,800,000
Capital Expenditure		421,300,000	399,600,000	321,900,000	218,200,000	173,500,000
EBITDA		1,226,100,000	16,000,000	775,700,000	1,130,300,000	1,089,000,000
Return on Assets %						
Return on Equity %						
Debt to Equity						

CONTACT INFORMATION:
Phone: 404 885-8000   Fax: 404 885-8682
Toll-Free: 800-685-5000
Address: 1550 Peachtree St., NW, Atlanta, GA 30309 United States

STOCK TICKER/OTHER:
Stock Ticker: EFX   Exchange: NYS
Employees: 11,400   Fiscal Year Ends: 12/31
Parent Company:

SALARIES/BONUSES:
Top Exec. Salary: $1,557,692   Bonus: $
Second Exec. Salary: $711,424   Bonus: $

OTHER THOUGHTS:
Estimated Female Officers or Directors: 1
Hot Spot for Advancement for Women/Minorities:

Sales, profits and employees may be estimates. Financial information, benefits and other data can change quickly and may vary from those stated here.

Esusu Financial Inc

esusurent.com

NAIC Code: 511210Q

TYPES OF BUSINESS:
Computer Software: Accounting, Banking & Financial
Rent Payment Data Capture & Reporting
Credit Bureau Reporting
Credit Building Solution
Rent Relief Fund

BRANDS/DIVISIONS/AFFILIATES:

CONTACTS: Note: Officers with more than one job title may be intentionally listed here more than once.
Samir Goel, Co-CEO
Wemimo Abbey, Co-CEO

GROWTH PLANS/SPECIAL FEATURES:
Esusu Financial, Inc. is a financial technology company that has developed a credit building platform for individuals in the U.S. who do not have histories with credit reporting agencies. Esusu encompasses automated features that report monthly rent payments to credit bureaus, boosting individual credit scores along the way. Approximately 3,500 individuals who previously did not have credit established prime scores in 18-month's time. Participants can view credit score improvements and obtain credit reports through the platform. To get started, Esusu sends an email and uses bank-grade security to confirm identity and for protecting data; once enrolled, renters continue to pay rent on time and consider applying for rent relief if falling behind on a payment. Esusu's rent relief fund is designed to provide rent relief for renters experiencing financial hardship. The fund is made possible via donations, which can also be accomplished through the esusurent.com website. Partners of Esusu include Equifax, TransUnion and Experian credit bureaus; Yardi, RealPage, MRI Real Estate Software, and entrata rent reporting platforms; and Target Foundation, Acumen, and The Global Good Fund philanthropic entities.

FINANCIAL DATA: Note: Data for latest year may not have been available at press time.

In U.S. $	2021	2020	2019	2018	2017	2016
Revenue						
R&D Expense						
Operating Income						
Operating Margin %						
SGA Expense						
Net Income						
Operating Cash Flow						
Capital Expenditure						
EBITDA						
Return on Assets %						
Return on Equity %						
Debt to Equity						

CONTACT INFORMATION:
Phone: 646-664-8947   Fax:
Toll-Free:
Address: 215 W 125th St., Ste. 410, New York, NY 10027 United States

STOCK TICKER/OTHER:
Stock Ticker: Private   Exchange:
Employees: 88   Fiscal Year Ends:
Parent Company:

SALARIES/BONUSES:
Top Exec. Salary: $ Bonus: $
Second Exec. Salary: $ Bonus: $

OTHER THOUGHTS:
Estimated Female Officers or Directors:
Hot Spot for Advancement for Women/Minorities:

Sales, profits and employees may be estimates. Financial information, benefits and other data can change quickly and may vary from those stated here.

Even (Even Responsible Finance Inc)

even.com

NAIC Code: 511210Q

TYPES OF BUSINESS:

Computer Software: Accounting, Banking & Financial
Money Management
On-demand Wage Pay
Software Development

BRANDS/DIVISIONS/AFFILIATES:

CONTACTS: *Note: Officers with more than one job title may be intentionally listed here more than once.*

David Baga, CEO
Quinten Farmer, Pres.
Stephen Taylor, VP-Finance
Samantha Goldman, CMO
Jenny Molyneaux, VP-Operations
Evan Goldschmidt, CTO
Jon Schlossberg, Chmn.

GROWTH PLANS/SPECIAL FEATURES:

Even Responsible Finance, Inc. is a software application designer and developer that has developed an on-demand wage payment platform called Even. By offering on-demand pay, companies help employees, which in turn helps the company via worker productivity, employer brand, retention and absenteeism. The on-demand pay platform gives employees visibility into their earnings, access to pay when they need it and more. For a flat monthly fee, Even's membership model also provides employees with tools to help them plan and save. The Even app provides an easy way to employees to check their next shifts and glance at their current earnings. The app's spending assistant takes the total dollar amount of upcoming bills and subtracts it from the bank balance for a broad picture of the user's account. Since most bills are due once a month, Even automatically finds and surfaces the bills becoming due during the current pay period, and shows the amount needed to cover those bills. This process gives employees a clear picture of what they need for bills until their next paycheck arrives. Even is available in all U.S. states, and results in 90 days usually show that employees go from spending more than they make to having money left over in their accounts.

FINANCIAL DATA: *Note: Data for latest year may not have been available at press time.*

In U.S. $	2021	2020	2019	2018	2017	2016
Revenue						
R&D Expense						
Operating Income						
Operating Margin %						
SGA Expense						
Net Income						
Operating Cash Flow						
Capital Expenditure						
EBITDA						
Return on Assets %						
Return on Equity %						
Debt to Equity						

CONTACT INFORMATION:

Phone: 510-350-7678   Fax:
Toll-Free:
Address: 1440 Broadway, Fl. 5, Oakland, CA 94612 United States

STOCK TICKER/OTHER:

Stock Ticker: Private   Exchange:
Employees: Fiscal Year Ends:
Parent Company:

SALARIES/BONUSES:

Top Exec. Salary: $ Bonus: $
Second Exec. Salary: $ Bonus: $

OTHER THOUGHTS:

Estimated Female Officers or Directors:
Hot Spot for Advancement for Women/Minorities:

Sales, profits and employees may be estimates. Financial information, benefits and other data can change quickly and may vary from those stated here.

Plunkett Research, Ltd.

Experian plc

www.experianplc.com

NAIC Code: 561450

TYPES OF BUSINESS:

Credit Reporting
Information & Database Management
Validation & Processing Software
Consumer Information Services
Financial Consulting
Analytics
Credit Protection

BRANDS/DIVISIONS/AFFILIATES:

Experian North America Inc
Experian Holdings Ireland Ltd
Experian Information Solutions Inc

GROWTH PLANS/SPECIAL FEATURES:

Experian is one of the leading credit bureaus in North America and the United Kingdom, providing the consumer information that is the basis for granting credit. The company also provides decision analytics, marketing data, and direct-to-consumer credit products. About one fourth of the company's revenue is generated outside North America and the United Kingdom, primarily in Latin America and Asia.

CONTACTS: *Note: Officers with more than one job title may be intentionally listed here more than once.*

Brian Cassin, CEO
Kerry Williams, COO
Lloyd Pitchford, CFO
Nadia Ridout-Jamieson, CCO
Jacky Simmonds, Chief People Officer
Joe Manna, CTO
Robert Nelson, Group General Counsel
Rick Gallagher, Group Dir.-Corp. Strategy & Dev.
Nadia Ridout-Jamieson, Dir.-Comm.
Nadia Ridout-Jamieson, Dir.-Investor Rel.
Richard Fiddis, Managing Dir.-Strategic Markets
Joy Griffiths, Global Managing Dir.-Experian Decision Analytics
Ricardo Loureiro, Managing Dir.-Experian Latin America
Joy Griffiths, CEO-Asia Pacific
Mike Rogers, Chmn.
Victor Nichols, CEO-Experian North America

FINANCIAL DATA: *Note: Data for latest year may not have been available at press time.*

In U.S. $	2021	2020	2019	2018	2017	2016
Revenue	5,372,000,000	5,179,000,000	4,861,000,000	4,662,000,000	4,335,000,000	4,550,000,000
R&D Expense						
Operating Income	1,063,000,000	1,185,000,000	1,157,000,000	1,164,000,000	1,085,000,000	1,087,000,000
Operating Margin %						
SGA Expense	417,000,000	378,000,000	342,000,000	328,000,000	322,000,000	349,000,000
Net Income	803,000,000	675,000,000	695,000,000	815,000,000	866,000,000	753,000,000
Operating Cash Flow	1,488,000,000	1,256,000,000	1,241,000,000	1,192,000,000	1,355,000,000	1,371,000,000
Capital Expenditure	422,000,000	487,000,000	439,000,000	431,000,000	399,000,000	339,000,000
EBITDA	1,806,000,000	1,633,000,000	1,527,000,000	1,547,000,000	1,581,000,000	1,588,000,000
Return on Assets %						
Return on Equity %						
Debt to Equity						

CONTACT INFORMATION:

Phone: 353 18469100   Fax: 353 18469150
Toll-Free:
Address: Newenham House Northern Cross, Malahide Road, Dublin, D17 AY61 Ireland

STOCK TICKER/OTHER:

Stock Ticker: EXPGY   Exchange: PINX
Employees: 17,560   Fiscal Year Ends: 03/31
Parent Company:

SALARIES/BONUSES:

Top Exec. Salary: $1,133,111   Bonus: $2,364,752
Second Exec. Salary: $900,000   Bonus: $1,872,000

OTHER THOUGHTS:

Estimated Female Officers or Directors: 5
Hot Spot for Advancement for Women/Minorities: Y

Sales, profits and employees may be estimates. Financial information, benefits and other data can change quickly and may vary from those stated here.

Feedzai Inc

NAIC Code: 511210Q

feedzai.com

TYPES OF BUSINESS:

Computer Software: Accounting, Banking & Financial
Financial Risk Solutions
Artificial Intelligence
Advanced Risk Management Platform
Big Data
Machine Learning
Technology Development
Software Development

BRANDS/DIVISIONS/AFFILIATES:

Revelock

CONTACTS: Note: Officers with more than one job title may be intentionally listed here more than once.

Nuno Sebastiao, CEO
Mariana Jordao, Sr. VP-Oper.
Curtis Smith, CFO
Nuno Pires, Head-Global Sales
Dalia Turner, VP-People
Paulo Marques, CTO
Pedro Barata, Chief Product Officer

GROWTH PLANS/SPECIAL FEATURES:

Feedzai, Inc. utilizes artificial intelligence to combat financial crime. The company has developed an advanced risk management platform powered by big data and machine learning, which scores trillions of dollars of transactions for the purpose of protecting global businesses. Because of this security platform, Feedzai customers can expand into new channels, geographies and payment types, and can build models to address their specific business needs. Feedzai's solutions also enable customers to make business decisions swiftly and effectively. Feedzai takes a four-strategy approach to fighting financial crime: prevention strategies that enable early-stage protection; detection strategies via data, cyber activity and customer history; remediation strategies for customers impacted by financial crime; and compliance and transparency strategies throughout the customer journey. Industries served by Feedzai include retail banks, payment processors, merchants, challenger banks and acquirers. Feedzai is headquartered in California, USA, with offices throughout the world, including Portugal, the U.K., Hong Kong, Australia, Singapore and Spain. During 2021, Feedzai acquired Revelock, an advanced biometric platform.

Feedzai offers its employees health insurance, remote work options, maternity/paternity programs and other benefits.

FINANCIAL DATA: Note: Data for latest year may not have been available at press time.

In U.S. $	2021	2020	2019	2018	2017	2016
Revenue						
R&D Expense						
Operating Income						
Operating Margin %						
SGA Expense						
Net Income						
Operating Cash Flow						
Capital Expenditure						
EBITDA						
Return on Assets %						
Return on Equity %						
Debt to Equity						

CONTACT INFORMATION:

Phone: 650 260-8924   Fax:
Toll-Free:
Address: 1875 S. Grant St., Ste. 950, San Mateo, CA 94402 United States

STOCK TICKER/OTHER:

Stock Ticker: Private   Exchange:
Employees: 500   Fiscal Year Ends:
Parent Company:

SALARIES/BONUSES:

Top Exec. Salary: $ Bonus: $
Second Exec. Salary: $ Bonus: $

OTHER THOUGHTS:

Estimated Female Officers or Directors:
Hot Spot for Advancement for Women/Minorities:

Sales, profits and employees may be estimates. Financial information, benefits and other data can change quickly and may vary from those stated here.

Plunkett Research, Ltd.

Fidelity Investments Inc

www.fidelity.com

NAIC Code: 523920

TYPES OF BUSINESS:

Mutual Funds
Human Resources Administration Services
Employee Benefits Services
Online Brokerage
Physical Branch Investment Offices
Clearing and Execution Products and Services
Real Estate Investments
Institutional Account Management and Services

BRANDS/DIVISIONS/AFFILIATES:

Fidelity Insitutional Asset Management
Fidelity Charitable

CONTACTS: *Note: Officers with more than one job title may be intentionally listed here more than once.*

Abigail Johnson, CEO
Jim Speros, Chief Creative Officer
Steve A. Scullen, III, Pres., Corp. Oper.
Lori Kalahar Johnson, VP-Online Strategy
Jacques Perold, Pres., Fidelity Management & Research Company
Charles Morrison, Pres., Asset Mgmt.
Nancy D. Prior, Pres., Fixed Income Div.

GROWTH PLANS/SPECIAL FEATURES:

Fidelity Investments, Inc. is one of the world's largest providers of financial services, serving 40 million individual customers. With approximately $11.8 trillion total customer assets and $4.5 trillion total discretionary assets under management, the company offers personal investment services, workplace investment services, institutional solutions and asset management. The personal investment division offers financial planning and retirement options such as independent retirement accounts (IRAs), annuities and managed accounts; brokerage and cash management products; college savings accounts; and other financial services for individual investors. The workplace investment division works with employers to build benefit programs for their employees. This segment provides recordkeeping, investments and servicing in relation to contributions, benefits, health and welfare and stock plans. For financial institutions, Fidelity provides technology and personalized service such as clearing, custody, investment products, brokerage and trading services to a wide range of financial firms. Fidelity Institutional Asset Management is a distribution organization dedicated to the institutional marketplace. It serves as a gateway to Fidelity's broad and deep institutional investment management capabilities, including U.S. equity, international equity, fixed income and asset allocation. In addition, Fidelity Charitable is an independent public charity that allows donors to establish a dedicated donor-advised fund to support their favorite charities in the short-term and create a systematic plan for longer-term philanthropic goals. Headquartered in Boston, Massachusetts, Fidelity is comprised of 12 regional offices and more than 200 investor centers in the U.S.

The company is owned approximately 49% by the founding family and 51% by current and former employees.

FINANCIAL DATA: *Note: Data for latest year may not have been available at press time.*

In U.S. $	2021	2020	2019	2018	2017	2016
Revenue	24,000,000,000	21,000,000,000	20,790,000,000	20,400,000,000	18,200,000,000	15,900,000,000
R&D Expense						
Operating Income						
Operating Margin %						
SGA Expense						
Net Income	8,100,000,000	7,200,000,000	6,840,000,000	6,300,000,000	5,300,000,000	3,450,000,000
Operating Cash Flow						
Capital Expenditure						
EBITDA						
Return on Assets %						
Return on Equity %						
Debt to Equity						

CONTACT INFORMATION:

Phone: 617-563-7000   Fax:
Toll-Free: 800-343-3548
Address: 82 Devonshire St., Boston, MA 02109 United States

STOCK TICKER/OTHER:

Stock Ticker: Private   Exchange:
Employees: 68,000   Fiscal Year Ends: 12/31
Parent Company:

SALARIES/BONUSES:

Top Exec. Salary: $ Bonus: $
Second Exec. Salary: $ Bonus: $

OTHER THOUGHTS:

Estimated Female Officers or Directors: 2
Hot Spot for Advancement for Women/Minorities:

Sales, profits and employees may be estimates. Financial information, benefits and other data can change quickly and may vary from those stated here.

Fifth Third Bancorp

www.53.com

NAIC Code: 522110

TYPES OF BUSINESS:
Banking
Mortgages
Trust Services
Insurance
Investment Services
Leasing
Payment Processing Services
Asset Management

BRANDS/DIVISIONS/AFFILIATES:
Fifth Third Securities
Fifth Third Insurance Agency
Fifth Third Private Bank
Fifth Third Institutional Services

GROWTH PLANS/SPECIAL FEATURES:
Fifth Third Bancorp is a diversified financial-services company headquartered in Cincinnati. The company has over $200 billion in assets and operates numerous full-service banking centers and ATMs throughout Ohio, Kentucky, Indiana, Michigan, Illinois, Florida, Tennessee, West Virginia, Georgia, and North Carolina.

Fifth Third Bancorp offers comprehensive benefits, retirement/savings options and employee assistance plans programs.

CONTACTS: *Note: Officers with more than one job title may be intentionally listed here more than once.*
Greg Carmichael, CEO
Melissa Stevens, Executive VP
Jamie Leonard, CFO
Mark Hazel, Chief Accounting Officer
Richard Stein, Chief Credit Officer
Jude Schramm, Chief Information Officer
Susan Zaunbrecher, Chief Legal Officer
Robert Shaffer, Chief Risk Officer
Kristine Garrett, Executive VP
Kevin Lavender, Executive VP
Margaret Jula, Executive VP
Lars Anderson, Executive VP
Timothy Spence, President

FINANCIAL DATA: *Note: Data for latest year may not have been available at press time.*

In U.S. $	2021	2020	2019	2018	2017	2016
Revenue		7,233,000,000	7,253,000,000	6,151,000,000	5,729,000,000	5,783,000,000
R&D Expense						
Operating Income						
Operating Margin %						
SGA Expense		2,848,000,000	2,827,000,000	2,502,000,000	2,364,000,000	2,319,000,000
Net Income		1,427,000,000	2,512,000,000	2,193,000,000	2,194,000,000	1,564,000,000
Operating Cash Flow		371,000,000	1,824,000,000	2,856,000,000	1,494,000,000	2,114,000,000
Capital Expenditure		358,000,000	304,000,000	134,000,000	231,000,000	312,000,000
EBITDA						
Return on Assets %						
Return on Equity %						
Debt to Equity						

CONTACT INFORMATION:
Phone: 800 972-3030   Fax: 513 579-6246
Toll-Free: 800-972-3030
Address: 38 Fountain Square Plaza, Cincinnati, OH 45263 United States

STOCK TICKER/OTHER:
Stock Ticker: FITB   Exchange: NAS
Employees: 19,872   Fiscal Year Ends: 12/31
Parent Company:

SALARIES/BONUSES:
Top Exec. Salary: $1,100,070   Bonus: $
Second Exec. Salary: $688,501   Bonus: $

OTHER THOUGHTS:
Estimated Female Officers or Directors: 4
Hot Spot for Advancement for Women/Minorities: Y

Sales, profits and employees may be estimates. Financial information, benefits and other data can change quickly and may vary from those stated here.

Finicity a Mastercard Company

www.finicity.com

NAIC Code: 511210Q

TYPES OF BUSINESS:
Computer Software: Accounting, Banking & Financial
Financial Technology
Financial Data Aggregation
Financial Data Verification
Digital Lending Solutions
Income and Payment Verification
Digital Payment Solutions
Digital Transaction History

BRANDS/DIVISIONS/AFFILIATES:

CONTACTS: Note: Officers with more than one job title may be intentionally listed here more than once.
Steve Smith, CEO

GROWTH PLANS/SPECIAL FEATURES:
Finicity, a Mastercard Company is a financial technology firm that offers an online platform for helping individuals, families and organizations to make financial decisions. The Finicity platform provides three core solutions: lending, money management and payments. The firm's lending solutions are Fair Credit Reporting Act (FCRA) compliant and occur digitally. Lend data services are categorized into: assets, providing lenders bank-validated insights into borrower financial assets in real-time; income, identifying and validating income streams for mitigating risk and supplementing decision-making processes; employment, providing employment verification from multiple data sources; cash flow, assessing and managing risk via smart data insights about the applicant's cash flow and other related financial trends; transaction, providing borrower transaction information, account balances, investment positions, credits/debits and more; statements, verifying customer address and other information via statement transactions; and scoring attributes, which are derived from transactions, payee types, payee streams, balances and other scoring analytics. Financial management solutions aggregate consumer-permissioned data via application programming interface (API) tools in order to present clean and categorized transaction histories (past two years) to be used for financial documentation and/or lending purposes. Last, Finicity's payment solutions verify bank account details, account owners and the balances needed to enable swift and secure money movement for new account onboarding, as well as for necessary funding and payments to be settled in real-time.

FINANCIAL DATA: Note: Data for latest year may not have been available at press time.

In U.S. $	2021	2020	2019	2018	2017	2016
Revenue						
R&D Expense						
Operating Income						
Operating Margin %						
SGA Expense						
Net Income						
Operating Cash Flow						
Capital Expenditure						
EBITDA						
Return on Assets %						
Return on Equity %						
Debt to Equity						

CONTACT INFORMATION:
Phone: 801 984-4200 Fax:
Toll-Free:
Address: 434 W. Ascension Way, Ste. 200, Salt Lake City, UT 84123 United States

STOCK TICKER/OTHER:
Stock Ticker: Subsidiary Exchange:
Employees: 700 Fiscal Year Ends:
Parent Company: Mastercard Incorporated

SALARIES/BONUSES:
Top Exec. Salary: $ Bonus: $
Second Exec. Salary: $ Bonus: $

OTHER THOUGHTS:
Estimated Female Officers or Directors:
Hot Spot for Advancement for Women/Minorities:

Sales, profits and employees may be estimates. Financial information, benefits and other data can change quickly and may vary from those stated here.

Finix Payments Inc

www.finixpayments.com

NAIC Code: 522320

TYPES OF BUSINESS:

Financial Transactions Processing, Reserve, and Clearinghouse Activities
SaaS - Payment Processing
Financial Technology
Digital Payments Management
Application Programming Interface Solution
Payout Management
Merchant Onboarding Solution
Developer Tools

BRANDS/DIVISIONS/AFFILIATES:

CONTACTS: *Note: Officers with more than one job title may be intentionally listed here more than once.*

Richie Serna, CEO

GROWTH PLANS/SPECIAL FEATURES:

Finix Payments, Inc. is a financial technology company that has designed a payments management solution specifically for software-as-a-service (SaaS) platforms and fintech companies. From startups to publicly-traded firms, Finix offers solutions needed to build payment experiences for their customers. The company application programming interface (API) helps businesses accept payments, manage payouts and onboard merchants, including ecommerce entities, all within a single source. Business users control permission access, customized fees, transaction limits and more. Finix offers both blended and interchange plus pricing for merchants. Transferring payments, storing data and ongoing audits are covered by Finix, which is PCI Level 1 compliant and is equipped with 3D secure authentication for enhanced fraud protection, KYC identity verification and GDPR/CCPA/SOC data processes. Solutions for developers include tokenized cards, automatic subscription billing and peer-to-peer payment solutions. Headquartered in San Francisco, California, Finix has an additional office in Chicago and many employees work remotely.

Finix offers its employees comprehensive health benefits, life insurance, equity share, paid time off and parental leave.

FINANCIAL DATA: *Note: Data for latest year may not have been available at press time.*

In U.S. $	2021	2020	2019	2018	2017	2016
Revenue						
R&D Expense						
Operating Income						
Operating Margin %						
SGA Expense						
Net Income						
Operating Cash Flow						
Capital Expenditure						
EBITDA						
Return on Assets %						
Return on Equity %						
Debt to Equity						

CONTACT INFORMATION:

Phone: 415-888-5080   Fax:
Toll-Free:
Address: 71 Stevenson St., Fl. 11, San Francisco, CA 94105 United States

STOCK TICKER/OTHER:

Stock Ticker: Private   Exchange:
Employees: Fiscal Year Ends:
Parent Company:

SALARIES/BONUSES:

Top Exec. Salary: $ Bonus: $
Second Exec. Salary: $ Bonus: $

OTHER THOUGHTS:

Estimated Female Officers or Directors:
Hot Spot for Advancement for Women/Minorities:

Sales, profits and employees may be estimates. Financial information, benefits and other data can change quickly and may vary from those stated here.

Fireblocks Inc

www.fireblocks.com

NAIC Code: 511210E

TYPES OF BUSINESS:

Computer Software: Network Security, Managed Access, Digital ID, Cybersecurity & Anti-Virus
Digital Asset Security Platform
Multi-Party Computation
Chip Isolation Technology
Application Programming Interfaces
On-Chain Settlement Solutions
Decentralized Finance App Solutions
Wallet-as-a-Service

BRANDS/DIVISIONS/AFFILIATES:

CONTACTS: *Note: Officers with more than one job title may be intentionally listed here more than once.*

Michael Shaulov, CEO
Stephen Richardson, VP-Product Strategy & Bus. Solutions
Anitha Gopalan, CFO
Yelena Osin, VP-Mktg.
Daphne Berger, VP-Human Resources
Idan Ofrat, CTO
Pavel Berengoltz, VP-Research & Dev.

GROWTH PLANS/SPECIAL FEATURES:

Fireblocks, Inc. has developed an easy-to-use digital asset security platform that helps financial institutions protect digital assets from theft or hackers. The platform does this by using multi-party computation (MPC) and patent-pending chip isolation technology to secure private keys, application programming interface (API) credentials and eliminate the need for deposit addresses. The all-in-one platform provides customers a way for running their digital asset business, including secure on-chain settlement, access to decentralized finance apps (DeFi or dApps), an MPC wallet-as-a-service that pushes transaction speeds faster than the industry average, anti-money laundering compliance, permissioned DeFi, tokenization, regulatory requirement management and a policy/workflow engine for managing transaction policies from anywhere, any time. Customers served by Fireblocks include banks, neobanks, exchanges, lending desks, over-the-counter exchanges and brokerages, market makers, prop traders and hedge funds. Based in the U.S., Fireblocks has operations worldwide, including the U.K., Israel, Hong Kong, Singapore, Germany, France and Switzerland.

FINANCIAL DATA: *Note: Data for latest year may not have been available at press time.*

In U.S. $	2021	2020	2019	2018	2017	2016
Revenue						
R&D Expense						
Operating Income						
Operating Margin %						
SGA Expense						
Net Income						
Operating Cash Flow						
Capital Expenditure						
EBITDA						
Return on Assets %						
Return on Equity %						
Debt to Equity						

CONTACT INFORMATION:

Phone: 646 978-9173   Fax:
Toll-Free:
Address: 500 7th Ave., New York, NY 10018 United States

STOCK TICKER/OTHER:

Stock Ticker: Private
Employees: 245
Parent Company:

Exchange:
Fiscal Year Ends:

SALARIES/BONUSES:

Top Exec. Salary: $ Bonus: $
Second Exec. Salary: $ Bonus: $

OTHER THOUGHTS:

Estimated Female Officers or Directors:
Hot Spot for Advancement for Women/Minorities:

Sales, profits and employees may be estimates. Financial information, benefits and other data can change quickly and may vary from those stated here.

Fiserv Inc

NAIC Code: 522320

www.fiserv.com

TYPES OF BUSINESS:
Financial Services
Investment Services
Online Banking
Electronic Billing & Payment
Software Applications & Investment Management Solutions

GROWTH PLANS/SPECIAL FEATURES:
Fiserv is a leading provider of core processing and complementary services, such as electronic funds transfer, payment processing, and loan processing, for U.S. banks and credit unions, with a focus on small and midsize banks. Through the merger with First Data in 2019, Fiserv now provides payment processing services for merchants. About 10% of the company's revenue is generated internationally.

BRANDS/DIVISIONS/AFFILIATES:
First Data
STAR

CONTACTS:
Note: Officers with more than one job title may be intentionally listed here more than once.

Frank Bisignano, CEO
Robert Hau, CFO
Denis OLeary, Chairman of the Board
Kenneth Best, Chief Accounting Officer
Lynn McCreary, Chief Legal Officer
Guy Chiarello, COO
Christopher Foskett, Executive VP, Divisional
Devin McGranahan, Other Corporate Officer
Suzan Kereere, Other Executive Officer
Byron Vielehr, Other Executive Officer

FINANCIAL DATA:
Note: Data for latest year may not have been available at press time.

In U.S. $	2021	2020	2019	2018	2017	2016
Revenue		14,852,000,000	10,187,000,000	5,823,000,000	5,696,000,000	5,505,000,000
R&D Expense						
Operating Income		1,388,000,000	1,594,000,000	1,526,000,000	1,522,000,000	1,445,000,000
Operating Margin %						
SGA Expense		5,652,000,000	3,284,000,000	1,228,000,000	1,150,000,000	1,101,000,000
Net Income		958,000,000	893,000,000	1,187,000,000	1,246,000,000	930,000,000
Operating Cash Flow		4,147,000,000	2,795,000,000	1,552,000,000	1,483,000,000	1,431,000,000
Capital Expenditure		900,000,000	721,000,000	360,000,000	287,000,000	290,000,000
EBITDA		5,090,000,000	3,207,000,000	2,304,000,000	1,967,000,000	1,856,000,000
Return on Assets %						
Return on Equity %						
Debt to Equity						

CONTACT INFORMATION:
Phone: 262 879-5000   Fax: 262 879-5275
Toll-Free: 800-872-7882
Address: 255 Fiserv Dr., Brookfield, WI 53045 United States

STOCK TICKER/OTHER:
Stock Ticker: FISV   Exchange: NAS
Employees: 44,000   Fiscal Year Ends: 12/31
Parent Company:

SALARIES/BONUSES:
Top Exec. Salary: $1,000,000   Bonus: $
Second Exec. Salary: $531,250   Bonus: $

OTHER THOUGHTS:
Estimated Female Officers or Directors: 1
Hot Spot for Advancement for Women/Minorities:

Sales, profits and employees may be estimates. Financial information, benefits and other data can change quickly and may vary from those stated here.

Flywire Corporation

www.flywire.com

NAIC Code: 522320

TYPES OF BUSINESS:

Payment Processing
Currency Exchange
Payments Processing
Invoicing

GROWTH PLANS/SPECIAL FEATURES:

Flywire Corp provides a secure global payments platform, offering its clients an innovative and streamlined process to receive reconciled domestic and international payments in a more cost effective and efficient manner. The company's solutions are built on three core elements namely a payments platform; a proprietary global payment network and vertical-specific software backed by its deep industry expertise.

Flywire offers on-the-job training, mentoring and development workshops; stock options; and travel opportunities.

BRANDS/DIVISIONS/AFFILIATES:

CONTACTS: *Note: Officers with more than one job title may be intentionally listed here more than once.*

Michael Massaro, CEO
Michael Ellis, CFO
Phillip Riese, Chairman of the Board
Peter Butterfield, Chief Compliance Officer
David King, Chief Technology Officer
Rob Orgel, COO
Sharon Butler, Executive VP, Divisional
John Talaga, Executive VP, Divisional

FINANCIAL DATA: *Note: Data for latest year may not have been available at press time.*

In U.S. $	2021	2020	2019	2018	2017	2016
Revenue		131,783,000	94,918,000			
R&D Expense		24,501,000	15,008,000			
Operating Income		-15,815,000	-17,457,000			
Operating Margin %						
SGA Expense		75,292,000	60,641,000			
Net Income		-11,107,000	-20,116,000			
Operating Cash Flow		-14,223,000	4,073,000			
Capital Expenditure		2,141,000	3,748,000			
EBITDA		-8,949,000	-13,377,000			
Return on Assets %						
Return on Equity %						
Debt to Equity						

CONTACT INFORMATION:

Phone: 617 329-4524   Fax:
Toll-Free:
Address: 141 Tremont St., #10, Boston, MA 02111 United States

STOCK TICKER/OTHER:

Stock Ticker: FLYW
Employees: 665
Parent Company:

Exchange: NAS
Fiscal Year Ends: 12/31

SALARIES/BONUSES:

Top Exec. Salary: $425,000   Bonus: $
Second Exec. Salary: $325,000   Bonus: $

OTHER THOUGHTS:

Estimated Female Officers or Directors:
Hot Spot for Advancement for Women/Minorities:

Sales, profits and employees may be estimates. Financial information, benefits and other data can change quickly and may vary from those stated here.

Forter Inc

NAIC Code: 511210E

www.forter.com

TYPES OF BUSINESS:

Computer Software: Network Security, Managed Access, Digital ID, Cybersecurity & Anti-Virus
Ecommerce Fraud Prevention
Fraud Detection Technology

BRANDS/DIVISIONS/AFFILIATES:

GROWTH PLANS/SPECIAL FEATURES:

Forter, Inc. is a fraud prevention company that provides related technology for online retailers and marketplaces. The firm's solutions include payment protection, account protection, smart routing, policy abuse protection, returns abuse protection, item not received (INR) abuse protection, second payment services directive (PSD2) compliance, payment service provider protection, fiat-to-crypto protection and loyalty program protection. Forter has processed more than $200 billion in transactions annually, protecting over 800 million consumers globally from credit card fraud, account takeover, identity theft and more. The company has office locations in the U.S., Israel, the U.K. and Singapore. Partners of Forter include worldpay, mastercard, Salesforce, SAP, CapitalOne, Adobe, among others.

CONTACTS: *Note: Officers with more than one job title may be intentionally listed here more than once.*

Michael Reitblat, CEO
Liron Damri, Pres.
Aaron Barfoot, CFO
Oren Ellenbogen, VP-Engineering
Lauren Vigliante, VP-People
Iftah Gideoni, CTO
Colin Sims, COO

FINANCIAL DATA: *Note: Data for latest year may not have been available at press time.*

In U.S. $	2021	2020	2019	2018	2017	2016
Revenue						
R&D Expense						
Operating Income						
Operating Margin %						
SGA Expense						
Net Income						
Operating Cash Flow						
Capital Expenditure						
EBITDA						
Return on Assets %						
Return on Equity %						
Debt to Equity						

CONTACT INFORMATION:

Phone: Fax:
Toll-Free: 800 537-0601
Address: 575 5th Ave., New York, NY 10017 United States

STOCK TICKER/OTHER:

Stock Ticker: Private   Exchange:
Employees: 470   Fiscal Year Ends:
Parent Company:

SALARIES/BONUSES:

Top Exec. Salary: $ Bonus: $
Second Exec. Salary: $ Bonus: $

OTHER THOUGHTS:

Estimated Female Officers or Directors:
Hot Spot for Advancement for Women/Minorities:

Sales, profits and employees may be estimates. Financial information, benefits and other data can change quickly and may vary from those stated here.

Forward Financing LLC

www.forwardfinancing.com

NAIC Code: 522291

TYPES OF BUSINESS:

Consumer Lending
Small Business Loans/Revenue-Based Financing
Online Loan Application
Working Capital Solutions

BRANDS/DIVISIONS/AFFILIATES:

CONTACTS: Note: Officers with more than one job title may be intentionally listed here more than once.

Justin Bakes, CEO
Michael Spinello, Pres.
Eugene Wong, VP-Finance & Strategy
Ohi Akhigbe, VP-Portfolio Risk & Analytics
Shannon Braley, VP-People
Brittney St. Germain, VP-Technology
Alexis Shapiro, VP

GROWTH PLANS/SPECIAL FEATURES:

Forward Financing, LLC is a financial technology company that provides working capital to small businesses underserved by traditional financing options. How it works: businesses qualify by having been in business in the U.S. for at least one year, making $10,000 or more in monthly revenue, and owners must have a 500+ credit scores; then apply for an application through the Forward Financing website, with information such as owner's name, social security number, business name, Tax ID number and last three month's business bank statements; Forward Financing will conduct a full, upfront underwrite and issue an informed decision (usually within a few hours); and if approved and if the customer accepts the approval and terms, funds are transferred into the business bank account that same day. If a customer is up-to-date with payments and has paid about half of the overall balance, they may qualify for a renewal. Forward Financing provides working capital to businesses in more than 700 industries, in every U.S. state.

Forward Financing offers its employees comprehensive medical benefits, professional development opportunities, 401(k), parental leave and company perks.

FINANCIAL DATA: Note: Data for latest year may not have been available at press time.

In U.S. $	2021	2020	2019	2018	2017	2016
Revenue						
R&D Expense						
Operating Income						
Operating Margin %						
SGA Expense						
Net Income						
Operating Cash Flow						
Capital Expenditure						
EBITDA						
Return on Assets %						
Return on Equity %						
Debt to Equity						

CONTACT INFORMATION:

Phone: Fax:
Toll-Free: 888 244-9099
Address: 53 State St., Fl. 20, Boston, MA 02109 United States

STOCK TICKER/OTHER:

Stock Ticker: Private   Exchange:
Employees: Fiscal Year Ends:
Parent Company:

SALARIES/BONUSES:

Top Exec. Salary: $ Bonus: $
Second Exec. Salary: $ Bonus: $

OTHER THOUGHTS:

Estimated Female Officers or Directors:
Hot Spot for Advancement for Women/Minorities:

Sales, profits and employees may be estimates. Financial information, benefits and other data can change quickly and may vary from those stated here.

FTX Trading Ltd

ftx.com/intl

NAIC Code: 523130

TYPES OF BUSINESS:

Digital Currency Exchange
Financial Technology
Cryptocurrency Trading
Cryptocurrency Exchange
Derivatives
Digital Trading Platform
Volatility Investment Instruments
Leveraged Tokens

BRANDS/DIVISIONS/AFFILIATES:

ftx.com
ftx.us

GROWTH PLANS/SPECIAL FEATURES:

FTX Trading Ltd. is a financial technology company founded in 2019, and developed an online cryptocurrency exchange specifically for traders. The ftx.com platform offers innovative products such as derivatives, options, volatility investment instruments and leveraged tokens. FTX Trading's mission was to develop a platform robust enough for professional trading firms and intuitive enough for first-time users. Partners and collaborations of FTX include, but are not limited to, Circle, True USD, Paxos, Fenwick and West, Proof of Capital, Sequoia, Paradigm Capital, Ribbit Capital, Multicoin Capital, Thoma Bravo, and Lightspeed Venture Partners. Headquartered in the Bahamas, FTX originated as a Bahamian cryptocurrency exchange, but began offering stock trading to U.S. customers in early 2022 (ftx.us).

CONTACTS:
Note: Officers with more than one job title may be intentionally listed here more than once.

Samuel Bankman-Fried, CEO
Constance Wang, COO
Dan Friedberg, Regulatory Officer
Nishad Singh, Head-Engineering
Gary Wang, CTO

FINANCIAL DATA:
Note: Data for latest year may not have been available at press time.

In U.S. $	2021	2020	2019	2018	2017	2016
Revenue						
R&D Expense						
Operating Income						
Operating Margin %						
SGA Expense						
Net Income						
Operating Cash Flow						
Capital Expenditure						
EBITDA						
Return on Assets %						
Return on Equity %						
Debt to Equity						

CONTACT INFORMATION:

Phone: 206 913 4300   Fax:
Toll-Free:
Address: Friar's Hill Rd., 11 Mandolin Pl., Saint John's, AG-04 Antigua And Barbuda

STOCK TICKER/OTHER:

Stock Ticker: Private   Exchange:
Employees: Fiscal Year Ends:
Parent Company:

SALARIES/BONUSES:

Top Exec. Salary: $ Bonus: $
Second Exec. Salary: $ Bonus: $

OTHER THOUGHTS:

Estimated Female Officers or Directors:
Hot Spot for Advancement for Women/Minorities:

Sales, profits and employees may be estimates. Financial information, benefits and other data can change quickly and may vary from those stated here.

Fundrise LLC

fundrise.com

NAIC Code: 523920

TYPES OF BUSINESS:

Online Real Estate Investment Funds
Real Estate Investment
Digital Investment Platform
Real Estate Management
Real Estate Investment Software
Technology Innovation and Development

BRANDS/DIVISIONS/AFFILIATES:

Rise Companies Corp

CONTACTS: *Note: Officers with more than one job title may be intentionally listed here more than once.*

Ben Miller, CEO

GROWTH PLANS/SPECIAL FEATURES:

Fundrise, LLC offers a real estate investment platform through a combination of investment expertise and technology. The company pairs its asset network with investors to acquire high-quality assets ranging from debt to equity, commercial to residential, and more. Fundrise has a strategy of acquiring assets for less than their intrinsic value, and typically less than their replacement cost. The company's team then works to increase the value of each asset over time via hands-on management and in partnership with local operators. Fundrise has acquired assets collectively worth over $7 billion, on behalf of its 300,000+ investors (from its 2010 founding to April 28, 2022). Investor returns are maximized through the firm's low-fee approach due to eliminating most intermediaries. Fundrise designs its own software and handles every piece of its real estate business in-house. Investors can create an account, choose their portfolio strategy and begin to watch their investment diversify across a series of investment funds tailored to the selected strategy. New assets may be added to the portfolio by Fundrise over time, with no additional investment required by the investor. The in-app newsfeed enables investors to view each asset in their portfolio and watch it evolve over time. Fundrise operates as a subsidiary of Rise Companies Corp.

FINANCIAL DATA: *Note: Data for latest year may not have been available at press time.*

In U.S. $	2021	2020	2019	2018	2017	2016
Revenue						
R&D Expense						
Operating Income						
Operating Margin %						
SGA Expense						
Net Income						
Operating Cash Flow						
Capital Expenditure						
EBITDA						
Return on Assets %						
Return on Equity %						
Debt to Equity						

CONTACT INFORMATION:

Phone: 202 584-0550   Fax:
Toll-Free:
Address: 11 Dupont Cir. NW, Fl. 9, Washington, DC 20036 United States

STOCK TICKER/OTHER:

Stock Ticker: Subsidiary   Exchange:
Employees: Fiscal Year Ends:
Parent Company: Rise Companies Corp

SALARIES/BONUSES:

Top Exec. Salary: $ Bonus: $
Second Exec. Salary: $ Bonus: $

OTHER THOUGHTS:

Estimated Female Officers or Directors:
Hot Spot for Advancement for Women/Minorities:

Sales, profits and employees may be estimates. Financial information, benefits and other data can change quickly and may vary from those stated here.

Gemini Trust Company LLC

gemini.com

NAIC Code: 523130

TYPES OF BUSINESS:

Digital Cryptocurrency Exchange
Cryptocurrency Exchange

BRANDS/DIVISIONS/AFFILIATES:

Gemini
Gemini Wallet
Gemini dollar
Gemini Earn
Gemini Credit Card
Gemini ActiveTrader
Gemini Clearing
Gemini Pay

CONTACTS: *Note: Officers with more than one job title may be intentionally listed here more than once.*

Tyler Winklevoss, CEO
Cameron Winklevoss, Pres.

GROWTH PLANS/SPECIAL FEATURES:

Gemini Trust Company, LLC is a software developer that has created Gemini, a cryptocurrency exchange and custodian that allows customers to buy, sell and store digital assets. More than 20 cryptocurrencies are used on Gemini, including bitcoin, bitcoin cash, ether, Litecoin and Zcash. Gemini is a New York trust company subject to the capital reserve requirements, cybersecurity requirements and banking compliance standards set forth by the New York State Department of Financial Services and the New York Banking Law. The Gemini exchange makes it simple to research the crypto market, buy bitcoin or other cryptos and build a portfolio for the future of money. Access to the tools needed to understand the crypto market and begin investing are through a single interface. Gemini is offered via online, mobile app and Gemini Wallet. Advanced products include trading, custody, clearing, Gemini dollar and payments. Gemini offers a crypto-native finance platform for institutions and retail investors. The platform offers multiple application programming interface (API) options, including WebSockets, FIX and public and private REST APIs to help institutions and traders access market data and trading services. Other products include Gemini Earn, Gemini Credit Card, Gemini ActiveTrader, Gemini Clearing, Gemini Pay and Gemini Mobile, among others. Partners of the firm include Samsung, TradingView, Brave, Nifty Gateway, and others. During 2021, Gemini announced its was expanding its operations in southeast Asia, with plans to establish satellite offices throughout the region, including Australia and Hong Kong.

Gemini offers its employees comprehensive health plans, 401(k), learning/development opportunities and a variety of company assistance plans and perks.

FINANCIAL DATA: *Note: Data for latest year may not have been available at press time.*

In U.S. $	2021	2020	2019	2018	2017	2016
Revenue						
R&D Expense						
Operating Income						
Operating Margin %						
SGA Expense						
Net Income						
Operating Cash Flow						
Capital Expenditure						
EBITDA						
Return on Assets %						
Return on Equity %						
Debt to Equity						

CONTACT INFORMATION:

Phone: 866-240-5113   Fax:
Toll-Free:
Address: 600 Third Ave., Fl. 2, New York, NY 10016 United States

STOCK TICKER/OTHER:

Stock Ticker: Private   Exchange:
Employees: 760   Fiscal Year Ends:
Parent Company:

SALARIES/BONUSES:

Top Exec. Salary: $ Bonus: $
Second Exec. Salary: $ Bonus: $

OTHER THOUGHTS:

Estimated Female Officers or Directors:
Hot Spot for Advancement for Women/Minorities:

Sales, profits and employees may be estimates. Financial information, benefits and other data can change quickly and may vary from those stated here.

Giact Systems LLC

www.giact.com

NAIC Code: 511210E

TYPES OF BUSINESS:
Computer Software: Network Security, Managed Access, Digital ID, Cybersecurity & Anti-Virus
Secure Payment Solutions
Identity Protection Solutions
Technology Innovation
Compliance Solutions

BRANDS/DIVISIONS/AFFILIATES:
London Stock Exchange Group plc
Refinitiv US Holdings Inc
EPIC Platform
g-AUTHENTICATE
g-VERIFY
g-IDENTIFY
g-MOBILE
g-OFAC

CONTACTS: Note: Officers with more than one job title may be intentionally listed here more than once.

Merlin Bise, Dir-Technology

GROWTH PLANS/SPECIAL FEATURES:
Giact Systems, LLC creates and delivers innovative technology solutions that protect companies and their customers from payments and identity fraud. The firm offers a comprehensive suite of enrollment, payment, identity and compliance solutions through a single platform, EPIC Platform. Use cases include account validation and authentication, identity verification, ongoing monitoring and account maintenance, securing payments, stopping unauthorized payments, complying with financial crime networks and such. Industries served by the Giact include banking, ecommerce, government agencies, insurance, lending, medium-sized businesses, retail, telecommunications, utilities and others. The company's technology solutions are deployed at over 1,000 companies ranging in size from Fortune 500 to sole proprietors. Other solution brands of Giact include gAUTHENTICATE, gVERIFY, gIDENTIFY, gMOBILE, gOFAC and gSCAN, among others. Giact operates as a subsidiary of Refinitiv US Holdings, Inc., itself a subsidiary of London Stock Exchange Group plc.

FINANCIAL DATA: Note: Data for latest year may not have been available at press time.

In U.S. $	2021	2020	2019	2018	2017	2016
Revenue						
R&D Expense						
Operating Income						
Operating Margin %						
SGA Expense						
Net Income						
Operating Cash Flow						
Capital Expenditure						
EBITDA						
Return on Assets %						
Return on Equity %						
Debt to Equity						

CONTACT INFORMATION:
Phone: 866 918-2409   Fax:
Toll-Free:
Address: 700 Central Expy S., Ste. 300, Allen, TX 75013 United States

STOCK TICKER/OTHER:
Stock Ticker: Subsidiary   Exchange:
Employees: 75   Fiscal Year Ends:
Parent Company: London Stock Exchange Group plc

SALARIES/BONUSES:
Top Exec. Salary: $ Bonus: $
Second Exec. Salary: $ Bonus: $

OTHER THOUGHTS:
Estimated Female Officers or Directors:
Hot Spot for Advancement for Women/Minorities:

Sales, profits and employees may be estimates. Financial information, benefits and other data can change quickly and may vary from those stated here.

Goldman Sachs Group Inc (The)

www.goldmansachs.com

NAIC Code: 523110

TYPES OF BUSINESS:
Investment Banking
Investment Banking
Global Markets
Asset Management
Wealth Management
Credit Cards
Online Banking

BRANDS/DIVISIONS/AFFILIATES:

GROWTH PLANS/SPECIAL FEATURES:
Goldman Sachs is a leading global investment banking firm whose activities are organized into investment banking (20% of net revenue), global markets (40%), asset management (25%), and consumer and wealth management (15%) segments. Approximately 60% of the company's net revenue is generated in the Americas, 15% in Asia, and 25% in Europe, the Middle East, and Africa. In 2008, Goldman reorganized itself as a financial holding company regulated by the Federal Reserve System.

CONTACTS: *Note: Officers with more than one job title may be intentionally listed here more than once.*
David Solomon, CEO
Stephen Scherr, CFO
Sheara Fredman, Chief Accounting Officer
Laurence Stein, Chief Administrative Officer
Kathryn Ruemmler, Chief Legal Officer
Brian Lee, Chief Risk Officer
John Waldron, COO
John Rogers, Executive VP
Denis Coleman, Other Corporate Officer
Elizabeth Hammack, Treasurer

FINANCIAL DATA: *Note: Data for latest year may not have been available at press time.*

In U.S. $	2021	2020	2019	2018	2017	2016
Revenue		44,559,000,000	33,274,000,000	33,256,000,000	29,419,000,000	28,053,000,000
R&D Expense						
Operating Income						
Operating Margin %						
SGA Expense		13,710,000,000	13,092,000,000	13,068,000,000	12,441,000,000	12,104,000,000
Net Income		9,459,000,000	8,466,000,000	10,459,000,000	4,286,000,000	7,398,000,000
Operating Cash Flow		-13,728,000,000	23,868,000,000	20,421,000,000	-17,742,000,000	5,570,000,000
Capital Expenditure		6,309,000,000	8,443,000,000	7,982,000,000	3,185,000,000	2,876,000,000
EBITDA						
Return on Assets %						
Return on Equity %						
Debt to Equity						

CONTACT INFORMATION:
Phone: 212 902-1000   Fax: 212 902-3000
Toll-Free:
Address: 200 West St., New York, NY 10282 United States

STOCK TICKER/OTHER:
Stock Ticker: GS   Exchange: NYS
Employees: 43,900   Fiscal Year Ends: 12/31
Parent Company:

SALARIES/BONUSES:
Top Exec. Salary: $1,850,000   Bonus: $6,660,000
Second Exec. Salary: $1,850,000   Bonus: $5,460,000

OTHER THOUGHTS:
Estimated Female Officers or Directors: 5
Hot Spot for Advancement for Women/Minorities: Y

Gravity Payments Inc

gravitypayments.com

NAIC Code: 522320

TYPES OF BUSINESS:

Financial Transactions Processing, Reserve, and Clearinghouse Activities
Small Business Credit Card Processing
Mobile Payments
Ecommerce Payments
Invoicing Services
Recurring Payment Services
Payment Devices
Merchant Financing

BRANDS/DIVISIONS/AFFILIATES:

Gravity Capital
El Server

GROWTH PLANS/SPECIAL FEATURES:

Gravity Payments, Inc. is a payments processing company for independent merchants, with a mission to lower costs. Gravity's services include credit card processing, mobile payments, ecommerce, invoicing, recurring payments, point-of-sale, payment devices, integrated payments, gift and loyalty programs and merchant financing (via Gravity Capital). The firm offers flexible payment solutions for developers, including integrating payment processing into present business management software of point-of-sale with the support of Gravity's full-service integration team. Developers can also integrate directly with cloud-based devices or through the company's Windows-based desktop solution, El Server. Gravity is open to partnerships for various purposes, including software integration and helping businesses grow via referral programs, affiliate marketing and business development strategies. Headquartered in Seattle, Gravity Payments has additional offices in Idaho and Hawaii.

CONTACTS: Note: Officers with more than one job title may be intentionally listed here more than once.

Dan Price, CEO

FINANCIAL DATA: Note: Data for latest year may not have been available at press time.

In U.S. $	2021	2020	2019	2018	2017	2016
Revenue						
R&D Expense						
Operating Income						
Operating Margin %						
SGA Expense						
Net Income						
Operating Cash Flow						
Capital Expenditure						
EBITDA						
Return on Assets %						
Return on Equity %						
Debt to Equity						

CONTACT INFORMATION:

Phone: 206 388-5900   Fax: 866 701-4700
Toll-Free:
Address: 5601 22nd Ave NW, Ste. 200, Seattle, WA 98107 United States

STOCK TICKER/OTHER:

Stock Ticker: Private   Exchange:
Employees: 208   Fiscal Year Ends:
Parent Company:

SALARIES/BONUSES:

Top Exec. Salary: $ Bonus: $
Second Exec. Salary: $ Bonus: $

OTHER THOUGHTS:

Estimated Female Officers or Directors:
Hot Spot for Advancement for Women/Minorities:

Sales, profits and employees may be estimates. Financial information, benefits and other data can change quickly and may vary from those stated here.

Greenlight Financial Technology Inc

greenlight.com

NAIC Code: 511210Q

TYPES OF BUSINESS:

Computer Software: Accounting, Banking & Financial
Debit Cards for Kids
Investment Education
Savings Education
Banking Education
Money Management
Financial Technology
Mobile App

BRANDS/DIVISIONS/AFFILIATES:

CONTACTS: *Note: Officers with more than one job title may be intentionally listed here more than once.*

Timothy Sheehan, CEO
Johnson Cook, Pres.
Brian Dong, CFO
Rachel Hamilton, CMO
Ben Swartwout, Chief People Officer
Sameera Rao, CTO
Will Yu, COO

GROWTH PLANS/SPECIAL FEATURES:

Greenlight Financial Technology, Inc. has developed and offers a way for kids and teens to bank and invest. Greenlight Financial itself is not a bank, banking services are provided by Community Federal Savings Bank. The firm offers debit cards for kids and teens to learn use and manage money, and parents can directly deposit funds for needs or as an allowance for doing chores or working hard. Up to 2% can be earned on savings, and debit cards reward 1% in cash back to savings when kids and teens display smart spending and money management. Interest strategies teaches kids and teens the power of compound growth. Kids can round up purchases to the next dollar and automatically add the change to their savings; and they can set a percentage of their allowance to go toward savings and then put it on autopilot. Families can also teach children to research and trade stocks and exchange traded funds (ETFs) for building long-term wealth. Parents approve each trade placed. Parents can use the app to invest in their child's future education or other goals. Personalized quizzes are offered for fund recommendations. Greenlight offers options cross all of its plans.

Greenlight Financial offers its employees comprehensive health benefits, 401(k), remote work, professional development opportunities, paid parental leave and flexible time off.

FINANCIAL DATA: *Note: Data for latest year may not have been available at press time.*

In U.S. $	2021	2020	2019	2018	2017	2016
Revenue						
R&D Expense						
Operating Income						
Operating Margin %						
SGA Expense						
Net Income						
Operating Cash Flow						
Capital Expenditure						
EBITDA						
Return on Assets %						
Return on Equity %						
Debt to Equity						

CONTACT INFORMATION:

Phone: 404 953-5925   Fax:
Toll-Free: 888-483-2645
Address: 303 Peachtree St., NE, Ste. 4300, Atlanta, GA 30308 United States

STOCK TICKER/OTHER:

Stock Ticker: Private   Exchange:
Employees: Fiscal Year Ends:
Parent Company:

SALARIES/BONUSES:

Top Exec. Salary: $ Bonus: $
Second Exec. Salary: $ Bonus: $

OTHER THOUGHTS:

Estimated Female Officers or Directors:
Hot Spot for Advancement for Women/Minorities:

Sales, profits and employees may be estimates. Financial information, benefits and other data can change quickly and may vary from those stated here.

Plunkett Research, Ltd.

GreenSky Inc

www.greensky.com

NAIC Code: 522291

TYPES OF BUSINESS:
Consumer Lending
Online Lending
Online Payments

GROWTH PLANS/SPECIAL FEATURES:
GreenSky Inc operates as a technology company. The company offers a proprietary technology infrastructure platform to supports the full transaction lifecycle, including credit application, underwriting, and real-time allocation. Its platform caters to merchants, consumers, and banks.

BRANDS/DIVISIONS/AFFILIATES:

CONTACTS: *Note: Officers with more than one job title may be intentionally listed here more than once.*
David Zalik, CEO
Andrew Kang, CFO
Angela Nagy, Chief Accounting Officer
Gerald Benjamin, Chief Administrative Officer
Kevin Goldstein, Chief Credit Officer
Steven Fox, Chief Legal Officer
Tim Kaliban, Chief Risk Officer
Ritesh Gupta, COO
Robert Partlow, Executive VP, Divisional
Jennifer Russell, Executive VP
Dennis Kelly, President, Divisional

FINANCIAL DATA: *Note: Data for latest year may not have been available at press time.*

In U.S. $	2021	2020	2019	2018	2017	2016
Revenue		525,649,000	529,646,000	414,673,000	325,887,000	263,865,000
R&D Expense						
Operating Income		52,540,000	120,953,000	152,790,000	145,599,000	119,811,000
Operating Margin %						
SGA Expense		147,141,000	129,698,000	94,754,000	81,786,000	59,523,000
Net Income		9,965,000	31,980,000	24,256,000	138,668,000	124,464,000
Operating Cash Flow		-468,101,000	153,327,000	256,426,000	160,394,000	121,943,000
Capital Expenditure		14,567,000	15,381,000	6,581,000	4,135,000	4,666,000
EBITDA		66,613,000	120,012,000	161,576,000	150,187,000	128,172,000
Return on Assets %						
Return on Equity %						
Debt to Equity						

CONTACT INFORMATION:
Phone: 678-264-6105   Fax:
Toll-Free: 866-936-0602
Address: 5565 Glenridge Connector, Ste. 700, Atlanta, GA 30342 United States

STOCK TICKER/OTHER:
Stock Ticker: GSKY
Employees: 992
Parent Company:

Exchange: NAS
Fiscal Year Ends:

SALARIES/BONUSES:
Top Exec. Salary: $625,000   Bonus: $312,500
Second Exec. Salary: $450,000   Bonus: $200,000

OTHER THOUGHTS:
Estimated Female Officers or Directors:
Hot Spot for Advancement for Women/Minorities:

Sales, profits and employees may be estimates. Financial information, benefits and other data can change quickly and may vary from those stated here.

Groww (Nextbillion Technology Pvt Ltd)

groww.in

NAIC Code: 523120

TYPES OF BUSINESS:

Securities Brokerage
Online and Mobile App Trading
Financial Investing
Stock Trading
Mutual Funds
Futures and Options
Brokerage Services
Financial Technology

BRANDS/DIVISIONS/AFFILIATES:

GROWTH PLANS/SPECIAL FEATURES:

Nextbillion Technology Pvt. Ltd. is a financial technology company based in India that has developed an investment platform called Groww. Investment types include mutual funds, stocks, futures, options, initial public offerings (IPOs) and fixed deposits. Opening a stocks account and maintaining it is free, but brokerage services are charged when an order is executed. The Groww platform has more than 30 million users in India who can learn how to select stocks, learn about mutual funds and how to diversify investments during market volatility. The company's technology ensures personal information and data is fully encrypted and secure. Users can invest anywhere, at any time across mobile and online devices.

CONTACTS: Note: Officers with more than one job title may be intentionally listed here more than once.

Lalit Keshre, CEO
Harsh Jain, COO

FINANCIAL DATA: Note: Data for latest year may not have been available at press time.

In U.S. $	2021	2020	2019	2018	2017	2016
Revenue	55,062,372	385,448				
R&D Expense						
Operating Income						
Operating Margin %						
SGA Expense						
Net Income	3,718,073	-10,547,976				
Operating Cash Flow						
Capital Expenditure						
EBITDA						
Return on Assets %						
Return on Equity %						
Debt to Equity						

CONTACT INFORMATION:

Phone: 91 091088-00604   Fax:
Toll-Free:
Address: Ste. 11, Fl. 2, 80 FT Rd., 4th Block, S.T Bed, Koramangala, Bengaluru, Karnataka 560034 India

STOCK TICKER/OTHER:

Stock Ticker: Private   Exchange:
Employees: Fiscal Year Ends: 03/31
Parent Company:

SALARIES/BONUSES:

Top Exec. Salary: $ Bonus: $
Second Exec. Salary: $ Bonus: $

OTHER THOUGHTS:

Estimated Female Officers or Directors:
Hot Spot for Advancement for Women/Minorities:

Sales, profits and employees may be estimates. Financial information, benefits and other data can change quickly and may vary from those stated here.

Plunkett Research, Ltd.

Guaranteed Rate Inc

www.rate.com

NAIC Code: 511210Q

TYPES OF BUSINESS:

Computer Software: Accounting, Banking & Financial
Digital Home Mortgages & Refinances
Financial Technology
Real-Time Mortgage Rates
Online Mortgage Qualification and Application

BRANDS/DIVISIONS/AFFILIATES:

FlashClose
Attorneys Title Guaranty Fund Inc

CONTACTS: *Note: Officers with more than one job title may be intentionally listed here more than once.*

Victor Ciardelli, CEO
Nik Athanasiou, COO
Suk Shah, CFO
Sanjay Gupta, CMO
Lizzie Garner, Chief People Officer
Dominick Marchetti, CTO
John Elias, Chief Revenue Officer & Strategy

GROWTH PLANS/SPECIAL FEATURES:

Guaranteed Rate, Inc. is a financial technology company that developed and offer digital mortgage services. The firm's online site provides a mortgage calculator that offers real-time rates and loan options without having to provide contact information. The online application process is easy and takes about 10 to 15 minutes to complete, and the secure transfer of documents takes place online as well. FlashClose is the company's technology that lets customers close the loan within minutes, from anywhere. Types of mortgage loans offered by Guaranteed include fixed-rate (15- or 30-year), adjustable rate (5-/7/10-year), home renovation loans, jumbo loans, government loans (FHA or VA), and interest-only loans. Other calculators provided on Guaranteed's site include closing costs, extra payments, home affordability, mortgage points and refinance mortgage. Guaranteed Rate comprises more than 850 branches throughout the U.S., serving all 50 states and Washington DC. In April 2022, Guaranteed acquired Attorneys' Title Guaranty Fund, Inc., a Chicago-based title insurance underwriter.

FINANCIAL DATA: *Note: Data for latest year may not have been available at press time.*

In U.S. $	2021	2020	2019	2018	2017	2016
Revenue						
R&D Expense						
Operating Income						
Operating Margin %						
SGA Expense						
Net Income						
Operating Cash Flow						
Capital Expenditure						
EBITDA						
Return on Assets %						
Return on Equity %						
Debt to Equity						

CONTACT INFORMATION:

Phone: 773-290-0505   Fax:
Toll-Free: 866 934-7283
Address: 3940 N. Ravenswood, Chicago, IL 60613 United States

STOCK TICKER/OTHER:

Stock Ticker: Private   Exchange:
Employees: Fiscal Year Ends:
Parent Company:

SALARIES/BONUSES:

Top Exec. Salary: $ Bonus: $
Second Exec. Salary: $ Bonus: $

OTHER THOUGHTS:

Estimated Female Officers or Directors:
Hot Spot for Advancement for Women/Minorities:

Sales, profits and employees may be estimates. Financial information, benefits and other data can change quickly and may vary from those stated here.

Guideline Inc

www.guideline.com

NAIC Code: 523920

TYPES OF BUSINESS:

Retirement Fund Management
Financial Technology
Retirement Investment Solutions
401(k) Plans
Simplified Individual Pension IRA Plans
Personal IRA Plans
Digital Investments
Money Management

BRANDS/DIVISIONS/AFFILIATES:

Guideline.com

CONTACTS: *Note: Officers with more than one job title may be intentionally listed here more than once.*

Kevin Busque, CEO
Jeff Rosenberger, COO
Aras Kolya, Chief Revenue Officer
Liz Mastrobattisto, Chief Compliance Officer
Christine Rimer, Chief Customer Officer
Qian Liu, Chief Data Officer
Mike Nelson, CTO

GROWTH PLANS/SPECIAL FEATURES:

Guideline, Inc. is a financial technology company and investment advisor that has developed and operates Guideline.com, a retirement investment platform. The company's technology enables the platform to automate many administrative tasks, integrate with leading payroll providers and build affordable retirement plans for the smallest of businesses. Guideline.com's 401(k) plan is designed for startups and small businesses, with features that can include traditional or Roth 401(k) plans, profit sharing, matching options and Safe Harbor plans. Employers can manage the 401(k) plans through the Guideline dashboard, and choose from a range of price points. The firm's simplified employee pension/individual retirement account (SEP IRA) plan is a retirement account that uses low-cost mutual funds and rebalances automatically. This plan has more than $6 billion of assets under management (AUM) and serves more than 30,000 small business clients. Guideline.com also offers a personal IRA plan, which is not tied to an employer, can be easier to withdraw from, and makes a good retirement option for people making present goals such as purchasing a home or planning for retirement. Personal IRA is designed for long-term growth and its investment portfolios rebalance automatically to help customers stay on track. There are no transaction fees for distributions, rollovers or other services under this plan. The estimated total AUM fees for Guideline's managed portfolios can be under 0.15%, and accounts start at $2 per month plus an annual 0.08% account fee. Headquartered in Texas, Guideline has other office locations in California and Maine, with plans to open another in Georgia (as of May 2022).

Guideline offers its employees comprehensive benefits, 401(k), stock options, professional development opportunities and other company programs and perks.

FINANCIAL DATA: *Note: Data for latest year may not have been available at press time.*

In U.S. $	2021	2020	2019	2018	2017	2016
Revenue						
R&D Expense						
Operating Income						
Operating Margin %						
SGA Expense						
Net Income						
Operating Cash Flow						
Capital Expenditure						
EBITDA						
Return on Assets %						
Return on Equity %						
Debt to Equity						

CONTACT INFORMATION:

Phone: Fax:
Toll-Free: 888 228-3491
Address: 1645 E. 6th St., Ste. 200, Austin, TX 78702 United States

STOCK TICKER/OTHER:

Stock Ticker: Private   Exchange:
Employees: 250   Fiscal Year Ends:
Parent Company:

SALARIES/BONUSES:

Top Exec. Salary: $ Bonus: $
Second Exec. Salary: $ Bonus: $

OTHER THOUGHTS:

Estimated Female Officers or Directors:
Hot Spot for Advancement for Women/Minorities:

Sales, profits and employees may be estimates. Financial information, benefits and other data can change quickly and may vary from those stated here.

Headnote Inc

headnote.com

NAIC Code: 522320

TYPES OF BUSINESS:

Financial Transactions Processing, Reserve, and Clearinghouse Activities
Payment Processing Platform for Legal Industry
Digital Payment Compliance
Accounts Receivable Management
Client Satisfaction Tracking Services
Recurring and Installment Payment Plans
Historic and Analytic Payment Data
Real-Time Payment Status Updates

BRANDS/DIVISIONS/AFFILIATES:

CONTACTS: *Note: Officers with more than one job title may be intentionally listed here more than once.*

Sarah Schaaf, CEO
Guy Barbaro, Head-Financial Oper.
Thornton Schaaf, Head-Product
Matt Crampton, CTO

GROWTH PLANS/SPECIAL FEATURES:

Headnote, Inc. is a financial technology company that provides compliant digital payments, accounts receivable (AR) management and client satisfaction tracking services and solutions for the legal industry. Headnote's compliant online payments solutions span: credit card and instant eCheck/ACH payments (for a flat fee); payment requests, website portal payments and manual credit card charges; recurring and installment payment plans on the schedule of the customer's choosing; and guaranteed payment security and full Payment Card Industry (PCI) compliance. The company's AR management and automation solution provides a personalized firm dashboard with real-time AR and payment activity that is updated automatically. It provides on-demand historic and outstanding payment and AR data at client/matter/firm-wide levels; automates collections via personalized, ongoing email reminders until invoices are paid in full; and offers recurring and installment payment plans. Headnote's client satisfaction tracking occurs through net promoter score (NPS) which: automatically surveys clients when they make a payment for services, asking on a 1-10 scale if they would refer the service provider; the feedback instantly appears on the firm's dashboard; overall rating is averaged over time; and any feedback provided can be analyzed during specific time periods or at the invoice/client/attorney level. Headnote provides a client activity tracker which lets them know if the invoice was received or opened; provides payment activity tracking, including whether the payment was received or if the client set up a payment plan; provides real-time status of all automated collection efforts; and provides historic receivables and payment data as well as predictive analytics on future receivables and cash flow.

FINANCIAL DATA: *Note: Data for latest year may not have been available at press time.*

In U.S. $	2021	2020	2019	2018	2017	2016
Revenue						
R&D Expense						
Operating Income						
Operating Margin %						
SGA Expense						
Net Income						
Operating Cash Flow						
Capital Expenditure						
EBITDA						
Return on Assets %						
Return on Equity %						
Debt to Equity						

CONTACT INFORMATION:

Phone: Fax:
Toll-Free: 888 893-5129
Address: 1 California St., Fl. 29 1 California St., Fl. 29, San Francisco, CA 94111 United States

STOCK TICKER/OTHER:

Stock Ticker: Private   Exchange:
Employees: Fiscal Year Ends:
Parent Company: Alpine Investors

SALARIES/BONUSES:

Top Exec. Salary: $ Bonus: $
Second Exec. Salary: $ Bonus: $

OTHER THOUGHTS:

Estimated Female Officers or Directors:
Hot Spot for Advancement for Women/Minorities:

Sales, profits and employees may be estimates. Financial information, benefits and other data can change quickly and may vary from those stated here.

Hippo Holdings Inc

NAIC Code: 524210

www.hippo.com

TYPES OF BUSINESS:
Insurance Agencies and Brokerages
Home Insurance
Smart Home Devices
Home Care Services
Home Maintenance Services
Claims Management

GROWTH PLANS/SPECIAL FEATURES:
Hippo Holdings Inc is a home insurance group that created a new standard of care and protection for homeowners. It provides insurance for computers, home offices, electronics, appliances, water backup, service line coverage among others.

BRANDS/DIVISIONS/AFFILIATES:
Hippo Insurance Services

CONTACTS: Note: Officers with more than one job title may be intentionally listed here more than once.
Assaf Wand, CEO

FINANCIAL DATA: Note: Data for latest year may not have been available at press time.

In U.S. $	2021	2020	2019	2018	2017	2016
Revenue		50,100,000				
R&D Expense						
Operating Income						
Operating Margin %						
SGA Expense						
Net Income		-125,000,000				
Operating Cash Flow						
Capital Expenditure						
EBITDA						
Return on Assets %						
Return on Equity %						
Debt to Equity						

CONTACT INFORMATION:
Phone: 650 294-8463   Fax:
Toll-Free: 877 838-8866
Address: 150 Forest Ave., Palo Alto, CA 94301 United States

STOCK TICKER/OTHER:
Stock Ticker: HIPO
Employees: 593
Parent Company:

Exchange: NYS
Fiscal Year Ends: 12/31

SALARIES/BONUSES:
Top Exec. Salary: $ Bonus: $
Second Exec. Salary: $ Bonus: $

OTHER THOUGHTS:
Estimated Female Officers or Directors:
Hot Spot for Advancement for Women/Minorities:

Sales, profits and employees may be estimates. Financial information, benefits and other data can change quickly and may vary from those stated here.

Hudson River Trading LLC

www.hudsonrivertrading.com

NAIC Code: 523110

TYPES OF BUSINESS:
Investment Banking and Securities Dealing
Quantitative Trading/High-Frequency Trading
Financial Technology
Automated Trading Algorithms
Advanced Mathematics
Electronic Trading Services
Liquidities

BRANDS/DIVISIONS/AFFILIATES:

CONTACTS: *Note: Officers with more than one job title may be intentionally listed here more than once.*
Jason Carroll, Managing Partner
Prashant Lal, Managing Partner
Oaz Nir, Managing Partner

GROWTH PLANS/SPECIAL FEATURES:
Hudson River Trading, LLC (HRT) is a financial technology company that researches and develops automated trading algorithms using advanced mathematical techniques. HRT was founded in 2002 by partners who graduated from Harvard and MIT with degrees in computer science and mathematics. Today, the company is also staffed with statisticians, physicists and engineers. HRT trades on nearly all of the world's electronic markets, and advocates for fair and transparent markets for everyone. As a liquidity provider, HRT's automated trading algorithms are designed to provide the best prices for its clients. The firm's diverse trading strategies enables them to provide substantial liquidity across a variety of time horizons. Headquartered in New York, HRT has additional locations in Colorado, Illinois and Texas, USA, as well as in China, India, Ireland, Singapore and the U.K.

HRT offers its employees on-site fitness rooms and classes, and chef-prepared meals and snacks.

FINANCIAL DATA: *Note: Data for latest year may not have been available at press time.*

In U.S. $	2021	2020	2019	2018	2017	2016
Revenue						
R&D Expense						
Operating Income						
Operating Margin %						
SGA Expense						
Net Income						
Operating Cash Flow						
Capital Expenditure						
EBITDA						
Return on Assets %						
Return on Equity %						
Debt to Equity						

CONTACT INFORMATION:
Phone: 212-293-1444   Fax:
Toll-Free:
Address: Three World Trade Ctr., 175 Greenwich St., Fl. 76, New York, NY 10007 United States

STOCK TICKER/OTHER:
Stock Ticker: Private   Exchange:
Employees: Fiscal Year Ends:
Parent Company:

SALARIES/BONUSES:
Top Exec. Salary: $ Bonus: $
Second Exec. Salary: $ Bonus: $

OTHER THOUGHTS:
Estimated Female Officers or Directors:
Hot Spot for Advancement for Women/Minorities:

Sales, profits and employees may be estimates. Financial information, benefits and other data can change quickly and may vary from those stated here.

Huobi Global Ltd

www.huobi.com/en-us

NAIC Code: 523130

TYPES OF BUSINESS:

Virtual Currency Exchange Services
Blockchain Development
Blockchain Technologies
Digital Asset Trading
Cryptocurrency Wallets
Industry Research
Brokerage Services
Crypto Lending Services

BRANDS/DIVISIONS/AFFILIATES:

Hbit Limited (Huobi Brokerage)
Huobi Pool
Huobi Chat
Huobi Wallet
Huobi Cloud
Huobi Eco Chain
Huobi DeFi Labs

CONTACTS: Note: Officers with more than one job title may be intentionally listed here more than once.

Leon Li, CEO

GROWTH PLANS/SPECIAL FEATURES:

Huobi Global Ltd. is based in the Seychelles archipelago of the Indian Ocean and was founded in 2013 as a blockchain company desiring to accelerate the digital economy via core blockchain innovation and technologies. Huobi operates across multiple sectors, including enterprise and public blockchains, digital assets trading, cryptocurrency wallets and industry research. Huobi's platform enables account members to purchase, sell and trade assets. Subsidiary Hbit Limited (also known as Huobi Brokerage) provides digital asset financial services, with ensured security and compliance, to institutional and high-net-worth clients throughout the world. Brokerage services include over-the-counter trading, and lending (including institution-level crypto asset lending). Other brands and entities under Huobi Global include Huobi Pool, Huobi Chat, Huobi Wallet, Huobi Cloud, Huobi Eco Chain and Huobi DeFi Labs. Huobi DeFi Labs is the group's platform for decentralized finance (DeFi) research, investment/incubation and ecosystem building, all dedicated to building a financial system in collaborations with the global crypto and DeFi community, presently and in the future. Huobi Global has offices in Korea and Japan.

FINANCIAL DATA: Note: Data for latest year may not have been available at press time.

In U.S. $	2021	2020	2019	2018	2017	2016
Revenue						
R&D Expense						
Operating Income						
Operating Margin %						
SGA Expense						
Net Income						
Operating Cash Flow						
Capital Expenditure						
EBITDA						
Return on Assets %						
Return on Equity %						
Debt to Equity						

CONTACT INFORMATION:

Phone: 248-3001216550   Fax:
Toll-Free:
Address: C/O A.C. Management Ltd., Ste. 10, Fl. 10, Mahe,

STOCK TICKER/OTHER:

Stock Ticker: Private
Employees:
Parent Company:

Exchange:
Fiscal Year Ends:

SALARIES/BONUSES:

Top Exec. Salary: $ Bonus: $
Second Exec. Salary: $ Bonus: $

OTHER THOUGHTS:

Estimated Female Officers or Directors:
Hot Spot for Advancement for Women/Minorities:

Sales, profits and employees may be estimates. Financial information, benefits and other data can change quickly and may vary from those stated here.

iCapital Network Inc

NAIC Code: 523910

www.icapitalnetwork.com

TYPES OF BUSINESS:

Online Private Equity and Hedge Fund Investment Platform
Financial Technology
Alternative Investments
High Net-Worth
Private Equity
Hedge Funds

BRANDS/DIVISIONS/AFFILIATES:

CONTACTS: *Note: Officers with more than one job title may be intentionally listed here more than once.*

Lawrence Calcano, CEO
Adrian Czebiniak, Chief Data Officer
Michael Kushner, CFO
Jon Ewing, CMO
Jennifer Ashley, Chief People Officer
Tom Fortin, CIO
Lawrence Calcano, Chmn.

GROWTH PLANS/SPECIAL FEATURES:

iCapital Network, Inc. is a financial technology company offering a platform for alternative investments, which are bought and sold through tech-based solutions for advisors, their high-net-worth client base, asset managers and banks. iCapital offers both alternative solutions and custom solutions, with access to a curated menu of private equity and hedge funds. Private investment opportunities span senior lending, real assets, junior and asset-backed lending and distress/special circumstances for capital appreciation/growth returns across real estate, buyouts, growth equity and venture capital. Headquartered in New York, iCapital Network has offices in North America, Europe and Asia. In March 2022, iCapital agreed to acquire the alternative investment feeder fund platform of Stifel Financial Corp., expanding the companies' existing partnership.

iCapital Network offers its employees comprehensive health coverage, 401(k), bonuses and equity incentives, short-/long-term disability and other benefits.

FINANCIAL DATA: *Note: Data for latest year may not have been available at press time.*

In U.S. $	2021	2020	2019	2018	2017	2016
Revenue						
R&D Expense						
Operating Income						
Operating Margin %						
SGA Expense						
Net Income						
Operating Cash Flow						
Capital Expenditure						
EBITDA						
Return on Assets %						
Return on Equity %						
Debt to Equity						

CONTACT INFORMATION:

Phone: 212 994-7400   Fax:
Toll-Free:
Address: 60 E. 42nd St., New York, NY 10165 United States

STOCK TICKER/OTHER:

Stock Ticker: Private   Exchange:
Employees: Fiscal Year Ends:
Parent Company:

SALARIES/BONUSES:

Top Exec. Salary: $ Bonus: $
Second Exec. Salary: $ Bonus: $

OTHER THOUGHTS:

Estimated Female Officers or Directors:
Hot Spot for Advancement for Women/Minorities:

Sales, profits and employees may be estimates. Financial information, benefits and other data can change quickly and may vary from those stated here.

iCheckGateway.com

ach.icheckgateway.com

NAIC Code: 522320

TYPES OF BUSINESS:

Financial Transactions Processing, Reserve, and Clearinghouse Activities
Financial Technology
Payment Processing Solutions
Cash Discount Programs
Hosted Payments
Virtual Terminal Payments
Email Invoicing
Payments Technology Developer Tools

BRANDS/DIVISIONS/AFFILIATES:

CONTACTS: *Note: Officers with more than one job title may be intentionally listed here more than once.*

Jason Estes, CEO

GROWTH PLANS/SPECIAL FEATURES:

iCheckGateway.com (ICG) is a U.S.-based business and provider of innovative payment processing technology solutions. ICG offers an extensive range of solutions, streamlining and enhancing business processes through a single payment platform. The firm's solutions include Automated Clearing House (ACH) processing, credit card processing, cash discount programs, hosted payment portals, interactive voice response (IVR) payments, small message system (SMS/text) payments, mobile payments, recurring payments, virtual terminals, email invoicing, check verification, plug-ins and developer tools, Payment Card Industry (PCI) compliance and fraud prevention. For developers, ICG offers installation and customization solutions. Developers can also try out live modules with existing software. Industries served by ICG include insurance, municipalities, utilities, TV broadcasting, medical billing, payroll, non-profit charities, finance companies, religious organizations, banking, leasing services and property management. iCheckGateway.com is a registered partner of Elavon, Inc., itself a subsidiary of U.S. Bancorp.

FINANCIAL DATA: *Note: Data for latest year may not have been available at press time.*

In U.S. $	2021	2020	2019	2018	2017	2016
Revenue						
R&D Expense						
Operating Income						
Operating Margin %						
SGA Expense						
Net Income						
Operating Cash Flow						
Capital Expenditure						
EBITDA						
Return on Assets %						
Return on Equity %						
Debt to Equity						

CONTACT INFORMATION:

Phone: Fax:
Toll-Free: 888 746-5741
Address: 13099 S. Cleveland Ave., Ste. 510, Fort Myers, FL 33907
United States

STOCK TICKER/OTHER:

Stock Ticker: Private   Exchange:
Employees: Fiscal Year Ends:
Parent Company:

SALARIES/BONUSES:

Top Exec. Salary: $ Bonus: $
Second Exec. Salary: $ Bonus: $

OTHER THOUGHTS:

Estimated Female Officers or Directors:
Hot Spot for Advancement for Women/Minorities:

Sales, profits and employees may be estimates. Financial information, benefits and other data can change quickly and may vary from those stated here.

IHS Markit Ltd

www.ihsmarkit.com

NAIC Code: 541910

TYPES OF BUSINESS:
Market Research
Information Technology
Data Science
Insights
Software
Consulting
Analysis

BRANDS/DIVISIONS/AFFILIATES:
S&P Global Inc

CONTACTS: *Note: Officers with more than one job title may be intentionally listed here more than once.*
Doulas L. Peterson, CEO-S&P
Jerre Stead, Chairman of the Board
Anurag Gupta, Executive VP, Divisional
Jonathan Gear, Executive VP, Divisional
Stephen Green, Executive VP, Divisional
Heather Matzke-Hamlin, Senior VP
Daniel Yergin, Vice Chairman

GROWTH PLANS/SPECIAL FEATURES:
IHS Markit Ltd. is an information company that leverages technology and data science to provide insights, software and data to customers. The firm serves a wide range of industries, including academic/education, aerospace and defense, agribusiness, automotive, chemical, construction, energy and natural resources, financial services, insurance, maritime/trade and retail, as well as climate and sustainability, economics and country risk, and engineering intelligence. HIS Markit unites comprehensive data, expertise and digital tools to help customers make informed decisions, identify growth, plan accurately, navigate uncertainty, build an advantage and more. Its engineering intelligence platform provides a single source for accessing technical knowledge that resides inside and outside the engineering-based organization, for problem-solving and decision support. IHS comprises experts, analysts and consultants that deliver guidance across business issues and geographies. The company maintains sales offices in more than 15 countries and serves customers in over 100 countries. In February 2022, IHS Markit was acquired by S&P Global, Inc. and announced it would be merging businesses over the next few months.

FINANCIAL DATA: *Note: Data for latest year may not have been available at press time.*

In U.S. $	2021	2020	2019	2018	2017	2016
Revenue	4,459,312,067	4,287,800,064	4,414,600,192	4,009,200,128	3,599,699,968	2,734,799,872
R&D Expense						
Operating Income						
Operating Margin %						
SGA Expense						
Net Income		870,700,032	502,700,000	542,300,032	416,900,000	152,800,000
Operating Cash Flow						
Capital Expenditure						
EBITDA						
Return on Assets %						
Return on Equity %						
Debt to Equity						

CONTACT INFORMATION:
Phone: 44-20-7260-2000   Fax:
Toll-Free:
Address: 25 Ropemaker St., Fl.4, Ropemaker Place, London, EC2Y 9LY United Kingdom

STOCK TICKER/OTHER:
Stock Ticker: Subsidiary
Employees: 5,000
Parent Company: S&P Global Inc

Exchange:
Fiscal Year Ends: 12/31

SALARIES/BONUSES:
Top Exec. Salary: $ Bonus: $
Second Exec. Salary: $ Bonus: $

OTHER THOUGHTS:
Estimated Female Officers or Directors:
Hot Spot for Advancement for Women/Minorities:

Sales, profits and employees may be estimates. Financial information, benefits and other data can change quickly and may vary from those stated here.

Immutable Holdings Inc

NAIC Code: 511210E

www.immutableholdings.com

TYPES OF BUSINESS:

Computer Software: Network Security, Managed Access, Digital ID, Cybersecurity & Anti-Virus

GROWTH PLANS/SPECIAL FEATURES:

Immutable Holdings, Inc. is a blockchain holdings company and Web3 venture studio managing industry-leading businesses in the blockchain space. Its current portfolio of businesses include: NFT.com, Immutable Asset Management, 1-800-Bitcoin, HBAR Labs, CBDC.com and Immutable Advisory.

BRANDS/DIVISIONS/AFFILIATES:

CONTACTS: Note: Officers with more than one job title may be intentionally listed here more than once.

Jordan Fried, CEO
Jeanna Liu, COO
Jordan Fried, Chmn.

FINANCIAL DATA: Note: Data for latest year may not have been available at press time.

In U.S. $	2021	2020	2019	2018	2017	2016
Revenue		391,399	234,548	252,581		
R&D Expense						
Operating Income						
Operating Margin %						
SGA Expense						
Net Income		-85,979	-226,898	-258,109		
Operating Cash Flow						
Capital Expenditure						
EBITDA						
Return on Assets %						
Return on Equity %						
Debt to Equity						

CONTACT INFORMATION:

Phone: 604 270-8881   Fax:
Toll-Free:
Address: 207 West Hastings Street, Vancouver, BC V6B 1H7 Canada

STOCK TICKER/OTHER:

Stock Ticker: HOLD   Exchange: NEOE
Employees: Fiscal Year Ends: 09/30
Parent Company:

SALARIES/BONUSES:

Top Exec. Salary: $ Bonus: $
Second Exec. Salary: $ Bonus: $

OTHER THOUGHTS:

Estimated Female Officers or Directors:
Hot Spot for Advancement for Women/Minorities:

Sales, profits and employees may be estimates. Financial information, benefits and other data can change quickly and may vary from those stated here.

Plunkett Research, Ltd.

Industrial & Financial Systems AB (IFS)

www.ifsworld.com

NAIC Code: 511210Q

TYPES OF BUSINESS:

Software Applications
Banking & Financial Software
Manufacturing Software
Application Service Provider
Enterprise Software Development
Enterprise Resource Planning
Management Solutions
Analytics

BRANDS/DIVISIONS/AFFILIATES:

Axios Systems
Customerville

CONTACTS: Note: Officers with more than one job title may be intentionally listed here more than once.

Darren Roos, CEO
David Phull, COO
Alastair Sorbie, Pres.
Constance Minc, CFO
Oliver Pilgerstorfer, CMO
Kate Bishop, Chief Human Resources Officer
Sal Laher, CIO
Jesper Alwall, General Counsel
Fredrik vom Hofe, Sr. VP-Bus. Dev.
Anne Vandbakk, VP-Corp. Comm.
Bengt Nilsson, Vice Chmn.
Dave Holroyd, Managing Dir.-IFS Defense
Jonas Persson, Chmn.

GROWTH PLANS/SPECIAL FEATURES:

Industrial & Financial Systems AB (IFS), based in Sweden, develops and delivers enterprise software for customers worldwide who manufacture and distribute goods, maintain assets and manage service-focused operations. The company's solutions include enterprise resource planning, enterprise asset management, service management, applications, aviation maintenance management, field service management and enterprise operational analytical intelligence. IFS supports more than 10,000 customers worldwide from a network of local offices. The firm's product development activities primarily take place in Sweden and Sri Lanka, and its consultancy business operates throughout the Americas, Europe, the Middle East, Africa and Asia Pacific. During 2021, IFS acquired Axios Systems, engaged in the service management space and strengthens IFS' IT service management and IT operations management capabilities; and acquired Customerville, a feedback platform that listens across the entire customer journey, blending technology, design and behavioral science to emulate how people share and respond to feedback.

FINANCIAL DATA: Note: Data for latest year may not have been available at press time.

In U.S. $	2021	2020	2019	2018	2017	2016
Revenue	747,821,170	880,312,000	668,000,000	585,964,000	513,133,000	401,379,000
R&D Expense						
Operating Income						
Operating Margin %						
SGA Expense						
Net Income			154,000,000	-27,373,200	-1,216,820	30,799,200
Operating Cash Flow						
Capital Expenditure						
EBITDA						
Return on Assets %						
Return on Equity %						
Debt to Equity						

CONTACT INFORMATION:

Phone: 46-13-460-3600   Fax: 46-13-460-40-01
Toll-Free: 888-437-4968
Address: Teknikringen 5, (Box 1545), Linkoping, 581 15 Sweden

STOCK TICKER/OTHER:

Stock Ticker: Private
Employees: 4,500
Parent Company:

Exchange:
Fiscal Year Ends: 12/31

SALARIES/BONUSES:

Top Exec. Salary: $ Bonus: $
Second Exec. Salary: $ Bonus: $

OTHER THOUGHTS:

Estimated Female Officers or Directors: 3
Hot Spot for Advancement for Women/Minorities: Y

Sales, profits and employees may be estimates. Financial information, benefits and other data can change quickly and may vary from those stated here.

Insurify Inc

insurify.com

NAIC Code: 524210

TYPES OF BUSINESS:

Insurance Agencies and Brokerages
Insurance Comparison Platform
Financial Technology
Insurance Quotes
Online Insurance Application
Online Insurance Payments
Online Insurance Management

BRANDS/DIVISIONS/AFFILIATES:

GROWTH PLANS/SPECIAL FEATURES:

Insurify, Inc. is a financial technology company that has developed and operates a virtual insurance platform offering auto, home and life insurance products. Users can compare quotes from a single source, obtain personalized quotes in five minutes or less, and purchase insurance online, mobile app or over the phone. Everything for insurance coverage can be accomplished online or through a call with an agent. More than 300 insurance companies offer insurance products through the Insurify platform, including Farmers, Nationwide, Travelers and Liberty Mutual. Insurify also provides access to exclusive rates and special discounts to its customers. The online platform offers information such as the cheapest insurance available, the best/recommended insurance available, the average cost of insurance and insurance information per U.S. state. Insurify is officially licensed and operates in all 50 states. Purchased insurance products can also be managed through Insurify. Investors of the firm include Viola, Motive Partners, Nationwide, MassMutual Ventures, Hearst Ventures, and MTech Capital.

CONTACTS: Note: Officers with more than one job title may be intentionally listed here more than once.

Snejina Zacharia, CEO

FINANCIAL DATA: Note: Data for latest year may not have been available at press time.

In U.S. $	2021	2020	2019	2018	2017	2016
Revenue						
R&D Expense						
Operating Income						
Operating Margin %						
SGA Expense						
Net Income						
Operating Cash Flow						
Capital Expenditure						
EBITDA						
Return on Assets %						
Return on Equity %						
Debt to Equity						

CONTACT INFORMATION:

Phone: 617 285-4467   Fax:
Toll-Free: 866 373-0443
Address: 222 Third St., Ste. 1320, Cambridge, MA 02142 United States

STOCK TICKER/OTHER:

Stock Ticker: Private   Exchange:
Employees: 100   Fiscal Year Ends:
Parent Company:

SALARIES/BONUSES:

Top Exec. Salary: $ Bonus: $
Second Exec. Salary: $ Bonus: $

OTHER THOUGHTS:

Estimated Female Officers or Directors:
Hot Spot for Advancement for Women/Minorities:

Sales, profits and employees may be estimates. Financial information, benefits and other data can change quickly and may vary from those stated here.

Plunkett Research, Ltd.

Intuit Inc

www.intuit.com

NAIC Code: 511210Q

TYPES OF BUSINESS:

Computer Software-Financial Management
Business Accounting Software
Consumer Finance Software
Tax Preparation Software
Online Financial Services

GROWTH PLANS/SPECIAL FEATURES:

Intuit is a provider of small-business accounting software (QuickBooks), personal tax solutions (TurboTax), and professional tax offerings (Lacerte). Founded in the mid-1980s, Intuit controls the majority of U.S. market share for small-business accounting and DIY tax-filing software.

BRANDS/DIVISIONS/AFFILIATES:

Credit Karma
ProConnect
QuickBooks
TurboTax
Mint
Lacerte
ProFile
Rocket Science Group LLC (The)

CONTACTS: *Note: Officers with more than one job title may be intentionally listed here more than once.*

Sasan Goodarzi, CEO
Michelle Clatterbuck, CFO
Brad Smith, Chairman of the Board
Mark Flournoy, Chief Accounting Officer
Marianna Tessel, Chief Technology Officer
Lauren Hotz, Controller
Kerry McLean, Executive VP
J. Chriss, Executive VP
Gregory Johnson, Executive VP
Laura Fennell, Executive VP
Scott Cook, Founder

FINANCIAL DATA: *Note: Data for latest year may not have been available at press time.*

In U.S. $	2021	2020	2019	2018	2017	2016
Revenue	9,633,000,000	7,679,000,000	6,784,000,000	5,964,000,000	5,177,000,000	4,694,000,000
R&D Expense	1,678,000,000	1,392,000,000	1,233,000,000	1,186,000,000	998,000,000	881,000,000
Operating Income	2,500,000,000	2,176,000,000	1,854,000,000	1,497,000,000	1,395,000,000	1,242,000,000
Operating Margin %						
SGA Expense	3,626,000,000	2,727,000,000	2,524,000,000	2,298,000,000	1,973,000,000	1,807,000,000
Net Income	2,062,000,000	1,826,000,000	1,557,000,000	1,211,000,000	971,000,000	979,000,000
Operating Cash Flow	3,250,000,000	2,414,000,000	2,324,000,000	2,112,000,000	1,599,000,000	1,401,000,000
Capital Expenditure	125,000,000	137,000,000	155,000,000	124,000,000	230,000,000	522,000,000
EBITDA	2,948,000,000	2,430,000,000	2,121,000,000	1,776,000,000	1,634,000,000	1,476,000,000
Return on Assets %						
Return on Equity %						
Debt to Equity						

CONTACT INFORMATION:

Phone: 650 944-6000   Fax: 650 944-3060
Toll-Free: 800-446-8848
Address: 2700 Coast Ave., Mountain View, CA 94043 United States

STOCK TICKER/OTHER:

Stock Ticker: INTU   Exchange: NAS
Employees: 10,600   Fiscal Year Ends: 07/31
Parent Company:

SALARIES/BONUSES:

Top Exec. Salary: $1,000,000   Bonus: $
Second Exec. Salary: $700,000   Bonus: $

OTHER THOUGHTS:

Estimated Female Officers or Directors: 5
Hot Spot for Advancement for Women/Minorities: Y

Sales, profits and employees may be estimates. Financial information, benefits and other data can change quickly and may vary from those stated here.

Jack Henry & Associates Inc

NAIC Code: 511210Q

www.JackHenry.com

TYPES OF BUSINESS:

Software-Data Processing
Financial Services Software
Data Processing
Integrated Computer Systems
Bank
Credit Union
Corporation

BRANDS/DIVISIONS/AFFILIATES:

Jack Henry Banking
Symitar
ProfitStars

GROWTH PLANS/SPECIAL FEATURES:

Jack Henry is a leading provider of core processing and complementary services, such as electronic funds transfer, payment processing, and loan processing for U.S. banks and credit unions, with a focus on small and midsize banks. Jack Henry serves about 1,000 banks and 800 credit unions.

CONTACTS: Note: Officers with more than one job title may be intentionally listed here more than once.

David Foss, CEO
Kevin Williams, CFO
Teddy Bilke, Chief Technology Officer
Gregory Adelson, COO
Matthew Flanigan, Director
Craig Morgan, General Counsel
Stacey Zengel, President, Divisional

FINANCIAL DATA: Note: Data for latest year may not have been available at press time.

In U.S. $	2021	2020	2019	2018	2017	2016
Revenue	1,758,225,000	1,697,067,000	1,552,691,000	1,536,603,000	1,431,117,000	1,354,646,000
R&D Expense	109,047,000	109,988,000	96,378,000	90,340,000	84,753,000	81,234,000
Operating Income	398,719,000	380,627,000	347,285,000	390,475,000	364,432,000	342,168,000
Operating Margin %						
SGA Expense	187,060,000	197,988,000	185,998,000	182,146,000	162,898,000	157,593,000
Net Income	311,469,000	296,668,000	271,885,000	376,660,000	245,793,000	248,867,000
Operating Cash Flow	462,129,000	510,532,000	431,128,000	412,142,000	357,322,000	365,116,000
Capital Expenditure	157,837,000	177,510,000	170,781,000	149,920,000	148,186,000	164,562,000
EBITDA	574,617,000	553,569,000	508,794,000	544,930,000	507,736,000	491,614,000
Return on Assets %						
Return on Equity %						
Debt to Equity						

CONTACT INFORMATION:

Phone: 417 235-6652   Fax:
Toll-Free: 800-299-4222
Address: 663 W. Highway 60, Monett, MO 65708 United States

STOCK TICKER/OTHER:

Stock Ticker: JKHY   Exchange: NAS
Employees: 6,717   Fiscal Year Ends: 06/30
Parent Company:

SALARIES/BONUSES:

Top Exec. Salary: $840,000   Bonus: $
Second Exec. Salary: $500,030   Bonus: $

OTHER THOUGHTS:

Estimated Female Officers or Directors: 3
Hot Spot for Advancement for Women/Minorities: Y

Sales, profits and employees may be estimates. Financial information, benefits and other data can change quickly and may vary from those stated here.

JPMorgan Chase & Co Inc

www.jpmorganchase.com

NAIC Code: 522110

TYPES OF BUSINESS:

Commercial Banks (Banking)
Mortgages
Investment Banking
Stock Brokerage
Credit Cards
Business Finance
Mutual Funds
Annuities

BRANDS/DIVISIONS/AFFILIATES:

JPMorgan Chase Bank NA
JP Morgan Securities LLC
MP Morgan Securities plc

GROWTH PLANS/SPECIAL FEATURES:

JPMorgan Chase is one of the largest and most complex financial institutions in the United States, with more than $3 trillion in assets. It is organized into four major segments-- consumer and community banking, corporate and investment banking, commercial banking, and asset and wealth management. JPMorgan operates, and is subject to regulation, in multiple countries.

JPMorgan Chase offers its employees comprehensive benefits, retirement options and assistance programs.

CONTACTS: *Note: Officers with more than one job title may be intentionally listed here more than once.*

Marianne Lake, CEO, Divisional
Jeremy Barnum, Other Corporate Officer
Mary Erdoes, CEO, Divisional
Douglas Petno, CEO, Divisional
Daniel Pinto, CEO, Subsidiary
James Dimon, CEO
Jennifer Piepszak, CFO
Nicole Giles, CFO, Divisional
Elena Korablina, Chief Accounting Officer
Lori Beer, Chief Information Officer
Ashley Bacon, Chief Risk Officer
Gordon Smith, Co- President
Stacey Friedman, General Counsel
Peter Scher, Other Corporate Officer
Robin Leopold, Other Corporate Officer

FINANCIAL DATA: *Note: Data for latest year may not have been available at press time.*

In U.S. $	2021	2020	2019	2018	2017	2016
Revenue		119,475,000,000	115,627,000,000	109,029,000,000	98,979,000,000	95,668,000,000
R&D Expense						
Operating Income						
Operating Margin %						
SGA Expense		37,464,000,000	37,734,000,000	36,407,000,000	33,909,000,000	32,876,000,000
Net Income		29,131,000,000	36,431,000,000	32,474,000,000	24,441,000,000	24,733,000,000
Operating Cash Flow		-79,910,000,000	6,046,000,000	14,187,000,000	-2,501,000,000	20,196,000,000
Capital Expenditure						
EBITDA						
Return on Assets %						
Return on Equity %						
Debt to Equity						

CONTACT INFORMATION:

Phone: 212 270-6000   Fax: 212 270-1648
Toll-Free: 877-242-7372
Address: 383 Madison Ave., New York, NY 10179 United States

STOCK TICKER/OTHER:

Stock Ticker: JPM   Exchange: NYS
Employees: 271,025   Fiscal Year Ends: 12/31
Parent Company:

SALARIES/BONUSES:

Top Exec. Salary: $750,000   Bonus: $8,700,000
Second Exec. Salary: Bonus: $8,100,000
$750,000

OTHER THOUGHTS:

Estimated Female Officers or Directors: 3
Hot Spot for Advancement for Women/Minorities: Y

Sales, profits and employees may be estimates. Financial information, benefits and other data can change quickly and may vary from those stated here.

Kabbage Inc

NAIC Code: 511210Q

www.kabbage.com

TYPES OF BUSINESS:
Computer Software: Accounting, Banking & Financial
Business Account Insights
Business Payment Solutions
Cash Flow Solutions
Checking Account

BRANDS/DIVISIONS/AFFILIATES:
American Express Company

CONTACTS:
Note: Officers with more than one job title may be intentionally listed here more than once.
Rob Frohwein, CEO

GROWTH PLANS/SPECIAL FEATURES:
Kabbage, Inc. is an American Express company that connects small businesses with account insights and cash flow solutions, such as payment processing and access to capital. Through its proprietary technologies, Kabbage Insights looks at the business' income history and expense trends via connected accounts, and provides a percentage likelihood of the balance falling below the projected target balance. The forecast is based on reviewing historic behavior and predicting the balance one month into the future. With the chart, businesses can select and view specific accounts or all accounts at once. Kabbage Payments enables the acceptance of credit and debit cards through invoices or a custom pay link. The payment is deposited into the businesses' bank account the following banking day. To set up an account, Kabbage asks for basic information about the business owner and the business, the bank account where deposits are received is connected and a sub-merchant agreement is then reviewed, electronically signed and accepted. Businesses can then start customizing invoices while Kabbage handles the back-end processes of the account. Card payments can be accepted by sending emailed invoices, via mobile point of sale or through a custom pay link (for any amount less than $10,000 per transaction). When the business' customer clicks the link, they can instantly make card payments with major cards such as MasterCard, Visa, Discover and American Express. Transactions are processed by 5pm eastern time and deposited in the business' bank account within two banking days. The deposit amount is the total of all payments processed minus Kabbage fees and the amount of any returns or chargebacks. During 2021, Kabbage launched Kabbage Checking, an account designed for U.S. small businesses, offering the flexibility of mobile banking, from in-app account management to mobile check deposits, as well as in-person cash deposits and free ATM access.

FINANCIAL DATA:
Note: Data for latest year may not have been available at press time.

In U.S. $	2021	2020	2019	2018	2017	2016
Revenue						
R&D Expense						
Operating Income						
Operating Margin %						
SGA Expense						
Net Income						
Operating Cash Flow						
Capital Expenditure						
EBITDA						
Return on Assets %						
Return on Equity %						
Debt to Equity						

CONTACT INFORMATION:
Phone: 678 580-2689   Fax:
Toll-Free: 888 986-8163
Address: 925B Peachtree St. NE, Ste. 1688, Atlanta, GA 30309 United States

STOCK TICKER/OTHER:
Stock Ticker: Subsidiary   Exchange:
Employees: Fiscal Year Ends: 12/31
Parent Company: American Express Company

SALARIES/BONUSES:
Top Exec. Salary: $ Bonus: $
Second Exec. Salary: $ Bonus: $

OTHER THOUGHTS:
Estimated Female Officers or Directors:
Hot Spot for Advancement for Women/Minorities:

Sales, profits and employees may be estimates. Financial information, benefits and other data can change quickly and may vary from those stated here.

KakaoPay Corp

www.kakaopay.com

NAIC Code: 522320

TYPES OF BUSINESS:
Credit Card Processing, Online Payment Processing, EFT, ACH and Clearinghouses
Financial Technology
Digital Payments Platform
Money Management Solutions
Document Management Solutions
Investment Funds Management
Loan and Insurance Comparison Services
Bank Rate and Fees Comparison Services

BRANDS/DIVISIONS/AFFILIATES:
kakaopay

CONTACTS: Note: Officers with more than one job title may be intentionally listed here more than once.
Won-geun Shin, CEO

GROWTH PLANS/SPECIAL FEATURES:
KakaoPay Corp. is a Korea-based financial technology company that has developed and operates the digital payments and money management platform, kakaopay. Payment and money related services and solutions provided through the platform include money transfer, payments, membership/club store payments (without the need for need for membership cards or coupons), personal finance management (managing all bank/finance assets in one place), document management, bill payment notification/bill management and investment funds management. Financial services such as viewing and comparing credit cards to obtain the best benefits, and choosing a bank and comparing account interest-bearing rates as well as fees. Kakaopy also provides loan comparison services, including credit rating check without affecting score, interest rate comparison, personal borrowing limit across multiple financial institutions and more. A wide range of insurance services and products are offered by Kakaopay, including insurance for hobbies and pets. Insurance applications can be filled out online, and insurance premiums are accessible through the platform.

FINANCIAL DATA: Note: Data for latest year may not have been available at press time.

In U.S. $	2021	2020	2019	2018	2017	2016
Revenue	5,154,801,960	3,818,970,780	2,651,317,158	2,163,379,984	1,846,903,817	1,213,694,445
R&D Expense						
Operating Income						
Operating Margin %						
SGA Expense						
Net Income	1,382,768,520	159,269,247	-295,283,011	14,262,887	117,139,147	54,255,650
Operating Cash Flow						
Capital Expenditure						
EBITDA						
Return on Assets %						
Return on Equity %						
Debt to Equity						

CONTACT INFORMATION:
Phone: 82 216447405 Fax:
Toll-Free:
Address: 152, Pangyoyeok-ro Bundang-gu, Seongnam-si, 13529 South Korea

STOCK TICKER/OTHER:
Stock Ticker: 377300 Exchange: Seoul
Employees: Fiscal Year Ends: 12/31
Parent Company:

SALARIES/BONUSES:
Top Exec. Salary: $ Bonus: $
Second Exec. Salary: $ Bonus: $

OTHER THOUGHTS:
Estimated Female Officers or Directors:
Hot Spot for Advancement for Women/Minorities:

Sales, profits and employees may be estimates. Financial information, benefits and other data can change quickly and may vary from those stated here.

Katipult Technology Corp

NAIC Code: 511210Q

www.katipult.com

TYPES OF BUSINESS:
Computer Software: Accounting, Banking & Financial

BRANDS/DIVISIONS/AFFILIATES:

GROWTH PLANS/SPECIAL FEATURES:

Katipult Technology Corp is engaged in providing enterprise software and software-related services. It operates as a financial technology company offering a cloud-based software infrastructure that allows firms to design, set up and operate an investment platform. The platform includes modules for various user types, including investors, issuers, administrators, and auditors, among others. It generates subscription revenue and integration revenue. Subscription revenue consists primarily of monthly recurring SaaS revenue earned by providing access to the Platform whereas Integration revenue consists of revenue arising from the provision of regulatory consulting, marketing consulting, and customization services to clients. It has a business presence in Canada, the U.K., and other countries.

CONTACTS:
Note: Officers with more than one job title may be intentionally listed here more than once.

Gord Breese, CEO
Karim Teja, CFO
Ben Cadieux, Chief Technology Officer
Brock Murray, Director
Pheak Meas, Director
Karan Khiani, Vice President, Divisional
Stephen Donovan, Vice President, Divisional
James Church, Vice President, Divisional

FINANCIAL DATA:
Note: Data for latest year may not have been available at press time.

In U.S. $	2021	2020	2019	2018	2017	2016
Revenue		1,035,484	1,268,645	961,689	892,186	626,050
R&D Expense		617,051	641,388	716,753		
Operating Income		-1,166,588	-956,194	-1,466,478	-386,839	137,447
Operating Margin %						
SGA Expense		1,357,356	1,482,179	1,459,413	981,814	378,565
Net Income		-1,473,544	-240,226	-1,627,414	-882,683	110,263
Operating Cash Flow		-796,828	-544,041	-1,102,999	-397,347	73,926
Capital Expenditure			785	2,355		2,810
EBITDA		-1,189,355	-26,692	-1,528,497	-870,572	138,355
Return on Assets %						
Return on Equity %						
Debt to Equity						

CONTACT INFORMATION:
Phone: 403 457-8008   Fax:
Toll-Free:
Address: 777 Hornby Street, Vancouver, BC V6Z 1S4 Canada

STOCK TICKER/OTHER:
Stock Ticker: FUND
Employees: 37
Parent Company:

Exchange: TSX
Fiscal Year Ends: 12/31

SALARIES/BONUSES:
Top Exec. Salary: $ Bonus: $
Second Exec. Salary: $ Bonus: $

OTHER THOUGHTS:
Estimated Female Officers or Directors:
Hot Spot for Advancement for Women/Minorities:

Sales, profits and employees may be estimates. Financial information, benefits and other data can change quickly and may vary from those stated here.

KE Holdings Inc

investors.ke.com

NAIC Code: 531210

TYPES OF BUSINESS:

Real Estate Brokers and Agents, Including Property Management,
RealtorsÂ® and Leasing Agents
Real Estate Platform

BRANDS/DIVISIONS/AFFILIATES:

GROWTH PLANS/SPECIAL FEATURES:

KE Holdings Inc is engaged in operating an integrated online and offline platform for housing transactions and services in the People's Republic of China. The company through its Beike platform reinvents how service providers and housing customers efficiently navigate and consummate housing transactions, ranging from existing and new home sales, home rentals, to home renovation, real estate financial solutions, and other services. It operates in three operating segments Existing home transaction services; New home transaction services; and Emerging and other services. The company generates maximum revenue from New home transaction services segment.

CONTACTS: *Note: Officers with more than one job title may be intentionally listed here more than once.*

Yongdong Peng, CEO
Wangang Xu, COO
Tao Xu, CFO
Yongdong Peng, Chmn.

FINANCIAL DATA: *Note: Data for latest year may not have been available at press time.*

In U.S. $	2021	2020	2019	2018	2017	2016
Revenue		11,035,070,000	7,204,463,000	4,485,126,000	3,993,377,000	
R&D Expense		387,961,600	245,992,500	105,044,900	39,424,140	
Operating Income		619,087,800	-225,572,100	-138,171,700	-88,570,990	
Operating Margin %						
SGA Expense		1,769,858,000	1,797,781,000	1,161,274,000	826,702,000	
Net Income		434,882,100	-341,873,500	-73,246,280	-89,937,370	
Operating Cash Flow		1,465,782,000	17,633,630	503,647,500	-1,010,838,000	
Capital Expenditure		138,876,100	110,068,600	84,993,420	90,055,580	
EBITDA		900,180,700	-8,665,570	52,723,650	112,205,400	
Return on Assets %						
Return on Equity %						
Debt to Equity						

CONTACT INFORMATION:

Phone: 86 1058104689   Fax:
Toll-Free:
Address: No. 2 Chuangye Road, Beijing, 100086 China

STOCK TICKER/OTHER:

Stock Ticker: BEKE
Employees:
Parent Company:

Exchange: NYS
Fiscal Year Ends: 12/31

SALARIES/BONUSES:

Top Exec. Salary: $ Bonus: $
Second Exec. Salary: $ Bonus: $

OTHER THOUGHTS:

Estimated Female Officers or Directors:
Hot Spot for Advancement for Women/Minorities:

Sales, profits and employees may be estimates. Financial information, benefits and other data can change quickly and may vary from those stated here.

Klarna Bank AB

NAIC Code: 522291

klarna.com

TYPES OF BUSINESS:
Consumer Lending
Online Payment Solutions
Ecommerce

BRANDS/DIVISIONS/AFFILIATES:
Klarna Inc
Klarna

CONTACTS: *Note: Officers with more than one job title may be intentionally listed here more than once.*
Sebastian Siemiatkowski, CEO
Linda S. Hoglund, COO
Niclas Neglen, CFO
David Sandstrom, CMO
Luke Griffiths, Chief Commercial Officer
Koen Koppen, CTO
David Fock, Chief Product Officer

GROWTH PLANS/SPECIAL FEATURES:
Klarna Bank AB is a Swedish banking company under the supervision of the Swedish Financial Supervisory Authority. The firm operates Klarna, a Swedish ePayment platform that provides online payment services to ecommerce merchants. Klarna has a customer base of more than 90 million and works with some 250,000 merchants across 17 countries. The firm offers direct payments, pay after delivery options and installment plans in a smooth, single-click purchase experience that lets consumers pay when and how they want. The purpose at Klarna is to simplify buying by making the process simple and safe for consumers and merchants. Klarna's investors include Sequoia Capital, Silver Lake, Bestseller Group, Draagoneer, Permira, Visa, Ant Group and Atomico. Subsidiary Klarna, Inc. is based in the U.S., with offices in Ohio and New York. In late-2021, Klarna Bank agreed to acquire PriceRunner, which offers product discovery, reviews and price comparison data.

Klarna Bank offers its employees a health subsidy, pension and retirement contributions, and on-the-job training.

FINANCIAL DATA: *Note: Data for latest year may not have been available at press time.*

In U.S. $	2021	2020	2019	2018	2017	2016
Revenue	1,520,008,579	1,220,800,000	766,759,000	606,525,000	550,718,000	438,864,250
R&D Expense						
Operating Income						
Operating Margin %						
SGA Expense						
Net Income	-783,792,507	-167,958,000	-96,704,700	11,708,600	42,054,900	13,981,638
Operating Cash Flow						
Capital Expenditure						
EBITDA						
Return on Assets %						
Return on Equity %						
Debt to Equity						

CONTACT INFORMATION:
Phone: 46-8-120-120-10   Fax:
Toll-Free:
Address: Sveavagen 46, Stockholm, 111 34 Sweden

STOCK TICKER/OTHER:
Stock Ticker: Private
Employees: 4,789
Parent Company:

Exchange:
Fiscal Year Ends: 12/31

SALARIES/BONUSES:
Top Exec. Salary: $ Bonus: $
Second Exec. Salary: $ Bonus: $

OTHER THOUGHTS:
Estimated Female Officers or Directors: 1
Hot Spot for Advancement for Women/Minorities:

Sales, profits and employees may be estimates. Financial information, benefits and other data can change quickly and may vary from those stated here.

Kraken (Payward Inc)

www.kraken.com

NAIC Code: 523130

TYPES OF BUSINESS:
Commodity Contracts Dealing
Cryptocurrencies Exchange
Financial Technology

BRANDS/DIVISIONS/AFFILIATES:

CONTACTS: Note: Officers with more than one job title may be intentionally listed here more than once.
Jesse Powell, CEO

GROWTH PLANS/SPECIAL FEATURES:
Payward, Inc. is a financial technology company that has developed and operates the cryptocurrency exchange platform called Kraken. Established in 2011, Kraken is one of the largest and oldest Bitcoin exchanges in the world based on euro volume and liquidity. Globally, Kraken's client base trades more than 90 digital assets and seven different fiat currencies, including GBP, EUR, USD, CAD, JPY, CHF and AUD. Kraken markets can be monitored and traded through the Kraken iOS and Android apps, and through the Cryptowatch iOS, Android and desktop apps. Features offered by Kraken span security, funding options, liquidity, margin trading, indices, futures, over-the-counter (OTC), account management, cryptowatch, a wide range of fees across structured products and staking. The platform is trusted by over 8.5 million traders and institutions, and offers professional, 24/7 online support. Kraken's platform offers a wide range of information to learn about buying cryptocurrency, including documents, blogs, videos and podcasts. The firm is backed by investors including Tribe Capital, SkyBridge, Hummingbird Ventures, Blockchain Capital, Digital currency Group, among others.

Ninety-percent of Payward employees work remotely.

FINANCIAL DATA: Note: Data for latest year may not have been available at press time.

In U.S. $	2021	2020	2019	2018	2017	2016
Revenue						
R&D Expense						
Operating Income						
Operating Margin %						
SGA Expense						
Net Income						
Operating Cash Flow						
Capital Expenditure						
EBITDA						
Return on Assets %						
Return on Equity %						
Debt to Equity						

CONTACT INFORMATION:
Phone: 916 267-4413   Fax:
Toll-Free: 855 777-7603
Address: 237 Kearny St., Ste. 102, San Francisco, CA 94108 United States

STOCK TICKER/OTHER:
Stock Ticker: Private
Employees:
Parent Company:

Exchange:
Fiscal Year Ends:

SALARIES/BONUSES:
Top Exec. Salary: $ Bonus: $
Second Exec. Salary: $ Bonus: $

OTHER THOUGHTS:
Estimated Female Officers or Directors:
Hot Spot for Advancement for Women/Minorities:

Sales, profits and employees may be estimates. Financial information, benefits and other data can change quickly and may vary from those stated here.

KuCoin (Mek Global Limited)

www.kucoin.com

NAIC Code: 523130

TYPES OF BUSINESS:

Digital Currency Exchange
Financial Technology
Cryptocurrency Exchange
Spot Trading Services
Margin Trading Services
Future Trading
Software Development Kits
Crypto Investment Projects

BRANDS/DIVISIONS/AFFILIATES:

KuCoin Labs
KuCoin Ventures

CONTACTS: *Note: Officers with more than one job title may be intentionally listed here more than once.*

Johnny Lyu, CEO

GROWTH PLANS/SPECIAL FEATURES:

Mek Global Limited is a financial technology company that has developed and operates a global cryptocurrency exchange called KuCoin. The firm's purpose for KuCoin was to make access, education and the purchase and trading of crypto available to everyone in the world. Today, KuCoin has more than 10 million registered users. The company leverages cutting-edge technologies to create services for improving accessibility to the blockchain industry. Products offered by KuCoin include spot trading, margin trading, futures trading, crypto lending, trading bots and asset management. KuCoin's website offers tools for beginners, as well as application programming interface (API) documentation, software development kids (SDK) and more for developers. KuCoin Labs is an investment and incubation program launched in 2018, bringing together crypto experts for market research, analysis, investment and incubation in the cryptocurrency industry. KuCoin Labs has diversified investments into early-stage projects. KuCoin Ventures supports crypto and Web 3.0 builders both financially and strategically via deep insights and global resources.

FINANCIAL DATA: *Note: Data for latest year may not have been available at press time.*

In U.S. $	2021	2020	2019	2018	2017	2016
Revenue						
R&D Expense						
Operating Income						
Operating Margin %						
SGA Expense						
Net Income						
Operating Cash Flow						
Capital Expenditure						
EBITDA						
Return on Assets %						
Return on Equity %						
Debt to Equity						

CONTACT INFORMATION:

Phone: Fax:
Toll-Free:
Address: 20 Science Park Rd., Singapore, 117674 Singapore

STOCK TICKER/OTHER:

Stock Ticker: Private   Exchange:
Employees: Fiscal Year Ends:
Parent Company:

SALARIES/BONUSES:

Top Exec. Salary: $ Bonus: $
Second Exec. Salary: $ Bonus: $

OTHER THOUGHTS:

Estimated Female Officers or Directors:
Hot Spot for Advancement for Women/Minorities:

Sales, profits and employees may be estimates. Financial information, benefits and other data can change quickly and may vary from those stated here.

Plunkett Research, Ltd.

Lemonade Inc
www.lemonade.com

NAIC Code: 524126

TYPES OF BUSINESS:
Direct Property and Casualty Insurance Carriers
Renters and Home Insurance
Property and Casualty Insurance
Term Life Insurance
Pet Health Insurance
Artificial Intelligence
Insurance App
Online Signup

BRANDS/DIVISIONS/AFFILIATES:
Lemonade App
Maya

GROWTH PLANS/SPECIAL FEATURES:
Lemonade Inc operates in the insurance industry. The company offers digital and artificial intelligence based platform for various insurances and for settling claims and paying premiums. The platform ensures transparency in issuing policies and settling disputes.

CONTACTS: *Note: Officers with more than one job title may be intentionally listed here more than once.*
Timothy Bixby, CFO
Daniel Schreiber, Chairman of the Board
Shai Wininger, Co-CEO
Adina Eckstein, COO
John Peters, Other Executive Officer
Jorge Espinel, Other Executive Officer

FINANCIAL DATA: *Note: Data for latest year may not have been available at press time.*

In U.S. $	2021	2020	2019	2018	2017	2016
Revenue		94,400,000	67,300,000	22,500,000		
R&D Expense						
Operating Income						
Operating Margin %						
SGA Expense		146,100,000	119,800,000	55,700,000		
Net Income		-122,300,000	-108,500,000	-52,900,000		
Operating Cash Flow		-91,700,000	-78,100,000	-40,800,000		
Capital Expenditure		4,400,000	3,300,000	700,000		
EBITDA						
Return on Assets %						
Return on Equity %						
Debt to Equity						

CONTACT INFORMATION:
Phone: 917 608-9499　　Fax:
Toll-Free: 844 733-8666
Address: 5 Crosby St., Fl. 3, New York, NY 10013 United States

STOCK TICKER/OTHER:
Stock Ticker: LMND　　　Exchange: NYS
Employees: 1,119　　　　Fiscal Year Ends: 12/31
Parent Company:

SALARIES/BONUSES:
Top Exec. Salary: $410,000　　Bonus: $
Second Exec. Salary: $300,000　　Bonus: $

OTHER THOUGHTS:
Estimated Female Officers or Directors:
Hot Spot for Advancement for Women/Minorities:

Sales, profits and employees may be estimates. Financial information, benefits and other data can change quickly and may vary from those stated here.

LendingClub Corporation

NAIC Code: 522291

www.lendingclub.com

TYPES OF BUSINESS:
Consumer Lending
Loans

BRANDS/DIVISIONS/AFFILIATES:
LendingClub Bank NA
Radius Bancorp Inc

GROWTH PLANS/SPECIAL FEATURES:
LendingClub Corp is a company engaged in operating an online lending marketplace platform that connects borrowers and investors for the provision of the loan facility. It offers investors access to an asset class that has generally been closed to many investors and only available on a limited basis to institutional investors. The company through the platform offer loan products such as personal, education and patient finance, small business and auto to interested investors. It generates a majority of the revenue from the transaction fees received from the platform's role in accepting and decisioning applications on behalf of the bank partners to enable loan originations.

LendingClub offers its employees medical and dental insurance and a 401(k).

CONTACTS: Note: Officers with more than one job title may be intentionally listed here more than once.
Scott Sanborn, CEO
Thomas Casey, CFO
John Morris, Chairman of the Board
Fergal Stack, Chief Accounting Officer
Brandon Pace, Chief Administrative Officer
Annie Armstrong, Chief Risk Officer
Bahman Koohestani, Chief Technology Officer
Valerie Kay, Other Executive Officer
Ronnie Momen, Other Executive Officer

FINANCIAL DATA: Note: Data for latest year may not have been available at press time.

In U.S. $	2021	2020	2019	2018	2017	2016
Revenue		243,509,000	655,204,000	595,436,000	487,649,000	426,052,000
R&D Expense						
Operating Income						
Operating Margin %						
SGA Expense		292,076,000	517,715,000	497,158,000	421,548,000	423,842,000
Net Income		-187,538,000	-30,745,000	-128,308,000	-153,835,000	-145,969,000
Operating Cash Flow		418,031,000	-270,644,000	-638,950,000	-590,814,000	545,000
Capital Expenditure		31,147,000	50,668,000	52,976,000	44,615,000	51,842,000
EBITDA						
Return on Assets %						
Return on Equity %						
Debt to Equity						

CONTACT INFORMATION:
Phone: 415-632-5600   Fax: 415-632-5611
Toll-Free: 888-376-6642
Address: 595 Market St., Ste. 200, San Francisco, CA 94105 United States

STOCK TICKER/OTHER:
Stock Ticker: LC   Exchange: NYS
Employees: 1,030   Fiscal Year Ends: 12/31
Parent Company:

SALARIES/BONUSES:
Top Exec. Salary: $354,167   Bonus: $100,000
Second Exec. Salary: $400,000   Bonus: $

OTHER THOUGHTS:
Estimated Female Officers or Directors: 3
Hot Spot for Advancement for Women/Minorities: Y

Sales, profits and employees may be estimates. Financial information, benefits and other data can change quickly and may vary from those stated here.

Plunkett Research, Ltd.

LexisNexis

www.lexisnexis.com

NAIC Code: 561450

TYPES OF BUSINESS:
Credit Bureaus
Data Mining Platforms
Legal Information
Business Information
Artificial Intelligence
Machine Learning
Risk Management Solutions
Risk Prediction Technologies

BRANDS/DIVISIONS/AFFILIATES:
RELX PLC
LexisNexis Legal and Professional
LexisNexis Risk Solutions

CONTACTS: *Note: Officers with more than one job title may be intentionally listed here more than once.*
Mike Walsh, CEO-Legal & Professional
Mark Kelsey, CEO-Risk

GROWTH PLANS/SPECIAL FEATURES:

LexisNexis sells data mining platforms via online portals to help uncover the information that commercial organizations, agencies and non-profits need about individuals, businesses and assets. The company operates through two divisions: legal and professional, and risk solutions. The LexisNexis Legal and Professional division combines legal and business information with analytics and technology to advance the way its customers work and to strengthen the rule of law. It delivers tools to customers by applying machine learning, natural language processing, visualization and artificial intelligence to its global legal database. The information is used by customers to increase productivity, improve decision-making and outcomes, and generate revenue. Solutions are provided for law firms, corporate legal teams, corporate teams, government organizations, news and media organizations and academic institutions. The LexisNexis Risk Solutions division provides information to help customers across industry and government assets predict and manage risk. This division's portfolio of brands span multiple industries and provides innovative technologies, information-based analytics, decision tools and data services. Risk solutions are offered to customers in more than 170 countries, and over 270 million transactions are processed globally every hour. Industries served include collection and recovery entities, financial services, government, healthcare, insurance, law enforcement, public safety, corporations and non-profits. LexisNexis itself is owned by RELX PLC, based in London, U.K.

LexisNexis offers its employees wellness programs, money management resources and other benefits.

FINANCIAL DATA: *Note: Data for latest year may not have been available at press time.*

In U.S. $	2021	2020	2019	2018	2017	2016
Revenue	2,200,000,000	3,000,000,000	2,700,000,000	2,500,000,000		
R&D Expense						
Operating Income						
Operating Margin %						
SGA Expense						
Net Income						
Operating Cash Flow						
Capital Expenditure						
EBITDA						
Return on Assets %						
Return on Equity %						
Debt to Equity						

CONTACT INFORMATION:
Phone: 800-543-6862   Fax:
Toll-Free: 866-237-2133
Address: 230 Park Ave., Ste. 7, New York, NY 10169 United States

STOCK TICKER/OTHER:
Stock Ticker: Subsidiary   Exchange:
Employees: 9,000   Fiscal Year Ends: 12/31
Parent Company: RELX PLC

SALARIES/BONUSES:
Top Exec. Salary: $ Bonus: $
Second Exec. Salary: $ Bonus: $

OTHER THOUGHTS:
Estimated Female Officers or Directors:
Hot Spot for Advancement for Women/Minorities:

Sales, profits and employees may be estimates. Financial information, benefits and other data can change quickly and may vary from those stated here.

LoanSnap Inc

www.goloansnap.com

NAIC Code: 522292

TYPES OF BUSINESS:
Mortgage Lending, Underwriting and Investment
Financial Technology
Digital Lending Services
Money Management Solutions
Refinancing
Home Equity Lines of Credit
Mortgage Lending

BRANDS/DIVISIONS/AFFILIATES:

GROWTH PLANS/SPECIAL FEATURES:

LoanSnap, Inc. is a financial technology company that has developed and operates a digital lending platform to help individuals save money. How LoanSnap works: a few personal finance questions need to be answered, the platform displays the individual's current money situation and provides refinance, home equity line of credit (HELOC) and mortgage options to help them save money overall. Individuals who choose to consolidate expenses through a new loan, LoanSnap guides and follows up with them via updates along the way. Some people obtain cash-out loans, therefore unlocking the value of the home to pay down expenses. LoanSnap is an Equal Housing Lender. The firm's lending process is fast and secure due to its smart loan technology that utilizes artificial intelligence to analyze a consumer's money situation as well as thousands of loans to present users with options, quickly. LoanSnap is licensed in many states throughout the U.S.

CONTACTS: Note: Officers with more than one job title may be intentionally listed here more than once.
Karl Jacob, CEO

FINANCIAL DATA: Note: Data for latest year may not have been available at press time.

In U.S. $	2021	2020	2019	2018	2017	2016
Revenue						
R&D Expense						
Operating Income						
Operating Margin %						
SGA Expense						
Net Income						
Operating Cash Flow						
Capital Expenditure						
EBITDA						
Return on Assets %						
Return on Equity %						
Debt to Equity						

CONTACT INFORMATION:
Phone: Fax:
Toll-Free: 888-680-5777
Address: 3070 Bristol St., Ste. 200, Costa Mesa, CA 92626 United States

STOCK TICKER/OTHER:
Stock Ticker: Private   Exchange:
Employees: Fiscal Year Ends:
Parent Company:

SALARIES/BONUSES:
Top Exec. Salary: $ Bonus: $
Second Exec. Salary: $ Bonus: $

OTHER THOUGHTS:
Estimated Female Officers or Directors:
Hot Spot for Advancement for Women/Minorities:

Sales, profits and employees may be estimates. Financial information, benefits and other data can change quickly and may vary from those stated here.

M&T Bank Corporation

www.mtb.com

NAIC Code: 522110

TYPES OF BUSINESS:
Banking
Mortgages
Insurance Services
Securities Brokerage
Leasing Services
Reinsurance
Investment Management
Cash Management

BRANDS/DIVISIONS/AFFILIATES:
Manufacturers & Traders Trust Company
M&T Bank
Wilmington Trust NA
M&T Insurance Agency Inc
M&T Realty Capital Corporation
M&T Securities Inc
Wilmington Trust Investment Advisors Inc
Wilmington Funds Management Corporation

CONTACTS: Note: Officers with more than one job title may be intentionally listed here more than once.
Rene Jones, CEO
Robert Brady, Director
Darren King, CFO
Michael Spychala, Chief Accounting Officer
Robert Bojdak, Chief Credit Officer
John D'Angelo, Chief Risk Officer
Michele Trolli, Chief Technology Officer
Richard Gold, COO
Kevin Pearson, Director
William Farrell, Executive VP
Michael Todaro, Executive VP

GROWTH PLANS/SPECIAL FEATURES:
M&T Bank is one of the largest regional banks in the United States, with branches in New York, Pennsylvania, West Virginia, Virginia, Maryland, Delaware, and New Jersey. The bank was founded to serve manufacturing and trading businesses around the Erie Canal.

M&T offers its employees health benefits, pension plans, retirement plans and employee assistance programs.

FINANCIAL DATA: Note: Data for latest year may not have been available at press time.

In U.S. $	2021	2020	2019	2018	2017	2016
Revenue		5,954,761,000	6,191,943,000	5,928,302,000	5,632,187,000	5,295,883,000
R&D Expense						
Operating Income						
Operating Margin %						
SGA Expense		2,066,399,000	2,035,804,000	1,906,500,000	1,821,803,000	1,815,782,000
Net Income		1,353,152,000	1,929,149,000	1,918,080,000	1,408,306,000	1,315,114,000
Operating Cash Flow		789,187,000	2,357,555,000	2,089,852,000	2,781,935,000	1,183,411,000
Capital Expenditure		172,289,000	178,049,000	97,676,000	78,966,000	107,693,000
EBITDA						
Return on Assets %						
Return on Equity %						
Debt to Equity						

CONTACT INFORMATION:
Phone: 716 842-5445   Fax: 716 842-5177
Toll-Free: 800-724-2440
Address: One M&T Plaza, Buffalo, NY 14203 United States

STOCK TICKER/OTHER:
Stock Ticker: MTB
Employees: 16,973
Parent Company:

Exchange: NYS
Fiscal Year Ends: 12/31

SALARIES/BONUSES:
Top Exec. Salary: $1,000,000   Bonus: $750,000
Second Exec. Salary: $765,000   Bonus: $598,000

OTHER THOUGHTS:
Estimated Female Officers or Directors: 11
Hot Spot for Advancement for Women/Minorities: Y

Sales, profits and employees may be estimates. Financial information, benefits and other data can change quickly and may vary from those stated here.

M1 Holdings Inc

NAIC Code: 523120

www.m1finance.com

TYPES OF BUSINESS:

Securities Brokerage
Online Trading Platform
Financial Technology
Investments
Banking
Rewards Credit Cards
Line of Credit Lending
Brokerage Services

BRANDS/DIVISIONS/AFFILIATES:

M1 Finance LLC
M1 Spend LLC
M1 Plus

CONTACTS: Note: Officers with more than one job title may be intentionally listed here more than once.

Brian Barnes, CEO

GROWTH PLANS/SPECIAL FEATURES:

M1 Holdings, Inc. is a financial technology company that offers a range of financial products and services through wholly-owned subsidiaries M1 Finance, LLC and M1 Spend, LLC. Core products and services are centered around investing, borrowing and spending, from a single digital platform. Users build and control their own investment portfolios for free, including retirement; have access to lines of credit based on their investments; manage cash through an integrated checking account; and receive up to 10% cash back when spending with select companies they've invested in. Brokerage products and services are offered by M1 Finance and are not Federal Deposit Insurance Corporation (FDIC) insured and not guaranteed by a bank. M1 Spend checking accounts and M1 Visa debit cards are furnished by Lincoln Savings Bank, which is a member FDIC. The company's rewards credit card is powered by Deserve, and issued by Celtic Bank, an FDIC member. In addition, M1 Plus is an annual membership that offers exclusive features and rewards to help users earn more, access more and receive more perks and discounts. M1 Plus products and services are offered through M1 Finance and M1 Spend, and include features such as lower rates, additional percentage earnings, custodial accounts and more.

M1 offers its employees comprehensive health and retirement benefits, stock options and paid time off.

FINANCIAL DATA: Note: Data for latest year may not have been available at press time.

In U.S. $	2021	2020	2019	2018	2017	2016
Revenue						
R&D Expense						
Operating Income						
Operating Margin %						
SGA Expense						
Net Income						
Operating Cash Flow						
Capital Expenditure						
EBITDA						
Return on Assets %						
Return on Equity %						
Debt to Equity						

CONTACT INFORMATION:

Phone: 312 600-6668   Fax:
Toll-Free:
Address: 200 N LaSalle St., Ste. 800, Chicago, IL 60601 United States

STOCK TICKER/OTHER:

Stock Ticker: Private   Exchange:
Employees: Fiscal Year Ends:
Parent Company:

SALARIES/BONUSES:

Top Exec. Salary: $ Bonus: $
Second Exec. Salary: $ Bonus: $

OTHER THOUGHTS:

Estimated Female Officers or Directors:
Hot Spot for Advancement for Women/Minorities:

Sales, profits and employees may be estimates. Financial information, benefits and other data can change quickly and may vary from those stated here.

Plunkett Research, Ltd.

MANTL (Fin Technologies Inc)

www.mantl.com

NAIC Code: 511210Q

TYPES OF BUSINESS:

Computer Software: Accounting, Banking & Financial
SaaS - Banking Software
Bank Account Onboarding
Financial Technology

BRANDS/DIVISIONS/AFFILIATES:

MANTL

GROWTH PLANS/SPECIAL FEATURES:

Fin Technologies, Inc. is a financial technology and software-as-a-service (SaaS) company that developed MANTL, a digital platform that opens consumer and business bank accounts. Primarily serving community and regional banks and credit unions, MANTL provides a seamless banking platform for the end-user while assisting bank staff on the back-end. MANTL works in-branch and online, enabling the opening of personal and business accounts in real-time, 24/7. MANTL offers no code, is configurable and underwriting compliant. The platform also integrates with other leading fintech platforms. Fin Technologies is privately held by investors such as Alphabet's CapitalG, Point72Ventures and D1 Capital Partners.

Fin Technologies offers its employees comprehensive health benefits, 401(k), professional development opportunities and other company programs and perks.

CONTACTS: Note: Officers with more than one job title may be intentionally listed here more than once.

Nathaniel Harley, CEO
Taina Biggs, Sr. Dir.-Communications
Lauren Slutsky, VP-People
Benjamin Conant, CTO

FINANCIAL DATA: Note: Data for latest year may not have been available at press time.

In U.S. $	2021	2020	2019	2018	2017	2016
Revenue						
R&D Expense						
Operating Income						
Operating Margin %						
SGA Expense						
Net Income						
Operating Cash Flow						
Capital Expenditure						
EBITDA						
Return on Assets %						
Return on Equity %						
Debt to Equity						

CONTACT INFORMATION:

Phone: 646-791-1757   Fax:
Toll-Free:
Address: 347 5th Ave., New York, NY 10016 United States

STOCK TICKER/OTHER:

Stock Ticker: Private   Exchange:
Employees: 112   Fiscal Year Ends:
Parent Company:

SALARIES/BONUSES:

Top Exec. Salary: $ Bonus: $
Second Exec. Salary: $ Bonus: $

OTHER THOUGHTS:

Estimated Female Officers or Directors:
Hot Spot for Advancement for Women/Minorities:

Sales, profits and employees may be estimates. Financial information, benefits and other data can change quickly and may vary from those stated here.

MarketAxess Holdings Inc

NAIC Code: 523120

www.marketaxess.com

TYPES OF BUSINESS:
Online Trading Platform
Technology Solutions
Online Corporate Bond-Trading Marketplace

BRANDS/DIVISIONS/AFFILIATES:
MarketAxess Technologies Inc
Open Trading
BondTicker
LiquidityBridge
LiquidityEdge
Regulatory Reporting Hub

GROWTH PLANS/SPECIAL FEATURES:
Founded in 2000, MarketAxess is a leading electronic fixed-income trading platform that connects broker/dealers and institutional investors. The company is primarily focused on credit based fixed income securities with its main trading products being U.S. investment-grade and high-yield bonds, Eurobonds, and Emerging Market corporate debt. Recently the company has expanded more aggressively into Treasuries and municipal bonds with the acquisitions of LiquidityEdge and MuniBrokers in 2019 and 2021, respectively. The company also provides pre- and post-trade services with its acquisition of Regulatory Reporting Hub from Deutsche BÃ¶rse Group in 2020 adding to its product offerings.

CONTACTS:
Note: Officers with more than one job title may be intentionally listed here more than once.

Richard Mcvey, CEO
Christopher Gerosa, CFO
Nicholas Themelis, Chief Information Officer
Christopher Concannon, COO
Scott Pintoff, General Counsel
Christophe Roupie, Other Corporate Officer
Kevin McPherson, Other Corporate Officer

FINANCIAL DATA:
Note: Data for latest year may not have been available at press time.

In U.S. $	2021	2020	2019	2018	2017	2016
Revenue		689,125,000	511,352,000	435,565,000	397,471,000	369,919,000
R&D Expense						
Operating Income		374,728,000	250,882,000	212,584,000	201,768,000	191,602,000
Operating Margin %						
SGA Expense		100,458,000	91,220,000	83,030,000	67,881,000	63,694,000
Net Income		299,377,000	204,902,000	172,852,000	148,089,000	126,172,000
Operating Cash Flow		404,489,000	265,935,000	223,917,000	168,035,000	80,289,000
Capital Expenditure		45,628,000	34,700,000	47,593,000	25,557,000	18,503,000
EBITDA		418,339,000	283,534,000	235,664,000	221,042,000	209,440,000
Return on Assets %						
Return on Equity %						
Debt to Equity						

CONTACT INFORMATION:
Phone: 212 813-6000   Fax: 212 813-6390
Toll-Free:
Address: 55 Hudson Yards, 15/Fl, New York, NY 10001 United States

STOCK TICKER/OTHER:
Stock Ticker: MKTX   Exchange: NAS
Employees: 676   Fiscal Year Ends: 12/31
Parent Company:

SALARIES/BONUSES:
Top Exec. Salary: $500,000   Bonus: $
Second Exec. Salary: $500,000   Bonus: $

OTHER THOUGHTS:
Estimated Female Officers or Directors: 2
Hot Spot for Advancement for Women/Minorities: Y

Sales, profits and employees may be estimates. Financial information, benefits and other data can change quickly and may vary from those stated here.

Marqeta Inc

www.marqeta.com

NAIC Code: 522320

TYPES OF BUSINESS:
Credit Card Processing Services
Merchant Payment Solutions
Card Issuance
Card Developing

BRANDS/DIVISIONS/AFFILIATES:

GROWTH PLANS/SPECIAL FEATURES:

Headquartered in Oakland, California, and founded in 2010, Marqeta provides its clients with a card issuing platform that offers the infrastructure and tools necessary to offer digital, physical, and tokenized payment options without the need for a traditional bank. The company's open APIs are designed to allow third parties like DoorDash, Klarna, and Square to rapidly develop and deploy innovative card-based products and payment services without the need to develop the underlying technology. The company generates revenue primarily through processing and ATM fees for cards issued on its platform.

Marqeta offers its employees health and wellness programs, 401(k) and a variety of company perks.

CONTACTS: *Note: Officers with more than one job title may be intentionally listed here more than once.*

Jason Gardner, CEO
Philip Faix, CFO
Seth Weissman, Chief Legal Officer
Randy Kern, Chief Technology Officer
Vidya Peters, COO
Lori McAdams, Other Executive Officer
Kevin Doerr, Other Executive Officer
Darren Mowry, Other Executive Officer
Renata Caine, Senior VP, Divisional
Brian Kieley, Senior VP, Divisional

FINANCIAL DATA: *Note: Data for latest year may not have been available at press time.*

In U.S. $	2021	2020	2019	2018	2017	2016
Revenue		290,292,000	143,267,000			
R&D Expense						
Operating Income		-47,087,000	-58,863,000			
Operating Margin %						
SGA Expense		142,997,000	101,323,000			
Net Income		-47,695,000	-58,200,000			
Operating Cash Flow		50,273,000	-15,428,000			
Capital Expenditure		2,375,000	4,908,000			
EBITDA		-43,589,000	-55,783,000			
Return on Assets %						
Return on Equity %						
Debt to Equity						

CONTACT INFORMATION:
Phone: 510 250-7939 Fax:
Toll-Free: 888 462-7738
Address: 180 Grand Ave., Fl. 6, Oakland, CA 94612 United States

STOCK TICKER/OTHER:
Stock Ticker: MQ Exchange: NAS
Employees: Fiscal Year Ends: 12/31
Parent Company:

SALARIES/BONUSES:
Top Exec. Salary: $350,000 Bonus: $14,668
Second Exec. Salary: $350,000 Bonus: $9,778

OTHER THOUGHTS:
Estimated Female Officers or Directors:
Hot Spot for Advancement for Women/Minorities:

Sales, profits and employees may be estimates. Financial information, benefits and other data can change quickly and may vary from those stated here.

MasterCard Incorporated

NAIC Code: 522320

www.mastercard.com

TYPES OF BUSINESS:
Credit Card Issuer
Transaction Processing Services
Global Payment Solutions
Credit Cards
Debit Cards

BRANDS/DIVISIONS/AFFILIATES:
MasterCard
Maestro
Cirrus

GROWTH PLANS/SPECIAL FEATURES:
Mastercard is the second-largest payment processor in the world, having processed $4.8 trillion in purchase transactions during 2020. Mastercard operates in over 200 countries and processes transactions in over 150 currencies.

MasterCard offers its employees medical, dental and vision coverage; life, disability and AD&D insurance; child care options; flexible work hours; adoption assistance; financial wellness programs; and personal services and discounts.

CONTACTS: *Note: Officers with more than one job title may be intentionally listed here more than once.*
Michael Miebach, CEO
Edward McLaughlin, Pres., Divisional
Sachin Mehra, CFO
Ajay Banga, Chairman of the Board
Sandra Arkell, Chief Accounting Officer
Timothy Murphy, Chief Administrative Officer
Raja Rajamannar, Chief Marketing Officer
Rich Verma, General Counsel
Craig Vosburg, Other Executive Officer
Michael Fraccaro, Other Executive Officer
Kevin Stanton, Other Executive Officer
Ajay Bhalla, President, Divisional
Raj Seshadri, President, Divisional
Gilberto Caldart, President, Divisional

FINANCIAL DATA: *Note: Data for latest year may not have been available at press time.*

In U.S. $	2021	2020	2019	2018	2017	2016
Revenue		15,301,000,000	16,883,000,000	14,950,000,000	12,497,000,000	10,776,000,000
R&D Expense						
Operating Income		8,163,000,000	9,696,000,000	8,374,000,000	6,743,000,000	5,912,000,000
Operating Margin %						
SGA Expense		2,771,000,000	3,128,000,000	2,903,000,000	2,631,000,000	2,266,000,000
Net Income		6,411,000,000	8,118,000,000	5,859,000,000	3,915,000,000	4,059,000,000
Operating Cash Flow		7,224,000,000	8,183,000,000	6,223,000,000	5,555,000,000	4,484,000,000
Capital Expenditure		708,000,000	728,000,000	504,000,000	423,000,000	382,000,000
EBITDA		8,720,000,000	10,477,000,000	7,849,000,000	7,113,000,000	6,114,000,000
Return on Assets %						
Return on Equity %						
Debt to Equity						

CONTACT INFORMATION:
Phone: 914 249-2000   Fax: 914 249-4206
Toll-Free: 800-627-8372
Address: 2000 Purchase St., Purchase, NY 10577 United States

STOCK TICKER/OTHER:
Stock Ticker: MA
Employees: 24,000
Parent Company:

Exchange: NYS
Fiscal Year Ends: 12/31

SALARIES/BONUSES:
Top Exec. Salary: $1,250,000   Bonus: $
Second Exec. Salary: $729,167   Bonus: $

OTHER THOUGHTS:
Estimated Female Officers or Directors: 2
Hot Spot for Advancement for Women/Minorities: Y

Sales, profits and employees may be estimates. Financial information, benefits and other data can change quickly and may vary from those stated here.

MicroBilt Corporation

www.microbilt.com

NAIC Code: 511210Q

TYPES OF BUSINESS:

Computer Software: Accounting, Banking & Financial
Consumer and Commercial Credit Bureau Data Access
Consumer Credit Reporting Agency
Risk Management Solutions
Financial Technology
Credit Scoring Tools
Bank and Identify Verification Solutions
Business Credentialing Solutions

BRANDS/DIVISIONS/AFFILIATES:

GROWTH PLANS/SPECIAL FEATURES:

MicroBilt Corporation is a registered consumer credit reporting agency that helps businesses assess and manage risk. The firm's products are provided through a single online portal, and include credit scoring tools, bank verification, identity verification, payment solutions, collection and recovery, background screening and business credentialing. MicroBilt also offers solutions and services to accommodate specific business needs, including small businesses, developer platforms, batch processing, credit and decisioning solutions, call-center services and customized solutions.

MicroBilt offers its employees comprehensive medical benefits, 401(k), life/disability/AD&D insurance, supplemental accident insurance and paid time off.

CONTACTS: Note: Officers with more than one job title may be intentionally listed here more than once.

Walt Wojciechowski, CEO

FINANCIAL DATA: Note: Data for latest year may not have been available at press time.

In U.S. $	2021	2020	2019	2018	2017	2016
Revenue						
R&D Expense						
Operating Income						
Operating Margin %						
SGA Expense						
Net Income						
Operating Cash Flow						
Capital Expenditure						
EBITDA						
Return on Assets %						
Return on Equity %						
Debt to Equity						

CONTACT INFORMATION:

Phone: 770 635-8428   Fax:
Toll-Free: 800 884-4747
Address: 1640 Airporrt Rd., Ste. 115, Kennesaw, GA 30144 United States

STOCK TICKER/OTHER:

Stock Ticker: Private   Exchange:
Employees: 185   Fiscal Year Ends:
Parent Company:

SALARIES/BONUSES:

Top Exec. Salary: $ Bonus: $
Second Exec. Salary: $ Bonus: $

OTHER THOUGHTS:

Estimated Female Officers or Directors:
Hot Spot for Advancement for Women/Minorities:

Sales, profits and employees may be estimates. Financial information, benefits and other data can change quickly and may vary from those stated here.

Microsoft Corporation

NAIC Code: 511210H

www.microsoft.com

TYPES OF BUSINESS:
Computer Software, Operating Systems, Languages & Development Tools
Enterprise Software
Game Consoles
Operating Systems
Software as a Service (SAAS)
Search Engine and Advertising
E-Mail Services
Instant Messaging

BRANDS/DIVISIONS/AFFILIATES:
Office 365
Exchange
SharePoint
Microsoft Teams
Skype for Business
Outlook.com
OneDrive
LinkedIn

CONTACTS: *Note: Officers with more than one job title may be intentionally listed here more than once.*
Satya Nadella, CEO
Amy Hood, CFO
Alice Jolla, Chief Accounting Officer
Bradford Smith, Chief Legal Officer
Christopher Capossela, Chief Marketing Officer
Christopher Young, Executive VP, Divisional
Kathleen Hogan, Executive VP, Divisional
Judson Althoff, Executive VP
Jean-Philippe Courtois, Executive VP

GROWTH PLANS/SPECIAL FEATURES:

Microsoft develops and licenses consumer and enterprise software. It is known for its Windows operating systems and Office productivity suite. The company is organized into three equally sized broad segments: productivity and business processes (legacy Microsoft Office, cloud-based Office 365, Exchange, SharePoint, Skype, LinkedIn, Dynamics), intelligence cloud (infrastructure- and platform-as-a-service offerings Azure, Windows Server OS, SQL Server), and more personal computing (Windows Client, Xbox, Bing search, display advertising, and Surface laptops, tablets, and desktops).

Microsoft offers its employees comprehensive benefits, a 401(k) and employee stock purchase plans; and employee assistance programs.

FINANCIAL DATA: *Note: Data for latest year may not have been available at press time.*

In U.S. $	2021	2020	2019	2018	2017	2016
Revenue	168,088,000,000	143,015,000,000	125,843,000,000	110,360,000,000	89,950,000,000	85,320,000,000
R&D Expense	20,716,000,000	19,269,000,000	16,876,000,000	14,726,000,000	13,037,000,000	11,988,000,000
Operating Income	69,916,000,000	52,959,000,000	42,959,000,000	35,058,000,000	22,632,000,000	21,292,000,000
Operating Margin %						
SGA Expense	25,224,000,000	24,709,000,000	23,098,000,000	22,223,000,000	20,020,000,000	19,260,000,000
Net Income	61,271,000,000	44,281,000,000	39,240,000,000	16,571,000,000	21,204,000,000	16,798,000,000
Operating Cash Flow	76,740,000,000	60,675,000,000	52,185,000,000	43,884,000,000	39,507,000,000	33,325,000,000
Capital Expenditure	20,622,000,000	15,441,000,000	13,925,000,000	11,632,000,000	8,129,000,000	8,343,000,000
EBITDA	85,134,000,000	68,423,000,000	58,056,000,000	49,468,000,000	34,149,000,000	27,616,000,000
Return on Assets %						
Return on Equity %						
Debt to Equity						

CONTACT INFORMATION:
Phone: 425 882-8080   Fax: 425 936-7329
Toll-Free: 800-642-7676
Address: One Microsoft Way, Redmond, WA 98052 United States

STOCK TICKER/OTHER:
Stock Ticker: MSFT
Employees: 163,000
Parent Company:

Exchange: NAS
Fiscal Year Ends: 06/30

SALARIES/BONUSES:
Top Exec. Salary: $541,875   Bonus: $3,500,000
Second Exec. Salary: $2,500,000   Bonus: $

OTHER THOUGHTS:
Estimated Female Officers or Directors: 4
Hot Spot for Advancement for Women/Minorities: Y

Sales, profits and employees may be estimates. Financial information, benefits and other data can change quickly and may vary from those stated here.

MoCaFi (Mobility Capital Finance Inc)

mocafi.com

NAIC Code: 511210Q

TYPES OF BUSINESS:

Computer Software: Accounting, Banking & Financial
Mobile Banking Platform
Financial Technology
Credit Scoring Solutions
Rent Bill Pay Services
Mobile Check Deposit Services
Financial Wealth Solutions

BRANDS/DIVISIONS/AFFILIATES:

MoCaFi Bank Account
MoCaFi Debit Mastercard

CONTACTS: *Note: Officers with more than one job title may be intentionally listed here more than once.*

Wole C. Coaxum, CEO

GROWTH PLANS/SPECIAL FEATURES:

Mobility Capital Finance, Inc. is a financial technology company that developed MoCaFi, a digital platform for banking, building credit and improving one's financial status. The MoCaFi Bank Account is the company's primary banking service, which is offered by Sunrise Banks NA, a member of the Federal Deposit Insurance Corporation (FDIC). Together, the MoCaFi Bank Account and the MoCaFi Debit Mastercard offers no fees on: rent bill pay reporting to Equifax and TransUnion; cash withdrawals at Allpoint or Wells Fargo automated teller machines (ATMs); mobile check deposits through the Ingo Money portal; and cash depositing on the VanillaDirect Load Store, including Rite-Aid, CVS, Walgreens, Dollar General and Family Dollar. MoCaFa does not check credit nor banking history in order to open an account; approval is based on the verification of personal identity. MoCaFi's bill pay feature enables users to add billers and issue checks directly from the app for paying rent and other bills, which automatically reports to the credit agencies and boosts credit scoring and payment history. MoCaFi partners with small minority-owned businesses to offer MoCaFi debit card holders up to 3% cash back on purchases. The MoCaFi platform uses spending, savings, credit score and personal development activity to assess how far users are from wealth and what is needed to get there.

FINANCIAL DATA: *Note: Data for latest year may not have been available at press time.*

In U.S. $	2021	2020	2019	2018	2017	2016
Revenue						
R&D Expense						
Operating Income						
Operating Margin %						
SGA Expense						
Net Income						
Operating Cash Flow						
Capital Expenditure						
EBITDA						
Return on Assets %						
Return on Equity %						
Debt to Equity						

CONTACT INFORMATION:

Phone: 646 653-5665   Fax:
Toll-Free: 800-342-7374
Address: 215 W. 125th St., New York, NY 10027 United States

STOCK TICKER/OTHER:

Stock Ticker: Private   Exchange:
Employees: Fiscal Year Ends:
Parent Company:

SALARIES/BONUSES:

Top Exec. Salary: $ Bonus: $
Second Exec. Salary: $ Bonus: $

OTHER THOUGHTS:

Estimated Female Officers or Directors:
Hot Spot for Advancement for Women/Minorities:

Sales, profits and employees may be estimates. Financial information, benefits and other data can change quickly and may vary from those stated here.

Modern Treasury Corp

www.moderntreasury.com

NAIC Code: 522320

TYPES OF BUSINESS:

Financial Transactions Processing, Reserve, and Clearinghouse Activities
Financial Technology
Business Payments Platform
Payment Ledger Automation
Virtual Account Payments Solutions
Payments Compliance Solutions
Payments Fraud Solutions

BRANDS/DIVISIONS/AFFILIATES:

CONTACTS: *Note: Officers with more than one job title may be intentionally listed here more than once.*

Dimitri Dadiomov, CEO

GROWTH PLANS/SPECIAL FEATURES:

Modern Treasury Corp. is a financial technology company that has developed a payment operations platform for businesses. The firm's products and solutions enable business teams to move and track money, automating the full cycle of money movement, from payment initiation to approvals to reconciliation. How it works: business customers connect their bank to Modern Treasury's platform; set up bank accounts, payment methods and counterparties; initiate payments to debit or credit counterparties and set up alerts for incoming payments; and payments are automatically reconciled to transactions as they are posted to the business' bank account. Once set up, ledgers can be created to represent accounts or to segregate funds (internal and external); the application programming interface (API) logs transactions as they occur within the ledger; and balances are updated in real-time. Virtual accounts can be set up using API or the web application for receiving payments directly into those accounts, and Modern Treasury automatically reconciles payments to the appropriate virtual accounts. Compliance and fraud programs can also be integrated with payments for staying compliant and for monitoring suspicious behavior, catching fraud and minimizing risk. Founded in 2018, Modern Treasury is backed by investors such as Altimeter Capital, Benchmark and Y Combinator. The firm has offices in San Francisco and New York City.

Modern Treasury offers employees a healthcare package, 401(k), paid parental leave and paid time off.

FINANCIAL DATA: *Note: Data for latest year may not have been available at press time.*

In U.S. $	2021	2020	2019	2018	2017	2016
Revenue						
R&D Expense						
Operating Income						
Operating Margin %						
SGA Expense						
Net Income						
Operating Cash Flow						
Capital Expenditure						
EBITDA						
Return on Assets %						
Return on Equity %						
Debt to Equity						

CONTACT INFORMATION:

Phone: 650-387-7162   Fax:
Toll-Free:
Address: 77 Geary St., Fl. 4, San Francisco, CA 94108 United States

STOCK TICKER/OTHER:

Stock Ticker: Private   Exchange:
Employees: 200   Fiscal Year Ends:
Parent Company:

SALARIES/BONUSES:

Top Exec. Salary: $ Bonus: $
Second Exec. Salary: $ Bonus: $

OTHER THOUGHTS:

Estimated Female Officers or Directors:
Hot Spot for Advancement for Women/Minorities:

Sales, profits and employees may be estimates. Financial information, benefits and other data can change quickly and may vary from those stated here.

Monzo Bank Limited

monzo.com

NAIC Code: 522110

TYPES OF BUSINESS:

Online Bank
Digital Banking Services
Banking Mobile App
Financial Technology
Finance Management Solutions
Savings Solutions
Bill Pay Solutions

BRANDS/DIVISIONS/AFFILIATES:

CONTACTS: Note: Officers with more than one job title may be intentionally listed here more than once.

TS Anil, CEO

GROWTH PLANS/SPECIAL FEATURES:

Monzo Bank Limited is an online bank based in the U.K. The Monzo online platform/mobile app provide a digital hub for managing finances for free. Budgeting tools are offered through the platform, and seeing what, where and how money is being spent by the user is made clear for the purpose of staying on track of one's financial journey. For example, Monzo has a Pots feature for segmenting money for different purposes, such as dividing income and placing money into a pot for bills, a pot for food and groceries, and a pot for saving for a car. Monzo's round up feature rounds up payments to the nearest dollar and puts the spare change into a pot, enabling users to save a little bit at a time. User accounts can be protected with Touch ID, Face ID, fingerprint or PIN. Mobile banking app facilitates access to banking services through Sutton Bank, which is a Federal Insurance Deposit Corporation (FDIC) member. The Monzo Mastercard debit card is also issued by Sutton Bank, pursuant to a license from Mastercard International Incorporated. Monzo accounts are FDIC insured up to $250,000.

Monzo Bank offers its employees health insurance, 401(k), paid vacation time and other company benefits and perks.

FINANCIAL DATA: Note: Data for latest year may not have been available at press time.

In U.S. $	2021	2020	2019	2018	2017	2016
Revenue	90,060,263	69,158,178	15,259,545	2,114,546		
R&D Expense						
Operating Income						
Operating Margin %						
SGA Expense						
Net Income	-180,540,913	-146,217,139	-62,668,435	-42,578,069		
Operating Cash Flow						
Capital Expenditure						
EBITDA						
Return on Assets %						
Return on Equity %						
Debt to Equity						

CONTACT INFORMATION:

Phone: 01144 2038720620   Fax:
Toll-Free:
Address: Broadwalk House, 5 Appold St., London, EC2A 2AG United Kingdom

STOCK TICKER/OTHER:

Stock Ticker: Private
Employees:
Parent Company:

Exchange:
Fiscal Year Ends: 02/28

SALARIES/BONUSES:

Top Exec. Salary: $ Bonus: $
Second Exec. Salary: $ Bonus: $

OTHER THOUGHTS:

Estimated Female Officers or Directors:
Hot Spot for Advancement for Women/Minorities:

Sales, profits and employees may be estimates. Financial information, benefits and other data can change quickly and may vary from those stated here.

Moomoo Inc

www.moomoo.com

NAIC Code: 523120

TYPES OF BUSINESS:

Securities Brokerage
Online Trading Platform
Wealth Management Solutions
Financial Technology
Stock Screening Solution
Investment Strategy

BRANDS/DIVISIONS/AFFILIATES:

Futu Holdings Limited
Futu Inc
Futu Singapore Ptd Ltd
Futu Clearing Inc
Futu Wealth Advisors Inc

CONTACTS: Note: Officers with more than one job title may be intentionally listed here more than once.

Leaf Hua Li, Chmn.-Futu

GROWTH PLANS/SPECIAL FEATURES:

Moomoo, Inc. is a financial technology company that offers a fully digitalized trading and wealth management platform. Moomoo stock trading platform is commission-free, is powered by professional-grade tools, provides real-time data and comprises fully integrated social functionalities. The app was designed to help identify stocks fast through a comprehensive stock screener, consisting of more than 100 stock indicators to locate investments that match the user's preferred strategy. Moomoo users can compare multiple stocks side-by-side across key dimensions such as price trends, price-to-earnings ratios and other indicators. Unlimited access to real-time financial news and lessons about trading are provided on the platform. Moomoo is wholly-owned by Futu Holdings Limited, and its investment products and services are offered by, but not limited to, the following brokerage firms: Futu Inc., which is regulated by the U.S. Securities and Exchange Commission (SEC); and Futu Singapore Pte. Ltd., which is regulated by the Monetary Authority of Singapore (MAS). Futu Clearing, Inc. is a broker-dealer; and Futu Wealth Advisors, Inc. is an investment advisor.

FINANCIAL DATA: Note: Data for latest year may not have been available at press time.

In U.S. $	2021	2020	2019	2018	2017	2016
Revenue						
R&D Expense						
Operating Income						
Operating Margin %						
SGA Expense						
Net Income						
Operating Cash Flow						
Capital Expenditure						
EBITDA						
Return on Assets %						
Return on Equity %						
Debt to Equity						

CONTACT INFORMATION:

Phone: 650-798-5700 Fax:
Toll-Free: 888 721-0610
Address: 720 University Ave., Ste. 100, Palo Alto, CA 94301 United States

STOCK TICKER/OTHER:

Stock Ticker: Subsidiary
Employees: 20
Parent Company: Futu Holdings Limited

Exchange:
Fiscal Year Ends: 12/31

SALARIES/BONUSES:

Top Exec. Salary: $ Bonus: $
Second Exec. Salary: $ Bonus: $

OTHER THOUGHTS:

Estimated Female Officers or Directors:
Hot Spot for Advancement for Women/Minorities:

Sales, profits and employees may be estimates. Financial information, benefits and other data can change quickly and may vary from those stated here.

Plunkett Research, Ltd.

Morgan Stanley

www.morganstanley.com

NAIC Code: 523110

TYPES OF BUSINESS:

Stock Brokerage/Investment Banking
Institutional Securities
Wealth Management
Investment Management

BRANDS/DIVISIONS/AFFILIATES:

E*TRADE Financial LLC
E*TRADE Financial Corp

GROWTH PLANS/SPECIAL FEATURES:

Morgan Stanley is a global investment bank whose history, through its legacy firms, can be traced back to 1924. The company has institutional securities, wealth management, and investment management segments. The company had about $4 trillion of client assets as well as nearly 70,000 employees at the end of 2020. Approximately 40% of the company's net revenue is from its institutional securities business, with the remainder coming from wealth and investment management. The company derives about 30% of its total revenue outside the Americas.

CONTACTS:
Note: Officers with more than one job title may be intentionally listed here more than once.

James Gorman, CEO
Robert Rooney, Other Corporate Officer
Jonathan Pruzan, CFO
Raja Akram, Chief Accounting Officer
Eric Grossman, Chief Legal Officer
Keishi Hotsuki, Chief Risk Officer
Edward Pick, Other Corporate Officer
Andrew Saperstein, Other Corporate Officer
Sharon Yeshaya, Other Corporate Officer
Daniel Simkowitz, Other Corporate Officer
Mandell Crawley, Other Executive Officer

FINANCIAL DATA:
Note: Data for latest year may not have been available at press time.

In U.S. $	2021	2020	2019	2018	2017	2016
Revenue		45,269,000,000	38,926,000,000	37,714,000,000	35,852,000,000	32,711,000,000
R&D Expense						
Operating Income						
Operating Margin %						
SGA Expense		23,753,000,000	21,691,000,000	20,339,000,000	19,566,000,000	18,252,000,000
Net Income		10,996,000,000	9,042,000,000	8,748,000,000	6,111,000,000	5,979,000,000
Operating Cash Flow		-25,231,000,000	40,773,000,000	7,305,000,000	-4,505,000,000	2,447,000,000
Capital Expenditure		1,444,000,000	1,826,000,000	1,865,000,000	1,629,000,000	1,276,000,000
EBITDA						
Return on Assets %						
Return on Equity %						
Debt to Equity						

CONTACT INFORMATION:

Phone: 212 761-4000   Fax: 212 761-0086
Toll-Free:
Address: 1585 Broadway, New York, NY 10036 United States

STOCK TICKER/OTHER:

Stock Ticker: MS
Employees: 75,000
Parent Company:

Exchange: NYS
Fiscal Year Ends: 12/31

SALARIES/BONUSES:

Top Exec. Salary: $1,000,000   Bonus: $9,887,500
Second Exec. Salary: $1,500,000   Bonus: $7,875,000

OTHER THOUGHTS:

Estimated Female Officers or Directors: 3
Hot Spot for Advancement for Women/Minorities: Y

Sales, profits and employees may be estimates. Financial information, benefits and other data can change quickly and may vary from those stated here.

Morningstar Inc

NAIC Code: 511120

www.morningstar.com

TYPES OF BUSINESS:
Investment Research
Online Financial Information
Financial Periodicals
Investor Relations Services
Stock and Mutual Fund Tracking and Ratings
Investment Advisory Services

BRANDS/DIVISIONS/AFFILIATES:
Morningstar Credit Ratings LLC
Morningstar Sustainability Rating
PitchBook Data Inc
Cuffelinks
FirstLinks
AdviserLogic

GROWTH PLANS/SPECIAL FEATURES:
Morningstar is a provider of independent investment research to financial advisers, asset managers, and investors. The company focuses its operations on two core sectors: data and research. It offers data on investments such as mutual funds, stocks, exchange-traded funds, closed-end funds, separate accounts, and variable annuities. Further, the company tracks real-time market data of equity, derivative, and currency exchanges and other investments. In its research operation, Morningstar offers analyst research on passive and active mutual funds, alternative funds, and college saving plans. Morningstar's largest share of revenue is generated in the United States of America.

Morningstar offers its employees medical, dental and vision coverage; flexible spending accounts; 401(k); and tuition reimbursement.

CONTACTS:
Note: Officers with more than one job title may be intentionally listed here more than once.

Kunal Kapoor, CEO
Jason Dubinsky, CFO
Joseph Mansueto, Founder
Patrick Maloney, General Counsel
Bevin Desmond, Other Corporate Officer
Haywood Kelly, Other Corporate Officer
Daniel Dunn, Other Executive Officer
Daniel Needham, Other Executive Officer

FINANCIAL DATA:
Note: Data for latest year may not have been available at press time.

In U.S. $	2021	2020	2019	2018	2017	2016
Revenue		1,389,500,000	1,179,000,000	1,019,900,000	911,700,000	798,600,000
R&D Expense						
Operating Income		215,200,000	189,600,000	215,800,000	169,800,000	180,800,000
Operating Margin %						
SGA Expense		478,400,000	388,600,000	296,300,000	264,100,000	202,800,000
Net Income		223,600,000	152,000,000	183,000,000	136,900,000	161,000,000
Operating Cash Flow		384,300,000	334,400,000	314,800,000	250,100,000	213,700,000
Capital Expenditure		76,700,000	80,000,000	76,100,000	66,600,000	62,800,000
EBITDA		433,600,000	327,300,000	333,700,000	277,800,000	297,100,000
Return on Assets %						
Return on Equity %						
Debt to Equity						

CONTACT INFORMATION:
Phone: 312 696-6000 Fax: 312 696-6009
Toll-Free: 800-735-0700
Address: 22 W. Washington St., Chicago, IL 60606 United States

STOCK TICKER/OTHER:
Stock Ticker: MORN Exchange: NAS
Employees: 9,556 Fiscal Year Ends: 12/31
Parent Company:

SALARIES/BONUSES:
Top Exec. Salary: $400,000 Bonus: $
Second Exec. Salary: $400,000 Bonus: $

OTHER THOUGHTS:
Estimated Female Officers or Directors: 3
Hot Spot for Advancement for Women/Minorities: Y

Sales, profits and employees may be estimates. Financial information, benefits and other data can change quickly and may vary from those stated here.

MX Technologies Inc

www.mx.com

NAIC Code: 511210Q

TYPES OF BUSINESS:

Computer Software: Accounting, Banking & Financial
Financial Data Aggregation
Financial Technology
Application Programming Interfaces (APIs)
Financial Connectivity Solutions
Money Management Solutions
Artificial Intelligent Financial Insights
Personalized Financial Tools

BRANDS/DIVISIONS/AFFILIATES:

CONTACTS: *Note: Officers with more than one job title may be intentionally listed here more than once.*

Shane Evans, Interim CEO
Brett Allred, Chief Product Officer
Brian Kinion, CFO
Felix Quintana, CIO
Kimberly Cassady, Chief People Officer
Brandon Dewitt, CTO
Ryan Caldwell, Chmn.

GROWTH PLANS/SPECIAL FEATURES:

MX Technologies, Inc. is a financial technology company that offers open finance application programming interfaces (APIs) to businesses for connectivity, data and experience purposes. The firm primarily serves finance, digital banking, payments, lending and cryptocurrency industries. Connectivity products and solutions by MX include customer-permissioned data sharing, data connectivity, account connectivity, money management, live status and metrics, as well as related developer logs into connectivity and data performance. Data products and solutions include data aggregation, account and identity verification, and data enhancement via machine learning and customer behavior. Experience products and solutions include artificial-intelligent (AI)-derived personalized financial insights, personal engagement tools, self-guided financial wellness tools, financial health scoring tools, and mobile banking applications for 24/7 access to finances. Professional services by MX are primarily utilized to help customers reach goals and maximize value via financial data.

FINANCIAL DATA: *Note: Data for latest year may not have been available at press time.*

In U.S. $	2021	2020	2019	2018	2017	2016
Revenue						
R&D Expense						
Operating Income						
Operating Margin %						
SGA Expense						
Net Income						
Operating Cash Flow						
Capital Expenditure						
EBITDA						
Return on Assets %						
Return on Equity %						
Debt to Equity						

CONTACT INFORMATION:

Phone: 801 669-5500   Fax:
Toll-Free:
Address: 3401 North Thanksgiving Way, Ste. 500, Lehi, UT 84043 United States

STOCK TICKER/OTHER:

Stock Ticker: Private   Exchange:
Employees: Fiscal Year Ends:
Parent Company:

SALARIES/BONUSES:

Top Exec. Salary: $ Bonus: $
Second Exec. Salary: $ Bonus: $

OTHER THOUGHTS:

Estimated Female Officers or Directors:
Hot Spot for Advancement for Women/Minorities:

Sales, profits and employees may be estimates. Financial information, benefits and other data can change quickly and may vary from those stated here.

National Cash Management Systems

www.ncms-inc.com

NAIC Code: 522320

TYPES OF BUSINESS:
Financial Transactions Processing, Reserve, and Clearinghouse Activities
Financial Software Development
Financial Technology
Electronic Payment Processing
Payment Fraud Solutions
Payment Integration Products
Credit Card Processing Solutions

BRANDS/DIVISIONS/AFFILIATES:

GROWTH PLANS/SPECIAL FEATURES:

National Cash Management Systems (NCMS) designs and develops customized electronic payment processing systems utilizing the Federal Reserve's Automated Clearing House (ACH) network. The firm offers ACH solutions via software, virtual terminals, integration products, payment gateway services and fraud-control tools. ACH processing solutions by NCMS include eCheck acceptance, high-risk ACH and eCheck accounts and payment integration. Fraud reduction services by NCMS include real-time check verification, account owner authentication, identity verification and negative verification. Credit card processing solutions span virtual terminal, online acceptance, high-risk merchant accounts and payment gateway solution. Alternative processing solutions include high-risk ACH and eCheck accounts, high-risk merchant accounts, international payment processing and eCheck processing.

CONTACTS: Note: Officers with more than one job title may be intentionally listed here more than once.
Scott Lewis, Pres.

FINANCIAL DATA: Note: Data for latest year may not have been available at press time.

In U.S. $	2021	2020	2019	2018	2017	2016
Revenue						
R&D Expense						
Operating Income						
Operating Margin %						
SGA Expense						
Net Income						
Operating Cash Flow						
Capital Expenditure						
EBITDA						
Return on Assets %						
Return on Equity %						
Debt to Equity						

CONTACT INFORMATION:
Phone: 214 544-2245   Fax: 214 544-2246
Toll-Free: 877 370-9645
Address: 6800 Weiskopf Ave., Ste. 150, McKinney, TX 75070 United States

STOCK TICKER/OTHER:
Stock Ticker: Private   Exchange:
Employees: Fiscal Year Ends:
Parent Company:

SALARIES/BONUSES:
Top Exec. Salary: $ Bonus: $
Second Exec. Salary: $ Bonus: $

OTHER THOUGHTS:
Estimated Female Officers or Directors:
Hot Spot for Advancement for Women/Minorities:

Sales, profits and employees may be estimates. Financial information, benefits and other data can change quickly and may vary from those stated here.

NationalACH

nationalach.com

NAIC Code: 522320

TYPES OF BUSINESS:

Financial Transactions Processing, Reserve, and Clearinghouse Activities
Financial Technology
Payment Processing Solutions
Payment Software Integration
High-volume Payment Processing
High-risk Merchant Payment Solutions
Cloud-based Payment Reporting
Tailored Merchant Payment Solutions

BRANDS/DIVISIONS/AFFILIATES:

GROWTH PLANS/SPECIAL FEATURES:

NationalACH is a financial technology company that provides Automated Clearing House (ACH), eCheck and debit/credit card payment processing services to U.S. and international businesses via banks. The firm specializes in payment processing for high-volume and high-risk merchants. Solutions offered by NationalACH include ecommerce, virtual terminal, check by phone, same-day ACH credit, recurring payments, and account management with cloud-based reporting. NationalACH offers safe payment processing solutions, including fully compliant Level 1 PCI-DSS security standards for businesses, tokenization, fraud prevention features and account verification. Tailored single source payment solutions span financial services, global ecommerce, debt collection, adult merchant accounts, digital media, direct response, high risk, high ticket, high volume, travel, nutraceutical, lenders, subscription/membership and payouts. NationalACH's payment platform easily integrates with customer websites.

CONTACTS: *Note: Officers with more than one job title may be intentionally listed here more than once.*

Tina Brandon, VP-Sales

FINANCIAL DATA: *Note: Data for latest year may not have been available at press time.*

In U.S. $	2021	2020	2019	2018	2017	2016
Revenue						
R&D Expense						
Operating Income						
Operating Margin %						
SGA Expense						
Net Income						
Operating Cash Flow						
Capital Expenditure						
EBITDA						
Return on Assets %						
Return on Equity %						
Debt to Equity						

CONTACT INFORMATION:

Phone: 702-323-5761   Fax:
Toll-Free: 866 224-7600
Address: 3773 Howard Hughes Pkwy., Las Vegas, NV 89169 United States

STOCK TICKER/OTHER:

Stock Ticker: Private
Employees:
Parent Company:

Exchange:
Fiscal Year Ends:

SALARIES/BONUSES:

Top Exec. Salary: $ Bonus: $
Second Exec. Salary: $ Bonus: $

OTHER THOUGHTS:

Estimated Female Officers or Directors:
Hot Spot for Advancement for Women/Minorities:

Sales, profits and employees may be estimates. Financial information, benefits and other data can change quickly and may vary from those stated here.

NerdWallet Inc

www.nerdwallet.com

NAIC Code: 519130

TYPES OF BUSINESS:

Internet Publishing and Broadcasting and Web Search Portals
Credit Card and Bank Comparison

GROWTH PLANS/SPECIAL FEATURES:

Nerdwallet Inc is a free tool to find the best credit cards, cd
rates, savings, checking accounts, scholarships, healthcare
and airlines. Consumers have free access to the firm's expert
content and comparison shopping marketplaces, plus a data-
driven membership experience.

BRANDS/DIVISIONS/AFFILIATES:

CONTACTS: Note: Officers with more than one job title may be intentionally listed here more than once.

Tim Chen, CEO
Lauren StClair, CFO
Kelly Gillease, CMO
Lynee Luque, Chief People Officer

FINANCIAL DATA: Note: Data for latest year may not have been available at press time.

In U.S. $	2021	2020	2019	2018	2017	2016
Revenue		245,300,000	228,300,000			
R&D Expense		50,900,000	46,000,000			
Operating Income		1,100,000	28,400,000			
Operating Margin %						
SGA Expense		172,000,000	137,800,000			
Net Income		5,300,000	24,200,000			
Operating Cash Flow		15,400,000	31,400,000			
Capital Expenditure		18,700,000	14,800,000			
EBITDA		17,100,000	38,400,000			
Return on Assets %						
Return on Equity %						
Debt to Equity						

CONTACT INFORMATION:

Phone: 415 549-8913   Fax:
Toll-Free:
Address: 875 Stevenson St., Fl. 5, San Francisco, CA 94103 United States

STOCK TICKER/OTHER:

Stock Ticker: NRDS
Employees: 587
Parent Company:

Exchange: NAS
Fiscal Year Ends: 12/31

SALARIES/BONUSES:

Top Exec. Salary: $450,000   Bonus: $
Second Exec. Salary: $398,333   Bonus: $

OTHER THOUGHTS:

Estimated Female Officers or Directors:
Hot Spot for Advancement for Women/Minorities:

Sales, profits and employees may be estimates. Financial information, benefits and other data can change quickly and may vary from those stated here.

Plunkett Research, Ltd.

235

NetSpend Holdings Inc

www.netspend.com

NAIC Code: 522210

TYPES OF BUSINESS:

Prepaid Debit Cards
Financial Technology
Prepaid Debit Cards
Money Management Solutions
Direct Deposit Services
Cashback Rewards
Business Payment Solutions
Application Programming Interfaces (APIs)

BRANDS/DIVISIONS/AFFILIATES:

Global Payments Inc
NetSpend
Skylight ONE

CONTACTS: Note: Officers with more than one job title may be intentionally listed here more than once.

Kelley Knutson, Pres.
Rick Cox, Sr. VP-Oper.
Beth Deck, Exec. VP-Finance
Shannon Johnston, CTO
Anh Vazquez, Exec. VP-Direct Channel

GROWTH PLANS/SPECIAL FEATURES:

NetSpend Holdings, Inc. is a financial technology firm that offers alternative products for individuals who don't have a traditional bank account or prefer to use alternative financial services, serving approximately 68 million consumers. For consumers, NetSpend offers two pre-paid debit cards for money management purposes, which are branded under the NetSpend or Skylight ONE names. No credit check, activation fee nor minimum balance is required for the debit cards. They are reloadable and offer cashback rewards. The NetSpend mobile and online app provides alerts when money, including direct deposits, is received. For businesses, NetSpend offers payments and financial service solutions, including end-to-end program management capabilities, bank and network partnerships, employer payments, card programs (including payroll cards), data insights, open application programming interfaces (APIs), enterprise-grade payment processing, developer tools for flexibility and control, money disbursement and movement, cash-in, retail distribution and more. NetSpend Holdings operates as a subsidiary of Global Payments, Inc.

NetSpend offers its employees comprehensive health benefits, 401(k), tuition and adoption assistance, paid time off and a variety of company programs, plans and perks.

FINANCIAL DATA: Note: Data for latest year may not have been available at press time.

In U.S. $	2021	2020	2019	2018	2017	2016
Revenue	869,859,900	836,403,750	857,850,000	817,000,000	700,000,000	663,579,000
R&D Expense						
Operating Income						
Operating Margin %						
SGA Expense						
Net Income						
Operating Cash Flow						
Capital Expenditure						
EBITDA						
Return on Assets %						
Return on Equity %						
Debt to Equity						

CONTACT INFORMATION:

Phone: 512 532-8200   Fax:
Toll-Free: 866-387-7363
Address: 701 Brazos St., Ste. 1300, Austin, TX 78701 United States

STOCK TICKER/OTHER:

Stock Ticker: Subsidiary   Exchange:
Employees: 681   Fiscal Year Ends: 12/31
Parent Company: Global Payments Inc

SALARIES/BONUSES:

Top Exec. Salary: $ Bonus: $
Second Exec. Salary: $ Bonus: $

OTHER THOUGHTS:

Estimated Female Officers or Directors: 1
Hot Spot for Advancement for Women/Minorities:

Sales, profits and employees may be estimates. Financial information, benefits and other data can change quickly and may vary from those stated here.

Next Insurance Inc

www.next-insurance.com

NAIC Code: 524126

TYPES OF BUSINESS:
Direct Property and Casualty Insurance Carriers
Online Insurance
Small Business Insurance Coverage
Certificate of Insurance
General Liability
Workers Compensation
Professional Liability
Commercial Property

BRANDS/DIVISIONS/AFFILIATES:

CONTACTS: *Note: Officers with more than one job title may be intentionally listed here more than once.*
Guy Goldstein, CEO

GROWTH PLANS/SPECIAL FEATURES:

Next Insurance, Inc. is a financial technology company that offers business insurance products for small businesses, which can be obtained and managed online. The firm's seven insurance policy categories include general liability, workers' compensation, professional liability/E&O (errors and omissions), commercial auto, tools and equipment, commercial property, and business owners' policy. Discounts are provided if policies are bundled. Instant quotes are provided online by stating the kind of business it is, and selecting the type of coverage desired. Certificates of insurance can be obtained swiftly through Next's online or mobile app. The firm offers live U.S.-based insurance support. Next insures a wide range of industries, including architect, auto services, beauty, cleaning, construction, consulting, contractors, education, engineers, entertainment, fitness, financial services, food services, real estate, retail and therapy. Headquartered in California, USA, the company has additional offices in Texas, New York and Massachusetts, as well as in Kfar Saba, Israel.

FINANCIAL DATA: *Note: Data for latest year may not have been available at press time.*

In U.S. $	2021	2020	2019	2018	2017	2016
Revenue						
R&D Expense						
Operating Income						
Operating Margin %						
SGA Expense						
Net Income						
Operating Cash Flow						
Capital Expenditure						
EBITDA						
Return on Assets %						
Return on Equity %						
Debt to Equity						

CONTACT INFORMATION:
Phone: Fax:
Toll-Free: 855-222-5919
Address: 975 California Ave, Palo Alto, CA 94304 United States

STOCK TICKER/OTHER:
Stock Ticker: Private   Exchange:
Employees: 750   Fiscal Year Ends:
Parent Company:

SALARIES/BONUSES:
Top Exec. Salary: $ Bonus: $
Second Exec. Salary: $ Bonus: $

OTHER THOUGHTS:
Estimated Female Officers or Directors:
Hot Spot for Advancement for Women/Minorities:

Sales, profits and employees may be estimates. Financial information, benefits and other data can change quickly and may vary from those stated here.

Plunkett Research, Ltd.

Nivelo Tech Inc

nivelo.io

NAIC Code: 522320

TYPES OF BUSINESS:
Financial Transactions Processing, Reserve, and Clearinghouse Activities
Financial Technology
Payments Risk Solutions
Digital Payment Security
Payment Compliance
Payment Threat Detection
Payment and Identity Verification
Direct Employer Payments and Debits

BRANDS/DIVISIONS/AFFILIATES:
Exposure Scan
Scorer Engine
Instant Payroll

CONTACTS: *Note: Officers with more than one job title may be intentionally listed here more than once.*
Eli Polanco, CEO

GROWTH PLANS/SPECIAL FEATURES:
Nivelo Tech, Inc. is a financial technology company that offers risk management products and solutions in regards to digital payments, including income payments. Nivelo's three core products for businesses include: Exposure Scan, Scorer Engine, and Instant Payroll. Exposure Scan enables businesses to uncover payment risks and discover payroll opportunities, which help prevent payment failures and maintain positive customer experience across all payment offerings. Exposure Scan also enables users to comply with National Automated Clearing House Association (NACHA) rules, and monitor credit or other fraudulent activity. Scorer Engine enables businesses to manage digital ACH credit and debit payment risk via real-time and adaptive threat detection technology. This product features embedded scoring via application programming interfaces (APIs), transaction flagging for a clear explanation and view of each transaction, ongoing account information and payment verification for 24/7 risk detection, workflow automation across human resource administrations and employees, customized rules and related alerts via email or small message systems (SMS). Last, Instant Payroll allows payroll companies of any size to receive instant debits from their employers within seconds without wires, which eliminates non-sufficient funds and non-collection errors. Exact timing and status of payroll funds is displayed through the platform. Instant Payroll is compatible with existing human capital management (HCM) payroll software. Businesses can expand employer prospects by offering instant payout options through Instant Payroll.

FINANCIAL DATA: *Note: Data for latest year may not have been available at press time.*

In U.S. $	2021	2020	2019	2018	2017	2016
Revenue						
R&D Expense						
Operating Income						
Operating Margin %						
SGA Expense						
Net Income						
Operating Cash Flow						
Capital Expenditure						
EBITDA						
Return on Assets %						
Return on Equity %						
Debt to Equity						

CONTACT INFORMATION:
Phone: 917-704-4969   Fax:
Toll-Free:
Address: 335 Madison Ave., Fl. 3, New York, NY 10017 United States

STOCK TICKER/OTHER:
Stock Ticker: Private   Exchange:
Employees: Fiscal Year Ends:
Parent Company:

SALARIES/BONUSES:
Top Exec. Salary: $ Bonus: $
Second Exec. Salary: $ Bonus: $

OTHER THOUGHTS:
Estimated Female Officers or Directors:
Hot Spot for Advancement for Women/Minorities:

Sales, profits and employees may be estimates. Financial information, benefits and other data can change quickly and may vary from those stated here.

Nu Holdings Ltd (NuBank)

NAIC Code: 522210

nubank.com.br/en

TYPES OF BUSINESS:

Credit Card Issuing
Digital Banking
Financial Solutions and Services
Mobile App
Interest-Earning Accounts
Payment Solutions and Services
Credit Cards
Individual and Business Banking

BRANDS/DIVISIONS/AFFILIATES:

NuBank
Nubank Mastercard
Nubank PJ

GROWTH PLANS/SPECIAL FEATURES:

Nu Holdings Ltd is engaged in providing digital banking services. It offers several financial services such as Credit cards, Personal Account, Investments, Personal Loans, Insurance, Mobile payments, Business Account, and Rewards.

CONTACTS: *Note: Officers with more than one job title may be intentionally listed here more than once.*

David Velez, CEO
Gabriel Silva, CFO

FINANCIAL DATA: *Note: Data for latest year may not have been available at press time.*

In U.S. $	2021	2020	2019	2018	2017	2016
Revenue						
R&D Expense						
Operating Income						
Operating Margin %						
SGA Expense						
Net Income						
Operating Cash Flow						
Capital Expenditure						
EBITDA						
Return on Assets %						
Return on Equity %						
Debt to Equity						

CONTACT INFORMATION:

Phone: 55-800-591-2117   Fax:
Toll-Free:
Address: Rua Capote Valente, 39, Sao Paulo, SP 05409-000 Brazil

STOCK TICKER/OTHER:

Stock Ticker: NU   Exchange: NYS
Employees: Fiscal Year Ends:
Parent Company:

SALARIES/BONUSES:

Top Exec. Salary: $ Bonus: $
Second Exec. Salary: $ Bonus: $

OTHER THOUGHTS:

Estimated Female Officers or Directors:
Hot Spot for Advancement for Women/Minorities:

Sales, profits and employees may be estimates. Financial information, benefits and other data can change quickly and may vary from those stated here.

Obopay Inc

www.obopay.com

NAIC Code: 522320

TYPES OF BUSINESS:

Consumer Payment Processing Software

GROWTH PLANS/SPECIAL FEATURES:

Obopay, Inc. develops software that allows customers to send and receive money using their mobile phones. Obopay offers software solutions in three segments: Mobiile Payment Solutions, providing an array of money management services under a single mobile payment platform; Business Solutions, providing quick, safe and secure services for business transactions; and Agent Solutions, providing a scalable service to develop distribution networks. The firm operates in the U.S. and India.

BRANDS/DIVISIONS/AFFILIATES:

CONTACTS: *Note: Officers with more than one job title may be intentionally listed here more than once.*

Shailendra Naidu, CEO
D. Padmanabhan, Chmn.

FINANCIAL DATA: *Note: Data for latest year may not have been available at press time.*

In U.S. $	2021	2020	2019	2018	2017	2016
Revenue						
R&D Expense						
Operating Income						
Operating Margin %						
SGA Expense						
Net Income						
Operating Cash Flow						
Capital Expenditure						
EBITDA						
Return on Assets %						
Return on Equity %						
Debt to Equity						

CONTACT INFORMATION:

Phone: 91 80 66732300   Fax:
Toll-Free:
Address: 150, Diamond District, Old Airport Rd., Fl. 6, Twr. C, Bangalore, 560008 India

STOCK TICKER/OTHER:

Stock Ticker: Private
Employees:
Parent Company:

Exchange:
Fiscal Year Ends:

SALARIES/BONUSES:

Top Exec. Salary: $ Bonus: $
Second Exec. Salary: $ Bonus: $

OTHER THOUGHTS:

Estimated Female Officers or Directors:
Hot Spot for Advancement for Women/Minorities:

Sales, profits and employees may be estimates. Financial information, benefits and other data can change quickly and may vary from those stated here.

On Deck Capital Inc

NAIC Code: 522291

www.ondeck.com

TYPES OF BUSINESS:

Consumer Lending - Small Business
Business Loans
Term Loans
Lines of Credit
SBA Paycheck Protection
Digital Platform
Technology

BRANDS/DIVISIONS/AFFILIATES:

Enoval International Inc
OnDeck

CONTACTS: *Note: Officers with more than one job title may be intentionally listed here more than once.*

Noah Breslow, CFO
Noah Breslow, Chairman of the Board
Andrea Gellert, Other Executive Officer

GROWTH PLANS/SPECIAL FEATURES:

On Deck Capital, Inc., a subsidiary of Enova International Inc., operates OnDeck an online platform that offers loans to businesses globally. Loan products include term loans, lines of credit, and Small Business Association (SBA) paycheck protection program loans. Short-term loans for small businesses are options for borrowers who need funds for a specific business investment, such as starting a new project, expanding, or making a large purchase that cannot be covered with a credit card. These loans are a type of installment loans in which OnDeck offers a one-time lump sum of cash which is paid back per the project timeline negotiated. Short-term loans are generally repaid in a year or less, but some OnDeck repayment options have terms up to 24 months. A business line of credit is a revolving loan that allows access to a fixed amount of capital, which can be used when needed to meet short-term business needs. Revolving lines of credit primarily range from $6,000 to $100,000. SBA paycheck protection program (PPP) loans are loan amounts up to 2.5-times the average monthly payroll cost (or up to 3.5-times for employers in the accommodation and food service industry), for a maximum of $2 million for second draw PPP loans and a maximum of $10 million for first draw PPP loans. These loans have a 1% fixed interest rate and no additional fees, including no origination fees or pre-payment penalties. Term lengths are up to five years.

FINANCIAL DATA: *Note: Data for latest year may not have been available at press time.*

In U.S. $	2021	2020	2019	2018	2017	2016
Revenue	442,000,000	425,000,000	399,816,000	351,300,992	353,291,008	258,455,008
R&D Expense						
Operating Income						
Operating Margin %						
SGA Expense						
Net Income			27,955,000	27,681,000	-11,534,000	-82,958,000
Operating Cash Flow						
Capital Expenditure						
EBITDA						
Return on Assets %						
Return on Equity %						
Debt to Equity						

CONTACT INFORMATION:

Phone: 888 269-4246   Fax: 800 363-1160
Toll-Free:
Address: 1400 Broadway, Fl. 25, New York, NY 10018 United States

STOCK TICKER/OTHER:

Stock Ticker: Subsidiary   Exchange:
Employees: 742   Fiscal Year Ends: 12/31
Parent Company: Enova International Inc

SALARIES/BONUSES:

Top Exec. Salary: $ Bonus: $
Second Exec. Salary: $ Bonus: $

OTHER THOUGHTS:

Estimated Female Officers or Directors:
Hot Spot for Advancement for Women/Minorities:

Sales, profits and employees may be estimates. Financial information, benefits and other data can change quickly and may vary from those stated here.

One Finance Inc

www.onefinance.com

NAIC Code: 511210Q

TYPES OF BUSINESS:

Computer Software: Accounting, Banking & Financial
Money Management Application
Digital Banking Platform
Debit Card
Deposits
Savings
Virtual Payment Cards

BRANDS/DIVISIONS/AFFILIATES:

Coastal Community Bank
Walmart Inc
Ribbit Capital
Hazel by Walmart
Even Responsible Finance Inc
ONE
Pocket

CONTACTS: *Note: Officers with more than one job title may be intentionally listed here more than once.*

Omer Ismail, CEO

GROWTH PLANS/SPECIAL FEATURES:

One Finance, Inc. is a fintech company that partners with Coastal Community Bank to provide a seamless digital platform (ONE) for managing one's money. ONE's financial services app enables users to get paid, spend, save and borrow through a single platform. How it works: consumers create a profile, identity is then verified and a ONE debit card is issued for verified accounts. ONE is Federal Deposit Insurance Corporation (FDIC) insured up to $250,000, and features encryption technologies to keep data secure. Applying for ONE does not impact credit scores. ONE customers can enable an Auto-Save feature, which automatically rounds up debit card purchases to the next dollar and then automatically transfer the difference into a savings Pocket that earns a 3.00% annual percentage yield (APY). By enabling Pocket Protector, available funds can be pulled from the Spend Pocket to cover transactions that may take a balance below zero. Therefore, Pockets help users manage money in a convenient way. ONE debit card holders have access to 55,000 fee-free AllPoint ATMs throughout the U.S. Virtual cards can be created, and provide a secure buffer between Pockets and any merchant data breach. In April 2022, One Finance is the surviving entity in a multiple fintech merger involving an investment vehicle (Hazel) funded by Walmart, Inc. and Ribbit Capital. That same month, Hazel acquired Even Responsible Finance Inc., which was to be merged into the ONE brand name.

FINANCIAL DATA: *Note: Data for latest year may not have been available at press time.*

In U.S. $	2021	2020	2019	2018	2017	2016
Revenue						
R&D Expense						
Operating Income						
Operating Margin %						
SGA Expense						
Net Income						
Operating Cash Flow						
Capital Expenditure						
EBITDA						
Return on Assets %						
Return on Equity %						
Debt to Equity						

CONTACT INFORMATION:

Phone: 530 304-5568   Fax:
Toll-Free: 855 970-1919
Address: 2407 J St., Ste. 300, Sacramento, CA 95816-4736 United States

STOCK TICKER/OTHER:

Stock Ticker: Private
Employees:
Parent Company:

Exchange:
Fiscal Year Ends:

SALARIES/BONUSES:

Top Exec. Salary: $ Bonus: $
Second Exec. Salary: $ Bonus: $

OTHER THOUGHTS:

Estimated Female Officers or Directors:
Hot Spot for Advancement for Women/Minorities:

Sales, profits and employees may be estimates. Financial information, benefits and other data can change quickly and may vary from those stated here.

OpenInvest

NAIC Code: 523920

openinvest.com

TYPES OF BUSINESS:
Portfolio Management
Financial Technology
Personalized Investment Strategies
Digital Investment Platform
Environmental, Social Governance (ESG) Funds
Separately Managed Accounts
Mutual Funds
Exchange Traded Funds

BRANDS/DIVISIONS/AFFILIATES:
JPMorgan Chase & Co
Private Bank and Wealth Management

GROWTH PLANS/SPECIAL FEATURES:

OpenInvest is part of JPMorgan Chase & Co.'s Private Bank and Wealth Management division, and offers an intuitive and personalized investing strategy. The company's digital investment platform features dynamic custom indexing, sustainability reporting, proxy voting, tax optimization and more. Investment strategies include environmental/social/governance (ESG) funds separately managed accounts (SMAs), mutual funds and exchange traded funds (ETFs). Investment causes of OpenInvest span causes such as reducing greenhouse gas emissions, divesting from prison industrial complexes, investing in women leaders, investing in heart health, supporting diversity and rights, divesting from fossil fuel produces, and investing in disability inclusion, among others.

CONTACTS: *Note: Officers with more than one job title may be intentionally listed here more than once.*
Conor Murray, CEO
Josh Levin, Chief Strategy Officer
Hanu Kunduru, Dir.-Engineering
Leigh Kloss, Head-Mktg.
Derek Smith, Head-DevOps
Jimmy Sun, CTO
Sarah Sung, Head-Sales

FINANCIAL DATA: *Note: Data for latest year may not have been available at press time.*

In U.S. $	2021	2020	2019	2018	2017	2016
Revenue						
R&D Expense						
Operating Income						
Operating Margin %						
SGA Expense						
Net Income						
Operating Cash Flow						
Capital Expenditure						
EBITDA						
Return on Assets %						
Return on Equity %						
Debt to Equity						

CONTACT INFORMATION:
Phone: 908 977-6171   Fax:
Toll-Free: 855 466-6545
Address: 2 Mint Plaza, Ste. 604, San Francisco, CA 94103 United States

STOCK TICKER/OTHER:
Stock Ticker: Subsidiary   Exchange:
Employees: Fiscal Year Ends:
Parent Company: JPMorgan Chase & Co

SALARIES/BONUSES:
Top Exec. Salary: $ Bonus: $
Second Exec. Salary: $ Bonus: $

OTHER THOUGHTS:
Estimated Female Officers or Directors:
Hot Spot for Advancement for Women/Minorities:

Sales, profits and employees may be estimates. Financial information, benefits and other data can change quickly and may vary from those stated here.

OppFi Inc

NAIC Code: 511210Q

www.oppfi.com

TYPES OF BUSINESS:
Computer Software: Accounting, Banking & Financial
Personal Loans Platform

BRANDS/DIVISIONS/AFFILIATES:

GROWTH PLANS/SPECIAL FEATURES:
OppFi is a leading financial technology platform that empowers banks to offer accessible lending products through its proprietary technology and artificial intelligence, or AI. OppFi's primary mission is to facilitate financial inclusion and credit access to the 60 million everyday consumers who lack access to traditional credit through best available products. The average installment loan facilitated by OppFi's platform is $1,500, payable in monthly installments and with an average contractual term of 11 months. Payments are reported to the three major credit bureaus.

CONTACTS: *Note: Officers with more than one job title may be intentionally listed here more than once.*
Todd Schwartz, CEO
Elizabeth Simer, Chief Strategy Officer
Pamela Johnson, CFO
Yuri Ter-Saakyants, Chief Technology Officer

FINANCIAL DATA: *Note: Data for latest year may not have been available at press time.*

In U.S. $	2021	2020	2019	2018	2017	2016
Revenue		291,014,000				
R&D Expense						
Operating Income						
Operating Margin %						
SGA Expense						
Net Income		77,516,000				
Operating Cash Flow						
Capital Expenditure						
EBITDA						
Return on Assets %						
Return on Equity %						
Debt to Equity						

CONTACT INFORMATION:
Phone: 312 212-8079   Fax:
Toll-Free: 855 408-5000
Address: 130 E Randolph St., Ste. 3400, Chicago, IL 60601 United States

STOCK TICKER/OTHER:
Stock Ticker: OPFI
Employees: 554
Parent Company:

Exchange: NYS
Fiscal Year Ends: 12/31

SALARIES/BONUSES:
Top Exec. Salary: $ Bonus: $
Second Exec. Salary: $ Bonus: $

OTHER THOUGHTS:
Estimated Female Officers or Directors:
Hot Spot for Advancement for Women/Minorities:

Sales, profits and employees may be estimates. Financial information, benefits and other data can change quickly and may vary from those stated here.

Optiver

NAIC Code: 523110

www.optiver.com

TYPES OF BUSINESS:

Investment Banking and Securities Dealing
Market Maker
Option Trader
Financial Technology
Digital Investments
IT Infrastructure Investments
Fintech Investments

BRANDS/DIVISIONS/AFFILIATES:

Optiver Holding BV

GROWTH PLANS/SPECIAL FEATURES:

Optiver is an option trader and market maker owned by Netherlands-based Optiver Holding BV. The company makes markets on many exchanges, and therefore aims to improve the markets in which it trades by continuously offering the narrowest bid-ask spread possible. This strategy enables Optiver to inject liquidity into the market by ensuring a willing buyer and seller for traded products are present, which subsequently allows investors to trade some of their risk onto Optiver. The company provides institutional investors worldwide with liquidity in equities, foreign exchange, fixed income and commodity products. Focus areas of Optiver include financial technology, information technology infrastructure and digital assets. Optiver has global locations in the Australia, China, the U.K. and the U.S.

CONTACTS: *Note: Officers with more than one job title may be intentionally listed here more than once.*

Jan Boomaars, CEO

FINANCIAL DATA: *Note: Data for latest year may not have been available at press time.*

In U.S. $	2021	2020	2019	2018	2017	2016
Revenue						
R&D Expense						
Operating Income						
Operating Margin %						
SGA Expense						
Net Income						
Operating Cash Flow						
Capital Expenditure						
EBITDA						
Return on Assets %						
Return on Equity %						
Debt to Equity						

CONTACT INFORMATION:

Phone: 31 20-708-7000   Fax:
Toll-Free:
Address: Strawinskylaan 3095, Amsterdam, 1077 ZX Netherlands

STOCK TICKER/OTHER:

Stock Ticker: Subsidiary   Exchange:
Employees: 1,390   Fiscal Year Ends:
Parent Company: Optiver Holding BV

SALARIES/BONUSES:

Top Exec. Salary: $ Bonus: $
Second Exec. Salary: $ Bonus: $

OTHER THOUGHTS:

Estimated Female Officers or Directors:
Hot Spot for Advancement for Women/Minorities:

Sales, profits and employees may be estimates. Financial information, benefits and other data can change quickly and may vary from those stated here.

Plunkett Research, Ltd.

Orum (Project Midas Inc)

orum.io

NAIC Code: 511210E

TYPES OF BUSINESS:

Computer Software: Network Security, Managed Access, Digital ID,
Cybersecurity & Anti-Virus
Risk Prediction at Individual ACH Transaction Level
Money Movement Technology Solutions
Customized Payment Solutions
Secure Money and Payment Transfer

BRANDS/DIVISIONS/AFFILIATES:

Momentum

CONTACTS: *Note: Officers with more than one job title may be intentionally listed here more than once.*

Tony Jin, Dir.-Bus. Oper.
Ashley Trebisacci, Sr. Mngr.-People
Brandon Hawkinson, Sr. Software Engineer

GROWTH PLANS/SPECIAL FEATURES:

Project Midas, Inc. does business as Orum and is a technology service provider for banks and non-bank financial institutions in regards to moving money. Orum's application programming interface (API)-based payments platform, Momentum, enables a smart, easy and swift way for institutions and financial innovators to move money. Momentum enables users to leverage Orum's compliance and fraud services and integrations, and allows them to customize payment experiences so that payments can be made through major payment rails at varying levels of risk, speed and cost. Momentum's embedded all-in-one platform is flexible and compatible with many configurations. Orum designed the money movement platform to deliver every transaction securely and reliably. Use cases include: creating tools so that consumers can easily execute or automate their financial plans; allowing users to fund their accounts and/or begin investment immediately; disbursing approved insurance claims to consumers within seconds; unlocking three-to-five days of working capital and simplifying business payments reconciliations; offering fast and low-cost instant payouts for workers at the end of each shift; and transferring approved loans to consumers instantly.

Orum offers its employees comprehensive health benefits, 401(k), and employee assistance plans and programs.

FINANCIAL DATA: *Note: Data for latest year may not have been available at press time.*

In U.S. $	2021	2020	2019	2018	2017	2016
Revenue						
R&D Expense						
Operating Income						
Operating Margin %						
SGA Expense						
Net Income						
Operating Cash Flow						
Capital Expenditure						
EBITDA						
Return on Assets %						
Return on Equity %						
Debt to Equity						

CONTACT INFORMATION:

Phone: 844 647-6491   Fax:
Toll-Free:
Address: 819 Broadway, New York, NY 10003 United States

STOCK TICKER/OTHER:

Stock Ticker: Private   Exchange:
Employees: Fiscal Year Ends:
Parent Company:

SALARIES/BONUSES:

Top Exec. Salary: $ Bonus: $
Second Exec. Salary: $ Bonus: $

OTHER THOUGHTS:

Estimated Female Officers or Directors:
Hot Spot for Advancement for Women/Minorities:

Sales, profits and employees may be estimates. Financial information, benefits and other data can change quickly and may vary from those stated here.

Paxos Technology Solutions LLC

paxos.com

NAIC Code: 523920

TYPES OF BUSINESS:

Portfolio Management
Cryptocurrency Brokerage
Financial Technology
Blockchain Infrastructure
Cryptocurrency Settlement Services
Stablecoin Services
Tokenization
Digital Asset Trading Services

BRANDS/DIVISIONS/AFFILIATES:

Paxos
PAX Gold
itBit

GROWTH PLANS/SPECIAL FEATURES:

Paxos Technology Solutions, LLC is a financial technology company that developed, operates and builds the Paxos regulated blockchain infrastructure platform for enterprise partners and investors. As an open financial system, Paxos holds physical and digital assets, builds technology that allows assets to be stored and moved on any blockchain, and enables the movement of assets through a network of products and services. The company's products leverage technology with bank-level oversight so that Paxos users can trade, settle and manage assets. Products offered by Paxos include cryptocurrency brokerage, settlement services for securities, settlement services for commodities, stablecoin as a service, PAX Gold digital token backed by physical gold (similar to Bitcoin), and itBit digital asset trading for institutional investors. Headquartered in New York, Paxos Technology has global offices in London and Singapore.

CONTACTS: *Note: Officers with more than one job title may be intentionally listed here more than once.*

Charles Cascarilla, CEO

FINANCIAL DATA: *Note: Data for latest year may not have been available at press time.*

In U.S. $	2021	2020	2019	2018	2017	2016
Revenue						
R&D Expense						
Operating Income						
Operating Margin %						
SGA Expense						
Net Income						
Operating Cash Flow						
Capital Expenditure						
EBITDA						
Return on Assets %						
Return on Equity %						
Debt to Equity						

CONTACT INFORMATION:

Phone: 855-217-2967   Fax:
Toll-Free:
Address: 450 Lexington Ave., Ste. 3952, New York, NY 10017 United States

STOCK TICKER/OTHER:

Stock Ticker: Private   Exchange:
Employees: Fiscal Year Ends:
Parent Company:

SALARIES/BONUSES:

Top Exec. Salary: $ Bonus: $
Second Exec. Salary: $ Bonus: $

OTHER THOUGHTS:

Estimated Female Officers or Directors:
Hot Spot for Advancement for Women/Minorities:

Sales, profits and employees may be estimates. Financial information, benefits and other data can change quickly and may vary from those stated here.

Payfare Inc

corp.payfare.com

NAIC Code: 511210Q

TYPES OF BUSINESS:
Computer Software: Accounting, Banking & Financial

BRANDS/DIVISIONS/AFFILIATES:

GROWTH PLANS/SPECIAL FEATURES:
Payfare Inc is a global fintech company offering mobile banking, instant payment, and loyalty-reward solutions. Its financial technology platform is providing financial inclusion and empowerment to next-generation workers around the globe with a full-service mobile bank account and debit card with instant access to their earnings and relevant cash-back rewards. Some brands that use Payfare include Lyft, Uber and DoorDash.

CONTACTS: *Note: Officers with more than one job title may be intentionally listed here more than once.*
Dan Poirier, CEO
Kevin Mills, CFO
Tom McCole, Chairman of the Board
Michel Cote, Founder

FINANCIAL DATA: *Note: Data for latest year may not have been available at press time.*

In U.S. $	2021	2020	2019	2018	2017	2016
Revenue		10,558,580	4,953,401	2,816,935	911,148	18,786
R&D Expense						
Operating Income		-12,616,140	-12,217,740	-9,530,725	-8,701,633	-3,322,538
Operating Margin %						
SGA Expense		11,443,500	10,742,920	8,861,931	8,690,305	3,302,730
Net Income		-20,665,760	-18,764,940	-10,524,120	-8,948,349	-3,640,179
Operating Cash Flow		-1,339,330	-8,881,633	-6,711,863	-4,472,627	-667,485
Capital Expenditure		570,678	851,373	862,772	541,743	286,580
EBITDA		-18,142,160	-11,396,600	-9,653,912	-8,591,939	-3,609,118
Return on Assets %						
Return on Equity %						
Debt to Equity						

CONTACT INFORMATION:
Phone: 905 626-8200   Fax:
Toll-Free:
Address: 40 University Ave., Ste. 551, Toronto, ON M5J 1T1 Canada

STOCK TICKER/OTHER:
Stock Ticker: PAY   Exchange: TSE
Employees: 60   Fiscal Year Ends: 12/31
Parent Company:

SALARIES/BONUSES:
Top Exec. Salary: $ Bonus: $
Second Exec. Salary: $ Bonus: $

OTHER THOUGHTS:
Estimated Female Officers or Directors:
Hot Spot for Advancement for Women/Minorities:

Sales, profits and employees may be estimates. Financial information, benefits and other data can change quickly and may vary from those stated here.

Payliance

NAIC Code: 522320

payliance.com

TYPES OF BUSINESS:
Financial Transactions Processing, Reserve, and Clearinghouse Activities
Payments Processing And Acceptance
Payments Verification
Debt Collection Services
Financial Technology
Debt Collection Software
ACH, Card and Check Processing
Risk Assessment Tools

BRANDS/DIVISIONS/AFFILIATES:

CONTACTS: *Note: Officers with more than one job title may be intentionally listed here more than once.*
John Cullen, CEO
Randy Yost, Dir.-IT Oper.
Steve Valachovic, Exec. VP-Sales & Bus. Dev.
John Gilbert, CIO
James Robinson, Dir.-Product

GROWTH PLANS/SPECIAL FEATURES:

Payliance is a financial technology company that develops and provides digital payment solutions for businesses and organizations. The all-in-one suite of solutions span payments, verification and recovery. Payliance offers Automated Clearing House (ACH), card and check-based payment and processing solutions, including high-volume same-day and next-day ACH, debit card and physical/remote checks for merchants and lenders. Payliance verification services include account verification and risk assessment tools for validating all payment types. Recovery services include debt collection software solutions, licensed collection agents and strategic re-presentment technology for scheduling payments when chances are good to collect. Payliance offers a payment guarantee when accepting and processing payments via Payliance. Other markets served by Payliance include buy now pay later, accounts receivable management, and sports gambling/online gambling.

FINANCIAL DATA: *Note: Data for latest year may not have been available at press time.*

In U.S. $	2021	2020	2019	2018	2017	2016
Revenue						
R&D Expense						
Operating Income						
Operating Margin %						
SGA Expense						
Net Income						
Operating Cash Flow						
Capital Expenditure						
EBITDA						
Return on Assets %						
Return on Equity %						
Debt to Equity						

CONTACT INFORMATION:
Phone: 614 944-5788   Fax:
Toll-Free: 800 634-4484
Address: 2 Easton Oval, Ste. 310, Columbus, OH 43219 United States

STOCK TICKER/OTHER:
Stock Ticker: Private   Exchange:
Employees: Fiscal Year Ends:
Parent Company:

SALARIES/BONUSES:
Top Exec. Salary: $ Bonus: $
Second Exec. Salary: $ Bonus: $

OTHER THOUGHTS:
Estimated Female Officers or Directors:
Hot Spot for Advancement for Women/Minorities:

Sales, profits and employees may be estimates. Financial information, benefits and other data can change quickly and may vary from those stated here.

PayPal Holdings Inc

www.paypal.com

NAIC Code: 522320

TYPES OF BUSINESS:

Payment Processing-Intermediary
Online Payment Systems
Web-Enabled Payments
Online Auction Technology
Credit Cards
Debit Cards
Account Management
Money Transfer

BRANDS/DIVISIONS/AFFILIATES:

PayPal
PayPal Credit
Braintree
Venmo
Xoom
iZettle
Hyperwallet
Honey

GROWTH PLANS/SPECIAL FEATURES:

PayPal was spun off from eBay in 2015 and provides electronic payment solutions to merchants and consumers, with a focus on online transactions. The company had 377 million active accounts at the end of 2020, including 29 million merchant accounts. The company also owns Xoom, an international money transfer business, and Venmo, a person-to-person payment platform.

CONTACTS: *Note: Officers with more than one job title may be intentionally listed here more than once.*

Daniel Schulman, CEO
John Rainey, CFO
John Donahoe, Chairman of the Board
Jeffrey Karbowski, Chief Accounting Officer
Louise Pentland, Chief Legal Officer
Aaron Karczmer, Chief Risk Officer
Jonathan Auerbach, Chief Strategy Officer
Sripada Shivananda, Chief Technology Officer
Peggy Alford, Executive VP, Divisional
Mark Britto, Executive VP

FINANCIAL DATA: *Note: Data for latest year may not have been available at press time.*

In U.S. $	2021	2020	2019	2018	2017	2016
Revenue		21,454,000,000	17,772,000,000	15,451,000,000	13,094,000,000	10,842,000,000
R&D Expense				1,071,000,000	953,000,000	834,000,000
Operating Income		3,428,000,000	2,790,000,000	2,503,000,000	2,259,000,000	1,586,000,000
Operating Margin %						
SGA Expense		6,573,000,000	5,197,000,000	2,764,000,000	3,647,000,000	3,264,000,000
Net Income		4,202,000,000	2,459,000,000	2,057,000,000	1,795,000,000	1,401,000,000
Operating Cash Flow		5,854,000,000	4,561,000,000	5,483,000,000	2,531,000,000	3,158,000,000
Capital Expenditure		866,000,000	704,000,000	823,000,000	667,000,000	669,000,000
EBITDA		6,463,000,000	4,025,000,000	3,229,000,000	3,064,000,000	2,310,000,000
Return on Assets %						
Return on Equity %						
Debt to Equity						

CONTACT INFORMATION:

Phone: 408-967-1000   Fax: 650-864-8001
Toll-Free:
Address: 2211 N. First St., San Jose, CA 95131 United States

STOCK TICKER/OTHER:

Stock Ticker: PYPL   Exchange: NAS
Employees: 26,500   Fiscal Year Ends: 12/31
Parent Company:

SALARIES/BONUSES:

Top Exec. Salary: $653,846   Bonus: $1,175,000
Second Exec. Salary: $1,038,462   Bonus: $

OTHER THOUGHTS:

Estimated Female Officers or Directors: 1
Hot Spot for Advancement for Women/Minorities: Y

Sales, profits and employees may be estimates. Financial information, benefits and other data can change quickly and may vary from those stated here.

Personal Capital Corporation

www.personalcapital.com

NAIC Code: 523930

TYPES OF BUSINESS:
Online Investment Advice
Wealth Management
Cash Management
Retirement Planning
Investing

BRANDS/DIVISIONS/AFFILIATES:
Desmarais Family Residuary Trust
Pansolo Holding Inc
Empower Holdings LLC
Personal Capital Advisors Corporation

CONTACTS: *Note: Officers with more than one job title may be intentionally listed here more than once.*
Jay Shah, Pres.
Vince Maniago, Chief Product Officer
James Burton, CMO
Allison Amadia, Head-Human Resources & Chief Compliance Officer
Fritz Robbins, CIO
Craig Birk, Chief Investment Officer

GROWTH PLANS/SPECIAL FEATURES:

Personal Capital Corporation offers an online personal wealth and cash management platform. The company has more than $23 billion assets under management and serves over 31,800 investment clients across all 50 U.S. states (as of March 2022). A team of licensed fiduciary advisors and online tools are provided for people interested in investing, and together identify investment opportunities. Alerts are provided as well. Online tools include financial tools, net worth, savings planner, retirement planner, investment checkup and fee analyzer. The platform's dashboard offers a way for investors to see, understand and manage their money all in one place, and their advisor leverages the information to provide personalized wealth management advice, including advice on after-tax returns. Specialties by Personal Capital include financial services, personal finance software, investment management, 401(k), banking, financial planning, registered investment advisory, wealth advisory, and portfolio management. Online/mobile cash management occurs by opening a no-fee bank account with Personal Capital, which allows large withdrawals, wires up to $1 million, direct deposit, account linking for monthly bills, unlimited monthly transfers and no minimum balance requirement. Subsidiary Personal Capital Advisors Corporation is a registered investment adviser with the Securities and Exchange Commission. Personal Capital Corporation operates as a subsidiary of Empower Holdings, LLC, itself a subsidiary of Pansolo Holding, Inc., a corporation controlled by the Desmarais Family Residuary Trust.

Personal Capital offers its employees comprehensive health benefits, 401(k), company discount program, short/long-term disability opt-in, career development and other programs.

FINANCIAL DATA: *Note: Data for latest year may not have been available at press time.*

In U.S. $	2021	2020	2019	2018	2017	2016
Revenue						
R&D Expense						
Operating Income						
Operating Margin %						
SGA Expense						
Net Income						
Operating Cash Flow						
Capital Expenditure						
EBITDA						
Return on Assets %						
Return on Equity %						
Debt to Equity						

CONTACT INFORMATION:
Phone: 650 556-1310   Fax:
Toll-Free: 855 855-8005
Address: 3 Lagoon Dr., Ste. 200, Redwood City, CA 94065 United States

STOCK TICKER/OTHER:
Stock Ticker: Private   Exchange:
Employees: Fiscal Year Ends:
Parent Company: Pansolo Holding Inc

SALARIES/BONUSES:
Top Exec. Salary: $ Bonus: $
Second Exec. Salary: $ Bonus: $

OTHER THOUGHTS:
Estimated Female Officers or Directors:
Hot Spot for Advancement for Women/Minorities:

Sales, profits and employees may be estimates. Financial information, benefits and other data can change quickly and may vary from those stated here.

Plunkett Research, Ltd.

Petal Card Inc

www.petalcard.com

NAIC Code: 522210

TYPES OF BUSINESS:
Credit Card Issuing
Financial Technology
Online Credit Underwriting
Credit Building Strategies
Credit Card Issuing
Banking History Credit
Credit Measurement

BRANDS/DIVISIONS/AFFILIATES:

GROWTH PLANS/SPECIAL FEATURES:
Petal Card, Inc. is a financial technology company that specializes in online credit underwriting to help individuals build credit, avoid debt and obtain a Petal credit card. Petal analyzes each user's banking history (income, savings and spending) and transforms it into a cash score as an alternative to measuring credit worthiness. This strategy allows more people to be approved with better rates, even if they've never had credit before. Once approved, Petal provides tools for building positive credit history and tracking the credit score. Petal credit card activity is reported to all three major credit bureaus. Petal card holders can set a budget and freeze the card at any time. Partners of Petal Card include VISA, Credit Karma, WebBank, Experian, TransUnion and Equifax.

CONTACTS: Note: Officers with more than one job title may be intentionally listed here more than once.
Jason Gross, CEO

FINANCIAL DATA: Note: Data for latest year may not have been available at press time.

In U.S. $	2021	2020	2019	2018	2017	2016
Revenue						
R&D Expense						
Operating Income						
Operating Margin %						
SGA Expense						
Net Income						
Operating Cash Flow						
Capital Expenditure						
EBITDA						
Return on Assets %						
Return on Equity %						
Debt to Equity						

CONTACT INFORMATION:
Phone: 917 267-2582   Fax:
Toll-Free: 855 697-3825
Address: 233 Spring St., Fl. 3, New York, NY 10013-1522 United States

STOCK TICKER/OTHER:
Stock Ticker: Private   Exchange:
Employees: Fiscal Year Ends:
Parent Company:

SALARIES/BONUSES:
Top Exec. Salary: $ Bonus: $
Second Exec. Salary: $ Bonus: $

OTHER THOUGHTS:
Estimated Female Officers or Directors:
Hot Spot for Advancement for Women/Minorities:

Sales, profits and employees may be estimates. Financial information, benefits and other data can change quickly and may vary from those stated here.

PitchBook Data Inc

NAIC Code: 511210Q

www.pitchbook.com

TYPES OF BUSINESS:

Computer Software: Accounting, Banking & Financial
SaaS - Data Covering Private Capital Markets
Financial Technology
Data and Analytic Tools
Customer Relations Management Integration
Technology Plug-ins and Extensions
Product Release Information

BRANDS/DIVISIONS/AFFILIATES:

Morningstar Inc
PitchBook Desktop
PitchBook Mobile

CONTACTS: *Note: Officers with more than one job title may be intentionally listed here more than once.*

John Gabbert, CEO
Rod Diefendorf, COO
Patrick Ross, VP-Finance
Paul Santarelli, VP-Sales
Amy Whaley, VP-People
Peter Escher, VP-Data Oper.
Paul Jaeschke, VP-Products

GROWTH PLANS/SPECIAL FEATURES:

PitchBook Data, Inc. is a financial technology company that provides market data and related solutions through its PitchBook platform. The software-as-a-service (SaaS) firm delivers data, research and technology covering private capital markets, benchmarks, startups and venture capital. Products provided by PitchBook include: PitchBook Desktop and PitchBook Mobile, offering access to PitchBook data and analytical tools, including company profiles, funds and investors; customer relations management (CRM) integration; Excel plugin for Office 365 and Mac; Chrome extension; direct data integration; institutional-grade private market access and research; and access to product releases to evaluate fund returns via PitchBook benchmarks tool. Solutions by PitchBook span private market intelligence, fundraising, deal sourcing, due diligence, business development, networking and deal execution. Headquartered in Washington, USA, the company has global headquarters in the U.K. and Hong Kong. PitchBook Data operates as a subsidiary of Morningstar, Inc.

PitchBook Technology offers its employees comprehensive health benefits, 401(k), savings accounts, professional development opportunities, paid time off and a variety of company plans, programs and perks.

FINANCIAL DATA: *Note: Data for latest year may not have been available at press time.*

In U.S. $	2021	2020	2019	2018	2017	2016
Revenue						
R&D Expense						
Operating Income						
Operating Margin %						
SGA Expense						
Net Income						
Operating Cash Flow						
Capital Expenditure						
EBITDA						
Return on Assets %						
Return on Equity %						
Debt to Equity						

CONTACT INFORMATION:

Phone: 206 623-1986   Fax:
Toll-Free:
Address: 901 Fifth Ave., Ste. 1200, Seattle, WA 98164 United States

STOCK TICKER/OTHER:

Stock Ticker: Subsidiary   Exchange:
Employees: Fiscal Year Ends:
Parent Company: Morningstar Inc

SALARIES/BONUSES:

Top Exec. Salary: $ Bonus: $
Second Exec. Salary: $ Bonus: $

OTHER THOUGHTS:

Estimated Female Officers or Directors:
Hot Spot for Advancement for Women/Minorities:

Sales, profits and employees may be estimates. Financial information, benefits and other data can change quickly and may vary from those stated here.

Plaid Inc

plaid.com

NAIC Code: 511210Q

TYPES OF BUSINESS:

Computer Software: Accounting, Banking & Financial
Online Banking
API Technology
A2A Payments
Digital Wallets

BRANDS/DIVISIONS/AFFILIATES:

CONTACTS: *Note: Officers with more than one job title may be intentionally listed here more than once.*

Zack Perret, CEO

GROWTH PLANS/SPECIAL FEATURES:

Plaid, Inc. is a financial services company that builds the technical infrastructure application programming interfaces (APIs) that connect consumers, financial institutions and developers. The firm also designs and delivers related data insight and analytic products. Plaid's financial products include transactions, authorization of accounts and routing numbers, bank balance in real-time, account-holder identification, investments (retirement, brokerage, health, education), assets via users' finances, and liabilities such as mortgage data, credit cards and student loans. The company's site offers information on how users can make the most of its products, including apps, in the areas of personal finances, lending, wealth, consumer payments, banking and business finance. For consumers, Plaid apps can securely connect financial accounts into a single place, which can also be retrieved and shared at the user's discretion. Financial data stored elsewhere can be deleted directly from Plaid's systems in order to keep everything in one space. There is no charge for connecting accounts.

Plaid offers its employees comprehensive medical benefits, 401(k), partnerships with SoFo, equity packages, learning development opportunities and more.

FINANCIAL DATA: *Note: Data for latest year may not have been available at press time.*

In U.S. $	2021	2020	2019	2018	2017	2016
Revenue	235,400,000	220,000,000	150,000,000			
R&D Expense						
Operating Income						
Operating Margin %						
SGA Expense						
Net Income						
Operating Cash Flow						
Capital Expenditure						
EBITDA						
Return on Assets %						
Return on Equity %						
Debt to Equity						

CONTACT INFORMATION:

Phone: 415 799-1354   Fax:
Toll-Free:
Address: 85 2nd St., Ste. 400, San Francisco, CA 94105 United States

STOCK TICKER/OTHER:

Stock Ticker: Private   Exchange:
Employees: 1,000   Fiscal Year Ends: 12/31
Parent Company:

SALARIES/BONUSES:

Top Exec. Salary: $ Bonus: $
Second Exec. Salary: $ Bonus: $

OTHER THOUGHTS:

Estimated Female Officers or Directors:
Hot Spot for Advancement for Women/Minorities:

Sales, profits and employees may be estimates. Financial information, benefits and other data can change quickly and may vary from those stated here.

Plastiq Inc

NAIC Code: 522320

www.plastiq.com

TYPES OF BUSINESS:

Financial Transactions Processing, Reserve, and Clearinghouse Activities
Credit Card Payment Platform
Financial Technology
Payable Automation Solutions
Payments Software Development Kit
Credit Card Acceptance Software
Invoice Solutions
Payments Processing Solutions

BRANDS/DIVISIONS/AFFILIATES:

Plastiq Pay
Plastiq Accept

CONTACTS: *Note: Officers with more than one job title may be intentionally listed here more than once.*

Eliot Buchanan, CEO
Noah Goldberg, Head-Oper.
Amir Jafari, CFO
Yi Sun, Chief Engineer & Architect
Angela Loeffler, Chief People Officer
Stoyan Kenderov, CTO
Eric Normant, VP-Product Engineering

GROWTH PLANS/SPECIAL FEATURES:

Plastiq, Inc. is a financial technology company that has built the Plastiq payments platform to offer businesses and individuals the freedom of choosing how they want to pay for supplies, products and services. The firm offers two core products: Plastiq Pay and Plastiq Accept. Plastiq Pay enables suppliers to be paid by credit card even where they are not accepted because the platform will send the payment on the Plastiq user's behalf the way the supplier prefers. Thus, Plastiq automates the user's payables and expands working capital. Plastiq Pay offers unlimited free bank transfers, and integrates with all major accounting software tools. Payment approval permissions can be set up to keep workflow streamlined. Plastiq Accept accepts credit cards, debit cards and bank payments with no processing fees. Payments can be collected online through a unique payment link; payments in ecommerce can be embedded with Plastiq's checkout software development kit (SDK); invoices can be paid instantly through a provided payment link; and payments can be processed via computer or over the phone/virtually. Plastiq payment solutions by industry span manufacturing, construction, freight/logistics, wholesale, schools and education, retailers and ecommerce, membership clubs, accountants and for individuals. Headquartered in San Francisco, California, the company has a global office in Vancouver, British Columbia.

FINANCIAL DATA: *Note: Data for latest year may not have been available at press time.*

In U.S. $	2021	2020	2019	2018	2017	2016
Revenue						
R&D Expense						
Operating Income						
Operating Margin %						
SGA Expense						
Net Income						
Operating Cash Flow						
Capital Expenditure						
EBITDA						
Return on Assets %						
Return on Equity %						
Debt to Equity						

CONTACT INFORMATION:

Phone: 866-313-9823   Fax:
Toll-Free:
Address: 447 Sutter St., Ste. 405, PMB 49, San Francisco, CA 94108 United States

STOCK TICKER/OTHER:

Stock Ticker: Private   Exchange:
Employees: Fiscal Year Ends:
Parent Company:

SALARIES/BONUSES:

Top Exec. Salary: $ Bonus: $
Second Exec. Salary: $ Bonus: $

OTHER THOUGHTS:

Estimated Female Officers or Directors:
Hot Spot for Advancement for Women/Minorities:

Sales, profits and employees may be estimates. Financial information, benefits and other data can change quickly and may vary from those stated here.

PNC Financial Services Group Inc

www.pnc.com

NAIC Code: 522110

TYPES OF BUSINESS:
Retail Banking
Financial Services
Retail Banking
Corporate Banking
Institutional Banking
Asset Management
Residential Mortgages
Loan and Lease Solutions

BRANDS/DIVISIONS/AFFILIATES:
PNC Bank NA
BBVA USA Bancshares Inc

GROWTH PLANS/SPECIAL FEATURES:
PNC Financial Services Group is a diversified financial services company offering retail banking, corporate and institutional banking, asset management, and residential mortgage banking across the United States.

PNC offers its employees health and life insurance, retirement and savings options and other benefits.

CONTACTS: *Note: Officers with more than one job title may be intentionally listed here more than once.*
William Demchak, CEO
Karen Larrimer, Executive VP
Robert Reilly, CFO
Gregory Kozich, Chief Accounting Officer
Gregory Jordan, Chief Administrative Officer
Michael Hannon, Chief Credit Officer
Kieran Fallon, Chief Risk Officer
E. Parsley, Executive VP
Michael Lyons, Executive VP
Stacy Juchno, Executive VP
Carole Brown, Executive VP
Deborah Guild, Executive VP
Richard Bynum, Executive VP
Ganesh Krishnan, Executive VP
Vicki Henn, Executive VP

FINANCIAL DATA: *Note: Data for latest year may not have been available at press time.*

In U.S. $	2021	2020	2019	2018	2017	2016
Revenue		16,798,000,000	17,827,000,000	17,132,000,000	16,329,000,000	15,162,000,000
R&D Expense						
Operating Income						
Operating Margin %						
SGA Expense		5,909,000,000	5,948,000,000	5,756,000,000	5,468,000,000	5,088,000,000
Net Income		7,517,000,000	5,369,000,000	5,301,000,000	5,338,000,000	3,903,000,000
Operating Cash Flow		4,659,000,000	7,363,000,000	7,840,000,000	5,699,000,000	3,635,000,000
Capital Expenditure						
EBITDA						
Return on Assets %						
Return on Equity %						
Debt to Equity						

CONTACT INFORMATION:
Phone: 412 762-2265   Fax: 412 762-5798
Toll-Free: 888-762-2265
Address: 300 Fifth Ave., Tower at PNC Plaza, Pittsburgh, PA 15222-2401 United States

STOCK TICKER/OTHER:
Stock Ticker: PNC
Employees: 59,426
Parent Company:

Exchange: NYS
Fiscal Year Ends: 12/31

SALARIES/BONUSES:
Top Exec. Salary: $1,192,692   Bonus: $
Second Exec. Salary: $700,000   Bonus: $

OTHER THOUGHTS:
Estimated Female Officers or Directors: 4
Hot Spot for Advancement for Women/Minorities: Y

Sales, profits and employees may be estimates. Financial information, benefits and other data can change quickly and may vary from those stated here.

Policygenius Inc

www.policygenius.com

NAIC Code: 524210

TYPES OF BUSINESS:
Insurance Agencies and Brokerages
Online Insurance Marketplace
Insurance Quote Comparison
Financial Technology
Licensed Insurance Agents

BRANDS/DIVISIONS/AFFILIATES:

GROWTH PLANS/SPECIAL FEATURES:

Policygenius, Inc. is a financial technology company that has developed an online insurance marketplace called Policygenius. The platform combines technology with real licensed agents to help people obtain the insurance they need. Policygenius compares quotes from multiple insurance companies within minutes. As an independent insurance broker, the firm gets paid a commission by insurance companies for each sale. Insurance commissions are pre-built into the price of an insurance policy; therefore, consumers are not charged an additional fee by Policygenius. Insurance products offered span life, home, auto, disability, renters, health, long-term care, pet and other insurance. Headquartered in New York, Policygenius has an additional office in North Carolina.

CONTACTS: Note: Officers with more than one job title may be intentionally listed here more than once.
Jennifer Fitzgerald, CEO
Francois de Lame, Chief Product Officer

FINANCIAL DATA: Note: Data for latest year may not have been available at press time.

In U.S. $	2021	2020	2019	2018	2017	2016
Revenue						
R&D Expense						
Operating Income						
Operating Margin %						
SGA Expense						
Net Income						
Operating Cash Flow						
Capital Expenditure						
EBITDA						
Return on Assets %						
Return on Equity %						
Debt to Equity						

CONTACT INFORMATION:
Phone: Fax:
Toll-Free: 855-695-2255
Address: 32 Old Slip, Fl. 30, New York, NY 10005 United States

STOCK TICKER/OTHER:
Stock Ticker: Private   Exchange:
Employees: Fiscal Year Ends:
Parent Company:

SALARIES/BONUSES:
Top Exec. Salary: $ Bonus: $
Second Exec. Salary: $ Bonus: $

OTHER THOUGHTS:
Estimated Female Officers or Directors:
Hot Spot for Advancement for Women/Minorities:

Sales, profits and employees may be estimates. Financial information, benefits and other data can change quickly and may vary from those stated here.

Poynt Company

poynt.com

NAIC Code: 522320

TYPES OF BUSINESS:
Financial Transactions Processing
Payment Terminal Solutions
Omnichannel
eCommerce
Merchant
Invoices

BRANDS/DIVISIONS/AFFILIATES:

CONTACTS: Note: Officers with more than one job title may be intentionally listed here more than once.
Osama Bedier, CEO

GROWTH PLANS/SPECIAL FEATURES:
Poynt Company has developed an open commerce platform that offers all-in-one payment solutions. The firm's payment products and services are primarily designed for merchants, resellers and developers. Poynt OS' open operating system can power any smart payment terminal worldwide. For merchants, Poynt Processing offers everything needed to run the business, including in-person, eCommerce and invoicing with card-on-file; point of sale payment processing; choice of smart terminals; integrated business software; business management tools (100% remote); third-party apps to meet business needs; and access to merchant cash advances. Poynt Processing activates instantly and funds the following day. Support is provided 24/7. For resellers, Poynt Processing's omnicommerce (in-store, eCommerce, invoices) payment solution offers payment processing, pre-installed core software applications, choice of smart terminal, third-party apps, instant onboarding, 1-2 day fulfillment, next-day deposits, and no hidden fees or contracts. Poynt's platform enables users to manage thousands of devices (printers, cash drawers, scanners), to troubleshoot from anywhere, and to build custom-tailored solutions. For developers, Poynt's open commerce platform integrates for easy distribution, including developer documents, application programming interface (API) references, and app creation. For original equipment manufacturers (OEMs), Poynt's solutions can bring omnicommerce cloud capabilities to any Android payment device, and enables merchants to accept payments across multiple channels using any device. A merchant portal is used for managing daily operations such as settlements, transactions, accounting and more; and provides access to a variety of business apps, from employee scheduling to inventory, from curbside pickup to gift cards. Poynt is headquartered in California, with an international headquarter in Singapore. The company is backed by Elavon, Google Ventures, Matrix Partners, National Australia Bank, NYCA Partners, Oak HC/FT Partners, Stanford-StartX Fund, and Webb Investment Network.

FINANCIAL DATA: Note: Data for latest year may not have been available at press time.

In U.S. $	2021	2020	2019	2018	2017	2016
Revenue						
R&D Expense						
Operating Income						
Operating Margin %						
SGA Expense						
Net Income						
Operating Cash Flow						
Capital Expenditure						
EBITDA						
Return on Assets %						
Return on Equity %						
Debt to Equity						

CONTACT INFORMATION:
Phone: 855-398-0833   Fax:
Toll-Free:
Address: 4151 Middlefield Rd., Palo Alto, CA 94303 United States

STOCK TICKER/OTHER:
Stock Ticker: Subsidiary
Employees:
Parent Company: GoDaddy Inc

Exchange:
Fiscal Year Ends:

SALARIES/BONUSES:
Top Exec. Salary: $ Bonus: $
Second Exec. Salary: $ Bonus: $

OTHER THOUGHTS:
Estimated Female Officers or Directors:
Hot Spot for Advancement for Women/Minorities:

Sales, profits and employees may be estimates. Financial information, benefits and other data can change quickly and may vary from those stated here.

Prodigy Ventures Inc

NAIC Code: 511210Q

www.prodigy.ventures

TYPES OF BUSINESS:
Computer Software: Accounting, Banking & Financial

GROWTH PLANS/SPECIAL FEATURES:
Prodigy Ventures Inc delivers Fintech innovation. The company develops software and services with emerging technologies for digital transformation, identity, and payments. Digital transformation services include strategy, architecture, design, project management, agile development, quality engineering, and staff augmentation.

BRANDS/DIVISIONS/AFFILIATES:

CONTACTS:
Note: Officers with more than one job title may be intentionally listed here more than once.

Jeffery Watts, CEO
Andrew Hilton, CFO
Thomas Beckerman, Chairman of the Board
Doug Woolridge, Senior VP
Natalie Mohammed, Vice President, Divisional

FINANCIAL DATA:
Note: Data for latest year may not have been available at press time.

In U.S. $	2021	2020	2019	2018	2017	2016
Revenue		12,536,120	15,960,390	13,301,180	9,531,082	8,651,796
R&D Expense		299,491	739,874	799,140	776,080	763,127
Operating Income		632,929	410,942	215,246	425,776	1,004,934
Operating Margin %						
SGA Expense		2,462,147	3,124,115	2,146,342	1,608,284	1,119,566
Net Income		411,975	269,517	137,851	272,828	704,027
Operating Cash Flow		816,968	874,918	-35,247	-488,561	1,062,539
Capital Expenditure		136,810	54,534	19,994	36,320	31,963
EBITDA		789,880	565,060	234,754	440,881	1,012,969
Return on Assets %						
Return on Equity %						
Debt to Equity						

CONTACT INFORMATION:
Phone: 416 488-7700   Fax:
Toll-Free:
Address: 77 King Street West, Toronto, ON M5K 1G8 Canada

STOCK TICKER/OTHER:
Stock Ticker: PGV
Employees:
Parent Company:

Exchange: TSX
Fiscal Year Ends: 12/31

SALARIES/BONUSES:
Top Exec. Salary: $ Bonus: $
Second Exec. Salary: $ Bonus: $

OTHER THOUGHTS:
Estimated Female Officers or Directors:
Hot Spot for Advancement for Women/Minorities:

Sales, profits and employees may be estimates. Financial information, benefits and other data can change quickly and may vary from those stated here.

Plunkett Research, Ltd.

Propel Inc

www.joinpropel.com

NAIC Code: 511210Q

TYPES OF BUSINESS:
Computer Software: Accounting, Banking & Financial
Low Income Finance Platform
Money Management Solutions
Debit Account
Debit Cards
Mobile App

BRANDS/DIVISIONS/AFFILIATES:
Providers

CONTACTS: *Note: Officers with more than one job title may be intentionally listed here more than once.*
Jimmy Chen, CEO
Jeff Kaiser, COO
Ram Mehta, CTO

GROWTH PLANS/SPECIAL FEATURES:
Propel, Inc. is a financial technology company that develops products to help low-income Americans improve their financial health. The firm's free app, Providers, is used by millions of Americans across the country every month for money management purposes. Whether it be paychecks, food stamps, electronic benefits transfer (EBT), unemployment income or disability income, Providers helps users make the most of their funds. Balances and spending can be easily seen on the app, informing users about how much they have and how much they can spend. Stores that accept EBT can be located through the app. Providers is available in all 50 states. Providers comes with a free debit account for managing money, and is accepted for no-fee at over 30,000 automated teller machines (ATMs). Instant transaction notifications occur through the app. Users need to update information on Providers if rent is raised or pay is cut so that adjustments on the application can be made, as well as providing help with finding a new job, obtaining discounts and coupons and more.

FINANCIAL DATA: *Note: Data for latest year may not have been available at press time.*

In U.S. $	2021	2020	2019	2018	2017	2016
Revenue						
R&D Expense						
Operating Income						
Operating Margin %						
SGA Expense						
Net Income						
Operating Cash Flow						
Capital Expenditure						
EBITDA						
Return on Assets %						
Return on Equity %						
Debt to Equity						

CONTACT INFORMATION:
Phone: 913-206-6362   Fax:
Toll-Free:
Address: 397 Bridge St. Fl. 8, Brooklyn, NY 11201 United States

STOCK TICKER/OTHER:
Stock Ticker: Private   Exchange:
Employees: Fiscal Year Ends:
Parent Company:

SALARIES/BONUSES:
Top Exec. Salary: $ Bonus: $
Second Exec. Salary: $ Bonus: $

OTHER THOUGHTS:
Estimated Female Officers or Directors:
Hot Spot for Advancement for Women/Minorities:

Sales, profits and employees may be estimates. Financial information, benefits and other data can change quickly and may vary from those stated here.

Plunkett Research, Ltd.

Public.com (Public Holdings Inc)

public.com

NAIC Code: 523120

TYPES OF BUSINESS:

Securities Brokerage
Online Trading Platform
Financial Technology
Online Investments
Stock Investments
Exchange Traded Funds
Cryptocurrencies
Investment Education Resources

BRANDS/DIVISIONS/AFFILIATES:

Public.com
Open to the Public Investing Inc

CONTACTS: *Note: Officers with more than one job title may be intentionally listed here more than once.*

Jannick Malling, CEO

GROWTH PLANS/SPECIAL FEATURES:

Public Holdings, Inc. is a financial technology company that has developed and maintains an online investment platform, Public.com. Users can build their investment portfolio across stocks, exchange traded funds (ETFs) and cryptocurrencies, with thousands of stocks and ETFs to choose from and more than 25 cryptos. Public.com enables users to search for investors who share the same interests, browse recent initial public offerings (IPOs), see which companies are reporting earnings soon, and other information. Following people and companies enrich user feed and presents fresh daily content. Most Public.com members are long-term investors; therefore, the app sends an annual notification/reminder to users to see if they desire to continue hold a specific investment or move it elsewhere. Public builds educational features into its app so that investors can learn along the way, with features including terminology definitions, and explanations for when a stock is moving. Customer support is offered through several ways, including online chat and speaking with real people. Securities are offered to self-directed customers via subsidiary Open to the Public Investing, Inc., a registered broker-dealer and member of FINRA & SIPC. Cryptocurrency trading is provided by Apex Crypto LLC, which is not a registered broker-dealer or FINRA member and is not affiliated with Public Holdings nor any of its subsidiaries.

Public offers its employees comprehensive health benefits, 401(k) and other company plans and perks.

FINANCIAL DATA: *Note: Data for latest year may not have been available at press time.*

In U.S. $	2021	2020	2019	2018	2017	2016
Revenue						
R&D Expense						
Operating Income						
Operating Margin %						
SGA Expense						
Net Income						
Operating Cash Flow						
Capital Expenditure						
EBITDA						
Return on Assets %						
Return on Equity %						
Debt to Equity						

CONTACT INFORMATION:

Phone: 646 462-4225   Fax:
Toll-Free:
Address: 1 State St. Plz., Fl.10, New York, NY 10004 United States

STOCK TICKER/OTHER:

Stock Ticker: Private   Exchange:
Employees: Fiscal Year Ends:
Parent Company:

SALARIES/BONUSES:

Top Exec. Salary: $ Bonus: $
Second Exec. Salary: $ Bonus: $

OTHER THOUGHTS:

Estimated Female Officers or Directors:
Hot Spot for Advancement for Women/Minorities:

Sales, profits and employees may be estimates. Financial information, benefits and other data can change quickly and may vary from those stated here.

Q2 Holdings Inc

q2ebanking.com

NAIC Code: 511210Q

TYPES OF BUSINESS:
Computer Software: Accounting, Banking & Financial

BRANDS/DIVISIONS/AFFILIATES:

GROWTH PLANS/SPECIAL FEATURES:
Q2 Holdings Inc. is a provider of cloud-based virtual banking solutions for regional financial institutions to deliver mobile banking services to retail and commercial end-users who wish to bank anywhere and anytime. Its solutions operate on an integrated tablet-first platform which provides financial institutions a comprehensive view of account holder activity, and meets the regulatory and security requirements applicable to the industry. The firm generates revenue from subscription-based arrangements for software offerings, typically for five years. A large majority of the firm's revenue is generated in the United States.

CONTACTS: *Note: Officers with more than one job title may be intentionally listed here more than once.*
Matthew Flake, CEO
David Mehok, CFO
R. H. Seale, Chairman of the Board
William Furrer, Chief Strategy Officer
Adam Blue, Chief Technology Officer
John Breeden, COO
Kim Rutledge, Executive VP, Divisional
Jonathan Price, Executive VP, Divisional
Barry Benton, General Counsel
Bharath Oruganti, Senior VP, Divisional
Anthony Hall, Senior VP, Divisional

FINANCIAL DATA: *Note: Data for latest year may not have been available at press time.*

In U.S. $	2021	2020	2019	2018	2017	2016
Revenue		402,751,000	315,484,000	241,100,000	193,978,000	150,224,000
R&D Expense		97,381,000	76,273,000	51,334,000	40,338,000	32,460,000
Operating Income		-86,111,000	-50,719,000	-27,705,000	-25,675,000	-29,411,000
Operating Margin %						
SGA Expense		145,441,000	121,106,000	93,772,000	78,349,000	68,276,000
Net Income		-137,620,000	-70,877,000	-35,397,000	-26,164,000	-36,354,000
Operating Cash Flow		-2,890,000	567,000	4,595,000	9,472,000	3,394,000
Capital Expenditure		24,667,000	14,325,000	13,331,000	13,285,000	17,364,000
EBITDA		-55,718,000	-34,617,000	-12,237,000	-11,408,000	-23,161,000
Return on Assets %						
Return on Equity %						
Debt to Equity						

CONTACT INFORMATION:
Phone: 512-275-0072   Fax:
Toll-Free:
Address: 13785 Research Blvd., Ste. 150, Austin, TX 78750 United States

STOCK TICKER/OTHER:
Stock Ticker: QTWO
Employees: 2,028
Parent Company:

Exchange: NYS
Fiscal Year Ends: 12/31

SALARIES/BONUSES:
Top Exec. Salary: $520,000   Bonus: $
Second Exec. Salary: $368,400   Bonus: $

OTHER THOUGHTS:
Estimated Female Officers or Directors:
Hot Spot for Advancement for Women/Minorities:

Sales, profits and employees may be estimates. Financial information, benefits and other data can change quickly and may vary from those stated here.

Q4 Inc

www.q4inc.com

NAIC Code: 511210K

TYPES OF BUSINESS:

Computer Software: Sales & Customer Relationship Management (CRM)

GROWTH PLANS/SPECIAL FEATURES:

Q4 Inc is a capital markets communications platform provider. The company's end-to-end technology platform facilitates interactions across the capital markets through its IR website products, virtual events solutions, capital markets CRM, shareholder and market analytics tools.

BRANDS/DIVISIONS/AFFILIATES:

CONTACTS: *Note: Officers with more than one job title may be intentionally listed here more than once.*

Darrell Heaps, CEO
Donna de Winter, COO
Warren Faleiro, CTO
Dorothy Arturi, Chief People Officer
Mark Ramsay, CRO

FINANCIAL DATA: *Note: Data for latest year may not have been available at press time.*

In U.S. $	2021	2020	2019	2018	2017	2016
Revenue		40,381,180	22,400,370	17,300,990		
R&D Expense		6,539,652	3,272,166	2,054,465		
Operating Income		-11,706,400	-9,616,348	-4,949,310		
Operating Margin %						
SGA Expense		22,332,080	16,338,050	10,864,600		
Net Income		-13,118,530	-11,053,110	-8,265,095		
Operating Cash Flow		-3,515,144	-6,091,543	-3,113,580		
Capital Expenditure		4,921,315	265,790	31,147		
EBITDA		-8,493,964	-8,926,593	-3,562,193		
Return on Assets %						
Return on Equity %						
Debt to Equity						

CONTACT INFORMATION:

Phone: 647 278-7959   Fax:
Toll-Free:
Address: 469-A King Street West, Toronto, ON M5V 1K4 Canada

STOCK TICKER/OTHER:

Stock Ticker: QFOR   Exchange: TSE
Employees: Fiscal Year Ends: 12/31
Parent Company:

SALARIES/BONUSES:

Top Exec. Salary: $ Bonus: $
Second Exec. Salary: $ Bonus: $

OTHER THOUGHTS:

Estimated Female Officers or Directors:
Hot Spot for Advancement for Women/Minorities:

Sales, profits and employees may be estimates. Financial information, benefits and other data can change quickly and may vary from those stated here.

Qonto (Olinda SAS)

qonto.com/en

NAIC Code: 522110

TYPES OF BUSINESS:

Online Business Banking
Financial Technology
Online Payments Platform
Business Accounts
Business Credit Cards
Money Transfer Services
Business Lending
Cash Surplus Investing

BRANDS/DIVISIONS/AFFILIATES:

CONTACTS: *Note: Officers with more than one job title may be intentionally listed here more than once.*

Alexandre Prot, CEO
Steve Anavi, Pres.

GROWTH PLANS/SPECIAL FEATURES:

Olinda SAS is a France-based financial technology firm that has developed and operates Qonto, an online payment platform for freelancers, associations and small/medium businesses. Founded in 2016, Qonto is regulated, approved and supervised by the Frenche Autorite de Controle Prudentiel et de Resolution (ACPR). Services offered through Qonto include business account setup, Mastercard business cards, SEPA and SWIFT transfers, all payment methods for sending/receiving in France and globally, automated bookkeeping, expense management, account connectivity solutions, business loans, business financing solutions, and cash surplus investment options. Multiple accounts can be created on Qonto with dedicated international bank account numbers (IBANs) to separate expense items, activities and create team budgets, etc. Share capital can be deposited into the user's Qonto online account. Customer service support is offered daily via chat, phone or email. Olinda has additional European offices in Berlin, Barcelona and Milan.

FINANCIAL DATA: *Note: Data for latest year may not have been available at press time.*

In U.S. $	2021	2020	2019	2018	2017	2016
Revenue						
R&D Expense						
Operating Income						
Operating Margin %						
SGA Expense						
Net Income						
Operating Cash Flow						
Capital Expenditure						
EBITDA						
Return on Assets %						
Return on Equity %						
Debt to Equity						

CONTACT INFORMATION:

Phone: 33 1 76 41 03 08   Fax:
Toll-Free:
Address: 20 bis rue La Fayette, Paris, 75009 France

STOCK TICKER/OTHER:

Stock Ticker: Private
Employees:
Parent Company:

Exchange:
Fiscal Year Ends:

SALARIES/BONUSES:

Top Exec. Salary: $ Bonus: $
Second Exec. Salary: $ Bonus: $

OTHER THOUGHTS:

Estimated Female Officers or Directors:
Hot Spot for Advancement for Women/Minorities:

Sales, profits and employees may be estimates. Financial information, benefits and other data can change quickly and may vary from those stated here.

Ramp Business Corporation

ramp.com

NAIC Code: 522210

TYPES OF BUSINESS:

Business Credit Card Issuing
Financial Technology
Business Money Management Software
Business Credit Cards
Credit Card Expense Control
Pre-Approved Cards
Workflow Software Solutions
Automated Account and Audit Solutions

BRANDS/DIVISIONS/AFFILIATES:

CONTACTS: *Note: Officers with more than one job title may be intentionally listed here more than once.*

Eric Glyman, CEO
Gene Lee, Chief Product Officer
Karim Atiyeh, CTO

GROWTH PLANS/SPECIAL FEATURES:

Ramp Business Corporation is a financial technology company that builds money management software and related solutions for businesses. Ramp's credit card software and solutions include: unlimited branded business credit cards (physical and virtual) acceptable anywhere; card merchant/vendor block and spend restriction features; account limit, time and/or category features; card management software updated in real-time; unlimited 1.5% cashback; no fees; cards run on VISA; and mobile ready. Business funds software and solutions include: high-limit business cards via Ramp proprietary underwriting capabilities; establishing flexible expense policies through Ramp's policy builder, which can be uploaded to Ramp for employees to sign; built-in security at every step of the credit card process; spend controls, whether for employee or merchant; and employee pre-approval cards. Ramp's workflow software and solutions include: deploying finance stacks, uniting all finances into a single platform, centralizing company spend, creating workflows, connecting HR systems, automating employee onboarding, collaborating via email/Slack/SMS, automating account and audit books, and utilizing integrations for streamlining work from approvals to accounting. Last, Ramp software and solutions that same time and money across receipt matching, expense categorizing, travel booking/expense/receipt automation, real-time expense reporting, transaction savings analytics and insights, and price intelligence for savings purposes. Primary integration platforms include NetSuite, QuickBooks, Sage, Xero, Slack and 1Password, but more than 1,000 integrations are acceptable with Ramp.

Ramp offers its employees comprehensive health benefits, personal growth opportunities, paid time off and competitive salaries.

FINANCIAL DATA: *Note: Data for latest year may not have been available at press time.*

In U.S. $	2021	2020	2019	2018	2017	2016
Revenue						
R&D Expense						
Operating Income						
Operating Margin %						
SGA Expense						
Net Income						
Operating Cash Flow						
Capital Expenditure						
EBITDA						
Return on Assets %						
Return on Equity %						
Debt to Equity						

CONTACT INFORMATION:

Phone: 855-206-7283   Fax:
Toll-Free:
Address: 71 5th Ave., Fl. 6, New York, NY 10003 United States

STOCK TICKER/OTHER:

Stock Ticker: Private   Exchange:
Employees: Fiscal Year Ends:
Parent Company:

SALARIES/BONUSES:

Top Exec. Salary: $ Bonus: $
Second Exec. Salary: $ Bonus: $

OTHER THOUGHTS:

Estimated Female Officers or Directors:
Hot Spot for Advancement for Women/Minorities:

Sales, profits and employees may be estimates. Financial information, benefits and other data can change quickly and may vary from those stated here.

Plunkett Research, Ltd.

Real Matters Inc

www.realmatters.com

NAIC Code: 511210Q

TYPES OF BUSINESS:
Computer Software: Accounting, Banking & Financial

GROWTH PLANS/SPECIAL FEATURES:
Real Matters Inc is a Canadian network management services provider for the mortgage lending and insurance industries. The company's platform combines proprietary technology and network management capabilities with tens of thousands of independent qualified field agents. Its operating segment includes U.S. Appraisal; U.S. Title and Canada. The company generates maximum revenue from the U.S. Appraisal segment. Its U.S. Appraisal segment provides residential mortgage appraisals for purchase, refinance, and home equity transactions through its Solidifi brand.

BRANDS/DIVISIONS/AFFILIATES:

CONTACTS: *Note: Officers with more than one job title may be intentionally listed here more than once.*
Brian Lang, CEO
William Herman, CFO
Jason Smith, Chairman of the Board
Ryan Smith, Chief Technology Officer
Kevin Walton, Executive VP, Divisional
Kim Montgomery, Executive VP, Subsidiary
Craig Rowsell, Executive VP, Subsidiary
Andrew Bough, Executive VP, Subsidiary
Robert Smith, Executive VP, Subsidiary
Loren Cooke, Executive VP, Subsidiary
Jay Greenspoon, General Counsel
Colleen McCafferty, Other Executive Officer
Victoria MacDonald, Other Executive Officer
Lisa Allen, Vice President, Divisional
Lyne Beauregard, Vice President, Divisional

FINANCIAL DATA: *Note: Data for latest year may not have been available at press time.*

In U.S. $	2021	2020	2019	2018	2017	2016
Revenue	504,107,000	455,945,000	322,537,000	281,451,000	302,976,000	248,547,000
R&D Expense						
Operating Income	51,748,000	65,370,000	16,986,000	-15,702,000	-15,358,000	-1,177,000
Operating Margin %						
SGA Expense	103,806,000	88,543,000	72,412,000	76,760,000	83,196,000	53,768,000
Net Income	32,992,000	41,991,000	8,958,000	-4,571,000	-24,014,000	-6,281,000
Operating Cash Flow	25,021,000	74,689,000	25,643,000	10,372,000	-8,523,000	4,191,000
Capital Expenditure	3,025,000	1,828,000	2,065,000	423,000	1,807,000	1,475,000
EBITDA	51,557,000	66,324,000	24,572,000	16,786,000	-10,042,000	7,639,000
Return on Assets %						
Return on Equity %						
Debt to Equity						

CONTACT INFORMATION:
Phone: 905 695-2684   Fax: 905 739-1222
Toll-Free:
Address: 50 Minthorn Boulevard, Markham, ON L3T 7X8 Canada

STOCK TICKER/OTHER:
Stock Ticker: REAL   Exchange: TSE
Employees: 3,355   Fiscal Year Ends: 09/30
Parent Company:

SALARIES/BONUSES:
Top Exec. Salary: $ Bonus: $
Second Exec. Salary: $ Bonus: $

OTHER THOUGHTS:
Estimated Female Officers or Directors:
Hot Spot for Advancement for Women/Minorities:

Sales, profits and employees may be estimates. Financial information, benefits and other data can change quickly and may vary from those stated here.

Refinitiv Limited

www.refinitiv.com

NAIC Code: 519130

TYPES OF BUSINESS:
Internet Publishing and Broadcasting and Web Search Portals
Financial Market Data
Financial Markets Infrastructure
Investments
Trading
Risk Analytics

BRANDS/DIVISIONS/AFFILIATES:
London Stock Exchange Group

GROWTH PLANS/SPECIAL FEATURES:
Refinitiv Limited is a London Stock Exchange Group business and a world-leading provider of financial markets data and infrastructure. Refinitiv serves more than 40,000 customers and 400,000 end users across 190 countries, powering participants across the global financial marketplace. The company provides information, insights and technology that enable customers to execute investing, trading and risk decisions. Solutions offered by Refinitiv cover a wide range of financial sectors, and include investment banking, corporate treasury, investing and related advisory services, financial crime, trading, wealth management, risk and compliance, Islamic finance, market data, cloud computing, regulatory services and sustainable environmental/social/governance (ESG) finance.

CONTACTS: *Note: Officers with more than one job title may be intentionally listed here more than once.*
David W. Craig, CEO

FINANCIAL DATA: *Note: Data for latest year may not have been available at press time.*

In U.S. $	2021	2020	2019	2018	2017	2016
Revenue	2,514,823,293	2,418,099,320	2,434,329,600	1,982,209,240	1,890,117,120	
R&D Expense						
Operating Income						
Operating Margin %						
SGA Expense						
Net Income		-43,447,040	-74,761,200	558,368,800	-80,947,200	
Operating Cash Flow						
Capital Expenditure						
EBITDA						
Return on Assets %						
Return on Equity %						
Debt to Equity						

CONTACT INFORMATION:
Phone: 4420 7250 1122   Fax:
Toll-Free:
Address: Five Canada Sq., Canary Wharf, London, E14 5AQ United Kingdom

STOCK TICKER/OTHER:
Stock Ticker: Subsidiary   Exchange:
Employees: Fiscal Year Ends: 12/31
Parent Company: London Stock Exchange Group plc

SALARIES/BONUSES:
Top Exec. Salary: $ Bonus: $
Second Exec. Salary: $ Bonus: $

OTHER THOUGHTS:
Estimated Female Officers or Directors:
Hot Spot for Advancement for Women/Minorities:

Sales, profits and employees may be estimates. Financial information, benefits and other data can change quickly and may vary from those stated here.

Plunkett Research, Ltd.

Regions Financial Corporation

www.regions.com

NAIC Code: 522110

TYPES OF BUSINESS:

Banking
Mortgages
Insurance
Securities Brokerage
Investment Services
Trust Services
Asset Management
Mutual Funds

BRANDS/DIVISIONS/AFFILIATES:

Regions Bank
Regions Equipment Finance Corporation
Regions Commercial Equipment Finance LLC
Regions Investment Services Inc
Regions Securities LLC
Regions Affordable Housing LLC
Ascentium Capital

GROWTH PLANS/SPECIAL FEATURES:

Regions Financial is a regional bank headquartered in Alabama, with branches primarily in the Southeastern and Midwestern United States. Regions primarily provides traditional commercial and retail banking and also offers mortgage services, asset management, wealth management, securities brokerage, insurance, and trust services.

Employee benefits include medical, dental, vision, life and disability insurance; a 401(k) plan; training and career development; employee assistance programs; and reimbursement accounts.

CONTACTS: *Note: Officers with more than one job title may be intentionally listed here more than once.*

John Turner, CEO
Ronald Smith, Other Corporate Officer
David Turner, CFO
Charles McCrary, Chairman of the Board
David Keenan, Chief Administrative Officer
Amala Duggirala, Chief Information Officer
Tara Plimpton, Chief Legal Officer
C. Lusco, Chief Risk Officer
Kate Danella, Chief Strategy Officer
Hardie Kimbrough, Controller
John Owen, COO
William Ritter, Other Corporate Officer
Scott Peters, Other Corporate Officer

FINANCIAL DATA: *Note: Data for latest year may not have been available at press time.*

In U.S. $	2021	2020	2019	2018	2017	2016
Revenue		6,225,000,000	5,820,000,000	5,821,000,000	5,654,000,000	5,596,000,000
R&D Expense						
Operating Income						
Operating Margin %						
SGA Expense		2,400,000,000	2,234,000,000	2,322,000,000	2,311,000,000	2,264,000,000
Net Income		1,094,000,000	1,582,000,000	1,759,000,000	1,263,000,000	1,163,000,000
Operating Cash Flow		2,324,000,000	2,581,000,000	2,275,000,000	2,281,000,000	1,954,000,000
Capital Expenditure		59,000,000	24,000,000	71,000,000	191,000,000	64,000,000
EBITDA						
Return on Assets %						
Return on Equity %						
Debt to Equity						

CONTACT INFORMATION:

Phone: 205 326-5807 Fax: 205 326-7459
Toll-Free: 800-734-4667
Address: 1900 Fifth Ave. N., Birmingham, AL 35203 United States

SALARIES/BONUSES:

Top Exec. Salary: $993,558 Bonus: $
Second Exec. Salary: $700,000 Bonus: $

STOCK TICKER/OTHER:

Stock Ticker: RF
Employees: 19,406
Parent Company:

Exchange: NYS
Fiscal Year Ends: 12/31

OTHER THOUGHTS:

Estimated Female Officers or Directors: 6
Hot Spot for Advancement for Women/Minorities: Y

Sales, profits and employees may be estimates. Financial information, benefits and other data can change quickly and may vary from those stated here.

Remitly Global Inc

NAIC Code: 522320

www.remitly.com/us/en

TYPES OF BUSINESS:
Electronic Funds Transfer Services
Electronic Financial Payment Services

BRANDS/DIVISIONS/AFFILIATES:

GROWTH PLANS/SPECIAL FEATURES:
Remitly Global Inc provides integrated financial services to immigrants, including helping customers send money internationally in a quick, reliable, and more cost-effective manner by leveraging digital channels. It supports cross-border transmissions across the globe. Its revenue is generated on transaction fees charged to customers and foreign exchange spreads between the foreign exchange rate offered to customers and the foreign exchange rate on the company's currency purchases.

Remitly offers its employees competitive benefits and company perks.

CONTACTS: *Note: Officers with more than one job title may be intentionally listed here more than once.*
Matthew Oppenheimer, CEO
Susanna Morgan, CFO
Robert Singer, Chief Marketing Officer
Karim Meghji, Chief Technology Officer
Joshua Hug, Co-Founder
Robert Kaskel, Executive VP, Divisional
Vishal Ghotge, Executive VP, Geographical
Saema Somalya, General Counsel
Rene Yoakum, Other Executive Officer

FINANCIAL DATA: *Note: Data for latest year may not have been available at press time.*

In U.S. $	2021	2020	2019	2018	2017	2016
Revenue		256,956,000	126,567,000			
R&D Expense		40,777,000	32,008,000			
Operating Income		-29,183,000	-50,602,000			
Operating Margin %						
SGA Expense		105,460,000	69,200,000			
Net Income		-32,564,000	-51,392,000			
Operating Cash Flow		-114,209,000	8,435,000			
Capital Expenditure		4,370,000	7,209,000			
EBITDA		-26,152,000	-46,867,000			
Return on Assets %						
Return on Equity %						
Debt to Equity						

CONTACT INFORMATION:
Phone: 206 535-6152   Fax:
Toll-Free: 888 736-4859
Address: 1111 3rd Ave., Ste. 2100, Seattle, WA 98101 United States

STOCK TICKER/OTHER:
Stock Ticker: RELY   Exchange: NAS
Employees: 1,800   Fiscal Year Ends: 12/31
Parent Company:

SALARIES/BONUSES:
Top Exec. Salary: $281,667   Bonus: $
Second Exec. Salary: $ Bonus: $

OTHER THOUGHTS:
Estimated Female Officers or Directors:
Hot Spot for Advancement for Women/Minorities:

Sales, profits and employees may be estimates. Financial information, benefits and other data can change quickly and may vary from those stated here.

Plunkett Research, Ltd.

Revelock (Buguroo Offensive Security SL) www.revelock.com/en

NAIC Code: 511210E

TYPES OF BUSINESS:

Computer Software: Network Security, Managed Access, Digital ID, Cybersecurity & Anti-Virus
Technology Development
Risk Management Solutions
Fraud Detection Solutions
Fraud Prevention Solutions
Remediation Solutions
Compliance Solutions

BRANDS/DIVISIONS/AFFILIATES:

Feedzai Inc

GROWTH PLANS/SPECIAL FEATURES:

Buguroo Offensive Security SL does business as Revelock and develops technology in regards to risk management. Revelock's end-to-end risk management platform delivers fraud detection, prevention, remediation and compliance without impacting user experience. The platform's capabilities help minimize tasks and concerns related to fraud and money laundering. During 2021, Buguroo and its Revelock brand name was acquired by Feedzai, Inc.

CONTACTS: Note: Officers with more than one job title may be intentionally listed here more than once.

Pablo de la Riva, CEO
Jose Carlos Corrales, Chief Product Officer
Javier Minguella, CFO
Pedro Asua, Dir.-Mktg.
Richard da Silva, VP-Sales (EMEA)
David Moran, CTO
Nicolas Severino, COO

FINANCIAL DATA: Note: Data for latest year may not have been available at press time.

In U.S. $	2021	2020	2019	2018	2017	2016
Revenue						
R&D Expense						
Operating Income						
Operating Margin %						
SGA Expense						
Net Income						
Operating Cash Flow						
Capital Expenditure						
EBITDA						
Return on Assets %						
Return on Equity %						
Debt to Equity						

CONTACT INFORMATION:

Phone: 34 91 22 94 349   Fax:
Toll-Free:
Address: Anabel Segua 16, Bldg. 3, Fl. 4, Alcobendas, Madrid 28108 Spain

STOCK TICKER/OTHER:

Stock Ticker: Subsidiary   Exchange:
Employees: Fiscal Year Ends:
Parent Company: Feedzai Inc

SALARIES/BONUSES:

Top Exec. Salary: $ Bonus: $
Second Exec. Salary: $ Bonus: $

OTHER THOUGHTS:

Estimated Female Officers or Directors:
Hot Spot for Advancement for Women/Minorities:

Sales, profits and employees may be estimates. Financial information, benefits and other data can change quickly and may vary from those stated here.

RIBBIT (Cash Flow Solutions Inc)

followthefrog.com

NAIC Code: 511210Q

TYPES OF BUSINESS:

Computer Software: Accounting, Banking & Financial
Artificial Intelligence Finance Analytics
Payments Solutions
Customer Onboarding
Payments Processing
Verification Solutions
Money Management Solutions

BRANDS/DIVISIONS/AFFILIATES:

RIBBIT
BankQUALIFY
BankVERIFY+
BankLOGIN+
BankTRANSACT
AIR

CONTACTS: *Note: Officers with more than one job title may be intentionally listed here more than once.*

Shawn Princell, CEO

GROWTH PLANS/SPECIAL FEATURES:

Cash Flow Solutions, Inc. is the parent company of RIBBIT, which offers artificial intelligent (AI) finance analytic and payments products and solutions for businesses and organizations. RIBBIT primarily serves lenders, billers, banks and fintechs, helping them make decisions regarding consumers and customers. RIBBIT offers four primary products: BankQUALIFY, which identifies account ownership, flags potential fraud and assesses payment affordability risk based on the six attributes of name, address, phone, email and account/routing number; BankVERIFY+, which provides predictive analytics on 99% of bank accounts via payment behavior and offers five action codes, namely A1 (best), A2 (good), A3 (okay), A4 (flag) and D1 (decline); BankLOGIN+, a patent-pending bank transaction analytics solution that automates financial and payment decisioning through insights across affordability, income verification, know your customer, and cash flow timing; and BankTRANSACT, which offers payment processing options such as Automated Clearing House (ACH), same-day ACH and real-time payments, and application programming interface (API) and/or tokenization can be utilized to enhance payment processing security. In addition, RIBBIT's AIR offering stands for affordability index report, in which businesses can use to educate consumers regarding their ability to pay and improve opportunities by providing insights into cash flow, payment behavior, recurring obligations and income analysis.

FINANCIAL DATA: *Note: Data for latest year may not have been available at press time.*

In U.S. $	2021	2020	2019	2018	2017	2016
Revenue						
R&D Expense						
Operating Income						
Operating Margin %						
SGA Expense						
Net Income						
Operating Cash Flow						
Capital Expenditure						
EBITDA						
Return on Assets %						
Return on Equity %						
Debt to Equity						

CONTACT INFORMATION:

Phone: 513 524-2320   Fax:
Toll-Free: 800 736-5123
Address: 5166 College Corner Pike, Oxford, OH 45056 United States

STOCK TICKER/OTHER:

Stock Ticker: Private   Exchange:
Employees: Fiscal Year Ends:
Parent Company:

SALARIES/BONUSES:

Top Exec. Salary: $ Bonus: $
Second Exec. Salary: $ Bonus: $

OTHER THOUGHTS:

Estimated Female Officers or Directors:
Hot Spot for Advancement for Women/Minorities:

Sales, profits and employees may be estimates. Financial information, benefits and other data can change quickly and may vary from those stated here.

Ripple Labs Inc

ripple.com

NAIC Code: 522320

TYPES OF BUSINESS:
Financial Transactions Processing, Reserve, and Clearinghouse Activities
Open Source Payments
Cryptocurrency
Blockchain Solutions
Tokenization
Finance Software
Financial Technology
Digital Transformation Solutions

BRANDS/DIVISIONS/AFFILIATES:
XRP Ledger
XRP
XRPL.org

CONTACTS: *Note: Officers with more than one job title may be intentionally listed here more than once.*
Brad Garlinghouse, CEO
Eric van Miltenburg, Chief Bus. Officer
Kristina Campbell, CFO
Eric Jeck, Sr. VP-Corp. Dev.
Kiersten Hollars, Sr. VP-People & Communications
David Schwartz, CTO
Devraj Varadhan, Sr. VP-Engineering

GROWTH PLANS/SPECIAL FEATURES:
Ripple Labs, Inc. is an enterprise blockchain company that has developed an opensource payments infrastructure that enables financial institutions, businesses, governments and developers to move, manage and tokenize value via cryptocurrency solutions. Ripple partners with customer to streamline underlying infrastructure, and work with regulators, governments and central banks to ensure payment solutions are optimized, secure and compliant. The company provides developer tools and support for building public blockchains through its XRP Ledger product. XRP Ledger and its native digital asset XRP were designed for speed, low cost, scalability and sustainability, thus allowing developers and entrepreneurs to seamlessly transform existing applications to unlock new user experiences across payments, decentralized finance (DeFi), non-fungible tokens (NFTs), identity, foreign exchange, tokenization and more. XRPL.org is a site for the XRP Ledger developer community, featuring tools, documents, events and other related resources. Solutions by Ripple include cross-border payments, crypto liquidity and central bank digital currency. Headquartered in the U.S., Ripple Labs has 15 locations around the world.

FINANCIAL DATA: *Note: Data for latest year may not have been available at press time.*

In U.S. $	2021	2020	2019	2018	2017	2016
Revenue						
R&D Expense						
Operating Income						
Operating Margin %						
SGA Expense						
Net Income						
Operating Cash Flow						
Capital Expenditure						
EBITDA						
Return on Assets %						
Return on Equity %						
Debt to Equity						

CONTACT INFORMATION:
Phone: 415 213-4838   Fax:
Toll-Free:
Address: 315 Montgomery St., Fl. 2, San Francisco, CA 94104 United States

STOCK TICKER/OTHER:
Stock Ticker: Private
Employees: 500
Parent Company:

Exchange:
Fiscal Year Ends: 12/31

SALARIES/BONUSES:
Top Exec. Salary: $ Bonus: $
Second Exec. Salary: $ Bonus: $

OTHER THOUGHTS:
Estimated Female Officers or Directors:
Hot Spot for Advancement for Women/Minorities:

Sales, profits and employees may be estimates. Financial information, benefits and other data can change quickly and may vary from those stated here.

Riskified Ltd

NAIC Code: 511210E

www.riskified.com

TYPES OF BUSINESS:
Computer Software: Network Security, Managed Access, Digital ID, Cybersecurity & Anti-Virus
KYC

GROWTH PLANS/SPECIAL FEATURES:
Riskified Ltd has built a next-generation eCommerce risk management platform that allows online merchants to create trusted relationships with their consumers. It primarily generates revenue by granting merchants access to its eCommerce risk management platform and reviewing and approving eCommerce transactions for legitimacy.

BRANDS/DIVISIONS/AFFILIATES:

CONTACTS:
Note: Officers with more than one job title may be intentionally listed here more than once.

Eido Gal, CEO
Naama Ofek Arad, COO
Aglika Dotcheva, CFO
Peter Elmgren, Customer Relations Officer
Dana Teplitsky, VP-Global Human Resources
Assaf Feldman, CTO

FINANCIAL DATA:
Note: Data for latest year may not have been available at press time.

In U.S. $	2021	2020	2019	2018	2017	2016
Revenue		169,740,000	130,555,000			
R&D Expense		36,642,000	25,041,000			
Operating Income		-6,808,000	-13,875,000			
Operating Margin %						
SGA Expense		62,990,000	54,522,000			
Net Income		-11,347,000	-14,175,000			
Operating Cash Flow		-3,120,000	3,843,000			
Capital Expenditure		2,961,000	2,532,000			
EBITDA		-5,448,000	-13,160,000			
Return on Assets %						
Return on Equity %						
Debt to Equity						

CONTACT INFORMATION:
Phone: 203 300-9264   Fax:
Toll-Free:
Address: 30 Kalischer St., Tel Aviv, 6525724 Israel

STOCK TICKER/OTHER:
Stock Ticker: RSKD   Exchange: NYS
Employees: Fiscal Year Ends: 12/31
Parent Company:

SALARIES/BONUSES:
Top Exec. Salary: $ Bonus: $
Second Exec. Salary: $ Bonus: $

OTHER THOUGHTS:
Estimated Female Officers or Directors:
Hot Spot for Advancement for Women/Minorities:

Sales, profits and employees may be estimates. Financial information, benefits and other data can change quickly and may vary from those stated here.

Plunkett Research, Ltd. — 273

Robinhood Markets Inc

www.robinhood.com

NAIC Code: 523120

TYPES OF BUSINESS:
Securities Brokerage
Online Trading

BRANDS/DIVISIONS/AFFILIATES:
Robinhood Financial LLC
Robinhood Crypto LLC

GROWTH PLANS/SPECIAL FEATURES:
Robinhood Markets Inc is creating a modern financial services platform. It designs its own products and services and delivers them through a single, app-based cloud platform supported by proprietary technology. Its vertically integrated platform has enabled the introduction of new products and services such as cryptocurrency trading, dividend reinvestment, fractional shares, recurring investments, and IPO Access. It earns transaction-based revenues from routing user orders for options, equities, and cryptocurrencies to market makers when a routed order is executed.

CONTACTS: *Note: Officers with more than one job title may be intentionally listed here more than once.*
Vladimir Tenev, CEO
Jason Warnick, CFO
Daniel Gallagher, Chief Legal Officer
Christina Smedley, Chief Marketing Officer
Baiju Bhatt, Co-Founder
Gretchen Howard, COO
Aparna Chennapragada, Other Executive Officer

FINANCIAL DATA: *Note: Data for latest year may not have been available at press time.*

In U.S. $	2021	2020	2019	2018	2017	2016
Revenue		958,833,000	277,533,000			
R&D Expense		215,630,000	94,932,000			
Operating Income		119,274,000	-105,521,000			
Operating Margin %						
SGA Expense		409,952,000	219,596,000			
Net Income		7,449,000	-106,569,000			
Operating Cash Flow		1,876,254,000	1,260,085,000			
Capital Expenditure		32,330,000	12,453,000			
EBITDA		129,212,000	-100,077,000			
Return on Assets %						
Return on Equity %						
Debt to Equity						

CONTACT INFORMATION:
Phone: 650-940-2700 Fax:
Toll-Free:
Address: 85 Willow Rd, Menlo Park, CA 94025 United States

STOCK TICKER/OTHER:
Stock Ticker: HOOD
Employees:
Parent Company:

Exchange: NAS
Fiscal Year Ends:

SALARIES/BONUSES:
Top Exec. Salary: $257,436 Bonus: $4,200,000
Second Exec. Salary: $400,015 Bonus: $450,000

OTHER THOUGHTS:
Estimated Female Officers or Directors:
Hot Spot for Advancement for Women/Minorities:

Sales, profits and employees may be estimates. Financial information, benefits and other data can change quickly and may vary from those stated here.

Roofstock Inc

NAIC Code: 523930

www.roofstock.com

TYPES OF BUSINESS:
Real Estate Investment Advice
Real Estate Investment
Real Estate Ecommerce Platform
Technology Solutions
Buy and Sell Real Estate

BRANDS/DIVISIONS/AFFILIATES:

CONTACTS: *Note: Officers with more than one job title may be intentionally listed here more than once.*
Gary Beasley, CEO
Michael Shoemaker, COO
Suresh Srinivasan, CMO
Navneet Arora, Chief People Officer
Amit Akhouri, CTO
Gregor Watson, Chmn.

GROWTH PLANS/SPECIAL FEATURES:

Roofstock, Inc. offers an ecommerce marketplace for investing in the single-family rental home sector. The company provides research, analytic and insight strategies for evaluating and purchasing these certified properties. Roofstock pre-inspects the rental properties and offers information regarding the property, tenancy, property management and more. Anyone can invest, first-time investors to global asset managers, all of which can evaluate, purchase and own residential properties throughout the world. Fractional ownership shares of fully-managed investment properties are also offered. Roofstock built its state-of-the-art technology to provide this service. How it works: investors state how much they want to spend, how much they want to place as a down payment and if they will be using cash or financing the purchase. If approved, investors search for a rental property, review the data offered, and can make an offer through the Roofstock site for free. If the offer is accepted, Roofstock charges a marketplace fee equal to 0.5% of the contract price or $500, whichever is higher. From that point, Roofstock's service and transaction team guides the investor through escrow until the transaction is closed. Rental owners can submit a listing by entering property information and uploading pictures. A free price estimate will be subsequently provided, and if accepted, Roofstock will perform due diligence before uploading the property onto the ecommerce site. Offers are managed completely online, and once the owner accepts a bid, Roofstock coordinates the transaction process from start to finish. Most transactions are completed within 30 days after the purchase and sale agreement has been signed.

FINANCIAL DATA: *Note: Data for latest year may not have been available at press time.*

In U.S. $	2021	2020	2019	2018	2017	2016
Revenue						
R&D Expense						
Operating Income						
Operating Margin %						
SGA Expense						
Net Income						
Operating Cash Flow						
Capital Expenditure						
EBITDA						
Return on Assets %						
Return on Equity %						
Debt to Equity						

CONTACT INFORMATION:
Phone: 510-250-7918 Fax:
Toll-Free: 800 466-4116
Address: 1600 MacArthur Blvd., Oakland, CA 94602 United States

STOCK TICKER/OTHER:
Stock Ticker: Private Exchange:
Employees: 200 Fiscal Year Ends:
Parent Company:

SALARIES/BONUSES:
Top Exec. Salary: $ Bonus: $
Second Exec. Salary: $ Bonus: $

OTHER THOUGHTS:
Estimated Female Officers or Directors:
Hot Spot for Advancement for Women/Minorities:

Plunkett Research, Ltd.

Secure Payment Systems Inc
www.securepaymentsystems.com

NAIC Code: 522320

TYPES OF BUSINESS:
Financial Transactions Processing, Reserve, and Clearinghouse Activities
Payment Processing Services
Reporting and Risk Management Tools
ACH Payments
Credit and Debit Card Processing
Account Validation Solutions
Risk Management Solutions
Gift and Loyalty Cards

BRANDS/DIVISIONS/AFFILIATES:
Payliance

CONTACTS: *Note: Officers with more than one job title may be intentionally listed here more than once.*
Linden Fellerman, Pres.
Richard Lobdell, VP-Finance & Admin.
Scott Kanter, VP-Mktg. & Sales
Rick Cone, VP-IT & Systems

GROWTH PLANS/SPECIAL FEATURES:
Secure Payments Systems, Inc. (SPS) is a payment processing and information services company that specializes in serving small-/mid-size retailers and service providers. SPS facilitates payment transfers by providing businesses with a full range of transaction processing, reporting and risk management tools so they can accept payments, pay vendors and/or transfer funds at point-of-sales or digitally. Products and services by SPS span Automated Clearing House (ACH) enterprise solutions, ACH payments, consumer financing, credit/debit card processing, account validation, risk management, check services, bill payment solutions, gift and loyalty cards, and lender ACH processing. Tools offered by SPS include marketing, secure messaging, point-of-sale equipment and related software. Just a few of SPS' many partners include Jefiti, FinMkt, Vergent Loan Management Software, Early Warning Systems, TeleCheck, microbilt, Solupay, nmi, Partner Payments, and nuvei. In February 2022, SPS was acquired by Payliance, with plans to combine the two organization, but terms of the combination were not disclosed as of this writing.

FINANCIAL DATA: *Note: Data for latest year may not have been available at press time.*

In U.S. $	2021	2020	2019	2018	2017	2016
Revenue						
R&D Expense						
Operating Income						
Operating Margin %						
SGA Expense						
Net Income						
Operating Cash Flow						
Capital Expenditure						
EBITDA						
Return on Assets %						
Return on Equity %						
Debt to Equity						

CONTACT INFORMATION:
Phone: 702 701-8433   Fax:
Toll-Free:
Address: 3993 Howard Hughes Pkwy, Ste. 390, Las Vegas, NV 89169 United States

STOCK TICKER/OTHER:
Stock Ticker: Subsidiary   Exchange:
Employees: 33   Fiscal Year Ends:
Parent Company: Payliance

SALARIES/BONUSES:
Top Exec. Salary: $ Bonus: $
Second Exec. Salary: $ Bonus: $

OTHER THOUGHTS:
Estimated Female Officers or Directors:
Hot Spot for Advancement for Women/Minorities:

Sales, profits and employees may be estimates. Financial information, benefits and other data can change quickly and may vary from those stated here.

Singularity Future Technology Ltd

NAIC Code: 518210

www.singularity.us

TYPES OF BUSINESS:
Virtual Currency Mining

BRANDS/DIVISIONS/AFFILIATES:

GROWTH PLANS/SPECIAL FEATURES:

Singularity Future Technology is a Nasdaq-listed company, revolutionizing blockchain supply management by focusing on innovative solutions for globally interconnected networks and establishing state-of-the-art crypto mining pools. Services include Thor Miner, an ASIC Certified crypto mining technology; Ming Pool, which allows customers to earn Bitcoin without self mining; and IDC, an instant electricity support program and stabilized data center. The firm's miners include the S99, S99 S, S99 Max and the S99 Pro.

CONTACTS: *Note: Officers with more than one job title may be intentionally listed here more than once.*

Yang Jie, CEO
Tuo Pan, CFO
Lei Cao, Chairman of the Board
Shi Qiu, Chief Technology Officer
Jing Shan, COO
Lei Nie, Vice President
ZhiKang Huang, Vice President, Divisional

FINANCIAL DATA: *Note: Data for latest year may not have been available at press time.*

In U.S. $	2021	2020	2019	2018	2017	2016
Revenue	5,151,032	6,535,956	41,771,048	23,064,564	11,445,613	7,310,540
R&D Expense						
Operating Income						
Operating Margin %						
SGA Expense						
Net Income	-6,823,343	-16,452,894	-6,533,844	459,051	3,624,892	-1,965,929
Operating Cash Flow						
Capital Expenditure						
EBITDA						
Return on Assets %						
Return on Equity %						
Debt to Equity						

CONTACT INFORMATION:
Phone: 718 888-1814   Fax: 718 888-1148
Toll-Free:
Address: 98 Cutter Mill Rd., Ste. 322, Great Neck, NY 11021 United States

STOCK TICKER/OTHER:
Stock Ticker: SGLY   Exchange: NAS
Employees: 43   Fiscal Year Ends: 06/30
Parent Company:

SALARIES/BONUSES:
Top Exec. Salary: $ Bonus: $
Second Exec. Salary: $ Bonus: $

OTHER THOUGHTS:
Estimated Female Officers or Directors:
Hot Spot for Advancement for Women/Minorities:

Sales, profits and employees may be estimates. Financial information, benefits and other data can change quickly and may vary from those stated here.

Socure Inc

www.socure.com

NAIC Code: 511210E

TYPES OF BUSINESS:

Computer Software: Network Security, Managed Access, Digital ID, Cybersecurity & Anti-Virus
Digital Identity Verification Solutions
Software and Technology Development
Identification Platform Solution
Automated Machine Learning
Fraud Risk Management Solutions
Know Your Customer (KYC) Solutions

BRANDS/DIVISIONS/AFFILIATES:

ID+

CONTACTS: *Note: Officers with more than one job title may be intentionally listed here more than once.*

Johnny Ayers, CEO
Rivka Gewirtz Little, Chief of Staff
Avi Aronovitz, CFO
Gary Sevounts, CMO
Scott Slipy, Chief People Officer
Pablo Abreu, Chief Product Officer
Rong Cao, Sr. VP-Technology

GROWTH PLANS/SPECIAL FEATURES:

Socure, Inc. has developed and delivers a platform for digital identity verification and trust, in real-time. Socure's ID+ platform leverages automated machine learning with over 300 sources of curated data to provide an instant, multi-dimensional view of identity verification and fraud risk at day zero. The company's identity engine encompasses know your customer (KYC), identity fraud detection and document verification across a streamlined strategy, reducing manual review efforts. Customers and industries served by Socure include banks, challenger banks, lenders, payments/remittance, investment and trading, telecommunications, healthcare and insurance. Among Socure's many investors include Flint Capital, Accel, Capital One Ventures, Synchrony Financial, SCALE, Two Sigma Ventures, Citi Ventures, Sorenson Capital, and FF Venture Capital.

Socure offers its employees comprehensive health benefits, 401(k), flexible spending accounts, fertility benefits, short-long-term disability and life insurance coverage, among other benefits.

FINANCIAL DATA: *Note: Data for latest year may not have been available at press time.*

In U.S. $	2021	2020	2019	2018	2017	2016
Revenue						
R&D Expense						
Operating Income						
Operating Margin %						
SGA Expense						
Net Income						
Operating Cash Flow						
Capital Expenditure						
EBITDA						
Return on Assets %						
Return on Equity %						
Debt to Equity						

CONTACT INFORMATION:

Phone: 866 932-9013 Fax:
Toll-Free:
Address: 885 Tahoe Blvd., Ste. 11, Incline Village, NV 89451 United States

STOCK TICKER/OTHER:

Stock Ticker: Private Exchange:
Employees: Fiscal Year Ends:
Parent Company:

SALARIES/BONUSES:

Top Exec. Salary: $ Bonus: $
Second Exec. Salary: $ Bonus: $

OTHER THOUGHTS:

Estimated Female Officers or Directors:
Hot Spot for Advancement for Women/Minorities:

Sales, profits and employees may be estimates. Financial information, benefits and other data can change quickly and may vary from those stated here.

SoFi (SoFi Technologies Inc)

www.sofi.com

NAIC Code: 522291

TYPES OF BUSINESS:

Consumer Lending
Mortgage Companies

BRANDS/DIVISIONS/AFFILIATES:

SoFi Money
SoFi Relay
SoFi Invest
SoFi Protect
SoFi Stadium

GROWTH PLANS/SPECIAL FEATURES:

SoFi is a financial services company that was founded in 2011 and is currently based in San Francisco. Initially known for its student loan refinancing business, the company has expanded its product offerings to include personal loans, credit cards, mortgages, investment accounts, banking services, and financial planning. The company intends to be a one-stop shop for its client's finances and operates solely through its mobile app and website. Through its acquisition of Galileo in 2020 the company also offers payment and account services for debit cards and digital banking.

CONTACTS: *Note: Officers with more than one job title may be intentionally listed here more than once.*

Anthony Noto, CEO
Richard Garside, Global Head-Oper.
Michelle Gill, CFO
Joanne Bradford, CMO
Jing Liao, Chief Human Resources Officer
Tony Donohoe, Chief Technology Officer
Tim Hutton, Chmn.

FINANCIAL DATA: *Note: Data for latest year may not have been available at press time.*

In U.S. $	2021	2020	2019	2018	2017	2016
Revenue		565,532,000	442,659,000	269,399,000		
R&D Expense						
Operating Income						
Operating Margin %						
SGA Expense		715,157,000	565,931,000	433,871,000		
Net Income		-224,053,000	-239,697,000	-252,399,000		
Operating Cash Flow		-479,336,000	-54,733,000	1,023,277,000		
Capital Expenditure		24,549,000	37,590,000	13,729,000		
EBITDA						
Return on Assets %						
Return on Equity %						
Debt to Equity						

CONTACT INFORMATION:

Phone: Fax:
Toll-Free: 855-456-7634
Address: 234 1st St, San Francisco, CA 94105 United States

STOCK TICKER/OTHER:

Stock Ticker: SOFI   Exchange: NAS
Employees: 1,977   Fiscal Year Ends: 12/31
Parent Company:

SALARIES/BONUSES:

Top Exec. Salary: $ Bonus: $
Second Exec. Salary: $ Bonus: $

OTHER THOUGHTS:

Estimated Female Officers or Directors:
Hot Spot for Advancement for Women/Minorities:

Sales, profits and employees may be estimates. Financial information, benefits and other data can change quickly and may vary from those stated here.

SpotOn Transact LLC

www.spoton.com

NAIC Code: 522320

TYPES OF BUSINESS:

Financial Transactions Processing, Reserve, and Clearinghouse Activities
Payment Processing Software
Financial Technology
Omnichannel Commerce Solutions
Integrated Business Streamlining Solutions
Digital Marketing Solutions
Customer Reach Solutions

BRANDS/DIVISIONS/AFFILIATES:

GROWTH PLANS/SPECIAL FEATURES:

SpotOn Transact, LLC is a financial technology company that offers payment processing software, systems and solutions. SpotOn serves the restaurant, hospitality, retail, enterprise, automotive, professional services, health and beauty industries. Products of the firm include payments across all types and channels (in-store, online, digitally), omnichannel commerce solutions for enterprise businesses, integrated software and services for streamlining business and increasing sales, and digital marketing solutions for reaching customers and enhancing customer experience. Headquartered in San Francisco, California, SpotOn Transact has additional offices in Illinois, Michigan and Colorado, USA, as well as Mexico City, Mexico and Krakow, Poland. SpotOn Transact LLC is a registered independent sales organization (ISO) of Merrick Bank, South Jordan, Utah, and Wells Fargo Bank NA, Concord, California.

CONTACTS: *Note: Officers with more than one job title may be intentionally listed here more than once.*

Zachary Hyman, Managing Partner
Matthew Hyman, Managing Partner

FINANCIAL DATA: *Note: Data for latest year may not have been available at press time.*

In U.S. $	2021	2020	2019	2018	2017	2016
Revenue						
R&D Expense						
Operating Income						
Operating Margin %						
SGA Expense						
Net Income						
Operating Cash Flow						
Capital Expenditure						
EBITDA						
Return on Assets %						
Return on Equity %						
Debt to Equity						

CONTACT INFORMATION:

Phone: 424 345-5211   Fax:
Toll-Free: 877 814-4102
Address: 100 California St., Fl. 9, San Francisco, CA 94111 United States

STOCK TICKER/OTHER:

Stock Ticker: Private   Exchange:
Employees: 1,600   Fiscal Year Ends:
Parent Company:

SALARIES/BONUSES:

Top Exec. Salary: $ Bonus: $
Second Exec. Salary: $ Bonus: $

OTHER THOUGHTS:

Estimated Female Officers or Directors:
Hot Spot for Advancement for Women/Minorities:

Sales, profits and employees may be estimates. Financial information, benefits and other data can change quickly and may vary from those stated here.

Spring Labs (Springcoin Inc)

www.springlabs.com

NAIC Code: 511210E

TYPES OF BUSINESS:

Computer Software: Network Security, Managed Access, Digital ID, Cybersecurity & Anti-Virus
Secure Information Transferring Between Businesses
Data Exchange Technology
Patented Tokenization Solutions
Identity Matching Technology
Data Permissioning
Data Protection Solutions
Advanced Cryptography Solutions

BRANDS/DIVISIONS/AFFILIATES:

CONTACTS: *Note: Officers with more than one job title may be intentionally listed here more than once.*

John Sun, CEO
Joel Eckhause, COO
Cris Neckar, Chief Information Security Officer
David Kravitz, Dir.-Research
Matt Smith, CTO
Adam Jiwan, Chmn.

GROWTH PLANS/SPECIAL FEATURES:

Springcoin, Inc. does business as Spring Labs and develops innovative ways to exchange data. Primarily, Spring Labs facilitates the secure sharing of sensitive data through patented tokenization and matching technologies. The company's platform consists of: transparent data permissioning, so that users can only share what they want to share; privacy protection, to ensure its customers and users retain control of their personally identifiable information (PII) data; and unlocking previously unavailable information via advanced cryptography, enabling companies to mutually benefit from sharing information without revealing any sensitive data. Spring Labs' secure data exchanges and clean rooms enable users to share sensitive information without revealing any underlying data. The firm's income stability indicators provide indices and more than 300 granular attributes to generate easy-to-use scores, allowing lenders to evaluate an application and improve underwriting, acquisition marketing and account and collections management processes. Spring Labs' know your everything (KYOx) is a digital passport that enables blockchain and smart contract applications to access off-chain data sources to create new, permission-controlled decentralized financial (DeFi) and Web3 services and applications.

FINANCIAL DATA: *Note: Data for latest year may not have been available at press time.*

In U.S. $	2021	2020	2019	2018	2017	2016
Revenue						
R&D Expense						
Operating Income						
Operating Margin %						
SGA Expense						
Net Income						
Operating Cash Flow						
Capital Expenditure						
EBITDA						
Return on Assets %						
Return on Equity %						
Debt to Equity						

CONTACT INFORMATION:

Phone: 310-494-6928   Fax:
Toll-Free:
Address: 4551 Glencoe Ave., Ste. 155, Marina Del Rey, CA 90292 United States

STOCK TICKER/OTHER:

Stock Ticker: Private
Employees:
Parent Company:

Exchange:
Fiscal Year Ends:

SALARIES/BONUSES:

Top Exec. Salary: $ Bonus: $
Second Exec. Salary: $ Bonus: $

OTHER THOUGHTS:

Estimated Female Officers or Directors:
Hot Spot for Advancement for Women/Minorities:

Sales, profits and employees may be estimates. Financial information, benefits and other data can change quickly and may vary from those stated here.

Square (Block Inc.)

www.squareup.com

NAIC Code: 522320

TYPES OF BUSINESS:
Mobile Credit Card Processing
Credit Card Readers
Point-of-Sale Terminals
Small Business Tools
Payment Software
Stock Trading Accounts
Bitcoin
Developer Platform

BRANDS/DIVISIONS/AFFILIATES:
Square
Tidal
Crew
Block

GROWTH PLANS/SPECIAL FEATURES:
Founded in 2009, Square provides payment acquiring services to merchants, along with related services. The company also launched Cash App, a person-to-person payment network. Square has operations in Canada, Japan, Australia, and the United Kingdom; about 5% of revenue is generated outside the U.S.

CONTACTS: Note: Officers with more than one job title may be intentionally listed here more than once.
Jack Dorsey, CEO
Amrita Ahuja, CFO
Ajmere Dale, Chief Accounting Officer
Sivan Whiteley, General Counsel
Alyssa Henry, Other Corporate Officer
Brian Grassadonia, Other Corporate Officer

FINANCIAL DATA: Note: Data for latest year may not have been available at press time.

In U.S. $	2021	2020	2019	2018	2017	2016
Revenue		9,497,578,000	4,713,500,000	3,298,177,000	2,214,253,000	1,708,721,000
R&D Expense		881,826,000	670,606,000	497,479,000	321,888,000	268,537,000
Operating Income		-18,815,000	26,557,000	-36,614,000	-54,206,000	-170,453,000
Operating Margin %						
SGA Expense		1,688,873,000	1,061,082,000	750,396,000	503,723,000	425,869,000
Net Income		213,105,000	375,446,000	-38,453,000	-62,813,000	-171,590,000
Operating Cash Flow		381,603,000	465,699,000	295,080,000	127,711,000	23,131,000
Capital Expenditure		138,402,000	62,498,000	62,787,000	26,097,000	25,833,000
EBITDA		357,122,000	102,155,000	24,347,000	-16,927,000	-132,708,000
Return on Assets %						
Return on Equity %						
Debt to Equity						

CONTACT INFORMATION:
Phone: 415-281-3976   Fax:
Toll-Free:
Address: 1455 Market St., Ste. 600, San Francisco, CA 94103 United States

STOCK TICKER/OTHER:
Stock Ticker: SQ
Employees: 8,521
Parent Company:

Exchange: NYS
Fiscal Year Ends: 12/31

SALARIES/BONUSES:
Top Exec. Salary: $468,750   Bonus: $
Second Exec. Salary: $468,750   Bonus: $

OTHER THOUGHTS:
Estimated Female Officers or Directors: 1
Hot Spot for Advancement for Women/Minorities:

Sales, profits and employees may be estimates. Financial information, benefits and other data can change quickly and may vary from those stated here.

Stash Financial Inc

www.stash.com

NAIC Code: 523120

TYPES OF BUSINESS:

Securities Brokerage
Financial Technology
Online Investments
Online Trading
Banking
Saving
Retirement
Money Management

BRANDS/DIVISIONS/AFFILIATES:

Stash Beginner
Stash Growth
Stash+
Stash Investments LLC

CONTACTS: Note: Officers with more than one job title may be intentionally listed here more than once.

Brandon Krieg, CEO
Ed Robinson, Pres.
Adriel Lares, CFO
Dale Sperling, CMO
Lynne Oldham, Chief People Officer
Cliff Hazelton, CTO
Chidi Achara, Chief Brand Officer

GROWTH PLANS/SPECIAL FEATURES:

Stash Financial, Inc. is a financial technology and related services company that offers an online platform called Stash, which provides access to investment and banking accounts through a variety of subscription plans. Stash was designed to include smaller investors, providing unlimited financial opportunity to underserved Americans, regardless of income. All-in-one subscription plans begin at $1 per month, and include: Stash Beginner, Stash Growth and Stash+. Stash Beginner is for first-time budgeters and investors; Stash Growth ($3/month) is for long-term savers and investors; and Stash+ ($9/month) is for families, debit card spenders and seasoned investors. These plans include fractional shares, no hidden fee banking, 19,000 free ATMs, a stock-back card (giving stock in the companies shopped at), budget and saving plans, money management app, advice and more. Free online education about Stash and investing is provided through the Stash website. Kids can also learn how to invest through Stash+ custodial accounts. As of May 2022, Stash had over 6 million users. Subsidiary Stash Investments, LLC is a registered Securities and Exchange Commission investment adviser.

FINANCIAL DATA: Note: Data for latest year may not have been available at press time.

In U.S. $	2021	2020	2019	2018	2017	2016
Revenue	100,000,000	75,000,000	43,000,000			
R&D Expense						
Operating Income						
Operating Margin %						
SGA Expense						
Net Income						
Operating Cash Flow						
Capital Expenditure						
EBITDA						
Return on Assets %						
Return on Equity %						
Debt to Equity						

CONTACT INFORMATION:

Phone: Fax:
Toll-Free: 800 205-5164
Address: 500 7th Ave., Fl. 8, New York, NY 10018 United States

STOCK TICKER/OTHER:

Stock Ticker: Private   Exchange:
Employees: 300   Fiscal Year Ends:
Parent Company:

SALARIES/BONUSES:

Top Exec. Salary: $ Bonus: $
Second Exec. Salary: $ Bonus: $

OTHER THOUGHTS:

Estimated Female Officers or Directors:
Hot Spot for Advancement for Women/Minorities:

Sales, profits and employees may be estimates. Financial information, benefits and other data can change quickly and may vary from those stated here.

Stripe Inc

stripe.com

NAIC Code: 522320

TYPES OF BUSINESS:

Payment Processing -Intermediary
Digital Payment Solutions
Application Programming Interfaces
Web Payment Solutions
Mobile App Payment Solutions
Customer Experience Tools
Data Analytics Solutions
Fraud Detection Solutions

BRANDS/DIVISIONS/AFFILIATES:

Stripe Connect
Stripe Sigma
Stripe Radar
Stripe Issuing
Stripe Terminal
Stripe Atlas
OpenChannel

CONTACTS: Note: Officers with more than one job title may be intentionally listed here more than once.

Patrick Collison, CEO
John Collison, Pres.

GROWTH PLANS/SPECIAL FEATURES:

Stripe, Inc. is an online payment platform designed for companies ranging from startups to enterprises. The firm serves millions of companies in over 120 countries, enabling them to receive payments in over 135 currencies and through various payment methods. Stripe offers a suite of application programming interfaces (APIs) that allow developers to easily integrate Stripe's payment platform into their web interface and mobile applications. Stripe's payments product accepts all major cards through its single, unified platform, and enables users to set up a marketplace and bill customers on a recurring basis. Businesses can design billing around customer/user experience (CX/UX) via embedded platform tools. Stripe Connect is the firm's payment platform and is designed to accept money and pay out to third parties; and provides a complete set of building blocks to support virtually any business model, including on-demand businesses, ecommerce, crowdfunding, travel and events. Stripe Sigma enables business teams to run operations more efficiently, to analyze data and to manage production. Stripe Radar makes it easy for handling everything involved in establishing an internet business. Radar fights fraud through its detection features via machine learning technology. Stripe Issuing is an API for creating, distributing and managing physical and virtual payment cards. Stripe Terminal is a programmable point of sale, extending the ecommerce presence into the physical world. It enables in-person payments for any business model via Stripe's pre-certified card readers, JavaScript and mobile SDKs, and cloud-based hardware management. In addition, Stripe Atlas is an easy-to-use platform for forming a company, helping the launch of a startup from anywhere in the world. Stripe is dual-headquartered in San Francisco and Dublin, with offices in London, Paris, Singapore, Tokyo and more. In December 2021, Stripe acquired OpenChannel, a provider of app marketplace software.

FINANCIAL DATA: Note: Data for latest year may not have been available at press time.

In U.S. $	2021	2020	2019	2018	2017	2016
Revenue	7,770,000,000	7,400,000,000	1,350,000,000	800,000,000	790,500,000	775,000,000
R&D Expense						
Operating Income						
Operating Margin %						
SGA Expense						
Net Income						
Operating Cash Flow						
Capital Expenditure						
EBITDA						
Return on Assets %						
Return on Equity %						
Debt to Equity						

CONTACT INFORMATION:

Phone: 650 427-9276   Fax:
Toll-Free: 888-963-8955
Address: 510 Townsend St., San Francisco, CA 94103-4918 United States

STOCK TICKER/OTHER:

Stock Ticker: Private
Employees: 2,650
Parent Company:

Exchange:
Fiscal Year Ends: 12/31

SALARIES/BONUSES:

Top Exec. Salary: $ Bonus: $
Second Exec. Salary: $ Bonus: $

OTHER THOUGHTS:

Estimated Female Officers or Directors:
Hot Spot for Advancement for Women/Minorities:

Sales, profits and employees may be estimates. Financial information, benefits and other data can change quickly and may vary from those stated here.

Suplari Inc

NAIC Code: 511210Q

suplari.com

TYPES OF BUSINESS:
Computer Software: Accounting, Banking & Financial
SaaS - Business Resource Management
Finance Software Solutions
Business Procurement Solutions
Artificial Intelligence
Machine Learning Technologies
Data Analytics
Financial Planning and Spend

BRANDS/DIVISIONS/AFFILIATES:
Microsoft Corporation
Suplari Intelligence Cloud
Suplari Connect
Suplari Agile Contracts
Suplari Agile Performance Management
Supplier Diversity Insights
Spend Analytics
Suplari for Finance

CONTACTS:
Note: Officers with more than one job title may be intentionally listed here more than once.
Nikesh Parekh, CEO

GROWTH PLANS/SPECIAL FEATURES:

Suplari, Inc. is a financial technology company that develops products and solutions that help global finance and procurement teams manage costs and cash flow via data, automated insights and predictive actions. Suplari's Spend Intelligence Cloud provides a single platform equipped with these artificial intelligent (AI) and machine learning (ML) features so that enterprises can rapidly assess, predict and change spend, investments and operations strategy in real-time. Other products by the firm include: Suplari Connect, for team collaboration and support; Suplari Agile Contracts, which enable businesses to manage contracts and identify savings opportunities via automation technology; Suplari Agile Performance Management, for planning, executing, measuring, budgeting and assessing financial performance via data and AI-generated automated insights; Supplier Diversity Insights, for automating and streamlining supplier diversity programs with Suplari supplier diversity insights; Spend Analytics, providing solutions for procurement and finance across supplier, departments and categories; Suplari for Finance, which forecasts financial planning and spend in order to improve accuracy and eliminate budget surprises; and Suplari for Procurement, offering AI-based, software designed to maximize every dollar of profit and discover every dollar of cost savings by analyzing current and historical data patterns. Suplari operates as a subsidiary of Microsoft Corporation.

Suplari offers its employees comprehensive health benefits, 401(k) and stock options.

FINANCIAL DATA:
Note: Data for latest year may not have been available at press time.

In U.S. $	2021	2020	2019	2018	2017	2016
Revenue						
R&D Expense						
Operating Income						
Operating Margin %						
SGA Expense						
Net Income						
Operating Cash Flow						
Capital Expenditure						
EBITDA						
Return on Assets %						
Return on Equity %						
Debt to Equity						

CONTACT INFORMATION:
Phone: 425 610-9496   Fax:
Toll-Free:
Address: 1700 7 Ave., Ste. 116, PMB #348, Seattle, WA 98101 United States

STOCK TICKER/OTHER:
Stock Ticker: Subsidiary   Exchange:
Employees: Fiscal Year Ends:
Parent Company: Microsoft Corporation

SALARIES/BONUSES:
Top Exec. Salary: $ Bonus: $
Second Exec. Salary: $ Bonus: $

OTHER THOUGHTS:
Estimated Female Officers or Directors:
Hot Spot for Advancement for Women/Minorities:

Sales, profits and employees may be estimates. Financial information, benefits and other data can change quickly and may vary from those stated here.

SVB Financial Group

www.svb.com

NAIC Code: 522110

TYPES OF BUSINESS:
Banking
Lending Services
Asset Management
Investment Banking
Online Banking
Trade & Foreign Exchange Services
Mutual Funds
Advisory Services

BRANDS/DIVISIONS/AFFILIATES:
Silicon Valley Bank

GROWTH PLANS/SPECIAL FEATURES:
SVB Financial Group provides loans and ancillary financial services to startups, private equity, and venture capital firms. The bank has four segments: Global Commercial Bank, SVB Private Bank, SVB Capital, and SVB Leerink. In addition to providing loans to venture-capital-backed startups, the company invests in private equity and venture capital funds of funds. The bank operates throughout the United States and maintains offices in the United Kingdom, Israel, China, and India.

SVB Financial offers comprehensive benefits, retirement options and employee assistance programs.

CONTACTS: *Note: Officers with more than one job title may be intentionally listed here more than once.*
Gregory Becker, CEO
Daniel Beck, CFO
Roger Dunbar, Chairman of the Board
Karen Hon, Chief Accounting Officer
Marc Cadieux, Chief Credit Officer
Michelle Draper, Chief Marketing Officer
Laura Izurieta, Chief Risk Officer
Philip Cox, COO
Michael Zuckert, General Counsel
Christopher Edmonds-Waters, Other Executive Officer
John China, President, Divisional
Michael Descheneaux, President, Subsidiary

FINANCIAL DATA: *Note: Data for latest year may not have been available at press time.*

In U.S. $	2021	2020	2019	2018	2017	2016
Revenue		3,919,849,000	3,259,500,000	2,601,022,000	1,940,856,000	1,574,751,000
R&D Expense						
Operating Income						
Operating Margin %						
SGA Expense		1,400,065,000	1,107,353,000	837,055,000	710,407,000	609,171,000
Net Income		1,208,368,000	1,136,856,000	973,840,000	490,506,000	382,685,000
Operating Cash Flow		1,445,487,000	1,164,129,000	933,562,000	580,099,000	437,977,000
Capital Expenditure		87,407,000	65,479,000	45,865,000	50,884,000	53,311,000
EBITDA						
Return on Assets %						
Return on Equity %						
Debt to Equity						

CONTACT INFORMATION:
Phone: 408 654-7400   Fax: 408 496-2405
Toll-Free:
Address: 3003 Tasman Dr., Santa Clara, CA 95054 United States

STOCK TICKER/OTHER:
Stock Ticker: SIVB   Exchange: NAS
Employees: 6,567   Fiscal Year Ends: 12/31
Parent Company:

SALARIES/BONUSES:
Top Exec. Salary: $995,385   Bonus: $
Second Exec. Salary: $748,654   Bonus: $

OTHER THOUGHTS:
Estimated Female Officers or Directors: 4
Hot Spot for Advancement for Women/Minorities: Y

Sales, profits and employees may be estimates. Financial information, benefits and other data can change quickly and may vary from those stated here.

Synchrony Financial

NAIC Code: 522210

www.mysynchrony.com

TYPES OF BUSINESS:
Credit Card Issuing
Consumer Lending
Commercial Loans
Auto Loans & Leases
Insurance
Mortgages
Home Equity Loans
Private Label Credit Cards

BRANDS/DIVISIONS/AFFILIATES:
Synchrony Bank
CareCredit

GROWTH PLANS/SPECIAL FEATURES:

Synchrony Financial, originally a spin-off of GE Capital's retail financing business, is the largest provider of private-label credit cards in the United States by both outstanding receivables and purchasing volume. Synchrony partners with other firms to market its credit products in their physical stores as well as on their websites and mobile applications. Synchrony operates through three segments: retail card (private-label and co-branded general-purpose credit cards), payment solutions (promotional financing for large ticket purchases), and CareCredit (financing for elective healthcare procedures).

CONTACTS: *Note: Officers with more than one job title may be intentionally listed here more than once.*
Thomas Quindlen, CEO, Divisional
Alberto Casellas, CEO, Divisional
Curtis Howse, CEO, Divisional
Bart Schaller, CEO, Divisional
Brian Doubles, CEO
Brian Wenzel, CFO
Margaret Keane, Chairman of the Board
David Melito, Chief Accounting Officer
Henry Greig, Chief Credit Officer
Paul Whynott, Chief Risk Officer
Carol Juel, Chief Technology Officer
Jonathan Mothner, Executive VP
Michael Bopp, Executive VP
Jeffrey Naylor, Independent Director
Roy Guthrie, Independent Director

FINANCIAL DATA: *Note: Data for latest year may not have been available at press time.*

In U.S. $	2021	2020	2019	2018	2017	2016
Revenue		15,456,000,000	17,913,000,000	17,134,000,000	16,008,000,000	14,421,000,000
R&D Expense						
Operating Income						
Operating Margin %						
SGA Expense		1,787,000,000	2,004,000,000	1,955,000,000	1,812,000,000	1,630,000,000
Net Income		1,385,000,000	3,747,000,000	2,790,000,000	1,935,000,000	2,251,000,000
Operating Cash Flow		7,487,000,000	8,990,000,000	9,342,000,000	8,916,000,000	6,823,000,000
Capital Expenditure						
EBITDA						
Return on Assets %						
Return on Equity %						
Debt to Equity						

CONTACT INFORMATION:
Phone: 203-585-2400 Fax:
Toll-Free: 866-419-4096
Address: 777 Long Ridge Rd., Stamford, CT 06902 United States

STOCK TICKER/OTHER:
Stock Ticker: SYF Exchange: NYS
Employees: 18,000 Fiscal Year Ends: 12/31
Parent Company:

SALARIES/BONUSES:
Top Exec. Salary: $1,175,000 Bonus: $2,232,500
Second Exec. Salary: $800,000 Bonus: $1,140,000

OTHER THOUGHTS:
Estimated Female Officers or Directors: 1
Hot Spot for Advancement for Women/Minorities:

Sales, profits and employees may be estimates. Financial information, benefits and other data can change quickly and may vary from those stated here.

Tala

tala.co

NAIC Code: 511210Q

TYPES OF BUSINESS:

Computer Software: Accounting, Banking & Financial
Financial Technology
Credit Building Solutions
Lending Solutions
Savings Solutions
Finance Education

BRANDS/DIVISIONS/AFFILIATES:

CONTACTS: *Note: Officers with more than one job title may be intentionally listed here more than once.*

Shivani Siroya, CEO
Jen Loo, CFO
Jori Pearsall, Chief Product Officer
Punam Brahmbhatt, Sr. VP-People & Programs
Nachiket Shiralkar, CTO

GROWTH PLANS/SPECIAL FEATURES:

Tala is a financial technology firm that has developed an accessible consumer credit product that instantly underwrites and disperses loans to people who have never had a formal credit history, all through a smartphone app. Loans range from $10 to $500. Tala is powered by advanced data science and consists of a modern credit infrastructure, looking at the customer's texts and call logs, merchant transactions, overall app usage and other behavioral data to build their credit profile. The application process takes minutes and money is either sent directly to the borrower's mobile money account or to other cash out options. Tala offers its mobile loans in Kenya, Philippines, Mexico and India. A minimal fee for each loan. Tala also provides savings accounts, tips and courses on growing a business, savings, credit and more. Investors of Tala include Upstart, the Stellar Enterprise Fund, RPS Ventures, the J. Safra Group, IVP, Revolution Growth, Lowercase Capital, Data Collective Venture Capital, ThomVest Ventures and PayPal Ventures.

Tala offers its employees comprehensive health benefits, professional development opportunities and more.

FINANCIAL DATA: *Note: Data for latest year may not have been available at press time.*

In U.S. $	2021	2020	2019	2018	2017	2016
Revenue						
R&D Expense						
Operating Income						
Operating Margin %						
SGA Expense						
Net Income						
Operating Cash Flow						
Capital Expenditure						
EBITDA						
Return on Assets %						
Return on Equity %						
Debt to Equity						

CONTACT INFORMATION:

Phone: Fax:
Toll-Free:
Address: 1633 26th St., Santa Monica, CA 90404 United States

STOCK TICKER/OTHER:

Stock Ticker: Private   Exchange:
Employees: Fiscal Year Ends:
Parent Company:

SALARIES/BONUSES:

Top Exec. Salary: $ Bonus: $
Second Exec. Salary: $ Bonus: $

OTHER THOUGHTS:

Estimated Female Officers or Directors:
Hot Spot for Advancement for Women/Minorities:

Sales, profits and employees may be estimates. Financial information, benefits and other data can change quickly and may vary from those stated here.

TD Ameritrade Holding Corporation

www.amtd.com

NAIC Code: 523120

TYPES OF BUSINESS:

Discount Stock Brokerage
Online Brokerage
Financial Planning
Clearing Services
Online Financial Trading
Technology Services and Solutions

BRANDS/DIVISIONS/AFFILIATES:

Charles Schwab Corporation (The)
TD Ameritrade Inc
TD Ameritrade Clearing Inc
TD Ameritrade Media Productions Company
Thinkorswim
ThinkTech

CONTACTS: *Note: Officers with more than one job title may be intentionally listed here more than once.*

Steve Boyle, CEO
Timothy Hockey, Director
Thomas Nally, Executive VP, Divisional
Steven Quirk, Executive VP, Divisional
Peter deSilva, Executive VP, Divisional
Ellen Koplow, Executive VP

GROWTH PLANS/SPECIAL FEATURES:

TD Ameritrade Holding Corporation provides securities brokerage services and technology-based financial services to retail investors and independent registered investment advisors. The company provides its services through online, telephone, branch and mobile channels. Products and services include: common and preferred stock, purchasing common and preferred stocks, American Depository Receipts and closed-end funds traded on any U.S. exchange or quotation system; exchange-traded funds (ETFs), offering ETFs from leading providers; mutual funds, from a portfolio of mutual funds from leading fund families; options, offering a range of option trades; futures, in a wide variety of commodities, stock indices and currencies; foreign exchange, with access to trading in over 75 different currency pairs; fixed income, offering a variety of Treasury, corporate, government agency and municipal bonds as well as certificates of deposit; annuities, both fixed and variable; education, offering a suite of free education for beginner, intermediate and advanced investors that is designed to teach investors how to approach the selection process for investment securities and actively manage their investment portfolios; new and secondary issue securities, offering primary and secondary offerings of fixed income securities, closed-end funds, common stock and preferred stock; margin lending, extending credit to clients who maintain margin accounts; cash management services, via third-party banking relationships offering FDIC-insured deposit accounts and money market mutual funds to clients as cash sweep alternatives; and U.S. market access in Asia, offering Singapore and Hong Kong access to U.S. markets and the ability to trade stocks, ETFs, options, futures and options of futures. Primary subsidiaries of TD Ameritrade include TD Ameritrade Inc. (brokerage services), TD Ameritrade Clearing Inc. (brokerage) and TD Ameritrade Media Productions Company (financial news network). In addition, Thinkorswim is an electronic trading platform, and ThinkTech is engaged in technology. TD Ameritrade Holding Corporation itself is a subsidiary of The Charles Schwab Corporation.

FINANCIAL DATA: *Note: Data for latest year may not have been available at press time.*

In U.S. $	2021	2020	2019	2018	2017	2016
Revenue	6,357,520,000	6,113,000,000	6,016,000,000	5,452,000,000	3,676,000,000	3,273,999,872
R&D Expense						
Operating Income						
Operating Margin %						
SGA Expense						
Net Income			2,208,000,000	1,472,999,936	872,000,000	842,000,000
Operating Cash Flow						
Capital Expenditure						
EBITDA						
Return on Assets %						
Return on Equity %						
Debt to Equity						

CONTACT INFORMATION:

Phone: 402 331-7856   Fax:
Toll-Free: 800-237-8692
Address: 200 S. 108th Ave., Omaha, NE 68154 United States

SALARIES/BONUSES:

Top Exec. Salary: $ Bonus: $
Second Exec. Salary: $ Bonus: $

STOCK TICKER/OTHER:

Stock Ticker: Subsidiary   Exchange:
Employees: 9,226   Fiscal Year Ends: 09/30
Parent Company: Charles Schwab Corporation (The)

OTHER THOUGHTS:

Estimated Female Officers or Directors: 4
Hot Spot for Advancement for Women/Minorities: Y

Sales, profits and employees may be estimates. Financial information, benefits and other data can change quickly and may vary from those stated here.

Plunkett Research, Ltd.

Tornado (Nvstr Technologies Inc)

tornado.com

NAIC Code: 523120

TYPES OF BUSINESS:
Securities Brokerage
Online Trading Platform
Investment Education
Stock Trading Solutions
Rewards for Investment Learning
Tailored Investment News

BRANDS/DIVISIONS/AFFILIATES:
Tornado

GROWTH PLANS/SPECIAL FEATURES:
Nvstr Technologies, Inc. operates Tornado, a hybrid investment platform. Users can buy, sell and trade through Tornado; can learn about investing through the app and earn rewards from Tornado while doing so; and can join conversations with leading investors to see what stocks they are buying and selling and compare investment strategies. Tornado also offers real-time news tailored to the user's interests and investments. Stocks can be explored and filtered per interests and goals, and investors can choose their own stocks or opt for a diversified set of exchange traded funds (ETFs) for more guidance. Tornado is registered with Financial Industry Regulatory Authority (FINRA) and the U.S. Securities and Exchange Commission (SEC), and a member of the Securities Investor Protection Corporation (SIPC). It has up to $37.5 million in insurance with Lloyds of London, among other insurance coverage.

CONTACTS: *Note: Officers with more than one job title may be intentionally listed here more than once.*
Bernard George, CEO

FINANCIAL DATA: *Note: Data for latest year may not have been available at press time.*

In U.S. $	2021	2020	2019	2018	2017	2016
Revenue						
R&D Expense						
Operating Income						
Operating Margin %						
SGA Expense						
Net Income						
Operating Cash Flow						
Capital Expenditure						
EBITDA						
Return on Assets %						
Return on Equity %						
Debt to Equity						

CONTACT INFORMATION:
Phone: 917-757-1722   Fax:
Toll-Free:
Address: 135 Madison Ave., Fl. 5, New York, NY 10016 United States

STOCK TICKER/OTHER:
Stock Ticker: Private   Exchange:
Employees: 60   Fiscal Year Ends:
Parent Company:

SALARIES/BONUSES:
Top Exec. Salary: $ Bonus: $
Second Exec. Salary: $ Bonus: $

OTHER THOUGHTS:
Estimated Female Officers or Directors:
Hot Spot for Advancement for Women/Minorities:

Sales, profits and employees may be estimates. Financial information, benefits and other data can change quickly and may vary from those stated here.

TradeStation Group Inc

www.tradestation.com

NAIC Code: 523120

TYPES OF BUSINESS:

Online Stock Brokerage
Financial Information
Stock Trading Software
Foreign Exchange Transactions
Futures Commission Merchant

BRANDS/DIVISIONS/AFFILIATES:

Monex Group Inc
TradeStation Securities inc
TradeStation Crypto Inc
TradeStation Technologies inc
TradeStation
You Can Trade Inc

CONTACTS: *Note: Officers with more than one job title may be intentionally listed here more than once.*

John Bartleman, CEO
Greg Vance, CFO
Michael Fisch, CTO
Marc J. Stone, Chief Legal Officer
William P. Cahill, VP-Brokerage Oper.
Takashi Oyagi, Chief Strategic Officer
Edward Codispoti, VP-Finance

GROWTH PLANS/SPECIAL FEATURES:

TradeStation Group, Inc. is an online brokerage firm operating through its wholly-owned subsidiaries, including TradeStation Securities, Inc.; TradeStation Crypto, Inc.; and TradeStation Technologies, Inc. Together, the group providers products and services under the TradeStation brand and trademark. Trading products include stocks, exchange traded funds (ETFs), an IPO trading platform, options, futures, futures options, crypto, mutual funds and bonds. Platforms and tools offered by TradeStation include desktop, web trading, mobile apps, simulated trading, order execution, a web application programming interface (API), and a trading app store, among others. In addition, wholly-owned You Can Trade, Inc. offers an online media publication service that provides investment educational content, ideas and demonstrations, and does not provide investment or trading advice, research or recommendations. You Can Trade operates under its own brand and trademarks. TradeStation itself operates as a wholly-owned subsidiary of Japanese online financial services provider, Monex Group, Inc. Headquartered in Florida, TradeStation Group has additional offices in Illinois, New York and Texas. In late-2021, TradeStation announced plans to go public through a business combination with Quantum Fintech Acquisition Corporation. Monex Group would retain 100% of its equity in TradeStation. Upon completion of the transaction (expected by mid-2022), TradeStation would list on the New York Stock Exchange under ticker symbol TRDE.

TradeStation offers its employees comprehensive health benefits, life and disability insurance, retirement savings plans, and a variety of employee assistance plans and programs.

FINANCIAL DATA: *Note: Data for latest year may not have been available at press time.*

In U.S. $	2021	2020	2019	2018	2017	2016
Revenue	218,652,000	188,639,000	181,131,000	188,196,000	167,752,000	154,353,000
R&D Expense						
Operating Income						
Operating Margin %						
SGA Expense						
Net Income	23,790,000	10,277,000	18,596,000	2,649,000	-4,103,000	-4,371,000
Operating Cash Flow						
Capital Expenditure						
EBITDA						
Return on Assets %						
Return on Equity %						
Debt to Equity						

CONTACT INFORMATION:

Phone: 954-652-7000   Fax: 954-652-7300
Toll-Free: 800-556-2022
Address: 8050 SW 10th St., Ste. 2000, Plantation, FL 33324 United States

STOCK TICKER/OTHER:

Stock Ticker: Subsidiary   Exchange:
Employees: 294   Fiscal Year Ends: 03/31
Parent Company: Monex Group Inc

SALARIES/BONUSES:

Top Exec. Salary: $ Bonus: $
Second Exec. Salary: $ Bonus: $

OTHER THOUGHTS:

Estimated Female Officers or Directors:
Hot Spot for Advancement for Women/Minorities:

Sales, profits and employees may be estimates. Financial information, benefits and other data can change quickly and may vary from those stated here.

TransUnion

NAIC Code: 561450

www.transunion.com

TYPES OF BUSINESS:
Credit Reporting

GROWTH PLANS/SPECIAL FEATURES:
TransUnion is one of the leading credit bureaus in the United States, providing the consumer information that is the basis for granting credit. The company also provides fraud detection, marketing, and analytical services. TransUnion operates in over 30 countries, and about one fourth of its revenue comes from international markets.

BRANDS/DIVISIONS/AFFILIATES:

CONTACTS: *Note: Officers with more than one job title may be intentionally listed here more than once.*
Christopher Cartwright, CEO
Todd Cello, CFO
Pamela Joseph, Chairman of the Board
Timothy Elberfeld, Chief Accounting Officer
Abhinav Dhar, Chief Information Officer
Heather Russell, Chief Legal Officer
Richard Mauldin, COO
John Danaher, Executive VP, Divisional
David Neenan, Executive VP, Divisional
Steven Chaouki, Executive VP, Geographical
Timothy Martin, Executive VP
Todd Skinner, President, Divisional
David Wojczynski, President, Divisional

FINANCIAL DATA: *Note: Data for latest year may not have been available at press time.*

In U.S. $	2021	2020	2019	2018	2017	2016
Revenue		2,716,600,000	2,656,100,000	2,317,200,000	1,933,800,000	1,704,900,000
R&D Expense						
Operating Income		568,000,000	607,800,000	512,500,000	464,700,000	300,500,000
Operating Margin %						
SGA Expense		860,300,000	812,100,000	707,700,000	585,400,000	560,100,000
Net Income		343,200,000	346,900,000	276,600,000	441,200,000	120,600,000
Operating Cash Flow		787,400,000	776,700,000	555,700,000	468,000,000	389,900,000
Capital Expenditure		214,100,000	198,500,000	180,100,000	135,300,000	124,000,000
EBITDA		950,000,000	976,200,000	787,900,000	698,100,000	556,100,000
Return on Assets %						
Return on Equity %						
Debt to Equity						

CONTACT INFORMATION:
Phone: 312-985-2860   Fax:
Toll-Free:
Address: 555 W. Adams St., Chicago, IL 60661 United States

STOCK TICKER/OTHER:
Stock Ticker: TRU   Exchange: NYS
Employees: 4,700   Fiscal Year Ends:
Parent Company:

SALARIES/BONUSES:
Top Exec. Salary: $971,154   Bonus: $951,639
Second Exec. Salary: $634,615   Bonus: $488,020

OTHER THOUGHTS:
Estimated Female Officers or Directors:
Hot Spot for Advancement for Women/Minorities:

Sales, profits and employees may be estimates. Financial information, benefits and other data can change quickly and may vary from those stated here.

TrueAccord Corp

www.trueaccord.com

NAIC Code: 511210Q

TYPES OF BUSINESS:

Computer Software: Accounting, Banking & Financial
Digital Debt Collection Solutions
Debt Recovery Solutions
Machine Learning Technology
Customer Engagement
Recovery and Collections Starter Kit

BRANDS/DIVISIONS/AFFILIATES:

TrueAccord Recover
TrueAccord Retain

GROWTH PLANS/SPECIAL FEATURES:

TrueAccord Corp. is a financial technology firm that offers a digital-first, machine learning collections and recovery platform for businesses and merchants. TrueAccord's artificial intelligent platform automatically improves and optimizes engagement over time, scaling efficiently to any collections or recovery volume. It reaches consumers through personalized messages across channels, and helps them resolve their debts and delinquencies. The platform's two primary solutions are branded as TrueAccord Recover and TrueAccord Retain. Industries served by TrueAccord include financial services, insurance, telecommunications, technology real estate, medical and utilities. TrueAccord's recovery and collections starter kit enables customers to build their own strategy, and includes tips, tricks, guides, calculators, cheat sheets and more.

CONTACTS:
Note: Officers with more than one job title may be intentionally listed here more than once.

Mark Ravanesi, CEO

FINANCIAL DATA:
Note: Data for latest year may not have been available at press time.

In U.S. $	2021	2020	2019	2018	2017	2016
Revenue						
R&D Expense						
Operating Income						
Operating Margin %						
SGA Expense						
Net Income						
Operating Cash Flow						
Capital Expenditure						
EBITDA						
Return on Assets %						
Return on Equity %						
Debt to Equity						

CONTACT INFORMATION:

Phone: Fax:
Toll-Free: 866 611-2731
Address: 16011 College Blvd., Ste. 130, Lenexa, KS 66219 United States

STOCK TICKER/OTHER:

Stock Ticker: Private   Exchange:
Employees: Fiscal Year Ends:
Parent Company:

SALARIES/BONUSES:

Top Exec. Salary: $ Bonus: $
Second Exec. Salary: $ Bonus: $

OTHER THOUGHTS:

Estimated Female Officers or Directors:
Hot Spot for Advancement for Women/Minorities:

Sales, profits and employees may be estimates. Financial information, benefits and other data can change quickly and may vary from those stated here.

Plunkett Research, Ltd.

Truebill Inc

www.truebill.com

NAIC Code: 511210Q

TYPES OF BUSINESS:
Computer Software: Accounting, Banking & Financial
Personal Finances Platform
Subscription Management Solution
Income and Spend Management
Savings Solutions
Credit Score Solutions
Budgeting Solutions
Financial Technology

BRANDS/DIVISIONS/AFFILIATES:
Rocket Companies Inc

CONTACTS: Note: Officers with more than one job title may be intentionally listed here more than once.
Haroon Mokhtarzada, CEO
Idris Mokhtarzada, CTO

GROWTH PLANS/SPECIAL FEATURES:
Truebill, Inc. is a financial technology company that provides a range of financial services and solutions to help individuals optimize financial health. Truebill's subscription management feature automatically finds subscriptions and bills on behalf of users to help them stop paying for things they no longer use or need. To improve one's income/spend ratio, Truebill provides a breakdown of finance income and spend as well as advice on how to improve it; and sends notifications about financial situations that may need attention. In regard to savings, the platform automatically scans bills to find ways to save; and Truebill negotiators will present best possible rates on bills, cards and such when users want them to. Truebill's smart savings accounts automatically analyze finance activity to determine optimal ways to save. Smart savings deposits are housed in the user's own account at Truebill's FDIC-insured banking partner. Smart savings accounts can be edited, paused, withdrawn from or closed at any time by the user. As for credit scores, Truebill provides access to the user's complete credit report and history. The credit score feature alerts about important changes that impact scoring and offers insights for understanding what everything means. Last, Truebill enables users to create a budget and then automatically monitors spending categories, and provides ways to help users stay on track for optimizing financial health and reaching financial goals. Truebill operates as a subsidiary of Rocket Companies, Inc.

Truebill offers its employees comprehensive health benefits, 401(k), life and short-/long-term disability coverage, paid time off and a variety of company plans and perks.

FINANCIAL DATA: Note: Data for latest year may not have been available at press time.

In U.S. $	2021	2020	2019	2018	2017	2016
Revenue						
R&D Expense						
Operating Income						
Operating Margin %						
SGA Expense						
Net Income						
Operating Cash Flow						
Capital Expenditure						
EBITDA						
Return on Assets %						
Return on Equity %						
Debt to Equity						

CONTACT INFORMATION:
Phone: 415 231-8180   Fax:
Toll-Free:
Address: 8455 Colesville Rd., Ste. 1645, Silver Spring, MD 20910 United States

STOCK TICKER/OTHER:
Stock Ticker: Subsidiary   Exchange:
Employees: Fiscal Year Ends:
Parent Company: Rocket Companies Inc

SALARIES/BONUSES:
Top Exec. Salary: $ Bonus: $
Second Exec. Salary: $ Bonus: $

OTHER THOUGHTS:
Estimated Female Officers or Directors:
Hot Spot for Advancement for Women/Minorities:

Sales, profits and employees may be estimates. Financial information, benefits and other data can change quickly and may vary from those stated here.

Truework (Zethos Inc)

www.truework.com

NAIC Code: 511210Q

TYPES OF BUSINESS:
Computer Software, Accounting, Banking & Financial
Employment & Income Verification
Mortgage and Lending Income Verification Solutions
Data Aggregation
Data Software
Verification Resources

BRANDS/DIVISIONS/AFFILIATES:
Truework

CONTACTS: *Note: Officers with more than one job title may be intentionally listed here more than once.*
Ryan Sandler, CEO

GROWTH PLANS/SPECIAL FEATURES:

Zethos, Inc. is a financial technology company that provides employment verification services through its Truework platform. Solutions by Truework are designed for varied industries, and span mortgage, consumer lending and pre-employment. Mortgage companies can close loans faster and increase borrower conversion during the underwriting process with Truework's easy-to-use web application and application programming interface (API), as well as related integrations that fit into any underwriting workflow. Consumer lenders across personal loans, auto loans and student loan refinancing can swiftly approve borrowers with its data verification solutions. The single platform provides instant approvals and broad coverage. Employment history can be verified through Truework for any U.S. employee, which comprises more than 35 million instant records nationwide and over 7 million in Truework's own network. Truework utilizes a multichannel approach, and employment verification requests are generally completed within seconds. How Truework works: pre-approvals are backed by verified income; access to income and employment data provides verification of employee; permissioned payroll data is embedded into the Truework platform in regards to customers issuing loans; and Truework teams processes manual verifications for hard-to-reach employers to help save time. Related resources are offered on the Truework website, including lenders, verifiers, employers, employees, employer directory and API documents.

Zethos offers its employees comprehensive health benefits, 401(k) and other company plans and perks.

FINANCIAL DATA: *Note: Data for latest year may not have been available at press time.*

In U.S. $	2021	2020	2019	2018	2017	2016
Revenue						
R&D Expense						
Operating Income						
Operating Margin %						
SGA Expense						
Net Income						
Operating Cash Flow						
Capital Expenditure						
EBITDA						
Return on Assets %						
Return on Equity %						
Debt to Equity						

CONTACT INFORMATION:
Phone: Fax:
Toll-Free: 833 878-3967
Address: 325 Pacific Ave., San Francisco, CA 94111 United States

STOCK TICKER/OTHER:
Stock Ticker: Private   Exchange:
Employees: Fiscal Year Ends:
Parent Company:

SALARIES/BONUSES:
Top Exec. Salary: $ Bonus: $
Second Exec. Salary: $ Bonus: $

OTHER THOUGHTS:
Estimated Female Officers or Directors:
Hot Spot for Advancement for Women/Minorities:

Sales, profits and employees may be estimates. Financial information, benefits and other data can change quickly and may vary from those stated here.

Truist Financial Corporation

www.truist.com

NAIC Code: 522110

TYPES OF BUSINESS:
Banking
Financial Services
Banking Services
Asset Management
Credit Cards
Insurance
Mortgage
Lending

BRANDS/DIVISIONS/AFFILIATES:
Truist Bank

GROWTH PLANS/SPECIAL FEATURES:
Based in Charlotte, North Carolina, Truist is the combination of BB&T and SunTrust. Truist is a regional bank with a presence primarily in the Southeastern United States. In addition to commercial banking, retail banking, and investment banking operations, the company operates several nonbank segments, the primary one being its insurance brokerage business.

CONTACTS:
Note: Officers with more than one job title may be intentionally listed here more than once.

Kelly King, CEO
Daryl Bible, CFO
Cynthia Powell, Chief Accounting Officer
Scott Case, Chief Information Officer
Ellen Fitzsimmons, Chief Legal Officer
Clarke Starnes, Chief Risk Officer
William Rogers, COO
David Weaver, Other Corporate Officer

FINANCIAL DATA:
Note: Data for latest year may not have been available at press time.

In U.S. $	2021	2020	2019	2018	2017	2016
Revenue		22,705,000,000	12,568,000,000	11,558,000,000	11,317,000,000	10,935,000,000
R&D Expense						
Operating Income						
Operating Margin %						
SGA Expense		8,419,000,000	4,970,000,000	4,313,000,000	4,121,000,000	4,106,000,000
Net Income		4,482,000,000	3,224,000,000	3,237,000,000	2,394,000,000	2,426,000,000
Operating Cash Flow		7,437,000,000	1,520,000,000	4,349,000,000	4,635,000,000	2,672,000,000
Capital Expenditure		815,000,000				
EBITDA						
Return on Assets %						
Return on Equity %						
Debt to Equity						

CONTACT INFORMATION:
Phone: 336-733-2000   Fax:
Toll-Free:
Address: 214 N. Tyron St., Charlotte, NC 28202 United States

STOCK TICKER/OTHER:
Stock Ticker: TFC
Employees: 52,641
Parent Company:

Exchange: NYS
Fiscal Year Ends: 12/31

SALARIES/BONUSES:
Top Exec. Salary: $1,200,000   Bonus: $
Second Exec. Salary: $1,100,000   Bonus: $

OTHER THOUGHTS:
Estimated Female Officers or Directors: 1
Hot Spot for Advancement for Women/Minorities:

Sales, profits and employees may be estimates. Financial information, benefits and other data can change quickly and may vary from those stated here.

Trulioo Inc

www.trulioo.com

NAIC Code: 511210E

TYPES OF BUSINESS:

Computer Software: Network Security, Managed Access, Digital ID, Cybersecurity & Anti-Virus
Digital Identity Network
Identity Verification Services
Data Sources
Identification Document Verification Solutions
Business Verification Solutions

BRANDS/DIVISIONS/AFFILIATES:

GlobalGateway
HelloFlow

CONTACTS: *Note: Officers with more than one job title may be intentionally listed here more than once.*

Steve Munford, CEO

GROWTH PLANS/SPECIAL FEATURES:

Trulioo, Inc. offers global online identity verification services. The company's marketplace for identity services and data sources is GlobalGateway, validating against 400+ data sources in nearly 200 countries across mobile networks, credit bureaus, banks, governments, utilities, consumer files, business registers and biometrics. Trulioo's products are grouped into three categories: identity verification, to compare identity data against independent data sources, to support Know Your Customer (KYC) processes, and to attain/retain customers; ID document verification, to run document checks, to deploy routing for increasing pass rates and to authenticate users via selfies; and business verification, to verify business details and owners, to obtain official company documents, and to verify over 330 million businesses. GlobalGateway can verify digital identities in developing countries such as Bangladesh, China, India, Indonesia, Mexico, Nigeria and Pakistan, as well as in countries where unbanked adults reside. Industries served by Trulioo include banking, cryptocurrency, foreign exchange, gaming, marketplaces/communities, payments, remittances and wealth management, among others. Headquartered in Canada, the company has a satellite office in Ireland, and expanding its teams throughout the U.S. In February 2022, Trulioo acquired HelloFlow, a Denmark-based firm that offers a no-code, drag-and-drop solution for client onboarding monitoring and digital workflow. Trulioo plans to use HelloFlow's technology to assist in onboarding new customers.

FINANCIAL DATA: *Note: Data for latest year may not have been available at press time.*

In U.S. $	2021	2020	2019	2018	2017	2016
Revenue						
R&D Expense						
Operating Income						
Operating Margin %						
SGA Expense						
Net Income						
Operating Cash Flow						
Capital Expenditure						
EBITDA						
Return on Assets %						
Return on Equity %						
Debt to Equity						

CONTACT INFORMATION:

Phone: 855 484-8800   Fax:
Toll-Free:
Address: 1200 - 1055 West Hastings St., Vancouver, BC V6E 2E9 Canada

STOCK TICKER/OTHER:

Stock Ticker: Private   Exchange:
Employees: Fiscal Year Ends:
Parent Company:

SALARIES/BONUSES:

Top Exec. Salary: $ Bonus: $
Second Exec. Salary: $ Bonus: $

OTHER THOUGHTS:

Estimated Female Officers or Directors:
Hot Spot for Advancement for Women/Minorities:

Sales, profits and employees may be estimates. Financial information, benefits and other data can change quickly and may vary from those stated here.

Trumid Financial LLC

www.trumid.com

NAIC Code: 511210Q

TYPES OF BUSINESS:

Computer Software: Accounting, Banking & Financial
Corporate Debt Trading Platform
Financial Technology
Data Aggregation
User Experience
User Interface
User Workflow
Data Analytics

BRANDS/DIVISIONS/AFFILIATES:

CONTACTS: Note: Officers with more than one job title may be intentionally listed here more than once.

Michael Sobel, Co-CEO
Ronnie Mateo, Co-CEO

GROWTH PLANS/SPECIAL FEATURES:

Trumid Financial, LLC combines technology, intuitive design and market expertise to deliver an easy-to-use trading solution. The Trumid platform offers a personalized user experience via customizable market data feeds, flexible protocols and quantitative models for liquidity purposes. Its data aggregation features provide access to a complete view of the market, and offers multiple data sources to help guide users along their trading journeys. Users can choose how and what they want to trade within the Trumid platform. Trumid Financial encompasses fixed income market experts that create products and workflow solutions specifically tailored to credit market participants. The company keeps its focus on user experience/user interface (UX/UI) and user workflow results when designing its products and solutions. Trumid's agile and flexible technology stack enables the quick reaction to market opportunities and client needs. Trumid provides aggregated market data and analytics to power its trade execution; and users are able to make informed trading decisions through its proprietary pricing service for corporate bonds at Fair Value Model Price (FVMP), which is about $20,000 USD.

Trumid Financial offers its employees comprehensive health benefits.

FINANCIAL DATA: Note: Data for latest year may not have been available at press time.

In U.S. $	2021	2020	2019	2018	2017	2016
Revenue						
R&D Expense						
Operating Income						
Operating Margin %						
SGA Expense						
Net Income						
Operating Cash Flow						
Capital Expenditure						
EBITDA						
Return on Assets %						
Return on Equity %						
Debt to Equity						

CONTACT INFORMATION:

Phone: 212 618-0300   Fax:
Toll-Free:
Address: 1411 Broadway, Ste. 2410, New York, NY 10018 United States

STOCK TICKER/OTHER:

Stock Ticker: Private   Exchange:
Employees: 115   Fiscal Year Ends:
Parent Company:

SALARIES/BONUSES:

Top Exec. Salary: $ Bonus: $
Second Exec. Salary: $ Bonus: $

OTHER THOUGHTS:

Estimated Female Officers or Directors:
Hot Spot for Advancement for Women/Minorities:

Sales, profits and employees may be estimates. Financial information, benefits and other data can change quickly and may vary from those stated here.

Trustly Group AB

NAIC Code: 522320

www.trustly.net/us

TYPES OF BUSINESS:
Financial Transactions Processing, Reserve, and Clearinghouse Activities
Financial Technology
Open Banking Payment Platform

BRANDS/DIVISIONS/AFFILIATES:
Nordic Capital

GROWTH PLANS/SPECIAL FEATURES:
Trustly Group AB is a financial technology company based in Sweden that has developed a unique payments platform. Trustly enables consumers to securely pay merchants online, from anywhere in the world, directly through their bank accounts. This payment method offers an alternative to card networks. How it works: users sign in to their open banking without leaving the merchant's site; there is no sign up, no card nor bank numbers to enter, and no billing info to provide; one agreement and one integration gives the business access to consumers in North America and across Europe, and sets the business up with integrated multi-currency functionality, enabling the Trustly platform to transact with consumers. Once Trustly approves a payment, it is fully guaranteed, with no chargebacks. Trustly is a Nacha Preferred Partner for online banking payment and verification. Trustly Group is privately-owned by Nordic Capital.

CONTACTS:
Note: Officers with more than one job title may be intentionally listed here more than once.

Oscar Berglund, CEO

FINANCIAL DATA:
Note: Data for latest year may not have been available at press time.

In U.S. $	2021	2020	2019	2018	2017	2016
Revenue	288,762,000	241,963,280				
R&D Expense						
Operating Income						
Operating Margin %						
SGA Expense						
Net Income						
Operating Cash Flow						
Capital Expenditure						
EBITDA						
Return on Assets %						
Return on Equity %						
Debt to Equity						

CONTACT INFORMATION:
Phone: 46 8 50521120   Fax:
Toll-Free:
Address: Radmansgatan 40, 5tr, Stockholm, SE-113 57 Sweden

STOCK TICKER/OTHER:
Stock Ticker: Private   Exchange:
Employees: 620   Fiscal Year Ends: 12/31
Parent Company: Nordic Capital

SALARIES/BONUSES:
Top Exec. Salary: $ Bonus: $
Second Exec. Salary: $ Bonus: $

OTHER THOUGHTS:
Estimated Female Officers or Directors:
Hot Spot for Advancement for Women/Minorities:

Sales, profits and employees may be estimates. Financial information, benefits and other data can change quickly and may vary from those stated here.

UAB JM Trading (Cryptomate)

www.cryptomate.net

NAIC Code: 523130

TYPES OF BUSINESS:
Virtual Currency Exchange Services
Financial Technology
Cryptocurrency Trading
Buy and Sell Crypto Platform

BRANDS/DIVISIONS/AFFILIATES:

GROWTH PLANS/SPECIAL FEATURES:
UAB JM Trading is a financial technology company that has developed and operates the Cryptomate platform for buying and selling cryptocurrency. With access to online banking via UK Faster Payments, coins can be sent to the user's wallet in as little as five minutes after placing an order. Cryptomate offers a wide selection of crypto, which are viewable on the platform's coins page. Types of crypto include, Bitcoin, Ethereum, XRP, Tether, Litecoin, EOS, Cardano, Dogecoin and TRON, among many others. How it works: those with a verified Cryptomate account choose the cryptocurrency they wish to purchase; enter email address and crypto wallet details; and make a payment through their online banking account. Once the order has been placed and payment received, users receive crypto coins to the wallet provided during the order. To sell cryptocurrency, users fill out an online form, specify how much of which coin they want to sell to Cryptomate, and the platform will reply with a competitive quote for the coins (usually on the same day).

CONTACTS: *Note: Officers with more than one job title may be intentionally listed here more than once.*
William Thomas, CEO

FINANCIAL DATA: *Note: Data for latest year may not have been available at press time.*

In U.S. $	2021	2020	2019	2018	2017	2016
Revenue						
R&D Expense						
Operating Income						
Operating Margin %						
SGA Expense						
Net Income						
Operating Cash Flow						
Capital Expenditure						
EBITDA						
Return on Assets %						
Return on Equity %						
Debt to Equity						

CONTACT INFORMATION:
Phone: 370-6-675-2135   Fax:
Toll-Free:
Address: J. Savickio g. 4-7, Vilnius, 01108 Lithuania

STOCK TICKER/OTHER:
Stock Ticker: Private
Employees:
Parent Company:

Exchange:
Fiscal Year Ends:

SALARIES/BONUSES:
Top Exec. Salary: $ Bonus: $
Second Exec. Salary: $ Bonus: $

OTHER THOUGHTS:
Estimated Female Officers or Directors:
Hot Spot for Advancement for Women/Minorities:

Sales, profits and employees may be estimates. Financial information, benefits and other data can change quickly and may vary from those stated here.

UP Fintech Holding Limited

ir.itiger.com/investor-relations

NAIC Code: 523120

TYPES OF BUSINESS:
Online Securities Brokerage
Online Trading
Brokerage

BRANDS/DIVISIONS/AFFILIATES:
Tiger

GROWTH PLANS/SPECIAL FEATURES:
UP Fintech Holding Ltd is an online brokerage firm focusing on Chinese investors. Its trading platform enables investors to trade in equities and other financial instruments on multiple exchanges of stocks and other derivatives. The company offers its customers brokerage and value-added services, including trade order placement and execution, margin financing, account management, investor education, community discussion, and customer support.

CONTACTS: *Note: Officers with more than one job title may be intentionally listed here more than once.*
John Fei Zeng, CFO

FINANCIAL DATA: *Note: Data for latest year may not have been available at press time.*

In U.S. $	2021	2020	2019	2018	2017	2016
Revenue		138,496,700	58,662,900	33,560,260	16,949,180	5,475,837
R&D Expense						
Operating Income		21,033,230	-10,174,250	-46,892,110	-9,015,210	-13,538,280
Operating Margin %						
SGA Expense		34,356,480	19,934,920	20,980,500	11,032,360	8,650,409
Net Income		16,064,790	-6,589,431	-43,207,730	-7,510,049	-10,758,450
Operating Cash Flow		535,281,000	243,309,100	-21,171,600	-8,510,634	-11,502,790
Capital Expenditure		978,142	1,317,435	1,684,382	585,016	440,305
EBITDA		21,961,650	-9,422,085	-46,418,380	-8,672,760	-13,342,520
Return on Assets %						
Return on Equity %						
Debt to Equity						

CONTACT INFORMATION:
Phone: 86-10-56216660   Fax:
Toll-Free:
Address: 18/Fl, Grandyvic Bldg., No.16 Taiyanggong Middle R, Beijing, 100028 China

STOCK TICKER/OTHER:
Stock Ticker: TIGR   Exchange: NAS
Employees: 1,134   Fiscal Year Ends: 12/31
Parent Company:

SALARIES/BONUSES:
Top Exec. Salary: $ Bonus: $
Second Exec. Salary: $ Bonus: $

OTHER THOUGHTS:
Estimated Female Officers or Directors:
Hot Spot for Advancement for Women/Minorities:

Sales, profits and employees may be estimates. Financial information, benefits and other data can change quickly and may vary from those stated here.

Upgrade Inc

www.upgrade.com

NAIC Code: 522291

TYPES OF BUSINESS:
Consumer Lending
Mobile Banking
Credit Cards
Debit Cards
Personal Loans
Auto Refinancing
Credit Score Solutions
Debt Consolidation

BRANDS/DIVISIONS/AFFILIATES:

GROWTH PLANS/SPECIAL FEATURES:

Upgrade, Inc. is a financial technology firm that provides online and mobile banking services, as well as affordable loans and cards. Upgrade offers free credit health tools for optimizing credit scores, along with resources that explain factors that influence credit scores, offer credit score simulated scenarios and provide customized recommendations. Upgrade offers a rewards checking account that provides cash back on expenses and low rates on loans and cards, and charges no AMT fees, no account fees and no transfer fees. A range of debit card options are provided, including those for average to excellent credit and those for improving credit. Lines of credit can be applied for toward the Upgrade card. Personal loans up to $50,000 at affordable monthly payments can be applied toward refinancing credit cards, debt consolidation, home improvement or major purchases. Car payments can be lowered through Upgrade's auto refinancing strategy.

CONTACTS: *Note: Officers with more than one job title may be intentionally listed here more than once.*
Renaud Laplanche, CEO

FINANCIAL DATA: *Note: Data for latest year may not have been available at press time.*

In U.S. $	2021	2020	2019	2018	2017	2016
Revenue						
R&D Expense						
Operating Income						
Operating Margin %						
SGA Expense						
Net Income						
Operating Cash Flow						
Capital Expenditure						
EBITDA						
Return on Assets %						
Return on Equity %						
Debt to Equity						

CONTACT INFORMATION:
Phone: 347 776-1730   Fax:
Toll-Free: 844 319-3909
Address: 275 Battery St., Fl. 23, San Francisco, CA 94111 United States

STOCK TICKER/OTHER:
Stock Ticker: Private   Exchange:
Employees: 540   Fiscal Year Ends:
Parent Company:

SALARIES/BONUSES:
Top Exec. Salary: $ Bonus: $
Second Exec. Salary: $ Bonus: $

OTHER THOUGHTS:
Estimated Female Officers or Directors:
Hot Spot for Advancement for Women/Minorities:

US Bancorp (US Bank)

NAIC Code: 522110

www.usbank.com

TYPES OF BUSINESS:
Banking
Lease Financing
Consumer Finance
Credit Cards
Discount Brokerage
Investment Advisory Services
Trust Services
Insurance

BRANDS/DIVISIONS/AFFILIATES:
US Bank NA
Elavon Inc

GROWTH PLANS/SPECIAL FEATURES:

As a diversified financial-services provider, U.S. Bancorp is one of the nation's largest regional banks, with branches in well over 20 states, primarily in the Western and Midwestern United States. The bank offers many services, including retail banking, commercial banking, trust and wealth services, credit cards, mortgages, and other payments capabilities.

U.S. Bancorp offers comprehensive benefits, retirement options and employee assistance programs.

CONTACTS: *Note: Officers with more than one job title may be intentionally listed here more than once.*
Andrew Cecere, CEO
James Kelligrew, Vice Chairman, Divisional
Terrance Dolan, CFO
Lisa Stark, Chief Accounting Officer
Katherine Quinn, Chief Administrative Officer
Mark Runkel, Chief Credit Officer
Jodi Richard, Chief Risk Officer
James Chosy, General Counsel
Elcio Barcelos, Other Executive Officer
Gregory Cunningham, Other Executive Officer
Dominic Venturo, Other Executive Officer
Gunjan Kedia, Vice Chairman, Divisional
Timothy Welsh, Vice Chairman, Divisional
Shailesh Kotwal, Vice Chairman, Divisional
Jeffry von Gillern, Vice Chairman, Divisional

FINANCIAL DATA: *Note: Data for latest year may not have been available at press time.*

In U.S. $	2021	2020	2019	2018	2017	2016
Revenue		23,226,000,000	22,883,000,000	22,181,000,000	21,852,000,000	21,105,000,000
R&D Expense						
Operating Income						
Operating Margin %						
SGA Expense		8,256,000,000	8,037,000,000	7,822,000,000	7,474,000,000	6,766,000,000
Net Income		4,959,000,000	6,914,000,000	7,096,000,000	6,218,000,000	5,888,000,000
Operating Cash Flow		3,716,000,000	4,889,000,000	10,564,000,000	6,472,000,000	5,336,000,000
Capital Expenditure						
EBITDA						
Return on Assets %						
Return on Equity %						
Debt to Equity						

CONTACT INFORMATION:
Phone: 651 466-3000   Fax:
Toll-Free:
Address: 800 Nicollet Mall, Minneapolis, MN 55402 United States

STOCK TICKER/OTHER:
Stock Ticker: USB   Exchange: NYS
Employees: 68,796   Fiscal Year Ends: 12/31
Parent Company:

SALARIES/BONUSES:
Top Exec. Salary: $1,200,000   Bonus: $
Second Exec. Salary: $725,000   Bonus: $

OTHER THOUGHTS:
Estimated Female Officers or Directors: 5
Hot Spot for Advancement for Women/Minorities: Y

Sales, profits and employees may be estimates. Financial information, benefits and other data can change quickly and may vary from those stated here.

ValidiFI LLC

validifi.com

NAIC Code: 511210Q

TYPES OF BUSINESS:
Computer Software: Accounting, Banking & Financial
Financial Technology
Banking Data Aggregation
Payment Data Aggregation
Account Validation Solutions
Payments Solutions
Fraud and Risk Management Solutions
Compliance Solutions

BRANDS/DIVISIONS/AFFILIATES:

GROWTH PLANS/SPECIAL FEATURES:
ValidiFI, LLC is a financial technology firm that has developed a digital platform that aggregates banking and payment data. ValidiFI provides seamless integrations to structured data and validated models to improve account openings, credit decisions, payments, fraud, risk and compliance. Institutions and businesses leverage the platform to enhance their offerings and support the digital process. ValidiFI's products include account validation, bank aggregation, bank account ownership, bank account validation, card account verification, lead conversion scoring and risk tools. These products offer solutions across credit, risk, identity, fraud, customer acquisition, account management, collections and payment recovery, compliance and know your customer (KYC).

CONTACTS: *Note: Officers with more than one job title may be intentionally listed here more than once.*
Oscar DiVeroli, CEO

FINANCIAL DATA: *Note: Data for latest year may not have been available at press time.*

In U.S. $	2021	2020	2019	2018	2017	2016
Revenue						
R&D Expense						
Operating Income						
Operating Margin %						
SGA Expense						
Net Income						
Operating Cash Flow						
Capital Expenditure						
EBITDA						
Return on Assets %						
Return on Equity %						
Debt to Equity						

CONTACT INFORMATION:
Phone: 754 209-2511   Fax:
Toll-Free: 754 260-2400
Address: 2300 Corporate Blvd., Ste. 241, Boca Raton, FL 33431 United States

STOCK TICKER/OTHER:
Stock Ticker: Private   Exchange:
Employees: Fiscal Year Ends:
Parent Company:

SALARIES/BONUSES:
Top Exec. Salary: $ Bonus: $
Second Exec. Salary: $ Bonus: $

OTHER THOUGHTS:
Estimated Female Officers or Directors:
Hot Spot for Advancement for Women/Minorities:

Sales, profits and employees may be estimates. Financial information, benefits and other data can change quickly and may vary from those stated here.

Varo Money NA

www.varomoney.com

NAIC Code: 522110

TYPES OF BUSINESS:

Online Bank
Financial Technology
Bank Accounts
Savings Accounts
Debit and Credit Cards
Cash Advances
Credit Score Solutions

BRANDS/DIVISIONS/AFFILIATES:

Varo Bank NA
Varo Advance
Varo Believe

CONTACTS: *Note: Officers with more than one job title may be intentionally listed here more than once.*

Colin Walsh, CEO
Jon Alferness, Dir.-Product
Thibault Fulconis, Dir.-Finance
Carolyn Feinstein, Dir.-Mktg.
May O'Neal, Dir.-People
Deep Varma, Dir.-Technology
Jakub Jurek, Dir.-Data

GROWTH PLANS/SPECIAL FEATURES:

Varo Money NA is a financial technology firm that was granted full regulatory approval to open Varo Bank NA in 2020. The firm was the first national bank charter granted to a U.S. consumer fintech, which enabled Varo to offer customers comprehensive, FDIC-insured banking services. Today, Varo Bank offers full-service online banking with no monthly fees, no transfer fees, no foreign transaction fees, no minimum balance and no Allpoint-branded ATM fees. There are some bank fees such as out-of-network ATM withdrawals, cash deposits through third-party money transfer services and over-the-counter cash withdrawals. Bank deposits are FDIC insured up to $250,000. Varo savings accounts offer automatic savings tools and high-interest for growing money. Savings accounts can be configured to receive a percentage of direct deposits, as well as change that has been rounded up to the nearest dollar on purchases. Varo Advance is a cash advance option for up to $100 to help account balances without being charged overdraft fees. Varo Believe is the company's credit card for building credit, and requires no minimum security deposit, no annual fee or interest, and no hard credit check to apply. Varo Believe enables users to spend through the card for things they normally purchase, and when they make on-time payments in full, they build a positive credit history. Credit scores can be checked through the Varo online/mobile platform.

Varo offers its employees comprehensive health benefits, 401(k), paid time off and other company programs and perks.

FINANCIAL DATA: *Note: Data for latest year may not have been available at press time.*

In U.S. $	2021	2020	2019	2018	2017	2016
Revenue						
R&D Expense						
Operating Income						
Operating Margin %						
SGA Expense						
Net Income						
Operating Cash Flow						
Capital Expenditure						
EBITDA						
Return on Assets %						
Return on Equity %						
Debt to Equity						

CONTACT INFORMATION:

Phone: 800 827-6526   Fax:
Toll-Free: 877 377-8276
Address: 100 Montgomery, Ste. 1201, San Francisco, CA 94108 United States

STOCK TICKER/OTHER:

Stock Ticker: Private   Exchange:
Employees: Fiscal Year Ends:
Parent Company:

SALARIES/BONUSES:

Top Exec. Salary: $ Bonus: $
Second Exec. Salary: $ Bonus: $

OTHER THOUGHTS:

Estimated Female Officers or Directors:
Hot Spot for Advancement for Women/Minorities:

Sales, profits and employees may be estimates. Financial information, benefits and other data can change quickly and may vary from those stated here.

Plunkett Research, Ltd.

Veem Inc

www.veem.com

NAIC Code: 522320

TYPES OF BUSINESS:

Financial Transactions Processing, Reserve, and Clearinghouse Activities
Electronic Funds Transfer Services
Global Payments Platform
Identity and Account Verification Solutions
Payments Processing
Business Invoicing Solutions
Mass Payments Solution
Payment Tracking Solution

BRANDS/DIVISIONS/AFFILIATES:

Veem Wallet
Mass Pay from Veem

CONTACTS: *Note: Officers with more than one job title may be intentionally listed here more than once.*

Marwan Forzley, CEO
Olivier Veyrac, VP-Bus. Dev.
Pramod Iyengar, CFO
Jeanette Yoder, Head-Mktg.
Esraa Hezain, Dir.-Human Resources
Ralf Dagher, VP-Engineering
Suhas Maskar, Dir.-Data & Analytics

GROWTH PLANS/SPECIAL FEATURES:

Veem, Inc. is a financial technology company that provides a global payments network designed for businesses. How Veem works: 1. Users complete an online account to start paying and invoicing businesses throughout the world, without subscription, setup nor hidden fees; 2. Connect bank account and verify identity; 3. Send, receive and invoice payments through an email address, and business partners then set up an account or allow the user to add their information on their behalf; 4. Veem notifies the business partner that there is a transaction waiting for them, and once they complete a one-time account setup and verification, the money can begin to move. Money can be tracked throughout the payment journey through Veem, which provides live updates and statuses. Payments are deposited directly to a bank account, debit card or Veem Wallet. Mass Pay from Veem is a solution that enables multiple payments to be sent at once. Integration features are available for accounting, developer and workflow purposes. Veem is open to partnerships. Headquartered in California, USA, Veem has global offices in Ontario, Canada and Shanghai, China.

FINANCIAL DATA: *Note: Data for latest year may not have been available at press time.*

In U.S. $	2021	2020	2019	2018	2017	2016
Revenue						
R&D Expense						
Operating Income						
Operating Margin %						
SGA Expense						
Net Income						
Operating Cash Flow						
Capital Expenditure						
EBITDA						
Return on Assets %						
Return on Equity %						
Debt to Equity						

CONTACT INFORMATION:

Phone: Fax:
Toll-Free: 877 279-2629
Address: 75 Broadway, Ste. 202, San Francisco, CA 94111 United States

STOCK TICKER/OTHER:

Stock Ticker: Private
Employees: 140
Parent Company:

Exchange:
Fiscal Year Ends:

SALARIES/BONUSES:

Top Exec. Salary: $ Bonus: $
Second Exec. Salary: $ Bonus: $

OTHER THOUGHTS:

Estimated Female Officers or Directors:
Hot Spot for Advancement for Women/Minorities:

Sales, profits and employees may be estimates. Financial information, benefits and other data can change quickly and may vary from those stated here.

Venmo

venmo.com

NAIC Code: 522320

TYPES OF BUSINESS:

Financial Transactions Processing, Reserve, and Clearinghouse Activities
Electronic Funds Transfer Services
Digital Payments Platform
Social Payments Platform
Credit Card
Rewards Card
Cryptocurrency
Crypto Trading

BRANDS/DIVISIONS/AFFILIATES:

PayPal Holdings Inc
PayPal Inc
Venmo Credit Card

CONTACTS: *Note: Officers with more than one job title may be intentionally listed here more than once.*

Andrew Kortina, CEO

GROWTH PLANS/SPECIAL FEATURES:

Venmo is a financial technology firm that provides the Venmo digital and social payments platform. Venmo enables users to pay, get paid, shop, gift and split expenses. With a Venmo Credit Card, holders can earn up to 3% cash back and send, spend and purchase cryptocurrency. Reward categories automatically updated based on what is purchased, making earnings and savings to grow. The Venmo Credit Card features a personalized QR code for making payments and getting paid. Various types of crypto are offered through Venmo, which can be used to buy, track and sell. Businesses with a Venmo profile can reach customers who prefer to pay through the app. Headquartered in California, Venmo has offices throughout the U.S., including Arizona, Illinois, Massachusetts, Nebraska and New York. Venmo operates as a subsidiary of PayPal Holdings, Inc. All money transmission is provided by PayPal, Inc.

Venmo offers its employees comprehensive health benefits and a 401(k).

FINANCIAL DATA: *Note: Data for latest year may not have been available at press time.*

In U.S. $	2021	2020	2019	2018	2017	2016
Revenue						
R&D Expense						
Operating Income						
Operating Margin %						
SGA Expense						
Net Income						
Operating Cash Flow						
Capital Expenditure						
EBITDA						
Return on Assets %						
Return on Equity %						
Debt to Equity						

CONTACT INFORMATION:

Phone: 855-812-4430   Fax:
Toll-Free:
Address: 2211 N. First St., San Jose, CA 95131 United States

SALARIES/BONUSES:

Top Exec. Salary: $ Bonus: $
Second Exec. Salary: $ Bonus: $

STOCK TICKER/OTHER:

Stock Ticker: Subsidiary   Exchange:
Employees: Fiscal Year Ends:
Parent Company: PayPal Holdings Inc

OTHER THOUGHTS:

Estimated Female Officers or Directors:
Hot Spot for Advancement for Women/Minorities:

Sales, profits and employees may be estimates. Financial information, benefits and other data can change quickly and may vary from those stated here.

Plunkett Research, Ltd. 307

Veriff Inc
www.veriff.com

NAIC Code: 511210E

TYPES OF BUSINESS:
Computer Software: Network Security, Managed Access, Digital ID,
Cybersecurity & Anti-Virus
Online Identity Verification
Automated Machine Learning Technology
Know Your Customer Verification
Identification Verification Software
Biometric Authentication
Assisted Image Capture Solutions
Proof of Address Document Solutions

BRANDS/DIVISIONS/AFFILIATES:

GROWTH PLANS/SPECIAL FEATURES:
Veriff, Inc. develops and delivers digital identity verification
solutions for connecting companies with verified persons. The
firm's products include full-service identity verification
solutions, automated machine learning, know your customer
(KYC) checks, identification verification software, biometric
authentication and reverification, assisted image capture
solutions and proof of address document solutions. Industries
served by Veriff include financial technology, mobility,
cryptocurrency, gaming, metaverse, education, healthcare and
human resource management. Use cases include age
verification, driver validation, new account onboarding,
customer identity management and access management.
Headquartered in Tallinn, Estonia, the company has a global
office in New York, USA.

Veriff offers its employees comprehensive health benefits,
stock options, learning and development opportunities and
other benefits.

CONTACTS:
Note: Officers with more than one job title may be intentionally listed here more than once.

Kaarel Kotkas, CEO
Indrek Heinloo, COO
Amish Mody, CFO
Duncan Steblyna, VP-Product
Kristina Lilleois, VP-People
Jaanus Kivistik, CTO
Tiit Paananen, VP-Engineering

FINANCIAL DATA:
Note: Data for latest year may not have been available at press time.

In U.S. $	2021	2020	2019	2018	2017	2016
Revenue						
R&D Expense						
Operating Income						
Operating Margin %						
SGA Expense						
Net Income						
Operating Cash Flow						
Capital Expenditure						
EBITDA						
Return on Assets %						
Return on Equity %						
Debt to Equity						

CONTACT INFORMATION:
Phone: 372 607 5050   Fax:
Toll-Free:
Address: 11 Niine, Tallinn, Harjumaa, 10414 EE Estonia

STOCK TICKER/OTHER:
Stock Ticker: Private
Employees: 350
Parent Company:

Exchange:
Fiscal Year Ends:

SALARIES/BONUSES:
Top Exec. Salary: $ Bonus: $
Second Exec. Salary: $ Bonus: $

OTHER THOUGHTS:
Estimated Female Officers or Directors:
Hot Spot for Advancement for Women/Minorities:

Sales, profits and employees may be estimates. Financial information, benefits and other data can change quickly and may vary from those stated here.

Verifi Inc

NAIC Code: 511210K

www.verifi.com

TYPES OF BUSINESS:
Computer Software: Sales & Customer Relationship Management (CRM)
SaaS - Electronic Payment and Risk Management Solutions
Dispute Management Services
Payment Protection Solutions
Ecommerce Management Services
Transaction Processing
Fraud Detection and Tracking
Notice Delivery

BRANDS/DIVISIONS/AFFILIATES:
Visa Inc

GROWTH PLANS/SPECIAL FEATURES:
Verifi, Inc. is a subsidiary of Visa, Inc. that offers dispute management services for seller, issuer and reseller businesses. Founded in 2005, Verifi provides end-to-end payment protection and management solutions, including ecommerce management. The firm processes over 20 billion transactions annually and serves more than 25,000 merchant and partners accounts internationally. Verifi's solutions span prevention, recovery, rapid dispute resolution, fraud notice delivery, dispute notice delivery, fraud rate tracking and more.

Verifi offers its employees comprehensive health benefits, 401(k), employee stock options, and pet insurance.

CONTACTS:
Note: Officers with more than one job title may be intentionally listed here more than once.

Sara Craven, CEO
Chris Marchand, VP-Bus. Dev.
Deborah Kurtz, VP-Finance
Greg Witten, VP-Sales
Toni Espera, Sr. VP-People Oper.
Jeff Sawitke, Chief Product Officer
Tony Wootton, Chief Revenue Officer

FINANCIAL DATA:
Note: Data for latest year may not have been available at press time.

In U.S. $	2021	2020	2019	2018	2017	2016
Revenue						
R&D Expense						
Operating Income						
Operating Margin %						
SGA Expense						
Net Income						
Operating Cash Flow						
Capital Expenditure						
EBITDA						
Return on Assets %						
Return on Equity %						
Debt to Equity						

CONTACT INFORMATION:
Phone: 323 655-5789   Fax: 323 655-5537
Toll-Free: 888 398-5188
Address: 8023 Beverly Blvd., Ste. 1, Box #310, Los Angeles, CA 90048 United States

STOCK TICKER/OTHER:
Stock Ticker: Subsidiary   Exchange:
Employees: Fiscal Year Ends:
Parent Company: Visa Inc

SALARIES/BONUSES:
Top Exec. Salary: $ Bonus: $
Second Exec. Salary: $ Bonus: $

OTHER THOUGHTS:
Estimated Female Officers or Directors:
Hot Spot for Advancement for Women/Minorities:

Sales, profits and employees may be estimates. Financial information, benefits and other data can change quickly and may vary from those stated here.

Virtu Financial Inc

www.virtu.com

NAIC Code: 523120

TYPES OF BUSINESS:
Electronic Stock Trading
Market Maker
Trading Solutions
Broker-Dealer
Trading Execution
Analytics
Technology

BRANDS/DIVISIONS/AFFILIATES:

GROWTH PLANS/SPECIAL FEATURES:

Virtu Financial Inc is a leading technology-enabled market maker and liquidity provider to the global financial markets. The company's operating segment includes Market Making; Execution Services and Corporate. It generates maximum revenue from the Market Making segment. The Market Making segment principally consists of market making in the cash, futures and options markets across global equities, options, fixed income, currencies, and commodities. Geographically, it derives a majority of revenue from the United States and also has a presence in Ireland; Singapore; Canada; Australia and Other Countries.

CONTACTS: Note: Officers with more than one job title may be intentionally listed here more than once.
Douglas Cifu, CEO
Sean Galvin, CFO
Vincent Viola, Chairman Emeritus
Brett Fairclough, Co-COO
Joseph Molluso, Co-COO
Robert Greifeld, Director
Stephen Cavoli, Executive VP, Divisional

FINANCIAL DATA: Note: Data for latest year may not have been available at press time.

In U.S. $	2021	2020	2019	2018	2017	2016
Revenue		3,239,331,000	1,530,082,000	1,878,718,000	1,027,982,000	702,272,000
R&D Expense						
Operating Income		1,509,059,000	113,461,000	803,271,000	188,503,000	215,252,000
Operating Margin %						
SGA Expense		97,499,000	142,349,000	76,236,000	90,407,000	23,039,000
Net Income		649,197,000	-58,595,000	289,441,000	2,939,000	32,980,000
Operating Cash Flow		1,060,884,000	168,771,000	714,595,000	290,574,000	239,599,000
Capital Expenditure		60,359,000	57,812,000	47,949,000	33,090,000	20,263,000
EBITDA		1,611,567,000	142,116,000	855,440,000	240,045,000	237,832,000
Return on Assets %						
Return on Equity %						
Debt to Equity						

CONTACT INFORMATION:
Phone: 212-418-0100   Fax: 212-418-0123
Toll-Free: 800-544-7508
Address: 165 Broadway, One Liberty Plaza, New York, NY 10006 United States

STOCK TICKER/OTHER:
Stock Ticker: VIRT
Employees: 973
Parent Company:

Exchange: NAS
Fiscal Year Ends:

SALARIES/BONUSES:
Top Exec. Salary: $273,973   Bonus: $3,750,000
Second Exec. Salary: $1,000,000   Bonus: $500,000

OTHER THOUGHTS:
Estimated Female Officers or Directors:
Hot Spot for Advancement for Women/Minorities:

Sales, profits and employees may be estimates. Financial information, benefits and other data can change quickly and may vary from those stated here.

Visa Inc

NAIC Code: 522320

www.visa.com

TYPES OF BUSINESS:
Credit Cards
Payments Technology
Payments Solutions
Chip Payment Technology
Debit Solutions
Prepaid Solutions
Credit Payment Solutions

BRANDS/DIVISIONS/AFFILIATES:
Visa Canada Corporaiton
CyberSource Corporation
Visa USA Inc
Visa International Service Association
Visa Worldwide Pte Limited
Visa Europe Limited
Visa Technology & Operations LLC
VisaNet

CONTACTS: *Note: Officers with more than one job title may be intentionally listed here more than once.*
Alfred Kelly, CEO
Vasant Prabhu, CFO
James Hoffmeister, Chief Accounting Officer
Kelly Tullier, Chief Administrative Officer
Lynne Biggar, Chief Marketing Officer
Paul Fabara, Chief Risk Officer
Ryan McInerney, President
Rajat Taneja, President, Divisional

GROWTH PLANS/SPECIAL FEATURES:
Visa is the largest payment processor in the world. In fiscal 2020, it processed almost $9 trillion in purchase transactions. Visa operates in over 200 countries and processes transactions in over 160 currencies. Its systems are capable of processing over 65,000 transactions per second.

FINANCIAL DATA: *Note: Data for latest year may not have been available at press time.*

In U.S. $	2021	2020	2019	2018	2017	2016
Revenue	24,105,000,000	21,846,000,000	22,977,000,000	20,609,000,000	18,358,000,000	15,082,000,000
R&D Expense						
Operating Income	15,807,000,000	14,092,000,000	15,401,000,000	13,561,000,000	12,163,000,000	9,762,000,000
Operating Margin %						
SGA Expense	2,524,000,000	2,475,000,000	2,755,000,000	2,579,000,000	2,391,000,000	2,054,000,000
Net Income	12,311,000,000	10,866,000,000	12,080,000,000	10,301,000,000	6,699,000,000	5,991,000,000
Operating Cash Flow	15,227,000,000	10,440,000,000	12,784,000,000	12,713,000,000	9,208,001,000	5,574,000,000
Capital Expenditure	705,000,000	736,000,000	756,000,000	718,000,000	707,000,000	523,000,000
EBITDA	17,380,000,000	15,073,000,000	16,057,000,000	14,031,000,000	12,813,000,000	8,941,000,000
Return on Assets %						
Return on Equity %						
Debt to Equity						

CONTACT INFORMATION:
Phone: 650-432-3200   Fax:
Toll-Free: 800-847-2911
Address: P.O. Box 8999, San Francisco, CA 94128-8999 United States

STOCK TICKER/OTHER:
Stock Ticker: V   Exchange: NYS
Employees: 21,500   Fiscal Year Ends: 09/30
Parent Company:

SALARIES/BONUSES:
Top Exec. Salary: $1,400,059   Bonus: $
Second Exec. Salary: $1,000,040   Bonus: $

OTHER THOUGHTS:
Estimated Female Officers or Directors: 6
Hot Spot for Advancement for Women/Minorities: Y

Sales, profits and employees may be estimates. Financial information, benefits and other data can change quickly and may vary from those stated here.

Plunkett Research, Ltd.

Voyager Digital Ltd

www.investvoyager.com

NAIC Code: 511210Q

TYPES OF BUSINESS:
Computer Software: Accounting, Banking & Financial

GROWTH PLANS/SPECIAL FEATURES:
Voyager Digital Ltd through its subsidiary operates as a crypto-asset broker that provides retail and institutional investors with a turnkey solution to trade crypto assets. The company offers investors execution, data, wallet, and custody services through its institutional-grade open architecture platform.

BRANDS/DIVISIONS/AFFILIATES:

CONTACTS: Note: Officers with more than one job title may be intentionally listed here more than once.
Stephen Ehrlich, CEO
Philip Eytan, Chmn.

FINANCIAL DATA: Note: Data for latest year may not have been available at press time.

In U.S. $	2021	2020	2019	2018	2017	2016
Revenue	175,056,000	1,149,903	87,318			
R&D Expense		2,615,227	3,319,653	36,297		
Operating Income	55,847,000	-8,840,650	-41,193,560	-1,150,808	-139,427	-101,344
Operating Margin %						
SGA Expense	119,209,000	7,219,423	37,941,610	1,112,731	139,427	101,344
Net Income	-51,488,000	-10,170,260	-30,808,870	-154,021	-139,427	-101,344
Operating Cash Flow	217,135,000	-4,518,679	-3,978,231	-1,416,962	-289,766	-21,069
Capital Expenditure		4,399	33,871	30,093		
EBITDA	56,158,000	-10,010,390	-30,789,250	-1,149,028	-139,427	-101,344
Return on Assets %						
Return on Equity %						
Debt to Equity						

CONTACT INFORMATION:
Phone: 212 547-8807   Fax:
Toll-Free:
Address: 33 Irving Plaza, New York, NY 10003 United States

STOCK TICKER/OTHER:
Stock Ticker: VOYG
Employees:
Parent Company:

Exchange: TSE
Fiscal Year Ends: 06/30

SALARIES/BONUSES:
Top Exec. Salary: $ Bonus: $
Second Exec. Salary: $ Bonus: $

OTHER THOUGHTS:
Estimated Female Officers or Directors:
Hot Spot for Advancement for Women/Minorities:

Sales, profits and employees may be estimates. Financial information, benefits and other data can change quickly and may vary from those stated here.

Wealthfront Corporation

www.wealthfront.com

NAIC Code: 523920

TYPES OF BUSINESS:
Portfolio Management
Financial Technology
Wealth Investment Strategies
Long-term Investing
Index Funds Investments
Sustainable Investments
Direct Indexing Investments
Banking and Line of Credit

BRANDS/DIVISIONS/AFFILIATES:

CONTACTS: *Note: Officers with more than one job title may be intentionally listed here more than once.*
Andy Rachleff, CEO

GROWTH PLANS/SPECIAL FEATURES:

Wealthfront Corporation is a financial technology company that develops solutions for building wealth. The Wealthfront platform is designed for long-term investment strategies and offers a diversified, customizable, portfolio. Once terms are selected by the investor, Wealthfront automates the portfolio to help maximize returns and minimize tax effects. Wealthfront charges a 0.25% annual advisory fee for its portfolios, which span: Classic, offering a globally diversified portfolio of low-cost index funds; Socially Responsible, which is designed around sustainability, diversity, equity and more; and Direct Indexing, for accounts over $100,000 and globally diversified to strategically invest in individual U.S. stocks to enhance tax savings. In partnership with Green Dot and other banks, Wealthfront offers banking services such as FDIC insurance and bill pay, as well as brokerage services for building wealth. Wealthfront users can borrow up to 30% of their portfolio through a line of credit, with applications available online.

Wealthfront offers its employees comprehensive health benefits, flexible working hours and other company plans and perks.

FINANCIAL DATA: *Note: Data for latest year may not have been available at press time.*

In U.S. $	2021	2020	2019	2018	2017	2016
Revenue						
R&D Expense						
Operating Income						
Operating Margin %						
SGA Expense						
Net Income						
Operating Cash Flow						
Capital Expenditure						
EBITDA						
Return on Assets %						
Return on Equity %						
Debt to Equity						

CONTACT INFORMATION:
Phone: 650 249-4258   Fax:
Toll-Free:
Address: 261 Hamilton Ave., Palo Alto, CA 94301 United States

STOCK TICKER/OTHER:
Stock Ticker: Private   Exchange:
Employees: 265   Fiscal Year Ends:
Parent Company:

SALARIES/BONUSES:
Top Exec. Salary: $ Bonus: $
Second Exec. Salary: $ Bonus: $

OTHER THOUGHTS:
Estimated Female Officers or Directors:
Hot Spot for Advancement for Women/Minorities:

Sales, profits and employees may be estimates. Financial information, benefits and other data can change quickly and may vary from those stated here.

Webull Financial LLC

www.webull.com

NAIC Code: 523120

TYPES OF BUSINESS:

Securities Brokerage
Online Trading
Investments
Retirement Planning and Investment
Brokerage Accounts
Technology
Online Tools and Analytics

BRANDS/DIVISIONS/AFFILIATES:

Hunan Fumi Information Technology Co Ltd
Webull

CONTACTS: Note: Officers with more than one job title may be intentionally listed here more than once.

Anthony Denier, CEO

GROWTH PLANS/SPECIAL FEATURES:

Webull Financial, LLC has developed and operates an online trading and investment platform called Webull. The platform charges no commissions and requires no deposit minimums. Users can diversify their portfolios through Webull's comprehensive suite of investment products, including stocks, fractional shares, options, exchange traded funds (ETFs) and American Depository Receipts (ADRs). Users can invest in thousands of stock companies and fractional shares with as little as $5 using Webull's trading tools and analytics. Options provide a strategic alternative to just investing in equity. ETFs diversify holding by investing in a group of stocks with the same convenience as trading a single stock. Digital currency investments span Bitcoin, Ethereum, Bitcoin Cash and Litecoin. Different types of brokerage accounts are available on Webull for various investment objectives, including saving for retirement with Webull Traditional, Roth or Rollover IRA; and individual brokerage accounts, which allow users to buy and sell securities and assets. Webull supports extended hours trading, including full pre-market (4:00 am-9:30 am ET) and after hours (4:00 pm-8:00 pm ET) sessions. The platform provides intuitive charts, multiple technical indicators and Level 2 Advance (Nasdaq TotalView) to help users analyze companies, trends and seize trading opportunities. Users have access to Webull's advanced and fully customizable desktop platform. They can consolidate watchlists, analyze charts, place orders and check positions across all Webull platforms (mobile, PC and web). When opening a Webull account, individuals must issue a government ID card comprising their photo, name and date of birth. Webull Financial is a member of SIPC, NASDAQ and NYSE. The firm is registered with and regulated by the Securities and Exchange Commission (SEC) and the Financial Industry Regulatory Authority (FINRA). Webull Financial is owned by Hunan Fumi Information Technology Co., Ltd.

FINANCIAL DATA: Note: Data for latest year may not have been available at press time.

In U.S. $	2021	2020	2019	2018	2017	2016
Revenue						
R&D Expense						
Operating Income						
Operating Margin %						
SGA Expense						
Net Income						
Operating Cash Flow						
Capital Expenditure						
EBITDA						
Return on Assets %						
Return on Equity %						
Debt to Equity						

CONTACT INFORMATION:

Phone: 917 725-2448   Fax:
Toll-Free: 888 828-0618
Address: 44 Wall St., Ste. 501, New York, NY 10005 United States

STOCK TICKER/OTHER:

Stock Ticker: Subsidiary   Exchange:
Employees: 170   Fiscal Year Ends:
Parent Company: Hunan Fumi Information Technology Co Ltd

SALARIES/BONUSES:

Top Exec. Salary: $ Bonus: $
Second Exec. Salary: $ Bonus: $

OTHER THOUGHTS:

Estimated Female Officers or Directors:
Hot Spot for Advancement for Women/Minorities:

Wells Fargo & Company

NAIC Code: 522110

www.wellsfargo.com

TYPES OF BUSINESS:
Banking
Credit & Debit Cards
Personal Trust Accounts Management
Mutual Fund Administration
Mortgages
Insurance Services
Investment Banking
Asset Management

BRANDS/DIVISIONS/AFFILIATES:
Wells Fargo Bank NA

GROWTH PLANS/SPECIAL FEATURES:

Wells Fargo is one of the largest banks in the United States, with approximately $1.9 trillion in balance sheet assets. The company is split into four primary segments: consumer banking, commercial banking, corporate and investment banking, and wealth and investment management. It is almost entirely focused on the U.S.

Wells Fargo offers its employees a 401(k) plan, tuition reimbursement, adoption assistance, discounted checking and savings accounts and scholarships for dependent children.

CONTACTS: *Note: Officers with more than one job title may be intentionally listed here more than once.*
Michael Weinbach, CEO, Divisional
Saul Van Beurden, Other Corporate Officer
Barry Sommers, CEO, Divisional
Mary Mack, CEO, Divisional
Perry Pelos, CEO, Divisional
Jonathan Weiss, CEO, Divisional
Charles Scharf, CEO
Michael Santomassimo, CFO
Steven Black, Chairman of the Board
Muneera Carr, Chief Accounting Officer
Amanda Norton, Chief Risk Officer
Scott Powell, COO
Ellen Patterson, General Counsel
Lester Owens, Other Corporate Officer
Derek Flowers, Other Corporate Officer
Ather Williams, Other Corporate Officer
Kleber Santos, Other Corporate Officer

FINANCIAL DATA: *Note: Data for latest year may not have been available at press time.*

In U.S. $	2021	2020	2019	2018	2017	2016
Revenue		72,340,000,000	85,063,000,000	86,408,000,000	86,273,000,000	86,728,000,000
R&D Expense						
Operating Income						
Operating Margin %						
SGA Expense		35,411,000,000	37,841,000,000	34,134,000,000	34,658,000,000	33,061,000,000
Net Income		3,301,000,000	19,549,000,000	22,393,000,000	22,183,000,000	21,938,000,000
Operating Cash Flow		2,051,000,000	6,730,000,000	36,073,000,000	18,722,000,000	169,000,000
Capital Expenditure						
EBITDA						
Return on Assets %						
Return on Equity %						
Debt to Equity						

CONTACT INFORMATION:
Phone: 866 249-3302   Fax:
Toll-Free: 800-869-3557
Address: 420 Montgomery St., San Francisco, CA 94163 United States

STOCK TICKER/OTHER:
Stock Ticker: WFC   Exchange: NYS
Employees: 268,531   Fiscal Year Ends: 12/31
Parent Company:

SALARIES/BONUSES:
Top Exec. Salary: $1,750,000   Bonus: $3,200,000
Second Exec. Salary: $2,500,000   Bonus: $

OTHER THOUGHTS:
Estimated Female Officers or Directors: 8
Hot Spot for Advancement for Women/Minorities: Y

Sales, profits and employees may be estimates. Financial information, benefits and other data can change quickly and may vary from those stated here.

Wise Ltd

wise.com

NAIC Code: 522320

TYPES OF BUSINESS:

Online Money Transfer Service
Financial Technology
Multi-Currency Bank Accounts
Payments Solutions
Money Conversion Solutions
Money Transfer Services
Debit Cards
Digital Cards

BRANDS/DIVISIONS/AFFILIATES:

CONTACTS: *Note: Officers with more than one job title may be intentionally listed here more than once.*

Kristo Kaarmann, CEO

GROWTH PLANS/SPECIAL FEATURES:

Wise Ltd. is financial technology company launched in 2011, offering multi-currency accounts for the movement of money worldwide. Wise digital accounts enable users and businesses to send and receive money/payments cheaper and easier than through regular banks. Accounts can convert and hold more than 50 currencies, holding multiple currencies is free and converting them is charged per the real exchange rate. There are no subscription charges for accounts. The Wise international debit card lets users spend abroad with the real exchange rate; and up to $100 in cash can be taken via ATMs abroad for a low fee. The Wise debit card can be used digitally (via online or mobile app), and works just like the physical card. Wise provides international money transfers online for a flat fee and percentage, which vary per transfer type. Large money transfer services are available per the real exchange rate and low fees. Tracking solutions are provided for money transfers. Headquartered in London, U.K., Wise has office locations throughout the world.

FINANCIAL DATA: *Note: Data for latest year may not have been available at press time.*

In U.S. $	2021	2020	2019	2018	2017	2016
Revenue	578,765,540	375,000,076				
R&D Expense						
Operating Income						
Operating Margin %						
SGA Expense						
Net Income	42,479,466	18,588,900				
Operating Cash Flow						
Capital Expenditure						
EBITDA						
Return on Assets %						
Return on Equity %						
Debt to Equity						

CONTACT INFORMATION:

Phone: 44786-493-2720   Fax:
Toll-Free:
Address: 56 Shoreditch High St., Tea Bldg., Fl. 6, London, E1 6JJ United Kingdom

STOCK TICKER/OTHER:

Stock Ticker: WISE
Employees: 2,419
Parent Company:

Exchange: London
Fiscal Year Ends: 03/31

SALARIES/BONUSES:

Top Exec. Salary: $ Bonus: $
Second Exec. Salary: $ Bonus: $

OTHER THOUGHTS:

Estimated Female Officers or Directors:
Hot Spot for Advancement for Women/Minorities:

Sales, profits and employees may be estimates. Financial information, benefits and other data can change quickly and may vary from those stated here.

Workday Inc

NAIC Code: 511210H

www.workday.com

TYPES OF BUSINESS:
Human Resources Software
Enterprise Financial Planning Software (ERF)
Analytics Software

BRANDS/DIVISIONS/AFFILIATES:
Scout REP
Workday Strategic Sourcing

GROWTH PLANS/SPECIAL FEATURES:
Workday is a software company that offers human capital management, or HCM, financial management, and business planning solutions. Known for being a cloud-only software provider, Workday is headquartered in Pleasanton, California. Founded in 2005, Workday now employs over 12,000 employees.

Workday offers its employees health plans, retirement plans and employee assistance programs.

CONTACTS: *Note: Officers with more than one job title may be intentionally listed here more than once.*
Robynne Sisco, CFO
Thomas Bogan, Vice Chairman, Divisional
David Duffield, Chairman Emeritus
Aneel Bhusri, Chairman of the Board
Richard Sauer, Chief Legal Officer
Christine Cefalo, Chief Marketing Officer
Luciano Gomez, Co-CEO
James Bozzini, COO
Doug Robinson, Co-President
George Still, Director
Sayan Chakraborty, Executive VP, Divisional
Pete Schlampp, Executive VP, Divisional
Leighanne Levensaler, Executive VP, Divisional
Emily McEvilly, Other Executive Officer
Ashley Goldsmith, Other Executive Officer
Barbara Larson, Senior VP, Divisional
Michael Stankey, Vice Chairman

FINANCIAL DATA: *Note: Data for latest year may not have been available at press time.*

In U.S. $	2021	2020	2019	2018	2017	2016
Revenue	4,317,996,000	3,627,206,000	2,822,180,000	2,143,050,000	1,569,407,000	1,162,346,000
R&D Expense	1,721,222,000	1,549,906,000	1,211,832,000	910,584,000	680,531,000	469,944,000
Operating Income	-248,599,000	-502,230,000	-463,284,000	-303,223,000	-376,665,000	-264,659,000
Operating Margin %						
SGA Expense	1,647,241,000	1,514,272,000	1,238,682,000	906,276,000	781,996,000	582,634,000
Net Income	-282,431,000	-480,674,000	-418,258,000	-321,222,000	-408,278,000	-289,918,000
Operating Cash Flow	1,268,441,000	864,598,000	606,658,000	465,727,000	348,655,000	258,637,000
Capital Expenditure	256,330,000	244,544,000	212,957,000	152,536,000	120,813,000	133,667,000
EBITDA	87,329,000	-147,484,000	-165,432,000	-133,263,000	-263,104,000	-171,030,000
Return on Assets %						
Return on Equity %						
Debt to Equity						

CONTACT INFORMATION:
Phone: 925-951-9000   Fax:
Toll-Free: 877-967-5329
Address: 6230 Stoneridge Mall Rd., Ste. 200, Pleasanton, CA 94588 United States

STOCK TICKER/OTHER:
Stock Ticker: WDAY   Exchange: NAS
Employees: 12,500   Fiscal Year Ends:
Parent Company:

SALARIES/BONUSES:
Top Exec. Salary: $471,712   Bonus: $453,735
Second Exec. Salary: $500,000   Bonus: $241,000

OTHER THOUGHTS:
Estimated Female Officers or Directors: 2
Hot Spot for Advancement for Women/Minorities:

Sales, profits and employees may be estimates. Financial information, benefits and other data can change quickly and may vary from those stated here.

Yapstone Inc

www.yapstone.com

NAIC Code: 522320

TYPES OF BUSINESS:
Financial Transactions Processing, Reserve, and Clearinghouse Activities
Payments Platform
Financial Technology
Online Payments
Pay Out Solutions
Fraud Detection and Prevention
Dispute Management
Plug-In Integrations

BRANDS/DIVISIONS/AFFILIATES:

CONTACTS: *Note: Officers with more than one job title may be intentionally listed here more than once.*
Frank Mastrangelo, CEO
Michael Orlando, COO
Elliott DeLoach, CFO
Adam DeMonaco, CIO & Security
Sunita Liggin, VP-Human Resources
Frank Salinas, CTO
Tom Villante, Chmn.

GROWTH PLANS/SPECIAL FEATURES:
Yapstone, Inc. is a financial technology company that has developed a payments platform for a variety of industries and markets. The firm was founded in 1999 with the goal of converting bills paid by paper checks into online electronic payments. Today, Yapstone processes more than $20 billion in payment volume every year. Yapstone's products enable businesses to accept online payments, pay out users, detect and prevent fraud, manage disputes, onboard seamlessly, improve conversions and monetize transaction through existing platforms, all from a single source. Businesses can leverage Yapstone's entire payments platform or plug into distinct features that fit business needs and requirements. Solutions span a range of industries, including travel, marketplaces, ecommerce, fintech, gaming, eLearning, over-the-top (OTT) content providers and digital asset exchanges. Headquartered in California, USA, Yapstone has an international office in Drogheda, Ireland.

Yapstone offers its employees comprehensive health plans, 401(k) and paid time off.

FINANCIAL DATA: *Note: Data for latest year may not have been available at press time.*

In U.S. $	2021	2020	2019	2018	2017	2016
Revenue						
R&D Expense						
Operating Income						
Operating Margin %						
SGA Expense						
Net Income						
Operating Cash Flow						
Capital Expenditure						
EBITDA						
Return on Assets %						
Return on Equity %						
Debt to Equity						

CONTACT INFORMATION:
Phone: 866-289-5977   Fax:
Toll-Free:
Address: 2121 N. California Blvd., Ste. 400, Walnut Creek, CA 94596
United States

STOCK TICKER/OTHER:
Stock Ticker: Private
Employees: 260
Parent Company:

Exchange:
Fiscal Year Ends:

SALARIES/BONUSES:
Top Exec. Salary: $ Bonus: $
Second Exec. Salary: $ Bonus: $

OTHER THOUGHTS:
Estimated Female Officers or Directors:
Hot Spot for Advancement for Women/Minorities:

Sales, profits and employees may be estimates. Financial information, benefits and other data can change quickly and may vary from those stated here.

Yodlee Inc

www.yodlee.com

NAIC Code: 511210Q

TYPES OF BUSINESS:
Computer Software: Accounting, Banking & Financial
Financial Technology
Data Aggregation
Data Analytics
Digital Financial Services
Fraud Reduction Solutions
Customer Activation
Financial Building

BRANDS/DIVISIONS/AFFILIATES:
Envestnet inc
Envestnet-Yodlee

CONTACTS: *Note: Officers with more than one job title may be intentionally listed here more than once.*
Arun Anur, COO
Marc Blouin, CFO
Brandon Rembe, Chief Product Officer
Jillian Munro, Dir.-Technology
Arjun Singh, Managing Director, Divisional
Joseph Polverari, Other Executive Officer
William Parsons, Other Executive Officer
Timothy O'Brien, Senior VP, Divisional
Thomas Hempel, Senior VP, Divisional
Eric Connors, Senior VP, Divisional
Arun Anur, Senior VP, Divisional

GROWTH PLANS/SPECIAL FEATURES:
Yodlee, Inc. is a financial technology company that offers its Envestnet/Yodlee data aggregation and data analytics platform. The firm powers cloud-based innovation for digital financial services, primarily serving fintechs and financial institutions. The Envestnet/Yodlee platform enables customers to help their consumers obtain better lending rates, lower fees, higher returns and other related benefits. The platform aggregates accounts for tens of millions of consumers worldwide, and the data improves via machine learning algorithms while also providing visibility into various and unique account types. Products by Envestnet/Yodlee are grouped into two categories: data/apps/and APIs, including aggregation, verification, enrichment, financial wellness and conversational artificial intelligence (AI); and analytics, offering solutions for investors and corporates. Industry solutions span retail banking, wealth management, payments, financial wellness, and financial technology (fintech) data aggregation and insights. Developer solutions include fraud reduction, customer activation and financial app building. Yodlee, Inc. operates as a subsidiary of Envestnet, Inc., a public American financial technology corporation. Envestnet/Yodlee has offices in the U.S., Australia, the U.K. and India.

Envestnet/Yodlee offers its employees comprehensive benefits, 401(k), life/AD&D/short-long-term disability coverage, an employee assistance program and other company plans, programs and perks.

FINANCIAL DATA: *Note: Data for latest year may not have been available at press time.*

In U.S. $	2021	2020	2019	2018	2017	2016
Revenue						
R&D Expense						
Operating Income						
Operating Margin %						
SGA Expense						
Net Income						
Operating Cash Flow						
Capital Expenditure						
EBITDA						
Return on Assets %						
Return on Equity %						
Debt to Equity						

CONTACT INFORMATION:
Phone: 650 980-3600   Fax:
Toll-Free:
Address: 999 Baker Way, Ste. 100, San Mateo, CA 94404 United States

STOCK TICKER/OTHER:
Stock Ticker: Subsidiary   Exchange:
Employees: 702   Fiscal Year Ends:
Parent Company: Envestnet Inc

SALARIES/BONUSES:
Top Exec. Salary: $ Bonus: $
Second Exec. Salary: $ Bonus: $

OTHER THOUGHTS:
Estimated Female Officers or Directors:
Hot Spot for Advancement for Women/Minorities:

Sales, profits and employees may be estimates. Financial information, benefits and other data can change quickly and may vary from those stated here.

Zelle

NAIC Code: 522320

www.zellepay.com

TYPES OF BUSINESS:
Financial Transactions Processing, Reserve, and Clearinghouse Activities
Electronic Funds Transfer Services
Bank to Bank Money Transfer

BRANDS/DIVISIONS/AFFILIATES:
Early Warning Services LLC

GROWTH PLANS/SPECIAL FEATURES:
Zelle is a money transfer platform owned by Early Warning Services, LLC. How Zelle works: access Zelle by enrolling an email or U.S. mobile number through a mobile banking app or with the Zelle app; enter the recipient's email address or U.S. mobile number; enter the amount to be sent; the recipient receives a notification explaining how to complete the payment; and when complete, the payment is sent. Therefore, Zelle moves money directly from bank account to bank account within minutes. Zelle is in more than 1,000 banking apps and is primarily free to use.

CONTACTS: *Note: Officers with more than one job title may be intentionally listed here more than once.*
Albert Ko, CEO

FINANCIAL DATA: *Note: Data for latest year may not have been available at press time.*

In U.S. $	2021	2020	2019	2018	2017	2016
Revenue						
R&D Expense						
Operating Income						
Operating Margin %						
SGA Expense						
Net Income						
Operating Cash Flow						
Capital Expenditure						
EBITDA						
Return on Assets %						
Return on Equity %						
Debt to Equity						

CONTACT INFORMATION:
Phone: 844-428-8542 Fax:
Toll-Free:
Address: 16552 N. 90th St, Scottsdale, AZ 85260 United States

STOCK TICKER/OTHER:
Stock Ticker: Subsidiary Exchange:
Employees: Fiscal Year Ends:
Parent Company: Early Warning Services LLC

SALARIES/BONUSES:
Top Exec. Salary: $ Bonus: $
Second Exec. Salary: $ Bonus: $

OTHER THOUGHTS:
Estimated Female Officers or Directors:
Hot Spot for Advancement for Women/Minorities:

Sales, profits and employees may be estimates. Financial information, benefits and other data can change quickly and may vary from those stated here.

Zillow Group Inc

NAIC Code: 519130

www.zillow.com

TYPES OF BUSINESS:
Online Real Estate Information
Real Estate Platform
Mortgage Loans
Artificial Intelligence
Machine Learning
Broker

GROWTH PLANS/SPECIAL FEATURES:
Zillow Group is an Internet-based real estate company that has historically focused on deriving ad revenue from third-party brokers on online marketplaces such as Zillow.com, Trulia, and HotPads. More recently it has shifted its focus to iBuying via the Zillow Offers platform.

BRANDS/DIVISIONS/AFFILIATES:
Zillow
Trulia
StreetEasy
HotPads
OutEast.com
Zestimates
Mortech
dotloop

CONTACTS: *Note: Officers with more than one job title may be intentionally listed here more than once.*
Richard Barton, CEO
Allen Parker, CFO
Lloyd Frink, Chairman of the Board
Jennifer Rock, Chief Accounting Officer
Aimee Johnson, Chief Marketing Officer
David Beitel, Chief Technology Officer
Jeremy Wacksman, COO
Bradley Owens, General Counsel
Dan Spaulding, Other Executive Officer
Errol Samuelson, Other Executive Officer
Stanley Humphries, Other Executive Officer
Arik Prawer, President, Divisional
Susan Daimler, President, Divisional

FINANCIAL DATA: *Note: Data for latest year may not have been available at press time.*

In U.S. $	2021	2020	2019	2018	2017	2016
Revenue		3,339,817,000	2,742,837,000	1,333,554,000	1,076,794,000	846,589,000
R&D Expense		518,072,000	477,347,000	410,818,000	319,985,000	273,066,000
Operating Income		35,412,000	-246,835,000	-45,628,000	12,589,000	-192,682,000
Operating Margin %						
SGA Expense		1,029,938,000	1,080,304,000	814,774,000	659,017,000	694,614,000
Net Income		-162,115,000	-305,361,000	-119,858,000	-94,420,000	-220,438,000
Operating Cash Flow		424,197,000	-612,174,000	3,850,000	258,191,000	8,645,000
Capital Expenditure		108,517,000	86,635,000	78,535,000	78,635,000	71,722,000
EBITDA		119,958,000	-97,218,000	-10,314,000	-46,334,000	-112,310,000
Return on Assets %						
Return on Equity %						
Debt to Equity						

CONTACT INFORMATION:
Phone: 206 470-7000   Fax:
Toll-Free:
Address: 1301 Second Ave., Fl. 31, Seattle, WA 98101 United States

STOCK TICKER/OTHER:
Stock Ticker: Z   Exchange: NAS
Employees: 5,504   Fiscal Year Ends: 12/31
Parent Company:

SALARIES/BONUSES:
Top Exec. Salary: $636,626   Bonus: $
Second Exec. Salary: $593,156   Bonus: $

OTHER THOUGHTS:
Estimated Female Officers or Directors: 2
Hot Spot for Advancement for Women/Minorities: Y

Sales, profits and employees may be estimates. Financial information, benefits and other data can change quickly and may vary from those stated here.

ADDITIONAL INDEXES

Contents:

Index of Firms Noted as "Hot Spots for Advancement" for Women/Minorities   **322**

Index by Subsidiaries, Brand Names and Selected Affiliations   **323**

INDEX OF FIRMS NOTED AS HOT SPOTS FOR ADVANCEMENT FOR WOMEN & MINORITIES

Ally Financial Inc
Alphabet Inc (Google)
American Express Company
Bank of America Corporation
Barclays PLC
Boursorama
Bread Financial Holdings Inc
Capital One Financial Corporation
Charles Schwab Corporation (The)
Citigroup Inc
Citizens Financial Group Inc
Discover Financial Services
E*Trade from Morgan Stanley
Envestnet Inc
Experian plc
Fidelity Investments Inc
Fifth Third Bancorp
Goldman Sachs Group Inc (The)
Industrial & Financial Systems AB (IFS)
Intuit Inc
Jack Henry & Associates Inc
JPMorgan Chase & Co Inc
LendingClub Corporation
M&T Bank Corporation
MarketAxess Holdings Inc
MasterCard Incorporated
Microsoft Corporation
Morgan Stanley
Morningstar Inc
PayPal Holdings Inc
PNC Financial Services Group Inc
Regions Financial Corporation
SVB Financial Group
TD Ameritrade Holding Corporation
US Bancorp (US Bank)
Visa Inc
Wells Fargo & Company
Zillow Group Inc

INDEX OF SUBSIDIARIES, BRAND NAMES AND AFFILIATIONS

Brand or subsidiary, followed by the name of the related corporation

Accelerated Payouts; **Actum Processing LLC**
ACHFileChex; **ACHWorks**
ACHWorks Checkout; **ACHWorks**
ACHWorks Virtual Terminal; **ACHWorks**
Acorns Early; **Acorns Grow Inc**
Acorns Later; **Acorns Grow Inc**
Acorns Sustainable Portfolios; **Acorns Grow Inc**
AdMob; **Alphabet Inc (Google)**
AdSense; **Alphabet Inc (Google)**
ADVANCE.AI; **Ekata Inc**
AdviserLogic; **Morningstar Inc**
AdvisorPeak; **Addepar Inc**
AffiniPay For Associations; **AffiniPay LLC**
Ai Extract; **Accelitas Inc**
Ai Life Save; **Accelitas Inc**
Ai Lift; **Accelitas Inc**
Ai Validate; **Accelitas Inc**
AIR; **RIBBIT (Cash Flow Solutions Inc)**
AIR MILES; **Bread Financial Holdings Inc**
AirPods; **Apple Inc**
Alchemy Amplify; **Alchemy Insights Inc**
Alchemy Build; **Alchemy Insights Inc**
Alchemy Monitor; **Alchemy Insights Inc**
Alchemy Notify; **Alchemy Insights Inc**
Alchemy Supernode; **Alchemy Insights Inc**
Ally Bank; **Ally Financial Inc**
Ally Corporate Finance; **Ally Financial Inc**
Ally Invest Advisors Inc; **Ally Financial Inc**
Ally Invest Forex LlC; **Ally Financial Inc**
Ally Invest Securities LLC; **Ally Financial Inc**
Ally Lending; **Ally Financial Inc**
Ally Ventures; **Ally Financial Inc**
American Express Company; **Kabbage Inc**
American Express Global Business Travel; **American Express Company**
American Express Travel Related Services Co Inc; **American Express Company**
Anchorage Custody; **Anchorage Labs Inc**
Anchorage Digital Bank NA; **Anchorage Labs Inc**
Anchorage Financing; **Anchorage Labs Inc**
Anchorage Governance; **Anchorage Labs Inc**
Anchorage Hold LLC; **Anchorage Labs Inc**
Anchorage Lending CA LLC; **Anchorage Labs Inc**
Anchorage Staking; **Anchorage Labs Inc**
Anchorage Trading; **Anchorage Labs Inc**
Android; **Alphabet Inc (Google)**
Apple TV; **Apple Inc**
Apple Watch; **Apple Inc**
Appriss Insights; **Equifax Inc**
Ascentium Capital; **Regions Financial Corporation**
Aspiration Zero; **Aspiration Partners Inc**

Attorneys Title Guaranty Fund Inc; **Guaranteed Rate Inc**
AuthenteCheck; **Actum Processing LLC**
Avant Credit Card; **Avant Inc**
Axios Systems; **Industrial & Financial Systems AB (IFS)**
Baidu Inc; **Du Xiaoman Financial**
BankLOGIN+; **RIBBIT (Cash Flow Solutions Inc)**
BankQUALIFY; **RIBBIT (Cash Flow Solutions Inc)**
BankTRANSACT; **RIBBIT (Cash Flow Solutions Inc)**
BankVERIFY+; **RIBBIT (Cash Flow Solutions Inc)**
Barclays International; **Barclays PLC**
Barclays UK; **Barclays PLC**
BBVA USA Bancshares Inc; **PNC Financial Services Group Inc**
Betterment Holdings Inc; **Betterment LLC**
BigCommerce Pty Ltd; **BigCommerce Holdings Inc**
Binance Chain; **Binance**
Binance Labs; **Binance**
Binance Smart; **Binance**
Bitkub Capital Group Holdings; **Bitkub Online Co Ltd**
Block; **Square (Block Inc.)**
Blockchain Intelligence Group; **BIGG Digital Assets Inc**
BlockFi Bitcoin Trust; **BlockFi Inc**
BlockFi Ethereum Trust; **BlockFi Inc**
BlockFi Litecoin Trust; **BlockFi Inc**
BlockFi Rewards; **BlockFi Inc**
BlockFi Wallet; **BlockFi Inc**
BNB; **Binance**
BondTicker; **MarketAxess Holdings Inc**
Boursorama Banque; **Boursorama**
Braintree; **PayPal Holdings Inc**
BrandLoyalty; **Bread Financial Holdings Inc**
Bread; **Bread Financial Holdings Inc**
Bread Financial; **Bread Pay (Lon Operations LLC)**
Bread Pay; **Bread Pay (Lon Operations LLC)**
Brex API; **Brex Inc**
Brex Card; **Brex Inc**
Brex Cash; **Brex Inc**
BTRS Holdings Inc; **Billtrust (BTRS Holdings Inc)**
Cadre; **Cadre (RealCadre LLC)**
Cadre Fund Co-Investments; **Cadre (RealCadre LLC)**
Capital One Bank (USA) National Association; **Capital One Financial Corporation**
Capital One National Association; **Capital One Financial Corporation**
CareCredit; **Synchrony Financial**
Cargon Insights; **Aspiration Partners Inc**
Carta Securities LLC; **Carta Inc (eShares Inc)**
CashNetUSA; **Enova International Inc**
Chainalysis; **Chainalysis Inc**
Chainalysis Business Data; **Chainalysis Inc**
Chainalysis Kryptos; **Chainalysis Inc**
Chainalysis KYT; **Chainalysis Inc**
Chainalysis Market Intel; **Chainalysis Inc**
Charles Schwab & Co Inc; **Charles Schwab Corporation (The)**
Charles Schwab Bank; **Charles Schwab Corporation (The)**

INDEX OF SUBSIDIARIES, BRAND NAMES AND AFFILIATIONS, CONT.

Charles Schwab Corporation (The); **TD Ameritrade Holding Corporation**
Charles Schwab Investment Management Inc; **Charles Schwab Corporation (The)**
Checkout LLC; **Checkout.com (Checkout Ltd)**
Checkout MENA FZ LLC; **Checkout.com (Checkout Ltd)**
Checkout SAS; **Checkout.com (Checkout Ltd)**
ChemFree Corp; **CoreCard Corp**
Chianalysis Reactor; **Chainalysis Inc**
Cirrus; **MasterCard Incorporated**
ClientPay; **AffiniPay LLC**
Clover; **Clover Network Inc**
Clover Dashboard; **Clover Network Inc**
Clover Online Ordering; **Clover Network Inc**
Clyde; **Clyde Technologies Inc**
Coastal Community Bank; **One Finance Inc**
COL Easy Investment Program; **COL Financial Group Inc**
COL Margin Account; **COL Financial Group Inc**
Comenity; **Bread Financial Holdings Inc**
CoreCard Software Inc; **CoreCard Corp**
CoreCard SRL; **CoreCard Corp**
CoreENGINE; **CoreCard Corp**
CPA Charge; **AffiniPay LLC**
Credit Karma; **Intuit Inc**
Credit Score Simulator; **Credit Karma Inc**
Crew; **Square (Block Inc.)**
Cross River; **Cross River Bank (CRB Group Inc)**
Cross River Bank; **Cross River Bank (CRB Group Inc)**
CSG Systems International Inc; **CSG Forte Payments Inc**
Cuffelinks; **Morningstar Inc**
Current Core; **Current (Finco Services Inc)**
Customerville; **Industrial & Financial Systems AB (IFS)**
CyberSource Corporation; **Visa Inc**
DailyPay; **DailyPay Inc**
Dave; **Dave Inc**
Deposit Chek; **Early Warning Services LLC**
Desmarais Family Residuary Trust; **Personal Capital Corporation**
digit; **Digit (Hello Digit LLC)**
Diners Club; **Discover Financial Services**
Discover; **Discover Financial Services**
Discover Network; **Discover Financial Services**
DocuSign Agreement Cloud; **DocuSign Inc**
DocuSign eSignature; **DocuSign Inc**
dotloop; **Zillow Group Inc**
Doxo; **Doxo Inc**
doxoDIRECT; **Doxo Inc**
doxoINSIGHTS; **Doxo Inc**
doxoPLUS; **Doxo Inc**
Dwolla; **Dwolla Inc**
Dwolla Balance; **Dwolla Inc**
E*TRADE Financial Corp; **Morgan Stanley**
E*TRADE Financial LLC; **Morgan Stanley**
Early Warning Services LLC; **Zelle**

Ekata Identity Engine; **Ekata Inc**
El Server; **Gravity Payments Inc**
Elavon Inc; **US Bancorp (US Bank)**
Empower Holdings LLC; **Personal Capital Corporation**
Enoval International Inc; **On Deck Capital Inc**
Envestnet | Analytics; **Envestnet Inc**
Envestnet | Enterprise; **Envestnet Inc**
Envestnet | MoneyGuide; **Envestnet Inc**
Envestnet | PMC; **Envestnet Inc**
Envestnet | Retirement Solutions; **Envestnet Inc**
Envestnet | Tamarac; **Envestnet Inc**
Envestnet | Yodlee; **Envestnet Inc**
Envestnet inc; **Yodlee Inc**
Envestnet-Yodlee; **Yodlee Inc**
EPIC Platform; **Giact Systems LLC**
ETRADE Capital Management LLC; **E*Trade from Morgan Stanley**
ETRADE Futures LLC; **E*Trade from Morgan Stanley**
ETRADE Securities LLC; **E*Trade from Morgan Stanley**
Even Responsible Finance Inc; **One Finance Inc**
Exchange; **Microsoft Corporation**
Experian Holdings Ireland Ltd; **Experian plc**
Experian Information Solutions Inc; **Experian plc**
Experian North America Inc; **Experian plc**
Exposure Scan; **Nivelo Tech Inc**
ExtraCash; **Dave Inc**
Feedzai Inc; **Revelock (Buguroo Offensive Security SL)**
Fidelity Charitable; **Fidelity Investments Inc**
Fidelity Insitutional Asset Management; **Fidelity Investments Inc**
Fifth Third Institutional Services; **Fifth Third Bancorp**
Fifth Third Insurance Agency; **Fifth Third Bancorp**
Fifth Third Private Bank; **Fifth Third Bancorp**
Fifth Third Securities; **Fifth Third Bancorp**
First Data; **Fiserv Inc**
FirstLinks; **Morningstar Inc**
FlashClose; **Guaranteed Rate Inc**
FTX Ventures; **Dave Inc**
ftx.com; **FTX Trading Ltd**
ftx.us; **FTX Trading Ltd**
Futu Clearing Inc; **Moomoo Inc**
Futu Holdings Limited; **Moomoo Inc**
Futu Inc; **Moomoo Inc**
Futu Singapore Ptd Ltd; **Moomoo Inc**
Futu Wealth Advisors Inc; **Moomoo Inc**
g-AUTHENTICATE; **Giact Systems LLC**
Gemini; **Gemini Trust Company LLC**
Gemini ActiveTrader; **Gemini Trust Company LLC**
Gemini Clearing; **Gemini Trust Company LLC**
Gemini Credit Card; **Gemini Trust Company LLC**
Gemini dollar; **Gemini Trust Company LLC**
Gemini Earn; **Gemini Trust Company LLC**
Gemini Pay; **Gemini Trust Company LLC**
Gemini Wallet; **Gemini Trust Company LLC**
g-IDENTIFY; **Giact Systems LLC**

INDEX OF SUBSIDIARIES, BRAND NAMES AND AFFILIATIONS, CONT.

Global Payments Inc; **NetSpend Holdings Inc**
GlobalGateway; **Trulioo Inc**
Gmail; **Alphabet Inc (Google)**
g-MOBILE; **Giact Systems LLC**
GoEnergy Inc; **Creek Road Miners Inc**
g-OFAC; **Giact Systems LLC**
Google Ad Manager; **Alphabet Inc (Google)**
Google LLC; **Alphabet Inc (Google)**
GooglePlay; **Alphabet Inc (Google)**
Gravity Capital; **Gravity Payments Inc**
Guideline.com; **Guideline Inc**
g-VERIFY; **Giact Systems LLC**
Hazel by Walmart; **One Finance Inc**
Hbit Limited (Huobi Brokerage); **Huobi Global Ltd**
HelloFlow; **Trulioo Inc**
Hippo Insurance Services; **Hippo Holdings Inc**
HomePod; **Apple Inc**
Honey; **PayPal Holdings Inc**
HotPads; **Zillow Group Inc**
Hunan Fumi Information Technology Co Ltd; **Webull Financial LLC**
Huobi Chat; **Huobi Global Ltd**
Huobi Cloud; **Huobi Global Ltd**
Huobi DeFi Labs; **Huobi Global Ltd**
Huobi Eco Chain; **Huobi Global Ltd**
Huobi Pool; **Huobi Global Ltd**
Huobi Wallet; **Huobi Global Ltd**
Hyperwallet; **PayPal Holdings Inc**
ID+; **Socure Inc**
Identity Chek; **Early Warning Services LLC**
Instant Payroll; **Nivelo Tech Inc**
InterPrivate III Financial Partners Inc; **Aspiration Partners Inc**
Intuit Inc; **Credit Karma Inc**
iOS; **Apple Inc**
iPad; **Apple Inc**
iPhone; **Apple Inc**
ISC Software; **CoreCard Corp**
itBit; **Paxos Technology Solutions LLC**
iZettle; **PayPal Holdings Inc**
Jack Henry Banking; **Jack Henry & Associates Inc**
JP Morgan Securities LLC; **JPMorgan Chase & Co Inc**
JPMorgan Chase & Co; **OpenInvest**
JPMorgan Chase Bank NA; **JPMorgan Chase & Co Inc**
Kabbage Inc; **American Express Company**
kakaopay; **KakaoPay Corp**
Klarna; **Klarna Bank AB**
Klarna Inc; **Klarna Bank AB**
KuCoin Labs; **KuCoin (Mek Global Limited)**
KuCoin Ventures; **KuCoin (Mek Global Limited)**
Lacerte; **Intuit Inc**
LawPay; **AffiniPay LLC**
Lemonade App; **Lemonade Inc**
LendingClub Bank NA; **LendingClub Corporation**
LexisNexis Legal and Professional; **LexisNexis**

LexisNexis Risk Solutions; **LexisNexis**
LinkedIn; **Microsoft Corporation**
LiquidityBridge; **MarketAxess Holdings Inc**
LiquidityEdge; **MarketAxess Holdings Inc**
Liveoak Technololgies Inc; **DocuSign Inc**
Lon Inc; **Bread Financial Holdings Inc**
London Stock Exchange Group; **Refinitiv Limited**
London Stock Exchange Group plc; **Giact Systems LLC**
LoyaltyOne; **Bread Financial Holdings Inc**
Lyons Commercial Data; **Autoscribe Corporation**
M&T Bank; **M&T Bank Corporation**
M&T Insurance Agency Inc; **M&T Bank Corporation**
M&T Realty Capital Corporation; **M&T Bank Corporation**
M&T Securities Inc; **M&T Bank Corporation**
M1 Finance LLC; **M1 Holdings Inc**
M1 Plus; **M1 Holdings Inc**
M1 Spend LLC; **M1 Holdings Inc**
Maestro; **MasterCard Incorporated**
MANTL; **MANTL (Fin Technologies Inc)**
Manufacturers & Traders Trust Company; **M&T Bank Corporation**
MarketAxess Technologies Inc; **MarketAxess Holdings Inc**
Mass Pay from Veem; **Veem Inc**
MasterCard; **MasterCard Incorporated**
Mastercard Incorporated; **Arcus Financial Intelligence Inc**
Mastercard Incorporated; **Ekata Inc**
Maya; **Lemonade Inc**
MedPay; **AffiniPay LLC**
Microsoft Corporation; **Suplari Inc**
Microsoft Teams; **Microsoft Corporation**
Mint; **Intuit Inc**
MoCaFi Bank Account; **MoCaFi (Mobility Capital Finance Inc)**
MoCaFi Debit Mastercard; **MoCaFi (Mobility Capital Finance Inc)**
Momentum; **Orum (Project Midas Inc)**
Monex Group Inc; **TradeStation Group Inc**
Morgan Stanley; **E*Trade from Morgan Stanley**
Morningstar Credit Ratings LLC; **Morningstar Inc**
Morningstar Inc; **PitchBook Data Inc**
Morningstar Sustainability Rating; **Morningstar Inc**
Mortech; **Zillow Group Inc**
MP Morgan Securities plc; **JPMorgan Chase & Co Inc**
Netcoins; **BIGG Digital Assets Inc**
NetCredit; **Enova International Inc**
NetSpend; **NetSpend Holdings Inc**
Network Partners; **Discover Financial Services**
NFT API; **Alchemy Insights Inc**
Nordic Capital; **Trustly Group AB**
NuBank; **Nu Holdings Ltd (NuBank)**
Nubank Mastercard; **Nu Holdings Ltd (NuBank)**
Nubank PJ; **Nu Holdings Ltd (NuBank)**

INDEX OF SUBSIDIARIES, BRAND NAMES AND AFFILIATIONS, CONT.

Office 365; **Microsoft Corporation**
OnDeck; **On Deck Capital Inc**
ONE; **One Finance Inc**
OneDrive; **Microsoft Corporation**
Open to the Public Investing Inc; **Public.com (Public Holdings Inc)**
Open Trading; **MarketAxess Holdings Inc**
OpenChannel; **Stripe Inc**
Oportun Financial Corporation; **Digit (Hello Digit LLC)**
Opportunity Zones; **Cadre (RealCadre LLC)**
Optiver Holding BV; **Optiver**
Orbipay; **Alacriti Inc**
OutEast.com; **Zillow Group Inc**
Outlook.com; **Microsoft Corporation**
Pangea; **Enova International Inc**
Pansolo Holding Inc; **Personal Capital Corporation**
PAX Gold; **Paxos Technology Solutions LLC**
Paxos; **Paxos Technology Solutions LLC**
PayBright; **Affirm Holdings Inc**
Payliance; **Secure Payment Systems Inc**
PaymentVision; **Autoscribe Corporation**
Paymode-X; **Bottomline Technologies Inc**
PayPal; **PayPal Holdings Inc**
PayPal Credit; **PayPal Holdings Inc**
PayPal Holdings Inc; **Braintree**
PayPal Holdings Inc; **Venmo**
PayPal Inc; **Venmo**
Peace of Mind; **Actum Processing LLC**
Personal Capital Advisors Corporation; **Personal Capital Corporation**
PitchBook Data Inc; **Morningstar Inc**
PitchBook Desktop; **PitchBook Data Inc**
PitchBook Mobile; **PitchBook Data Inc**
Plastiq Accept; **Plastiq Inc**
Plastiq Pay; **Plastiq Inc**
PNC Bank NA; **PNC Financial Services Group Inc**
Pocket; **One Finance Inc**
Private Bank and Wealth Management; **OpenInvest**
ProConnect; **Intuit Inc**
ProFile; **Intuit Inc**
ProfitStars; **Jack Henry & Associates Inc**
Providers; **Propel Inc**
Public.com; **Public.com (Public Holdings Inc)**
PULSE; **Discover Financial Services**
QuickBooks; **Intuit Inc**
Radius Bancorp Inc; **LendingClub Corporation**
RealCadre; **Cadre (RealCadre LLC)**
Refinitiv US Holdings Inc; **Giact Systems LLC**
Regions Affordable Housing LLC; **Regions Financial Corporation**
Regions Bank; **Regions Financial Corporation**
Regions Commercial Equipment Finance LLC; **Regions Financial Corporation**
Regions Equipment Finance Corporation; **Regions Financial Corporation**

Regions Investment Services Inc; **Regions Financial Corporation**
Regions Securities LLC; **Regions Financial Corporation**
Regulatory Reporting Hub; **MarketAxess Holdings Inc**
RELX PLC; **LexisNexis**
Returnly; **Affirm Holdings Inc**
Revelock; **Feedzai Inc**
REWARD; **DailyPay Inc**
RIBBIT; **RIBBIT (Cash Flow Solutions Inc)**
Ribbit Capital; **One Finance Inc**
Rise Companies Corp; **Fundrise LLC**
Robinhood Crypto LLC; **Robinhood Markets Inc**
Robinhood Financial LLC; **Robinhood Markets Inc**
Rocket Companies Inc; **Truebill Inc**
Rocket Science Group LLC (The); **Intuit Inc**
Round-Ups; **Acorns Grow Inc**
S&P Global Inc; **IHS Markit Ltd**
SAP Concur; **Concur Technologies Inc**
SAP SE; **Concur Technologies Inc**
Scorer Engine; **Nivelo Tech Inc**
Scout REP; **Workday Inc**
Seal Software Group Limited; **DocuSign Inc**
Secondary Market; **Cadre (RealCadre LLC)**
SeedInvest; **Circle Internet Financial Limited**
SharePoint; **Microsoft Corporation**
Side Hustle; **Dave Inc**
Silicon Valley Bank; **SVB Financial Group**
Simplic; **Enova International Inc**
Simplify; **Actum Processing LLC**
Skylight ONE; **NetSpend Holdings Inc**
Skype for Business; **Microsoft Corporation**
SmartWasher; **CoreCard Corp**
Societe Generale Group; **Boursorama**
SoFi Invest; **SoFi (SoFi Technologies Inc)**
SoFi Money; **SoFi (SoFi Technologies Inc)**
SoFi Protect; **SoFi (SoFi Technologies Inc)**
SoFi Relay; **SoFi (SoFi Technologies Inc)**
SoFi Stadium; **SoFi (SoFi Technologies Inc)**
South Mountain Merger Corp; **Billtrust (BTRS Holdings Inc)**
Speedpay; **ACI Worldwide Inc**
Spend Analytics; **Suplari Inc**
Square; **Square (Block Inc.)**
STAR; **Fiserv Inc**
Stash Beginner; **Stash Financial Inc**
Stash Growth; **Stash Financial Inc**
Stash Investments LLC; **Stash Financial Inc**
Stash+; **Stash Financial Inc**
StreetEasy; **Zillow Group Inc**
Stripe Atlas; **Stripe Inc**
Stripe Connect; **Stripe Inc**
Stripe Issuing; **Stripe Inc**
Stripe Radar; **Stripe Inc**
Stripe Sigma; **Stripe Inc**
Stripe Terminal; **Stripe Inc**

INDEX OF SUBSIDIARIES, BRAND NAMES AND AFFILIATIONS, CONT.

Suplari Agile Contracts; **Suplari Inc**
Suplari Agile Performance Management; **Suplari Inc**
Suplari Connect; **Suplari Inc**
Suplari for Finance; **Suplari Inc**
Suplari Intelligence Cloud; **Suplari Inc**
Supplier Diversity Insights; **Suplari Inc**
Symitar; **Jack Henry & Associates Inc**
Synchrony Bank; **Synchrony Financial**
TD Ameritrade Clearing Inc; **TD Ameritrade Holding Corporation**
TD Ameritrade Clearing Inc; **Charles Schwab Corporation (The)**
TD Ameritrade Holding Corporation; **Charles Schwab Corporation (The)**
TD Ameritrade Inc; **TD Ameritrade Holding Corporation**
TD Ameritrade Inc; **Charles Schwab Corporation (The)**
TD Ameritrade Media Productions Company; **TD Ameritrade Holding Corporation**
TerraZero Technologies Inc; **BIGG Digital Assets Inc**
Thinkorswim; **TD Ameritrade Holding Corporation**
ThinkTech; **TD Ameritrade Holding Corporation**
Tidal; **Square (Block Inc.)**
Tiger; **UP Fintech Holding Limited**
Tornado; **Tornado (Nvstr Technologies Inc)**
TradeStation; **TradeStation Group Inc**
TradeStation Crypto Inc; **TradeStation Group Inc**
TradeStation Securities inc; **TradeStation Group Inc**
TradeStation Technologies inc; **TradeStation Group Inc**
TrueAccord Recover; **TrueAccord Corp**
TrueAccord Retain; **TrueAccord Corp**
Truework; **Truework (Zethos Inc)**
Truist Bank; **Truist Financial Corporation**
Trulia; **Zillow Group Inc**
TurboTax; **Intuit Inc**
Universal Payments (UP); **ACI Worldwide Inc**
US Bank NA; **US Bancorp (US Bank)**
USD Coin; **Circle Internet Financial Limited**
Variant Equity Advisors; **Certegy Payments Solutions LLC**
Varo Advance; **Varo Money NA**
Varo Bank NA; **Varo Money NA**
Varo Believe; **Varo Money NA**
Veem Wallet; **Veem Inc**
Venmo; **PayPal Holdings Inc**
Venmo Credit Card; **Venmo**
VeriCheck Inc; **ACHWorks**
Visa Canada Corporaiton; **Visa Inc**
Visa Europe Limited; **Visa Inc**
Visa Inc; **Verifi Inc**
Visa International Service Association; **Visa Inc**
Visa Technology & Operations LLC; **Visa Inc**
Visa USA Inc; **Visa Inc**
Visa Worldwide Pte Limited; **Visa Inc**
VisaNet; **Visa Inc**

Walmart Inc; **One Finance Inc**
watchOS; **Apple Inc**
Webull; **Webull Financial LLC**
Wells Fargo Bank NA; **Wells Fargo & Company**
Wilmington Funds Management Corporation; **M&T Bank Corporation**
Wilmington Trust Investment Advisors Inc; **M&T Bank Corporation**
Wilmington Trust NA; **M&T Bank Corporation**
Wizard Brands Inc; **Creek Road Miners Inc**
Wizard Entertainment Inc; **Creek Road Miners Inc**
Wizard World Inc; **Creek Road Miners Inc**
Workday Strategic Sourcing; **Workday Inc**
Xoom; **PayPal Holdings Inc**
XRP; **Ripple Labs Inc**
XRP Ledger; **Ripple Labs Inc**
XRPL.org; **Ripple Labs Inc**
You Can Trade Inc; **TradeStation Group Inc**
YouTube; **Alphabet Inc (Google)**
Zelle Network; **Early Warning Services LLC**
Zestimates; **Zillow Group Inc**
Zillow; **Zillow Group Inc**

INDEX OF SUBSIDIARIES, BRAND NAMES AND AFFILIATIONS, CONT.

A Short FinTech, Cryptocurrency & Electronic Payments Industry Glossary

2FA: See "Two-Factor Authentication."

5G Cellular: A wireless technology that is expected to produce blinding download speeds of one gigabyte per second (Gbps), and perhaps as high as 10 Gbps. The first specifications for 5G were agreed to by the global wireless industry from 2017 to 2019. Significant rollout was expected to begin in the early 2020s. While certain 5G features can be used to boost speeds of earlier 4G networks, a true rollout requires major investment in new cellular infrastructure and systems.

A2A: Account-to-account.

Account Aggregators: Companies that operate online platforms that can connect to consumers' and businesses' bank accounts and investment accounts in order to verify account ownership, enable online payments, study an individual's spending and conduct other financial transactions online.

ACH: See "Automated Clearing House (ACH)."

ACH Fraud: During an electronic funds payment transaction process, hackers gain access to the information on either side of a transaction, and pose as one of the parties with the intent to receive payment fraudulently.

Advanced Encryption Standard (AES): A U.S. government recognized standard for secure and classified data encryption and decryption. It was originally known as Rijndael.

AES: See "Advanced Encryption Standard (AES)."

AI: See "Artificial Intelligence (AI)."

Analytics: Generally refers to the deep examination of massive amounts of data, often on a continual or real-time basis. The goal is to discover deeper insights, make recommendations or generate predictions. Advanced analytics includes such techniques as big data, predictive analytics, text analytics, data mining, forecasting, optimization and simulation.

Anti Money Laundering (AML): Regulations requiring banks, investment firms and certain other companies to take steps to ascertain that their clients are not using accounts to launder money that was illegally obtained.

API: See "Application Programming Interface (API)."

Application Programming Interface (API): A set of protocols, routines and tools used by computer programmers as a way of setting common definitions regarding how one piece of software communicates with another.

Applications: Computer programs and systems that allow users to interface with a computer and that collect, manipulate, summarize and report data and information. Also, see "Apps."

Applied Research: The application of compounds, processes, materials or other items discovered during basic research to practical uses. The goal is to move discoveries along to the final development phase.

Apps: Short for applications, apps are small software programs designed to run primarily on mobile devices such as smartphones and tablets. Also known as "mobile apps."

Artificial Intelligence (AI): The use of computer technology to perform functions somewhat like those normally associated with human intelligence, such as reasoning, learning and self-improvement.

Automated Clearing House (ACH): Electronic funds transfers that are commonly used for regularly recurring payments. For example, a consumer or business can elect to have a recurring bill payment sent to a vendor or supplier via ACH each month. The rules and procedures are different from bank wires. (Also, see "Wire Transfer".)

B2B: See "Business-to-Business."

B2C: See "Business-to-Consumer."

B2E: See "Business-to-Employee."

B2G: See "Business-to-Government."

BaaS: See "Banking-as-a-Service (BaaS)."

Back-Office: Generally considered to include such areas as accounting, human resources, call centers, financial transaction processing. A back-office application is a software program designed to handle back-office tasks. Also, see "Business Process Outsourcing (BPO)."

Bank Regulation: The formulation and issuance by authorized agencies of specific rules or regulations, under governing law, for the conduct and structure of banking.

Banking-as-a-Service (BaaS): Bank-like services, sometimes white-labeled or cobranded, that nonbanks can utilize to offer accounts, loans or payment services to their customers. Also called BaaS, such services are usually distributed by actual banks to client websites via APIs (Application Programming Interfaces).

Basic Research: Attempts to discover compounds, materials, processes or other items that may be largely or entirely new and/or unique. Basic research may start with a theoretical concept that has yet to be proven. The goal is to create discoveries that can be moved along to applied research. Basic research is sometimes referred to as "blue sky" research.

Behavioral Targeting: An advertising method that attempts to target ads to individual consumers based on their history of activities or purchases.

Big Data: The massive sets of data that are generated and captured to a growing extent by a wide variety of enterprises. For example, the digitization of health care records is creating big data sets. Likewise, consumer activities on an extremely popular website like Facebook create big data sets. A growing trend will be the generation of big data sets by remote wireless sensors. The challenges created by big data include the steps of data capture, storage, visualization and analysis. The opportunities include targeted online advertising: greater efficiency in health care, energy, business and industry, as well as intelligent transportation systems and better outcomes in health care.

Biometrics: The use of a user's physical attributes to enable login to a network or account. Biometrics may include iris scans, fingerprints, facial images or other features, rather than relying on passwords or PIN codes that can be more easily hacked.

Bitcoin: A digital (virtual) cryptocurrency launched in 2009. Bitcoin utilizes blockchain technologies. See "Cryptocurrency."

Bitcoin Wallet: A software program in which Bitcoins can be accessed by the owner, via a private key (number).

Blockchain: A technology that records ownership of Bitcoin and similar cryptocurrencies. Records of transactions made in these cryptocurrencies are maintained across multiple computers linked in a peer-to-peer network.

Blockchain Wallet: A digital wallet that allows users to manage, monitor and conduct cryptocurrency. Blockchain Wallet is provided by Blockchain.

Branding: A marketing strategy that places a focus on the brand name of a product, service or firm in order to increase the brand's market share, increase sales, establish credibility, improve satisfaction, raise the profile of the firm and increase profits. Also, see "Brand."

Broker/Dealer (Broker-Dealer): A firm that is licensed to buy and sell mutual fund shares and other securities with the public.

Business-to-Business: An organization focused on selling products, services or data to commercial customers rather than individual consumers. Also known as B2B.

Business-to-Consumer: An organization focused on selling products, services or data to individual consumers rather than commercial customers. Also known as B2C.

Business-to-Employee: A corporate communications system, such as an intranet, aimed at conveying information from a company to its employees. Also known as B2E.

Business-to-Government: An organization focused on selling products, services or data to government units rather than commercial businesses or consumers. Also known as B2G.

Call Center: A department within a company or a third-party organization that manages inbound and outbound telephone calls. This organization usually processes orders, provides technical support and/or provides marketing support. Call centers are frequently provided on an outsourced basis by service firms in lower-cost nations.

Card-Not-Present: A credit or credit card transaction that is made without the physical presence of the card itself, such as an online purchase. Such transactions are more likely to be fraudulent.

CFPB: See "Consumer Financial Protection Bureau (CFPB)."

Challenger Bank: See "Neobank."

Chat Bot: Like a voice assistant, chat bots are services accessed through a digital chat interface. A chat bot is intended to enable a website to interface in a non-human manner to provide instant service to customers and visitors. Chat bots can be connected to artificial intelligence in order to provide reasonable answers to common customer questions or needs. ChatterBot is a dialog engine for creating chatbots.

Check Clearing: The movement of checks from the banks or other depository institutions where they are deposited back to those on which they are written, and funds movement in the opposite direction. This process results in credits to accounts at the institutions of deposit and corresponding debits to accounts at the paying institutions. The Federal Reserve participates in check clearing through its nationwide facilities, though many checks are cleared by private sector arrangement.

CHIPS: See "Clearinghouse Interbank Payment System (CHIPS)."

Clearing House: An association of banks that permits the clearing of checks drawn on member banks.

Clearinghouse Interbank Payment System (CHIPS): An automated clearing system used primarily for international payments. This system is owned and operated by the New York Clearinghouse banks and engages Fedwire for settlement.

Cloud: Refers to the use of outsourced servers to store and access data, as opposed to computers owned or managed by one organization. Firms that offer cloud services for a fee run clusters of servers networked together, often based on open standards. Such cloud networks can consist of hundreds or even thousands of computers. Cloud services enable a client company to immediately increase computing capability without any investment in physical infrastructure. (The word "cloud" is also broadly used to describe any data or application that runs via the Internet.) The concept of cloud is also increasingly linked with software as a service.

Consumer Financial Protection Bureau (CFPB): An agency mandated by U.S. legislation to oversee and regulate the issuance of financial products like mortgages, credit cards, personal loans and retirement plans. The bureau has a large budget that does not require Congressional approval. The budget is funded by the Federal Reserve. The agency has the authority to enforce its rules on banks with more than $10 million in assets.

Consumerization: An approach to new product and services development focused on quickly determining and fulfilling the needs of individual consumers. This may be demand-driven development as opposed to technology-driven. Consumerization also may be a business development model based on first fulfilling the needs of consumers with the hope that demand for a new product or service will then broaden to include businesses, government and other enterprises.

Contactless Payment: The use of "smart" credit cards or advanced cell phones to make payments. Chips, which may be RFID or may be chips designed especially for payment purposes, wirelessly transfer credit or debit account information to cash registers, ticket stands or vending machines. ExxonMobil's popular SpeedPass system, used at gasoline pumps, is an example based on RFID.

Content Aggregator: A content aggregator collects content and distributes it to subscribers, network operators or other content companies.

Cookie: A piece of information sent to a web browser from a web server that the browser software saves and then sends back to the server upon request. Cookies are used by web site operators to track the actions of users returning to the site.

CORE Banking: A backend computer system that processes daily transactions in a central location, regardless of where they occur among a bank's branches or online sites.

CRM: See "Customer Relationship Management (CRM)."

Crowdfunding: Raising money online from the public in order to support a cause or help launch a new product/service.

Cryptoasset: Digital assets such as Bitcoins.

Cryptocurrency: A digital (virtual) currency that is encrypted for security. Cryptocurrencies are housed within decentralized systems based on blockchain technology. Bitcoin is a leading example.

Cryptocurrency Exchange: An exchange that enables the purchase and trading of cryptocurrencies. Also called Digital Currency Exchange (DCE).

Crypto-token: A type of cryptocurrency that represents particular tradable digital assets found on a blockchain.

Customer Relationship Management (CRM): Refers to the automation, via sophisticated software, of business processes involving existing and prospective customers. CRM may cover aspects such as sales (contact management and contact history), marketing (campaign management and telemarketing) and customer service (call center history and field service history). Well known providers of CRM software include Salesforce, which delivers via a Software as a Service model (see "Software as a Service (Saas)"), Microsoft and Oracle.

Cybersecurity: Practices and technologies that help protect computers, networks and data from being compromised, hacked or taken over by outside parties, such as via ransomware, phishing or a computer virus. Cybersecurity tools include software, such as antivirus, and hardware, such as firewalls.

Cyberspace: Refers to the entire realm of information available through computer networks and the Internet.

Data Mining: Analyzing large sets of data in order to find patterns. Machine learning is often utilized.

Day Trade: Also known as a daylight trade. The purchase and sale or the short sale and cover of the same security in a margin account on the same day.

De Novo Bank: A recently established banking institution.

Decentralized Finance (DeFI): The use of a blockchain network to deliver financial products and track their ownership. This enables buyers, lenders and sellers of financial products to transact directly with each other (peer-to-peer), rather than going through a middleman such as a traditional financial institution.

Debit Card: A card that resembles a credit card but which debits a transaction account (checking account) with the transfers occurring contemporaneously with the customer's purchases. A debit card may be machine readable, allowing for the activation of an automated teller machine or other automated payments equipment.

DeFI: See "Decentralized Finance (DeFI)."

Demographics: The breakdown of the population into statistical categories such as age, income, education and sex.

Depository Institution: A financial institution that obtains its funds mainly through deposits from the public. This includes commercial banks, savings and loan associations, savings banks, and credit unions. Although historically they have specialized in certain types of credit, the powers of nonbank depository institutions have been broadened in recent years. For example, NOW accounts, credit union share drafts, and other services similar to checking accounts may be offered by thrift institutions.

Development: The phase of research and development (R&D) in which researchers attempt to create new products from the results of discoveries and applications created during basic and applied research.

Digital: The transmission of a signal by reducing all of its information to ones and zeros and then regrouping them at the reception end. Digital transmission vastly improves the carrying capacity of the spectrum while reducing noise and distortion of the transmission.

Digital Currency: Electronic payment methods used to purchase goods and services over the internet. Includes cryptocurrencies and virtual currencies.

Digital ID: Data that can confirm the identity of the user of a network, shopping cart or online system.

Digital Wallet: An app that enables a consumer to store encrypted bank account, debit card and credit card information. A technology called tokenization is typically used. (See "Tokenization.") The user is then enabled to check out in retail stores (via smartphone and specially equipped cash registers/POS) and online, without the need to enter payment account data. Biometric data such as a fingerprint is often used to ID the user on a smartphone. On a PC, account login is typically required. The end result is enhanced payment data security, plus reduced time checking out, as the consumer doesn't need to key-in account numbers, which often leads to errors on small screens. Top digital wallets include Apple Pay, Google Pay and LG Pay.

Direct Deposit: A method of payment which electronically credits a checking or savings account.

Discount Broker: A broker or brokerage firm that executes buy and sell transactions at commission rates lower than a full-service broker or brokerage.

Disintermediate: A business or distribution model that bypasses the middleman in marketing or retailing. For example, a web site that enables end-consumers to purchase apparel direct from a designer or manufacturer, bypassing retail stores and traditional catalogs, is attempting to disintermediate the supply chain.

Disruptive: A new technology or business model that unexpectedly threatens to displace existing products or services. For example, the manner in which email has disrupted standard postal service. By some estimates, in order to be disruptive, a new service or product must provide most of the value of existing methods, and ideally even enhanced value, while reducing costs and/or speeding delivery.

Distributed Ledger: A strategy of utilizing networks of computers to record transactions, documents and ownership records. Unlike traditional databases, such ledgers have no central data location or administration.

Distributed Ledger Technology (DLT): A blockchain-enabled database of transactions. It can be shared across multiple sites or nodes. Any changes to the ledger are instantly copied to all participating sites. Also, see "Blockchain."

Dividend: The distribution to shareholders, in cash or stock, of part of a company's earnings, cash flow or capital.

Dividend Reinvestment Plan: The automatic reinvestment, typically without incurring brokerage commissions, of shareholder dividends into additional shares of stock. Plans sometimes provide for share purchases at a discount to the market price. Dividend reinvestment plans let shareholders accumulate stock over time using dollar cost averaging.

DLT: See "Distributed Ledger Technology (DLT)."

Earn to Play: See "Play to Earn Games."

E-Commerce: The use of online, internet-based sales methods. The phrase is used to describe both business-to-consumer and business-to-business sales.

Ecosystem: In online platforms, an ecosystem is a business strategy wherein numerous complimentary services and tools are offered that create high levels of convenience for the user, who only has to login once to conduct multiple tasks. The ultimate ecosystem may be WeChat, based in China, which offers instant messaging, social media, streaming entertainment, payment services, access to government services, shopping and a very wide variety of additional services. In FinTech, Square (owned by Block), is an excellent example, where features include credit card processing, business marketing, and, within the related Venmo app, P2P payments, investments, debit cards and much more.

Effective Interest Rate: Also referred to as annual percentage rate (APR), this is the cost of interest on a yearly basis expressed as a percentage. It includes up-front costs paid to obtain the loan and is, therefore, usually a higher amount than the interest rate stipulated in the mortgage or loan. It is useful in comparing various loan programs that have different rates and points.

EDI: See "Electronic Data Interchange (EDI)."

EFT: See "Electronic Funds Transfer (EFT)."

eIDV: See "Electronic Identity Verification (eIDV)."

Electronic Data Interchange (EDI): An accepted standard format for the exchange of data between various companies' networks. EDI allows for the transfer of e-mail as well as orders, invoices and other files from one company to another.

Electronic Funds Transfer (EFT): Moving money from one account to another via electronic means.

Electronic Identity Verification (eIDV): The use, in real-time, of public and private databases to confirm an individual's identity, for account setup or sometimes for login security. eIDV uses information such as Social Security number, cellphone account ownership records, credit bureau records and address records.

Embedded Finance: Including financial services or tools within non-financial platforms and websites. For example, the offering of bank-like services (such as lending or payments) by retailers or distributors.

Embedded Insurance: Including insurance services or tools within non-insurance platforms and websites. For example, the offering of insurance coverage by automobile dealers or manufacturers.

Embedded Investments: Including investment services or tools within non-investment platforms and websites. For example, the offering of stock trading within payments platforms like Block.

EMEA: The region comprised of Europe, the Middle East and Africa.

Encryption: A means of securing digital data using an algorithm and a key/password so that it is unreadable without the correct key.

Equities: A term used to describe stock investments in corporations as opposed to debt investments in corporations (bonds).

Ethereum: A brand of virtual currency.

ETF: See "Exchange Traded Fund (ETF)."

ETN: See "Exchange Traded Note (ETN)."

EU: See "European Union (EU)."

EU Competence: The jurisdiction in which the European Union (EU) can take legal action.

European Community (EC): See "European Union (EU)."

European Union (EU): A consolidation of European countries (member states) functioning as one body to facilitate trade. Previously known as the European Community (EC). The EU has a unified currency, the Euro. See europa.eu.int.

Exchange Rate: The price of a country's currency in terms of another country's currency.

Exchange Traded Fund (ETF): A basket of stocks designed to mirror a particular index, such as the NASDAQ 100, while trading like shares of stock on an exchange. Some ETFs track narrow indexes that represent specific industrial sectors, or even more limited areas such as indexes covering gold or real estate investment trusts. A few ETFs are actively managed by stock pickers and do not track indexes. ETFs were designed to compete with mutual funds and index funds. One large difference is that mutual funds are priced only once daily. The price of an ETF fluctuates throughout the day, accurately reflecting the value of the underlying stocks in the basket at any time of day. ETFs have low operating costs and may offer income tax advantages over index funds.

Exchange Traded Note (ETN): Debt securities pioneered by Barclays Bank, and also issued by firms such as Merrill Lynch. They are listed on stock exchanges and can be bought and sold in secondary markets. ETNs have a set maturity date, but typically do not pay periodic interest payments as standard bonds do.

Expense Ratio: The comparison of the cost of operating a property, business or organization to its gross income.

Extensible Markup Language (XML): A programming language that enables designers to add extra functionality to documents that could not otherwise be utilized with standard HTML coding. XML was developed by the World Wide Web Consortium. It can communicate to various software programs the actual meanings contained in HTML documents. For example, it can enable the gathering and use of information from a large number of databases at once and place that information into one web site window. XML is an important protocol to web services. See "Web Services."

Facial Recognition: Software that is capable of identifying a person his/her facial features to an image of that face. In account login verification, it is part of a strategy known as biometrics.

Fair Credit Reporting Act: A consumer protection law that regulates consumer credit report providers. For example, the act sets up procedures for correcting mistakes on an individual's credit record, provides certain restrictions on publishing credit reports and generally governs a consumer's rights.

FASB: See "Financial Accounting Standards Board (FASB)."

FDIC: Federal Deposit Insurance Corporation, a U.S. government agency that guarantees funds deposited at member banks up to a specified amount per account.

Federal Reserve Bank (FRB): One of the twelve operating banks of the U.S. Federal Reserve System, located throughout the U.S. These banks operate 25 branches and carry out Federal Reserve functions, including the nationwide payment clearing system, distribution of the nation's currency, regulating member banks and serving as the banker to the U.S. Treasury. See "Federal Reserve System."

Federal Reserve District (Reserve District or District): One of the twelve geographic regions served by a Federal Reserve Bank. See "Federal Reserve System."

Federal Reserve System: The central banking system of the United States. It regulates the money supply, sets interest rates and attempts to keep inflation under control. It is responsible for the short term interest rates know as the Discount Rate and the Federal Funds Rate. It operates 12 branch Federal Reserve banks throughout the United States and it regulates national banks and monetary transactions between banks.

Financial Accounting Standards Board (FASB): An independent organization that establishes the Generally Accepted Accounting Principles (GAAP).

Financial Institution: An institution that uses its funds chiefly to purchase financial assets (loans, securities) as opposed to tangible property. Financial institutions can be classified according to the nature

of the principal claims they issue. See also depository institution.

Financial Technology (FinTech): A term used to broadly describe the utilization of advanced computer and communication technologies to enable more streamlined financial transactions for both consumers and businesses. FinTech service may include banking, insurance, investing, mortgages, credit cards, debit cards and related services. Typically, FinTech services are disruptive to established, traditional means (such as physical, store-front banks and offices), and are delivered to users via convenient smartphone apps.

FinTech: See "Financial Technology (FinTech)."

Forex: Foreign Exchange, or the conversion of the currency of one nation into that of another. For example, the exchange of U.S. Dollars for the Euro. Also known as "FX."

FRB: See "Federal Reserve Bank (FRB)."

Freemium: A business model in which a product or service (usually a digital game, software or web service) is offered at no charge to the user, but advanced features and services are promoted for purchase.

GAAP: See "Generally Accepted Accounting Principles (GAAP)."

Gamification: The use of game design and practices to enhance non-game content in order to attract users and increase engagement. For example, the use of games in online advertising and marketing, or the use of games in online education.

GDPR: See "General Data Protection Regulation (GDPR)."

General Data Protection Regulation (GDPR): Regulations that govern the collection and processing of personal information from individuals who live in the European Union (EU).

Generally Accepted Accounting Principles (GAAP): A set of accounting standards administered by the Financial Accounting Standards Board (FASB) and enforced by the U.S. Security and Exchange Commission (SEC). GAAP is primarily used in the U.S.

Generation M: A very loosely defined term that is sometimes used to refer to young people who have grown up in the digital age. "M" may refer to any or all of media-saturated, mobile or multi-tasking. The term was most notably used in a Kaiser Family Foundation report published in 2005, "Generation M: Media in the Lives of 8-18 year olds." Also, see "Generation Y" and "Generation Z."

Generation X: A loosely-defined and variously-used term that describes people born between approximately 1965 and 1980, but other time frames are recited. Generation X is often referred to as a group influential in defining tastes in consumer goods, entertainment and/or political and social matters.

Generation Y: Refers to people born between approximately 1982 and 2002. In the U.S., they number more than 90 million, making them the largest generation segment in the nation's history. They are also known as Echo Boomers, Millennials or the Millennial Generation. These are children of the Baby Boom generation who will be filling the work force as Baby Boomers retire.

Generation Z: Some people refer to Generation Z as people born after 1991. Others use the beginning date of 2001, or refer to the era of 1994 to 2004. Members of Generation Z are considered to be natural and rapid adopters of the latest technologies.

Geofencing: The practice of setting virtual boundaries around a physical location and targeting mobile device users within those areas for a variety of purposes including search and rescue, advertising and social interaction.

Global Payment Innovation (GPI): A process started by payments organization SWIFT to enhance standards and speeds for processing cross-border payments.

GPI: See "Global Payment Innovation (GPI)."

Hadoop: An open source, big data storage and analysis technology.

Hash Rate: The speed at which a Bitcoin miner solves Bitcoin code.

Health Savings Account (HSA): A plan that combines a tax-free savings and investment account

(somewhat similar to a 401k) with a high-deductible health coverage plan. The intent is to give the consumer more incentive to control health care costs by reducing unnecessary care while shopping for the best prices. The consumer contributes pre-tax dollars annually to a savings account (up to $2,850 for an individual or $5,650 for a family, as of 2007). The employer may or may not match part of that contribution. The account may be invested in stocks, bonds or mutual funds. It grows tax-free, but the money may be spent only on health care. Unspent money stays in the account at the end of each year. The consumer must purchase an insurance policy or health care plan with an annual deductible of at least $1,000 for individuals or $2,000 for families.

HSA: See "Health Savings Account (HSA)."

Hybrid Cloud: A data strategy where some applications and data are moved to cloud-based systems, while highly sensitive data or certain functions are kept on client-owned systems.

Hyperledger: The framework for blockchains of distributed data.

ICO: See "Initial Coin Offering (ICO)."

IDaaS: Identity-as-a-Service. Services, based in the cloud, that manage user authentication on a network or online service.

IFRS: See "International Financials Reporting Standards (IFRS)."

Individual Retirement Account (IRA): An investor-established, tax-deferred account set up to hold funds until retirement.

Industry Code: A descriptive code assigned to any company in order to group it with firms that operate in similar businesses. Common industry codes include the NAICS (North American Industrial Classification System) and the SIC (Standard Industrial Classification), both of which are standards widely used in America, as well as the International Standard Industrial Classification of all Economic Activities (ISIC), the Standard International Trade Classification established by the United Nations (SITC) and the General Industrial Classification of Economic Activities within the European Communities (NACE).

Initial Coin Offering (ICO): The event when a supply of cryptocoins is first offered to investors.

Initial Public Offering (IPO): A company's first effort to sell its stock to investors (the public). Investors in an up-trending market eagerly seek stocks offered in many IPOs because the stocks of newly public companies that seem to have great promise may appreciate very rapidly in price, reaping great profits for those who were able to get the stock at the first offering. In the United States, IPOs are regulated by the SEC (U.S. Securities Exchange Commission) and by the state-level regulatory agencies of the states in which the IPO shares are offered.

Instant Payments: Transfer of funds from one party to another in near real-time, with little to no lag for crediting of the funds to the receiver's account.

Insuretech: A term used to describe the use of online systems to simply the process of selling and maintaining insurance policies. The end goal is frequently to reduce costs, steps and middlemen.

Intellectual Property (IP): The exclusive ownership of original concepts, ideas, designs, engineering plans or other assets that are protected by law. Examples include items covered by trademarks, copyrights and patents. Items such as software, engineering plans, fashion designs and architectural designs, as well as games, books, songs and other entertainment items are among the many things that may be considered to be intellectual property. (Also, see "Patent.")

Interexchange Carrier (IXC or IEC): Any company providing long-distance phone service between LECs and LATAs. See "Local Exchange Carrier (LEC)" and "Local Access and Transport Area (LATA)."

International Financials Reporting Standards (IFRS): A set of accounting standards established by the International Accounting Standards Board (IASB) for the preparation of public financial statements. IFRS has been adopted by much of the world, including the European Union, Russia and Singapore.

Internet of Things (IoT): A concept whereby individual objects, such as kitchen appliances, automobiles, manufacturing equipment, environmental sensors or air conditioners, are connected to the Internet. The objects must be able to identify themselves to other devices or to databases. The ultimate goals may include the collection and processing of data, the control of instruments and machinery, and eventually, a new level of synergies, artificial intelligence and operating efficiencies among the objects. The Internet of Things is often referred to as IoT. Related technologies and topics include RFID, remote wireless sensors, telecommunications and nanotechnology.

IP: See "Intellectual Property (IP)."

IRA: See "Individual Retirement Account (IRA)."

KBA: See "Knowledge Based Authentication (KBA)."

Know Your Customer (KYC): A standard in financial industries that requires financial firms to gather and verify substantial amounts of information before accepting new customers, and then to maintain valid information on those customers. The intent is to reduce fraudulent activities.

Knowledge Based Authentication (KBA): A security measure that identifies end users by asking them to answer security questions in order to log into an account or network.

KYC: See "Know Your Customer (KYC)."

LAC: An acronym for Latin America and the Caribbean.

LDCs: See "Least Developed Countries (LDCs)."

Least Developed Countries (LDCs): Nations determined by the U.N. Economic and Social Council to be the poorest and weakest members of the international community. There are currently 50 LDCs, of which 34 are in Africa, 15 are in Asia Pacific and the remaining one (Haiti) is in Latin America. The top 10 on the LDC list, in descending order from top to 10th, are Afghanistan, Angola, Bangladesh, Benin, Bhutan, Burkina Faso, Burundi, Cambodia, Cape Verde and the Central African Republic. Sixteen of the LDCs are also Landlocked Least Developed Countries (LLDCs) which present them with additional difficulties often due to the high cost of transporting trade goods. Eleven of the LDCs are Small Island Developing States (SIDS), which are often at risk of extreme weather phenomenon (hurricanes, typhoons, Tsunami): have fragile ecosystems: are often dependent on foreign energy sources: can have high disease rates for HIV/AIDS and malaria: and can have poor market access and trade terms.

LINUX: An open, free operating system that is shared readily with millions of users worldwide. These users continuously improve and add to the software's code. It can be used to operate computer networks and Internet appliances as well as servers and PCs.

M2M: See "Machine-to-Machine (M2M)."

M2M2P: Machine-to-machine-to-people. Also, see "Machine-to-Machine (M2M)."

Machine-to-Machine (M2M): Refers to communications from one device to another (or to a collection of devices). It is typically through wireless means such as Wi-Fi or cellular. Wireless sensor networks (WSNs) will be a major growth factor in M2M communications, in everything from factory automation to agriculture and transportation. In logistics and retailing, M2M can refer to the advanced use of RFID tags. See "Radio Frequency Identification (RFID)." The Internet of Things is based on the principle of M2M communications. Also, see "Internet of Things (IoT")."

Machine Learning (ML): The ability of a computer or computerized device to learn based on the results of previous actions or the analysis of a stream of related data. It is a vital branch of Artificial Intelligence that uses advanced software in order to identify patterns and make decisions or predictions.

Management Fee: The amount paid by a mutual fund for an investment adviser's services.

Margin Account (Stocks): An account at a stock brokerage that can be leveraged. A loan in the margin account is collateralized by the stock owned by the account. In the event that the stock's value drops by a sufficient degree, the owner is asked either to put more cash into the account or to sell part of the stock.

Market Segmentation: The division of a consumer market into specific groups of buyers based on demographic factors.

M-Commerce: Mobile e-commerce over wireless devices.

Merchant Services: Credit card transaction processing services, typically provided by a retail bank. Merchant services include the processing and clearing of credit card transactions and the forwarding of the funds received to the client's bank account.

Microloan (Microlending): A microloan is a type of lending being practiced mainly in emerging nations. The idea is to provide a small amount of capital, typically less than $300, so that an entrepreneur may buy equipment to start or enhance a small business. For example, these loans are often used to buy sewing machines for a home-based apparel business, equipment for a small food stand, or animals for a family farm. This practice is also described as microlending or microfinance.

Millenials: See "Generation Y."

ML: See "Machine Learning (ML)."

Mobile Apps: See "Apps."

Money Market Fund: A mutual fund that specializes in investing in short-term securities, typically bonds and commercial paper with a duration of 30 to 180 days. These funds usually offer the investor a low initial investment, with some check-writing privileges, and are used to park short-term cash.

Multi-Factor Authentication: A strategy wherein additional levels of ID are required after a username and password have been provided. For example, the requirement that the user enter a code that has been pushed to him/her via a text message.

NACHA: The national organization that enables ACH payments via the ACH (Automated Clearinghouse) Network. The network connects all U.S. financial institutions, enabling secure and efficient movement of money and information directly from one bank account to another. ACH payments are commonly used for regularly recurring payments. For example, a consumer or business can elect to have a recurring bill payment sent to a vendor or supplier via ACH each month. The rules and procedures are different from bank wires. (Also, see "ACH" and "Wire Transfer".)

Near Field Communication (NFC): Short-range wireless connectivity that enables communication between devices that are touching or brought within several centimeters of each other. For example, NFC enables cell phones and special credit cards to act as smart payment cards when waived at point-of-sale terminals.

Neobank: A FinTech firm that offers bank-like services, such as checking, savings, debit cards and possibly investments, but does not have, or is not focused on, physical banking offices. Neobanks are sometimes called "challenger banks." They provide convenient apps for their users. They may actually own a bank charter, but more often offer their services in partnership with third-party banks.

Network Effect: A phenomenon whereby each additional user added to a system brings disproportionately greater utility to the existing user base. Excellent examples include the telephone, fax machine and social media. This is a business effect that can rapidly and exponentially grow a user base.

Network Effect: A phenomenon whereby each additional user added to a system brings disproportionately greater utility to the existing user base. Excellent examples include the telephone, fax machine and social media. This is a business effect that can rapidly and exponentially grow a user base.

NFC: See "Near Field Communication (NFC)."

OCC: See "Office of the Comptroller of the Currency (OCC)."

Office of the Comptroller of the Currency (OCC): An independent bureau of the Treasury Department and the oldest federal financial regulatory body. The OCC oversees the nation's federally chartered banks and promotes a system of bank supervision and regulation that: promotes safety and soundness by requiring that national banks adhere to sound management principles and comply with the law: and encourages banks to satisfy customer and community needs while remaining efficient competitors in the financial services market.

Open Banking: A business strategy that enables financial firms to quickly assemble new services and tools for their customers, via software APIs.

Open Banking: A business strategy that enables financial firms to quickly assemble new services and tools for their customers, via software APIs.

Open Source (Open Standards): A software program for which the source code is openly available for modification and enhancement as various users and developers see fit. Open software is typically developed as a public collaboration and grows in usefulness over time. See "LINUX."

P2P Payments: See "Peer-to-Peer Payments."

PaaS: See "Payments-as-a-Service (PaaS)."

Patent: An intellectual property right granted by a national government to an inventor to exclude others from making, using, offering for sale, or selling the invention throughout that nation or importing the invention into the nation for a limited time in exchange for public disclosure of the invention when the patent is granted. In addition to national patenting agencies, such as the United States Patent and Trademark Office, and regional organizations such as the European Patent Office, there is a cooperative international patent organization, the World Intellectual Property Organization, or WIPO, established by the United Nations.

Payment Gateway: Technology that gathers credit card, debit card or other types of payment account details at the time of sale/payment, and seamlessly transmits that information to a payment processing orgainzation so that funds eventually get deposited to the vendor's bank account.

Payment Service Directive Two (PSD2): Regulations that force European payments processors and gateways to utilized advanced customer and account authentication at the time of payment in order to reduce fraud.

Payments-as-a-Service (PaaS): Payments functions, such as ACH routing and account owner verification, offered as a plug-in service to websites and platforms that have a need to rapidly deploy payments abilities to their customers.

PCI Compliance: Privacy and antifraud regulations to ensure that credit card data protected. Also known as Payment Card Industry Compliance.

Peer-to-Peer Payments: Systems or apps, such as Zelle and Venmo, that enable one party to pay another party outside of traditional banking and credit card services.

Play to Earn Games: A category of online games where players can earn tokens, cryptocurrency or NFTs for playing. The allure is that the players can trade these earnings or sell them for cash. Blockchain software is typically running in the background. A pioneer in this field is Axie Infinity, which operates on the Ethereum blockchain.

Point-of-Sale (POS): A cash register with the capability to scan a UPC code, electronically record a sale and accept payment via multiple means, including the scanning of a credit card or digital wallet. It may utilize NFC, near field communications, to read cards and digital wallets.

Portal: A comprehensive web site for general or specific purposes.

Portfolio: A collection of securities (stocks or bonds) owned by an individual or an institution, such as a mutual fund.

POS: See "Point of Sale (POS)."

Predictive Analytics: See "Analytics."

Private-Label Credit Card: A system in which credit cards have the store's name on them, but the accounts receivable are sold to a financial institution.

Protocol: A set of rules for communicating between computers. The use of standard protocols allows products from different vendors to communicate on a common network.

PSD2: See "Payment Service Directive Two (PSD2)."

R&D: Research and development. Also see "Applied Research" and "Basic Research."

Radio Frequency Identification (RFID): A technology that applies a special microchip-enabled tag to an individual item or piece of merchandise or inventory. RFID technology enables wireless, computerized tracking of that inventory item as it moves through the supply chain from factory to

transport to warehouse to retail store or end user. Also known as radio tags.

Real Time Payments: See "Instant Payments."

Real-Time Payments (RTP): A real-time payments system is composed of technology that enables instantaneous money transfer between banks and banking systems.

Request to Pay (RTP): A messaging service that is designed to work alongside existing payments infrastructures. It allows the paying customer more control than direct debit does. Relying on account-to-account (A2A) payments, it also eliminates costly printed checks and credit card transactions.

Robo Advisor: See "Roboinvesting."

Roboinvesting: The use of computer algorithms, which may include machine learning and/or artificial intelligence, to maintain and trade investment accounts. Each account is set up by software based on the goals and needs indicated by the user when the account is established. Maintenance fees tend to be very low, and the investments made are often focused on ETFs.

Routing Number: See "Wire Transfer."

RTP: See "Request to Pay (RTP)."

SaaS: See "Software as a Service (SaaS)."

Scalable: Refers to a network that can grow and adapt as the total customer count increases and as customer needs increase and change. Scalable websites (and the hardware and software behind them) are extremely vital to rapidly-growing online services. Scalable networks can easily manage increasing numbers of workstations, servers, user workloads and added functionality.

Security: A common name for a stock, bond, debt instrument, preferred stock or other investment unit sold by a company, a mutual fund or a government.

SEPA: Single Euro Payments Area.

Service Level Agreement (SLA): A detail in a contract between a service provider and the client. The agreement specifies the level of service that is expected during the service contract term. For example, computer or Internet service contracts generally stipulate a maximum amount of time that a system may be unusable.

Sharia (in banking): The set of Islamic rules that govern activities of all types, Sharia strictly limits the use of interest payments. Instead, many business deals in Islamic societies must be structured on creative lease, rent or other alternative contracts, rather than interest-bearing loans or bonds, in order to be acceptable.

Single Sign-On: A system that permits a user to use one set of login credentials, such as a username/password, to access multiple applications, such as databases, within an organization. It is appropriate as a high-level login in enterprises that are running many different types and brands of software.

SLA: See "Service Level Agreement (SLA)."

Smart Contract: Self-executing contracts where an agreement between buyer and seller are written into lines of code. Such contracts utilize blockchain.

Social Media: Sites on the Internet that feature user generated content (UGC). Such media include wikis, blogs and specialty web sites such as MySpace.com, Facebook, YouTube, Yelp and Friendster.com. Social media are seen as powerful online tools because all or most of the content is user-generated.

Software as a Service (SaaS): Refers to the practice of providing users with software applications that are hosted on remote servers and accessed via the Internet. Excellent examples include the CRM (Customer Relationship Management) software provided in SaaS format by Salesforce. An earlier technology that operated in a similar, but less sophisticated, manner was called ASP or Application Service Provider.

Strong Customer Authentication (SCA): A technology that ensures that online payment transactions are secure and that fraud is significantly reduced. SCA took effect beginning in 2022.

Sweep Account: A bank or deposit account that automatically sweeps excess funds into an interest earning account at the end of each business day.

Tokenization: A technology whereby a digital wallet app will request from the issuing bank a token, a unique identification number, to represent vital account information for payment via credit card, debit card or bank account. The digital wallet then encrypts the newly tokenized card, making it ready for use. When a user taps their mobile device on a POS terminal or pays within a mobile app, the digital wallet responds with the token and a cryptogram which acts as a one-time-use password. Account security is thus greatly enhanced.

Two-Factor Authentication: A strategy wherein two levels of ID are required after a username and password have been provided. For example, the requirement that the user enter a code that has been pushed to him/her via a text message.

UI: See "User Interface (UI)."

Unified Payment Interface (UPI): An app that enables users to transfer money, developed by the National Payments Corporation of India (NPCI).

UPI: See "Unified Payments Interface (UPI)."

User Experience (UX): An overall interaction that a user has with a product or service: the human-device interaction is a key point of differentiation for most tech companies.

User Generated Content (UGC): Data contributed by users of interactive web sites. Such sites can include wikis, blogs, entertainment sites, shopping sites or social networks such as Facebook. UGC data can also include such things as product reviews, photos, videos, comments on forums, and how-to advice. Also see "Social Media."

User Interface (UI): The software and hardware that enable humans to interact with machines: typically a great user interface is a key differentiator for companies. For example, Windows is a user interface that enables users to access computers.

Vendor: Any firm, such as a manufacturer or distributor, from which a retailer obtains merchandise.

Web Services: Self-contained modular applications that can be described, published, located and invoked over the World Wide Web or another network. Web services architecture evolved from object-oriented design and is geared toward e-business solutions. Microsoft Corporation is focusing on web services with its .NET initiative. Also see "Extensible Markup Language (XML)."

Web3: Not to be confused with the Semantic Web (which has, from time-to-time in the past, been called Web 3.0), a version of the world wide web based on blockchain technology. Also known as Web 3.0.

Wire Transfer: A bank wire, or wire transfer, is an electronic method whereby money is transferred from one financial institution to another. Wire transfers are nearly immediate. There is typically a fee involved. The banks involved are identified by unique routing numbers so that the money can be sent to the correct place. In the U.S., routing numbers may also be referred to as ABA numbers. One unique attribute is that only the sender can initiate a wire. ACH payments are similar but operate under different rules. (See "ACH".)

XML: See "Extensible Markup Language (XML)."

Zero Trust: A strategy wherein networks should never automatically assume that anything either within or outside the network is valid or trustworthy. This requires continual user authentication at a higher level. That is, access to an account or a network should not be provided until authorization and identity are well verified. This verification can be against a database of multiple ID factors. For example, a user with a verified user name/password should be attempting access from a device that is typically utilized by that person, in a geolocation that is typical and from an IP address that is not blacklisted. Any access attempt that doesn't pass such real-time tests should be forced to pass through additional verification steps.

CPSIA information can be obtained
at www.ICGtesting.com
Printed in the USA
JSHW030742240622
27253JS00006B/18